The Order of Ethics
and
The Ploy of Consciousness

GW00801667

by
Gregory Heritage

THE ORDER OF ETHICS AND THE PLOY OF CONSCIOUSNESS

Blog and Contact Information: **Millennium Vigil** - millenniumvigil.org

To protect happiness and goodness sometimes requires the sacrifice and duty of living in a shell of misery and frustration. Sometimes this involves the chilling burden of restraining oneself from committing mistakes of compassion. But then something profoundly good and pure grows from this by finding happiness in the happiness of others. And everything comes to a blissful moment of peace in all parts of the self and the world – one achieves true happiness, where the tormented self is released of the suffering of not being happy, choosing to suffer to create goodness in the world that is only ever felt in the spirit of virtue, where one becomes free from a cruel fate by making good on it and seeing how the world makes good on suffering through you. And if all else fails, at least you can find solace in the courage that at least you did everything you could, at least you found a moment of true happiness beyond the veil of a life consumed with fear, misery, and cruelty. True happiness, in this life and age, comes through blissful misery. To be happy you must be a certain type of person, and that life will always be bittersweet. But this is the greatest peace and the highest happiness that can be achieved.

Contents

Contents

Introduction

Like anyone, I have questions. No given answer is truly satisfying and distraction is unfulfilling. Times are changing quickly, with technological advancement and ethical values of modern societies shaping emerging generations. Yet where our material capacities and intellectual resources have flourished, it seems the nature of mankind is much the same and struggling with its new challenges. Where changes in values and attitudes are underdoing conditioning by a transforming world, a foundational aspect of human nature may seem deficient, immature, if not damned.

Morality is in crisis. Ethics and morality are distorted, confused, warped, meaningless; other times they are left to the mercy of subjectivity lacking the function and power of justice. Mankind is struggling to adapt quickly to shifts in environmental conditioning; normative guidance and ethical understanding are needed more than ever. Ethics and morality need to be revised and reformed with a concrete utility and clear vision in light of the extraordinary insights found across scholarly work. But efforts in moral philosophy, especially their primitive colloquial forms, have been insufficient and inadequate for providing effective guidance on action and living. There are fundamental questions that need to be addressed concerning how we ought to act and live in a globalised world, which may be reaching its threshold of sustained effective growth.

As a young man entering adulthood and accepting responsibility for my actions and way of living, I have questions and concerns of a profound and practical nature. Where values and norms were once straightforward and convenient, such tradition no longer suffices and satisfies. Where morality and purpose are reduced to subjective incoherence, we are led to confusion and disorder. Yet this design of disorder is at the core of rapid change in attitudes, values, and morality, serving as the foundation of progress through antagonism between discord and order.

I want order, insight, and purpose where I find none, moving me down a path of self-exploration and pursuit of insight and value, to find that even the most insightful old tales only shed light on a partial truth. No philosophy I have hitherto familiarised myself with explored and accounted for the entirety of the human condition, restricting themselves to individualistic interpretations and schools of thought. Above all, no convention or norm of the past is prepared or adequate in coherently interpreting moral wisdom from life in the modern world. Thus began an impulsive, obsessive, and reactionary pursuit of new enlightenment on how to live, act, and what is worth living for. And so where gimmicks have emerged in the past, it is only a matter of time another one is found. With this ambition comes an extensive project on ethics as both normativity and its metaphysics.

These pages hold a new line of thought which will challenge many conceptions of the modern world and the nature of humanity, to then find, and structure, a different ethic, morality, and philosophy. The purpose of this writing is to contribute towards humanity's global ethics in a beneficial and constructive manner, to offer a viable, realistic alternative to greatly conflicted moralities, and to offer a different path or ideal to those who may seek it. My reflection on, and analysis of, ethics and morality began in my own confusion, through which I have come to an impression that much of the purpose of human endeavour and action is poorly understood and often taken for granted. The foremost question that arises is why we do what we do and to what end. The ambition of this work is to advance morality beyond its past of default, inadequacy, deficiency, and corruption.

I am painfully aware of sceptical attitudes towards knowledge and the over-confidence of people's claims to truth. I don't hold 'the truth'. I am merely offering another perspective developed through constant self-doubt and extensive meditation on the subjects I shall discuss – foremost on morality and ethics. The value I ascribe to my work rests with a fairly simple foundation – people's pursuit of well-being. By consistently referring to this relatively straightforward notion, by referring to its authority over behaviour, I believe I have been able to construct a coherent thought worth turning into a project of this size in its multidimensional implications.

This is not a light-hearted and simplistic read. Simplicity will not do ethics and morality the justice they demand, and interpretations of the truth are never uncomplicated. I will do my best to avoid use of unnecessarily complex language. However, by revising the foundation of ethics and structuring a new philosophy and thought, the use of terminology will evolve to become more intricate and increasingly technical; as of Section 3, the devil is in the details.

Every word used will be deliberately crafted with wide-ranging meanings and implications. Even in differentiating between words such as *mankind* and *humanity* I will refer to different concepts and ascribe to them different meaning. In time, even using terms within a single sentence tied to a single word, such as between *of* and *for*, will reach out to very different thoughts.

While the basic interpretation will remain straightforward, greater insight will be found in the details of the wording. This original work will not be a summary or simplification, yet the essence of arguments and main points will tend to be highlighted throughout. A reader's guide will accompany this work in the form of a blog as a practice of the author's moral responsibility (see the cover page for a link to *Millennium Vigil* - the digital presence and brand of heritin ethics and heritism as a practice of the heritin tradition to help and educate people on ethics and morality). The terms used will be found in origin of this work, with many notions and concepts borrowed and revised through prior studies that will be helpful but unnecessary to understand the main points. Although, some topics instrumental for greater understanding of this work, notably its metaphysics of the mind and anatomy of logic and reason, will require dedication and specific terms, above all in Section 4. But even then I will take some ideas and fundamentally revise them to find an alternative interpretation.

The ambition of this project is to make its content accessible to all those willing. So along this dedicated study will be elements of basic introductions to ideas, and even though incomplete, they will suffice for the gist of things. That said, some complex ideas and certain arguments will require a great deal of technicality and intricate wording. Certain arguments cannot be simplified further without diluting the point sought to be made. With sufficient perseverance, this work alone and use of the internet will suffice.

The nature of this work is ambiguous, diverse, and fluid. Its implications will be serious for both the person and academia. However, despite the elements of dedicated study and its technical nature, this is not intended to be an extensive academic essay. Due to the nature of the topics and themes discussed, as with any moral philosophy, this work will offer guidance and serve as a sort of self-help book. I shall borrow many technical and colloquial terms to then revise them and integrate them into a single interpretation in this philosophy and its foundational principle thoughts. I will write in commentary to my experiences, which have been crucial to the formation of this philosophy. There is the theory, but there is also the close-knitted story of its conception to serve the dual nature of ethics. I, like any other person, am a case study of and for ethics, part of a shared narrative in which we are all our own protagonists.

I was born half-Russian and half-English. I have visited and lived in many places because of my father's career as a journalist. My engagement with politics began at an early age and my studies of politics and philosophy at university expanded my understanding and deepened my knowledge. Study of philosophy and experience of society have fostered insight into the fundamental relation between philosophy and the social sciences. These two areas of study and endeavour will become intertwined in this work to form a conceptual framework to unite and bridge philosophy of morality and ethics with social and natural sciences. My experiences, circumstances of my life, and my education have ignited many thoughts.

As the learned reader will be aware, the state of human endeavour is overshadowed by much conflict and discord. Mankind, if not in a state of conflict, often lives in a fragile peace and superficial solidarity. I am not torn between my Western and Russian heritage, as I have lived and grown in both worlds. Yet I have never truly committed to either, leaving me to embrace mankind and its many societies in common humanity with no strict allegiances but to those of my morality and conscience. I have in many ways become an outsider to both societies and cultures, whilst being familiar and only partially integrated into both, but embracing all beyond the convention of identity. It should not come as a surprise that I understand and see things very differently. Circumstances of my predicament have nourished a fluidity in culture, normativity, thought, identity, and spirit. I have, perhaps, a unique experience and insight growing up: from my experiences of life, society, people, and culture in Russia and England, then life in a deeply divided society in Israel – a country and society torn by violence.

Violence – a disease of the mind and a poison of the spirit – lingered with me throughout much of my life after it profoundly affected me in Israel. I have grown up with affliction of violence, anger, hate, and fear at the core of my being and it had overshadowed much of my life, whereby something very different in essence grew from what was torn out. These features of experience will serve as points of insight that find a new way of thinking beyond the restrictive state of fear ascriptive to violence and reactionary anger. It will not come as a surprise that this work aspires to peace and progress rather than destructive conflict.

Morality is too often weak; its contradictory theories and practices have become a destructive, conflicting reality. Impressions on the mind, knowledge, and feeling are not separate aspects of life as some theories might suggest. To discuss these central themes of life separately is to ignore what it is to act and be alive in the first place. The causal connections of mankind's endeavours are interlinked, and there is a common foundation to us all and to the ethics that govern and exemplify our behaviour. There is a fundamental unity in the functions of organic mechanisms that produce the structures we model and inhabit. Appreciating this not only sets its own distinctive agenda, but also serves as ethical guidance. In time, this work will encompass and integrate ethics into a single, centred framework and model. Morality of our base nature, which guides global endeavour, is inconsistent, conflicted, unclear, undisciplined, and often petty. Through such a conceptual lens one can begin to see and appreciate things differently, then act with greater fulfilment, ambition, and dedication.

Mankind still lives in a world of international anarchy and disunity, threatened by many challenges looming on the horizon of mankind's future. Many of these issues are symptomatic of ethics, with the core of our ambitions, desires, and actions being problematic and of concern for ethical study. In many respects, the nature of mankind is its own problem. The misanthrope and cynic might defer to apathy, unfulfilling hedonism, and destructive policy, yet insight is minimal through a veil of despair. Then, under the given veil of restrictive thought and identity, narrow insight offers little for greater interest of mutual benefit. Ethics and morality are inherent to the sociopolitical, with challenges to international order having a more profound cause in relation to conflict in morality itself.

To overcome this challenge will require much more than political, social, and economic resolution and redemption. One must defer to a more fundamental device of power as *moral authority* at the core of actions themselves. The progressive power of morality and idealism may be scorned at, yet with a new perspective it will become known as an integral parallel, if not the only true currency of all matters of living and action extending to government affairs as well. These are but some of the issues that will have to be addressed and studied in a detailed and comprehensive revision of ethics and morality.

The foundation of this philosophy, explored in Section 1, will orientate around the thought that all matters of actions stem from their function of the pursuit of well-being. Through this basic thought, I will strip down attitude of morality to its foundations in Section 1 and carry on in Section 2 to evaluate the foundation of morality. For the reader most concerned with commentary concerning the social structures of ethics, Section 2 and Part 3 of Section 3 will be of the most interest, yet to appreciate them fully requires basic understanding of Section 1 and Parts 1 and 2 of Section 3. Then, in Section 3, I will find a morality by developing an alternative foundation for ethical practice through a revised interpretation of our fundamental ambition detailed in Sections 1 and 2, to improve on the deficiency of common moral functions and dispositions. I will attempt to find a morality and ethic capable of encompassing the many issues the modern world faces, to offer a valid and meaningful theory of ethics and moral philosophy.

There may be some elements of my theory that might initially come across as counter-intuitive, impractical, or even radical. However, in time these impressions should be dissolved as I revise some presupposed intuitions and structure them into coherent thoughts and ambitions, to then improve on them. The scope of this large project is due to the ambition I have set myself to fundamentally revise morality and ethics, integrate them with a metaphysical account of reason and logic and understanding of the conscious mind, and explore ethics through a distinctive model and understanding – a comprehensive subject I will refer to as *structural ethics*. Structural ethics is the social science of ethics and the art of morality studying the structures borne of our behaviour and habits, shaping all aspects of human behaviour in accordance with the function and purpose of actions.

Structural ethics has been inspired by many ideas in philosophy and social science, all of which cannot be coherently referenced to. Structural ethics as the social science of ethics has been partly inspired by Philip Brey's technological structural ethics in philosophy of engineering and technology[1]. However, structural ethics as a *discipline* of the social science of well-being is fundamentally different to Brey's technological structural ethics. Structural ethics as a discipline structures and systematises actions, values, desires, and behaviour and influences on behaviour, from the conscious mind to environmental variables, and isn't intended to *only* compliment individual ethics – the ethical study of people and behaviour, according to Brey. Structural ethics studies all aspects of behaviour relevant to behaviour's intended goals and well-being, to then inform normative guidance and moral philosophy, as well as structure normativity. As such, structural ethics is broader in its vision and application than technological structural ethics.

Many of the themes to be discussed in this book will engage elusive axioms of common sense and intuition taken for granted, but making intuition and common sense coherent in logically structured thought is in itself a challenge with incredible rewards. The centrepiece of this project's originality might be found in Section 1 and how *action* is defined in respect of morality and ethics. It is around this fundamental thought concerning the nature of morality that it evokes a wealth of intuition creating the content of these pages. Through a simple and deceptively straightforward thought, ethics can be understood and accounted for very well. Then, these intuitions thrive to develop into a comprehensive account of ethics, morality, and the anatomy and structure of their mechanisms in the mind in terms of abstract phenomena of mentality, physical substance of the body, and environmental conditioning. Ethics can begin to bridge natural and social sciences with coherent understanding and theory, to dissolve the view of philosophy as mere opinion deprived of structure or capacity of action to address and balance perceived opinion or immature thought. I begin this work with a normative and metaphysical account of the functionality of ethics and morality through the mind. I dedicate Section 4 to a deeper exploration of the metaphysics of the mind and consciousness to propose a concrete account of the place of logic and reason in the mind and world. Then, I am forced to discuss integral questions of the nature of consciousness to fully account for the structured mechanisms of behaviour.

Beyond the metaphysics of ethics and morality, which will play an imperative role in the following normative theories and then their applied ethics, this project will centre on a deceptively simple personal question: Are fear and suffering good, and should we give in to fear or resist it? The entire study of ethics in this project will centre on the theme of the significance and moral quality of not giving into fear and suffering as a force of subjugation. Fear and aversion to pain have profound impacts on our lives, and ethics guided by these functions and parameters have been instrumental for us. However, I will come to extensively argue that the utility of these guiding ethical principles has in many ways expired. I then dedicate myself to a massive undertaking of revising and restructuring ethics from their basic foundation and develop ethics in a new direction fulfilling human potential, a direction interpreting and emphasising familiar intuitions lacking nourishment and maturity by a deficient ethic.

During this exploration, which has been a journey of self-reflection and development for myself, I have learnt a great deal on the metaphysics of morality and ethics that will become key points for thoughts on the structures of ethics. The metaphysical account of ethics I offer will seek to revive objective morality and ethics, to then also revive a firm and categorical account of Natural Law serving as a Constitution of

Natural Law and moral law. Due to the nature of the themes I explore and as a result of the essence of the ethic formulated, this discussion of ethics will become very personal and, in sum, *spiritual*. This is something that would be expected from posing a personal question of what is morally better and greater – giving into fear and pain, or seeking to overcome it. I will argue in favour of the latter, posing the journey to overcome and conquer fear as a profound endeavour that will reach into the core of the self and being alive, granting extraordinary insight.

It begins with a Fundamental Principle...

Section 1:

Systems of Ethics and a Fundamental Principle

Chapter 1:

Metaphysics of Ethics as Functions of Actions

The world, philosophy, and people are odd things, with a variety of words being appropriate to describe the many faces and features of people and their ways of thinking. Things can be simple, to then produce complexity defying all sense. There is an extraordinary amount of information concerning the world and living that it is hard to believe that anything can be intuitively made sense of, and yet we persist with our stubbornness. Our self-awareness is a gift we struggle to grasp. Mankind has accomplished some truly incredible things, but also succeeded in causing a lot of havoc. We have channelled our minds into the world to create objects that arouse sentiments and passions, tools that let us set foot in places we had not even imagined in our dreams, to become capable of destroying the planet we live with. We can go even further to build a more hopeful world and live to become greater than the slave our first nature trapped us in, grow to live a life brightened by the liberty of our humanity and its virtues. One must begin to ask what the function of action and living is in the first place.

Why do we live? Why do we continue pushing ourselves rather than keeling over and withering until death takes us? Why do we strive towards goals? Why do we set aims? Why do we give ourselves purpose? Why do we even get up in the morning? What's the point of doing an action in the first place? What is this *goal-directive behaviour*? All living creatures seem to be beings of 'doing', and all acts of life are tangled in the strings of the grand puppeteer identified as *ethics* that guide and set the agenda for actions. So what is the role of ethics in our lives? To understand and employ ethics and morality one must first understand their function as actions. It may seem that a simple question has been overlooked: Why do we perform actions and why should we act? What is the purpose of actions? Why live? Then, to further appreciate ethics we must study the metaphysics and pathology of actions: How do actions come about and what is the origin of the first 'action'? How are actions executed in the body and mind? Studying these themes has led me to a total revision of ethics, the product of which is this extensive work on the many dimensions and aspects of ethics.

This much is evident: our ethics serve as guidelines of actions in accordance with our *will*, which is the sum machination and dynamic that sets and executes *goal-directive behaviour*. What we desire to achieve is what dictates the execution and performance of action and the corresponding standards adopted and integrated. All that is of the *will* underlying actions, known first (deceptively) in its simpler form as intention and deliberation, is *ambition* by a goal set in mind. For example, a person who values honesty as a virtue will strive to live honestly and adopt a moral standard that honesty is worthy of action. Such a statement is straightforward and self-evident; however, the topic I want to concentrate on is an analysis of the nature of our will as goal-directive dynamics in ethics, for an action is only ever performed with an ambition, even if the ambition is veiled by its intuitive sense and reason for action.

All living things want something and have a particular goal; if they don't, or have already succeeded in their ambition, then no action or process would occur to achieve satisfaction of a desire or goal, because the existence of a will implies there is an ambition to pursue. Even if a living creature lacks a mind or a form of consciousness and lacks the concept of 'wanting', perhaps a plant or bacteria, it nevertheless physically manifests a form of movement. In this respect, is it possible to find a singular function that governs all other desires and processes of a living being? Is there a single fundamental principle that dictates all ethics? Is there a fundamental catalyst for the execution and performance of actions as movement of the body and mind? I will demonstrate that it is possible to deduce a universal function of the will and contingent actions that lays the foundation for ethics and morality. Doing so would be sensible by analysing the actions and behaviour of living things.

Most living things are governed by an ambition pursued as a function of their nature, notably linked to survival. The evolution of life through natural selection has shaped functions of living things. This notion can be clearly seen as an exemplifying cause behind much of the behaviour and many of the actions of living things, or at least the developmental trends of evolving bodies can be found to exemplify much behaviour related to the ambition or function of survival. Common animals could be argued to mainly strive for survival, or it could be said that survival is the only thing they can strive for. Humans also ordinarily conduct their actions in a relatable fashion.

However, people's ethics are exceedingly more complex. Actions are often performed without deliberation; sometimes the continuity of actions serves only as a function of surviving trends of behaviour without deliberate intent. The intention behind certain actions might not be survival, yet the appropriate behaviour does sustain survival by a design of selective adaptation and fortune. *Nature* – hereon a capitalised term used to denote the sum sphere of living things and their link to the rest of physical substance and moving elements of the world – is constituted by a mechanism of shaping life through natural selection and forces affecting adaptation. Our bodies and minds have developed in line with this model and function. But where the body acts in a manner sustaining itself and the mind, the ambition of survival is only a part of the guiding will implementing actions.

Actions and thoughts are shaped by the capacities of the mind inherited and conditioned by the environment, a presiding force being that of natural selection and survival. Yet it is clear that we act in a reflexive and automatic manner reciprocal of our inherited functions of the body and mind. People are not robots of deliberative reason where an action is performed on the basis of a conjured and made-up ambition; rather, we act in accordance with inherited functions and intuitions invoked by the mind. Essentially, we act on a *feeling* corresponding to functions of the anatomy of our minds. Some drink wine because they enjoy it, yet that function of pleasure is only enabled by the anatomy of the body and mind capable of sensing the pleasure, a capacity cultivated through development of our bodies through evolution and the continuity of conditioning. We have children because functions of the mind invoke an intuition that beckons actions corresponding to reproduction, or functions of the mind invoke reproductive behaviour leading to the continuity of life by means of sustainable actions.

Here we draw up certain thoughts on the nature of goal-directive behaviour of actions: first, they correspond to functions of the body and mind, and second, the catalyst of actions is more sophisticated than empty functions lacking *feeling* or *awareness* in our actions. Actions correspond to functions exemplified through their *mental states* such as emotions. Actions serve the purpose of fulfilling an ambition set by a function. We know these functions through the most basic intuitions of conscious self-awareness. *Intuitions* are considered in this work to be quick, automatic, basic thoughts mostly of subconscious origin. The thought 'I am hungry, I should eat' is an example of an intuition.

If each action serves a function, then what function is foundational to the model and formula of actions by goal-directive behaviour? What product moves systems of ethics to conduct and implement actions? As suggested above, the function may seem to be the continuity of actions, yet the continuity of actions only occurs through a mode of actions and ethics able to sustain relevant functions, deliberately or not. But it is clear that it is not the nature or essence of goal-directive behaviour to merely deliberately sustain continuity for continuity's sake, to survive for the sake of survival, to sustain life for life's sake, *to act for action's sake.*

The continuity of prevailing functions in relation to their respective actions, such as survival, comes as a result of that which enables the continuity and sustainability of actions. Actions – in terms of their effect on awareness as part of their function, automatic or deliberative – pursue an ambition and goal precedent to the action itself, superceding the action in its ambition. An action is only produced by a foundational principle that exemplifies causal change producing the action or thought, by a foundational principle acting as a conduit of systematic variables giving cause to a function leading to the action itself. There must be an ambition causing the action, just as there must be an ambition bound to conscious awareness and functions of the mind guiding an action and being part of an action, but not simply *being* the action. We act not for the sake of action, but for what the action does, what it produces for the *ethical agent* as an ethical catalyst and conduit causing an *action* to occur. We act for and in our *ethical interest.*

To gain insight into the function of actions one must first understand what actions are. Much discussion can be had on the topic, but for the current purpose I shall not delve into specific literature. Broadly speaking, actions can be understood to involve *movement* with a key qualification of deliberation or intent in the execution and design of movement. For instance, one might intuitively suppose that making a cup of tea is an *action*. In contrast, a plant arguably does not perform any form of action as deliberate movement, rather it merely thrives and moves if the conditions are accommodating. Where the flower points towards a brighter light, a more complex organism achieves continuity of living and sustainable behaviour through more sophisticated movements as actions. Where life evolved from simpler organic constructs, a movement becomes an *action* through an intricate system of variables through a central processing system such as the brain.

There is a distinction between reactions as automatic movements and actions as intentional movements. A simple cell may perform a basic function and movement without intent, yet where an organ processing information adjusts the variables through awareness of one's surroundings, movement changes in a fundamental way to perform *actions*. Where animals may commonly act contingent on the functions of basic instincts, the actions of people are performed through a more sophisticated system of functions involving deliberation on informational variables integrating environmental awareness into the assessment of appropriate action.

What is clearest in such a model is that we act in respect of prompts to action. If our bodies experience pain, we react to it momentarily and then adopt a sustainable approach and broader reaction to pain as actions that avoid or resolve pain. Environmental stimuli provide the brain and mind with information relevant to decision-making and actions. Sometimes we follow a deliberative approach as complex thought on action, or we simply react reflexively or through actions of subconscious origin. All functions of behaviour serve a purpose in accordance with relevant information. For example, actions and reactions that avoid painful mental states are only invoked by the function implementing such actions. 'Fight or flight' actions and reactions can exercise unpredictable power on the mind to implement actions of questionable rationale and sense. But the determination of the actions taken in accordance with the fight-or-flight instinct occurs in terms of the function of the body implementing the corresponding movement in action and thought.

Here we can begin to appreciate that intentional movements as actions, even thoughts themselves, are subjects of the functions of cognitive and bodily behaviour. Functions as features of a mechanical and deterministic mind guide mental processing in terms of thoughts and intuitions in accordance with variables and inputs conditioning an ambition contingent on a *function*. Where information and related functions, such as thoughts, can be purely hypothetical, irrelevant, detached, and random, actions are distinct in that they channel and involve information relevant to the action itself. A thought might not be contextual to the immediate environment, yet relevant information will shape an action.

Actions serve functions, regardless of whether they are reactionary or deliberative. The reflex is a conditioned movement sustaining its pattern of behaviour, while a deliberative action appears necessary for more complex and continued trends of behaviour such as those of life-long consequence. But what does any function do? What is the principle that exemplifies all models of functions in living things? For basic creatures, functions of behaviour and of the mind are what enable continuity of existence such as with the plant reaching towards light. For deliberative creatures like people, these functions take on much greater forms through thought and intuition contingent on mental states as the sum of functional information.

Survival is a prominent, if not dominant, feature of people's behaviour. However, there are clear examples where people's actions are not moved by unilateral functions of survival and are only bilaterally derivative from the instinct of survival. A point that will be reiterated throughout this work, a life not worth living will cease in its unsatisfied form; a depressive person in pain will commit suicide – cease all action – if the mind is set to it, or the person will strive to move beyond the depressive state. Furthermore, as a basic thought experiment, actions and existence do not necessarily have to be or exist, yet to exist requires that which enables and sustains existence. It is theoretically conceivable that we could withhold action in certain circumstances or that we or somebody else could have not existed. A self-condemning action in terms of its respective function might serve a form of social survival through natural selection, yet this function is not necessarily of a fundamental interest to the person that surrenders the life he or she finds not worth living. The cause of suicide could be unfulfilled functions invoking suffering in the mind, yet the action itself for the individual is not one of survival.

There is a broader function in actions than simple continuity of actions, integrating a necessary element sustaining actions beyond the action itself, or at least this is the case for deliberative actions. A life not worth living might end itself, suggesting action involves other elements than just a concern for continuity. The continuity of life itself requires a contingent element giving *sense* and *feeling* to the continuity of a virtue worth continuing, of action and ambition worth sustaining. Then, the continuity of actions requires capable functions reciprocal of sustainable actions such that there is a function of the mind and body capable of sustaining a pattern of behaviour and the perceived worth of an action's ambition.

The pursuit of happiness is commonly interpreted to be a directive of action. Many seem to want happiness in some form or another, so they act according to this ambition. It would thus be intuitive to suggest that the function of deliberative actions could be a form of happiness. One must then ask what happiness is, but the sum of the question, whether happiness is conceived as joy, pleasure, or inner peace, can be simplified with the suggestion that happiness is a mental state. In respect of prior discussion, happiness as a mental state and feeling must therefore be or have a function – a mechanism enabling it. The question of what is the fundamental function remains unclear.

Deliberative actions striving for a particular mental state are contingent on a function, for example that which makes us happy, but the distinction between deliberative action and automatic movement is unclear. We may intentionally act in pursuit of happiness, yet our bodies may react and actions may be caused by subconscious influences in a mode of movement that is superficially subservient to the ambition of being happy. But then neither are reactions performed with the deliberate intent of survival. What is a deliberative action?

Actions are always conditional in terms of their accessible information and relevant instigating factors. Where we sense pain, we react. Where we do not sense pain, or do not think about pain, we may act irrespective of pain. Where reactions may lack deliberation and rational sense, one has to ask what constitutes and formulates deliberation in actions (in contrast to reactions). If intentional actions are conditional to available information, which works through a complex function of multidimensional influences of deliberation on actions, then actions are arguably no more than complex reactions. The function of deliberative actions engages multiple aspects of the body and mind, channelling information towards a sophisticated and complex reaction that we perceive as an intentional *action*. In sum, where actions work contingent on functions and conditions of stimuli and prompts to action, they can be qualified as not very distinct from sophisticated reactions. Details of this theme and the implications of deterministic actions and mental functions will be explored in Section 4.

While the study of ethics may concern itself with deliberative actions, it is imperative in the study of ethics to account for actions also as *sophisticated reactions*. One may simplify ethics in terms of deliberative actions, such as the intentional pursuit of happiness, yet this would not fully grasp the nature of actions as mechanisms and functions of the body and mind, notably as functions dealing with complex informational awareness of the environment as that which feeds into the senses and perceptions known in conscious awareness. Anything and everything beyond the first point of familiarity as conscious awareness is environmental as the sum of information in respective mental states. In the context of this project, *mental state(s)* will be a specific term used to refer to what we experience in conscious awareness as sensation, perception, and feeling.

The significant point to be raised is that where the function of automatic movement may seem to be unclear, i.e. they are mere functions that were able to sustain their continued service without intent, the same issue may apply to deliberative actions. Where we may be tempted to simply look at ethics in terms of actions and not functions or reactions, in doing so we would not appreciate the greater picture or involve greater insight on the essence of actions, reactions, and functions. It may seem as though actions and reactions are essentially random, meaningless, and only conditionally and circumstantially purposeful. Therefore, we can also exemplify the will as no more than its ascriptive nature in terms of the functions that pertain to the will.

The deliberation and intent of an action are no more than a conglomerate of functions linked in a central information-processing faculty. The centrepiece of this thought and argument is that all actions are always conditional and circumstantial to the triggers of those actions and their respective functions, whether desires, ambitions, informational states, thoughts, or intuitions.

What we have now in consideration of the functions of actions (as reactions) is that they are subservient to functions reflecting mental states, while there can also be complex reactions eluding conscious awareness such as reflexes or instinctive reactions. Furthermore, the continuity of actions is only a byproduct or function of being able to act in the first place, with continuity only occurring as a function the enables continuity.

It may seem as though we have reached a complete stupor, a total incoherent mess. However, this way of thinking equally allows us to formulate all actions and reactions in terms of *states of being*. Mental states as reflections of mental and bodily functions necessarily imply that there *are* such functions. *Being*, as a form of activity and existing functions, can involve latent and dormant functions to be actualised by a respective prompt. But where an action or reaction only occurs by the function enabling it, it means there is a state of *being* even if its mental states elude memory and immediate conscious awareness, because the function enabling an action will necessarily have to be active in order for the consequence (of the function) to occur.

All movements, as actions or reactions, intentional or not, are functions of being concerned with matters of being. All functions employ themselves as states of being *for* states of being. All functions work in tandem with what exists, even if only in terms of functions of thought yet to be actualised. Actions are enabled through, and dedicated to, the functions of states of being. But for a function to be sustainable and continue it must qualify for effective and able functions as actions and reactions. A function that does not do itself or its host an effective service will not be able to sustain itself. Therefore, it becomes a necessary criterion of functions to be effective if the behaviour of functions is to succeed and continue.

Functions serve their host to seek and strive for gains, profit, and *maxims of interest* in and through actions by whatever the mind deems to be worthy of ambition. Since all functions are extensions and utilities of states of being, and their concern is success and effectiveness of behaviour and living, this suggests there can be only one function key to states of being – of *well-being, of flourishing*. The key function in actions and reactions is the living thing's pursuit of well-being. It is not sufficient for a living thing to simply be; functions necessitate effective being where one's functions pertaining to being and existence are effective. The function of a living thing necessitates an integral category of well-being. All the actions and ambitions of a living thing strive for, and function in relation to, well-being and flourishing.

The nuanced aspects of the discussion thus far were in service to the dedicated reader, but the main point can be noted in a basic and intuitive sense. All actions strive for well-being; everything we do complies with a guiding ambition of pursuing well-being. The odd thing, however, is that this fundamental guiding function of actions is commonly taken for granted. The familiar pursuit of happiness is an exemplified function of living and action that strives for well-being. When we aren't happy, we try to be; when we're in pain, we strive to not be in pain. Ethics are the systems of actions, such as in terms of actions' respective functions, with morality being the consideration of the norms and parameters of interest and the concern to pursue and fulfil our ambitions.

It is crucial to make a note here that there is a key distinction between *morality* and *ethics*. Ethics as a subject and study concerns itself with the systems of morality and actions, that which produces and is responsible for the functions corresponding to morality as manifestations of ethical dynamics in the body that is able to act or move. Morality, on the other hand, concerns itself with the practice of actions, which fulfils the functions and ambitions understood through the systems of ethics. Where all actions and ambitions concern themselves with well-being, ethics is the area of understanding the systems, anatomy, and metaphysics of the moving body's function and pursuit corresponding to the concern of well-being. Morality is an area dedicated to the norms and practical concerns of *how* to achieve well-being in relation to the systemic features of well-being, which is exemplified through ethics. Ethics study actions and their systems, while morality dedicates itself to which actions fulfil their function – lead to or produce well-being. This core function of the pursuit of well-being through actions is better known in simpler empirical terms by observing behaviour. Illustrations would be useful to appreciate the function of living things as pursuing well-being.

It's usual for people to exploit their natural advantages and characteristics, be it looks, skills, or talents, to further their will as the ambition to flourish. Leaders may deny truths or 'justly' deceive their followers with witty words and charming appearances to further their own interest whether they are of a selfish nature or deceptively made to look benevolent, all to employ a course of action leaders believe is for the best. We eat because we want to live; we live because we want to live well. We excel because we want to better our circumstances. We avoid pain because we don't want to be in pain. The drug addict will manipulate others, betray those who care for him or her, and may use any opportunity to satisfy the desire to receive pleasure. The high of a drug is what the hedonistic mind may believe is, and senses as, well-being. In all behaviour a pattern begins to emerge of an underlying will and function that is deterministic of ethics.

There is an even more intriguing category of people to evaluate. What of the ethos of the insane, or of the sceptic and nihilist? Is there any form of progression through unbound morality or through delusion? Living without rules – or to put it more critically, living by a rule of having no rules – grants an individual freedom of action that conventional morality would restrict. If a person's sentiments and intuitions dictate moral conduct, whatever the philosophy behind it, then he would not follow through with the immoral acts a nihilist may be prone to. An insane and deluded individual may not think through his or her actions and act on compulsion of mental disorders. Ignoring common morality would grant the nihilist and lunatic a justification and motive to fulfil his or her desires unregulated by morality. However, even with rationality distorted by madness and the lack of concern for morality by the nihilist, the individual nevertheless pursues an idea of well-being. If there was no aim, even if elusive to concise reasoning and conscious awareness, then no action would be undertaken. In such a manner, even the nihilist and madman adopt attitudes or moralities that guide their venture of flourishing.

If all the examples I have explored and any other hypothetical cases are investigated, one could reach a conclusion from the emerging pattern that a fundamental will and ambition is that of pursuing well-being, flourishing, and fulfilment. Even thoughts serving a function strive for the core of all ambition, will, and function to live well. Therefore, I will outline a *Fundamental Principle of Living Beings and Actions – all living beings' actions function in accordance with, and are determined by, the pursuit of well-being; all actions are functions of the will to flourish*. I shall refer to this principle for most part simply as *the Fundamental Principle*.

The two noted criteria of the Fundamental Principle go hand in hand but exemplify two distinctive features of the Fundamental Principle. First, the determination of actions by the pursuit of flourishing entails a deterministic understanding of ethics and, with it, a major theme of metaphysics of the fundamental will to flourish in accordance with *functions* and *mechanisms* of the body and mind which produce movement as an action pursuing a certain end. The will to flourish is not a mere abstraction, and morality and ethics are grounded in deterministic, causal aspects of the physical, material substance of the world causally responsible for the functions of the mind.

Second, the framework of actions as *functions* of the will to flourish is extremely important. Actions are not mere random events or phenomena – they are deterministic and are manifestations *of* the will to flourish; actions are only enacted, enabled, or manifest themselves as the will to flourish and its endeavour prompting a pursuit. While the intention of an action and the act itself may seem two distinct elements, the Fundamental Principle and its fundamental will are intrinsically bound to actions and the two – actions and the will – are one and the same. Actions and the will of an action are conceptually different things, yet in ethics the two are metaphysically bound and conceptually distinct only as part of two criteria of states of the phenomena of pursuing well-being, with actions being a manifestation of the will to act and the will being inherent to actions themselves.

To illustrate this point, when I write an essay I do so with the intent to fulfil a particular objective, such as to prove a point, with the intent and the will to act being part of the activity itself as an actualised function. One may think or suppose that the will prompting the activity (of writing an essay) is somewhat distinct to the act of writing itself; my intent or will to write is different to the engagement and activity of writing. The point raised is that the two aren't actually metaphysically separate and the concepts are only 'two sides of the same coin'. So, while the action is enabled by a will to act, the action itself is the manifestation of its will.

As I reflect on and analyse ethics I am not simply talking about an abstract, mental phenomenon of the will or intent of an action; I am studying the physical phenomenon of the act itself as a manifestation of a concrete will encompassing relevant functions of behaviour. The bio-chemical reactions underlying functions of the brain responsible for the conduct of the mind, the brain's electrical activity, are the dynamics of ethics and actions as manifestations of the physical processes responsible for a 'will' to flourish, to be well. An action is a manifestation prompted by its will and, at the same time, the embodiment of its will. The processes that move my hand to write an essay exemplify the will and function to do so. Yet the physical processes also behold the will of the action, whereby without a will – a force moving an action – there could be no act of a living thing. Things can simply happen, but events and movements of living things do not happen without contingent forces acting as catalysts to the respective events.

In the physical processes of living bodies there is a distinctive, bilateral feature regulating and guiding its activity as part of the physical process itself. To describe actions as *functions* of the fundamental will to flourish, along with its intuitive suggestion, means to say that actions embody their will and are moved by a bilateral force influencing and mediating them, whereby they become different to the ordinary events of inanimate objects by virtue of having a guiding intent of purpose (to pursue flourishing). Actions are functions of the processes that instigate them and functions are embodiments of their processes, to which all actions function by their original catalyst, of processes leading to and/or pursuing flourishing. Actions function as the body and mind's pursuit of flourishing. However, the action is not detached from its will, whereby the will continues and extends into the manifestation of the function of the will. A more detailed, comprehensive account of the metaphysics of the Fundamental Principle and its fundamental will is deeply contextual on further study in later parts of this project.

The idea of the Fundamental Principle of Living Beings and Actions is not completely original and relates to Aristotle's naturalism and virtue ethics[1,2], but with an alternative interpretation. One issue that cannot be overlooked is that views on flourishing as morality and attitude vary greatly by individual conditioning and circumstance, thereby giving rise to the subjectivity of morality corresponding to the viability of well-being in relation to the judgement of individual circumstances. This is ultimately a normative concern of moral philosophy, yet the relevance of personal, subjective experience of well-being is integral to ethics and action.

What is well-being and flourishing as a mental state? As a state of being or function pursuing a state of being, well-being is a species of sensation, feeling, and intuition, but not in an ordinary sense. Well-being is never of a simple sort defined by a single emotion, sensation, or feeling. Rather, states of flourishing are known in sum as intuition, as awareness of a state of self. States of well-being are comprehensive mental totals of functions and conscious awareness. Both deliberative actions and automatic reactions affect states of the self, yet no single function as a mental state corresponds to a 'sensation' of well-being. Flourishing is evoked in sum total states of the self and being, known in conscious awareness of fulfilled states in relation to complex, cross-level, cross-sphere, multidimensional functions. For instance, pleasure does not in itself lead to well-being, but rather the pleasurable mental state can grant a sum of experience and sensation as emotionally fulfilling, just as it may also overshadow suffering. This sum of experience and awareness will be noted in terms of *spirit* and *spirituality* – a comprehensive sense, feeling, and awareness of states of being as *living*.

Quality of living can be hard to exemplify in concrete terms, with a relevant notion perhaps being best suited in terms of a most intuitive, yet oddly fluid, concept. We are in tune with states of well-being through basic intuitions, with *conscious awareness* of these states being key. Yet the summary of such awareness cannot be pin-pointed to a single function, but must rather be encompassed in a comprehensive sense of conscious experience of living as a multidimensional concept. A mental state on its own might serve a singular dimension of the self, but only in a summarised state of being exemplified as, and known through, *spirit as conscious awareness* can well-being be appreciated. Only fulfilled spirit qualifies well-being. States of flourishing are distinguished by intuition and sensation, as much as by reflective thought, producing a general state of one's living and relevant conscious awareness – *spirit.*

Well-being is not measured by a single criterion of qualification, as states of well-being encompass a variety of contributing factors for one's sense of living. This summary of the sense of living and state of being in conscious awareness is defined in terms of, and qualified as, *spirit.* The ambiguity of what constitutes well-being is not an ambiguity of the term itself, or at least not in this sense. Rather, the dubiety of what constitutes flourishing and well-being is a matter of normative ethics and qualification of spirit. Anyone can have a sense of flourishing and well-being, yet it is a matter of normative ethics to establish which mode of flourishing is the most fulfilling. We can all know for ourselves what we find fulfilling, as states of well-being are clearest to us in intuition when they are known through mental states representative of particular functions. But structuring the actions of fulfilling spirit in a coherent framework clearly isn't simple; this is an enormous task to which much of this project is dedicated.

Concerning ambiguity in the conditioning of well-being, many functions account for a general sense of being. For example, the paranoid schizophrenic will see conspiracy and delusions because of the active conditioning of their troubled mind. Consequently, the schizophrenic can only sense well-being within the confines of his or her perceived world and is limited by it. Moreover, cultural relativism of normative ethics and metaethics may tell us that people are experimenting and constantly adapting through modes of well-being. Yet in the case of successful forms of actions and behaviour, one can begin to exemplify greater forms of well-being and modes of action, indicative of an achievable greater success depending on the circumstances. Extreme deviations in moral conduct do not reject the underlying governing principle and function to strive for well-being. Furthermore, the formulation of the Fundamental Principle will not necessarily deny moral subjectivity, to instead account for perceived subjectivity. It will become apparent as a repetitive theme that the subjectivity of morality is only a product of its complexity in relation to individual circumstances and conditions, which doesn't deny the possibility of moral truths – truths of well-being and good spirit.

A relevant concern is that there are instances when people may know what the best course of action is, yet they do not pursue it. The Ancient Greeks knew this form of weakness of will and acting against one's interests as *akrasia.* For example, the addict who wishes to give up her choice of drug might not have the resolve to change her ways. Elements of the functions of the mind move the will to its respective actions, whereby functions contributing to the assessment of actions may conflict and a certain element will ultimately hold sway. While the addict attempts to change his or her way of life, conditioning of the self and mind propagate a pattern of behaviour and thought familiar to a sense of well-being. The matter of conflicting functions contributing to the qualification of the best action will feature throughout this work.

It is worth noting the parallel where, although pleasure may present itself as a state of well-being, the total state of the self, such as moments of lucidity from pleasure, reveal that the self is not flourishing, whether because there is no pleasure or because the habit of pleasure is destructive. Essentially, we pursue what we (our minds and corresponding functions) deem to be the most valuable in the present circumstance, yet the determination of what is taken to be worthy is not straightforward or simple, according to which we are at the mercy of the mind's determinate judgement. This becomes a key feature of the manifestation of our will as a function to pursue flourishing.

Another point worth noting is the association of beliefs with the Fundamental Principle. Beliefs as elements and functions of information are also influenced by, as well as influence, the pursuit of flourishing. The nihilist who sees no meaning in life, and is miserable because of this, flourishes by existing with this private truth, because to him living according to the truth is better than living in illusion. There are exceptional cases when people form or accept a belief independent of their intentional desire to do so. We form beliefs through functions of the mind, just as the mind can only understand things by the determination of a function, not by intentional deliberation to choose to understand something. We may reject to believe or embrace certain knowledge, or we may interpret information differently, but ultimately much of this is deterministic of relevant functions. Beliefs as features of information then become integral to actions as functions respective of informational input. Machinations and determination of the mind are central to states of well-being. Hence, there is a notable feature of the determination of well-being and mental functions corresponding to well-being that defy any deliberation or choice. The matter of reason and belief in the determination of ethics and morality, however, will feature in proceeding Chapters.

The Fundamental Principle entails self-interest in actions in terms of the effect of behaviour on states of well-being, this selfishness seemingly being antithetical to morality. If matters of morality and ethics are all about self-fulfilment, and if self-fulfilment is essentially all about how something is experienced, then it follows that we are egotistic, selfish creatures. The pursuit of self-interest, exemplified by *ethical egoism*, is not intrinsically wrong and is perhaps best understood in amoral, ethical terms as a function of actions.

However, there is a major difference between self-interest and selfishness, because self-interest as the ambition to flourish consists of many dimensions, factors, and conditions, whereas selfishness may commonly be one-dimensional and of unilateral ethical interest. For example, the desire for one's community to flourish at a cost to the self can be a form of self-interest, just as sacrifice of community for personal gain is moved by self-interest. Nonetheless, there is a distinction to be made between selfishness and selflessness.

Selflessness is traditionally a virtue, a benevolent force in ethics that can produce positive effects (of flourishing) for those around a selfless person. But the pursuit of virtue or acting in virtue as selflessness is fundamentally tied to the pursuit of flourishing, hence it is within the parameters of self-interest. I will explore at greater depth in later work how benevolence and interest in global well-being are, indeed, a virtue. For the present context, however, a basic illustration can suffice. An action will have consequences, which will affect states of affairs and thus people's states of being. An action causing suffering tends to reflect and propagate through people and circumstances; 'what goes around, comes around'. Actions also affect the state of self by conditioning thinking and the internal environment of prevailing attitudes and respective functions. In this sense, greater self-interest would be best achieved through accommodating positive internal and external environments, with the normative details to be discussed in later work.

Selfishness, in the sense of it being self-centred in one's narrow ambition, is then a meagre and lesser ambition of the pursuit of flourishing. Selfishness is a mere manifestation of the lack of mindfulness, of narrow vision, and of limited cognitive foresight. Selfishness, in terms of sustainable, grand self-interest, in comparison to what may be qualified as selflessness or a charitable character, is nothing more than foolishness or stupidity in the ambition of flourishing. Self-interest itself is not inherently wrong or morally abhorrent, or may even be considered entirely amoral, but how such ambition and intent is employed is a matter of moralising and judgement.

Defining morality in terms of ethics and human endeavour as fundamentally egotistic may suggest a counter-intuitive understanding of morality. If we are mere seekers of value and interest, does morality not become reducible to the relentless pragmatism of maximising value, with moral conviction and ideals being established parameters of well-being? I would argue this is the foundation of ethics and morality, according to which corresponding normativity and morality is structured. We are relentless value-maximisers and pursuers of ethical interest, but this can manifest itself with great diversity. Actions are a means to an end – a utility – in terms of the directive of the ethical interest to flourish. Actions achieve this end by affecting the external environment as states of affairs and the internal environment of consciousness. Actions are responses and functions of their author's categorical ambition to flourish. Hence, the purpose of actions is to affect the experience of living of the being causing and invoking an action. Actions are all about shaping our experience and quality of living.

It is easy to question the rationality of people. To act and function in pursuit of interest, however, does not necessarily mean we act in an appropriate rational and deliberative manner. Cognitive biases, from tendencies of simplification, loss-aversion, to the negativity bias, may be interpreted as degrading to our quality of rationality, further undermining the capacity for deliberative action and proper or effective morality. The subconscious mind and automatic, non-deliberative actions, such as those influenced by cognitive biases, seem to devastate the argument of the primacy of rationality. If we tend to act more in an impulsive and deterministic manner, with rationality having a lesser effect and being at the mercy of conditional influences of the functions of behaviour such that we have no real freedom in our actions and thoughts, then morality could seem to be reducible to nihilism or irrelevance as a study, as automatic, subconscious, and mechanical actions are primary. Embracing cognitive biases and rejecting a basic understanding of rationality, however, can give insight, forming a coherent and clear vision of the functional model of actions and goal-directive behaviour. By studying cognitive biases, one can understand more about the structured, mechanical nature of ethics and actions, with an illustrative example serving to bring together the above points of discussion.

The *negativity bias* emphasises worse elements in a situation by focusing attention to bad things. Media is a staunch example of this attribution in people's cognitive biases where news outlets profit more from people's tendency to see negativity rather than positivity, with comedians profiting from the latter, contingent on reaction to the former. Biases are not necessarily permanent without ways around them, yet they serve to exemplify the deterministic and functional nature of the mind and actions. Information available to judgement and complex functions of actions greatly condition the course of action. This little function of the negativity bias can shape worldviews, attitudes, and subsequently actions and their modelled structures of activity in terms of society. But while this may seem degrading to the sense of rationality, the negativity bias can be exemplified to serve a distinct function.

By paying attention to the bad we see more of what needs to be improved. This function can serve a purpose, while also becoming deficient and failing itself if inconsistent or incompatible with conditions of circumstance – becoming *corrupt*. In evolutionary terms of bodily and mental functions, there is a distinct qualification in the negativity bias where it has served to bring attention – highlight information – to the mind responsible for causing actions responding to the environment, even if unconsciously. Alternatively, where people may be subject to a positivity bias, they might reject valid negative elements of an object of concern. By losing positivity to negativity, sense of living – spirit – is perhaps worse off than it previously was, manifesting itself as a *loss-aversion bias* – a notion exemplifying, briefly, people's tendency to favour security and avoiding losses rather than the uncertainty of profiting even if profit promises greater sum gains. The processes of the Fundamental Principle can be interpreted as underlying biases in the functions of the mind as well.

The negativity bias, in tandem with the loss-aversion bias, highlight something integral to the human condition and our mental faculties. The information we receive and emphasise in actions tends to correspond to *functions*. We believe and act according to mechanisms, allowing to formulate a driving model of actions in terms of functions where being and activity are governed by the principle that we pursue well-being and ethical profit through our actions and functions. But to whatever degree, it is clear that there is a distinct and prominent functional nature in people's behaviour, applying to actions and the antecedent conditioning of an action in relation to mental functions such as beliefs.

Concerning the implications of cognitive biases, the features of emphasising negativity and loss serve as an indicator of a central function in the pursuit of well-being – security from, and aversion to, *suffering*, with suffering defined by *negative or loss of ethical interest*. Where there is flourishing, there will also be suffering as the lack of well-being. *Suffering* will be considered and defined in this project as the opposite of well-being and states of flourishing. Security from suffering, notably as aversion to physical and mental *pain*, is evidently, without further analysis, a key feature of the functions of behaviour and ethics. Much of this project will be dedicated to analysing the merit and utility of suffering and pain-aversion as security in well-being over gains in ethical interest. This notion in the functions of ethics will be remarked as a key term with the capitalised term *Fear*. Aversion to suffering and pain as security from loss in well-being – fear of uncertainty and pain – is the ethical function of *Fear*. Human behaviour is inherently defined by the pursuit of ethical gain – well-being. For example, behaviour is usually influenced and conditioned more by positive affirmation and reinforcement than by punishment, with certain exceptions. Fear is a restriction, a condition, a defence mechanism that is learnt through the experience of pain and suffering. Sometimes this is good, and sometimes not. However, it is exactly that – *conditional*, subservient to other core desires and goals.

In light of these related features of the fundamental will and function to flourish and pursue well-being, one can conclude the following version of the Fundamental Principle. The centrepiece of this project is this formal *Fundamental Principle of Living Beings and Actions – all living beings' actions and the dynamics of mental functions move in accordance with, and are determined by, the pursuit of the greatest or highest mode of well-being and flourishing, with the determination of mental functions subject to mental states and functions of the mind in accordance with relevant and available influence on the will; all actions are functions or contingencies of the will to flourish.*

Drawing on this Fundamental Principle and its association with spirit as awareness of states of being, the final, brutal, and most accurate test of any ethic and morality is simple: How does one feel and how does an action and its consequence make one feel? If an action and way of living is fulfilling, then it is fulfilling and suffices as well-being. But if one is dissatisfied, wants more, or an ambition is unfulfilling or instigates unsustainable behaviour, then a state of being is not fulfilled, which might manifest itself as a diminished state of well-being, yet not as an outright rejection of a flourishing state. Routine and habit offer distraction from questions that are seemingly irrelevant to the immediate concern of habit. It can, indeed, be a good thing to follow a direction of immediate occupation or default normativity, but there are notable limits to this focused vision and ambition. When our occupation and endeavour is unfulfilling and when we suffer, we begin to reflect, think, plan. It is good and fulfilling to pursue a focused function, yet sometimes this may lack purpose, vision, ambition, and dedication. This is where meditations on philosophy begin, the coherence of which can be found through a *Fundamental Principle* corresponding to all functions of actions and living. The implication of this Fundamental Principle as a groundwork in ethics and morality will be explored further in the rest of Section 1.

Chapter 2:

Logic and Reason of the Fundamental Principle

For all the virtues of modernity, we still struggle to understand morality, and it appears that our efforts render moral standards a misleading game of words. Relativity has sown confusion in actions, yet the functions of actions have succeeded nonetheless. Some may subscribe to subjectivity in simple terms of having no defining ground for particular actions, then act nonetheless. Some may consider morality as a mere restraint on desire, thereby failing to appreciate the presence of desire and intention in moral or immoral actions. Some may consider morality subjective in terms of incessant arbitration of sentiment and intuition in moral dispositions. On closer inspection, one cannot deny or overlook the major component sowing doubt in moral objectivity in terms of the failure of rationale. It may seem there is little-to-no sense or rational structure in the morality of actions. Most notably, David Hume's discourses on ethics and morality[3] are among the most prominent, especially in challenging objective morality in terms of the ascription of good and bad to facts and knowledge. We may say or think an action or thing is 'good', yet convention may seem to elude the definitive and structured reason for this mode of thinking and action. This Chapter will consider the matter of ascription of ethical values corresponding to moral evaluation, mainly by challenging Hume's *is-ought distinction* or *fact-value gap*, other implications of the *Naturalistic Fallacy*, as well as exploring the nature of *reason* and *logic* in actions and functions of the mind.

David Hume's arguments of the fact-value gap or is-ought distinction reciprocate conventional thought regarding the nature of conflicting and logically unclear attribution of good and bad in actions, mental states, and objects. On a brief note, an interpretation of Hume's argument holds that we can get facts about the world through the senses or through science, but moral values are not found in the same manner; moral values or 'oughts' are nothing like the facts observed. Rather, we attribute values to what we observe, with observations being fundamentally different in their essence to values. Such a thought will strike a chord with the sceptic and fit in with the view of subjective opinions on ethical values and moral rules.

A person may see incredible value and beauty in one thing, while another sees nothing of worth. One may think honesty is a good thing, while another person values blamelessness above all else; yet few can concretely account for why these convictions and actions occur. In a sense, Hume's critique of moral objectivity may be understood to claim that the world of facts is, as such, free of any values; the values are just our attitudes towards the facts and both faculties are mutually exclusive in reason or logic. This *fact-value gap* paradigm can be understood as a model of functions where rationality and sentiment (fact and value) are not functionally synchronised, with rationality eluding the function of value and sentiment.

In a simple illustration, one might try to explain why they like or enjoy something, or why they follow conventional manners of action or behaviour by social conditioning, yet not concretely and systematically formulate why they think and act the way they do. In short, there seems to be a divide and *desynchrony* between rationality and sentiment, manifesting itself in both directions as lack or excess of either rationality or sentiment. The fact-value gap is similar to Hume's Law of the *is-ought distinction*, which challenges moral objectivity by arguing that it is logically invalid to deduce an 'ought' from an 'is' statement – it is invalid to derive a conclusive moral evaluation (ought) from premises that are purely descriptive. The is-ought distinction exemplifies the same issue as the fact-value gap, but in a different manner, so that where there is an informational state as *is* (as being), an *ought* (a value claim of how this should be) is not clearly logically binding. As Hume wrote[4]:

> "In every system of morality, which I have hitherto met with, I have always remark'd, that the author proceeds for some time in the ordinary way of reasoning, and establishes the being of a God, or makes observations concerning human affairs; when of a sudden I am surpriz'd to find, that instead of the usual copulations of propositions, is, and is not, I meet with no proposition that is not connected with an ought, or an ought not. This change is imperceptible; but is, however, of the last consequence. For as this ought, or ought not, expresses some new relation or affirmation, 'tis necessary that it shou'd be observ'd and explain'd; and at the same time that a reason should be given, for what seems altogether inconceivable, how this new relation can be a deduction from others, which are entirely different from it. But as authors do not commonly use this precaution, I shall presume to recommend it to the readers; and am persuaded, that this small attention wou'd subvert all the vulgar systems of morality, and let us see, that the distinction of vice and virtue is not founded merely on the relations of objects, nor is perceiv'd by reason."

Why should the act of killing people be deemed wrong? Why ought one not kill? Why ought one to kill? To preserve social cohesion and stability, but then to what end? These questions have been known to lack coherence, yet many such discussions have been elusive to, as well as taken for granted, the fundamental function of actions to pursue well-being – the Fundamental Principle of Living Beings and Actions. This foundation of actions structures not only what forms actions take, but also, perhaps most importantly, *why* they occur at all. The strength of the argument of the Fundamental Principle is that its intuitive ease comes through empirical observation and practical wisdom of people's conduct. One can then know and understand that all functions, including morality as values and convictions guiding actions, stem from the ambition of pursuing well-being exemplified by and in actions themselves. Hence, the Fundamental Principle can provide coherence and structure to all matters of ethics and their manifestations as morality.

Ethics and morality serve as functions to guide actions and behaviour, encompassing values in terms of beliefs and convictions, as discussed in Chapter 1. So how do we form values? Does sentiment dictate values or does logic have a role? These questions are best answered with a practical evaluation. For example, how and why could a person form a value and belief that 'cats are evil'? A person who forms the value that 'cats are evil' is implicitly of the opinion that cats are in some way of an ethically negative interest, potentially harmful to one's well-being. In contrast, some may view it as irrational to consider cats evil, because cats can appear rather passive and harmless. But why might a person form such a conviction? For the sake of argument, one could consider that a past experience of a cat, such as a cat scratching the person during childhood, created a negative impression of the species, consequently forming a belief that cats are harmful. Impressions of fear, anxiety, and pain are influential on people's formation of values and beliefs contingent on something harmful as ethically negative. A value favouring aversion reacting to a source of suffering, such as an agitated cat, draws on action to avoid cats, therein protecting oneself from being scratched by a cat. Scratches cause harm and bleeding, which the body senses through a mental state of pain. Pain can then aid the body by triggering a contingent protective response and function, adapting to the experience of suffering caused by a specific external stimulus. In this case, the fear of cats is not wholly irrational, as it serves to protect a person's interests, with the reaction being an efficient mode of action compared to slower actions of extensive deliberation.

Cognitive biases are major features of the interpretation and formulation of values. For instance, the negativity bias can serve a function emphasising growth and improvement, even though any function can be influenced by a variety of factors and take on corrupted forms of action by undermining interests emphasised by the function (the bias) itself. The negativity bias can detract from well-being, yet its focus on aversion to pain can serve to guide actions in accordance with a value to protect oneself from a source of harm or to address it by relinquishing complacency. Focusing on the bad in the world, such as by watching the news and paying more attention to suffering, can highlight information concerning a danger and threat, although action can manifest itself in a less helpful manner. The values of seeing the bad can serve to bring attention to pain which can then be amended through action. In a similar fashion, the loss-aversion bias can serve to emphasise security in our desires and behaviour in terms of respective values and feelings favourable of security. By mediating risk-taking behaviour through the loss-aversion bias, in tandem with the negativity bias, endeavour and behaviour can manifest itself by a predominant tendency of secure and stable growth, rather than chaotic, uncertain growth of big-losses and big-gains. So we can see that values in tandem with observations can function in accordance with the pursuit of well-being.

The illustrations outlined should serve to highlight the functional nature of values in relation to observable information, in other words that values form contingent on facts. Hume's fact-value gap may argue that there is a rift or 'bridge' between the 'realm of facts' and the 'realm of values', yet we form values nonetheless, and rather coherently, on the basis of information relating to matters of well-being. One doesn't even need to provide a concrete anatomical or pathological account of how exactly the mind formulates values and 'ought' statements; it is sufficient to highlight the fact that values form contingent on information relevant to considerations of well-being, abiding functions of the mind to pursue well-being through and in actions.

One can challenge the idea that there are natural properties relevant to well-being in objects of interest. However, this is ultimately irrelevant, because it is clear that we ascribe values to facts relating to concerns of well-being. Essentially, values form contingent on facts through functions and relations of ethical interests of well-being, determined by one's rationale and general feelings of the self and one's state of living. We embrace information to formulate values in relation to our concerns for well-being. Clearly, values can be understood coherently and intuitively through the innate conceptual lens of the concern for well-being relating to awareness of circumstance. If we did not, one could speculate that actions would be incoherent in their purpose in relation to being – existing and moving – and environmental conditions. This, however, clearly isn't the case, as actions follow goal-directive behaviour.

Here it is imperative to explore the power of the functional implication of the Fundamental Principle. *Reason* in functions of value-formulation can be noted to accompany goal-directive behaviour contingent on the function or mechanism of the fundamental will to flourish. Ethical values and respective moral principles guiding behaviour are *thoughts*, principles of conduct *formulated* and *structured* in the mind. We strive for well-being; hence, we act by this mechanism invoking actions in the first place, consciously or not.

If a point of information becomes relevant to action, whether in terms of the complex cascade of deliberation or as a sensory stimulus triggering a reaction, then reason of the mind as thought and *structures of logic* take information into account of how to act or whether to act at all. If our thoughts and intuitions come to embrace the knowledge that something is harmful to us, then we act according to this information as a reaction or a deliberative action contingent on conscious or subconscious parameters of behaviour through values as codes of morality, experience, wisdom, and insight into well-being. If something is deemed good to us, then we pursue it; if something is sensed to be bad, then we avoid it or resolve it. The structure of reason in the model of value-formation is found contingent on the concern of well-being exemplified through the Fundamental Principle. If something is found to be worthy of virtue, then action will be reasonable in pursuing it for the good of well-being. Rational models of values and their reasoning can be coherently accounted for in terms of values' function to serve the interests of well-being, subsequently triggering relevant actions.

The facts we observe in the world inform us of our surroundings, from which our minds then formulate values and conditions of actions as their morality on how we can act to live in the best way possible with respect to the experienced environmental conditions. It can be demonstrated how and why values and parameters of morality form logically within systems of ethics structured in terms of the Fundamental Principle. If a course of action, habit, or manner of behaviour is deemed to nourish spirit with sensed well-being, then pursuing that positive state of being is logical in terms of the function to pursue well-being through action. Hence, moral statements and values can be, and are, logically bound to the facts we observe in the world, bridging observable facts and values synthesised in the mind. Therefore, subjectivity in moral values in terms of the division between facts and values, as noted with Hume's fact-value gap, is mistaken in its implication that morality and values cannot be found or structured coherently in terms of facts and reason. This challenge also applies to the closely-related Hume's Law of the is-ought distinction, such that prescriptive statements attach to descriptive statements through ethical and logical functions and relating interests of well-being. Deliberate actions use knowledge to condition and adjust functions of behaviour in accordance with the desire for well-being, tempered by, or appealing to, our sensations, perceptions, and feelings.

While a goal-directive model of behaviour in terms of the concern for well-being can provide a basic account of how values form contingent on facts, there are more complex nuances that have to be addressed. For one, confusion in morality and lack of logical structure in morality is evident in unconscious competing desires and respective narratives of goal-directive behaviour that we are not strictly aware of. We want to live well and we strive to act accordingly, even if what we sense as being good for us is known not to be good in the long-term. Indeed, it is relevant to note that subjects of logic and rationale, such as thoughts, are in their own right inherently amoral; thoughts only begin to have moral significance and judgement when relevant to information conditioning actions.

Thoughts themselves and facts can be amoral, yet in the context of actions and relevance to well-being they begin to carry a contingency of ethical value to the interest of well-being. The model of actions as functions of behaviour abiding the pursuit of ethical interest as well-being can be intuitive, coherent, and clear through mindful observation. Yet it may come across as odd that values form automatically and subconsciously in an almost *sub-logical* form, with reason simply manifesting its creations of logic in the shape of autonomous faculties of the mind not requiring incessant deliberation and thought in formulating at least some values. So while there are still many themes to discuss on the complex issue of moral subjectivity, one must first account for the functional nature of sentiments and feelings and their influence on ethical and moral dispositions.

How is the behaviour of emotions linked to the Fundamental Principle? Why do bodies have emotions? What functions do sentiments and feelings fulfil? Different emotions have different roles, but the basis of their function is the same – an evolutionary advantage tested by Nature to maximise flourishing relating to the ethics and morality of survival. Fear prevents us from carrying out dangerous actions to protect ourselves. Grief makes us learn from our mistakes. Hate pushes us to remove competition and other threats. Anger gives strength and vigour. Pleasure and happiness make us feel like we are flourishing, driving us to indulge them. Love makes us protect and bond with those we see as special. Compassion makes us contribute to the prosperity of a community. All these examples of sentiments can be associated with certain functions in service to the ambition to flourish through a variety of approaches and strategies. Sentiments can manifest and apply themselves in many ways, as both useful or damaging, yet this disparity does not negate the primary function of pursuing well-being, even if our judgements and values do end up failing us.

How then does our mind determine reaction and apply sentiment? Sentiments can serve evolutionary functions, with the structure of their functions formulated coherently through the determination of interests relevant to well-being. As with the example of the aggressive cat, one can exemplify the reason and logic behind the aversive sentiment as the fear of cats. For instance, a structure of logic or reason can be noted in patterns of behaviour averse to dangers contingent on sentiments and intuitions of fear and anxiety. By being cautious of a source of potential harm we can act more appropriately to secure the interest of well-being. Instincts have definitely served living creatures in terms of survival responding to environmental pressures shaping our state of living. Even though instincts are not necessarily deliberative in their functions, their functions still persist in sparking reactions and tempering actions by providing certain information and utilities of behaviour such as nervousness, anxiety, and stress.

Now, sentiments, emotions, and feelings are not a form of reason or logic in themselves. However, they do function in terms of structures of logic like deliberate actions but with respect to environmental stimuli prompting reactions. Just as actions are a tool of the body and mind used to achieve the primary interest of well-being through operations of the mind and reason, reactions operate in the same fashion. The difference in reactions and behaviour directly related to basic instincts is that they are operationally simpler, more direct, considering a narrower scope of information. Reactions can be logically structured just as deliberate actions, perhaps even more coherently in terms of goal-directive behaviour exemplifying an end in functions of instinct such as survival. Even though it is not obvious and intuitively or empirically clear, we can structure reactions and the projection of sentiment contingent on the functions of the body and mind pursuing well-being. So even though reactions might not be a form of reason or logic, their functional basis can be highlighted, albeit in arguably abstract terms, to flow in a reasoned and logical framework contingent on the function of the Fundamental Principle.

Setting aside the question of whether mental states have functional power in themselves, one can at the very least, in the present context, describe the functions of structures of reason that underlie reactions. Conscious mental states, such as emotions, might not have distinct power of their own to directly influence behaviour (see Section 4). However, conscious mental states can be instigated by functions of reason responding to stimuli producing the corresponding mental states and their conscious appearances. Emotions may simply be the products of the functions of reason and logic, being convenient summaries of mental states in terms of their constructs of the body's and brain's functions. While this theme will be discussed in greater depth in Section 4, it is sufficient to point out that regardless of the nature of emotions' and mental states' power in the determination of action, they nevertheless follow the function of the Fundamental Principle.

The divided functional spheres of reason and rationale can be classified in two levels: *base* and *high reason*. Base-reason is reason of the base functions of the mind, in particular those corresponding to emotional reactions and instincts. This form of reason may for the most part be reactionary and non-deliberative. For instance, the reasoning which exemplifies functions relating to instinct, such as the fear of cats because cats may cause harm, is a mechanism of reason responsible for ethical values corresponding to sentiments and basic reactions.

An issue with categorising a sphere of base-reason is that it might not be clear whether reason simply exemplifies why and how we act, or whether reason actually underlies processes of the mind corresponding to conscious experiences of emotions. Relevant points to consider are, firstly, that we are not always clear of the reasons and intentions behind actions, such as with impulsive reactions; and secondly, we may often appear to act according to conscious deliberation. However, intent can be distorted by neglected, buried, and unfelt sentiments, with actions being produced contingent on the functions of the mind producing an emotion that, while not consciously acknowledged, continues to exert subconscious influence on the determination of actions. The functions of reason underlying instincts, however, can also greatly influence deliberative reason by setting the agenda which deliberative reason and rationale serve or compliment, at times inadequately.

On the other hand, *higher* or *high-reason* is that of complex, computational, and analytic thought commonly attributed to deliberation and ascriptive of the convention of rationality, encompassing mathematical, scientific, and philosophical thought. Together, the faculties of reason form the *body or anatomy of reason – the psyche*, alternatively to be referred to as *all-reason*. While actions and the mind may operate through specific faculties and organs, actions and thoughts simultaneously engage multiple aspects of the body, mind, and psyche. For instance, philosophical thought may be of a functional primacy in accordance with high-reason, yet the purpose of such thought is in service of an ambition or agenda set by base-reason such as to pursue survival.

A question arises regarding the nature of the human condition. Are we rational? We certainly aren't fully deliberative creatures, and if we were wholly deliberative and rational, this would likely be behaviourally inefficient. After all, reactions can be much quicker and ultimately more functionally rewarding than slow, inefficient deliberative actions, with notable and clear cases of corrupted actions and reactions – that is, ethical functions that are inefficient, impaired, or broken, producing behaviour that cannot fulfil its goal.

That said, if reason can be demonstrated to underlie all functions, even if the products of functions, such as mental states, are not a form of, but functionally structured by, reason or logic, then perhaps we can be understood as functionally wholly rational, yet not deliberative. This work will consider all creatures to be behaviourally wholly rational in relation to a mechanical understanding of the mind and functions of the Fundamental Principle. Reason and degrees of rationality, even if reactive and unconscious, can be seen to underlie all functions of the body and mind. However, the diversity of reason's functions is extensive and can stem from, as well as follow, multiple functions of reason, higher or baser, at the same time within a single action. Accounting for the complexity of reason in actions is part of ethical insight and understanding that can structure coherent morality; doing so, however, is not simple and requires the study and analysis of a lot of information.

It is worth distinguishing between *reason* and *logic*. Reason can be shown in premises and sentences to correspond to certain functions. For instance, reasoning can be shown to underlie a model of actions such as: 'I did so because I wanted what is best for me'. In this single sentence, however, there are many points of information and constituencies of reason. Another form of reasoning can be illustrated numerically as '2+2=4.' While the nature of words and numbers may appear different, their essence as an *object or point of meaning* follows the same nature as the composition of meaning or information. The individual components forming a structure of *reason* will be referred to in the context of this project as *logic – the substance of reason.*

The distinction between reason and logic may seem arbitrary, yet this qualification will be central to the discussions of their nature in Section 4 looking at philosophy, metaphysics, and the structures of the mind, consciousness, reason, and logic. As a brief illustration, the nature of the term '2' can correspond to certain sensations and stimuli, with the *causal qualification* of a thought '2' residing in mechanical structures of the mind appealing to a *substance of logic* corresponding to the notion of '2' and correlating physical, non-abstract functional manifestations of said thought. These themes, however, only serve to provide a formal account of the systems of ethics that are not central to moral deliberation drawing on the certainty of the Fundamental Principle.

The main point of these detailed and complex arguments is simply that if the mind and body operate systematically, deterministically, and mechanically, then all functions must operate in a similar fashion. Even emotions and instinctive reactions must then operate mechanically. The Fundamental Principle can serve to illustrate a structure of all movement, intentional or reflexive. Concern for wellness, and the function to pursue well-being, provide a logical focal point for the structures of actions and reactions, with the latter being understood more in terms of the evolutionary development that enabled sustainable, non-deliberative movement of the body. If reason provides the resource for illustrating the structures of actions, then one can discuss the mechanisms of actions in terms of *reason,* even when reason is obscure and automatic. There is mechanical order in the functions of the mind and body, with actions and reactions usually being responses to respective stimuli. These causal categories and qualifications of stimuli that affect actions can be illustrated in terms of reason. Functions are utilities and services of, by, and for the Fundamental Principle, as all functions of the mind respective of actions and reactions are utilities for producing well-being.

The observation of a lion charging at a person is a form of fact, yet if an action or reaction is to be executed, then the observed fact becomes integral to conditioning respective movement. Reason can illustrate, note, and exemplify the processes of thinking and automatic functions of the mind corresponding to actions and reactions in terms of the grounding Fundamental Principle. The individual components of reason corresponding to a function, such as the individual features of a premise, are considered with the dedicated term *logic* – the equivalent of the substance of reason. Functions can be obscure in their logical structure, notably of an instinctive nature, and so it becomes helpful to distinguish between functional categories of reason – high and base.

While the mechanisms of functions do not operate in abstract terms of logic and reason, they *can* be outlined in terms of reason and logic. Just as the natural sciences may defer to mathematical constructs to describe natural phenomena and processes, the same can be done for the functions of living beings and actions in terms of reason and logic. Whether or not these are mere abstractions or concrete, actual, or *real* elements of the world is somewhat irrelevant to the functions themselves. Thus, the Fundamental Principle exemplifying functions of the psyche can also serve to illustrate logic and reason underlying and corresponding to the constructs of functions. Therefore, *reason* is considered as a tool for making sense of actions and their functions, hailing as a key feature of ethics and morality.

The anatomy of reason as part of the metaphysics of the mind is integral to greater understanding of ethics, beyond its simple conception in terms of actions and reactions and their moral evaluation or ethical implications, for systems of ethics and actions can only be understood through examining reactions and innate functions as part of deliberative actions. Discussions thus far should point to a most profound implication: ethics and morality are *functional* and *deterministic.* Systems and principles of ethics and morality are not pulled out of thin air and are not synthetic, purely abstract, subjective elements. Ethics and morality correspond to fundamentals of living things and their innate capacities, including those of the human condition. Reason can serve to exemplify functions of human behaviour. Where mathematics can serve to exemplify patterns noted in the natural sciences, logic provides the foundation of reason that exemplifies trends in behaviour and mental processing. All movement as action and reaction then becomes coherent in terms of a conceptual foundation in reference to the Fundamental Principle.

One comes to the essence of the argument: behaviour is not of an abstract structure, but is of an actual naturalistic, functional, and deterministic structure. Ethics and morality don't simply emerge randomly and selectively through incoherent and acausal mental states; actions and reactions follow a structured and deterministic function. Naturalists in ethics may attempt to ground morality and ethical judgements through a certain *telos* as a purpose of actions. The Fundamental Principle can serve to take this notion further to not only provide a complimentary *telos,* but also provide a conceptual fundamental to exemplify *all* behaviour and their ethical structure. According to the Fundamental Principle, ethics of actions to pursue well-being are not only a purpose; actions towards well-being are an actual *deterministic function*, are an *absolute directive of living and behaviour.* We have no choice in our actions and behaviour but to strive to fulfil the purpose actions serve – to pursue of well-being. The Fundamental Principle draws on, or leads to, a very strict account of actions as deterministic, functional, structured, and causal. Actions aren't intentional towards an end but are actual manifestations of an end or function invoking actions in the first place – the pursuit of well-being.

In short, where an appeal in ethics to teleology may be dismissed, the implications of the Fundamental Principle take the argument further to exemplify actions and reactions in terms of a functional essence of all movement of substance, whether of intent or not, such that there can only ever be a foundational function in any form of behaviour. All and any movement of substance as action and reaction can only ever by exemplified and made sense of in terms of their function as deterministic and non-deliberative.

This account of actions and systems of ethics may be appealing to evolutionary psychologists. First of all, it may provide an idea on the evolution of the first action and development of the faculties of reason, with the essence of reason being bound to qualifications of causal structures and respective processes of reason and the parallel substrate of logic (again, see Section 4). Second, if one is to understand actions, then that person must also account for the most natural and organic form of actions as reactions. If one is to account for actions, then that person must consider the essence of the first action, which could not be more than anything but a simple, non-deliberative movement that led to an evolved form of informed reaction.

On this note, it would be worth discussing some contextual matters of literature on ethics, especially those reflective of Hume's theories. For one, while some may assume the is-ought distinction, known as 'Hume's Law', denies any possibility of validly deriving an ought from an is, Hume's Law can be interpreted to claim that some moral judgements can be formed, but perhaps not purely logically without a given moral and ethical premise[5]. Hume's Law can be understood to mean that for a factual statement to be integral to a moral judgement, it requires (as part of a model of ethics) an ethical principle or assumption to be relevant or somewhat logically grounding[6]. Providing a relevant, credible, and concrete source for a moral judgement, however, has been notoriously difficult. Here is an example explored in the relevant literature[7]:

1. Torturing people for fun causes great suffering (factual premise).
2. It is wrong to cause great suffering (moral premise).
3. Therefore, torturing people for fun is wrong (moral conclusion).

Justifying and validating premise (2) is, or has been, difficult. Intuition and sentiment may dictate that the validity of statement (2) is correct, yet this validity is subjective to the circumstances of judgement and the character of each individual, hence lacks coherent and binding logical structure. By appealing to the Fundamental Principle, one can understand any moral premise in terms of its ethical features, and then formulate a logical claim derived through the function invoking the judgement in the first place. Any action or inaction is moved by a function to pursue positive states of being. To formulate a coherent and valid judgement corresponding to the function of a moral premise, such as the premise that 'it is wrong to cause great suffering', requires an understanding of what the moral premise does. According to the Fundamental Principle, moral standards as codes of conduct are parameters of actions guiding endeavour towards satisfaction of the function to pursue positive ethical interest through actions. A moral premise that 'it is wrong to cause great suffering' is a contingency element of behaviour serving the function that pursues well-being. By considering and testing whether causing people great suffering evokes states of well-being can then lead to rigid and coherent structuring of ethics in terms of behaviour's effects on states of being. Ethical terms composing moral statements and claims correspond to systems of ethics in terms of functions beholden to a model of goal-directive behaviour. All behaviour is bound to its functional structure exemplified by the Fundamental Principle; thus, if behaviour is to be conditioned with logical structures guiding and serving the functions of actions, then moral premises, norms, and standards arise to serve deliberation on competing interests and desires.

If goal-directive behaviour can serve to distinguish between what actions we should perform towards a conceived end, with the grand ambition of all behaviour being that of the pursuit of well-being, then a logical structure of morality can be implemented and found in terms of the Fundamental Principle. If causing people suffering does not serve one's own ends of nurturing states of well-being, then it is logical (and mechanically and functionally consistent) that one wouldn't and ought not to torture people. If logic in statements and premises is a measure or qualification of consistency, then it is logical that morally evaluating behaviour can give structure to morality. For moral premises such as (2) to be logical and relevant, one needs to subject the claim to a test of whether a mode of behaviour will produce well-being.

One needs a binding ethical premise to logically form a valid moral judgement. There needs to be a point of reference for a logical conclusion of a moral judgement. If moral judgements are guides and recommendations for actions, then the Fundamental Principle is the necessary point of reference. Goal-directive behaviour is integral to the functions that enable actions. For instance, government policy can be a rather straightforward manifestation of goal-directive behaviour: the agenda sets the precedence for policy. Morality concerning individual actions, however, does not appear to be of such clear agenda and goals. The nature of actions is to pursue well-being. Therefore, morality's agenda is to pursue well-being. The formal structure of the functional argument can be illustrated as bellow:

1. Of the foundation of ethics:
    i. Functions (mechanisms) of the psyche give cause for behaviour.
    ii. Behaviour corresponds to a function.
    iii. Goals are functions of behaviour.
    iv. Goals correspond to actuated and enabling functions.
    v. Active functions are states of being – of existing movement.
    vi. Goals are functions of states of being.
    vii. States of being require effective and sustainable functions.
    viii. Effective functions correspond to behaviour enabling and sustaining states of being.
    ix. Functional states of being require wellness (as effectiveness) of their functions.
    x. Therefore, behaviour corresponds to functions striving for well-being.

2. Of the systems of moralising:
   i.   Morality is a guide or recommendation for action (how one ought to act).
   ii. If (1), then actions strive for well-being.
   iii. If (i) and (ii), then the morality of actions concerns goals of well-being.
   iv. Therefore, morality serves as guidance for achieving well-being.

Without the Fundamental Principle, logical moral premises seem obscure and counter-intuitive. According to the Fundamental Principle, illogical moral premises seem impossible and counter-intuitive, as all behaviour can be exemplified in terms of ethical interest in well-being. There is always a reason explaining people's behaviour and why someone does what he or she does. As for the nature of intuitions determining morality, this matter will be reserved for the following Chapter. For now, one can conclude that moral knowledge is possible as premises, claims, thoughts, and intuitions concerning values in mental states and behaviour pursuing well-being. All mechanisms of the mind, from thoughts to the processes invoking mental states of sentiment, are functions of logic and reason. This functional and mechanical account of behaviour and mental processing can describe morality and ethics as part of behaviour in a logical structure grounded on the essence of behaviour and movement as the pursuit of well-being and the continuity of being. Morality has the functional role of guiding behaviour and actions, hence any moral value claim of *ought* or *ought not* is a logical function concerning well-being. Values can be derived from, or ascribed to, facts because any knowledge relevant to the concern of well-being becomes *moral knowledge* as *practical insight* and *ethical wisdom* on that which makes us flourish and live in fulfilled spirit. Since all actions and behaviour are a mechanism of the pursuit of well-being, then it is logical to consider knowledge as an element influencing functions of the mind corresponding to ethical interests of well-being, i.e. values and attitudes. Because actions and their mediation through thought and morality are concerned with the pursuit of well-being, formulating the logic of actions in terms of well-being gives moral claims and premises a coherent and valid logical structure. Therefore, morality can have meaning and a logical structure in terms of the Fundamental Principle.

Chapter 3:

Meaning in Ethics and Morality

Moral premises are meaningful as logical constructs and functions describing the desire for well-being. Moral knowledge is objective and coherent as wisdom in terms of what affects our quality of life. Since morality can be logically structured through functions corresponding to deterministic behaviour in line with the Fundamental Principle, then 'right and wrong' and 'good or bad' in ethics and morality might be meaningful and definable terms. This Chapter will establish the meaning of key terms for ethical and moral discourse, as well as give further insight into the systems of ethics and the nature of states of well-being.

Firstly, it would help to settle a linguistic dichotomy in ascribing meaning to moral terms by addressing George Edward Moore's *open question argument* or *Naturalistic Fallacy*. Briefly, the argument maintains that moral properties, such as of goodness, cannot be ascribed to natural properties or to an 'ought' statement or claim[8]. The argument draws on an analytic paradox where equating something with 'goodness', such as 'flourishing is good', would be suggest a tautology such that the contextual moral premise becomes 'good is good' or 'flourishing is flourishing'. It is not clear that a moral property 'x' (e.g. well-being) is self-evidently the way it is, in other words for well-being to be good. Essentially, without a logically grounding principle, it is not clear how anything is self-evidently logically good, as per the convention of moral scepticism and subjectivity. Consequently, it seems that moral claims, such as 'well-being is good', are open to further questioning and are inconclusive.

There are a number of responses to the Naturalistic Fallacy, with the Fundamental Principle offering another area of insight. All words and sentences are functions with their own logical qualifications – that is, meaning. Words, like *well-being* and *goodness,* have their own meaning and influence on thought. Every word and premise has contextual meaning through respective functions of logic and information. Every word and sentence denotes and exemplifies certain meaning. 'Well-being is good' is not a tautological claim but a very contextual one with its own functions of meaning. Words can mean different things in different contexts to postulate a certain claim or premise, to structure unitary meaning in a sentence. Yet each individual word would usually have its own meaning, regardless of whether the concept exemplified by a word is complex or simple.

The word 'good' generally means or is suggestive of *positivity*. If someone says certain behaviour is *good,* he or she means to show approval. Similarly, one can have a positive undertone when saying to a dog: 'bad boy!' to highlight positivity in naughty but desirable behaviour, for example if it's amusing. Then we also use the term *bad* to describe negative and perhaps undesirable states, such as 'a bad day' being a *day* shrouded with certain negativity, or 'bad dog!' being an expression of disapproval. In this sense, the word *good* has contextual, fluid meaning. In contrast, the word *well-being* can have a synonym or variant equivalent to *flourishing*, yet it is a rigid concept. It serves to exemplify a certain meaning corresponding to a sense of *well-being*, even though that sense can correspond to different sensations. In the context of the premise 'well-being is good', the terms *well-being* and *good* serve different functions. They are not analytically equivalent.

A critic may respond by arguing that language can be subjective in meaning, but this is ultimately arbitrary because meaning, no matter how it is presented, is singular and unipolar in its logical qualification. The meaning of something single as '1' or 'one' is the same despite its numerical or grammatical appearance. Language can be rigid and structured through meaning, otherwise if meaning was fluid and wholly subjective, then no meaning, language, discourse, or knowledge would be possible. But while at least an appearance of knowledge and meaning persists, it is sufficient to dismiss an argument that difference in language and terminology accounts for the validity of the premise '*x* is good'. Consequently, it becomes a matter of defining morality respective of intuition and logical structure to establish the meaning of its key terms.

Practical insight dictates that matters of well-being are not arbitrary. Our actions adapt to different experiences and impressions. There is a clear distinction in the mind between pleasure and pain, between what is good and bad for our state of being. Differentiating between the quality of being (or life) as good or bad serves a meaningful function to ascribe positivity and negativity, regulating behaviour in terms of ethical interest (to flourish). The claim 'well-being is good' serves to moralise *well-being* – a phenomenon of being and living – by highlighting its positivity. Well-being on its own, like any thought, is amoral until it becomes relevant to the concerns of the ethical interest to pursue well-being. In this context, then, functions qualify ethical interests by indicating positivity or negativity. But where the claim 'well-being is good' is not tautological, as the function of each individual term is contextually different, it is *axiomatic*. To our most basic intuitions, as exemplified by behaviour and actions, even if faulty and corrupt, everything is of practical concern for ethical interest. We know well-being to be *good* because this is the goal and function of actions and behaviour in the first place.

Moore's argument is right in its implication that a systemic ethical claim ascriptive of goodness would be axiomatic and intuitive, yet achieving this point of intuitive familiarity and logical coherence is subject to greater testing and experimentation. Where *well-being* is a central ethical notion as part of the function of ethics and morality, its constituent elements, such as particular experiences and specific behaviour as actions, can be subject to greater validation in terms of negativity or positivity in states of being.

Moral principles, claims, attitudes, or propositions relate to our outlooks on standards of flourishing. Considering flourishing as a product and premise of actions can give meaning to moral discourse, which is henceforth reducible to discussions on what course of action, what attitudes, what principles, and what sort of behaviour produce flourishing within a set of conditions. If we are wrong, we suffer because of developments in the world not in our favour. Memory, experience, *a posteriori* knowledge (knowledge from experience), and trial-and-error methods of learning are extremely relevant to considerations of morality as guidelines for well-being. The quality or property of goodness arises with us engaging with the world, whereby considerations of what actions fulfil the greatest promise of our fundamental will to flourish have significant context and meaning. The property of goodness arises from our engagement with the world in a meaningful way that serves as a beacon guiding our actions. The conscious mind devises morality and prescribes it to matters of Nature to differentiate greater and lesser flourishing, something that becomes natural to us as part of a natural system of our being. We give value, meaning, and reality to our own sense of piety, but piety of Nature is amoral until conscious life looks inward to give piety use – a utility. Goodness and moral language is not strictly a *property* of Nature, but a *contingency* feature of living beings' activity and function giving substance to moral properties. This process is part of the function of ethics and morality bound in a logical structure rooted in the Fundamental Principle.

The qualification of states of being and the actions that affect them is a logical function contingent on the fundamental interest of well-being. To say that 'well-being is good' is to qualify *goodness* of being as *good*, yet not to say the being is itself *good*. There is clear potential for differentiation in states of being and actions contingent on a function to produce positive states of being. Quality of life can be good or bad, but quality of life itself is an amoral object of meaning until a relevant function is employed. Evaluation is integral to moralising, with different functions suggesting and employing different meanings. Moral language and discourse is ascriptive of functions and behaviour that necessarily serve the pursuit of flourishing, carrying specific contextual meaning in terms of the logic that cause reflection on behaviour and state of being. Therefore, Moore's Naturalistic Fallacy is mistaken, because it misconceives ethics (without a grounding element of logic in respect of the Fundamental Principle exemplifying all behaviour) and the nature of moral discourse.

One may be able to morally define, distinguish, and qualify behaviour, actions, and states of being. As mentioned already, *good* and *goodness* serve to denote positivity. Positivity in actions, in terms of the Fundamental Principle, would be positivity of a function and action – what generates and qualifies as *well-being*. To claim that something is *moral*, as opposed to *immoral*, in the context of qualifying actions, is to approve of certain behaviour and actions. Since actions are functions affecting states of being, and morality is tasked with guiding actions towards the goal of *well-being* – a state of good living, of positive ethical interest – then positive values in ethics and morality are those that lead to flourishing. Therefore, one can conclude that *good* in ethics and moral statements has a meaning corresponding to the positive effect on that which produces flourishing and positive being. Whether it is an attitude, principle, ethic, or action that is subject to moral evaluation, goodness indicates the positivity of a function, feature, or utility corresponding to the pursuit of flourishing.

With this qualification of *goodness* comes a dilemma, because this definition implies that every ethic is technically good. Since *good* is equivalent to *flourishing*, and every action produces some degree of well-being in accordance with the Fundamental Principle, then technically every action is good. One might claim that murder is bad, yet murder might serve the interests of the person carrying out the murder. To an external arbiter and judge, the survival of one creature at a cost to another is one creature surviving nonetheless; if survival is the end goal, then something succeeds and may be good. Morality may seem arbitrary because well-being is greatly conditional on individual circumstance, with every action serving the conditional end of nurturing states of well-being. Base and high faculties of reason may enforce a mode of conduct against or in favour of greater interest through determination of the body and multidimensional environmental and mental influences. But no action can occur without a contingent function enabling it and without a certain goal or service of the function, intentional or not. Every action corresponds to a state of being with the function of striving for well-being. So, by definition and practical insight, every action is one that pursues flourishing and produces well-being in various degrees, meaning that every action is *technically* good.

While every action produces a degree of flourishing, it is also the function of behaviour, as part of the nature of the pursuit of flourishing, to pursue the *greater or highest* form of well-being. We don't simply strive for something; we seek to maximise ethical interest in particular circumstances. Perceptions, judgements, and ambitions corresponding to greater interests, however, are subject to qualification and conditioning beyond only deliberation and mindful 'rational' control. It is clear that we do distinguish between degrees of well-being, facilitating the essence of morality and trends in behaviour. There is a functional reason why we prefer certain conduct to another. Consideration of goodness in ethics and morality can be qualified in terms of effective and sustainable well-being, of a comparatively greater or higher good. The normative implications of this formulation of good actions are multiple and significant, setting the tone for key concepts and core thoughts of a philosophy respective of the Fundamental Principle. The point that all people strive for what their determination in relation to the fundamental will deems to be greater flourishing is valid and will serve as a core principle in ethical discourse.

Subjectivity of morality is clearly observable, but it is a superficial reality that serves to outline the different modes of development of people and measures of well-being. Under different conditions, circumstances, and different qualities of character, certain moral principles may have greater weight than others. It may be difficult to definitively conclude an absolute moral principle or truth of well-being, but not impossible. A variety and richness of piety means the liberty of values producing flourishing in different contexts can develop moral understanding and corresponding standards and principles.

Furthermore, understanding that people pursue what they think is best for them is imperative to understanding people and can facilitate a variety of traditional virtues such as empathy, acceptance, tolerance, and wisdom. In the whole mess of moral disparity thought of as subjectivity, yet actually a matter of complex theorising and intuition on morality largely distorted by base-reason lacking sophistication and discipline, objective moral claims can be found, developing and improving our understanding of ethics. But in all the *good* we conceive and live by, a reigning supreme moral truth of *the Highest Good – Summum Bonum –* can be found, which will be central to this project's interpretation of ethics and morality.

While everything is a degree of well-being, there are degrees of qualification and differentiation between greater and lesser fulfilment, known foremost through practical ethical wisdom. Since we all pursue the greatest well-being and satisfaction of spirit, then we strive for the *Highest Good* of well-being, even though it is conditional and circumstantial in relation to a variety of contributing factors affecting states of being in a given environment.

There are definitive answers to questions of well-being, for any sense of well-being is relevant to life experiencing flourishing. The Highest Good is the paragon of fulfilment and flourishing, setting conditions for *Natural Law* and *moral law* of the prospects, functions, mechanisms, rules, and principles of flourishing.

An example of Natural Law and moral law, which I will analyse in more depth later on, is that of a self-consuming, unsustainable mode of morality, say that of the addiction of a hedonist. Morality in addiction destroying the self will eventually consume its moral agent, whereby a sustainable morality, that which does not exceed consumption of pleasure into derogation, will continue and be more sustainable than self-consumption in addiction. Some trends and rules persist in the human ambition to flourish, as is noticeable in larger scales of ethical dynamics and functions through society, as with the fall of empires and the rise of civilisations. These are the basic definitions of Natural Laws and moral laws. If the function of actions strives for well-being as effective, sustainable, and rewarding movement and being, then there are conditions relevant to greater well-being. These qualifications, however, must consider both reason, such as estimation of sum goodness in relation to, for example, criteria of continuity and sum pleasure over a lifetime, and the arbitration of *spirit* corresponding to how something *feels*.

The next step is the definition of *bad*. I could just leave the definition of bad as 'the opposite of good; actions that do not evoke the greatest flourishing', but it's not as simple as that. If I attempt to define *bad* as I did with *good*, then it would hold the meaning (within ethics) of actions that are negative, which do not create the greatest flourishing. However, there is far more to it than this. The Fundamental Principle is another objection to our freewill, because our beliefs concerning flourishing create ethics and contingent moralities that are believed to be the most fulfilling in certain situations and environments. For example, a starving child in a ghetto will adopt the ethic of doing anything he can to get food, and this ethic would be regulated by his innate foundational belief of acting based on instinct and survival, then further conditioned by the environment of his habitat and his experiences. This notion, as well as the implications of the subconscious structures of logic as those of base-reason, demonstrate that our ideas on the greatest flourishing are *determined* to be what they are, just as our actions are determined, implying we are actually determined to pursue a way of flourishing that is logically and intuitively most superior and promising in our minds.

In other words, I am claiming that when people know what is *good*, they will live by it, but only if they genuinely conceive this *good* in thought and intuition and if it is greater than any other known *good*. Who are we to say that stealing is wrong to a starving victim of poverty? Those unfamiliar with experiences of grave suffering likely have insufficient insight to say otherwise, because they don't know what it may have been like to truly starve because of faults not necessarily one's own. This thought creates a problem for the definition of *bad*, because there is no straightforward way to argue that an individual's attitude and his or her values are negative to well-being since that view is in place for a logical reason, implying it is to a degree good for the individual.

An individual's values and principles are what he or she has come to understand and sense to be a viable degree of flourishing. This is relatively similar to the criticisms mentioned with the attempt to define *good* with respect to the arbitrary qualification of degrees of goodness, and the response is similar – there may be a view on flourishing that is greater, yet it is a matter of establishing its nature. The issue with weighing the moral quality of wrongful values and actions is that they are varying degrees of lesser good. At what point does a lesser good become tolerable, acceptable, or compatible with the Highest Good? This question of evaluating what is morally bad is a matter of compatible values, those that can comply with parameters of producing positive ethical interest.

The greatest flourishing does not necessarily mean that acts of lesser moral quality are *wrong* if they form acceptable and compatible moral standards with positive ethical influences. This then becomes a matter of practical and normative ethics rather than of metaethics, it becomes a matter of *justice* and *righteousness*. But it can be argued now that the greatest flourishing does not necessarily negate greater flourishing in relation to other morality, especially considering that conflict could arise if the greatest flourishing disallows other good flourishing, resulting in considerable suffering, thus putting that particular notion of the greatest flourishing under scrutiny. This is an issue of tolerance.

To conclude the nature of morally bad actions, a *bad action* can be primarily considered in terms of that which produces lesser well-being and not the greatest well-being in respective conditions and circumstances of actions and being. To qualify a measure between good and bad on a spectrum of well-being is the task of normative ethics, and while this may be challenging, it is not impossible. *Bad* in morality suffices as a term qualifying lesser ethical interest, yet its attribution and use should be done cautiously and mindfully.

Morality always has developed and always will have to develop as the environment changes; morality has to *adapt*. Our moral reasoning has to adapt along conditioning of the body and mind. Nothing is inherently absolutely evil – everything is a degree of good. Where an action is destructive to others, it serves a purpose to the author of the action, even if not fulfilling of the culprit's greater interests. Where an object exerts force negative to living beings' interests, the object is amoral until logic provides an appropriate function. Ascription of evil itself may serve a constructive purpose in the pursuit of wellness. What is motionless and has no power is deemed amoral. That which destroys serves an end, especially if guided by intent. What was right before is uttered wrong another time. The value of the Highest Good changes with Nature, which shifts the quality, value, weight, and power of piety. The determination of what ethic or moral practice is right or wrong is set by the Natural Laws weighing in on the conditions a living being faces.

Ultimately, it is up to Nature to construct what is good or bad through its organic and deterministic function in accordance with our influence on the world, and all we can really do is act in our best judgement to identify the boundaries of good. At times, these judgements can come easily through dedicated study and pursuit of wisdom and insight; at other times, constructive moral effect and endeavour is too constricted because of the lack of available information, and greater effort becomes required for even the slightest progress. However, it is premature for me to study the Natural Laws and their minor forms as moral laws, yet it's important to have noted their relevance in ethics.

Here it would be wise to reflect on why exactly morality has been subjective. If goodness were a mere matter of well-being, and well-being did correspond to specific functions, then wouldn't it be clear and intuitive what the Highest Good of flourishing is? Morality would be clearer in terms of goal-directive behaviour, but the convention of behaviour in terms of any goal-directive behaviour enabling action through a corresponding function is multipolar, complicated, and distorted. There are many goals and many forms of well-being, and all of them are intuitive when sensed. All morality seems to strive for well-being, but this manifests itself differently. The main perpetrator of this distortion can be understood as part of confused intuition and goal-directive behaviour respective of the base faculties. We may consider survival to be the ultimate end, yet there are immeasurable influences factoring into the success of survival and continuity. Furthermore, quality of living is not defined by life for life's sake, but by a life rich in good spirit. A certain function may enable a state of being, yet this is only a partial fulfilment lacking satisfaction. Instinct can cause us to act in many ways and generate many narrow points of morality valuing pleasure or continuity, peace or violence, power or joy, family or wealth, and so on. But often these are only partial elements contributing to a whole experience of living and its quality.

There are many forms of well-being, with some more appropriate to certain conditions. The base faculties of instinct and contingent functions of the body and mind have profoundly influenced behaviour since the birth of human nature. But as times change, so do the circumstances of our environment. Instinct only has a partial and conditional influence on the directives of our states of being. Where instincts correspond to many different areas of life and push behaviour and desire in many directions, the state of well-being will be muddled, distorted, confused, and *desynchronised*. High-reason as mindful thought can only do so much to fulfil desires and guide actions, for without the foundation of fulfilment in terms of emotion and the anatomy of base-reason, living by pure rationale without any spirit, is not a life worth living, as this is a life deprived of meaningful living, existence without *sense* of being. But with all intuitions of well-being, especially those restricted in terms of base faculties, there might not be a unifying intuition with no 'greatest' or 'highest' directive of well-being. The pursuit of well-being is built on desire. All desires are derivative of the desire for well-being. We appease this desire in many ways, but only some satisfaction is truly satisfying. This is the purpose of morality, complicated and seemingly subjective where we don't know what we want – where values, interests, desires, and information compete – and where the fulfilment of desires is habitual and misleading. Morality satisfies the main desire; morality is the order of desire.

Nothing is inherently evil; everything is a degree of good. Thus, the moral is of the most promising good, of the quality that is most useful to us. Structuring the systems of intuitions into a coherent ethic, however, is a monumental task of normative ethics, studying many aspects and manifestations of intuitions and senses of being and well-being, including influences on states of being and well-being.

On this note, one comes to recognise the troubling aspect of considering well-being as the defining feature of ethics and morality. If morality is qualified by the sum of mental states, whether emotions or intuitions, noted with the concept of *spirit*, then isn't morality ultimately subjective nonetheless? Everybody senses and experiences their own degrees and forms of well-being respective of individual circumstances and conditions of living. Then isn't moralising experience of well-being reducible to a principle of 'to each his own'? The evident disparity and wealth of narrow impressions of well-being, such as with intuitions grounded in the base faculties, serves to highlight the matter at hand. It seems that defining morality in qualitative intuitions and sensations, which are ultimately subjective to individual conscious awareness, doesn't resolve much. Grounding objectivity in morality through sense of flourishing and well-being, inherently bound to sensation, perception, sentiment, and intuition, may be regarded as a spoiled effort. This metaethical dissatisfaction is an example of the normative issue comparable to the subjectivity of valuing and qualifying different pleasures – how can we argue that one pleasure is morally better than another?

Binding morality to the intuitions of sentiments and emotions can leave gaps in reasoning and reduce discourse to exchange of biased opinion. However, a grounded substance of reason forms the foundation of sensible, less-abstract intuition. Furthermore, intuitions that correspond to functions of the mind's anatomy have their universal properties in ethics. We know through awareness of our state of being when we are suffering or flourishing, when we are in pain or satisfied. However, if morality and well-being are based on the determination of spirit bound only to emotion and instinct, then morality will lose its objectivity.

The unique capacity of self-awareness and mindfulness in humanity grants us the affirmative intuition of awareness of self which qualifies degrees of flourishing and suffering. The nature of reason in mankind, formed of two distinct faculties, gives us a dimension of flourishing distinct to that of any base creature only capable of behaviour and satisfaction through instinct. Mankind has the capacity for base fulfilment *and* higher fulfilment. The latter of higher pleasures is not intended as mere elitism in pleasure or satisfaction of quasi-intellectual tastes. The higher pleasures exemplified are discernible in their relation to the spirit of humanity that is of greater complexity and sophistication than a creature bound to its base condition.

There is something more than satisfaction, contentment, and happiness. For instance, the capacity of people to be in a state of inner peace, surpassing the sphere of narrow satisfaction of base faculties, is an example of other imperatives for people's fulfilment. This illustration is not intended to argue that inner peace is the Highest Good, but it does serve as an example that there are spheres of fulfilment in people that surpass conflicting fulfilments of spirit bound to lonesome instincts. The relation between high-reason and base-reason, particularly in terms of goal-directive behaviour, is central to moral and normative deliberation. Nonetheless, addressing the issue of objective morality in terms of the qualification of sensation is not a simple argument.

Throughout this work I will build towards an understanding of reason and spirit that is based on more than base qualifications of sensed fulfilment in terms of emotion and instinct, but it is not blind rationale without spirit or of guilt-ridden perceived 'higher' pleasures. The complex nature of the human psyche of both baser and higher faculties inherits in us all a capacity of spirit to flourish beyond base and high pleasures and modes of fulfilment. True fulfilment comes in liberty of spirit satisfied in all that it finds good – in balance of reason and our desires and goals.

Pain is a primary example of a fundamental intuition of the human condition, serving to exemplify the universals of moral intuition contingent on the pursuit of wellness. Flourishing may intuitively qualify itself as the absence of suffering or as fulfilment greater than the sense of pain. However, the human psyche is more complex than simplistic and narrow intuitions in respect of unilateral base fulfilment. Our inherent capacities of high-reason, even if only immature and lacking wisdom and insight, mediate desires and influence fulfilment through their channels of reason secondary to base faculties. Being moved by constant craving and desire, pursuing ambition that does not alleviate the root of suffering, such as with blind and heedless pursuit of social status, power, and luxury for the sake of wanting more and more to evade insecurity and weakness, always leaves a person ultimately dissatisfied and limited in virtue of character, starving the spirit of greater potential. By craving things we cannot have, by pursuing things we can never achieve, by wanting more than we need, desire loses clarity and functional purpose, leading to dissatisfaction as corrupt functions of intuition.

Dissatisfaction is the spirit's and psyche's mode of invoking intuition to tell us that something is wrong, that we are not doing well. All dissatisfaction and frustration because of a lack of sensed well-being always has two dimensions of reason:

higher and baser. But as with pain, frustration also serves as a universal in moral intuition to indicate states of being. This will become much clearer in retrospect of my extensive analysis of moral sense bound to fear of pain, suffering, and death and sensed fulfilment qualified by base faculties lacking harmony with high-reason. In short, human intuition and many phenomena of mental states provide sufficient ground for objective universals for moral consideration concerning the quality of flourishing and well-being. Intuitions are built on a foundation that can be sensibly and coherently described through reason and accounted for through metaphysics. All functions of behaviour, including behaviour of thought, are structured through reason. Therefore, intuitions can be structured in terms of reason as well. After all, without concrete intuition of directing an action there can be no action or ambition to act; there can be no effect of an action without an antecedent catalyst to a cause.

Intuitions of good and bad are part of the human condition and part of nature. Any assignment of language to mental states, thoughts, and intuitions is not without a concrete aspect in Nature associated with the substance of logic moving reason and the mind. Intuition is natural and part of Nature, not a mere abstraction devoid of a reality creating it. Even if we cannot feel or experience people's state of being, if reciprocal functions of intuitions are invoked, such as through empathy, we can appreciate similar experiences, which is meaningful in moral context.

To put things into perspective, all intuitions and thoughts serve a purpose and are spurred by a designated consideration and class of flourishing. The intuition of hunger serves the purpose of alleviating hunger and sustain living, fully consistent within a paradigm of reason pertaining to survival and aversion of pain. All intuition and reason can be traced to an original catalyst for particular actions correspond- ing to a framework of normative guidance. The Fundamental Principle exempli- fies a fundamental will driving and constituting behaviour and actions in pursuit of conditional well-being. The fundamental will then operates within a framework of normative guidance through set objectives and goals of fundamentals guiding inter- ests – through an *ethos* constituting the framework of the will and the dynamics and structures of ethics, morality, and the will. Intuitions and reason are all bound to a fundamental of ethics and morality consistent with a specific ethos. Intuitions and actions in a framework of ethics are *structured* in accordance with an ethical *system*. I will dedicate later work to exploring the prevalence of a common operational ethos – an ethos of aversion to pain and suffering through fear. Yet, for now, it is important to note that intuitions can be understood and structured in a framework of a corre- sponding ethos as a core systemic directive, e.g. of aversion to pain and suffering.

All intuitions and reason can be considered and analysed in a framework of a corresponding ethos. If ethics can be systematically accounted for and structured, such as with reflection on actions and corresponding reasons for acting, if one can form a coherent structure of core variables and influences in goal-directive behav- iour, then intuitions can be moralised. Well-being as the sum of mental states in relation to spirit may only be finally qualified in an individual subjective sense, yet the mechanisms that enable these states can be structured by appealing to their func- tional logic and reason. In any instance of goal-directive behaviour, both the goal and the way of achieving that goal and satisfying the desire can be evaluated. A goal and desire can be examined to see if it is worth pursuing, if it will lead to something good, by looking at the antecedent reasons for the desired end and the desire itself. One simply has to keep asking the 'why' question to understand why a person is behaving the way he or she is. Why do you want what you want? What do you want to achieve? Why do you think it will make you feel better? Then, the directive of pursuing a desire through certain behaviour and corresponding values can be evaluated and moralised. The nature of bad habits that one wants to get rid of is a perfect and straightforward example for the case being argued.

The essence of the response to the subjectivity of values and moral language in terms of the qualification of spirit through intuition of well-being is that these experiences are structured and subject to conditioning by Natural Law. Aversion to pain – Fear – can be defined as a core directive of ethics and the directive to flourish. There is certain behaviour that is universal to the human condition. Our psyche is malleable and we are adaptive, yet some fundamentals do not change, notably those of our experience of relief and liberty of spirit. At the core of all intuitions one can structure a model of ethics through a respective ethos. Then, through extensive study and reflection we can empirically observe which behaviour is sustainable and which isn't. This, along with sincere and mindful self-reflection, can provide the necessary criteria of evaluation to form coherent and valid judgements based on intuitions.

As an illustration, the self-destructive habit of an addict may not be sustainable, therefore thought to be wrong. However, the addict may feel that he or she is indeed flourishing. Yet the cause of addiction is often veiled, of a state of being that a person cannot live without synthetic alteration of perception and sense of living. Is living in momentary extreme pleasure in the shadow of pain intuitively better than a gratified life of peace and joy not depending on harmful addiction? Isn't living without suffering better than a life momentarily distracted from suffering? It is by the nature of the Fundamental Principle that the latter is clearly better. But establishing clear intuitions and structuring respective ethics and morality is not easy or simple, hence why subjectivity is perceived in complexity.

Being mindful and ready to consider any operational ethos from which normative guidance and action is mediated and derived from is crucial to understanding, and formulating, structured, coherent, and objective accounts of intuitions. Through a corresponding ethos guiding the pursuit of flourishing, intuitions can be given a coherent structure. As explored with the case of the intuitions of hunger and pain, intuitions are formed consistently through a certain ethos guiding behaviour such as seeking fulfilment by avoiding pain and discomfort. Conflict in intuitions of aversion to pain, reflecting conflict and complexity of morality, is wholly contingent on the inherent problematic nature of an ethos of fulfilment through aversion to pain and suffering, which depends on the given circumstances and is conflicted when prescribed to normativity and morality. What works for one person might not work for another as relief from pain, thereby creating an inherently contradictory ethos that is then reflected in the structures of behaviour engaging with contradictory and conflicting intuitions and senses of flourishing that oppose one another. One's ambition to alleviate pain causes greater pain to another, which reflects back onto another person and produces an exhaustive cycle and dynamic of aversion to pain that never gets complete satisfaction or resolution by an inherently contradictory and conflicted ethos. Intuitions and moral sense have structure through a corresponding ethos – a corresponding system of ethics – but the conflict in intuitions and dilemmas in morality are exemplary of the limits of human cognition and the contradictions of our intuitions corresponding to the basis of intuition on part of the dynamics of reason.

Living well is qualified more by intuition and awareness of one's own state than by any hypothetical thoughts considering, qualifying, or constituting well-being. Sensations, sentiments, and feelings can be elusive qualifiers of the proper state of self; they can deceive and warp perceived reality. Thoughts can adjust sentiments and mediate perceptions of reality through attitudes. However, thought alone will never suffice for the sense of well-being. Intuition constitutes the self-awareness of states of living through reason and sentiments, sensations, and perceptions. Intuition relates to the faculty of mindfulness that crosses many boundaries of reason and its functions and products. Intuition is made up of its own logic and manner of reason, yet it is flexible, malleable, and at its own liberty of mindfulness, while equally drawing on the content of the thought. Intuition has its own substance corresponding to the metaphysics of ethics and morality; it functions in conjunction with mindfulness and all states binding all faculties of reason. Intuition of morality and well-being requires fulfilment in terms of both sentiment and rationale. Flourishing is found both by feeling and in reflection.

However, intuitions can and should be contested, and it is not an inherent good that an intuition is functional and ultimately benevolent. Testing and revising intuitions is a turbulent, complex, difficult, and sometimes painful ordeal. As I will show, the nature of morality and ethics has changed and requires profound revision including of our moral intuitions. Throughout this project I will extensively re-evaluate the nature, function, and piety of our intuitions, to then reformulate them, build on them, and alleviate the ones that are conflicted. This can be an extremely counter-intuitive, disturbing, and chaotic ambition, yet it is not fruitless or meaningless and is very much susceptible to mediation and adjustment through the ambition to flourish.

Intuitions are a coherent part of ethical reality – of *naturalism*. I will evaluate and explore morality through reason and intuitions, especially those corresponding to our sentiments, emotions, and feelings central to spirit. However, I will also take such discourses further and implement intuitive reasoning in common sense and practical wisdom in my moral deliberations and studies. I shall do so both indirectly and directly throughout this work. The metaphysics of morals explored in detail in Section 4, building on its former Sections, will provide a detailed and comprehensive model for the intricacies of systems from which ethics arise, in particular with reference to the structure and anatomy of reason and its automatic, reflexive functions as intuitions.

There is, however, a distinction between intuition, intuitive reasoning, and reason. Intuition entails the most basic form of thought, which is often taken for granted such as in the form of 'you just know it', something perhaps often strongly entwined with the faculties of base-reason. Intuition encompasses automatic and quick manifestations of reason, right or wrong. Intuitions can be qualified as simple forms of thought. The qualification of pain as bad and pleasure as good, for example, is a case of *intuition*. *Intuitive reasoning* is a thought process not produced in an instantaneous manner of intuition, but rather that of a thought-process guided by the fundamentals of intuition, reciprocating, resembling, or perhaps even embodying the very essence of common sense.

Reasoning, however, is much more complex and cognitively demanding. When intuitions conflict and intuitive reasoning exhausts its given potential, we naturally defer to *reasoning*. Reasoning has the potential to penetrate all spheres of the mind, even the processes of base faculties moving sentiments and instincts as reflexive logic. These elements of moralising, ethical analysis, and deliberation on actions are imperative for practical morality – that is, morality engaged in activity and not mere hypothesising or theory-building which practical morality follows.

In terms of the degrees of sensed wellness, we must distinguish between what is *good* and what is *right*. Goodness, as is common in utilitarian ethics, is much more 'grounded', much more immediate, much more evocative. Goodness relates to the feelings accompanying actions, to their *spirit*. Righteousness and rightness, on the other hand, are those more concerned with reasoning and (often) moral directives of dedicated high-reason. Doing what is right might not conform to immediate intuitions taken for granted; righteousness may defy immediate feelings of emphasised base-reason such as joy.

However, doing what is right is that which maximises goodness beyond immediate circumstances and feelings. Righteousness may defy immediate intuition, but it will, or is intended to, assist cognition concerning extended intuition. Denying oneself immediate fulfilment, denying an immediate good, can serve to maximise goodness overtime. Righteousness or rightness is the continuity and sustainability of goodness, although righteousness is unsustainable if it does not evoke definitive fulfilment and goodness. Doing what is right is contingent on its fulfilment and is sustained only by its power to nourish goodness. This, as with duty, is often undermined by impatience and undisciplined character and faltering mindfulness. Righteousness, as all goodness, is sometimes undermined by the limitations of cognitive capacities and wisdom. Thus, for any normativity to be effective and for its 'good' to be positive, effective, and sustainable, its righteousness must be in accordance with goodness and positive fulfilment.

In time, I shall come to posit an ethos by which righteousness and immediate appeal to duty evoke their own form of goodness that, when disciplined and practised, provides immediate fulfilment of a greater quality. Long-term and short-term interest and pleasure are best combined for the Highest Good. This will be part of my framework for normative guidance, which will combine pleasure, duty, and virtue; goodness, rightness, and character.

In Section 3, Part 1, I will revise some dominant normative theories in ethics and morality. The balance or measure of goodness and rightness will depend primarily on relevant virtues and characteristics embodied in the moral agent experiencing the effects (the spirit) of actions and who embodies the habits of behaviour producing actions affecting states of self and environment. The Aristotelian *Doctrine of the Mean*[9] may be commonly dismissed as ineffective, an impotent tool for normativity, as it supposedly does not tell us what to do[10]. One can defer to the Fundamental Principle to formulate the utility of the Doctrine of the Mean as a tool or mode in morality and living by which we can achieve greater fulfilment and well-being through balance in desires. For one, if behaviour is mechanical and conditional in terms of the psyche and state of mind, then the habits producing behaviour are conditioned by behaviour itself, with habits perpetuating themselves. Character and the psyche are central to actions and morality. Accordingly, there must be balance in behaviour and desires for their functions to be fulfilling and good, in whatever form that balance manifests itself. It is as if there is a universal Law of Nature that balance and moderation are key in all things. This might be what Aristotle originally intended in his Doctrine of the Mean – that moderation as balance is key to well-being and fulfilment.

Much of Aristotle's argument following the Doctrine is derivative of intuition and intuitive reasoning – of *practical wisdom*[11]. However, deliberative reasoning is perhaps not as strong for the argument in the way that the arguments are somewhat founded on unexplored intuitions that are taken for granted. This form of moderation is key to synchrony and harmony between goodness and righteousness. We should pursue 'feel-goods', but sustainably – in other words, in moderation. This is what the Doctrine of the Mean will signify in this project. It is central to the balance between rightness and goodness leading to greater fulfilment, to balance between sentiment, intuition, and thought – to be balanced in spirit. For the mind to adopt a conviction of what is good and right, subsequently assigning meaning to mental states and concepts through linguistic tools furthering the ambition of the Fundamental Principle, it has to follow synchrony of intuition, intuitive reasoning, and reason. Goodness and righteousness must meaningfully satisfy fundamental elements of ethics embodied and driven by the mind and its character. This necessitates agreement in intuition and reason, synchrony between rationale and sentiment, harmony between base and high faculties of reason.

The *character* of the mind, in respect of the mind's mechanical nature, is considered to be the dominant influence on shaping behaviour, actions, and the thoughts of a person. The underlying reason and logic of the psyche are universal and are amorphous; however, they adopt rigid forms through state of mind, through mechanisms of the mind. The *character* of a person is considered to be the manifestation and activity of the functions of reason embodied by the mind, with trends in people's behaviour exemplifying their character. Balance and synchrony in spirit of flourishing are central to meaningful morality and ethics. It is imperative to enjoy and learn to love doing what is right, especially when it is not immediately pleasant or sensed as good or joyous, which shall come through an ethos that receives pleasure from virtue, strength, and nobility of doing what is right, especially in defiance of pain and discipline under pressure.

Here arises a crucial point for meaningful and functional morality and ethics, one I believe has been neglected for far too long. Base and high functions of reason compound the mind into what it is, with high-reason performing a complex and diverse function that is able to adjust base-reason and shape character. But the two faculties are not distinct or detached, and their foundation cannot be changed. Any morality should understand and extensively study systems of ethics – the metaphysics and anatomy of morality. The anatomy of morality *cannot be changed*, as the mind and human psychology cannot be fundamentally changed, only adjusted, influenced, channelled, manipulated, and certain features, characteristics, and tendencies emphasised. High-reason allows us to perform such functions and operations. Morality can be found, designed even, and values structured.

However, high-reason alone cannot guide living and cannot provide or constitute good living. It is impossible to separate high-reason from base-reason in morality, and good living can never be achieved by neglecting one fundamental aspect of human pathology. All-reason must be in harmony, balanced, and fulfilled; good living in free spirit must consider all meaningful things arising in the mind and complete all elements of the psyche to nourish good spirit. How to achieve this, however, is a normative and moral question, and not a systemically ethical one. We must work with the psyche we have, and all spheres of our pathology must be fulfilled if we are to achieve good living. It is delusional to suppose that the fundamental nature of mankind can be changed; we can only work with what we have and exploit its many assets and utilities. Yet none should underestimate just what people can do, nor neglect the potential and ambition stored in us, which is in many ways restricted and suffocated through distortion of accentuated base-reason lacking discipline and developed capacity of high-reason. The normative framework, outlined later in this project, will do just that – use tools, functions, and assets (all are ethical and moral *utilities*) available in our anatomy of ethics in relation to relevant psychology, mentality, and spirit. Human nature cannot be erased, but it can be changed and moulded through its own innate flexibility and potential, through desire to change. But any such undertaking requires a harmonious approach directing and synchronising both base and high faculties of the psyche, then of spirit.

If the theory of the metaphysics of reason in ethics stands, then the bilateral dynamic of reason should exemplify that base-reason can influence high-reason and vice versa. No doubt, this is true. Sentiment and instinct can influence calculative thought, such as with the doctor having to decide who to save in an emergency, and mindful thought can dismiss fears, as with the dismissal of the primal fear of lightning. However, effective dynamics of reason can only ever be achieved when they are at liberty to interact with one another freely. Obstruction and ill-mindfulness in the dynamics and faculties of reason desynchronise influences on actions and the psyche. All bodies of reason are important in ethics, but to achieve synchrony the two faculties must be at liberty to organically interact with one another.

A healthy mind is crucial to well-being, as it affects the state of mind producing actions and influences the state of self, sensed in spirit. Only with true fulfilment and satisfaction of the two faculties of reason – of sentiment and rationale – can greater flourishing be achieved. The Doctrine of the Mean becomes extremely relevant. Only when the influences of thoughts are symbiotic and self-sufficient can they lead to greater fulfilment. Only in liberty of reason in terms of the will to flourish can a synchronised dynamic of greater flourishing be achieved and can the will to flourish influence and mediate both faculties of reason. Achieving this is easier said than done, and this founding thought will be explored at greater depth throughout this work and will serve as an imperative of ethics and morality to guide flourishing.

For now, I will conclude my discussion on the nature of the Fundamental Principle of Living Beings and move on to its effects on ethics and morality. The implications of the principle I outlined above are beyond just ethical matters, but much uncertainty surrounds the topic. Therefore, I will renew the study of this principle and its metaphysics in the final Fourth Section of my work.

Another point that must be made, or at least will be greatly beneficial for proceeding arguments and ideas, is the function of this Fundamental Principle. When the entire human mind is stripped of its attributes, including beliefs, behaviour, and perception, the essence of being alive is left with the Fundamental Principle. This principle is what pulls the strings, determines functionality, moves the direction of flourishing, and is causally responsible for living. It is a mechanical system at the essence of being alive. As such, I will often refer to this fundamental will to flourish as the *soul*, as it is the definition and the foundation of a living thing.

The soul is something beyond just a logically deduced principle or belief – it is both a mental and physical substance at the heart of our existence, or it is an entity as a principle of substance that shapes our entire existence and the world around us. The will to flourish is almost like a physical law governing our conscious minds. At what point does material turned into molecules and cells begin to function towards flourishing? Begin to *act*? Begin to *think* about *acting*? When does our *need to flourish* occur? When do we begin to have a *'will'*? How does material form consciousness and create the building blocks of the function of flourishing? There are microorganisms and other life forms, such as plants, which only flourish if the conditions are right, just follow chemical reactions, but are not capable of the conscious actions human beings and other creatures are capable of. Chemical and physical laws of interaction, when absolutely reduced, may seem to struggle to give a comprehensive account of how the Fundamental Principle, and intention of the will to flourish and sustain oneself, come into existence. In Section 4, the Fundamental Principle will be applied to a discussion of philosophy of mind and of the very nature of consciousness, the implications of which are very interesting.

A Summary

Section 1 is crucial for this project. Because of its importance I will outline a basic summary of key thoughts and terms. Some readers may not wish to focus on the details of technical arguments and discussions on metaethics. Furthermore, it may not be the concern of some to delve into the specifics of theory and may simply wish to study other themes of this work, requiring at least a basic understanding of the adopted stance on ethics and morality. If there are any questions concerning some of these terms and notions, refer back to the respective segments of Section 1. This Section discussed the *systems* of ethics. It is important to keep in mind that greater complexity arises from contingent structures of ethics and the metaphysics antecedent to ethics as a consequence of the anatomy of the psyche and of the conscious mind; those themes are discussed in other Sections of this project.

First, *the Fundamental Principle of Living Beings and Actions.* This concept is absolutely key – a *fundamental* of behaviour and actions. There are two definitions offered. The basic formulation is as follows: – *all living beings' actions function in accordance with, and are determined by, the pursuit of well-being; all actions are functions of the will to flourish.* This formulation, at first glance, simplifies the most basic of intuitions of behaviour and actions – that we strive for what we think is good for our well-being.

However, there are many aspects of behaviour that are exemplified by the Fundamental Principle, binding metaphysics and systems of actions (and ethics) to the causal structures of actions produced by behaviour and the ambition to flourish. The Fundamental Principle is the grounding point between the consequences of actions and what causes and invokes actions in the first place.

Due to the complex nature of actions and behaviour, particularly with respect to the mechanisms that invoke and shape them, a *formal* Fundamental Principle is put forward: *all living beings' actions and the dynamics of mental functions move in accordance with, and are determined by, the pursuit of the greatest or highest mode of well-being and flourishing, with the determination of mental functions subject to mental states and functions of the mind in accordance with relevant and available influence on the will; all actions are functions or contingencies of the will to flourish.*

This definition draws on the nuances of the axiomatic intuition and thought that living things strive for well-being through actions and behaviour.

With the advent and insight of modern technology and investigative methods, particularly the sciences, we can understand human behaviour as being deterministic and causally structured and coherent. For instance, psychology and neuroscience draw on structured mechanisms operating the brain and the conscious mind attached to the brain's physiology. While further relevant questions are raised, to be settled in Section 4, if there was no causal structure in behaviour and thought, whether grounded in a physical structure in terms of the brain or in abstract structures of the mind in relation to a foundational epiphenomenal 'will', then the study of actions and behaviour would arguably be impossible. Yet we do have knowledge and coherent insight on behaviour.

The formal Fundamental Principle accounts for these features of the will to flourish – the *fundamental will* or the *soul* – to explain the deterministic conditioning of actions. We may act on what we sense to be the greatest available well-being such as through pleasure. The mind qualifies and considers many factors and variables that affect state of mind and sense of well-being. There are disparities in our perceptions of well-being, shown in terms of structured influences relating to the conditioning of the mind. Disparities and variation in the perception and sensation of flourishing and corresponding actions is accounted for by the functional structure of the mind that processes information, such as experience and impression, relevant to actions and the concern for well-being. The influence of the Fundamental Principle is noted to also condition rationale, thoughts, and beliefs, such as with cognitive biases and selective beliefs. Yet we do not have much deliberate control over what we think and believe – these are simply functional processes of the mind; our will is at the mercy of the way the mind works. This is the reason a formal outline of the Fundamental Principle is necessary to structure the systems and dynamics of ethics. But in short, the essence of the argument is basic in terms of the evident structures of actions and behaviour that strive for well-being; our thoughts, intuitions, and senses may betray our interests, just as our judgements may be mistaken, yet these faults are part of the arbitrary conditioning and degrees of perceived well-being and respective functions of the mind and body.

The Fundamental Principle is intended to be in itself an *amoral* idea – that is, without relevant application, the concept simply describes the core of the systems of actions and behaviour. *Ethics* is distinguished specifically as an area of study concerning the *systems* and *structures* of behaviour and actions. Ethics does not concern itself with moralising, rather it studies that which leads to *normative ethics* – the moral evaluation (moralising) of actions and behaviour. Ethics studies what produces, shapes, and influences morality.

Morality, on the other hand, is the study of *practical ethics* to form and set the parameters and rules for actions and behaviour (introducing information for the mind's deliberation on, and determination of, actions) to fulfil their function exemplified through ethics. Morality is the study and development of conduct to fulfil the ambition of actions in the first place – to flourish. For example, 'one ought not to harm people' is a moral claim subject to moral evaluation, yet the nature of the term 'ought' or what constitutes 'harm to people' is an ethical matter.

The two are closely related and functionally complimentary, yet the distinction serves to offer some clarity by focusing on specific matters of interest. Furthermore, since all ethical matters are grounded on the Fundamental Principle and the interests of well-being, ethics is the study and wisdom of that which makes us flourish, and morality is the formulation of insight into practice to enable us to flourish through guidance of behaviour and actions. Therefore, where moral concerns may have been dismissed, the questions of how we ought to act – of morality – are the epitome of all practical concerns. Since all endeavour is moved and ruled by the ambition to achieve well-being, and ethics and morality are the studies of well-being and how to achieve it through actions and behaviour, then morality is fundamentally central to everyone and every practical concern. With this implication, the study of, and moralising, all spheres of human endeavour as causal structures of the pursuit of well-being, from material utility, society, culture, and politics, become central to morality.

The deterministic and functional nature of actions and behaviour allows us to structure and exemplify them in terms of *reason*. Reason is key to the study of ethics and the application of morality. There are two parallels to ethics: what we can exemplify and the corresponding underlying functions. We can use reason to describe the world or ascribe things to our surroundings, yet there is the equal parallel of how things really are. The mind follows its own causal structures, which can be described in terms of reason. Yet the causal qualifications of those processes themselves as parts of distinct elements of mechanisms are constituents of reason. We can exemplify behaviour in goal-directive behaviour and respective reasoning, but in these causal structures of the material of bodies there are distinct rules and categories of causes and causation. Just as mathematical equations can describe the structures of Nature, reason can do the same with regards to behaviour and all mental processes.

However, where the abstraction of reason may seem conventional, the deterministic and functional structure of behaviour suggests there is a substance that underlies mental causal categories. One thought is bound to another in a form of reasoning through its substance of *logic*. Laws of logic cannot be broken, just as structures of the material world follow Laws of Nature. The mathematical ascriptions to physical processes are reciprocal of the devised understanding of logic as the non-abstract substance underlying causal qualifications that govern the physical behaviour of the body, its brain, and the mental functions of the mind. In this sense, logic establishes interconnected structures of logic into that which we exemplify in terms of *reason*. This project embraces reason and logic as more than mere abstract and mental epiphenomena and instead considers them as concrete features of the world, material, and consciousness. This is what allows us to structure and make sense of behaviour and ethics.

Logic and reason underlie all functions of the mind. Where beliefs and thoughts form through reason, the arguments implied by the Fundamental Principle take this further to suggest that the mechanisms of emotional responses, yet not the actual conscious mental states of emotions, are structured through, and can be exemplified in terms of, reason. We are directly aware of some processes of reason in deliberate conscious thought, yet others are more elusive and automatic. Sometimes rationale may be restricted to deliberative reasoning in conscious awareness, yet often there are veiled, subconscious processes of reasoning that produce spontaneous thoughts and actions. Therefore, a distinction and qualification in the faculties of reason are introduced: *high-reason* and *base-reason*.

High-reason is of the conventional understanding of reason as deliberative, calculative, conscious, such as that of philosophical, scientific, and mathematical thought. Base-reason, on the other hand, is automatic and mostly of a practical concern. Instincts are a primary example of the base faculties of reason. We often react and function automatically, almost as if we are in auto-pilot where reflexive, reactionary reason has taken care of certain things. We are not usually directly aware of these processes of reason as they are automatic, reflexive, and instinctive. This makes it a rather sceptical undertaking to study the processes of base-reason and makes it counter-intuitive to suppose at a simple glance that the mechanisms bound to instincts are found on logic and reason. And yet instincts can be structured in a coherent and rational sense in terms of goal-directive behaviour grounded in the core function of the Fundamental Principle.

This brings one to consider the role of intuitions in reasoning and the study of ethics and morality. We often function in terms of intuition. Where morality may seem questionable, we act nonetheless. Intuition has a profound, if not dominant, influence on actions and behaviour. The discussion of ethics and morality or any goal-directive behaviour may commonly be based on intuitions that are misunderstood or the validity of intuitions is taken for granted. The Fundamental Principle revolves around the most basic but illusory intuition of all ambition and endeavour being enacted through the interest of well-being. Intuitions are automatic and reflexive functions of reason, often those corresponding to the mechanisms that evoke mental states. Common sense, as part of intuitive reasoning, is a primary example of intuition. Intuitions, as forms of reason corresponding to basic operations of the mind, are central to ethics and morality. Intuitions are not abstract and merely epiphenomenal manifestations of the mind, but are actual concrete formulations of reason. Formulating relevant logical constructs, however, is not always easy. Yet intuitions are key to understanding ourselves, the mind, and behaviour. By systematically and structurally accounting for intuitions, we can formulate a comprehensive account of goal-directive behaviour and particular functions of actions. This allows us to understand and evaluate intuitions and their bearing on the state of being and contingent goal-directive behaviour.

As an example introduced in Section 1 and to be discussed all throughout this project, *Fear* – aversion to pain and suffering – is a foundational intuition and function in accordance with the pursuit of well-being. Where we reflect on the foundations of intuitions, we can begin to analyse which sorts of behaviour and actions are most fruitful to our goals as functions of actions in the first place. Then, summing up intuitions and all mental states and mental functions, *spirit* – the sum awareness of the state of being *alive*, encompassing many spheres of behaviour and experience – is the ultimate qualifier of well-being and the success of actions.

It may seem that subjective experience distorts the objectivity of ethics and morality, yet the intuitions that pertain to the state of spirit *can be* structured into forms of logic. By grounding all states of well-being on a foundation of actions in relation to an ethos, such as Fear, we can objectively formulate what behaviour best serves our goals and is most fulfilling with respect to a goal and sense of well-being causing certain actions as extensions of goals, directives, and desires. The study of behaviour provides sufficient insight into the state of mind and its reasoning that allows us to understand whether or not one is truly satisfied in spirit of good living – of well-being.

Moral claims, statements, and propositions are obligated to the core function to pursue well-being. Subsequently, some key terms conventional to morality and ethics are noted. A *morally good* action is one that nourishes states of flourishing and well-being. A *right* action is one that nourishes and sustains *greater sums of goodness* beyond the immediate sensation or intuition of immediate *goodness*.

Bad and *wrong* actions are the opposites of goodness and rightness, but the matter is not as straightforward. All actions strive for a state of well-being, and although some may falter and be functionally deficient – be *corrupt* – they nonetheless produce some degree of well-being, even if much less. So a guiding thought is also that nothing that can be classified as purely *evil* – everything is but a degree of goodness. Yet there are definitive classifications of greater or lesser degrees of goodness and structures of well-being, with sustainability being but one such category of goodness affecting the sense and intuition of well-being. This calls on a cherished notion of the highest possible form of well-being in a given situation – *a Highest Good*.

Since we all strive for well-being, with wellness being greatly conditioned by circumstances and the environment, in all spheres of Nature there are possible highest potentials of goodness. The Highest Good is the pinnacle of goodness and wellness, an absolute of mind and spirit, a truth of morality and Natural Law. It is an entirely different matter whether or not we can actually achieve the Highest Good, yet by definition we are functionally bound to the pursuit of the Highest Good – we are all inherently capable of good. But even though the good is greatly conditional in terms of circumstances, its ultimate form as the Highest Good – known through spirit as sense, sentiment, intuition, and rationale in complete harmony and synchrony of the clearest intuitions – is only achievable through the human condition fulfilling both faculties of reason as the harmony of all-reason. The journey through and towards the insight of the Highest Good becomes the beginning and motive of the rest of this project to find moral knowledge and ethical wisdom. Here is the structuring of ethics and the pursuit of the Highest Good.

Section 2:

Structures of Ethics and the Mode of Base Morality

Part 1:

A Model of the Dynamics of Mutual Effect

Chapter 4:

A Model of Structural Ethics

Actions and behaviour are driven by the pursuit of well-being. It is quite extraordinary how the bond of organic material forming cells and organs moves actions that then shape the environment. Each individual is a conduit of the fundamental will to flourish; every person exerts force on the world, for even inaction enables certain influences to persist or become emphasised. The systems of ethics inevitably give rise to structures of ethics. Through every individual arise other *spheres* and *dimensions* of ethics as effects of actions corresponding to respective systems.

For one, society and civilisation are an inevitable consequence of the successes of mankind as social creatures. The directive to strive for well-being has transformed mankind into a conglomerate of ethical force, which serves the utility of maximising our interests. For instance, even the selfish profiteer requires consumption by others to accumulate wealth. Through our capacities, such as ingenuity and reasoning, we build cities, dedicate labour, fulfil roles, and serve a function, whether in the liberty of our talents or the necessity of circumstance.

Ethics as a study extends beyond only practical actions and encompasses all human endeavour. Ethics and morality are primary and central to all human ambition, as all ambition is that of well-being. The concern of ethics reaches, encompasses, and formulates matters and issues of all its spheres arising from the individual, binding people to the structures of ethics in the combined form of society, economics, politics, governance, labour, consumption, and other civic aspects of ethics.

If one is to be taken seriously in the pursuit of the Highest Good and moral wisdom, all its spheres must be studied, from antecedent metaphysics to the causal structures created by our desires. From every living being arises a causal cascade through each action or inaction, formulating a *structure of ethics*. To account for what is best for our ethical interests and to formulate morality, one ought to study the global causal cascades of actions and reactions. States of well-being are significantly conditioned by environmental circumstances, yet where some may see mere luck, causal machinations and their structures with respect to each and every action give rise to the *fortunes* of structural ethics as the effects of the determinations of actions and states of being. But all actions are *ethical dynamics* as mechanisms of the will exerting force that shapes the world. A structure of goal-directive behaviour and its causes arises to form the mutually binding global, localised, external, and internal *ethical environment*. But due to the deterministic and causally dualistic nature of actions and the fundamental will, shaped and conditioned by the influences of ethical environment, all spheres of structural ethics are inherently bound to one another.

Each particulate of force as information relevant to the thoughts that influence actions, whether something perceived to be as simple as the choice of what to eat for breakfast, is part of the causal cascade of actions. The causal interconnectedness of behaviour links a single thought to a global consequence. In this nearly incomprehensible scope of information and the dynamics of behaviour, in the global and universal scope of human endeavour concerned with well-being, consisting of the actions of each and every soul, the structures of ethical environments are formed. The scope of relevant knowledge and information is immeasurable, bridging natural and social sciences to a central interest of well-being. But if one is to understand ethics and apprehend the wisdom of the Highest Good, then one must commit to a study across the spheres, levels, and dimensions of the structures of ethics; one must study both the individual and community with equal weight and their mutually affecting ethical force.

To illustrate the nature of the study of structural ethics, choices in consumption as consumer habits, such as driving to work rather than walking, can have a minor global consequence as an individual instance, but a consequence nonetheless. Consider that choice in the millions and we get a cascade of an ethic in terms of its actions and relevant influences, such as values, determining said actions. The choice of driving or walking to work is established through conditions influencing behaviour through the Fundamental Principle and respective values.

However, one choice may ultimately be better than another. Concern for the natural environment may ascribe virtue to walking to work, while concerns for efficiency and time give merit to the choice of driving to work. Each respective choice, however, is determined by the content of the mind and influence of the ethical environment. But each sphere of influence is multipolar and multidimensional, compounding relevant variables into a causal structure of behaviour and its reflective conditioning by the effects of the ethical environment shaped by other actions. Understanding these processes and morally evaluating them by considering ethical interests and values is the service and prerogative of *structural ethics*.

With respect to the concern for well-being, we intrinsically consider multiple spheres of relevant information. The choice to exercise may be motivated by both the concern for health and the gratification of pleasure. A lazy attitude can result from exhaustion as the excess of exercise and may demand the need for rest. Where exercise relates to health, this aspect of an individual, such as of a national leader, might have significant influence on an ethical environment by shaping the mental state of a major ethical actor. All of this can be encompassed in terms of the concern for well-being.

To study ethics and perform moral evaluation, one ought to consider all spheres and far-reaching influences relevant to ethical interests. This relatively straightforward example of the consequence of the effect of health on people in positions of power should illustrate the scope of structural ethics. But to fully account for morality and ethics, one must engage in an empirical study of behaviour and consider the relevant influences affecting the mental states of sensed well-being or suffering. Trends in behaviour, such as with consequences and the reciprocal shaping of future actions by past experiences and consequences, are necessary for structuring and understanding ethics and to formulate relevant morality as lessons from consequences. Therefore, a significant element of ethics becomes empirical study as a social science that equally considers natural sciences factoring in, for example, the pathology of the brain, psychology, and the nature of the conscious mind.

Structural ethics as a social science accordingly studies what makes us better off and experiments with moral truth. But because our states of being are affected by many spheres on many fronts of causes and respective catalysts of those causes, the study of ethics binds individual life experiences with relevant factors of ethical environment that affect living conditions. All aforementioned spheres of influences on the determination and consequences of actions are relevant to moral evaluation of what leads to flourishing. Thus, the subject of *structural ethics* is conceived.

First, an issue of behaviour relating to the *agency-structure problem* ought to be mentioned. The agency-structure problem is the issue of how fundamentally interlinked levels of human behaviour and social structures affect each other. It is clear that ethical environment, such as society, affects human behaviour, yet it is the human agent that reacts to the environment and constitutes that same environment. Then, also, one has to account for how an action responds to first impressions of an environment, in other words, how a first action could've reacted to a state of environment antecedent to the action itself. This issue is central to matters of individual and social decision-making.

The proceeding discussion is not intended to provide a solution to the agency-structure problem for social sciences, yet it should provide some clarity with regards to normative functions conditioning people's actions in terms of the pursuit of well-being. The main point of the issue is to explain the relation between ethical functions in localised (individual) dynamics and their sum causal cascades of respective structures (ethical environments, local or global). While this model of the dynamics of mutual ethical effect between individuals and environment might be applied to other social sciences, the ambition of this project is deliberately restricted to structural ethics.

However, the implications of an ethical account of the agency-structure problem will be applicable to the considerations of related human activity and society's many dimensions. The issue raised by the agency-structure problem is how exactly each sphere affects and relates to the other. How and to what degree does the individual affect a structure, and how and to what extent does a sum sphere of actions, particularly ethical environment, influence and shape individual behaviour? All such questions must consider the mutual dynamics of ethical effect on states of well-being.

Structures and their agents affect one another. For example, society is shaped by its individuals, yet society also influences people's behaviour through social norms. One cannot deny that there is intuitive merit to conforming to social norms for the benefits of social living. However, equally, one cannot simplify the matter, as there have been many times when social norms were wrong, as well as individuals often being wrong in their convictions. Both people and society can get moral values wrong, but maxims of ethical interest can only be achieved through functional synchrony of mutually constructive effects towards well-being between structure and agency.

Where one may distinguish between which aspect, structure or agent, has greater effect on the other, it is also intuitive to suggest that any observation of these tangents of causes and effects are conditional and circumstantial. In different times and circumstances, agents and structures can affect each other differently. The relation is mutual, and so are the dynamics of their dualistic, reflective effects. There are many observations to be made and many interpretations to be proposed. Yet any validity of an interpretation can conform to a model of agent-structure dynamics where the relation of causal effect is compatible with a flexible understanding of observable relations between ethical causes and effects and their dimensions and categories. Society and people shape each other in many ways, and so any description of this relation would be correct in its own right, even if it does not account for the whole truth or only provides one interpretation where available insight is limited. Any theory describing human behaviour could be valid and correct, but pin-pointing the extent of any trend of behaviour, such as a social norm, is more ambiguous.

In terms of considering ethical tangents as causal structures of behaviour, just as a single line in a square has different properties to the square itself, the same idea applies to the study of human psychology and behaviour on a mass scale. But if the degree of effects is dualistic and conditionally arbitrary, how can we possibly provide a definitive model to understand how agents and structures interact? How can we make sense of the exact processes of interaction between agents and structures and relating effects on values and well-being?

Any structure is characterised by its individuals and Natural Laws. But how much power do individuals really have? Sometimes structures can be rigid and influence individuals to conform. Yet it is the individual conforming that gives the structure its form. An individual refusing to conform can then either succeed or suffer. There have been times when individuals and a select few have caused significant social change, as is seen with many historic revolutions and shifts in global shares of power. Then, also, rigid structures have crushed any unsuccessful dissent. In these dynamics of forces, social and natural, at the centre is the degree of ethical force. With sufficient resolve and support, a revolution can be successful. Without virtue supporting a revolutionary movement, such as wise, able, and organised leadership, the ethical force might not be sufficiently rigid in terms of other elements of a causal cascade. Any categorisation of an ethical force, cause, and effect can be exemplified through the notion of a *qualified ethical value*.

When sociopolitical dynamics are studied, it is not always easy to apply quantified analysis to understand them. Quantifiable data, such as polls and surveys, are relevant, yet there are certain social and ethical influences that simply cannot be quantified definitively without ambiguity. Therefore, attempts to understand ethical dynamics would benefit more from qualitative or *qualifying* values of any degree of effect. Where the subject of ethics is primarily concerned with well-being, the qualification of well-being is ultimately grounded in the judgement of spirit – to how we feel we are living. We might be able to appeal to natural science to quantify neural correlates of sensed well-being in mental states and their physiological counter-part, but to do so on a mass scale with entire societies is practically impossible. Nevertheless, it is intuitive and reasonable to conceive dynamics of structural effects in terms of qualitative ethical values as sum effects of, for example, neural activity and psychology relating to behaviour.

This conceptual view appeals to the norms, goals, and moral codes we value and how they affect well-being and ethical environment. Then this notion can be established in a structured form as a qualification of morality and norms in terms of ethical values as *values* of well-being and sustainable and effective behaviour. *Ethical values* are qualitative categories of the effects of behaviour and influences of ethical environment, which are quantitatively related to the causal force exerted by people's behaviour. Currency serves to estimate the value of something, with underlying ethical values having estimable degrees of force on the state of mind determining the sense of well-being. Then again, all information is inherently qualitative and categorised, summarising quantitative elements. So, for instance, liberally democratic societies may value civil liberties and human rights as norms and *ethical values* that pertain to, sustain, and are a continuation of, individual and social well-being. But considering that the success of any social norm is almost always causally multipolar and multidimensional – combining political, social, economic, civic, cultural, and intellectual factors and more – these dynamics are virtually unquantifiable in many circumstances. The exceptions are the prevalence of certain attitudes enabled by civic functions such as people's political and moral culture expressed through democratic mandate and self-determination. Therefore, one can defer to ethical valuation as a source of coherence in ethical norms and their effects on structures and individuals.

Ethical values interact and change. Concerning all the phenomena relevant to ethical interests, the mass causal cascades of human activity and our natural and social environments are in a constant state of flux between incomprehensible scopes of cause and effect. Even where some people gain a share of insight into structural effects, it is sometimes difficult to translate these insights into coherent and concise understanding in the form of common sense. Quantifying such forces is practically impossible, but it is possible to qualify them with respect to analysis and consideration of ethical structures and relating forces and values. Formulating a concise model to illustrate and explain cause and effect in the structures of ethics is incredibly complicated with respect to the enormous scope of information and interacting ethical values; the complete relation between culture, society, politics, and economics is practically impossible to grasp.

However, certain patterns and trends can be observed and exemplified. Ethics, or any social science, may seem wholly subjective, but the nature of this qualitative study and its scope of information makes it virtually impossible for us to be completely precise. Subjectivity is an excuse of complexity. However, if ethical values, which are fundamental of human interest and are functions of the psyche, integral to all goal-directive behaviour and activity, are found and made to be objective, then ethical valuation can become more coherent. We can identify dominant ethical influences and dynamics, then find better and clearer understanding of the systems of ethics. To do so requires appeal to the Fundamental Principle's role and manifestation in isolated patterns of behaviour to define a particular goal or function of behaviour. Where there is the Fundamental Principle instantiating a fundamental Natural Law of behaviour, its contingent manifestation in behaviour as an ethical core or *ethos* (as a primary sum goal of behaviour of the maximum ethical interest), and in relation to states of ethical environment, greatly conditions specific modes and manifestations of the direction of the pursuit of flourishing. For example, when behaviour is clearly unsustainable but its motivating factors are understood, structural dynamics of this behaviour can be studied and evaluated. If the behaviour related to addiction is properly understood, then we can make predictions of how a person will behave and what the potential consequences of their behaviour will be.

Fear is a fundamental intuition and mode of behaviour as an aversion to pain and suffering; Fear is the ethical core and *ethos* of the pursuit of well-being in terms of aversion to pain and suffering. It is a fundamental and undeniable core rule of ethics that to flourish we must pursue states of flourishing, whereby an intuition of dissatisfaction and ill-flourishing as *suffering* is categorical for sensing the opposite of wellness. Often we only live with a sense of well-being as momentary distraction or relief from suffering, live *in* suffering, but never complete succeed *from* suffering; often we sense well-being through suffering and do not appreciate well-being in its purest form. If we are suffering or are otherwise dissatisfied, the psyche will do anything to move past such a state, with settling for, or making peace with, a state of suffering being forms of the pursuit of well-being.

A prevalent feature of an ethos of Fear is *base morality* – an ethic and morality with emphasised features of base faculties of reason, with the directives of behaviour and reason set primarily by base-reason, particularly in terms of instinct, where the functions and directives of high-reason are only supplementary. Mankind can express strong predispositions and tendencies for irrationality as behaviour dominated by instincts, characterised by people's actions that are not in their greatest interests, are not controlled, and are not *mindful* – that are reactionary and whose intentions and desires aren't clear or premeditated. Irrationality can be made sense of in terms of a faculty of reason reciprocal of the functions of instincts and reasoning in behaviour according to instincts. Base-reason can enact primary behaviour, with high-reason only serving a supplementary influence, such as through deliberation, to fulfil goals set by base-reason. But where the primacy and focus of morality is in terms of base-reason, where high-reason has no autonomy or its own goals, the psyche primarily functions in terms of base values and their *base morality*. Where scorn may be ascribed to such a view of human activity as demeaning and animalistic, concern for status – a concern of instinct itself – is not inherent to the idea. Rather, the term *base* is deliberately used to describe the *default* or *basic* nature of behaviour and ethical conduct.

The problem with this base mode of behaviour, however, is that it can be very susceptible to contradictions, uncontrolled competing desires, and the vulnerability of an impressionable psyche. Instincts lead to reactions and set the goals of behaviour that become problematic for living and the intended goal of behaviour. For example, the desire for love, contradicted by a simultaneous fear of being hurt by falling in love and the fear of being vulnerable, complicates the pursuit of love. High-reason does not have a significant role where it is unable to sort out what goes on in one's mind, to balance desires, habits, and reactionary behaviour. High-reason, as per a traditional view of rationality, can produce self-control and mindful behaviour, different to the behaviour, concerns, or interests dominated by instincts, blind impulses, and reactions – behaviour of base morality. Where we are hurt, the mind automatically implements habits of thinking and reacting, with the processing of experiences and emotions largely being automatic, reflexive, and unconscious. The mechanical and self-deterministic nature of the mind produces an *impressionable* psyche that is heavily influenced and shaped by experiences, by *impressions*.

However, the impressionability of the base faculties of the psyche and the psyche's tendency to react are also what make base morality's behaviour adaptive and flexible. This adaptive feature has both good and bad aspects. An adaptive system of the mind, reasoning, and identity greatly susceptible to emotions and prone to reactions of instincts, familiar as irrationality, does not do itself a service in terms of base morality itself. Impressionability and fluid adaptiveness can lack rigid mechanisms of effective adaptation and learning, as is commonly known with people mishandling traumatic experiences by developing self-destructive habits. The directives of base morality, such as to not be in pain, are then undermined by base morality's own fundamentals of behaviour where avoiding pain through other instincts only distracts from pain but never allows that pain to heal.

The greatest problem of the ethos of Fear is that aversion to pain, combined with impressionability and a tendency for reaction, leads to a personal ethic and state of mind avoiding pain without actually confronting the source of pain, without relieving pain. Then, for example, a morality that confronts pain and deals with it effectively through a directive of Fear necessarily involves greater self-control – greater influence of high-reason. This 'higher' morality of Fear is different to base morality of Fear, and it is abundantly clear that the higher form is much rarer and intuitively more rewarding. Part 2 of Section 2 is dedicated to exploring and evaluating the structures of base morality. Section 3 will then improve on the weaknesses and flaws of base morality.

To understand the role of base morality, it would be useful to explore its origin and development. Mankind has evolved from a far more intellectually basic creature. A creature concerned with inward exploration and intellectual development lacking practical application would not be functionally equipped, or able, to flourish in a brutish environment of Nature. A philosopher sitting on a rock thinking all day without hunting, gathering, or farming would not have survived. A balance seems to have been necessary for survival through sustained growth and development, particularly in terms of technology. Instincts and their primary mode of reason and mental orientation, such as attitudes and what we think about and focus on, have definitively served an end and as an effective and *good* function, because we are still alive and have achieved progress.

Now, however, the primacy of instinct does not always serve our greater interests. Modern civilisation was impossible in our past state until proper and effective conditioning influenced and shaped human nature to enable and sustain modern society. Instincts and base morality have been instrumental for human development. Where instincts are primary or dominant, the pursuit of well-being in terms of survival and Fear becomes a core ethical function. Instincts and base morality are fundamentally concerned with pain-aversion and survival. Aversion of suffering and death, as opposed to reckless and risky behaviour of putting oneself in harm's way, was successful. The aversion of pain, suffering, and death is a core aspect and intuition of behaviour and the ethics that exemplify such behaviour. Therefore, Fear is a core ethos. The main point of this argument is simply that instinct has served a purpose and the path of development, through instinct's core features of survival and Fear, has prevailed and is still a major part of everyday life. Where Fear is a core feature of people and their behaviour, so too will it affect ethical structures and environment.

If the core of a structure of ethics is established on a particular directive of behaviour, in this case Fear, then relevant causes, effects, and values can be structured in relation to the fundamentals of behaviour, ways of thinking, and ethical interests such as in terms of instinct, survival, and Fear. For example, the study of political science and international relations is a discipline making sense of the nature of politics. The global arena of international relations is a mass causal cascade of different interacting forces.

To describe this state some scholars employ a particular conceptual lens to qualify states of affairs. A core concept in the study of politics is the view that the international system is *anarchic*. Some may argue this is unchangeable, others that it can be changed, while others say this structure is what we make of it. Someone even with basic understanding of politics will see that international politics is, indeed, ridden with features of state-orientated survival, of an international anarchy, and practical or selective lawlessness. A conventional and direct manifestation of the Natural Law of natural selection may be argued to still be fundamental to international anarchy. Where individuals or society are concerned and occupied with survival, so too will social structures and nation-states, producing an international system with prevalent and inherent features of people's and nations' fundamental directives of survival often relating to the primacy of instinct.

However, as is known in intuitive common sense, how one survives and senses well-being varies greatly in terms of a directive of instinct. Some value pleasure as the epitome of satisfaction, others wealth, while others find fulfilment in family. But where these modes of fulfilment are given primacy in terms of base morality, and their success is arbitrary and none are morally perfect, many different and complex ethical values contend in a single structure of ethics. A structure of ethics defined primarily by base morality, built on a shaky foundation of Fear and instinct, is intrinsically unstable, yet it has been very adaptive due to its inherent disorder. One must then question whether such a function is actually good anymore, as it is clear that the modern world lacks the order and structure it needs to be more effective and efficient in producing well-being.

Values contend, but where their primacy is set by instinct and base morality, governed by highly unprescriptive and circumstantial forces, this adaptiveness may lack the binding rigidity necessary for effective sustainability. A morality of social contract, lacking definitive power of binding ethical value, or is subject to a rationale detached from emotional fulfilment and immediate satisfaction of spirit, is a weak approach to giving an ethical structure its firmness. All these features point towards the fundamental role of mental and psychological functions in the dynamics of ethical values.

In short, only effective and truly good values, proportional or sufficiently potent in comparison to competing ethical values, enable continuity of corresponding ethical effects – are able to sustain themselves. Whether an ethical value will succeed depends on the function of the value and its corresponding actions. A function of behaviour, thought, and value can only succeed by Natural Law if it has sufficient value and force to sustainably react, and interact, with other ethical values in a global causal cascade. But to say or study whether or not a value will succeed involves examining its function and related causes and effects.

To evaluate whether a certain ethical function has sufficient value and force can be done through empirical observation and thought experiments. If a person was to shoot themself in the head with a gun, he or she wouldn't survive. If this mode of ethics is subject to a test of universalisability (to see whether it is a universally applicable value), then this ethic would most likely not be sustainable.

However, any test of universalisability is usually more complicated than it would first seem. If all bad people shot themselves in the head, with only good people remaining, then that might theoretically seem like a universalisable ethic. But if one is mindful of ambiguous tangents, then ethical valuation becomes more complicated, such as with people who think they're bad, when they really aren't, killing themselves.

Empirical observation gives valuable clues regarding the effects and sustainability of some modes of behaviour, thereby granting insight for ethical valuation. The final test is then the intuition of spiritual reflection as the evaluation of whether or not one is fulfilled, which can be done interpersonally as well as by studying a function of behaviour, or by reflecting on one's behaviour. If one strives to acquire all the wealth in the world, it is reasonable to assume that this person will never achieve his or her goal. If the goal of excessive wealth-accumulation is a directive of base morality, which it usually is as part of well-being through financial and social security, then it is contingent on Fear. But where Fear prevails and manifests itself in an excessive, if not corrupt, form of intentional overcompensation of security, then this ethic will reflect back onto the mind functioning in accordance with a ceaseless and unsatisfiable directive of security and Fear. Because the person will never be practically or spiritually fulfilled, one can safely conclude that an ethic of excess wealth-accumulation and desire for security is flawed, unsustainable, or even functionally corrupt. Similarly, a person who values security above all else, a person that is unable to appreciate the immediate goodness around him or her because of the distraction of, and lust for, excess security, will never be fulfilled or happy, because the foundation of his or her behaviour as thought and action cannot provide the sought-after relief.

The same manner of analysis and thought can be applied to study and evaluate the dynamics of suffering. A basic intuition concerning suffering is that we seek relief – *freedom from suffering* – when we suffer. This fundamental of ethics then guides actions and morality in many directions. One particularly common mode of morality in dealing with suffering is to project it onto others. This behaviour can manifest itself as a simple expression of pain or it can take on a corrosive, spiritually toxic, and mentally draining form as a personal inability to handle suffering, with the individual in pain subsequently resorting to project pain onto others to give oneself relief through a sense of control over suffering.

The problem with such an ethic and its causal tangent is that, where we are unable to deal with our own suffering and we project it onto others, we don't necessarily actually relieve suffering at its source or let ourselves heal. Furthermore, we cause harm by projecting our pain onto others, which then propagates a vicious dynamic as the *cycle of suffering*, creating an ethical environment of suffering that will inevitably, to some degree, affect everyone. Without truly relieving the source of suffering and pain, we can never flourish to the fullest extent as the relief and freedom from pain – *spiritual liberty from suffering*.

One can put forward a valid and very intuitive ethical value – but elusive in practice lacking mindfulness in, and understanding of, behaviour – that causing others harm is less fulfilling of our interests than truly relieving suffering. As one may see, the functions of behaviour and their intuitions can be structured and evaluated in terms of ethical interests relevant to the fundamental concern of well-being. This model will henceforth provide the conceptual tools necessary for a study of structural ethics as the study of well-being in terms of both individual and environmental factors.

Where the individual behaves according to the functions of the psyche, these functions are set and mediated by ethical values. The determination of ethical values' quality is subject to the causal cascade and structure of values and their relation to Natural Law and moral law. Different actions can use, involve, and affect different values, yet the functional effectiveness of any value is subject to the Laws of Nature. We know that certain behaviour is not as good as other behaviour.

The notion of Natural Law conceives a greatest or highest value – a parameter, condition, and principle – in any given structure, sphere, and environment of ethics, those which cannot be broken and are supreme in their value and force. We know that certain causal trends are good or bad through the insight of Natural Law, which in basic terms is reducible to common sense. For example, if a society cannot produce sufficient food, it will starve, wither, and potentially be exploited by a rival. On an individual level and in localised ethical environments, Natural Laws are much simpler and ethical values are easier to identify.

However, in larger considerations of ethical environment and causal cascades, such as in global terms, many mutually affecting values may distort the understanding of Natural Law, for every sustained function is enabled by a sufficient force. Periods of ultimately unsustainable actions can be extended and enabled by other supporting ethical values and resources, just as trends of ultimately sustainable actions may prevail over negative ethical values where goodness is, in sum, greater than badness. The abundance of goodness produces progress and growth; the excess of badness leads to degeneration; any idleness, as equal effects of good and bad, manifests itself as stagnation. But in any structure or system, the *Highest Good* is the sum greater value as a moral truth in all and any condition and circumstance. These structural phenomena are examples of the Natural Laws in ethics.

Where the study of behavioural functions and ethical values can be applied to the individual, it is also applicable to structures consisting of individual agents. The problem is that the global scope of ethical values and forces is much greater than the individual level. But by appealing to the Natural Laws governing and exemplifying all ethics – their dynamics of cause and effect – we can form coherent understanding of the structures of ethics. Where Natural Laws provide insight into the goodness and effectiveness of certain behaviour, the same conceptual model can theoretically be applied to greater levels of fluctuating and mutually affecting values and functions, although this can be practically difficult.

With respect to the agency-structure problem, the extent and level of effect is conditioned by the quality of a value and relevant Natural Law. However, these conditions, at least in an ethical and normative sense, can be accounted for by studying the functions involved and relating them to known Natural Laws. For example, a person conforming to social norms may increase his or her chances of surviving and prospering in society. A nonconforming person, however, might not flourish in an environment incompatible with his or her values and moral disposition. Yet where the environment is not hostile and is tolerant, the plurality of values can survive even if it does not flourish. Where a social norm becomes inconsistent with the demands of an ethical environment, the structure related to the value may suffer and be weakened.

Throughout history the most enduring civilisations have fallen because of conflicting ethical forces and values. But where the structure of an expansive social norm once flourished, a fault in its structure can become corrupted and cause calamity for the entire sphere. A previously minor ethical force, however, can then flourish through proper ethical and normative adaptation in the absence of a previously competing ethical force. Where the Natural Laws of natural selection applied in the wild, the same can also exemplify certain trends of change in civilisation and society. Ethics, norms, and morality change, evolve, adapt, or wither in a similar functional model to living beings.

However, where natural selection of living creatures works mainly in terms of bodies and causal structures of the natural environment, structural (ethical) dynamics operate through ethical values respective of the functions of behaviour and other levels of causes encompassing society and its spheres. The Natural Laws relevant to natural selection in the natural environment influence the structures of ethics as values contingent on the living things that shape an ethical environment and its structure. Referring to a clear Natural Law and function of behaviour can tell us whether corresponding behaviour will succeed in its ambition and desire.

For example, a democratic society may elect a certain form of government based on certain values; but where those values contradict the global state of environment, as in the values are poorly adapted to competing ethical forces, then democratic performance will be poor, negating ethical interests of well-being. Some may argue this is the case for the United Kingdom's decision to leave the European Union, where values of the electorate produced a result against ethical conditions set by the Natural Law of value-adaptation. The desire for well-being through autonomy may come at a cost to financial security and material capabilities, such as less funding meaning less military capabilities, undermining autonomy itself. Therefore, the value corresponding to the desire for autonomy, and the consequence it produced, is maladapted and functionally bad or corrupt. Subsequently, both the structure and its agents lose ethical interest – they suffer.

In conclusion to the issue of the dynamic effects between agency and structure, observable tangents of cause and effect vary and are conditional. Sometimes individuals thrive by conforming to structural norms; sometimes individuals and a structure thrive through reciprocal nourishment; other times entire structures collapse and are rebuilt with different founding values and principles. What we know with certainty is that individuals compose and affect the structure encompassing the effects of individual behaviour. Where the functions of behaviour move the individual, the same effects influence the relevant ethical structure. Prevailing and effective ethical values sustain their corresponding structures.

However, in complex structures of values and forces, a definitive and concise account of values can be extremely difficult, as is seen with the *problem* of agency-structure interaction. But in normative and ethical terms, by looking at the functions of behaviour and relevant values and norms, the functions of behaviour can be illustrated in terms of values, allowing us to account for their interactions. Then, by appealing to principles of behaviour and their values' relation to Natural Law, we can observe how an ethical value acts or interacts. That being said, this understanding of effects in agent-structure interaction is found through a model of analysing structural ethics with respect to the functions of the psyche and is primarily concerned with *ethical* study.

The Natural Laws are central to the considerations of the quality and scope of normative effects in an ethical structure and environment. A nation may have flourished in a post-war world by being able to provide for other nations that could not provide for themselves, as the victorious nations' resources were drained after years of conflict. The wealth of the resourceful nation guaranteed its long-term security and dominant position in the world through monopolies, debt, and favour.

However, where the rich nation's inherited values were of another time, and sufficient value wasn't given to ethical progress and adaptation, old values no longer applied to a new environment and global structure of competing values, with great wealth only buying bad values time in their decay. As the times changed, the rich nation wasn't able to dominate anymore, with its self-assured conviction being blind to a new reality. The structure characterised by the primacy and correctness of newer ethical functions and values, contradictory to present values, leads to the structure's inefficient and ineffective performance, subsequently leading to the suffering of individuals.

As an illustration, consider two nations: one embraces and integrates all people, while the other segregates. The attitudes and values of people producing an internally segregated society will suffer from inevitable ethical inefficiencies such as conflict, hostility, insecurity, and unhappiness. The attitudes and values of a racist person are a consequence and continuation of fear and vices such as insecurity, perpetuating suffering. This suffering will affect behaviour and project itself onto ethical environment. An environment of suffering will be subject to the influences of suffering. For example, a group of people, such as youths, that feel that their country has let them down will suffer, with their despair then influencing the state of ethical environment and contributing to instability. The united and socially harmonious nation will suffer less domestic issues and will consequently focus on other concerns, as well as effectively implement its human resources. Therefore, in this case, the socially harmonious society and nation will have an advantage over a nation suffering from internal divide and related domestic issues.

The Laws of Nature are logical structures of values in the dynamics – causes, effects, and consequences – of behaviour relevant to the causal structures of related values, of a causal tangent of behaviour with a structure resembling the model of effective behaviour with the greatest possible good outcome and influence. The Natural Law concerning the relief from suffering requires resolution of the source of suffering. The disproportionate value of security at a cost to goodness through other values, such as being happy with what one has when it is more than enough, produces behaviour that is unable to relieve the source of suffering – in this case, the fear of the vulnerability of insecurity.

Continued fear of vulnerability leads to avoiding vulnerability, building defences around it, without actual addressing it or growing stronger from it. Where a nation and society are obsessed with security, their fundamental insecurities and their antecedent values are not given sufficient attention. Their Fear leads to actions of fearful character and spirit, with reactions committed in fear seldom being wise or proportional. To determine the quality of a value and predict its effects, then establish the effects of, on, and between structures and individuals, one must appeal to the systems of ethics and their Natural Laws. By knowing and understanding the influence of a Natural Law, we can predict and make sense of its effects on a structure and people, then relate its effects between structures and agents.

The nuances of the application of this model of ethical analysis will be shown through its application in future Chapters. In short, where we understand human nature and its behaviour and psychology, then relate it to the Natural Laws and moral laws as objective understanding of the logic active in behaviour and subsequent causal structures of behaviour, we can begin to make sense of how states of the individual and states of ethical environment interact and affect each other. How this account of agency-structure interaction might be applied to other social sciences is not in the scope or concern of this project.

Natural selection and the adaptation of norms and ethical values provides systemic insight into the trends of ethical functions. There are dynamics and mechanisms as Natural Laws concerning the adaptation and development of values and dispositions. Ideas, values, and norms influence people's behaviour, which then affect society and civilisation. Good behaviour and activity lead to progress, growth, and well-being; bad civic and ethical activity produce stagnation and decay. Democratic performance is a straightforward example of the effects of values on the states of societies and nations. The Cold War's end with the retreat of communism and its regime's dissolution is another case of the effects and dynamics of ethics and the adaptation of values. Civil and social liberty enables a greater chance for a society and nation-state to adapt to its ethical environment, while also increasing the risk of maladaptation by enabling greater influence of competing values. Authority and order, on the other hand, can provide durability in order to survive in immediate circumstances, while potentially undermining the flexibility necessary for adaptation and long-term survival. Due to the complex nature of ethical causal cascades, there is always a delicate balance between durability and flexibility, rigidity and malleability. This is fundamental to the very nature of competitive politics, which is meant to balance progress and stability, growth and conservation, liberty and authority. But the two always go hand in hand, or else if the balance of Natural Law is neglected, any structure pays the costly price of the failure to adapt and suffers from corrupt behaviour (behaviour in which the goal and directive are fundamentally deficient in their function and are unachievable or unsustainable).

Progress is necessary for greater stability, just as sensibility is necessary for balanced development. The foundation of this function of fluctuating ethical values in terms of primary concerns and interests – that is, progress or stability, growth or conservation, degrees of liberty or authority – is fundamentally subject to individuality and people's behaviour under Natural Law. This fundamental, systemic feature of ethics' structures is the *adaptive cycle of values.* This Natural Law is at the core of ethical structures and human activity, especially in terms of the sociopolitical sphere. Poor values and principles of behaviour shaping democratic performance lead to poor choices and bad judgements, causing social deficiency and suffering. A nation with other civic orientations and with a more righteous and virtuous moral culture and its prevailing values is more likely to succeed, and its democratic performance would accordingly be more effective. The sphere of bad values suffers, while the sphere of good values thrives. In the end, the values that are better adapted to the state of ethical environment will succeed and grow, while values producing bad behaviour decay with their hosts.

This mechanism will feature prominently in the proceeding discussions of Section 2 and throughout this project. The main point I will build towards is that, where certain values have served a positive function up until now, their utility is diminishing and becoming corrupt in their now excessive vulnerability to environmental conditioning. Morality and people's psyche and character are not wholly equipped to confront modern ethical challenges. But few traditions that fostered the modern world are fundamentally able to effectively meet the demands of an emerging post-modern world, with those that do often lacking binding normative power. The many challenges to human civilisation necessitate a step forward in ethical and moral progress to solve the fundamental problem of structures built on now largely corrupt, sometimes devastatingly so, ethical functions – Fear and base morality. But to do so requires morally empowering people and supporting good aspects of ethical structures, yet it can be very tricky to influence people's behaviour and it is impossible to change those who do not want to change.

People's views differ greatly on pretty much everything. Some values are proportionally appropriate to certain conditions, while at the same time incompatible under other circumstances. Often facts are convoluted with opinions and are distorted by impressions, feelings, and their intuitions. In a more formal account, base-reason often warps facts, insight, knowledge, and wisdom through narrow, fearful thoughts manipulating outlooks. Cognitive biases serve a purpose, yet their use is limited where they are unable to handle increasingly complex information and where people lack the discipline to be mindful. Facts distorted by the impressionable opinions and shallow wisdom are of narrow insight. But combining the study of ethics and values with a level-head and patience enables the diversity of interpretations, making progress possible. Progress thrives with liberty.

However, often there is too much distortion and confusion surrounding facts and insights by the presence of initial impressions that usually act as biases rather than effective conceptual lenses. Nevertheless, feelings and opinions as narrow insights and simplistic intuitions are reflections of some degree of reality. How one feels is valid, even if distorted and only a partial reflection of the whole truth. But to pursue the insight of moral and ethical truth, to unveil the Highest Good, requires patience, sincerity, and discipline to study both intuition and reason, to understand sentiment and thought, one's own and others'. The intuitions of feelings and sentiments are valid and central to ethical and moral insight, but intuitions are only partial and incomplete without further mindful analysis, reflection, and reasoning.

The point of structural ethics is intended to formulate the qualifying criteria of ethical forces and values, particularly in relation to the adaptive cycle of values. Ethical forces and values can be distinguished between *organic* and *synthetic. Organic* ethical forces, functions, and dynamics are conceived as being self-regulating, self-produced, and at liberty in exercising their influence and to run their natural course. The adaptive cycle of values as a feature of Natural Law is an example of an organic ethical dynamic. A good analogy of ethical organicism is comparing it to a river's flow. Just as water flows in its own right, so too does human behaviour in accordance with the functions of the psyche inherited through conditioning by Nature. Where prevalent functions, such as the physical laws that govern the behaviour of a river's flow, might be self-sufficient, self-produced, and self-regulating, these forces in the structures of ethics can be classified as *organic.*

Attempts to influence a river's course can be disastrous or constructive; the same can be said for human activity. Philosophy as a utility of reason shaping mentality and state of mind can influence human behaviour. Influences on the mind can transmute into the structures of ethics. Where a self-producing function is organic, such as with instinctive behaviour, it can be influenced. Reasoning, as the input of information conditioning human behaviour and altering thoughts, can be an example of a non-organic ethical force – of a *synthetic* ethical force, function, and dynamic.

The synthetic nature of alternative variables in organic ethical functions does not mean that synthetic elements of ethical structures are incompatible with Natural Law. The influence of synthetic ethical elements and functions, such as ingenuity producing tools and civic states, has been central to adaptation and development. The implicit danger, such as with the analogy of a river's flow, is that synthetic intervention might not abide dominating organic influences, to which Natural Law will respond through self-regulation.

Collapses of empires and regimes, such as of the Soviet Union, can be attributed to the poor implementation of synthetic ethical elements in structures of ethics. The incompatibility of values with Natural Law produces consequences where organic influences begin to override unbefitting and weak synthetic influences, unless the synthetic element compliments or becomes part of the organic. For example, societies may function in accordance with prevailing values. People's desires and interests set the precedence for their behaviour and the structures they produce. Striving to influence this with incompatible and disruptive values, or seeking to overrule a prevailing function through synthetic ethical intervention, will only lead to disaster. Attempts at social engineering that contradict human nature in a given state of ethical environment and moral culture will always fail; synthetic functions must be relevant and proportional to primary organic ethical dynamics. To move a heavy box requires enough force for it to be moved; handling the box carelessly can cause it to tip over and its contents to shatter. Trying to defy prevalent organic features of the human condition, such as by denying or neglecting emotions in favour of excess rationality, can twist and warp the dynamics of reason to desynchronise rationale, leading to suffering, confusion, dissonance, and distortion of the mind and spirit. Then again, this sort of synthetic conditioning of organic dynamics can be progressive and constructive, as is clear with the advantages and insights provided by the scientific method – an inherited organic function of pattern recognition and reasoning transformed into a dedicated synthetic utility.

The measure of synthetic successes is subject to trial and error, as can be explored through the adaptive cycle of values. The mindful reader can begin to see the intuitive application of these classifications of ethical dynamics with respect to functions in structures of ethics and the relation between agents and structures. The conceptual distinction between native (organic) and foreign or emerging (synthetic) ethical forces and elements in a structure of ethics is crucial to understanding and applying ethics, because these concepts are key to qualifying dualistic effects between structures and its agents.

To further illustrate organic-synthetic functions and dynamics in structural ethics, plants serve as another good analogy. To grow a plant requires nourishment by the following main criteria: food, water, light, heat, and protection from environmental harm. Care for a plant can be categorised as an organic function of the synthetic human activity to grow crops. People's search for food is organic, while farming is synthetic behaviour arising in relation to the search for food. The plant can grow self-sufficiently (organically) through the provided basic nourishment. However, a plant's growth is affected by environmental hazards such as slugs or the weather. This is where 'synthetic' tools, foreign to the plant's organic (natural) state, can be implemented to enable its growth and fruition. One may use pesticides to get rid of parasites, which is a synthetic influence on the plant's natural growth. If strong wind breaks a plant, there may be devices to fix and strengthen the structure of the plant to withstand harsh weather. Certain utilities might be primarily synthetic, such as pesticides or a stick supporting the plant's body. But with measured and tested application, synthetic utilities could prove useful, complimentary, then necessary.

The same can apply to the sociopolitical sphere through social engineering implementing synthetic utilities, such as morality, influencing people's behaviour. Fire gave way to electricity to power our homes, with our use of electricity now being necessary for modern life where it was once completely alien. Purely synthetic ethical elements can become organic. Even though synthetic functions and dynamics may seem foreign, they are always combinations of inherently organic elements, compatible with other organic dynamics only when their functions and respective values are causally harmonious.

Globalisation has had an unprecedented influence on the global community. Faster ethical interaction and ever-closer ethical environments, with respect to their globalised structures of ethical dynamics, have created a rapid shift and transmutation in ethics, possibly even evolution of ethics on a scale the global community has never experienced.

Look at how values have transformed over the past century alone, especially after the World Wars: universal human rights have been declared, traditions have shifted dramatically with emerging generations, racial and cultural intolerance has receded (in some communities, at least). Globalisation is an extraordinary phenomenon in ethics. The global community, with respect to the globalisation of interacting ethical values on a massive scale and at a rapid pace, is arguably experiencing a vigorous period of ethical conditioning and adaptation. Ethical values are turbulently and swiftly changing, and each nation and society is one way or another experiencing the global effects of mass ethical adaptation. Societies are actively influenced by cataclysmic synthetic forces.

There is an abundance of ethical and normative diversity, contradiction, distortion, confusion, and even conflict. But this blossoming diversity of ethics, attributive of a state of the psyche strained by the seditious and fiery influences of competing high-reason through synthetic forces – as is seen with the effects of easily accessible biased information, mass media, and social media – is as perilous as it is fascinating. Formations of reason are virulently growing through an explosion of nourished diverse organic forces enabled by a combined synthetic catalyst, most notably in terms of technology and great material wealth. Organic sequences of reason and meaning are booming with the expansion of our material capacities and technological abilities.

It becomes a great challenge to make sense of the foundation of this change in the psyche and subsequent global ethical structures. While the catalyst of this rapid development has been coming for a long-time, the Millennial generation stands at its forefront and may be defining in the direction human civilisation goes and the mental and ethical development humanity undertakes. But as was mentioned previously, this stage of the adaptive cycle of values is turbulent and of an unstable foundation; one can either retreat or push forward. To perform the latter, to sustain and bolster positive ethical values, as well as to establish the degree of their piety, requires new insight and an appropriate conceptual lens – that of a structured and functional account of ethics synchronising the ethical dynamics of individual and structural behaviour.

In short, change in the global structure is rapid, but adaptation is not. Where positive values and functions are implemented, they may lack affirmative power and binding function. Where organic dynamics are booming in their scope and spheres, their constituency elements and functions are troubled by a diversity of synthetic ethical forces. Where positive ethical functions do manifest and continue, many corruptive and negative ethical values disrupt what is positive, with positive development too commonly, but far from absolutely, only barely succeeding negative values and inefficiencies. Too much progress is held back by the sins of the past, and the structure of ethical dynamics is too inefficient for the greater interest of the Highest Good, yet not wholly ineffective. Where it may seem as though all is hopeless, that one will never overcome suffering and dissatisfaction, that no happiness will ever last, that the world will end and human civilisation will crumble, another account could simply attribute such pessimism to the negativity bias and impressionable, undisciplined, and unmindful thought.

There is plenty that is good, even if this is not one's immediate fortune. Some simple things we take for granted are actually some of our best achievements, bringing us closer to the Highest Good as moral truth and being fulfilled through the effects of moral behaviour. But few would probably disagree that there is also a lot that is wrong in the world. Even though the good is sufficient and is prevalent, the Highest Good is not, and too much deficiency and ethical and moral dysfunction and corruption persist, whether as innocent but tragic ignorance, or as malicious and despicable vice of weak and petty character. While there is a destined future, a better one would only be secured with a proper response to immediate global ethical conditioning. Old cycles would be better off suppressed, diminished, or out-rightly broken to secure a better future. Structural ethics as a subject is a means to fulfilling this ambition, primarily as a service to the individual through moral wisdom.

Before one can attempt to solve problems, those problems need to be identified. In the proceeding Part 2 of Section 2 will be a comprehensive account and criticism of the modern structures of ethics. However, first, one must ask which level of analysis, in terms of agency and/or structure, should be taken. Considering the nature of the subject, both structural and individualistic ethical features, elements, functions, and dynamics have to be studied. However, this is best done by starting with one trend in a structure and moving down the its line of reasoning in functions of behaviour. This leads to studying both society and individuals, with the pinnacle of the level of analysis being perhaps rather surprising – nation-states.

In terms of causal structural cascades, with individuals being at the core of ethical functions, nation-states serve as central sum conduits of mass functions and effects of reason. The nation encompasses and heavily influences, as well as represents, an ethical environment, especially in terms of a society's moral culture reflecting its state of government.

As was discussed earlier, individual dispositions pursuing survival shape nation-states, which then reflects society as a whole. The behaviour and activity of power, and people's relation to, or experience of, power, highlights dominant values in terms of their effects and consequences. The state of society and government reflects people's attitudes, with the failure of proper and fair representation of the public being a symptom of a deficient system enabled by people not changing it. The influence of finances and lobbying of political movements are contingent ethical causal tangents of consumer behaviour, providing insight for ethical study.

Even so, nation-sates, while integral, will not be central to structural ethical study – the functions of ethics, in terms of values and reason, are. But this analysis and study is only coherent, but not simple, through a conceptual lens structuring goal-directive behaviour in terms of core systems of behaviour. This universal function is exemplified by the Fundamental Principle of Living Beings and Actions – that all actions, behaviour, and living things function in accordance with the pursuit of well-being. This conceptual framework of the structures of ethics can be formally termed as a *functionalist* or *normativist* view of structural ethics and relating implications in other spheres of study.

Structural analysis begins with exploring the capacities which instigate further opportunities of actions – material utility and the economic sphere. It is important to state that the proceeding discussions will concern themselves exclusively with ethics and normativity relating to the economic sphere, but not of economics in the traditional sense. A certain aim of structural ethics relating to economic factors is to account for why and how the ethical disposition for financial and material security prevails. It is intuitive to suppose that people want financial security to ensure that they have enough to eat and drink to survive.

This directive of ethics can manifest itself with a wild variety – from risk-taking behaviour to secure greater wealth, to complete rejection of conventional measures of wealth. Then it becomes possible to evaluate ethical trends and moralise (morally evaluate) them. This will also apply to the sociopolitical. The state of normativity and morality is questionable in the global dynamics of society and politics. Yet even though it may be intuitive as to why this is the case, it needs a formal account if these faults are to be amended. By foregoing the role of morality and normativity and their sphere of power, we have lost out on something impeccable, but understandably so due to the intuitive, yet elusive, nature of ethics. For instance, what can morality effectively do for national security and prevention of social strife? It will become apparent that normativity and morality, especially the power they naturally evoke through organic ethics, is a fundamental power that few have been able to capitalise on sufficiently without the coherence of ethical insight.

Naturally, and because of my degree of familiarity, much of my discussion will revolve around the competing values between Russia and the West, to then serve a dual purpose of a testament to common understanding, which may be of particular interest to some readers. There is a lot of decent literature and academic work done on the politics of Russia and the West, but mine will be mainly ethical and a sociocultural commentary. All such matters and their evaluation will be the ambition of the proceeding Chapters of this Section.

Part 2:

An Evaluation of Base Structures

Chapter 5:

Ethical Dynamics in Material Utility and the Primacy of Security

Material utility as material resourcefulness (wealth) and capacity (such as technology) has a profound effect on people, societies, civilisations, and ethics. It would come as no surprise that economic spheres of human activity are ethically significant in terms of their influence and value. The world has changed dramatically with the advent of extraordinary material capacities through technology and resources. Only through industrialisation and modernisation could the globalised mass ethical structure have arisen. The dynamics of ethics and corresponding values shift dramatically with the functions of material utilities. This trend can be observed with the displacement of "warrior ethics" by "welfare rather than glory" values describing transitions of societies towards post-industrial, modern democratic societies[1,2]. There is an evident distinction between pre-modern values of 'war and glory' and modern materialistic values favouring peace, security, and stability. This trend in ethical transition can be accounted for in psychological and behavioural terms where a sufficient degree of material stability and well-being produces loss-aversive behaviour.

This is consistent with the functional cognitive element of risk-assessment and loss-aversion. For instance, Prospect theory highlights the cognitive function that loss hurts more than comparative gains satisfy, in that after significant loss people become more risk-prone to regain what was lost[3]. Where modern materialistic societies achieve greater degrees of peace and stability, people become less prone to risk losing their gains. Consequently, a prevailing ethical tangent fosters a 'welfare' or materialistic ethical structure. This is then comparable to other spheres in modern societies where pain and poverty lead to risk-prone behaviour, which may be characterised by crime, hunger for success, or self-destructive habits. It is intuitive to suggest that when a person has little-to-nothing to lose, he or she will take greater risks than those with something to lose. These are just some examples of the central ethical dynamics of material utilities. But where, why, and how do these ethical functions form? How functionally good are they? What is their foundation?

With respect to Prospect theory, emotions are considered to have significant impact on risk-assessment and behaviour responding to loss, as the sense of loss can be more mentally evocative and painful than the comparative sense of satisfaction through gain[4]. These trends of behaviour, of course, are not absolutes. The element deserving the most focus is the role of emotions.

As was previously argued in Section 1, emotions correspond to base functions of the psyche with respect to instincts. Base functions of behaviour and their ethics and moralities can have a profound effect on the use of material utilities. It is quite obvious that money – a material utility – is of great significance to people. The imperative role of currency is both evocative and rationally engaging, as material wealth is imbued with both emotional and rational concerns, often with one aspect prevailing over the other. Material wealth is subsequently granted imperative ethical value and significance by the causal power it has on well-being. Accordingly, we can outline a central functional role of material utility in terms of base-reason. Material utility is significant with respect to its potential to produce ethical security and stability – conditions of well-being.

This, however, is intuitive. We need financial security in much of our activity. People work for money to lead stable and secure lives, as material wealth is causally contingent on the security of well-being through sustainable access to food, water, and comfort. A common ethical norm of the value of material utilities is quite obvious. People generally prefer security and stability, achievable and qualified by different categories of ethical values and attitudes. Material wealth is a means to this end. This function of behaviour and the ethics it produces give rise to the observable structure of ethics of base morality and its sphere of material utility.

A Natural Law in these functions is clear with regards to the foundation of corresponding behaviour – if people don't have material security, with material resources being central to well-being in terms of the food and water we consume to sustain life, then people risk becoming exposed to greater strife and suffering. If a person doesn't eat or drink enough, he or she dies; if an ethic does not meet such ends and fails to satisfy the necessities for life through an effective directive, the host of values suffers or perishes. A nation with lesser material and technological capacities will be more vulnerable than a more advanced nation. Material utility is central to the security of well-being, with security being a contingency of Fear. This is a basic Natural Law of material utility.

A structure built on a foundation valuing and pursuing stability and security then begs the question of the effectiveness of this mode of ethics. Often material security is related to the sum of security, but misunderstanding the nature of security can undermine or betray broader ethical interests as well as the interests of security. An ethic pursuing material security and wealth can lead to excess, as can be ascribed to deeply materialistic societies that might lack social cohesion and stability by the fault of unrestrained competition and a corrupt sense of security. One has to evaluate the merit and piety of the function of base morality in its structural form which jeopardises the structure itself.

Some consumer habits directly threaten our long-term interests by, for example, damaging the environment and following unsustainable hedonistic habits of consumption which further imbalance social powers by granting financial lobbies great, unmediated power. Furthermore, one has to question the merit of a base ethic of security and stability where it profoundly influences nation-states and governments to pursue material security by the desires of the people it serves, in the process jeopardising security in terms of peace by prioritising the value of material wealth involving costly long-term consequences. All such ethical issues, questions, explanations, and moral evaluations concerning material wealth and resources in ethics will be explored in this Chapter.

As the issue is intrinsically complicated, the questions and issues raised will not be clear-cut. This work will not commit to a 'keyboard crusade' and this Chapter will not provide any notable suggestions for solutions to global challenges. In fact, some elements of this work will highlight the merit and goodness of problematic material ethical dispositions such as national and individual preferences for material security. After all, material security is good for stable growth and progress. The conclusion will be that the issues of base morality that influence material utility are very complex and delicate and are at the mercy of individual ethical dispositions and functions.

In short, the main point will be that people are largely responsible for their own suffering through instability and insecurity, because the ethic that governs corresponding behaviour in its base form is fundamentally challenging and contradictory. Fear has served an invaluable end in producing a structure valuing security and stability, yet its functional manifestation through base morality ultimately contradicts its primary interest – stability and security. But because people and their organic ethical dispositions are central to the prevalent structure, there is no easy solution other than an ethical one in conjunction with the material which would have to meet both emotional and rational concerns and influences on behaviour. An element of an ethical value must overcome, or be on par with, the value given to material utility and security and stability. But to perform a cross-sphere study of base ethical structures would be best achieved by building on, and exploring the foundation of, base morality's relation to material capacities in focused spheres and observable causal structures.

At the core of the pursuit of security and stability is Fear. Material utilities and capacities have grown along related causal trends of behaviour and their ethics. First of all, one ought to highlight some basic great achievements of the ethics of Fear. Fear and base morality have led to incredible development of health and medicine, comfort of living, merged the globalised world, as well as made it possible for mankind to explore the fundamentals of existence through science. But these developments have also been accompanied by negative aspects and inefficiencies. Those neglected and left behind in the pursuit of progress can undermine and pull back the rest. Communities struggling while others thrive can threaten all progress. A collapsed or struggling economy and society in one part of the world can affect everyone else.

The progress for a few is not necessarily worth its virtue when the rest have to suffer. Technological breakthroughs allowed us to treat grave illnesses, but also enabled technology that changed the nature of conflict where a lunatic can now single-handedly commit atrocities and massacres with the pull of a trigger or the push of a button. Material utilities are at the core of all these developments, with ethical dispositions, such as of Fear, producing them. The basic framework is that Fear can lead to a lot of good, such as by invoking compassion helping those in pain and motivating people to progress, while being greatly overshadowed by its darker undertones further exacerbated by the biases of Fear.

The same model of the functions of Fear applies to the material sphere of human endeavour. However, where the good has historically outbid the bad, enabling development and growth, this balance is not clear anymore. Whatever challenges and horrors we have overcome, the nature of modern problems and issues is more complex and global. Many questions are raised concerning the sustainability of human consumption and the effective balance of material utilities. But these issues become even more complex with the governance of the people causing the problems in the first place, with a Natural Law of Fear and base morality necessitating security for the state and social survival. A measure of gridlock arises in the contradictions of base ethical structures of security. At the core of these dilemmas are individuals and the functional rules and principles that govern their ethics.

The individual pursues material security by the conditioning of Fear. Fear and its base morality ensure security that does a great service to people by providing sufficient food to eat, sufficient time and resources to enjoy living, to keep us warm when we are cold, to nurture children, and to nourish future generations to allow humanity to achieve new feats. Fear and its focus of base morality by-and-large does us a service and has unequivocally produced a lot of good, even with the contingent negative effects of the corruption of Fear.

However, the effects and functions of Fear are sometimes corrosive and too corrupt. Even though security and base morality serve a purpose and have good functions, there are negative aspects. In modern terms of massively interconnected ethical dispositions and behaviour, negative aspects of human activity can be significant enough to undermine sum goodness and greater ethical interest. Where the individual pursues security in well-being, with material utility being paramount, this feeds into a structure of related behaviour to create an environment necessitating material security, with Fear sometimes taking hold of people. This creates an ethically toxic environment.

The clearest example of the negative effects of Fear's base morality on security through material wealth is what happens with material insecurity and socioeconomic collapse. When people's security of well-being is threatened, Fear can lead to actions of questionable sense and of an instinctive disposition. In the past this most likely would have served an effective role. But where the power of money excites emotions and rationale tied to instincts, base morality is functionally orientated on instinct, with high-reason having little effect on instinct's reason. Where our security is threatened, we can do foolish and impulsive things that contradict our own greater interests.

Material capacities enable, as well as reciprocate, the ethical dynamics that drive the ambitions of actions. Material capacities are central to the physical causality through which ethical tangents operate. Without sufficient material utility, a contingent physical process, whether it is feeding the body or fuelling a vehicle, will not occur. If one cannot provide energy for a lorry to move, whether in terms of the driver or the engine, then the lorry will not fulfil its function. If a lorry cannot move, it will not do the service of transporting goods. If goods aren't delivered, stores will not receive supplies and people will not be able to obtain necessary products from said store. These processes occur on a massive and global scale with financial and economic collapses as fundamental disturbances in the dynamics of material utilities. Where people cannot easily obtain the materials necessary for sustaining life, base morality of survival adapts and invokes other measures of fulfilling its directive. This can give rise to ethical dispositions of crime to obtain necessary material, or it may give rise to charitability and generosity. The foundation of base morality serving instinct's reason of survival launches ethical values, norms, and attitudes in many directions by the conditioning of an unfavourable ethical environment.

Fear can move people to pursue their own ends of survival and well-being at a cost to others. When such an ethical disposition plants itself in a person's psyche, it springs further actions in similar character. Individual occupation and valuation of material security moves people to do everything they can to secure well-being. Where this ethical dynamic thrives in hostile environments of economic strife and collapse, the resurgent society is subject to extensive prevailing forces of ethical dynamics orientating on survival and disproportionate material security. Where a person experiences trauma and great fear, or learns a powerful lesson of powerlessness in insecurity, these memories shape his or her character. An ethical trait embodies and activates the pursuit of greater material security. An individual may then pursue advantageous social positions to secure wealth through honest work or through the opportunity to extort money by means of corruption. If a person does not have access to such means, or where a corrupt individual gets in the way of material security, Fear's instinct can invoke other, more extreme measures of security at a cost to others. Where people have nothing to lose but everything to gain, and suffering is powerful enough, people can become violent. Where material insecurity disempowers people and leaves them without any notable control over their lives, measures of security and control find other paths for satisfaction. Subsequently arises the trend of violence and poverty, of material wealth's possession over people who had no confident security during the development of their character. One may scorn such vice and immorality, but where matters of survival are dominant, it is not difficult to understand why, with reference to a model of Fear and base morality, people act the way they do. If a person's poverty is not the person's fault, such as in the case of a child born to poverty, life finds a way to sustain itself, thus fostering the ethical dynamics of the primacy of survival.

Where the dynamics of survival secure their place in a structure of ethics, they impress their function on the conditions of Natural Law and their sum by the Highest Good. A government can become characterised by faulty operating elements as corrupt individuals stealing funds and neglecting the public. Where a community's well-being is neglected and it is disempowered by an individual seeking security where he or she was once disempowered, a turbulent cycle in ethical values manifests itself as instability, disorder, and even revolt or revolution. People take advantage of periods of instability and ineffective laws to secure what they can to survive and for their instinctive fears to be appeased. In doing so, that same instability may continue where the primacy of survival and the need for material security prevents the establishment of effective structures of greater stability. The ethical dynamics that prevailed in a period of instability and turmoil continue in their function until they are neutralised and settled, affecting a society and state and enabling respective ethical values that contradict greater sum interests of a changing ethical environment. But these ethical dispositions may then leave those unwilling or unable to commit to extremes materially insecure. Self-serving individuals committed to extreme values cause ethical and material imbalance, undermining social synchrony and effective ethical rigidity. The concern of survival and the primacy of instinct, however, trump greater sensibilities and sow selfish ethical dispositions that erode effective socioeconomic environments. While there are ambiguities in this illustration of the ethical dynamics of survival in terms of socioeconomic turmoil, this should suffice to highlight the intuitive, but not absolute, trend in behaviour where individual insecurity leads to structural ethical deficits and troubles.

Similar ethical trends can be seen in the 2007-2008 Great Recession. Economic strife and insecurity caused global damage to growth and development, with the primacy of individual security out-valuing the concern for structural or social security. The former may seem to serve the security of the individual more according to a base sense of security, such as by seeing more numbers in a bank account rather than seeing a healthy socioeconomic environment. But the consequence of this ethical attitude is a structure susceptible and vulnerable to the instability of Fear, harming many more people and eventually oneself as an inhabitant of this environment. But a more extreme case of material, economic, and ethical instability can be observed in Russia's emergence from its communist phase.

Restructuring Russia's era of communist social engineering into a democratic free market country accompanied great social strife and upheaval. The consequence of the rapid transitioning period in the 90s following the late-communist Perestroika (literally 'rebuilding') made Russia what it is today, a transition that arguably still isn't finished. Russia still faces major issues of widespread corruption and crime. It is sensible to suggest that less crime and corruption is better for the general public and social and national development where the functions of order and governance are effective, proportional, and proper. However, it isn't easy to break the cycles that shaped a generation and the social trends and mannerisms corresponding to systematically imbedded instability and insecurity. Russia has experienced much instability in its history, which has reflected onto its people and their values and culture. Base morality and the ethics of survival are so ingrained and organic that they can hinder greater ethical interests where base morality is unmindful and predominantly reactive. Western countries have thrived through stability and liberty. In contrast, instability and insecurity experienced by other countries have left them more vulnerable and comparatively less able than advanced nations. Countries outside of the sphere of developed liberal democracies could theoretically thrive and have greater social cohesion and stability, then on growth and development. But ethical trends that sustained individuals and allowed people to thrive in periods of insecurity prevailed and found a place in their environment. With respect to the Natural Laws that govern such behaviour through Fear, the functions of behaviour in Fear prevail for a reason, in the process potentially undermining the interest of a better environment. These cycles and dynamics of Fear are not easily broken, and so they exert a powerful force on the many spheres of the structures of base morality.

A particular reason for mentioning Russia's economic strife following the dissolution of the Soviet Union is to develop understanding of the conditioning Russians experienced and, most importantly, subsequent ethical dynamics that followed. For the present context, and key for future discourse, there is one matter that must be discussed. The Soviet Union was heavily militarised, with the military further having a central cultural role as part of national identity and pride[5]. With the Soviet Union's dissolution and subsequent socioeconomic upheaval, military personnel would've experienced pressures of material insecurity, as did most of the general public.

Due to the cultural role of the military for Russia's national identity, and following the fundamental shift in power and structure of a post-communist world, Russians also had to endure a quite literal identity crisis with the loss of their 'great power' status[6,7]. The constructivist (political theory) approach, which emphasises the role of history, society, culture, and identity in international relations, can tell us a lot about the dynamics of ethics. Where social roles and the sense of self or meaning are lost, morality falls back to its common roots of basic instinct. Socioeconomic instability following the Soviet Union's dissolution was further inflamed by internal power vacuums exploited by criminal and opportunistic syndicates and a massive military force without binding leadership that led to people doing what they had to in order to survive in a hostile and desperate environment. The communist regime already had a prevalent underground, shady criminal syndicate operating to serve the interests of corrupt government officials[7] that preyed on the general public across Soviet countries. This inadvertently facilitated an infestation of organised crime and corruption across Russia's infrastructure[8] to the point of becoming 'casualised' and becoming a normal part of everyday life, even to some degree as a business ethic of 'getting things done'. Where military personnel and war veterans, with some veterans mentally disturbed by the war in Afghanistan, were left without a source of income or binding authority, organised crime took advantage of these people and their abilities[9]. The influx of military personnel in need of employment was made even worse with the 'Great Retreat' of the Soviet (Russian) military having to leave ex-Soviet Republics[10]. Newly independent nations understandably wanted to secure their independence, with Soviet troops being a cause of uncertainty by a regime that had notoriously implemented severe and authoritarian militaristic policies.

While the truth of the latter point is dualistic and complicated, its politics are sufficiently real in terms of their effects on mass psyche in relation to the emotional responses portraying a degree of reality, as is seen with how easily past grievances are provoked in the post-communist world, whether it is missile defences[12], gas and oil[13], or perceived desecration of historic cultural symbols[14]. The sudden surge of migration back to Russia, on top of major domestic issues, meant that relocated ex-soldiers faced serious social struggles, including: unemployment, housing shortages, poverty, and even problems of reintegration into local communities[15]. All these factors combined into a massive cross-national dynamic of extremes of the ethics of instinct and survival. And so ensued a turbulent time of crime and violence, with such behaviour characterised by the base morality of instinct and well-being as the security of survival. These experiences and their instability still affect Russian society, even if only as impressionable memories, with the fear of instability leading to stern measures of attempts to secure stability. Material security, as the security to survive and live well, is causally central to the ethical dispositions and functions that enabled and exacerbated social strife in Russia. This mode of Fear still affects Russia, most notably as corruption and crime, and there are no simple or easy solutions.

The dysfunctional element of these modes of ethics and their base morality is their futility and deceitful nature. Selfishness shrouds judgement in Fear which then undermines greater interest, with Fear consuming spirit and forever leaving one to live in the suffering of Fear. Not only do these ethical dispositions tend to foster an unfavourable environment and state of living, but they also betray the individual ethical agent. This is an important point concerning all matters of Fear's corruption – by pursuing and appeasing security in Fear without fundamental resolution and satisfaction, the sense of security will never be fully achieved and one will never be fulfilled. The pursuit of disproportionate security inherently only leads to insecurity, because the obsessive need for security is itself a function of insecurity. Therefore, material security as an excess and corrupt ethical function does not serve greater security or fulfilment. Again, there is no simple solution, because the dynamics of these ethical functions are organic and deeply ingrained into base morality, with organic and synthetic functions becoming easily susceptible to the character vulnerable to the negative elements of Fear.

The 90s were a dark time in Russia's history and have had a powerful effect in shaping ethical dynamics and environments. Crime and violence were brutish means of survival where synthetic structures of law abandoned the streets. Thugs thrived in this environment and some of them even came to own much of Russia's wealth, leaving Russia with its continued state of deep inequality, which isn't only a characteristic of Russian society. But in this economic turmoil people had to endure the way they could. Specialists and well-educated people had no means of earning money. Stores couldn't get supplies and sometimes there wasn't enough food. People had to sell things and food in streets just to earn a bare penny; some still do. Material insecurity in tandem with Fear is susceptible to instability and disarray. Insecurity and suffering lead to moral extremes, such as violence, by the ethical dispositions contingent on the functions of Fear. Reason may highlight other prospects and ethical interests, but when instinct exercises its evocative power over the psyche, base morality prevails. Morality as the functional code guiding actions is contingent on all experiences. Morality forms through justifications of base sensibility and reasoning. Justifying killing, violence, or crossing the law is just as much a mode or form of morality – are values – as are the functions of reason that restrict such actions. Ethical adaptation and the structures of morality and ethics do not operate through idealism; the structuring of ethics and the moralities created by ethical structures are organic in terms of the influences of ethical environment. Base-reason is often central to these functions of ethics and not always for the better. But to provide an incentive that over-powers the evocative functions of instincts and Fear is not simple.

Themes of behaviour in relation to material utility and their ethics would benefit from greater study to pin-point the effects of material states on judgement, behaviour, and their guiding values and ethics. However, to make note of the dangers and terrors of material insecurity does not require deeper study simply because these insecurities and their behaviour are intuitive. This allows for a comparative understanding of ethics related to material utilities in more stable and prosperous ethical environments.

Where it may seem as though Fear prevails in extremes of material insecurity, dynamics moving away from insecurity also prevail in comparatively more stable environments, with the concern for stability at times giving rise to an illusion of stability. Fear becomes corrupt in ethical functions obsessed with material security and short-term stability and comfort, as the corresponding directive cannot provide the satisfaction sought after. In particular, Fear's corruptive functions are present in consumer habits and their ethics.

People need material resources to live. We consume to sustain what we value – life and comfort; security is a means of achieving this. Security is perceived through its intuitions and senses, most notably as comfort and relief. Many people strive for comfort as a qualifying degree of well-being. Comfort, stability, and security are intuitive measures of fulfilment and well-being, but not absolutes of well-being. Furthermore, peace and stability have proven to be good ethical values and aspirations by virtue of progress and stability. Comfort, stability, and security are good, but only in measure of their sustainability. While Fear can drive ethics towards facilitating stability and comfort, sometimes its function undermines greater long-term continuity of stability and security by a fundamentally corrupt function of ethics.

The negativity bias is odd in its selective function. While people can react strongly to terrible news and shock, they also tend to turn a blind eye to strife or lose attention without constant stimulation, which at times gives way to apathy and desensitisation. The exact trends of these functions and their ethical accord are deeply circumstantial and conditional, which can nevertheless be accounted for by a systemic ethical directive of Fear. The functions of reason prioritise what they value most, which can be ascribed to selective awareness and concern. Often this valuation prioritises immediate pressing concerns, which is not without a coherent rational account of dealing with immediate troubles, even if through means of aversion and deflection through an attitude that pretends everything is 'fine'. People tend to behave more in response to their immediate environment rather than distant concerns. When short-sighted prioritisation and the security of comfort are combined into a structural ethical tangent, a subsequent ethic is formed where the immediacy of comfort and security undermines greater sustained security. Where Fear prioritises comfort, the greater sum of the ethical interest of comfort is neglected by a failure to address greater discomfort with comparatively less sacrifice. This can be fundamentally attributed to much of consumer ethics.

The main point being made is that Fear, as a directive valuing stability, security, and comfort, can undermine its own values in the long-term by immediate interests and comforts sensed to be more valuable and satisfying than sum greater discomfort. Fear can at times object to our greater interests by the fault of the primacy of immediate comfort and security. People don't always, perhaps don't usually, prefer or strive for discomfort and difficulty – an ethical function of Fear – or at least not with the direct intent to suffer for suffering's sake. Consequently, the preference for immediate comfort can be valued more than difficulty and discomfort, the repercussions of which can undermine greater stability and security.

For example, ignoring problems, such as social or environmental issues, is not usually the best approach to handling problems, whereby this function corresponding to Fear becomes corrupt in its utility. A person's inability to directly see the consequences of unsustainable consumption, or only feeling abstract consequences of a person's behaviour such as through inflation, often leads to unmindful behaviour focusing on the immediate moment. An immediate craving is more evocative than a rational concern that is not felt. These are no absolute trends in ethics, yet the functions of observed behaviour can be seen to be quite pervasive across many notable ethical spheres. This becomes more intuitive and apparent through empirical observation.

People's preference for stability, security, and comfort is often at odds with those same desires. People may be reluctant to make personal sacrifices and subject themselves to discomfort in order to achieve greater gains in sum maxims of ethical interest. The ethic of awareness averse to discomfort and pain, such as of ignoring a problem and ascribing it to others as their fault or as 'not one's problem', in particular with socioeconomic issues and disparities in the experience of socioeconomic environments, is corruptive and selfish. Living with a narrow and self-centred view and understanding of ethical environment can block unpleasant and inconvenient thoughts concerning significant issues.

However, in doing so, one does not solve the problem and continues to inhabit an environment which inherits the corruptive functions of a troubled sphere, especially on a national level. Then, avoiding discomfort restricts one's own ambition, strength, capacity, and potential, which can be good and bad. Poverty in one sphere of a society will reflect onto other spheres, notably as violent crime; ignoring and neglecting these issues, which may be convenient for some, only enables these corrosive ethical dynamics to fester and affect the entire ethical environment. Then, the evocative concerns raised by the negativity bias easily overwhelm the fragile, immature, undisciplined, and unmindful character and mind in a corruptive way when people fail to see sense and reason, betraying their own interests and values.

With respect to material utility, it doesn't take long to find cases of corruption and the great normative power material utility exercises on behaviour and ethical and moral determination. This is observable on many levels, from the individual to conglomerate enterprises and nation-states. States will turn a blind eye to some normative issues of other nations' conduct in order to win favour and access to resources vital for domestic satisfaction and security. Material enterprises, such as corporations – institutions designed to produce and profit as a measure of sustainability and security – implement a morality valuing profit at the centre of policy and activity, at times with considerable social and even political consequences. Institutions might willingly favour the primacy of material utility as wealth and profit over other dimensions of ethical value such as social harmony and justice.

The individual may easily condemn the perceived immorality of an enterprise and national policy, but the matter is not usually clear-cut and simple. Institutions focused on material utilities alone can fail to profit from other dimensions of values and interests corresponding to greater sum measures of security and material utility by misunderstanding the fundamental nature of ethics. Material resources are only *one* dimension of well-being, even though an imperative one.

Material utility and security are imperative for people's welfare and stable social dynamics and environments. The driving force for the development of material utility comes as consumption and production by the individual and the enterprises producing goods for consumption. The ethics of consumption are constituted by a wide variety of determining factors and their utility, from necessity to commodity, survival and the sustainability of survival through the enjoyment of life, and comfort and status. Material utility, especially in its form of currency, is imbued with great power contingent on Fear and base morality with respect to their capacity to provide comfort and security.

One notable aspect of social living is status, according to which wealth is often considered as a means of social security in relation to status. But a simple argument illustrating the deficiency of this value of status is that pursuing personal status can defer funds from social investment, which could have otherwise alleviated greater concern for security through social cohesion and harmony. For example, rather than trying to distract oneself from suffering perpetuated by the world, it may be more fulfilling to empower oneself and do something more constructive such as amending the source of suffering, for example by taking the time to inform yourself before you vote.

However, these corrupt aspects of Fear's function are more ambiguous than the present context would allow to explore without side-tracking from the main argument. The point outlined in the deficiency of sum security by the primacy of personal security reflects onto conglomerate policies and ethics. Personal and selfish (as narrow-minded) valuation of material wealth and security can object to greater vision and ambition where valuing material wealth for its own sake can blind one to the greater potential of material utility and its accumulation. What is the worth of great wealth if it isn't given power? Similarly, where corporations lose out from ethical mismanagement by neglecting employees and consumers, so too do individuals lacking resolve and ambition fail to achieve greater ambitions and fulfil greater interests by enabling despicable company policies and behaviour.

It is imperative to understand the Natural Laws of competitive environments, including corporations. Base morality and its structure of Fear that value a certain type of ethical security breed competitiveness and intrinsic uncertainty. In theory, where there are competing values, potentially anyone could be a rival or threat. Where an ethical agent, as an individual or institution, fails to comply with the rules of competition in the corresponding ethical environment, a value carried by another agent can succeed, with the 'big guy' beating the 'little guy', with the strong conquering the weak.

This line of competitive reasoning is not without a coherent function. Where an agent or dynamic fails to comply with the laws of competition, as is ascriptive of Fear, both will suffer by neglecting the parameters of security. This arguably drives much of corporate ethics, with material security also acting a principle of direct security of institutional, then individual, survival. One could further rationalise and justify this primacy of security as a necessity for sustaining companies providing employment for the public and goods for the general public, which feeds into the narrative of state concern for material security over other factors contributing to social security and harmony. If a company collapses, its sphere of employment, providing wealth for individuals, also diminishes. For other companies to capitalise on unemployment to expand their output potential, or for employment to be substituted by another employer, is a greater uncertainty than a healthy and profitable enterprise, which is accordingly in the interest of the public, the employer, nation-state, and ethical environment. And so corporate ethics of the primacy of survival, often measured and qualified by profit, and its systemic ethical attributes of Fear shape the sphere of competitive material utility, which quite clearly has advantages and disadvantages.

However, while total evaluations of the vice or virtue of modes of material utility are not currently the main concern, discussions of the faults of certain modes of material utility and their rigidity and organic dynamics will serve the ends of showing the limits of Fear as a guiding ethic. Even if the negativity of Fear is not pervasive or greater than its goodness, the effectiveness and efficiency of particular ethical functions are best served by improving the inefficiencies and negative aspects of an ethic. Building towards this requires understanding of the issues in specific spheres of ethics such as with material utility and the relations between consumers, enterprises, and nation-states.

Issues in materialistic ethics and corruption in financial enterprises are not uncommon. Notions of problems in materialistic ethics are intuitive in retrospect of the potential unsustainability of related behaviour in terms of the natural environment and non-renewable resources, even if opportunities to develop more efficient and effective technologies and consumer habits, at immediate cost to the environment, are relevant to these evaluations.

Furthermore, corruption in financial dealings, notably private firms lobbying governments to protect the values and interests of monopolies, are other examples of issues in common trends of materialistic ethics in consumer habits. Private lobbies can influence the judgements of legislators and government representatives to influence ethical dynamics in the sociopolitical for and/or against certain concerns and interests, whether to protect or neglect the environment, protect jobs or ensure survival of an enterprise, secure national interest through material and technological assets, or neglect the community to the point of democratic revolt and objectively unsound electoral decisions.

Where material utilities and currency have tremendous power for any ethical environment and its constituents, whether as extensive or basic levels of wealth, money is a factor of power. Currency corresponds to the ability of an ethical function to survive and continue its effect. For instance, if the liberal democratic normative sphere, such as some European nations, was more stringent in its emphasis of certain norms including human rights, it could theoretically foster greater contention or even conflict. If this sphere had greater material capacity than its opponent, such as in terms of military resources and technological assets, then it might succeed in waging a conflict, whether success is qualified as socioeconomic or military victory. If an institution and agency could speak the words but not back them up, then instigating conflict could be devastating for itself. Despite the many ambiguities, this illustration should be sufficient to highlight the relevance and power of material utilities.

This same model of ethical values and respective material capacities applies to institutions such as corporations. Any ethical function is pervasive only in so much as its corresponding material effect is sustainable and effective, with material substance often being a focal point of the adaptive functions of ethics utilising material resources as a continuation and extension of values and behaviour according to values. Material utility is in many ways the blood of ethics, the body which is sustained and moved by the mind embodying ethics. Where deficiencies in materialistic ethics are found, these ethical trends only prevail by the power granting them their continuity through hosts and agents of respective values – people, through their behaviour, giving power to an ethical function and perpetuating its consequences.

A company can lobby a certain interest group and ethical value. This can affect entire nations and communities by influencing powers centralised in the state. But institutional agencies, such as corporations, only have the power to lobby through funds and a group agreeing to the offered funding – through values guiding and permitting this behaviour. At the core of these interactions is the consumer – the person giving material power to a lobbying group and putting up with a representative's failure to promote electoral interests directly through mandate and not bilaterally and synthetically through empowering private groups. Then, the individual susceptible to Fear receiving wealth through corrupt means neglects greater social interests and development and fails to nourish an empowered, balanced, progressive, and adaptive community by the lack of effective funding.

Sometimes these ethical effects are enabled by commodity consumption that is not essential to life, yet is valued for good living, such as security of social status lacking the moral empowerment of virtuous autonomy. Other times, however, the necessity of material utility is maliciously corrupted and used against people's interests.

Where a material resource is a necessity, such as food and water, a conglomerate enterprise responsible for the resource's accessibility and delivery can turn sustainable enterprise into abusive profiteering and hold disproportionate power over the consumer. In this case there is no direct or simple solution to contradictions in the functions of Fear. Competitive markets can be mediated by appealing to people's values, to structure greater interests and desires of the consumer, to empower people to consume mindfully according to their own greater interest. The suffocated freedom of consumption is not solvable through the progressive power of reason empowering the judgement of a consumer to sort out his or her priorities.

Furthermore, lobby groups and the unintended consequences of foolishness can spread misinformation or deliberately lie in order to propagate a certain interest and value. This trend can especially be ascribed to media and information outlets either feeding off its viewers' desires, or promoting certain interests. But in a competitive environment, lobbying can be crucial to company success and survival.

To think that lobbying the government is achievable without lobbying the consumer is a mistake. Satisfying consumer interests comes in material and ethical terms. People who lean towards environmentally friendly consumption are more likely to follow corresponding consumer habits. In an age of fast-moving, easily accessible, and globalised information, ethics can become a valuable asset to material enterprise by facilitating another dimension of competitiveness by following people's interests and ethical concerns – their values. In a highly competitive environment, the quality of a product can also be valued in terms of people's desires and concerns. With ethics and morality being objective and it being possible to structure values by their measure of virtue and piety, such as in terms of social and environmental issues, people's conduct can be guided by appealing to their values which competitive enterprise can capitalise on. But this specific topic will be left for a much later discussion.

Where an ethical function is corrupt and deficient, such as private material interests neglecting social issues, the entire sphere of the ethical environment becomes in some form neglected, causing imbalance, potential degeneration, and functional inefficiencies. Even social cohesion or national security becomes undermined when an official of questionable moral character susceptible to lobbying neglects public interests, which then blows up into riots and crime in impoverished and neglected communities. Fear and base morality, in this respect, has a very notable deficient attribute of valuing immediate and short-sighted vision of security and comfort. But where rationale is clear, base morality is deficient in its immediate sense, intuition, and feeling of comfort generally being more appealing than, but not as rewarding as, struggle and sacrifice. There are many exceptions to these prevailing tangents, with base morality valuing struggle. However, these exceptions are clearly rarer than the norm.

To think that discomfort and sacrifice are unrewarding, or that rationale is devoid of, or irrelevant to, sentiment and intuition, is a fundamental misconception. The ethical value of material currency as a binding power over rationale and emotion is a testament to the imperative role of both faculties of the psyche and sense of well-being. The spiritual and mental effects of the concern for survival and related instincts are organically powerful, which is not a bad thing. However, survival itself is fundamentally challenged by the foundation of some of its prevalent functions, for even a seemingly minor and innocuous catalyst can have tremendous effect on a globalised ethical structure. The concern for survival and security hinders greater prosperity and satisfaction by portraying threats and insecurities where there are none or giving too much attention to insignificant ones, with the value and manner of security failing to effectively correspond to actual insecurities and the root cause of suffering. But then even the values and moralities that are able to surpass the evocative corruption of Fear in base morality are often only delicate virtues.

All behaviour is a function and mechanism produced by reason setting the narrative of goal-directive operations. Material utility is fundamental to sustainable ethical dynamics and functions just as food and water are necessary for sustaining the body. With greater dynamics in structures of ethics, enabled by greater material capacities, the relevance of material utilities becomes instrumental for the qualification and determination of ethical values. The primary utility of material resources in ethics is the provision of security, stability, comfort, and development. Morality conditions actions with respect to the ethics of behaviour, according to which Fear primarily values security and comfort in its determination of morality. Base morality shapes conduct and the direction and structure of our desires and ambitions. Base morality is founded on intuitions and the senses of immediate well-being, of basic forms of satisfaction such as not feeling hungry, being entertained, feeling joy and pleasure, and so on. This is an organic ethical function of the human psyche mainly behaving in terms of instincts.

However, due to the generally narrow scope of people's concerns and interests in terms of the base faculties, focused on a sense of being characterised by immediate sensations, the globalisation of ethics struggles where people's values have insufficiently adapted to confront global problems related to impulsive, instinctive behaviour lacking moral discipline, coherence, and wisdom. Focusing on immediate satisfaction to distract from a dissatisfying and depressing life, acting in accordance with immediate comforts in contradiction to greater long-term interests, while far from condemnable behaviour and behaviour that is understandable and deserving of compassion where it attempts to alleviate profound suffering, are all problems of base morality. But in this submission to Fear mankind does not rise in virtue beyond suffering, maintaining a state of suffering. Base morality alone is incapable of sustainably motivating behaviour to fulfil greater desires and interests beyond immediate base concerns.

Security in Fear demands that we preserve stability, comfort, and security as a directive of well-being. But without acknowledging and coherently structuring the dynamics of ethics, such as in terms of the effect of poverty on people, the interests of material and ethical security are undermined by a selfish attitude and narrow scope of interest that doesn't consider variables relevant to the immediate negative effects of the problem being ignored. Where people's focus on security is dominated by immediate sensations and in basic terms of currency and status, these aspects of base morality's ethics are often mindless when it comes to the sums of ethical environment where one neglected sphere will have repercussions. For instance, where a nation lacks inward investment into educating its electorate, voter determinations can yield foolish policy decisions. Where liberty is not given to people, the lack of self-determination festers in its suffering and can lead to revolt and conflict.

The structures of ethics are fundamentally causally interlinked, whereby greater security can only ever be achieved through disciplined conduct mindful of global ethical environment. Base morality often only provides a very basic and simplistic sense of well-being that doesn't universally satisfy the challenges of modern structures of ethics. Base morality cannot fulfil a person whose mind, heart, and baser self are fundamentally broken and in pain that cannot be resolved through instinctive behaviour, as base morality's directive will follow broken and unachievable desires. Base morality is built on values and behaviour that focuses on sensations and instincts, ordinarily of immature fulfilment and lacking the capacity and virtue to behave in a way that produces greater goodness. A binding intuition of both faculties of the psyche in synchrony of interests, desires, values, concerns, and sense of fulfilment would be best.

To mediate impulses and discipline behaviour, and to encourage the pursuit of greater long-term interests, the mind and spirit must be fulfilled in the moment of the action being performed and be stronger than depressive influences of pain and suffering. Only this form of behaviour can fortify values and activity satisfactory of global interests such as those concerning the issues of sustainability and the natural environment. Only by making the moment of choosing discomfort for the sake of greater interests more rewarding than the base satisfaction of simple pleasure, with the corresponding sense of fulfilment having to be greater than the impression of pain, can its values be sustainable and its interests acted on. Only by making the activity of flipping a switch to save energy more rewarding and by helping people to stop making pointless and vain purchases, mediating unsustainable consumption, can an ethic of material utility become sustainable.

How can morally right behaviour be made to feel better, to be more appealing, and to be more fulfilling than immediate goodness and pleasure? How does the sense of any goodness in actions arise, what is it found on, and can it be changed? Consumer behaviour and the use of material utilities are excellent topics to study in consideration of these questions. Our understanding of ethics, morality, and reason and their power has hitherto been insufficient for such developments, which this project will seek to amend.

Before these discussions are misinterpreted, they have been restricted to ethical concerns, not economic policy or ideology. The narrative thus far was that ethics is of central relevance to material utility. Criticism of the implementation of Fear in material utility does not concern materialistic ethics as a whole. Material wealth, security, and stability are instrumental for growth, development, and progress, which are then essential for greater stability, security, and comfort.

However, excessive concern over material utility blindsided to other spheres and dimensions of ethical value can contradict the function pursuing greater stability and security. Where Fear becomes overbearing and excessive in its function, it becomes corrupt and betrays its ethical agent or sphere. Fear can facilitate progress and caution, but it can also do the opposite. Even a seemingly minor vice produces character and future actions of immorality that harm ethical environment and run deficits in ethical value by facilitating suffering. Often, however, by the nature of vice, the corruption of Fear primarily acts against the individual. Base morality invokes the value of security and stability, according to which conduct can begin to pursue wealth and status as means of fulfilling ethical interests. But the foundation of such behaviour, which values greater wealth for wealth's sake without greater ambitions and values corresponding to the worth of self as a character and not mere object, is an unsteady, unstable, and insecure foundation. Consequently, the attitude projects itself onto ethical environment and necessitates a cycle of suffering where people are deceived into thinking greater value is found in blindly pursuing security through wealth.

The desire for sufficient wealth is an excellent, wise, and understandable value, especially where one suffered from financial insecurity, as well as a prized utility for facilitating good living. I have suffered from financial insecurity; at one point I starved for a week, surviving on a bit of bread a day and sugared water. Financial security is crucial for good living. But where basic, sufficient, and adequate levels of material security, stability, and comfort are achieved, overvaluing their relevance to the state of living according to the directive of Fear and base morality is corruptive because it reduces people's ambitions to meagre excess of instinct lacking the ambition of higher virtues as greater aspirations than values diminishing character, power, and spirit. Pursuing and valuing vain displays of wealth can manifest itself as a common ethic. But in pursuing this excess one merely reduces themselves to the enslavement of Fear and a worth of self subservient to Fear without greater ambition of notable virtue and meaning.

The ambition to develop enterprise and accumulate wealth by a directive to grow in strong character, however, is of much greater virtue. By pursuing an excess of Fear by Fear itself one will never be satisfied, because the function of the ethic itself is contradictory. However, effective material utility and its resourcefulness are instrumental to greater ambitions of development and progress, producing greater security and stability. This balance does organically arise, as its absence can sow discord and stagnation. Yet base morality quite notably suffers from disparities in its dynamics of material utility. The main subject of this critique of base morality's ethic of material utility is that its functions suffer from imbalances and inefficiencies, whereby the misrepresented primacy of material value can hinder the greater sums of ethical interests of well-being. But it is not the distribution of wealth that is necessarily functionally corrupt; the ethical question primarily concerns itself with how material utility is employed for greater interest, and this is evidently problematic in modern ethical spheres and a globalised world.

Negative aspects of material utility in base morality, especially with reference to the primacy of security, comfort, and stability, don't only persist in consumer habits, the inefficiency of misapplication of excess wealth, and concentrated ethical functions amplified by disproportionate power through wealth (particularly lobbying). People's value of security according to a base moral sense fundamentally influences and shapes the dynamics of the sociopolitical. This brings me to touch on a final concern of base morality's sphere of material utility with respect to the sociopolitical and nation-states, which will then be the next area of discussion. People's sense of security in terms of the primacy of immediate awareness shapes government policy. Where economic hardship affects society, this will inevitably reflect onto the performance of the state. A democratic nation may undergo democratic transition; a cautious authoritarian regime may implement new policies; negligent authoritarian regimes can experience riots and civil war. For the present context, I shall focus on democratic dynamics with respect to the ethics of material utility.

Governments are forced to adapt to the demands of the people it serves. It is quite evident that people of different nations and communities tend to mainly prioritise personal national security and stability. These dynamics are fully consistent with international competition as state survival and material security and prosperity. However, where one nation thrives, this can come at a cost to others. In theory, it is intuitive to suggest an idea where greater balance in material wealth between nations might facilitate greater international security and material independence, especially in terms of energy. However, where Fear and its uncertainty is prevalent – a sensible organic dynamic in ethics with a valid function – an idealisation of selflessness is impractical and naive with respect to the associated risks. Furthermore, certain liberal schools of thought argue that economic interdependence is key to greater security by making the mutual costs of conflict too great and unsustainable, whereby the significance of material utility to national interests by the will of its constituencies fosters mutually compatible normative values and dynamics, creating what is called a 'zone of peace'.

The structural ethics normativist approach can account for the dynamics which produce mutually compatible and complimentary functions of ethics in accordance with their respective values. Material utility in base morality has a powerful effect on mediating behaviour, whereby morality and ethics form contingent on material concerns. Where societies, cultures, and people are influenced by these fundamental forces, their normative functions become compatible through reciprocal interests and values such as peace, security, stability, and prosperity. This way of thinking is commonly attributed to liberal political theory, which can be shown to guide many aspects of liberally democratic politics and foreign policy. But where the concern of material utility in Fear creates its species of ethical structures, which evidently have generally been successful with respect to the survivability and prosperity of Western liberally democratic nations, a foundational aspect of uncertainty and caution in insecurity can undermine the rigidity of such structures. Where the electorate is dissatisfied with economic performance and its welfare, the public applies pressure on the state to adapt and innovate. A nation's pursuit of wealth can, but doesn't always, come at a cost to others. Mutual interest sometimes gives way to the pressure of personal interest, applicable to the dynamics of individual and institutional behaviour by their respective organic functions and Natural Laws. The primacy of security in immediate environment, notably on a national level, fosters competitiveness, whereby individuals and governments follow suit. A zone of peace is thus only as sustainable as material concern is satisfied among the general public of a liberal democracy.

For a nation to sacrifice its own interest and comfort for the privilege of others is brave or insane. With uncertainty of international competitiveness and domestic concern for well-being, greater cooperation and collaboration is difficult, if not impossible. A liberal zone of peace by its ethical dynamics can foster peace, yet it does not and cannot always universally sustain that peace, stability, and security by the foundations of Fear. But where Fear has its shortcoming here, negligence in Fear can be devastating and regressive. International peace, security, and stability are far from ideal in the liberal zone of peace, but they are worth their credit in hindsight of much conflict in human history. But we ought not to settle for this, and on a personal note I do not believe this is all people are worth – of mere security based on narrow ambition of Fear lacking ambition rising above Fear. However, for any ethical and normative development to occur where greater collaboration and mutual trust succeeds seems to be a distant possibility.

Nation-states are the central conduits of the dynamics of ethical functions with respect to any concentrated ethical environment, such as community or society, or at least this is the case in reference to the centralised nature of society and the power of government as a hub of concentrated functions of ethics and individual concerns for well-being (with the study of the mind and psyche being another dimension of insight by virtue of the influences on mass behaviour). The individual concern of a person for material security and welfare influences government policy in a fundamental way, with both good and bad aspects. Any government needs to serve the wishes of its people for material security and comfort, as is a fundamental disposition of base morality. But in doing so this can come at a cost to other nations, feeding a cycle of adaptive policies and values. Base morality can thus be quite fragile in its long-term greater security and stability.

Sometimes people's sense of security, such as with status and validation, betrays their own greater interests. These sorts of fundamental self-inflicted contradictions and conflicts are what centres of power, such as governments, have to deal with, whereby fundamental inefficiencies prevail. Governments inherently do not possess the power to fundamentally and radically influence people's behaviour, especially as the power of law is usually only synthetic and of non-binding social contract moral authority. Only a different organic form of power can fundamentally aid human endeavour by appealing directly to the interests of well-being and mediate conduct through morality – a normative, moral influence by the progressive power of reason. This power, however, is only partial to governments and the state, private lobbies, or similar institutions that are forced to capitalise and utilise prevalent dynamics. Dominant organic ethical forces are always of the people, not with the state or other institutions established through the agents of a structure. But without coherent moral authority, a structure and its economic, social, and political spheres will suffer from fundamental inefficiencies, at the core of which is the individual and the moralities that guide them.

To formulate a model of value, interest, and incentive, which surpasses focused base morality and enables and empowers certain desirable behaviour, requires the structuring of relevant ethical dynamics. It is difficult for people to find an authority of trust and fundamental consular power, and without proper understanding of ethics and morality this has been neglected and practically inconceivable. Then, reckless and unprepared attempts at social engineering, ethical machination, and ploys of morality, stripped of respect for the organic nature of ethics and its liberty, can cause ever-greater damage.

To the sceptic of the 'progressive power of reason' as normative and moral power, reason is fundamental to human behaviour. People reason with themselves to improve their condition and state, with others' advice helping to guide and motivate. The choice of consumption can shift dramatically with a person's decision to lose weight; a person's value of sustainable environment and consumption can influence their decisions. With proper conditioning and measures, reasoning can influence people's behaviour and mentality. Yet achieving a coherent and comprehensive understanding of the human psyche and its ethics is not simple; the relevance of material utility and the primacy of security in terms of Fear should demonstrate this.

To structure a sound and relevant institution of reason which people can trust is not easy, with relevant ambiguities and complexities making it difficult for specialised people to account for everything, no less the individual to make sense of it all themself. Logically structuring the ethical functions of material utility and the primacy of security in Fear should have provided some clues with regards to the foundational nature of the problems of human activity.

To illustrate this point, people's primary value of material security moves governments to measure comparative gains which would fulfil the interests of sum utility by satisfying the greatest number of people. People may criticise governments and corporations for immoral conduct, but people are at the heart of their own faults by the ethics that govern their dispositions, values, and actions. But in order to steer away from the natural grief and disheartenment of such tragic conclusions, with self-reflecting base morality perhaps fostering tendencies of misanthropy and discouragement, a clearer view suggests insight that the mechanical dynamics of reason formulating ethics are central to the causal trends of behaviour. This understanding then opens up a rich world of understanding and possibility.

Consumer and enterprise behaviour, reciprocal of materialistic ethics, can commonly be simplistically scrutinised. Yet while some aspects of the root of the problem are dualistic and complex, some are more straightforward in people's moral attitudes and behaviour. The primacy of security and comfort defined by the intuitions of base morality in consumer habits invoke dynamics of ethics where immediate stimulation is valued more than greater sums of ethical interest.

This applies to both enterprise and the individual consumer. Where it may seem as though material utility is the end in itself, currency can be structured with clarity in terms of the service provided by material utility to base morality and the ethics of survival and instinct. The structure built on these systemic functions has prevailed and the nature of incentives can be overbearing in terms of its values of base morality. The incentive of security and comfort, while not intrinsically wrong or bad, in its base form contradicts itself by withholding action in greater ambition and interest. The core of base morality's incentive of survival and satisfaction of instinct's intuitions is restricted in its capacity and ambition. High-reason that performs rational estimation and calculation does not rule over the most evocative states of being and the spirit of instinct and sentiment, and neither should rationale reject, neglect, or diminish the role of instinct and sentiment, which will become much more apparent as a utility in later discussions.

Consumers need to be empowered through ethical functions that maximise ethical interest and sum gains in terms of both the agent and institution. Perhaps quite surprisingly, a conclusion to be made is that people's materialistic ethics, governed by the primacy of security and comfort neglecting greater ambitions of power and strength, somewhat reciprocal of 'warrior ethics', hinder further sustainability and effectiveness of materialistic ethics. Material utility has been crucial to human progress and development, while also being overshadowed by many inefficiencies. At the core of such dynamics in material ethics is every individual constituting the structure of corresponding ethics and their functions of reason. Consumer habits are at the centre of conflicted and inefficient dynamics in the structures of ethics of Fear. Corporations and nation-states may be demonised, but it is ultimately people that give institutions power through the exchange of ethical interests.

Society is commonly a headless leviathan of tremendous ethical and material force which states and institutes can only monopolise on and slightly adjust in a dual-sided relationship. Even where a society may have a figure-head of concentrated normative or moral authority, which is only enabled through trust and the people who bestow value on a leader, lacking coherence and sense in the dynamics of ethics' structures restricts leaders' vision and judgement. So even if consumer habits had a central figurehead to mediate and empower their judgement, a centrepiece of authority without coherent vision and understanding is doomed to fail as a maladaptive synthetic dynamic. But while people can only fulfil their interests in personal ambition and action, they similarly can't do this alone and without a directive of binding ethical value as incentive and power. Only through power to fulfil personal ambition and interest, as unyielding resolve and willingness to sacrifice and suffer in order to achieve greater sum gains, can people fulfil greater interests in material utility such as by not enabling companies with undesirable ethical values and policies to survive. But in the preference for security and comfort relinquishing ambition, discipline, and individual normative power, an imbalance in the dynamics of ethics forms in a way that a conflicted structure characterised by malevolent ethical functions damages the rest.

Companies and states use what they can and what is available, including people's desires, according to which it is people's behaviour and their values and interests that set the mode of a structure's performance and function. Fear is its own source of inefficiency and vice. Whether or not this is ultimately sustainable is not something I can comfortably conclude, but one can nevertheless form a confident conclusion that a structure of ethics of Fear and base morality with respect to material utility suffers from significant disadvantages and corrupt ethical functions. People and their values are the cause, with a solution being the development of material utility, such as more environmentally friendly and materially sustainable projects, on top of fundamental ethical and moral development as growth in the virtue of character capable of effective behaviour corresponding to a globalised, material world. Concerning the latter, this aspect of the progressive power of reason, however, has not kept up the pace of development, and we are suffering for it.

Chapter 6:

Genealogy of Ethics

The subject of ethics studies, qualifies, evaluates, and judges behaviour through a model of goal-directive behaviour in terms of the functions of reason. Empirical observations and insights of the other sciences concerned with human activity are key to ethical and moral valuation. If one is to study ethics and put forward a theory accounting for the structures of ethical functions, then it is crucial to make sense of observable human activity. One ought to ideally account for why and how the dynamics of ethics and values manifest themselves the way they do. For instance, the ethos of Fear, which values pain-aversion and security from suffering, can be intuitive in terms of evolutionary development and an indirect imperative goal of survival and continuity.

However, as is usually the case, there are many ways of theorising and interpreting empirical observations. Sometimes interpretations of behaviour can become mere abstractions parading as sensible theories. Even though explanations may possess intuitive and reasonable validity, metaphysical and abstract explanations may lack reliable, informative, and testable insights. Philosophical interpretations and theories are ridden with partial and incomplete truths, often satisfying only simplistic understanding without achieving full understanding. But the truth exemplified as the Highest Good is usually a combination of partial truths and complex dynamics of ethical values. The Highest Good is never simple. For instance, socialist theories of material utility and social justice may apply to one sphere of ethical values and character compatible with socialist political and economic philosophy. However, in other spheres this same manner of thinking and respective values are alien and incompatible.

The purpose of structural ethics is to provide a model of studying behaviour and human activity, to offer a process and way of thinking and analysing to give clarity and insight, to then formulate responsive, accurate, concrete, and adaptive guidelines for behaviour. But to do so one must provide a framework for the empirical study of behaviour and ethics, to then evaluate and judge behaviour. Discussions thus far should suffice in introducing a way of thinking that befits empirical observation and related ethical valuation. Empirically objective ethical study must account for why ethical values and morality manifest themselves the way they do such as with moral and cultural relativism. This brings me to consider the subject of the *genealogy of ethics* as a study of ethics' development.

With respect to the authority of the Fundamental Principle, ethics is reducible to the concern for, and the dynamics of, well-being. As such, ethics can never be a fully scientific or empirical discipline in the traditional objective sense, because the qualification of well-being is subjective. But where the self can sense degrees of well-being, as is part of the nature of behaviour to succeed suffering and strive for well-being, this translates into wisdom as empirical ethical insight. This insight informs us of the mechanical and deterministic nature of the human psyche. With respect to the structure of the mind, there is an explanation for all desires, mental states, and emotional reactions in terms of reason. Experiences of well-being and their functions, while consciously subjective like any experience, have concrete structure in terms of the substance corresponding to reason. Therefore, subjective experiences of well-being can be objectively evaluated in terms of their goal-directive functions and degrees of well-being, meaning moral evaluation is not subjectively incoherent or abstract.

There is a reason for why we sense a degree of well-being, the behaviour of which and its desires reflecting the nature of perceived well-being. The well-being sensed during a synthetic pleasure relating to the high of a false sense of achievement and confidence is nothing compared to the pleasure experienced by a character of real achievement and strength. Furthermore, the oddity of ethics means its wisdom and insight can be transferred through reason building on other empirical impressions. One can appreciate an ethical value that pertains to a sense of well-being without appreciating the actual experience of well-being. An experience and emotion can be related to without feeling the particular emotion, borrowing from a related impression. For instance, experiencing pain and recovery from pain can be related to and understood by others without experiencing the exact same thing. The pain of a broken bone in one part of the body can be related to the pain of a different broken bone in another person.

Reason has influence over moral discussions because it engages shared functions of reason as mechanisms of behaviour and the deterministic mind. People experience life differently. Yet by virtue of the inherent human condition, the functions of the mind will nonetheless respond to set trends and core functions. Base faculties of the mind are notable in their familial role in human behaviour and well-being. For instance, engaging base elements of the psyche can universally give rise to common values such as in the case of the appreciation of pleasure and its mechanisms. Human nature is structured in a way that makes it possible for people to universally acknowledge the pleasantness of true love once even its glimmer has been experienced, or the pain of suffering and loss. The sense of well-being, which ethics and morality are concerned with, is objective to the individual, with objectivity in structures of ethics being found through understanding the functions of people's psyche and the intuitions of desires. Objectivity in ethics can be established and found by understanding people's needs, desires, goals, ambitions, and states of mind, the functions of which are concrete in reason and can be studied accordingly.

Ethics encompasses a broad range of relevant factors to well-being, for everything from medicine to the economy affect states of well-being as states of affairs (of the external environment) and states of self (of the internal environment, of the mind and spirit). Where empirical insight is imperative for the concerns of well-being with respect to practical ethical wisdom and reliable knowledge, ethical valuation is primarily philosophical. Questions of what is most valuable to the self is fundamentally of a philosophical nature. But then there are the wisdoms and insights of practical ethical wisdom that tell us what is fulfilling and what is not – information that is empirical and subject to introspective testing and analysis. This is what makes ethics appear subjective and rather mysterious, as the complexity of the dynamics of well-being and states of affairs are often of immeasurable complexity that elude personal wisdom and the capacity for proper judgement without assistance from those adept in ethical valuation.

However, even the most revered sages earn their wisdom through experience and may struggle with proper ethical valuation. Yet this complexity is humbling for all and binds good faith through common introspection and meditation on the many fundamental questions all share such as with the question of happiness. But because there are definitive trends in what makes people happy, such as healthy lifestyles, and in terms of desires and inclinations conditioned by experience and environment, there is a concrete role of objective ethical study as an instrument for achieving well-being. The central tenant of the argument is that the functions of reason in the psyche can be exemplified and studied in a coherent objective and empirical manner. But where philosophical questions abound as a foundation of insight, wisdom, and methodology, the scientific method is itself an intellectual tool borne of philosophical utility. By studying goal-directive behaviour and exemplifying its reason through a model of the metaphysics of structural ethics and the anatomy of reason, ethics can benefit from the utility of empirical study and broader theorising without committing further mistakes.

There is always a reason why people are the way they are, why they act as they do, and value what they value. This is what allows us to study the empirical aspect of ethics and make objective ethical claims referring to the structure of the human psyche and its developed characteristics. Many disciplines studying human nature and behaviour already exist, which are instrumental for ethics. Then, even subjects exploring the nature or relation of well-being are based on deeply philosophical matters of what constitutes well-being. For instance, medicine studies health, yet the nature of health can be somewhat amorphous. Structural ethics serves to bridge this divide between empirical and analytic practical concerns and formulate ethical and moral claims encompassing factors relevant to well-being. However, there is no simple formula for the general practice of such a discipline, as there is no definitive recipe for a method studying ethics.

The dual nature of ethics as philosophical and scientific is innate. That being said, ethics becomes a way of thinking reciprocal of its study encompassing empirical and metaphysical examination. This is the method of structural ethics. Where one may question how to study the human mind and psyche, the physiology and anatomy of reason, then ethical values, dynamics, mechanisms, and moral claims, structural ethics is *a* method. For example, the development of the value of security through Fear and the primacy of instinct and survival have been illustrated and discussed in the previous Chapter, befitting the subject area of the genealogy of ethics in terms of the development of values and their structural forms. But then this method must be applied to individuals and their environments to fully account for and understand ethics. The necessity for the development of this method and its aspect of a genealogy is to develop understanding of, for instance, cultural moral relativism, to begin shifting through ambiguities, complexities, and learning to make concrete and objective claims from empirical observations.

Cultural moral relativism relates to the observation that in different cultures there are different ethical values and moral formulations. Relativism is an organic ethical dynamic of adaptation. A traditional practice may have initially served a valued utility in a certain environment, which continued as an unbefitting or irrelevant ethical value in a new age. These developments can be accounted for by structuring values and behaviour in relation to their genealogy of development in terms of well-being.

Killing an animal may have been necessary for our ancestors to survive, while the nature of needs in modern societies has changed in that some people have the liberty to choose not to eat meat and nonetheless live well.

However, where it may seem as though relativism is inherent to ethical study and is a devastating argument to objectivity, relativism can be understood in terms of points of objectivity in respective ethical environments. Virtues can be relative to environments and conditions experienced by people, nonetheless objective in their specific conditioning by ethical dynamics. Morality is objective to relative demands in specific environments creating particular conditions for, and parameters of, well-being. However, residual values as traditions of the past commonly affect present states, for better or worse. Shifting through ethical values and disparities in morality by studying their development and consequences becomes crucial to ethics.

Traditions of studying human behaviour, such as evolutionary psychology, can at times appear rather abstract and metaphysical. This is especially applicable to ethical studies and philosophy in general. The concern raised is to make a cautionary point that ethics should not be reduced to a pseudoscience where an explanation is merely abstract. Human behaviour can be odd and complex, with a rich diversity of explanations, notably those relating to instinct and survival, offering only partial theories. This is not intended to shun any such work, but rather to highlight the notable limitations of these methods and their ways of thinking and analysis for the sake of caution and precision. A mechanical and deterministic understanding of the human psyche and the metaphysics of morals proposed in this work allow for a more structured method of studying behaviour.

However, any empirical observation will raise ambiguities and different explanations, demanding strong theories. Such is a work hazard of developing explanations for why things are the way they are. Even claims of how things are and subsequent claims of how things ought to be have been granted too much leniency in public moral and philosophical folklore parading as wisdom. Political philosophies are especially guilty of these stupors, methodically formulating only partial truths and minor observable trends in ethical dynamics. There is a time and place and an amorphous reality to any ethical value; only concise empirical observation and strong theorising can properly account for the development and manifestation of ethics.

The relevance of these aspects of ethics is imperative, the neglect of which can be devastating. The *genealogy* of ethics will be shown to be instrumental in the narrative of normative and ideational social, political, and economic developments. Misunderstanding ethics is in many ways equivalent to misunderstanding people, the potential consequences of which should be intuitive. Understanding what makes people tick, on the other hand, can be very rewarding and insightful. To implement the structural ethics method of explaining behaviour and the development (genealogy) of values, I shall perform a comprehensive analysis of Russians and their culture and ethics in terms of attitudes and values. Russians may seem an odd and peculiar sort, but it is one I am quite familiar with.

The Russian mentality can commonly be characterised by irrationalism, impulsiveness, fatalistic attitudes, emotional openness, and bizarre mannerisms of questionable sanity. Sometimes it may seem, even to Russians, as though it is impossible to rationally understand the Russian spirit and mentality. To some degree, a historic culture has arisen trying to describe this mentality and set of emotional trends that a person may struggle to make sense of rationally. Art has flourished in trying to describe the Russian spirit without rational explanation. In defiance of such tradition, studying the Russian mentality and spirit will be a particularly useful example of a study of the genealogy of ethics. The proceeding discussion shall affirm rationality in the perceived impossibility of mindful rationality in the oddness of Russians.

To an outsider, Russia and Russians can come across as very bizarre. Some aspects of this reputation are fair; much of it is simple misunderstanding and an affirmation of bias which can turn into negative impressions. But then all cultures joke about stereotypes. Emergent post-communist generations in Russia and their dispositions are to some degree in stark contrast to a long history of an alternative modernity in Russia during its Soviet phase. Furthermore, Russia is still adapting to a radical shift in its social, economic, and political environment, whereby one can argue that Russia has not yet completed a full transition away from its communist era without 'baggage'. People's visceral memory of the instability and insecurity of the 90s, as well as the many challenges Russia still faces in terms of its transitioning period, including corruption, is a testament to the residual ethical dynamics stemming from generations of a communist era. At the core of these phenomena are ethical dynamics. Where instability was at its peak in the 90s, the past couple of centuries and the wars Russia fought, on top of vicious authoritarian rule, have ingrained an ethical culture and mentality accustomed to degrees of instability. This instability and at times harsh environment have without a doubt had a profound influence on shaping much of Russian mentality.

In contrast, Western societies, or at least according to my insight of English society, have enjoyed comparatively much greater stability. But as of recent years, this stability is very questionable at its core – in both Russia and the West. Perhaps the best testament to the contrast between Russian and English moral culture is in my own case where after a life in Russia and moving across many countries, acclimatising to life in England, even in South-East London with a less-glamorous reputation to the rest of London, was a difficult and long process. Things are very different between English and Russian societies, mentalities, and cultures, the cause of which is without a doubt related to their fundamental differences in historic development. But where there are evident trends observable in the respective developments of ethics – such as with transitions into post-industrial, modern democratic societies and subsequent shifts in social needs, relatable to Maslow's hierarchy of needs[16] – the same general dynamics of functions of the human psyche should apply universally.

While there will obviously be disparities in cultural, ideational, and ethical mannerisms, their core as part of fundamental elements of stable and sufficiently prosperous ethical environments should more-or-less be consistent. If economic and social stability endured long enough, such as with transition into modernity and prevalent satisfaction of individual and societal needs, then greater comparative degrees of ethical stability and satisfaction of spirit (as well-being) should abound. It is the long disruption to such trends in much of Russian history over the past century that has shaped its evident ethical features as a distinct Russian mentality, or at least distinct to the foreigner. Examining this genealogy of ethics should help to understand ethical attributes and developments, as well as further highlight the imperative value of stability in individual and social ethical dynamics.

With respect to impressions of Russian mentality by observable behaviour, it is easy to understand the reputation for oddness. It doesn't take much to find various images and videos on the internet portraying peculiar and even ridiculous life in Russia. Whether it is 'dashcam' videos of attempted insurance fraud and familiar chaos on Russian roads, whether it is people doing only borderline successful feats of folk engineering, whether it is drunkards or persons of impoverished backgrounds doing outlandish things, or whether a comical situation becomes so common that a ludicrous story becomes casualised and normal. To some, life in Russia can certainly appear backwards in some respects, and no doubt there are elements of life in Russia that do no correlate with economic and social development of more advantageous societies. Sometimes, the only natural responses summing up the sentiment are: "What?" and "Really?!"

Not all impressions of Russia are fair. Like any society, there are good and bad aspects, oddities and normalities, trends and anomalies. Like any society with a sphere of impoverished and poorly educated people living in harsh or hostile environments, there will be a seemingly universal correlate of crime, extremism, violence, pain, instability, substance abuse, thriftiness, resourcefulness, and so on. Due to Russia's sheer geographic size and wealth disparity, the division between classes and between urban and rural people is particular evident. One might try to focus on addressing one aspect of an impression, but such matters are usually mere impressions of biases lacking greater vision and understanding. There is no evident particular feature, perhaps like alcoholism or malicious racism, that needs to be discussed until it becomes extremely prevalent, of the mentioned not being definitive to Russian identity or requiring an outcry of defence because they do not in fact dominate life in Russia as absolute trends of behaviour. Such thinking serves to reflect the general point of the negativity bias where vocal and evocative abnormalities can dominate perception, whereby the quiet and common normality is taken for granted as the standard norm familiar to expectation.

It appears as a common phenomenon, from watching the news to seeing an individual's actions, that biases shape and hinder perception. Biases do not necessarily mean prejudice, yet they do tend to deceive. Russia sometimes gets an odd reputation by a perhaps quite unusual phenomenon – Russians joking about themselves. In any evocative viral video, one usually pays attention to what is happening in the frame in accordance with the function of the biases of perception. On the other side of the frame is the recorder, and in Russia's case, in relation to a very prevalent mannerism of Russian social culture, it is somebody realising something ridiculous and laughing about it. In retrospect, Brits and Russians have something very in common in terms of humour, especially when it comes to dark humour. But while impressions of Russia and Russians will inherently be subjective and no single view will be concrete regarding Russia's (or any society's) diversity, one notable feature of life in Russia particularly stands out – peoples' common impulsiveness, rashness, and emotional openness.

To qualify a prevalent trend in Russians' behaviour, it can be summarised as normatively fatalistic, ascriptive of the words: "Shto budet, to budet" (what will happen, will happen). This goes hand in hand with a particular mannerism among Russians of 'building life' – setting and pursuing goals, actively improving quality of living. A notable feature of life in Russia, or at least compared to England, is its swiftness. Life moves and progresses quickly in Russia, especially in terms of marriage and family and getting through the business of everyday errands. There are too many notable aspects of Russian culture and mentality to perform a comprehensive analysis.

However, the role of quick-paced living in ethical studies is tangible to a stubborn and rash 'building of life'. An example of this attitude is people jumping on any opportunity and investment, whether it is a house or a job, and if the risk doesn't go well, worry about that later and sort it out later. This is but one aspect of a broader ethical dynamic of impulsiveness. Even corruption, specifically everyday corruption intended to serve the efficiency of daily errands and as a business ethic, is an example of an attitude where people are very open to taking risks. People might get into a lot of trouble for corruption, yet they persist in a casualised manner, even and especially bureaucrats. These mannerisms can be traced back to a useful mentality during periods of instability, especially during the Soviet Union's dissolution, where quick decisions were crucial for success.

As was discussed previously, the economic and social upheavals following Russia's transition away from its communist phase were frightful and disastrous. It should be very intuitive how impulsive and opportunistic attitudes prevailed where instability left people with little-to-nothing to lose. In the largely prevalent free-for-all, opportunism and thriftiness were invaluable ethical utilities, which surely many picked up on. A contrasting thought is that without opportunistic and quick decisions, people would have potentially lost out on even the basic necessities for survival. Simply put, it is impossible not to exemplify the profound effect the socioeconomic turmoil of the 90s has had on Russia's ethical dynamics and mentality, whether in shaping or nurturing them. Many of these functions of the psyche and behaviour can be understood in terms of Fear, instinct, and the value of security, which are inherently ethically intuitive. In times of instability, uncertainty, and hardship, impulsive and rash ethical values and dispositions can prevail.

However, instability is much more ingrained in Russian culture and mentality than only because of the 90s. The Second World War was devastating to all, but while the comparison of suffering is inappropriate, as all suffering is relevant, Russia was in a particularly dire situation, which reflected into its maximum utilitarian policies. Through great sacrifice, blood, and defiance, Russia prevailed. The harsh memory of the losses and sacrifices of the Great Patriotic War (as it is known in Russia) became part of Russia's culture and mentality. Where the Soviet military was central to national pride and identity, these ethical values, built on memories of glory and sacrifice, facilitated a significant presence of patriotism as a strong ethical dimension of identity, mentality, and value. The identity of Russians as protectors, fighters, and guardians against Nazism and capitalism was largely elementary to communist Russia's history.

These attitudes are comparable to liberal democratic nations' values as protectors and champions of liberty, justice, and human rights. The only difference was ideational and normative, yet the ambition shared fundamental similarities of doing something meaningful. After all, has a wealthy and opportunistic nation ever settled for idleness and menial ambition? Instability during and after the Second World War is familiar to Russian mentality, which was then subject to another great test during the dissolution of the Soviet Union. Russian patriotism is borne of conquering the odds, of defiant stubbornness, of sacrifice, strength, and courage. Unity as rallying around the flag to protect the nation and its people was the most natural course for an organised solution to strife and instability.

While Russians did experience degrees of stability through an alternative modernity during its communist era, much of this stability was built on vivid impressions of suffering and instability, subsequently fostering respective ethical values. The current focus of study should not highlight the ideational feature of Russian patriotism, but should rather focus on the ethical dynamics corresponding to significant elements of Russian mentality. Instability and suffering have shaped much of Russians' ethical values, dispositions, and respective mentalities. Even in Russia's communist era of degrees of stability and comfort, Russian mentality and ethics were still vividly built on familiarity with turmoil and strife.

The development of ethics accustomed to instability can be traced back even before the Second World War. Russia had experienced many revolutions in its history, a cycle that seems to have only partially been alleviated, but not resolved, over the past decades. The Russian Empire basically turned into a Soviet quasi-empire of an authoritarian liberty to be free from capitalism respective of communist rhetoric. Russia experienced many wars and its people suffered greatly, even before the 20th century, as did much of Europe. But with respect to civic and ethical development, Russia took a drastically different path to much of the West in terms of communist ideology – a grand experiment in social engineering, which ultimately failed. Yet another feature influencing Russian mannerism and mentality is the country's sheer size and division in power. While Russia's monarchical, communist, and sovereign democratic governments led its people, it is clear that there have always been rifts between the people and the state.

A simple analogy to this point is the peasant or farmer doing his work somewhere in the countryside and only faintly hearing some news of revolution. The peasant or farmer will get on with his everyday life as best he can, to what he is accustomed to as a person of a humble background. Even now, there are observable phenomena of people getting along with their lives while the government does something in the background. The case of corruption among the general public is especially notable in its ethical value of borderline ignoring the authorities.

This brings me to highlight another prominent feature of Russians' mentality with respect to familiarity with instability as people's familiarity with transitions in government and their epiphenomenal impacts on everyday life. A person in poverty will not necessarily feel the turmoil of a failing economy and sudden government transition, as this person might not be sufficiently active or integrated to be affected by socioeconomic change. Similarly, even in advanced democratic societies, governments change and people sometimes don't feel a significant impact on everyday life. This is especially evident in Russian society and mentality, whereby people have become largely accustomed to relying on themselves and other people through social networks. Where there was little currency for resources, personal connections were pivotal for doing well in Russian communist and post-communist social and ethical environments. People learnt to, or became familiar with, relying on themselves and the people around them, not necessarily the government or authorities. The two ethical aspects – relying on connections and the self, on top of centuries of periodic instability – compiled into an ethic where quick-living and rashness became ethical norms. These trends in Russia's development greatly influenced people's attitudes and mentalities, with spontaneity, impulsiveness, and fatalism (expressed as casualised attitudes towards the present and future in the form of attempts to make the best of what one immediately has) being the norm.

To understand and account for the Russian mentality and its ethical dynamics, one must also account for the mass psychology of Russians' general openness or emotional openness. Russians in particular may have a reputation for quirkiness with respect to their tendency to be emotionally open and straightforward, similar to the sincerity of a simple and easy-going person. This 'simplicity' of character is intended as simplicity in straightforwardness and sincerity, nothing derogatory. Sometimes people are deceitful, manipulative, and emotionally convoluted. People have different norms and tendencies in dealing with emotions and inclinations, with Russia in some respect having somewhat of a tradition of being much more straightforward and non-complicated in this respect. Rather than pursuing twisted and complicated schemes, a Russian may simply go for a drink or throw a punch. Of course, no such phenomena are absolutely ascriptive to Russians alone or that they necessarily still prevail as much as may have been previously observable in Russian culture and tradition. Nevertheless, these aspects of Russian mentality are notable and can be ascribed to the sense of irrationality in terms of impulsiveness in Russians' ethical mannerisms.

Some might suggest a thought that this tendency is for genetic reasons, but perhaps a better explanation would be in terms of social culture, mass psychology, and an ethical environment more accustomed to emotional openness and impulsive outbursts. In contrast, Brits might have a reputation for the 'stiff upper lip', a habit of politeness, and a love for drinking. But while any such phenomena are not universal or are only prevailing norms, there must be developmental reasons for why certain attitudes prevailed. These aspects of the genealogy of ethics is perhaps better explained in sociocultural terms rather than deeply-rooted biological ones.

Too many factors would be relevant for the analysis of why Russians are emotionally open and impulsive. Subsequently, the ethical attributes and morality of these dispositions are complex. For instance, an ethical value tolerant or understanding of sometimes aggressive drunkenness can be rather common. Similarly, violent outbursts or episodes of open crying can be common and normal among some spheres of life in Russia. Of course, many such phenomena are amplified by alcohol. But due to the pain causing such bouts, an aura of mutual understanding arises, whereby people are both emotionally hectic but also very open.

This correlate of pain in common experiences of similar pain, also of a trend of dealing with pain through substance, leads to mutual reflection on pain itself. With many periods of strife and trial, people were most aware of theirs and others' pain. While emotional openness cannot be ascribed to mutual pain as a lone or even dominant factor of development in mass psychology and contingent ethical dynamics, one can see how mutual familiarity with pain fosters a culture accepting openness through common understanding. But where the convention is to some degree accustomed to such behaviour, so too will contingent ethical values, with morality being susceptible to perceived irrationality and impulsiveness. It is no wonder that in a culture exposed to strife, grief, war, and revolution, with a history of broken hierarchies and fundamental upheavals, behaviour changes through pain, with institutions crumbling while the people endure. Where a culture may have had an ingrained tradition of sternness, further upheld by a hierarchy and enduring authority, Russia's culture and genealogy largely experienced less continuous and stable authority. And so people looked to themselves and followed their own determination and tradition.

I will concede that some elements of the discussion on Russia's genealogy of ethics thus far has had some major weaknesses as abstract and unconcise arguments, which was cautioned in the beginning of this Chapter. The genealogy of ethics works on the individual level by reflecting on old memories and impressions that shaped the psychological state of a person. On a social and national level, this same method of thought becomes much more complicated. Ideally, discourse would benefit from clearer empirical observations and study. However, the present discussion must be settled with a mere introductory example of a genealogy of ethics demonstrating how and why certain trends in ethics arise, or even question a trend's reality or prevalence. Biases in the impressions of normativity and behaviour commonly produce simplifications.

However, there are some notable aspects of normativity and ethics in Russia which feed into a rather clear general picture of the ethics that exemplify people's behaviour. Of those notable characteristics, impulsiveness, emotion, and elements of fatalism shine clear. Now, to settle the question of rationality, the aforementioned attributes in Russians' behaviour and mentality should become intuitively rational in terms of base-reason and Fear. The soldier who sacrificed himself for his family, friends, people, and country, did so in a dire moment of desperate defiance, for if the soldier was to die anyway, at least he would die in final moments of courage and virtue standing against adversity. The parent committing great risks to better the lives of his or her children in harsh circumstances, parents who jumped on any opportunity to earn money and setup advantages for their children, did so with little else to lose, according to the memory of the regret of lost opportunities. The humble and well-spirited old man living in the countryside will say and do much in good faith while tending to his potatoes and cabbages, living in a partial reality of news on the radio, yet in great spirit of the Russian countryside and tradition, occasionally swigging a little vodka to get the blood rushing and appetite going.

Where there has been hardship, there have been many who shared it, in doing so becoming open and sincere to one another, rallying against adversity. Where ethics and rationale are occupied with the concern for well-being, all mentalities and behavioural dispositions contingent on respective values have been integrated for a reason. In many respects what Russia is today has arisen from an ethical dynamic of a people accustomed to suffering and instability. Impulsiveness and strong emotional responses can be seen to be rational in respect of unstable ethical environments. Where scepticism remains, one needs only to remember that whatever functions of reason worked in Russia's ethical dynamics and mentality, the bottom-line is that those functions of behaviour succeeded – Russians survived, endured, and grew. Whether these dynamics are sustainable or effective anymore is another question. This brings me to considering some fundamental values and ideologies as extensions of normativity in Russian politics and society.

A fascinating period of Russia's development is its cataclysmic change since the 90s. Russia has transformed through the millennial and late-period Soviet generations. Russia has always had a rich tradition and culture. Now, with new generations of people and values, things have changed more than ever. Lost culture is reviving in some respects and evolving in others, then also stunted by corruption. These aspects of life and ethics in Russia may have been rather misunderstood or misrepresented, but there is a distinct element of modernity in urbanised Russia. While at times rather scrupulous and reclusive to general awareness among foreigners, there is a distinctive presence of Western-oriented (at least culturally), modern, even liberal, urbanised communities borne of a period of stability and sufficient wealth resembling a middle-class. This is further consistent with empirical observation of domestic public opinion, where modern materialistic attitudes have been sufficiently prevalent to enable preferences for comfort, stability, and economic welfare[17]. Observable 'principles of social order' between 2002 and 2012 demonstrate that people have come to largely (7 to 3 ratios of public opinion) priorities individual, personal interests over the state's interests[18].

Simply put, there are clear impressionable and empirically confirmable trends where distinct groups in Russia herald a prevailing ethic reciprocal of modernity as a preference for welfare and stability and truly 'welfare rather than glory'[19]. This ethic is characterised by internally-oriented, non-imperialistic priorities of protecting personal interests[20] rather than brash and impulsive expressions of pain as vices of 'great power through conquest' complexes. Moreover, there is a pronounced trend of Russian youths – that is, millennials – wanting and valuing the same things as their Western European counterparts, influenced by the draw of Western culture[21]. Where Western societies experienced quick shifts in ethical values through progressive new generations, similar phenomena, but not necessarily of the same orientation, are observable among Russians. But past traditions, mannerisms, cultures, and aspects of mass psychology remain.

A rather simple but significant clue with regards to Russia's state of ethics and society are people's common manners. A reputation may have been formed where even though Russians can be generous, have good intentions, and be of good faith, they nevertheless won't necessarily be polite or smile. Excessive smiling was once usually considered to be a characteristic of a simpleton, as being joyous without cause was a sign of ignorance or something else. But during my recent travels to Russia and speaking with Russians, in contrast to the period when I lived there, while smiles aren't everywhere, gentleness, kindness, and politeness have become (comparatively) much more common, at least in urban areas. Life in Russia has not been cushioned for many, but this has changed greatly since the beginning of the new millennium. Simple mannerisms of behaviour such as those mentioned highlight ethical development towards something more aligned with ethical modernity.

Where ethical modernity reaches its peak and the nature of needs transforms, so too does the nation and society, leading to the common challenges of modern society such as those encountered by Western societies including the consequences of excessively materialistic societies. Russian mentality and social culture are odd, but it is empirically confirmable that changes are occurring, complying with the model of changes in ethical values through periods of stability and instability with respect to the functions of Fear and their focus on base morality and instinctive reason.

At the forefront of these ethical developments are their normative, namely political and ideational, dimensions. Ethics can be classified as the subject area concerning itself with the metaphysical and empirical levels of the systems of ethics with respect to fundamental concerns for, and dynamics of, well-being. Normativity, on the other hand, relates to practiced ethical values and their morality in specific civic, social, political, and economic forms.

To illustrate this point, changes in ethical values, such as racism giving way to tolerance, are systemic features of ethics, whereas the social values and attitudes relating to racism belong to the subject area of normativity. Normativity relates strongly to morality, but with the distinction that normativity is morality prevalent and applied in its secondary form in terms of society, politics, economics, and so forth. Before I delve into a dedicated study of Russian politics to explore its normativity and ethics, the ideational contingency of ethical values – of fundamental normativity – must be explored. Specifically, the nature and question of Russian patriotism.

Examining nation-states, mass psychology, and general socioeconomic dynamics is crucial for the study of ethics and normativity. Governments reflect the moral culture and social state of their populace. Even a representative neglecting the public for personal gain, enabled by intrusively propagated interests of wealthy private lobbies or selfish interests, is a reflection of a social dynamic enabling this behaviour of lobbies and representatives through consumer conduct or personal attitudes normalising these states of government and society. The exploration of Russia's genealogy of ethics showed how nation-states and governments are extremely relevant to the study of ethics in terms of attitudes producing normativity adhering to public interests. Nations are a focal point of primary factors in an ethical environment – of government, society, economics, and culture. Looking at the normativity of nation-states and respective prevalent ethics among the public should provide some clues regarding the state of ethical environment. The degree of extreme views and attitudes among the public are a particular representation of social strife and spiritual and mental suffering – all representative of ethical deficiency. The ideational-normative sphere, as part of moral culture, in this sense, becomes important for understanding ethics and its development. Public attitudes, built on morality and corresponding normativity, reflect onto their governments.

The genealogy of Russia's value and idea of patriotism is based on many struggles including wars and revolutions. Prevailing over many perils, especially the Second World War, forced the people to unite. A legacy of glorious victory left its mark on values of heroism, courage, and perseverance. Russians are hardy and adaptive. But for the ordinary person, ideals were simpler in terms of defiance against an immediate, present, and real threat. Communist and early post-communist generations sometimes demonstrate a great love of their country. Some aspects of this attitude may be ascribed to a patriotic education, or to a strong culture calling back home, or to a strong draw of the remarkable and distinct spirit of Russia.

Russia has a long history and rich culture, which has reflected onto its enduring, resilient, and stubborn people. Patriotism is the value of this love of country. This, however, is not necessarily a love of nation and state. As Vladimir Putin, Russia's political patriarch, said himself: "Patriotism is love of the Fatherland" ('Lubov k Otechestvu')[22]. An odd but deceptively familiar trend in this ideology and normativity is love of country, land, tradition, culture, and people, with the government and state being mere formalities of minor relevance to a person's spirit and morality. American tradition of small government is similar where patriotism as the love of country eclipses the authority of the state. Russians might pride themselves on their patriotism, but this patriotism should be seen as exclusive to the normativity of nationalism.

Without digressing into the specifics of political philosophy, there are some key distinctions between patriotism and nationalism. To consider a point raised by Vladimir Putin, patriotism may be interpreted as love of country without prejudice or hostility towards other people[23]. In Western terms, such a classification is more familiar of civic nationalism – a non-xenophobic form of nationalism. In Russia's case, its normativity is better described as civic nationalism. Some incidents have left an evocative impression of Russians as ethnic nationalists[24], further exacerbated by the annexation of Crimea in 2014. Indeed, there has been a notable presence of neo-Nazis and racist hate groups in Russia[25,26].

However, where shock is exciting, any impression is better accounted for through empirical study. For one, a safe majority of people in Russia find anything related to Nazism as despicable and disgraceful, with Russian neo-Nazi hate groups being rejects. Russia is inherently pluricultural and ethnically diverse; any malicious and serious racism as policy and driving ideology, as opposed to casualised and humorous folk racism, is inimical to Russian identity.

This is distinct to other attitudes of nationalism. Trends in aspects of nationalism are empirically ambiguous[27]. There are no particular demographic groups in Russia with (ethnic) nationalist tendencies[28], just as Russia in general cannot be defined with ubiquitous xenophobic tendencies[29]. Furthermore, Russian nationalism of recent memory in terms of the Ukraine conflict is by-and-large empirically more associative of 'rally-around-the-flag' behaviour against perceived foreign threats without deep-rooted anti-Western attitudes[30], not expressions of neo-imperialistic ambitions. Therefore, Russia is more aligned with civic nationalism – known in Russia as patriotism.

A more technical and normatively significant difference between patriotism and (civic) nationalism are the specifics of their attitudes. For instance, take the following thought: "The difference between patriotism and nationalism is that a patriot is proud of his country for what it does, and the nationalist is proud of his country no matter what it does."[31] Of the two, it seems true patriotism is of genuine liberty, or rather a liberty to love. Russian patriotism is mainly a love of country and its rich spirit. As such, the nation-state is a mere bureaucracy of the normativity of social activity found on spirit bound to environment. This is more ascriptive of Russian tradition where people are for most part engaged with their own living and appreciation of culture, tradition, and spirit. This, however, has little-to-nothing to do with the state. In such terms, perhaps quite surprisingly, Russians can be described as rather libertarian.

A simple test of this libertarianism is Russians' prevalent knack for bending the laws and exploiting corruption for non-malicious means of surviving. With much strife and plenty of revolutions, it should come as no surprise that ethical dispositions of autonomy and self-sufficiency would give way to idealism and normativity more ascriptive of libertarianism rather than nationalism. In these crucial distinctions, one must question what role love has between country and nation, patriotism and nationalism. If patriotism is love of country, then is this love not supposed to be free? Is Russia's love of country and prevalent libertarianism among common folk under high castles of red walls not a sign of a fundamental normativity of liberty? These questions would beckon soul-searching and normative examination. While the claim is not that Russians are distinctively patriotic or libertarian rather than nationalistic, there is ambiguity, sufficiently so that Russia's mentality and its ideational normative expression is not simple or straightforward. Either philosophical-normative path is fair in its own right, but one view that cannot be ignored is that a love of country – patriotism – is inherently characterised by liberty in normativity, as a forced and oppressed love is something very different and twisted. The choice between patriotism and (civic) nationalism belongs to the individual, and nothing can inherently move the soul beyond its concern for well-being.

At the heart of Russia's authoritative regime of 'sovereign democracy' is supposedly patriotism, or what would perhaps be better described as civic nationalism. The claim of libertarian tendencies in Russian normativity may seem antithetical to its trend of ultraconservative governments of illiberal democracy. For one, everyday life in Russia is not one of oppression and suffering at the hands of authority (for most part, at least). If it is an authoritarian regime, it is a smart one catering to satisfy the public enough for them to be engaged in, or distracted by, opportunities or the business of everyday life. Then, also, many people in Russia might not be aware of shady dealings as much as Western audiences are.

For the present context, a foundation of Russia's authoritative government, as well as the normativity of its ideology, ought to be considered along the claim of libertarian tendencies among the people and the distinction between patriotism and nationalism. If people are so autonomous, independent, and characteristically libertarian, with a cultural rather than pathological knack for bending the laws and rules, then why have Russians elected and supported a strong and authoritative government?

Disorder, instability, and suffering moved people, as suffering usually does, to value and elect security. This is a reasonable, rational, and often good response, a part of the continued cycle of values between liberty and authority. Russia's illiberal government and its ideology is found on a platform of stability and security. People were suffering and it seemed only a stern authority could fix the many problems in Russian society. It is intuitive and natural to suppose that where people are so independent, only a strong leader and figurehead could bind common endeavour. Enter, Vladimir Putin.

Vladimir Putin and the normative ideation of authority and strength was borne of people's disquiet in suffering by the perils of the 90s. At the time, it looked like there was no other option. Furthermore, Putin's government's platform and implementation of policy was clearly successful in the short-term (to be discussed in the following Chapters). An ideology might suppose that sovereign democracy is rooted in a long-standing tradition or culture preferring strong, authoritative leadership, from tsars to dictators. There certainly is such a trend, but the nature and psyche of contemporary Russia is very different.

Discussions thus far can point to a much more coherent and concise explanation for Russian mentality – dissatisfaction with, and aversion to, instability and degeneration. People's tendency towards corruption is a strong indicator of people's defiance or disregard of 'strong authority'. Furthermore, to take for granted some future points, Putin's administration is quite cautious of public dissatisfaction. A solid critique of the normativity of sovereign democracy and nationalism, as opposed to patriotism, is the matter of people's dissatisfaction with a strong leader when that leader does not serve their interests.

This is empirically observable in a fall in support for Putin's governance before the Ukraine conflict[32] and just after the questionably legitimate 2012 presidential elections, evident with the subsequent mass protests in Moscow. A strong-man attribute of Russian politics is definitive, but only in so much as is common for any people to want a strong, confident, and capable leader. Furthermore, these normative orientations are only a manifestation of a dominant value seeing a strong personality in authority as a means to an end of securing stability and order. In short, Russia's seemingly authoritative preference is only a manifestation of a value as a means to an end and is not an inherent normative trait of its culture.

The libertarian dimension still holds, but how prevalent it is can only be confirmed with greater empirical study, which is not my current profession or ambition. But as can be seen from these discussions, the genealogy of ethics is pivotal to normativity and ideals, as well as mass culture and psychology. A mistake and misassessment in prevailing normativity, known better through studying the genealogy of ethics in respective spheres and environments, can be dire to policy direction and government effectiveness. This matter will be explored in the proceeding Chapter.

A final point to make regarding Russia's genealogy of ethics, instrumental to understanding Russia's society and politics, is the role of status and respect in Russian ethics and normativity. All prior discussions of this Chapter should come full circle and highlight the obsessively valued utility of status in Russian society. However, the value of status is found everywhere, from dynamics between individuals to interactions between nation-states. In some spheres, however, the role of status is exacerbated like a wound festering with suffering and vice. Fear can bread insecurity as a utility intended to motivate self-improvement turned malevolent through feeble character subdued by pain. Where the social animal of mankind is moved by instinct, emotion, and base-reason, status and the desire for respect and self-affirmation become key values to any individual.

First, it would be useful to consider the nature of status as an ethical and social utility in relation to psychology. Emotion and status are fundamentally linked[33], with the structural ethics account offering insight with regards to such dynamics of the psyche and functions in terms of base-reason as the morality of instinct. Status as a rank has much to offer in social groups and society as a whole, notably: as an asset for access to greater social and material goods[34]; gratification and nurture of self-esteem, positive self-image, and respective emotions and 'feel-goods'[35]; greater social (or even international) legitimacy and authority, providing a robust basis for normative power[36]; as well as the intuitive utility of higher status and elitism to achieve a sense of hierarchy, control, and security, which is especially evident in the Russian 'strong-man authority' mentality reciprocal of 'not messing with the big guy'. Status and the dynamics of respect have instrumental value to ethics and the human psyche in relation to the psyche's base, instinctive faculty. One may morally evaluate the effects and relevance of these dynamics of base-reason, but ethical study must ultimately admit the imperative role of most people living in accord of base morality and psychological needs for self-validation, decency, respect, and some dignity. This is just how people are, but in some environments the value of status is affluent and monopolised in strictly hierarchal and communitarian orders.

Neglect of status and positive self-identity can lead to conflict[37], which applies to both individual and structural levels of dynamics in ethical values and interests. Frustration abounds in the neglect of, or weakness in, status, as status is often perceived to be a reflection of identity and self-worth, with social base morality often forming a sense of self through the perceptions, validations, and judgements of others. Such trends are universal to the structures of base morality, with Russia and many other middle economies and developing societies still bearing an emphasised socioethical dynamic valuing status and hierarchy. Other nations, countries, and people also abide these conventions of base morality, with glorification in social media being of the same principle. But normatively speaking, status has a distinctly special role in its internal sociopolitical dynamics and foreign policy ambitions.

The final remark of the formal introduction of the subject of the genealogy of ethics is the reason for the value of status in Russian society. The drunken question of 'do you respect me?' ('ti menya uvazhayesh?') or the online persona furiously typing abuse in public chat are somewhat common in Russia's folk psychology and culture. The dynamics of these values can be accounted for in psychological terms of basic needs of self-affirmation and positive self-identity. Receiving appraisal from others, in whatever form, is a means to that end of psychological desire and socioethical value. When identity is in pain, of weak confidence, and of minor virtue, the sense of self struggles. Discussions of Russian mentality and value throughout this Chapter should already compose relevant intuitions of the role of status, its ethical values and developments, and some of Russia's unhealthy desire for status.

Understanding why people value what they value (in ethical terms concerned with well-being) was the ambition of this introductory work on the genealogy of ethics. The lack of dependable access to material resources, lack of social cohesion and effective institutional authorities, lack of security and stability, impressions of a hostile and aggressive social environment, a conflicted legacy of identity and loss of national pride and status, and the necessity of connections and networks for success, all factored into a focused primary value in Russian dynamics of ethics prizing status. I will conclude the Chapter on the genealogy of ethics with this point, to move on to other studies of the social, political, and economic dynamics shaped by normative orientations and ethical values. As was hinted previously, there are some notable oddities in Russian political culture, especially between nationalist, patriotic, and libertarian tendencies. An evaluation of this will be crucial to a general understanding of base morality and subsequent evaluation.

Chapter 7:

Vectors of Authority in Fear

Any study of Russia can be mired with controversy. Biases and impressions abound even among the most seasoned scholars. But where Western groups may quickly condemn and criticise Russia's government, or Russian authorities and 'specialists' respond critically and blather their 'insights' of subpar academic work of a lesser grade than that of a first-year social science student, they often do so with minor insight and understanding. But the nature of political professions seldom allows for clever design under swift prompts demanding a decision – a luxury no nation usually has.

Some criticisms of both the West and Russia are fair, others are not. Yet rarely is analysis of Russia's politics level-headed and its critique performed on Russians' own terms. There is plenty decent literature written on the subject of Russian politics and society, which informed and inspired this study. Nevertheless, many questions and answers are incomplete.

Political analysis features in ethical studies because it relates to states of normativity, with the neglect of normativity and morality being costly for nation-states. Russia will serve as a good case study of the consequences of neglecting normativity, as well as introduce some major normative and moral problems in global states of affairs. If the function of the state is to survive and protect its constituents, then noble virtue may lose out to Machiavellian ploys and brutalities of selfishness. These losses, I argue, have been a mistake of ignorance, with the veil of Fear denying far greater ethical interest.

Any study of Russia's politics cannot overlook Vladimir Putin – the centrepiece, the patriarch, the man. But where one might eagerly brandish him a tsar or lavish him as a fulcrum of authority and the main character on the stage, this is a mistake. Even Putin, in all his glory and infamy, is at the mercy of the audience – of society's leviathan that is the public and electorate. Where it may seem as though the cases of electoral fraud discount serious concern over public opinion, the learned reader will know the attention given by Putin's administration to domestic opinion. Putin's government fears instability more than the public itself, for not only will it wreck Putin's legacy and it will be his and his acquaintances heads that will roll, it will also destabilise the country once more. At the heart of the man's ambition is patriotic duty and value, or at least this might have been the intention before the first sin. This normative orientation is core to all ambition, desire, design, purpose, and identity of Russian authority. No matter how this attitude may seem to have been warped and twisted, there is still part of the government's spirit and soul that is moved by a predicate of love and care for the homeland – patriotism. Whether reality meets virtue and morality is the matter to be discussed.

Putin and his government came to power in a time of turmoil entering the new millennium. The people suffered after decades of ineffective, if not incompetent, leadership and government. The ambitions of the elites were consumed with vice, only to become cannibalised by their own greed and lust for significance at odds with the general public. Instability, insecurity, strife, and disarray were the platform on which stern authority rose time and time again, repeating the cycle inherent to the ethics moving mankind. This is where Putin and his authoritative government came to be. After generations of failures and blunders, a leader came with confidence, ability, ambition, motivation, and competence. These virtues, however, may have turned to excess and become vices, for it is in the sheer ability of Putin and his government to influence the nation that may have become the root of many of Russia's problems now. Like the parent cradling his child, failing to let the child learn, the child enters the unknown world with little under his or her belt but the memories of a sheltered life, unfit for the challenges ahead. Security – a foundation of progress – may be losing out to its greater sums by lack of development facilitating greater security through adaptation and innovation.

To give some context of the dangers of Russia's instability, where there was chaos and a not-too-distant immediate threat of economic and social collapse, a failed Russian state or civil war will have catastrophic repercussions. First, and perhaps most importantly, never has a nuclear superpower collapsed. One can only speculate where these devastating resources would end up if authority was lost and mankind's vice of instinct gave way to the extreme influences of Fear. If the highly militarised nation broke down more so than in the nineties, and even worse if civil war broke out, surrounding regions would suffer. Who is to say that other nations might not jump on the opportunity to occupy the country to capitalise on power-shares and resources? Many uncertainties are inherent to such cases, but a broken Russia would be a great detriment to all of mankind. So if there is a question to be asked whether it is better for Russia to be subject to a stern authority to guarantee some stability, or for liberty in uncertainty to prevail, in terms of a sum estimation of world interests and utilitarian maxims of human rights, it would be best to secure the most viable ethical interests.

However, greater security can only ever be guaranteed through progress and a stronger foundation of stability, which one may argue is what Russia now needs. Even though Russia is not completely poorly governed, its social state is not of despair under oppression, and hostility and fear do not cloud Russia's social atmosphere, there is only so much uncompetitive politics can do. The contemporary model of Russian governance is not useless or without its merits, but it is not adequately functional, nor competitive enough with some Western models that are in sum terms developmentally miles ahead and more competitive[38].

Putin and Russia are mired with allegations and strings of corruption. A meticulous account of corruption in Putin's past during his administrative years in St. Petersburg are recounted in Karen Dawisha's "Putin's Kleptocracy" (2014). It is quite clear that Putin has a history of corrupt dealings. But a normative aspect of this association is complex. First, it is not clear that he, at the time, had any greater aspirations than of a deputy mayor trying to make ends meet like any other person in tough circumstances. As Dawisha put it: "Russia was full of people at the highest level who were immersed in the corrupt politics of the 1990s, and it is hard to imagine anyone surviving and getting ahead without taking a bribe."[39] While condemnation is easy, a moderate response is one of unimpressive mediocrity on behalf of the man that now aspires to greatness, undistinguished in giving into the pressure most people shared. However, the odd thing is also that by being so familiar with the grime and muck of Russia's underbelly exposed in the country's fall, Putin possessed the experience and qualification to get things done in a state of rampant corruption.

To give credit where it is due, even if virtue is warped, Putin did answer the call of patriotic duty to bring order, stability, and security to Russia when his ambition was granted the post of presidency. And so begun an age of consciously amoral politics in Russia, no different to most of the world anyway. Individual philosophy and idealism don't imply virtue. The insight Putin possessed to some degree made him apt for the great challenge ahead, the successes and limitations of which are significant.

When some people find it odd that Putin can be revered as a 'glorious leader', this value was fostered over decades of superficially effective policy, or ones that at least gave the appearance of stability sufficient for the emergence of a potentially successive generation and attitude. Of course, the notorious lack of freedom in the press and authority's thin skin to criticism, responding to criticism with often excessive and questionable means, also helped consolidate such a reputation. However, apparently, this policy orientation at least nourished stability and security by cracking down on dissent, as is the usual guise of defensive authority.

That being said, there are degrees of intellectual disparity and freedom of thought among Russia's public. Stubborn defiance of authority and people's continued criticisms are something censure could never extinguish, even during periods of much greater oppression. There is no universal consensus among the electorate that is completely supportive of Putin. But one thing does unite Russia's electoral dynamics – Putin, as of yet, in a state of non-competitive politics by virtue of manipulation and personal competence, seemed for a long time as the most viable choice. Some are genuinely supportive of Putin; many simply settle for him. But after years upon years of hard work and securing some sense of stability, this is jeopardised by a foreign intervention that back-fired by only producing a legitimate rally-around-the-flag response among Russia's public and from within Russia itself. But these stirrings in patriotism are exactly what helped Russia throughout its turbulent history and what Putin's politics have normatively tried to achieve, which then has a real potential to bring people back to the country and motivate them to build it.

This is a dual element of Putin's normative politics where evoking a sense of status and 'greatpowerness' of Russia returning to the international arena as a significant player dominates domestic politics. Contingent on this is the pride of Russian self-awareness and identity as citizens of a great country, an ethical dynamic which applies to some American traditions as well. But while this certainly does have an effect on Russian mass psyche, Russians quite clearly, from personal impression and poll studies, note that they are pro-normative of 'soft power' (as opposed to militaristic hard power)[40]. But a fundamental disparity in this normativity and ideology is the modern, materialistic orientation of people's values preferring stability and prosperity as opposed to glory. A surge in patriotism, unless subject to far greater extremes that will only beckon hostility and instability, will not serve the effective role of an incentive lifting the nation as would real material and social opportunities. Russia has truly moved far away from its Soviet past; Putin's government has presided over this transformation, but it does not represent it.

Building on an understanding of the normativity obsessed with status, a stern criticism is implicit. The notorious case of Russia's state-sponsored doping of athletes throughout the Olympic games is a key example of Russia's government's state of normativity. First, there are some ambiguities in the case. Not every athlete necessarily cheated. Russian and English media were hectically split in polarities of opinion. While Western media and audiences were no doubt moved by a familiar impression of Russian crookedness, there are simple points to consider in this case study. The burden of proof was on Russia to prove it was not guilty, and a satisfactory response was not put forward except common rantings of conspiracy. English media, however, tends to have greater standards of accountability than Russian media, so it would be generally wiser to trust the former, which can be equally and fairly critical of domestic affairs than the biased and poorly-informed opinions of a foreign menacing state. But more convincingly, Russia's trend of disproportionate desire for status is sufficient to account for a likely motivation leading to doping and cheating for the sake of status. As a government policy, this is far more likely.

Now, cheating would have served the purpose of earning medals at the Olympics and uplifting people's spirits back home, but not satisfying people's concerns with economic and social opportunities. Status in international affairs and social dynamics only serves as a utility when acknowledged or 'legitimised' through others' perceptions[41]. And so, these policies were employed under a normative guideline of begging for others' respect at a cost to genuine personal virtue of real achievement. If virtue and sense of self were strong enough, Russia would not care so much about what other states saw in its achievement, through which people are infinitely happier. Thus, the policy of cheating was one of vice and cowardice, begging for status rather than earning its achievement, only bringing shame and dishonour to what could be great.

Fear and corrupt base morality are at fault, holding individuals and society back, as well as depriving the fulfilment of confidence and ambition rising above obsessive concerns over validation by others, producing self-improvement and growth of virtue. Deflecting blame then only facilitates negative reactions and stirs negative sentiments, the potential of which can eventually become deep-rooted hostility. But the worst part of such an ethic is its deprivation of opportunity to grow from admitting fault and vice. Where vice is not admitted, its causal tangents continue with their detrimental, corrosive, and corruptive effect undermining virtue and strength, weakening society and the state. Yet it would commonly be a nightmare for any government to admit such faults and vice, because society is punishing.

The other significant normative aspect of this case study is the general utilitarian attitude in Russian policy. A Russian saying comes to mind: 'Hotelos kak luchshe, poluchilos kak vsegda' ('wanted what was best, turned out as usual'). Policy sought to maximise value and interest, to foster well-being, or at least to a degree facilitating complacency or sufficient satisfaction opposing protests and riots. But it didn't turn out so well, with foreign powers rightfully discrediting and dishonouring Russia's government, and Russia's government undermining Russia's image. Similar outcomes have abounded in much of politics even beyond Russia, whereby in the pursuit of what was thought to be best one loses sight of what is truly important. As is common by looking at the general picture and the greater good, micro aspects composing the whole sphere of morality and normativity lose out, at times degrading the macro sphere of normativity. This has presided over much of Russian government domestic policy, whereby, although evidently not useless or ineffective, it is of limited vision, creativity, potential, and long-term prospect.

There were, and still are, many profound challenges to post-communist Russian domestic issues, with no clear, simple, or even political solutions being viable. In this turmoil, Putin's government did what it could in its best judgement. Where any criticism and scepticism is applied, one has to ask the basic, but essential, mindful question of: "What would you do?" Under such pretences, in a state of disarray, 'legal nihilism'[42], insecurity, and instability, Putin committed to illiberal means to secure some form of a free market democracy, which now hardly resembles a genuine liberal democracy. Media and the press are 'conditioned' with strong authoritative interventions, elections are rigged and manipulated, opposition politics is superficial and uncompetitive (much by their own fault of incompetence overshadowed by Putin's successes), corruption is unsolvable in the current model, bureaucracy is excessive, development is mediocre and of minimal global competitiveness[43], population demographics show major suffering[44], and socioeconomic trends are of restricted opportunity in that the most opportune of the population are emigrating[45]. There have been economic developments over recent years, and Russians are sturdy and resourceful, and competing information leads to different conclusions on Russia's state of society and economy, particularly in terms of the latter.

However, fundamental challenges nonetheless remain. But where any criticism applies, at the very least one ought to give credit where it is due that where stability and security have been sustained for long enough, a great leap forward may come from an emerging, transformed new socioethical sphere – notably in terms of the urbanised middle class[46]. There were no simple solutions and the government did what it could. Now, sins of the past are catching up.

A major success of Putin was to leash the suddenly powerful emerging oligarchy following a capitalist's dream of the open markets of the 90s. This is where class equality rocketed into class division within moments. An elite, often crooked, cunning, and vicious, privatised much of the country's wealth for itself. Wealth distribution wasn't appropriate and opportunities did not resemble fair competition of truly free markets. Russia became subject to the same social ills that affect other societies of major wealth disparities, especially where private firms and lobbies own pivotal assets to modern life such as the media. Where competitiveness gave way to monopolies and villainous characters obsessed with wealth and status (of which not all opportunists were of the sort), both Putin and the oligarchies were in varying degrees crooked, vicious, and ruthless. Ultimately, political power and machination, combined with unlawful means and expertise, consolidated Putin's victory and put chains on most oligarch's political ambitions. But where some might speculate that characters of ambition among the oligarchs were, indeed, of a good nature, the shadow of such virtues are personal, malicious, and petty motivations. As such, following a libertarian tradition, no faction or party could be trusted, but it seemed Putin had greater normative power to appeal to patriotism than private lobbies.

A competition took place between private lobbies and an emerging political elite, and for better or worse, Putin won. Stability and security were found on these class struggles and competitions among elites. If one is to speculate and look at traditions of people's materialistic and status-driven concerns reciprocal of many issues the West faces, Putin might have been the better option to secure order and stability in Russia at the time. However, this might end up coming at an unsustainable cost. But at least time was bought for a new stage and chance of stability and development, or at least their potential.

Putin rewarded loyalty and created a new circle of elites supposedly bound to normative patriotic concern. A long study of Russia's corruption and Putin's involvement[47] suggests an unconstitutional socioeconomic 'farming' of new elites. Essentially, it may seem as though he is not simply rewarding loyalty and enriching his 'cronies', but that he is also shaping a new elite of oligarchs bound to a centralised patriarchal authority. This is quite fascinating as a socioeconomic experiment in contrast to the West. In the West there are monopolies and social elites bound to a free market; these elites can influence the political landscape through lobbies.

Russia, on the other hand, has a centralised political lobby that influences others. This is the odd nature of Russia's state capitalism. Russia's government, or rather its informal 'outside-the-law' agencies or institutions, does the lobbying. Some aspects of Putin's or his associates' involvement in corruption can be encapsulated in these terms. It is worth considering that Putin doesn't consider corruption as a bad thing if it gets the job done[48], much like the general public, especially among uncertainty, thievery, and corruption in the public which the government itself has to deal with, resorting to trusted people and friends (associative of nepotism) as a means to an end[49].

These attitudes, however, are in fact quite common in Russia as a sort of business ethic, whereby corruption isn't considered to be corruption if it's not for mere personal gain and if it simply speeds up inefficient bureaucracies and faces up to the realities of a struggling populace experiencing extreme and unrealistic wealth distribution, notably among civil servants such as the police. But as is always the case, whether intended or not, a strong centralised authority leads to corruption and graft, which is the everyday reality of Russia's somewhat neglected public[50].

But to address the matter of corruption in state capitalist dealings, surely it would be best to assign and manage publicly owned corporate interests and policies through parliament and not mere presidential commands? Surely this seems more respectful of public concern and interest? Working outside of the constitutional framework has served its purpose for Putin's government and has secured some stability where the constitution and law were themselves flawed and impotent. Perhaps this was the only way to secure stability and order for growth to resume in a manner that can enable a stronger foundation for future stability and growth. But now this legacy has become a trap, for sudden de-corruption could have negative effects on government policy and affairs. This point, however, is ambiguous and consists of many topics yet to be discussed.

Concrete evaluations of this state-economic model, whether inherently corrupt or not, is worth examining. While it is not a perfect socioeconomic model, it served a definitive end and provided degrees of stability and growth on the back of non-renewable resources. Russia has progressed significantly since its period of the 90s. However, this growth has been limited and its potential perhaps exhausted. Where an exhaustive bureaucracy is ingrained and law enforcement services are deficient and underfunded, on top of an already prevalent norm of corruption, this only facilitates greater corruption and neglect of public funds. Following suit, funds in any project get sucked in by the machinations of corrupt interests and become excessive, further serving as a potential deterrent to investment, in Russia's case made manifest[51].

It may seem as though, despite the drawbacks, a profit can be made. Indeed, as was said, Russia's society and economy has grown since Putin took charge. No matter the challenge, Russia has somehow survived, and most likely will. However, its economy, then also society, has not relished in the most efficient and promising growth; Russia has not been able to fulfil its true economic and social potential. This point, however, have been raised by the government itself, especially under Medvedev's presidency. Sadly, greater development and innovation did not succeed. But this is not for lack of potential.

The Soviet Union had a history and culture of progressive science, which has carried a legacy into contemporary Russia while inspiring much talent. Russia unequivocally has the talent and potential for technological advancement[52], but investment has been neglected, squandered, and lost[53,54], in many respects due to corruption. Russia's potential is not fulfilled. At the core of this failure is the normativity of mass psychology as familiarity with, and often necessity of, corruption. In sum, a toxic environment of Fear is produced necessitating and emphasising corruption and graft which neglect society.

Fear has its quasi-beneficial element of corruption as the police officer providing enough for his or her family. But the greater structural element of this Fear is the venal and petty Fear of obsession with status and excess wealth which hinders Russia's potential and its society's welfare. One aspect of a solution is increasing civil service pay, the effectiveness of civil services, and stabilising wealth disparities. But an elite of incompetent ministers consumed by vice and unable to innovate policy and competitive governance, leaves a stagnant system of governance which feeds off corruption as a parasite leeching on nation and society.

Another point to mention with regards to the economy is the (re)development and state investment into the military industrial complex, whereby the military industrial complex has become a major part of Russia's economy. Where a centralised authority is preoccupied with perceptions of foreign threats and realist outlooks characterised by a Cold War mentality, understandably the government would invest into military development.

Now, under the current model and administration, military industrial lobbies might not exercise great influence on state policy. If this cap was suddenly removed and profiteers and warmongers capitalised on opportunity and potential domestic hostilities towards perceived foreign threats, a scepticism and caution which Putin's administration certainly stirred up, then what? A nation driven by a military economy without a strong authority restricting military financial lobbies is not good for anyone. But balancing these market forces and keeping the industry under a strict leash are imperative policy directives, for blind trust in people's virtue is not a universally sustainable policy.

The broader question of how to mediate market forces remains. Russia has an entrenched elite with monopolies, and the country's wealth distribution is obscene and unhealthy. It is not a matter of philosophical debate when public services are neglected by the lack of funding and graft in that even civil servants only barely get by without a truly living wage. This is unsustainable and only fosters deeply ingrained instability. For one, better wealth distribution can be achieved through greater development of a strong consumer base, a middle class, and a more competitive and fair free market environment, which requires degrees of liberalisation. But excess bureaucracy and its contingent corruption, as well as opportunist criminals, undermine these developments, even if economic and business development are achievable and possible in sum terms.

The sustainability of this model is ultimately questionable, just as is the sustainability of some Western models when private lobbies undermine effective governance and policy ingenuity. But there is another way – through normative power of moral authority advising consumer values and interests, respectful of the fundamentals of liberty in consumer habits and free market dynamics. This, however, will be a topic in later work and is an innovation that has not been available in the past. Even in this work it will only be a suggestive and introductory topic.

Russia's government's choices at the beginning were restricted and limited, at least practically. The future is the same, with stagnation and limited progress being concrete reality, even though Russia will survive and will grow (at some point). Economic reform took place in a framework of an established oligarchy influencing and manipulating, if not abusing, the political landscape. Upsetting the order of a strong centralised authority by injecting greater liberties may empower groups of lesser national and public interest than Putin's administration, especially if new political elites are less competent than Putin. If stability is lost, and neglect becomes greater, then Putin's administration may seem as the more promising choice. But then Putin's strategy of harvesting a new elite has many of its own drawbacks.

The regime is authoritative and centralised; it will take one weak leader among the political elite succeeding Putin for the system to crumble. If the history of authoritarian regimes has declared anything, it is that it takes one weak link for a regime to fall. By then, however, a sufficiently virtuous and liberally compatible populace in Russia may initiate and sustain a successful democratic transformation. But the ambiguities are diverse to the extent that the hypothesised outcome is mired with uncertainty and danger. A change in the middle class and from within the electorate is the most sustainable solution. But this would be best achieved through business and economic development in favour of new opportunities for philanthropists, notably by reducing bureaucratic pitfalls and minimising insufficient funding caused by corruption and other risks. This, however, entails the risk of granting alternate lobbies both good and bad political potential. Ultimately, greater liberalisation would be a better theoretical outcome, but whether reality is compatible with such idealisation is not clear. And so the democratic determination of the people will be the arbiter of Russia's future.

Liberalisation also requires transformation in the media. Russia's media is widely owned, or heavily influenced, by pro-Kremlin groups. In the beginning, during Russia's first stage of liberalisation after an era of communist policy, certain groups massively capitalised on media outlets. Some of them were not in favour of Putin. The West experiences such phenomena when opinions and interests of media moguls influence the availability of information. Putin took another turn of centralising media and enabling selective political bias. A much more positive model of the utility of the media is based on standards and rules, such as not to deliberately spread misinformation, that all agencies must follow, which in practice occurs in varying degrees. Russia did not have the opportunity in the beginning to effectively implement such policies. To establish security and stability, as well as to suppress dissent and genuinely destabilising factions, Russia's government under Putin largely took charge over, or heavily influenced, the media. This may seem as a liberal's nightmare, as well as indicate clear-cut authoritarian policy.

One concern in particular drives authoritative mediation of national news – fear of external threats. This can come across as a typical excuse of any authoritarian regime, and no doubt there is a degree of truth to this. But considering how critical foreign outlets can be of Russia's government, a centralised authority would understandably be cautious of granting liberty to such information. Then again, there are some such liberties in Russian media, including the internet, but only of an alternative liberty to that of Western media. The bottom-line of these informational outlets, as was seen with the Crimea crisis, is that foreign media can vastly misunderstand

Russia's deeply complex and divided politics.

Then again, complexity has rarely given pause to the voice of ignorance and the desire to be vocal for the sake of attention. Russia has faced extreme challenges which the traditions of liberal democracy aren't clearly able to solve. Russia was facing significant instability and uncertainty, which an authoritative figure, for at least some time, managed to alleviate, but for most part only as a plaster covering a haemorrhaging wound. Foreign intervention did run the risk of misinforming the public and electorate against their better judgement. But while one might argue this was malicious and deliberate, a more moderate response would be to suggest rather that foreign media simply did not possess the qualification or insight to properly understand post-communist Russian politics and society, especially if the country was to be run by persons of selfish interest such as some oligarchs.

Another major factor in Russia's chokehold over the media is the matter of Putin's past and corruption as a species of normatively ambiguous top-down political lobbying. Putin has quite evidently engaged in, or has been closely affiliated with, cases of corruption, but understandably so. If such word got out, it would seem as though Putin's future would be over and his legacy finished. In truth, however, it may surprise some just how aware many Russians are of Putin's inner dealings and 'business philanthropy'. Subsequently arises the common Russian rhetoric driving electoral behaviour: 'this guy has already thieved enough; if you vote for someone else, the new person will just steal before doing something in return'.

It may seem Putin has scored a good balance in these terms. But if word got out and public sentiment was stirred enough against Putin, then instability and revolution would be real possibilities, entailing great uncertainty and possibly danger for Russia. Russia is a complicated place with quirky politics. Misunderstanding its issues and challenges will not lead to anything good. Centralising the media and authority may seem a means to an end to block perceived malicious intent and ploys by external agencies and threats. But Russia's greatest challenges are domestically rooted and much more immediate than foreign threats. Whether authoritative measures over the media are a sincere truth in protective policy, or a self-justified excuse of thin skin and selfish ambition, is most likely a dualistic reality. Media restrictions serve the end of managing information enough to enable general lobbying performed by the state that shares familiarities with basic corruption. Liberalising the media will open up the administration and regime to greater criticism – some fair, others not – while also potentially threatening degrees of stability and security, especially if the darker allegations of Putin's involvement in manipulative plots are revealed to be true such as state sponsored assassinations.

The faults of policies restricting the freedom of information are numerous and significant. The guise of security and stability blocking mass circulation of information restricts greater security and stability by diminishing accountability. There is the necessity of controlling information for security purposes, but Russia's government's policy has extended this significantly and to a detrimental point. For one, the government and corrupt officials and agencies cannot be held to account properly without freedom of information accessible to the public. As is intuitive, knowing cases of corruption is instrumental to addressing corruption. Only liberty of the media can help fully hold the government to account, but this entails risks. Biased media warps reality and deceives viewers with little-to-no decency or respect for self-determination and judgement. Some people may truly be foolish and cannot properly appreciate factual information, but it is the role of specialists worthy of trust to inform the public where information is complex and ambiguous. Russia's state-sponsored or state-run media has taken this to the extreme where factual information is only elementary.

Russia is far from the only sphere guilty of bastardising news and information. Considering the costs of corruption to Russia, which are not necessarily the fault of Putin's administration's machinations but rather a consequence of Putin's prioritisation of state concern, limited transparency and accountability pays a heavy toll. However, which cost is ultimately greater – restricted or greater liberty – may be rather ambiguous for now, and Putin's sovereign democracy model of government might yet demonstrate something interesting and fruitful beyond its short-term, immediate solutions in dire situations. But as time passes, strong leadership becomes older and weaker, and new leadership becomes subject to petty squabbles among hungry elites – all practically inevitable variables. It becomes a question of whether Russia's state of corruption is sustainable in the near future, and empirical observation points to development reaching its threshold under the current model, meaning it has to adapt. Liberalisation and conventions which have served Western societies well have their merits, but their implementation has notable challenges the case of Russia, which may change dramatically with the emergence of new generations.

Committing electoral fraud is one of the greatest normative wrong-doings of Putin's administration, but perhaps not for reasons one would first assume. Part of the motivation for this manipulation is personal ambition, while the other more interesting aspect is 'patriotic' concern for the welfare of the country. While the electorate is in sum terms the ultimate arbiter and source of power for Putin's authority, many machinations have taken place to sway public opinion. A sudden rift in the political landscape runs the chance of undoing significant progress achieved over the past decades, as well as plunging the country into deep divide of revolution if authority is negligent. A combination of factors contributed to the normative outlook that enabled the policy of the manipulation of elections by the state. The most notable factors were the concern for security and stability, caution over perceived foreign threats that the judgement of the political patriarch may think the public underestimates, and the common high of power's control and status. An aspect of related normativity is ascriptive of a patriotic tradition of doing what one thinks is best for the country. But by rigging and manipulating elections, people's liberty and self-determination were undermined.

Putin as a vector of authority and centralised normative force was moved by a protective concern over the country and its people, even if as a mere facade. But this over-protectiveness of an abusive nanny state can disrupt change and adaptation through learning from mistakes and vice. People enabled Putin's administration and its normativity for self-interested reasons, support that worked with varying degrees of success. People's preference for stern authority and a strong-man leadership was their choice, even if the circumstances of this choice were manipulated by other coercive forces.

However, where a choice was taken away from people or made on their behalf, such as is the case with electoral fraud, this is an act against the people's virtue of self-determination, even if said judgement is not the soundest. Electoral fraud is an act against the people and the country, of a normative spirit relatable to treason. By taking away liberties from the country's people, even if not all or most of them, is still unpatriotic, as serving to aid the state over the people is normativity of state-oriented nationalism or normative statism where state interests are valued more than direct interests of the people. And now the country suffers the penance of excessive authority as the lack of liberty and opportunity to grow and develop.

One may ask whether love means protecting something from itself or letting it make its own choice. If a mistake means learning from a mistake and growing in virtue, then this is the right choice with respect to the justice of greater well-being. One may contend whether protection or greater liberty was right at the time of great instability and strife, but such a future is not fulfilling of Russia's potential. We come to identify a common corruptive phenomenon in base morality and Fear – the *mistake of compassion* and the *mistake of attachment*.

Rather than suggesting that compassion and attachment are wrong, their excess leads to terrible vice and becomes poisoned with Fear. By wanting what was best for something valued, while only having a sense of piety in terms of Fear and unmindful attachment, that value itself becomes betrayed by the lack of virtue. Putin was compared to Adolf Hitler following the annexation of Crimea and the crisis in Ukraine[55,56]. Such demonisation would understandably be very provocative among Russians. But one normative and ethical similarity can be highlighted.

Hitler is branded evil, but the greatest lesson from his vices may be commonly overlooked and wisdom lost. Hitler was driven by a deranged mind moving ambition on a national scale. In his view, the ambition was just and right, as is common for people to make excuses and justifications for themselves by the fear of personal weakness and imperfection. Hitler was clearly very attached to his ambitions and their promise to the nation. In the end, he betrayed his country and left it in rubble with a bloody stain on its history. The blindness of attachment to ambition and supposedly wanting what is best for the country leads one's judgement astray and leaves it consumed with Fear, according to which then one can only see through vice. By valuing something to obsessive and exhaustive lengths, such as with unhealthy attachment, one can become consumed with Fear. This certainly has its advantages in protecting people and loved ones, yet in terms of the sociopolitical this excess can be extremely corruptive, making one commit mistakes of compassion by holding back suffering and subsequently growth from suffering.

So, if Putin is indeed a patriot and is driven by love of country, his mistakes of compassion are such that Russia has been neglected and betrayed of its own greater interest by a self-absorbed protective value. Choices against the compulsion of attachment and compassion can be difficult, dire, and crippling, as is the case with undisciplined and dominant base morality, but these choices are sometimes necessary for greater well-being and the Highest Good. Righteousness demands sacrifice, for only the strongest and virtuous herald the Highest Good.

The normativity of the vices of mistakes of attachment may be associated with perception and judgement blinded by Fear and consumed by values of the 'greater good' lacking coherent morality. This is a dangerous normative attitude, and Russia's politics has especially suffered from it and will continue to do so in the future. The lack of open media undermines accountability and can be detrimental to competitive politics fostering ingenuity and adaptation.

That being said, Putin's governance has by no means been ineffective without strong internal competition biting the administration's back to keep it going, pushing it forward. Much of Russian parliamentary opposition is superficial as mere strawman parties subservient to Kremlin lobbies, with real opposition groups being disorganised and at times unqualified and often simply incompetent and unfit for governance and leadership. Within such structures of governance arises a very sinister and potentially disastrous vector of power that even Putin or any centralised authority will be unable to effectively mediate and control.

Russia experienced a dreadful crime wave following the Soviet Union's dissolution which consisted of desperate individuals with military experience and resources making a living in lawless streets. With Putin's promise of stability and security, swift action had to be taken. The government, or its informal and aconstitutional administration, employed federal security and intelligence services to control organised crime and crime-state syndicates where criminals and thugs managed to brutalise their way into government office positions[57]. Security services integrated criminal syndicates and kept them under some control, inevitably corrupting the institution itself in its desperation, turning some elements of Russia's government into what may be described as a 'mafia state'[58].

Where evaluations apply, at least this was some sort of control, the improvement of which may be very difficult. Any top-down witch-hunts and purges would escalate violence and further destabilise Russia when it was already lacking effective policing and funding. As foolish as it may seem, in desperate times it is not difficult to see the merit of such a policy. Of course, covering this up and hiding it from the general public would be instrumental to success, coupled with corruption or tolerance of corruption as means to a greater end. The consequences, however, are quite disturbing. People with extensive resources and power are able to exercise their corrupt interests, following the example of their higher-ups, and rob, extort, and blackmail citizens.

I am personally familiar with a case of a wealthy young Russian man who has been subject to security service surprise 'investigations' followed by attempts of blackmail and extortion. What sort of faith would a person have in the state when such occurrences and vectors of authority are given liberty? The real consequence was of a young man once eager to fulfil patriotic duty losing hope in the nation and seeking to live elsewhere. This is the hidden but prevalent aspect of the aforementioned policy of dealing with crime.

Another and more problematic contingency of such a policy is what happens when policy becomes serious about dealing with corruption. Where a source of luxury for an already corrupt agency consumed by vice is threatened, the corrupt agency will continue its unjust and immoral ways to make sure it remains untouchable. If an opposition group or individual become serious enough and pose a threat to corrupt aspects of government, it's only a matter of time until corrupted institutions and groups with power react. An opposition may try to stir up popular movement, but the corrupt security service agent will most likely disregard any democratic concern and will threaten, harm, maim, or kill a perceived threat. This poses a great danger to Russia and Putin's administration. If a popular figurehead is serious about opposing corruption is assassinated, society's anger will lead to riots, revolts, and potentially revolution. Public opinion will be split between pro-Putin and anti-government groups blaming the state for murder and subverting the democratic process. War most likely wouldn't be the outcome, but minor conflicts and deep social contentions will arise, and any such uncertainties are a great risk for the country's stability.

Putin and his legacy of stability and security will be threatened by these aspects of Russia's society and corruption in government. A messianic leader championing liberty may seem a good prospect, but a centralised authority of such dynamics of societal change towards greater liberalisation may in itself become a great threat to Russia if the movement's head is severed, leaving a split husk of pain, anger, and hatred.

A wise and sensible leadership of non-violent virtue and willing to commit personal sacrifice, however, can inspire change and development. But persons of such virtues of composure, empathy, understanding, and patience in Russia's political landscape, notably among the opposition, are effectively null.

If such a person did arise, he or she would most likely be severely hurt or killed. But in such sacrifice a social movement will be empowered and Russian defiance will flourish. To quote Obi-Wan Kenobi from "A New Hope" of the Star Wars franchise: "If you strike me down, I shall become more powerful than you can possibly imagine." And so a vector of virtue will end, but its value will correct many vices and its power will spur new virtues. This outcome is mired with uncertainty that would be better off avoided by both Russia's public and the government. Cooperation and top-down mediation of corrupt agencies would be the most promising, but such a rapport may seem almost impossible.

In this context, one must again appreciate the necessity and imperative value of a well-established middle class of diverse specialisation, ability, and a will to govern the country. Only through a populace of able capacity to form leadership and effective governance will Russia succeed with greater liberalisation and a brighter future of growth, development, and hope. Under Putin's administrations, the foundation of such a sociopolitical and normative resource has been emerging, but he will not be able to guarantee or enact a better future – only the people can.

Here arises a profound criticism of base morality and Fear. People elected for Russia's status quo in hope that the government will enact change for the better, yet the government is itself in a pitfall of policy utilities. Only competitiveness can solve this and branch out opportunities with a people willing to endure more uncertainty, insecurity, and instability, to take potentially great risks for a better future for all. Liberalisation and institutional modernisation have much to offer in this respect. But the electorate must pursue such an ambition and pressure the government to change, as well as embody and enable transformation. This is a difficult choice, and it might not even be a necessary one. But change has to happen, and the current state of Russia's society and politics isn't fit for the task without changing itself and its normativity and values leading to hopeful ambition. But Fear holds people back.

Attachment to security and stability can lead to the loss of its value and effectiveness in producing well-being. This has been argued to be the case for Russia, yet it applies almost globally. The structures of normativity and ethics in terms of Fear and base morality are not the most promising or fulfilling of our interests. Designed and orderly ethical development may have once seemed absurd, but the study of structural ethics is the means to such an endeavour. All ethical endeavour draws on moral and ethical truth revered as and through the Highest Good. There is a choice beyond Fear and base morality. Many traditional ethics have aspired to achieve freedom from pain and fear, but could not structure this endeavour into a concise and complete philosophy compatible with the challenges of modernity. Society and its centralised dynamics of authority are corrupted and undermined by Fear, but this need not be the case. However, any such change can only occur if people are willing to pursue greater ambition and become empowered by virtue and follow a new sense and value of morality. But then even advanced and developed societies in the West struggle with many social issues that aren't being resolved because of people's complacency, ignorance, and moral weakness.

It is time to address the epitome of the vices of Russia's state and the state's corrupt vectors of authority. Corrupt elements in Russia's security and civil services are

evident. They may pose a threat to reform and development surpassing the degenerative state of corruption. Putin's normativity has by all measures not been able to
utilise patriotism to alleviate symptoms of corruption. In part because he himself has
become a symptom of moral decay. Certain case studies point to a grave presence
of vice in Russia's government that is quite appropriately described as a disease of
the mind, spirit, morality, and character. In the culmination of the desire for power,
mistakes of attachment, obsession with status, and ignorance of morality, vice cannibalises itself. Russia's government under Putin's administration has committed despicable acts unworthy of the virtue of leadership and proper governance. State-sponsored or state associated murders of its own citizens, whether sanctioned by Putin's
administration or not, is nonetheless a dire failure on its part.

First, the notorious killing of Alexander Litvinenko. To some in Russia he was a
traitor and a whistleblower who exposed corruption in the federal security service.
It is not particularly important to discuss the weight of his crime, self-capitalising
deed, or dutiful act, as the aftermath and response is most interesting. According to
the view of Russia's government, Litvinenko was a traitor. However, he was a whistleblower, but not a terrorist. The moderate response to Litvinenko's alleged transgression would have been a legal one, whereby the perpetrator is put on fair trial. But this
clearly wasn't enough for some people in Russia.

Consider the nature of Litvinenko's murder: certain groups hated him, he was
seen as a traitor (inciting anger), he was poisoned with radioactive material (which
might not have been easily accessible), his death was slow and painful, and someone really went out of his way to make the death resonate with an evocative message. There was heavy emotion in the crime, almost as if someone was lashing out
in anger. Where Litvinenko's perceived treachery was that of a traitor, his actions
defied authority and status. The hallmarks of Litvinenko's murder as an act of vengeance and Russia's evident obsession with status fits the framework of the act being
sponsored by government affiliated groups. Treason is a mark of failure on behalf of
the normativity and moral authority of a nation and country. The punishment was
organised and extremely well sponsored – after all, obtaining radioactive material
doesn't seem to be an easy task.

This case demonstrates the character of significant elements of Russia's government, and the state failing to hold itself to account only enables such vice and depravity. Whether Putin himself was involved is somewhat ambiguous, but considering the nature of the crime, it is sensible to suggest that in some form or another
he must have had some connection to the assassination. The alternative account of
this state-sponsored crime is weakness of the state in relation to it failing to prevent such a high-profile incident, with the crime's links to Russia's government being
substantial. But if Russia had nothing to hide, or thought it was just and right in its
policies, even if difficult to understand, then it could defend itself rather than resort
to extreme measures.

Litvinenko's allegations were scandalous and perhaps even unbelievable, denial
and counter-claims would have worked with sufficient normative power and moral
sensibility. Putin, however, does not have this power, and in the international arena
his power is by-and-large of a distorted image that does not inspire trust or good
faith. Putin has little-to-no normative power of note or worth, whereby Russia's criticism of international affairs and other nations is just as blindsided as Russia's perceived criticism by others. Criticism by Russia is normatively diminutive when competitive domestic politics of, say, the United Kingdom is more than able to address its

flaws without Russia's foreign policy rantings and conspiracy theories. If Litvinenko really did strike a nerve with the more scandalous allegations of Putin's and the FSB's involvement in staged bombings that served as the basis of Putin's security-hawk virtue that helped him get elected, then there are much greater questions to be asked.

In such contexts, it becomes even more apparent why silencing free media becomes a state policy. In summary, Putin's virtue as a patriot is easily dismissed, because enabling murder of a country's own people, rewarding and permitting thievery of the nation's own citizens, and objecting to people's self-determination, even in the slightest degree, are not acts of love for country and people.

In fairness, one might counter-argue that Putin was not involved at all. Alternatively, one might argue that these were 'necessary' sins in desperate times, and that Putin's administration needed cooperation and support from security services to achieve greater ends. But more recent cases of Russia's broken normativity can be examined, which are perhaps the most abhorrent.

As was discussed with the case of Russia's state-sponsored doping, the government clearly has a knack for machination and plots, consistent with Putin's qualification and history involving security and intelligence services. Such characteristics extended to Russia's foreign policy in Syria. Russia sent troops and volunteers to protect its interests in Syria[59], just as other factions sent military personnel to protect their interests. Nothing in such a policy would be inherently surprising or normatively distinguishable. Patriotic ambitions were concerned with protecting national interests – fair enough, all countries share this concern.

However, something is especially worrying about how this military policy was employed. Russia sent in mercenaries consisting of Russians. The mercenaries got paid a decent sum to go fight, but then many ended up dead[60]. Of course, such consequences would be inevitable. But the nature of the policy is morally controversial. People from impoverished backgrounds needed work, and so they became easy recruits. These recruits were sent to fight on the frontline and on 'suicide missions', while Syrian Army troops merely went in to 'clean up'[61].

To formulate the structure of this normativity and rephrase the policy, it goes as such: poor people are lured in with money and are then sent to die. Sending in a professional army is one thing, but mercenaries constituted by desperate individuals is not the same, especially when they are sent to die. If this is Russian patriotism, then it is a bastardisation and brutalisation of a people no different to its previously more oppressive authoritarian regimes. And so, as has always been the case with negligent authority, the cycle of revolution and upheaval will continue. Putin's administration and Russia's defence ministry were without a doubt involved in such affairs. This is an example of Russia's government's orientation of normativity, which provides clues of what the shadow of its past looks like. This is not patriotism, and this is not what Russia is worth.

But then what would you do? Russia seeks to protect its national interests which it may perceive to be at odds with NATO encroachment and US foreign interests. Obsession with this threat leads Russia to only threaten and betray itself in its Fear. But this trend of behaviour and corruption is too common in base morality, and terribly so. Then Russia's government tries to win popularity among the electorate by fostering patriotic attitudes through appeal to the status of a great power – of Russia being a major player in global human endeavour. Yet, as was discussed, Russia's public's normativity orientates more on materialistic and modern values at odds with Russia's government's only major political resource of hard power – military power.

It is easier to criticise than offer viable solutions. In these complexities and in terms of the primacy of ethical value placed in security, which is an ethical orientation that the public enables, morality loses out to its base form of Fear. For instance, rather than silencing journalists and undermining liberty and the democratic process, would it not be best to be transparent in presenting challenges and the solutions offered? Isn't respecting people's liberty and the country's determination a true act of patriotism? For if faith in people is abandoned, then this is as much an act of condemnation. But indeed, political solutions are limited, and only normative appeal to the general public can fulfil greater goals and ambitions.

The government and military may send off young people to protect home, but in their distance of troubled times and contained spheres of fighting, with the reach of whizzing bullet being far from the comfort of a sheltered home, there are things any citizen can do back home. People who are not fighting abroad can embrace civic responsibility of virtue to improve on suffering and vice by confronting immorality and accepting personal responsibility in behaviour. This can be achieved with fairly straightforward disciplines by not supporting morally deficient practices and unsustainable behaviour, by not enabling private lobbies to undermine effective governance, by participating in the electoral process, or even something as simple as paying one's taxes. These attitudes then also apply to the society-to-state level. It ought to be the public's choice whether young people from impoverished backgrounds are sent to die for the sake of national interests, or whether the public should prioritise other interests such as making sure citizens at home can live decently and well.

This is not a statement of liberal philosophy when any threat of destabilisation and excessive authority undermine everyone's interests. It is, however, a matter of normative and ethical evaluation when such policies are employed and threaten the country and nation. If protecting a country's national interests by exploiting its vulnerable populace and sending young people to needlessly die is the state of normativity, then any moral claim surpasses the delusions of political philosophy, which has concrete sociopolitical consequences contingent on the ethical. Where a state performs immoral deeds to support public favour, it loses moral authority over the morally conscientious, which can then lead to apathy, abandonment (such as emigration), hostility, and social divide. But people and Fear are central to this, with the lack of coherent ethics and morality contributing to the moral confusion and distortion of global society, through which all mankind suffers.

The normativity of warrior glory ethics associative of Russia's 'patriotic' motivation is unbefitting of the virtue of empathy and unity in morality greater than a self-cannibalising Fear. But neither are 'modern' materialistic values of material security and stability wholly effective in addressing those fundamental ethical values. From a structural ethics point of view, development must move towards an adaptive hybrid and truly post-modern ethic characterised by values and interests beyond the restraints of Fear's dominant ethos and base morality.

To conclude the discussion of the relation between state performance and normativity, I shall leave the following quotes by Aung San Suu Kyi: "It is not power that corrupts but fear. Fear of losing power corrupts those who wield it and fear of the scourge of power corrupts those who are subject to it."[62] This familiar dynamic in ethics then leads to the common phenomenon ascriptive of Russia's state of society, politics, economics, and normativity with the following thought: "It is little wonder that in any society where fear is rife corruption in all forms becomes deeply entrenched."[63] Corruption is a great challenge to Russia, the root mechanism or cause of which is the corruption of Fear through base morality of unmediated instinct, blind compulsion, and immoderate aversion to pain. Russia needs to modernise and surpass its troubled past. But for modernisation and development to truly occur, fundamental ethical and normative change is necessary, which has been happening to some extent in Russia's public.

One may debate what constitutes modernity – whether it is post-industrial economics or living conditions of a society. A structural ethics point of view considers modernity in terms of the relation between agency and structure. Where a society or sphere of ethics is moved by vectors of authority centred in personas and individuals – that is, in agents – then its social contracts and parameters of normativity and ethics are centralised in an inherently vulnerable authority. Rule of law and institutional organisation sharing authority in greater harmony between the state and public are structures of ethics where a synthesis has occurred in the normativity of an agency binding to the ethical environment and the agency shaping the environment rather than deferring vectors of authority to the authoritative primacy of rule through individuals. Modernity is characterised by people able to self-govern without an imposing authority of individual agency coercing a way of life and common endeavour, even if the authoritative individual may be just and right in doing so. Modernity is balance and harmony in ethical values within a sphere of ethics between agency and structure, whereby a moral authority that binds all people and rules over them through shared principles and cooperation, not through one individual's ambition. But this modernity is only sustainable through a foundation of appropriate virtue, liberty, and development.

Sociopolitical modernity in terms of the primacy of common law and institutions binding vectors of authority to moral law is built on cultural modernity. A community and populace of able and competent specialists provide the resources and power of change towards innovation and progress. Materialistic dynamics of ethics are especially effective in their power to cause change and development by providing opportunities and the resources that drive ingenuity. Liberty becomes essential to such dynamics, with liberty then becoming stronger itself. Where an ethical environment, such as Russia's, resorts to the normativity of strong personality and individual leadership, it cannot truly modernise and fulfil its greater potential through the liberty of ingenuity to grow and flourish. Only sufficient vectors of normative and moral power within the sphere of an ethical environment can empower the values of reform, regeneration, and prosperity. Only people can achieve this, and only virtue and morality can empower and guide them towards this end. And so, the prospects of ethical modernity become real and promising, but only morality greater than the pressure of Fear can succeed.

While bottom-up sociopolitical transformation begins with normative growth, patriotism will have to take on the form of passing the torch of leadership, where authoritative leadership passes the flame to greater liberty of people's ambitions. In light of some suggestive criticisms, Russia's administration probably still has a heart of patriotism, even though tainted, and the courage to fulfil the people's wishes. It may seem as though Russia's spirit and character has been wholly compromised by Fear, but this is far from the case, and Russians have overcome much worse. A stable and peaceful transition into a new era of stability and security in Russia, defying its history of violence and insurrection, is in all people's interests. Even though Russia's government is mired with vice and corruption, virtue might still be appealed to. But such conviction is always a matter of bias and faith in people's goodness.

It might seem as though a turbulent and divisive democratic revolution is the only option, but collaboration and common efforts to secure a better future for the country and global human civilisation are most befitting of Russia's potential. Rather than fighting and rebelling against the government, a true testament to a new generation of normativity and virtue would be to compete in policy over Russia's future without heralding needless violence and conflict. Where the pain of loss and injustice can be visceral, overcoming such suffering is the mark of new virtue breaking of the cycle of suffering that has plagued Russia for too long, but this requires virtue surpassing the vices of Fear.

These dynamics are far from exclusive to Russia alone, as they are inherent to the base morality of Fear. Putin has had a role in Russia's regeneration. Even in the future, Russia may still need strong authoritative leadership to hold the federation together without reckless secession that would jeopardise security and stability across the region and fragment its pluricultural society. The question concerning the Middle East and the Caucuses to the south of Russia are imperative for Russian interests, and a naive and loose approach will not be fruitful. Putin's utility as a guiding authority is expiring, and sins of the past are exercising their penance. A final act of great courage and virtue to pass on the torch with respect for the people's choice would not only mark character of true patriotism, but will also denote a character of great virtue in the history of mankind that succeeded endless, vicious, and corrosive cycles of suffering, rising above the vices of man's Fear, worthy of true humanity. Alas, the virtues of mankind are weak under Fear, and rekindling hope, courage, and strength can be difficult even in oneself.

The difficulties of effective morality in global affairs, driven by the inherently contradictory and deceptive base morality of Fear, undermine humanity as a whole. Moving away from state-orientated normativity, I will next turn my attention to international affairs and notably foreign policy as an associative element of normativity to discuss base morality's problems, limitations, and merits.

Chapter 8:

The Order of Fear

Competitive international relations and global human activity are borne of the adaptive cycle of values and the evolution of normativity. This ethical structure, however, inherits many risks, dangers, and uncertainties. Fear and base morality are foundational to the prevalent global structure of ethics and ethical environment. Through behaviour and Natural Law arise the tendencies of states to pursue survival and welfare. Global politics and international relations are found on the base morality of Fear, and for good reason. Global structures of Fear have sustained mankind and enabled cautious nations to endure.

However, Fear also manifests itself in excess as vice. Great empires have crumbled for many reasons, with contributing causes always being domestic values and policies or competing foreign values and attitudes. The state is concerned with the primacy of security in survival and well-being – a feature of the primary value of aversion to pain in base morality. As such, the state is the centre of mankind's Fear and is a major channel of Fear in global endeavour, with structural forces being heavily influenced by individuals in positions of power, making the normativity and ethics of states particularly rigid in terms of their structural influences.

The individual in power subject to Fear will react accordingly if he or she is morally weaker than Fear. If survival is the end, then only two distant realities are possible – domination or cooperation, with each ethical path interacting and expanding in different ways. These two dynamics are caused by human behaviour and are subject to the Natural Laws that regulate them and the characters that enact corresponding ethics. Subsequently, normativity and ethics profoundly influence global mechanisms that affect states of well-being.

Mutually compatible and cooperative solidarity in normative values can enable, sustain, and strengthen peace, prosperity, and security. Normativity praising human rights and modern values of stability and peace, ascriptive of liberal schools of political thought, tend to be values upheld by liberal democracies. The success of Western nations and societies can be accounted for in terms of political ingenuity, innovation of liberal democracy, and ethics of stability and security strongly bound to material interests.

This normativity enables a liberal 'zone of peace' of the normativity of civil society, human rights, rule of law, peaceful values of welfare, and liberal democracy. The incentives of security, stability, and peace in accordance with Fear possess a distinctively positive and constructive aspect of base morality in relation to facilitating a liberal zone of peace through corresponding ethics and normativity. However, Fear and instinct can also significantly undermine greater peace, as was argued in Chapter

5 with respect to insecurity in material utility.

Fear can equally foster and undermine peace and stability, yet its intrinsic aspect of survival often serves as a shaky foundation for stable and adaptive structures. Many aspects of global civilisation have modernised, yet the character of mankind hasn't kept up developmental pace. Where values are subject to a whole new form of environmental conditioning in a modern world of previously unimaginable standards of living, the global modern ethical structure may be maladaptive if sustainability is not achieved.

Common ethical interest underlies mutually compatible normativity. While ethical elements of conflict and order in ethical development interact differently, their causal influences on the sociopolitical sphere can be exemplified in terms of the relation between *liberal* and *realist* thought. A generally more pessimistic and cynical view of politics might validate policies according to the primacy of survival in a dogged world of mankind's 'civilisation', with international law and institutions being mere technicalities or selective assets for personal ambition.

Rather than idealise states of affairs with hope, as may be the case with liberal interpretations, the normativity of international realism – the view that emphasises anarchy, selfishness, competition, and conflict in world politics – organically produces or reciprocates values of uncertainty and distrust, of insecurity and fear. This normative orientation may favour supremacy and domination as the guarantor of peace and survival, whereby cooperation only serves the end of state survival, unbound to greater values than the primitive attitudes of survival and related ethics. Realism is the most direct, primitive, and cynical manifestation of base morality and Fear, conforming to the ordinary elements of ethical values derivative of instincts.

The dual aspects of discord and order in the values of the ethical structures of Fear feature prominently in the modern world, especially between liberal democracies and other species of regimes. However, mutual solidarity of common normativity is inherently formally stronger than circumstantial normativity of simpler common interests. Any axis of convenience will lose out to an alliance of idealised ambitions and common ground, but only in so much as the physical capacity of this competing normativity meets the demands of environmental circumstances.

Both of these ethics are rooted in Fear, following the adaptive cycle of values. Fear can incentives security and stability, while also plunging us into war through uncertainty and lack of conviction in binding authority and common interest. Fear can cloud judgement to the point that its primacy of security undermines greater security, potential, and growth. This Chapter will evaluate the global state of affairs of the structures of ethics built on Fear; this Chapter will evaluate the ethical order of Fear.

Ethics are the ghostly functions of substance's movement. As forces of ethics compound our world and interact through conduits of substance – that is, living things – values and parameters of these forces compete. The study of the sociopolitical is intrinsic to the study of the structures of ethics, as sociopolitical ethics – normativity – is fundamental to the guidance of actions and policy. The competition of values, reciprocal of another dimension of natural selection, has shaped the world, and always will. While some may ignore the role of conventional morality in politics, ethics in politics is fundamental to agenda-setting (as goal-directive behaviour).

The subjectivity of morality is a result of complexity in desires and distortion of interests and values. Where security is the primary goal, its concern becomes a function of democratic states abiding public interests. Societies develop differently; different normativity shapes the state of the world. Interactions and contentions between liberal democracies and other types of regimes are the clearest examples of ethical dynamics as competing normativity in the modern, globalised, developing world. The common state of heated contention between Russia and the West, the role of China in the world, and the emerging world of multipolarity (diversity and greater balance) in global power-shares with respect to emerging major countries (BRICS), are prime cases for the study of normativity in terms of the guiding values and interests of states and their sociopolitical cultures. States only survive and flourish by adapting. Knowing which normativity, values, policies, and civic utilities benefit different circumstances is the gift of ethics to the social sciences, and the study of ethics thrives from the insight extracted from the social sciences and natural sciences. For now, the discussion will focus on the utility of Fear that rules nation-states and their societies.

To gouge the dimension of normativity in the sociopolitical, it can be understood to borrow from the constructivist theoretical approach in the study of political theory. For example, Mutually Assured Destruction (MAD) arguably prevented nuclear disaster during the Cold War. The normative account in an interpretation of Fear makes sense of this policy behaviour by virtue of people's cognitive and behavioural disposition towards instinct and survival, explored through the genealogy of ethics and base morality. Fear prevented global destruction, yet it also caused the conflict in the first place.

This dual function of Fear prevented oblivion, yet necessitated ever-greater risks and threats to sustain some existence of a status quo – overall a fragile balance. With the dissolution of the Soviet Union, hope was restored for global peace. Major contributing factors to this outcome were people's ambition for self-determination and self-consuming normativity of corruption in communist regimes.

Now, however, peace struggles again. Where at fault was once contention between NATO and the Warsaw Pact, present day contention is of elementary power and Fear's uncertainty over the intent of those with power. All states pursue survival, the most valuable utility for which is power. However, with great power comes supremacy and the potential to dominate, which frighten less powerful and less affluent nations. The nature of man has only changed on the surface by the values adopted, notably as human rights and civil society. However, the essence of base morality and Fear remains, manifesting itself as a world mired with incivility, lawlessness, and even tribal barbarism amplified by modern technologies.

Global culture only changes with the normativity and spirit of the individual, but the power to adapt through normativity gives supremacy of virtue to nations worthy of strong ethics that enable successful civic utilities and performance. Nations survive and thrive for a reason, with those reasons usually being strengths and virtues for a given amount of time in set conditions of ethical environment.

To highlight the main point raised throughout the proceeding Chapter, consider the Ukraine Crisis following 2014. All parties involved had contending values and interests. Each faction was right and wrong in their own way, and all intended well, yet were deceived by the vices of Fear, whether as bling ego, arrogance, or weakness of character.

The following claim may come across as surprising, but NATO and Russia share some fundamental similarities in their normativity and policy direction. One goal of NATO's intervention in the Kosovo War and subsequent bombing of Yugoslavia in 1999 was a swift response to prevent further genocide. The 2011 NATO intervention in Libya led by France and the United Kingdom was also motivated by the goal of preventing another genocide, to potentially prop up moderate pro-Western and liberally democratic political groups, and to secure some stability in a neighbouring region.

Neither of the two missions had the most successful results, yet an attempt was made; 'wanted what was best, but turned out as usual'. Now, consider Russia's support for pro-Russian forces in the Donbass. The conflict in Ukraine was of a deep social and ethnic divide. As is common for people, emotions and tempers went wild, instigating bloody conflict. A dimension of Russia's foreign policy in Ukraine was partly a clear concern for preventing ethnic genocide, which eventually escalated the conflict and perhaps caused more deaths and suffering, but these points are speculative. Russia's objection and cautionary reaction to NATO's bombastic intervention in Yugoslavia was not necessarily of a sinister desire to neglect people, but rather a disbelief that military intervention and destruction of infrastructure was the best course of action.

Judging by the consequences of NATO's mission in Yugoslavia, it's unclear whether this was the right approach in reflection of the consequences. The consequences included the conflict in Ukraine, which was partly exacerbated by the distrust sown after the Yugoslavia mission and further amplified by other NATO and Western intrusive policies such as in Libya. Biases and cultural backgrounds fostered divide in common interest, further amplified by the common normativity of people's attitudes of 'us versus them' and blaming others.

This relates strongly to the fundamental attribution error cognitive bias[64], which, briefly, characterises people's tendency to protect their sense of self and ego by attributing their faults to the constraints of circumstances, while other people's failures in similar circumstances are attributed to their dispositions of character (e.g. vices). Accordingly, contention between the West and Russia can be accounted for in simpler terms of misunderstanding and the corruptive biases of behavioural functions of Fear. Yet neither party distinctively possesses the virtue of patience and understanding to put in constructive effort where the demands and stresses of unforgiving and rapidly developing circumstances allow for quick implementation of well-designed strategies.

In doing so, people fail to recognise their faults, fostering greater divide and unnecessarily conflicting policy goals and interests. The Ukraine Crisis can be attributed to the faults of every party involved, yet none possessed the virtue to fully admit their vices and mistakes, for this is a perceived weakness. Then, misunderstanding and contention arise when they don't need to. This is a particular concern of evaluating the normativity of Fear and base morality in international affairs.

A wealth of literature is available on the subject of international relations and foreign policy analysis. However, normative evaluations are sometimes sparse and undedicated. Competing accounts are available with regards to evaluating policies, nations, and states of affairs. There are many ways to look at a single event, often subject to fundamental views and biases. Differences in vision, interests, values, priorities, and worldviews have loomed over relations between the West and Russia[65].

A significant element of such concerns is the West's liberalism as liberal democracy and Russia's illiberal sovereign democracy and ultraconservativism. Both sides are in different stages of development and are subject to different domestic and foreign influences. Naturally, there will be competing values and interests. While both blocs are concerned with stability and security, in Russia – by virtue of Putin's administration, its legacy, and a terrible not-too-distant past – the concern for stability is emphatic, coming at a cost to potential progress.

As was discussed in the previous Chapter, challenges to Russia's modernisation, development, and greater liberalisation are many and concrete. For Russia to become a real liberal democracy and truly modernise with effective rule of law, political culture, and civic performance that doesn't need strong-man authoritative governance, a lot of work remains to be done. It cannot happen on a whim, and some degrees of progress have been achieved. But more time is needed. Some of Western nations' intrusive, borderline impulsive, poorly planned, and incompetently strategised blind support for pro-Western popular movements, such as the Colour Revolutions in Eastern Europe and the Arab Spring, at times caused greater instability. Subjecting Russia to similar pressures and ploys is risky, at times counter-productive, and perhaps even dangerous, as the Eastern European and Eurasian regions need stability for their countries to develop further. A destabilised Russia mired with conflict is a detriment to all of mankind.

Some may ask the question: 'Who needs a strong Russia?' The simplest of answers is that a strong Russia should facilitate a stable Russia. An unstable Russia will lead to refugees, conflict, and crime that will affect surrounding regions, which Europe cannot afford and China would not prefer. If security in the Caucuses to Russia's south is undermined and jeopardised, another sphere of Islamist radicalism, as is familiar to Chechnya and Dagestan, will emerge, complicating US and European foreign interests. The same concerns apply to Russia. However, by the demands of circumstance, Russia could not implement effective liberal democracy. As such, misunderstanding and miscommunication prevail to the detriment of both spheres of mankind.

At the heart of such dynamics is relational normative power. To fulfil Russia's interests, order over progress had to be achieved. Europe's interests are normative in exporting liberal democracy and securing stability and peace around its borders, as well as encouraging economic prosperity and integration. Each faction's normativity responding to their respective demands of circumstance achieve different goals and possess distinct utility. For Russia, it is some sort and degree of stability. But Europe had been developmentally beyond such elementary concerns.

Indeed, Europe's model had much to offer: it has experienced peace for a while since its chaotic 20th century, it has great opportunities, fairly stable social environments, the highest living standards, good environmental standards, and decent labour norms and rules[66]. Considering the success of liberal democracies following the Western model and the survival of NATO and Western normativity over the Soviet communist model, it is understandable that the West would assume its political, economic, and normative model is superior[67]. Furthermore, much empirical evidence, as was noted above, supports the Western model with respect to its many elements of progressiveness, stability, and prosperity.

These concrete evaluations, however, would benefit from greater study, which is not the present goal. From an ethical standpoint and personal impression and experience from both sides of the fence between life in Russia and England, both models of normativity have their merits and virtues. However, in simpler psychological and spiritual terms, as well as general observations of social cohesion, life in England is, indeed, better. Suffering prevails in both spheres, yet its efficacy is softer and calmer in some parts of England. Both normative and ideational models are from perfect, and both Russia and the UK require a great deal of work to become unreal utopias of happiness. Yet the UK is arguably ahead by virtue of standards of living and the UK's many progressive social aspects, even despite its blunders of recent years.

While prospects in Russia might be limited, their demands in the West, even if available, are costly; I would know by the student debt I have. Nevertheless, I am extremely happy for the opportunity I received and the lessons I have learnt. Simple things like education and even restricted opportunities, taken for granted by many people accustomed to such norms, support a general statement that Western normativity and its effects on policy are better in sum terms. People may give the most attention to negative aspects and may dislike mundanity. Yet from a perspective of someone who has travelled a lot and lived in many places with little sustenance of stable social and ethical environments, life in England has treated me much better than anywhere else, even though I still had to, and still do, endure certain struggles. A seemingly simple thing like the National Health Service (the NHS), with decent medical care, shows for the extraordinary living conditions in England. This is why one can safely conclude that life in the West is better in many of its own ways, even though far from perfect and not without many faults. Therefore, one can claim that Western normativity is more successful and advanced.

Western normativity is only successful and more advanced because it has developed. Other nations, such as Russia, experience different conditions and pressures, or at least in sum terms. Therefore, civic utilities and normative values will differ across developmental stages, and for good reason. The fault of Western normativity is sometimes presuming that the model can be applied easily and effectively. But the intentions are to promote human rights and improve living standards for fellow people, on top of other self-interest to promote global peace, prosperity, stability, and security for all people's interests. Western policy is moved by self-interest and its genuine dimension of trying to help others, as is the case with the promotion of human rights. But in doing so, undisciplined morality, the function of which can be easily corrupted by Fear and immoderate instinct, warps the impression of normativity and erodes its moral authority.

People try to help, yet they often make mistakes. Where the stakes are high in the global arena and where impressions of Fear are easily evoked, mistakes have lasting consequences. Following suit, Russia has serious concerns with Western foreign policy in relation to the many mistakes Western countries have made. A normative divide has been fostered between the West and Russia through Fear and caution. Russia's policy is then moved by caution over what it sees as encirclement by NATO, intrusive foreign policies, and disastrous decisions of factions with great power.

Russia's domestic concerns of security and stability are antithetical to sometimes unsophisticated Western policy. Russia, at least, can and should only develop liberal democracy on its own terms by nourishing reciprocal normativity and political culture from within. Intervention, rather than soft assistance, will not perform the service necessary for Russia's ethical, social, and political development. In these rifts of normativity and common understanding, Russia forms the impression of a belligerent and neo-Imperialistic West, the leading power being the United States. Consequently, Russia reacts with an ambition of holding back a force that it thinks is destabilising and unhelpful, the constant affirmation of which fosters at times hostile sentiment and malicious impression. Everyone thinks they are the good guys, because the concerns of ego's social instinct and the functions of Fear make it so.

However, Fear and its vices and biases then also block the virtues of understanding and patience which could facilitate true and lasting peace. The foundation of these flaws are people and the public that enables flawed states of affairs. Thus, only occasionally does messianic leadership of great virtue arise, which, even so, only pales under the great forces of the structures of ethics, their Natural Laws, and the Highest Good. One might claim that both the West and Russia mean well, but the normativity that propagates values through actions and policies can easily contradict itself through the lack of mindfulness and discipline under the pressures of Fear, succumbing to the vices of Fear.

Good intentions have been twisted by Fear, and moral sense and virtues have been lost to Fear; the order of Fear has been corrupted on a fundamental level. Both factions are at moral fault; few bear the virtues to accept this, and even fewer herald the virtues to succeed vice. This Fear may be sustainable, but it is not fulfilling of greater ambition with respect to achieving world peace and collaborative efforts for greater mutual growth and prosperity.

A controversial aspect of the global ethical structure of Fear is the presence of a superpower – the United States of America. America heralds the status of a champion of liberty, democracy, and human rights, or so it has been claimed. Yet its many actions have contradicted its normativity through both domestic and foreign policies. For one, Fear prioritising the concern for security encouraged values of the primacy of state security. Accordingly, the National Security Agency (NSA) mass surveillance program was granted justification, arguably encroaching on civil liberties. However, the question remains concerning which of the two – civil liberties or the prevention of loss of life (or risks thereof) – is more important, with Fear and concerns over immediate survival favouring the latter – security and stability.

Neither is inherently bad, yet there are conditions for their effective utility. Considering the many domestic social issues in the United States, notably those exacerbated by poverty, inequalities, market monopolies, and poor governance that is no different to corruption, often rooted in issues of political culture and limited education, its normative power is easily questioned. Naturally, other countries pick up on this, then disproportionally inflate impression with biases. US foreign policies, like all countries' foreign policies, have been mired with imperfect and flawed decisions, at times detrimental to its image as a benevolent superpower.

Of course, some US foreign policies can be ascribed to the value of status in relation to the normativity of champions of freedom and the most powerful nation on Earth, just as Russia's foreign and domestic policy imbues status with great value. Where values and status contend and conflict, power struggles arise and peace is destabilised. This brings into consideration the general question of power in the dynamics and structures of global affairs.

Dominance over other nations carries the burden of others' caution and mistrust. Where a nation is able to exercise great power over another, Fear excites caution. Then, the nation of greater power becomes uncertain of emerging potential threats that desire power for security. This is the common dynamic between China and the United States, as is seen with the continued disputes over territory in the South China Sea. Base morality and Fear move values according to the interests of territory and resources for the purpose of security and power. Mutual distrust and concerns of security subsequently provoke Fear and enable and emphasise the ethical use of Fear – to avoid suffering. Fear possesses the benevolent utility of incentivising and encouraging progress and development, which has unequivocally led to the improvement of mankind. But where mutual mistrust continues, caution and insecurity also provoke conflict and contention. Fear is often a messy and chaotic ethical directive – a guiding interest in goal-directive behaviour; its threatening nature in the modern world is especially troubled.

We are all victims of our vulnerability under Fear; we all suffer in Fear. When others act with malice borne of Fear, the same Fear is excited in us, to the detriment and debasement of us all. This is the order of Fear, and it is corruptive. Mankind is not strong enough to usurp its fate and succeed the order of Fear, yet.

China's normativity at odds with Western orientations of ethics can pose a threat to Western livelihood, prosperity, and even liberal democracy. This statement is not one of certainty and is designed with ambiguity. China is not for a fact concerned with a directive of undermining the West and liberal democracy. Rather, the country simply wants what is best for itself, to serve its national interests, which is a more straightforward and direct goal than of liberal democracies pursuing global normative ambitions of changing the world.

Conflict is not inevitable and not a given. However, the odds between Western and Chinese normativity, with specific reference to human rights and civil liberties, emerging Chinese power might threaten the West. Even without direct intent, China's affluence and power could undermine Western normativity if the West fails to keep up developmental pace, which can occur through internal divide and unaddressed domestic issues of poor governance. If one side fails to adapt and prosper, it will suffer and degrade. Furthermore, uncertainty in relations between the West and China are inherent in terms of both sides' unpredictability of actions. We don't know what will happen in the future that may set both factions at odds. Then, an even greater uncertainty is how each side will respond. Fear among both is a threat, as we ourselves don't necessarily know how we will act or what will happen globally. These same uncertainties preside over all change in global power-shares with developing countries classified as 'BRICS' (Brazil, Russia, India, China, and South Africa).

The world is changing, and shares in power are shifting and their values evolving. The Western model is, indeed, not self-evident to be universal, yet its civic utility in advanced and developed societies and economies has much to offer. All utilities and values may have their merit in particular conditions and circumstances; all have their advantages and disadvantages. With change in the dynamics of political power, values can contend, compete, and conflict. These dynamics and their Natural Law of Fear may pose a great threat to mankind. We do not know with certainty how we will react to one another, and people do foolish things when threatened.

Surely there is something better in store for human ambition than a state of common Fear? What if people from all countries were willing to make their own sacrifices for mutual gain and a sum better sphere for living in peace and common security and stability? Relatable progress has been made in terms of the natural environment, issues of sustainability, and climate change. One must ask whether cooperation or secluded dominance is better for well-being, with both entailing risks and uncertainties. But if one is to favour global peace and harmony in power, then he or she must be prepared to make sacrifices for the common good, but if and only if this complies with Highest Good and successful virtue. This could potentially mean surrendering luxurious lifestyles and comforts, and living a somewhat materially diminished quality of life with less impulsive and sporadic consumer habits, granting its own greater rewards. People must ask themselves what is more valuable and whether they possess the virtue and ambition to pursue greater interests. Time will tell.

Challenges in established orders of power are dangerous; power vacuums are more dangerous. The US presides as a superpower during change in the global political and normative environment. Multipolarity of powerful nation-states will most likely emerge during America's era of dominance. Considering some blunders in

US foreign policy, its reactions to multipolarity might be counter-productive and dangerous, with Fear spurring reactive and instinctive policies lacking greater virtue.

However much the US is criticised and its track record is far from perfect, never has a superpower of this magnitude been even slightly as benevolent. Compared to major inequalities and established orders of power throughout history, America's supremacy has not been one as terrible as colonialism, mass genocide, wars for power, and systematic disregard for human rights, or at least this has been the case up to a certain point. The US is serving its own interests, but evidently many such interests benefit human civilisation. The Western model of liberal democracy has prevailed for a long time and enabled mankind to achieve incredible things.

Western normativity is progressive, adaptive, and generally successful in many respects, even though far from perfect. The United States goes out of its way to protect itself and other nations alike, to guard and protect its normativity with hopes of bettering mankind, or had done for some time. Of course, many aspects of these good intentions behind normativity can be questioned. But for the present context, consider that the US has helped many other nations, even if this help was not perfect or properly implemented. At least some good has come out of this directive of policy.

Negligence in policy-implementation has had negative consequences on perceived US intentions, as well as undermined the cause of liberal democracies valuing human rights and civil liberties. At a crucial point in the development of global civilisation, when other nations are becoming more capable and more powerful, the normativity that has prevailed in securing greater degrees of peace in Europe and has allowed the West to flourish may be crucial for international security, material interdependence and prosperity, and global peace in an otherwise very risky time.

Fear can jeopardise these ambitions. Western culture might not be universally applicable, yet peaceful transition in power and economic development should be paramount for concerns of well-being. But strengthening such values and virtues is imperative, and a state can only do so much in its Fear and basic function. A more balanced distribution of power, as with multipolarity, could be good in terms of encouraging, through necessity, greater collaboration and greater balance in competition of normativity and values, subsequently human adaptation.

For instance, greater pressure from other countries to make Western policy-makers to be more cautious would be beneficial for political strategy. Yet this could also lead to conflict if unbalanced and if the value of peace and cooperation is forgotten, which is evidently potentially preventable through economic interdependence in some cases where material concerns are greater than other interests. But Fear in power still remains a threat by undermining common values and normativity as a consequence of people's uncertainty and distrust. Only truly common normativity can bypass this, with base morality being effectively served through material concerns and nourished functions preferring stability and a healthy sense of happiness. Fear cannot promise this commonality, nor sustain it, for Fear will instigate uncertainty and indulge corruptive base morality.

Certain aspects of the discussion above may come across as unconcise. This is part of the systemic vice of Fear. In the reality of careful study and objective information it is near impossible to envisage a world of peace, harmony in power, and mutual prosperity. A world without the reign of Fear is unintuitive to mankind, yet only by rising above the order of Fear can we achieve the liberty of humanity. The normative sphere of liberal democracy and genuine respect for human rights might be, to this day, the only prospective model for achieving greater ambitions. However, this model itself suffers from many fundamental flaws.

For example, China may aspire to the prosperity and living conditions of the West. This is a good aspiration, as peace and social harmony of good living and the eradication of poverty are imperative for global well-being. However, for the populations of China, India, and Russia to live in as much excess as Western societies is mind-boggling with respect to sustainability and the availability of resources. Sheltered lives of base morality in modern societies are at times delusional and mad in their habits.

This is by no means a new thought, as culture is adapting and learning to branch out away from the mainstream and basic form of materialistic society and culture. As was discussed, however, materialism and consumerism have very positive attributes. But where a life that lacks stimulation and fulfilment clings to self-obsessive consumption of material and indulges in the pursuit of novelty, where this life lingers in the shadow of Fear without ambition moving past such idle states subdued by complacency and aversion to pain, it is a life of suffering, even if veiled. Concern of happiness moves normativity to adapt, yet the contingent global dynamics are rigid. It is a bothersome and crucial question of whether the Western model of excess and blind hedonism is sustainable, and whether it is even worth its supposed promise of happiness and fulfilment. But soul-searching is not the job of governance.

Materialism and consumerism serve economic models. Affluent nations, by virtue of their consumers, grow their material capacities, which then translate into technological development, social innovation, and political resources. For one, greater wealth can lead to greater military capability. An undeniable element of the survival of liberal democracy and the West is military prowess. Jeopardising economic success, such as by radically undermining material utility and consumer ethics, can be devastating for the world order, for human rights, for liberal democracy, and global peace. This doesn't even touch on the matter of environmental concerns. Smart consumerism might be the answer, yet the ethical question remains of how to incentives people or appeal to their desires. The civic utility of consumerism and materialism is only enabled and amplified by the will of the people and their guiding ethics. Furthermore, sensibility is favourable of this model, despite its many imperfections. But people's ordinary Fear and base morality undermining greater progress are the natural and organic contingency of the genealogy of instinctive ethics.

The directive of consumerism led to the present ethical environment, yet the ethic cannot address its own challenges, which are becoming increasingly problematic in terms of excess, unsustainability, and waste. Mankind is not yet above the structural forces of Fear reigning over it. And while Fear gratifies in many respects, it also holds back our greater interests.

Then again, risky policies borne of negligence and naivety can expose weaknesses that would be exploited by others. Mankind is weak and vulnerable under Fear, and the empowerment of virtue has not flourished, and prevailing standards of normativity are not sufficient to confront modern challenges and prospects of entering a world of fulfilling ambitions of the true Highest Good such as of global peace, prosperity, and happiness. Political goals are mired with impossibilities found on contradictory values as moral ideals and in practice. Liberal democracy and human rights are promising, yet the Fear and base morality that moves them also threaten liberty and humanity from within. Development of the mind, character, and spirit through morality is imperative for greater fulfilment of the interests of base morality – security, stability, prosperity, peace, well-being, and happiness. However, base morality is no longer enough to fulfil its own interests. A new vision is needed – a new ethic, a new directive, a new morality, a new incentive, new satisfaction, and new happiness applicable to, and viable in, the globalised modern world that could deliver humanity to normative post-modernism.

Consider another dimension of the same problem that the state cannot solve or effectively address, the cases which will also explore the role of normativity in global politics of human endeavour. Russia's perception of NATO encirclement and encroachment is evident, and NATO has indeed enlarged. Primitive sentiments of distrust, impressions of hostility, and a perceived or projected desire to dominate portray a negative image of NATO activity. Little study has been dedicated to the normative dimension of the contention between the West and Russia.

Why did NATO enlarge against Russia's vocal opposition, and why did other nations join (as NATO membership is entirely voluntary)? Why could post-communist Russia not sustain the security structure of the Warsaw Pact? Some may explore realist interpretations in terms of encroachment, underhand political manipulations, or ploys of an authoritarian regime emphasising a foreign threat. However, a distinctive normative element is crucial to make sense of the root of shifts in values, interests, alignments, and power.

The dissolution of the Soviet Union was primarily a consequence of domestic troubles. Russia notably suffered during its period of 'reconstruction' and reformation into a federation away from communism. However, Russia was not economically, socially, or politically able to preserve its once great power[68], least hold itself together. The disintegration of the Soviet bloc led to power vacuums and regional imbalances where Russia was surrounded by much weaker states seeking autonomy and independence, which naturally entailed risk of conflict[69].

Furthermore, the newly independent ex-Soviet client states in Eastern Europe sought to consolidate their autonomy and liberty, and understandably so. While accounts of communist rule over its client states may contend, a safe claim is that, by the nature of Soviet communism, client states did not have full autonomy of liberal democracy. Some may ascribe oppression and authoritative military policy to Russia, yet a better description would perhaps be in general terms of a tendency for sociopolitical domination by an established communist philosophy and its resourcefulness outcompeting other normativity. After all, even though communist Russia's strength was its size and wealth overbearing its neighbours, the philosophy and normativity that transformed Russia and mobilised it, while maintaining unity, is a testament to the temporary power Russia had. Nonetheless, the Soviet dread was oppressive to its member states[70], at least by virtue of not being a liberal democracy.

The communist regime in varying degrees also stifled Russia's own culture, such as with agricultural communities, religion, and general cultural and intellectual development, even though the regime fostered another dimension of Russian culture. In this context, it is understandable that major social and even ethnic rifts would occur between Russia and some of its ex-client states. Where Russian ultranationalists and ethnic nationalists, dreaming of neo-imperialism, gained traction in Russia's turbulent period after communist dissolution, neighbouring countries were extremely cautious of their regional hegemon. Hence, Eastern European countries in particular sought to branch out and find a new place in the world with their newfound independence and with hope of a better future. With the successes of the West's and Western Europe's model, new countries looked Westward rather than to a struggling

Russia in hopes of finding greater welfare.

In terms of security concerns, the US and its European NATO allies were concerned with the security gap threatening European peace and stability. This was wise in reflection of the conflicts in the Baltics, instability in the Caucuses, and to a degree even the Ukraine conflict. Consequently, it seemed logical for NATO to fill in the security vacuum in the interests of Europe, Russia, and the broader region[71].

NATO was the most promising choice at the time to offer stability in the region and provide security during a period of transformation. Furthermore, the United States provided Russia with assistance to reform in hopes of a new sphere of compatible normativity and liberal democracy. Europe was able to entice and assist newly independent Eastern European countries to become integrated into the sphere of liberal democracy, competent governance, economic prosperity, and social harmony. While the successes of Europe's integrative policies were not perfect, they did have some major successes in securing some peace and welfare in Eastern Europe. It must be kept in mind that NATO is a defensive organisation founded on common consensus and strongly in favour of liberal democratic norms that consolidate the security apparatus and alliance.

The West has engaged in attempts of social engineering by sponsoring pro-Western liberal democratic political movements such as with the Colour Revolutions surrounding Russia[72]. Where political lobbying of foreign countries' democratic processes is involved, of course this will evoke cautionary reactions. Material support for pro-Western, pro-liberal democratic political movements may be necessary for their sociopolitical success. Yet in doing so these policies perhaps unfairly intervene in the domestic politics of other nations and sow discord in the political structure, but most importantly undermine the moral authority and normative power of these movements where they are perceived to be intrusive and meddling, especially in reference to Russia.

As was discussed, challenges to Russia's greater liberalisation are profound; a reckless policy of foreign involvement can be disastrous for the world if it leads to a once again unstable Russia. A notion in Russian political culture that foreigners simply don't understand Russia is relevant in many respects, yet its philosophy is not without a rational, structured account. The same applies for Russia's potential involvement in Western politics, whether the US or Europe. Where such meddling in government performance is influenced by foreign groups and in light of perceived aggression from both sides, a divide consumes mutual understanding and normativity. NATO's directive is defensive by design and not of any neo-imperialist sort. But the foreign policies of its individual member states can project an image, subsequently normativity, of distrust and intrusiveness, which undermines its own cause and virtue.

Russia may perceive an aggressive and intrusive West, a reaction that some elements of Western foreign policy can easily incite. But the foundation of common misconceptions and biases has been found on the strengthening and territorial spread of the NATO alliance. Russia may see the spread of NATO as encroachment and in a realist's vision of domination and quasi-imperial debauchery. By failing to account for the simple normative aspects of Russia's newly independent neighbours concerned with Russia's great military power, Russia's legacy of imperialism, and lingering dreams of certain vocal and mentally unsound minorities in Russia, blame has been misplaced and misunderstanding has arisen.

Russia did not have the capacity and resources to secure regional stability and it took a long time for Russia to get back on its feet. Russia still isn't able to guarantee its own long-term prosperity, growth, security, and stability, least even hint at offering something viable for its neighbours and ex-allies. NATO plugged in the security gap and the European model provided its Eastern neighbours what Russia could not. This can almost be analogously summarised as the dynamic of a failed relationship that led to an unsatisfied partner getting in bed with another lover who could provide and satisfy. People's orientation of pursuing well-being and valuing greater degrees of certainty and security led to each faction and group to go its own way.

No one is at fault in this; each country is a victim of unfavourable circumstances and is suffering from a rift in common understanding and normativity. This is an unnecessary conflict and state of contention. But rather than addressing the regional source of seemingly conflicted interests – Eastern European countries concerned with their security and a titanic military power on their borders – Russia and the West go at each other's throats without solving normative and fundamental political concerns in the region. Fear and instinctive base morality block greater awareness and judgement of the situation where leadership is subject to unforgiving pressure. Fear is holding back each faction from fulfilling their greater interests of looking beyond primitive grievances and hostile impressions. Peace and cooperation are possible, but Fear denies the courage for these grand ambitions to become realities.

How can greater normativity and policy be achieved? Leadership of government will only ever respond to people's directives and will. Only through moral power appealing to people's normativity and culture can peace be consolidated from within to influence greater global spheres. The vision and scope of this work is ambitious, but by no means is it directly intended for government leadership. Neither is it dedicated exclusively to scholars, whose role in constructive criticism and further study would be greatly valued and appreciated. These discussions are dedicated to the individual reader and citizen. Only in change of each individual's world by agreeable normativity serving his or her interests and bettering people's circumstances can enduring peace be achieved. This, however, above all needs ethical and moral development and growth, rather than compelling intervention on seats of power provided only by the weight of people's conscience and public interests, values, and concerns.

The dangers and threats of continued contention are many. The occasional brink of war is only a short-term flare of symptoms of an otherwise troublesome ill. Russia's perception of a foreign threat may be a guise serving a manipulative authoritarian regime. However, it is not difficult to put oneself in Russia's shoes and understand its reasoning and concerns. The same can be said for Western policy directives and their underlying normativity. Russia needs to develop to guarantee its future stability and security, which is in all people's interests, especially regionally. Liberalisation and modernisation are key for Russia's growth, yet the challenges are many. The perception of a foreign entity undermining Russian security might simply be a facade for a corrupt kleptocracy and authoritarian regime, yet it may equally be a real and prevalent sentiment.

Russia will not liberalise under its political patriarchy of authoritative men while the administration is convinced of the existence of serious threats from near-abroad. The media will not liberalise while the government cannot permit truly competitive information distribution in a state of heightened security and near-war. Consequently, accountability will be minimal and political competitiveness will be stagnant. Without the certainty of peace in international relations between the West and Russia, as well as lingering excesses of corruption, Russia will not receive the investment it needs for the fulfilment of its potential to then truly break the cycle of revolution and strife. If Russia does not overcome its many obstacles and does not modernise, it will suffer, experience future turmoil, and expire. Where the authoritative administration and new aristocracy loses a clear and unifying head – its patriarch – and where competition of ambitions and petty motivations ruled by Fear preside over the social and political landscape, it is only a matter of time before Russia tears itself apart again. In a time of great uncertainty and global challenges to all mankind, this is not something that can be dismissed or afforded. Yet Russia is but one of many subjects of Fear.

Russia may aspire for a balanced world of multipolarity – of greater political competitiveness. Foreign policy disasters may be subverted and avoided where clear heads and common interests lead to mutual respect and the acceptance of international laws. Russia's own malice and pettiness can be held to account in a more stable world order. Where China's emerging great power could pose a threat, another ally would be useful for global security and competing voices able to exercise influence and reminding the value of peace, calm, and cooperation. Russia may seek a new place in the world with a new identity. Where it once fought a perceived capitalist threat and now defies a hegemon's power over past grievances, perhaps a new identity of a modern Russia is worthier of its virtue as a fighter for peace and cooperation.

A great risk comes with shifts in power of an emerging multipolar world. Russia may see itself as benefitting from this through the West's position of power being balanced by other global ethical actors. Yet Russia does not possess the normativity to form concrete alliances through fundamental common interests. In fact, much of Russia's political resources are only military and to some degree economic such as oil and gas, which are far from compelling. In doing so, Russia is unable to pursue its own goals of balancing and stabilising world power dynamics. While other nations build economic ties with less hostile and arguably less problematic countries, Russia loses out.

Make no mistake that Russia's and China's ties are not necessarily of normative compatibility or mutually reciprocal interests. Without binding normativity and with conflict of interests, China and Russia could eventually descend into war. China and Russia are not a promised alliance. Russia's folklore culture might even be more sceptical of Asians than Europeans and Americans. If China is to become aggressive or insistent on its ambitions and interests, the West could benefit from another ally. Furthermore, Europe would benefit greatly from a constructive partner securing its Eastern region all the way up to China, providing a buffer zone in dealing with the turbulent Middle East and the Caucuses. If Russia was to modernise and liberalise and become more normatively compatible with the West, both Russia and the West would benefit greatly, domestically and internationally.

To mediate shifts in global power of a multipolar order of normativity, Russia could become a central balancing agent of authority. Russia might never join the European Union and NATO, but neither is this a necessity or a reason for denying Russia's potential and hopeful future of modernisation and greater liberalisation characterised primarily by the rule of law, economic prosperity, and effective, accountable, fully democratic governments. Then again, modernisation is ultimately Russia's choice, and Fear is holding Russia back, just as Fear undermines humanity.

Russia could become an alternative sphere of liberal democracy, a neutral state of libertarian foreign policy respectful of (or perhaps even apathetic to) other nations' state of normativity and political culture, thereby not causing the damage of Western policies while serving as a paragon of the virtues of political modernism and liberal democracy. A neutral Russia interested in global peace and prosperity is an appealing and achievable possibility. If mankind is to succeed over its many present challenges, perhaps this could be key to global well-being and sustainable development unhindered by major conflict. Russia can solve its domestic problems and perceived threat of intrusive and hegemonic powers by playing at the West's own normative game but in another yard without hostility, yet with Russia's own image. Russia's normative, cultural, and political change could inspire many and help global growth and progress, yet Russia is not necessary for the conceived ambitions and is but one of many possibilities for achieving a promising and hopeful post-modern ethical structure.

These biases concerning Russia are based only on a greater familiarity with it than other societies and nations. But first, to achieve any such dream would require people to move past their Fear and pursue promising and fulfilling ambition – a universal ethical challenge. Only by succeeding Russia's primary normativity of Fear's excessive security undermining social, political, and economic progress can its potential be fulfilled through modernisation and liberalisation. No state or any one person can achieve this – only an ethic and its moral authority can. The West can then assist through tacit support and through patience, calm, cooperation, understanding, and normatively mindful policy and relations. But an incentive stronger than Fear's and base morality's intuition, binding rationale and sentiment, is necessary for such developments, or at least for a push in a new and hopeful direction.

The escalation of conflicting relations found on Fear and misunderstanding have led to some of the worst humanitarian crises of recent times – namely, Ukraine and Syria. While the source of conflict was first of all domestic and internal, caused by deep social and ethnic divide made volatile with poverty, neglect, and much suffering, intervention by global and local superpowers driven by their own interests brought in a new dimension of suffering and destruction. At its root – Fear.

There is little necessity for extensive discussion on the case studies mentioned, for there are sufficient good literature and studies that have been done on the subjects. However, the ethical and normative dimension hasn't received as much attention. The civil war in Ukraine and Russia's intervention in its immediate neighbourhood widely evoked an understandable reaction of perceiving Russia as resurgent, neo-Imperialist, assertive, aggressive, and threatening. But from the other side of the fence matters were not as simple, and the regime felt threatened, neglected, and its cultural, social, and national interests were forced into a state of contention with eager, yet not inherently wrong, Western policies. Nevertheless, each perspective is elusive to the narrow and simplistic vision of mindless base morality and the tragic clout of Fear. People and institutions felt threatened, and so their minds were blinded with fear, leading to careless mistakes of good intent. All involved are guilty of negligence.

However, this blame becomes worse in greater Fear that led to the bloodshed in Syria. Where Russia was once seen as resurgent, somewhat menacing, its normative entity degraded much further. Western alliances may have supported more moderate groups, yet in Russia's view, in support of the preferred legacy of a regime with closer ties to Russia since the Cold War under Assad's family, any pro-Western factions, liberally democratic or not, were a potential threat.

In Russia's view, Syria became a proxy war, and any faction that is pro-Western or hostile to the government, or simply mindless genocidal lunatics, were branded with the superficial and arbitrary term *terrorists*. Russia most likely perceived any anti-government cells as threats to Russia's national interests and therefore as 'terrorists'. But in Russia's pursuit of its interests in Syria, Fear eroded Russia's normative reputation further into an abomination that turned a blind eye to blatant brutality, genocide, and atrocity. People may pass the blame on each other, such as with Russia on Western mistakes that accidentally violated the ceasefire. But rather than reflecting on the mistake and allowing patience and virtue to prevail, Fear consumed all sides and they descended into conflict once again.

Putin may seek to protect and secure Russia, give it a worthy place in the international arena and to balance US influence. Yet under the legacy of his character lost to the morality of Fear and debased by instinct, by which most figures and all societies are afflicted, the necessity of desperate policy and vision blinded by Fear have lost any notable normativity, leaving only menial national assets and utilities that can only influence through conflict and contention.

The immediate global effect of this deep-rooted Fear on both sides is the massive death toll and suffering in Syria, as well as global inefficiency where collaboration is choked. Looking backward at the origins of understandable deviations in interests and priorities, the present state of needless contention is heart-breaking, for it is not at all unresolvable or fundamental – only over-shadowed by a great Fear. A shame, frankly.

The bottom-line is that the vector of authority in Russia's ethical sphere is normatively and morally compromised against its own good. But the global structural dynamic of Fear needlessly and reversibly poisons humanity, virtue, and goodness. And so humanity withers, the world decays, and people die and suffer. A rift in common understanding, values, and interests, sown by mankind's own Fear and the primacy of corrupt base morality, warps good intent and disturbs common good faith to the point of mutual loss. Russia needs help or at least time and some space, for all our sakes. Yet its own actions and subsequent reactions performed under a veil of terrible and petty Fear led to everyone's loss.

But where despair, apathy, and anger may settle in, it is useful to think in a different way to common instinct and narrow vision of base morality – hate not the sinner, but the sin. Hope may be dying; good faith might be lost. And even though time is running out, there is still a choice, an opportunity. But Fear and its convention of instinct's primacy in morality cannot fulfil our greater interests. Something must change, but that change can only happen within the individual and people's character and spirit; *ethical* and *moral* development beyond Fear and focused base morality is necessary for Fear's and base morality's own fundamental interests.

Chapter 9:

Discord of Reason

The discussions in Section 2 thus far have centred primarily on the structural level of ethical states of affairs. Now, attention should be turned back to the systemic level – to the psyche of people. Fear and base morality are prevalent socially and globally, with their fundamental disadvantages and limitations as ethical utilities having been noted – namely, the excessive desire for security leads to greater insecurity. However, evaluation of the personal dimension has been rather faint.

While problems in the global picture persist, the main issues arise with very personal challenges of individuals living in, and adapting to, the modern world. The relevant main theme will be summarised as the discord of reason between rationale and sentiment, between high-reason and base-reason in a diverse and rapidly changing world and ethical environment, change which many weren't, and still aren't, fully prepared for. A new challenge to individual concerns for states of well-being has manifested – a headless world lacking a binding and coherent morality creating order.

At this point I may only write as a single part of the millennial generation, yet I know I am far from alone. The proceeding Chapter will in many ways reflect depressive memories, yet balance them with insights of different mental states in accord of reason and mindfulness. Where the mind and base morality were borne of instinct and hostile environments demanding immediate survival and constant stimulation, the world has changed. A fundamentally different environment affecting our minds and spirit has arisen.

Over many generations, the structure of ethics has followed the sovereignty of Fear and the functions of base morality. Progress and development have been achieved; perhaps Fear was the only thing that made development possible and sustainable. However, the ethics of Fear and their primacy of functions in terms of base morality can be very inefficient.

Conflict, contention, vice, selfishness, biases lacking mindfulness and discipline, and a lack of coherent and promising moral authority have undermined human progress. Adaptiveness and competition are necessary for certain forms of development, and the modern world might not have been possible without Fear and base morality. But their limitations and vices are not necessarily sustainable. The challenges human civilisation faces are many and dire, whether concerning the environment, over-population, conflict, famine, or disease. A history of mistakes is punishing younger generations, sowing a rift in trust, good faith, and virtue. Present and future generations may be on the brink of the greatest challenges mankind has ever had to face, conditioned by moments that may be decisive for mankind's future. Negativity presides where an unhinged negativity bias and common vices shroud judgement, leaving many to cradle themselves without confronting the source of suffering and ill. Fear is corrosive and base morality is functionally insufficient to fulfil Fear's directive or greater maxims of the soul's imperative of well-being. Many are not spiritually equipped for effective and fulfilling life in a truly modern world, and society as a whole may suffer from disagreement leading to needless divide and contention instigated by vices of base morality.

Challenges to our livelihood were significant and demanding in the past; we succeeded by virtue of Fear. Now, modernity allows more people than ever to live peaceful, wealthy, stable, and secure lives, or only on the face of things. However, new challenges are emerging. A life lacking stimulation and engagement is often unfulfilled. Where time allows people to think and where boredom settles in, we are left to our thoughts. So we ponder life, philosophise, and remember embarrassing moments while trying to fall asleep.

Where stability and peace have been achieved – the dream of base morality's incentive – this can lead to stagnation and emptiness. And in our idleness, we become mad. Where we have abided Fear through base morality and life was engaged by constant pain and suffering, the mind and spirit were active, undeterred by mundane concerns. But where this pressure subsides and stimulation is lacking, the spirit withers and living becomes empty. We cling to experience and novelty, pursuing more and more stimulation to fulfil the primary desires and functions of the base faculties. Then, some might only continue this cycle until death puts them to rest, to distract themselves until the inevitable end without fundamental fulfilment, peace, and sense of achievement in life. Yet there are certainly great things in these forms of living, as is seen with the rich fulfilment of love or the bittersweet peace found in healing from heartbreak and by overcoming other suffering. However, where life is bound to ceaseless pursuit of stimulation and distraction, even if as the most fulfilling sentiment of love, the shadow of Fear always lingers in the back of the mind, detracting from lingering moments of satisfaction.

The concerns and primacy of base morality may have once reigned supreme and served our interests well. But where stability and times of peace allowed for culture and introspection to flourish, new needs awakened and new ways of thinking were discovered. Where base morality is fulfilled, the higher faculties look for a new occupation and foster needs of their own. People need engagement and stimulation in living; eventually, this can lead to the need of a purpose and meaning as part of a greater goal.

Religion might be designed by high-reason. Some may worship and envisage a caring and loving deity, one that fulfils some basic needs of people. People might have a fundamental need to be loved, and so a benevolent God engages their faith to fulfil their needs. Some may want a grand purpose, more than the momentary distraction and stimulation, something that can ease existential concerns and address the fundamental questions of living. Yet times have changed, and the conventions of past traditions do not suffice for modern challenges, for they are idols of expired times and are borne of different circumstances.

For example, some may not need to be loved to live and function, whereby the utility of a loving God expires. The scare of a mundane life of nine-to-five cleric jobs may drive some people mad, feeding negative attitudes towards life. God, religion, and old values of emphasised and dissatisfied base morality are not universal utilities in dealing with the concerns of modern life.

Base morality can invoke positive stimulation, distracting from negative feelings, while still retaining the self-corruptive feelings of hating a mundane life. Sense of meaning and purpose becomes lost, and the spirit suffers. Even the value of survival and care for continued existence may deteriorate where living is unfulfilled, further cutting away at effective ethical value and motivation to live. People need goals, directives, meaning, and purpose. Base morality and Fear have led to a point of development where modern structures of ethics have been found with a wealth of utilities to enrich, engage, and nourish life. Nevertheless, fundamental challenges remain by the very nature of the directive – well-being in terms of Fear, survival, and instinct.

While perfect living conditions have not been achieved, the time has come where many successes have been achieved such that a new ethical directive is necessary to sustain our achievements and growth. Fear and base morality cannot universally sustain what they themselves have created, and the value and effectiveness of their functions is deteriorating. Base morality created the extraordinary modern world and its outstanding quality of living. Yet the same industriousness and drive that created this state of affairs cannot promise its sustainability and the sustainability of the natural environment.

Incoherence in moral judgements reduced to subjectivity have sown normative divide and disproportionally competing values without clear and coherent evaluation. Too many problems arise from this, and one has to question the sustainability of amorality. Global society cannot carry on like this, of morality reduced to blind sentiment and instinct lacking the coherence of binding rationale, discipline, and mindfulness engaging our fundamental desires and interests. Then, no binding moral authority, as religion once might have been, can effectively and compellingly move progressive cultural and moral development.

Progress has been achieved, yet too many inefficiencies and problems arise in normativity when people presume Fear benefits their interests most, when desires and behaviour are based on blind values of headless instincts failing to achieve their own unfulfillable goals. One may simply ask: 'What is the point of survival? To live while it lasts? To enjoy life?' Value is found where positivity is sensed. Yet Fear fundamentally undermines this positivity if its ethics are based on distraction and the lack of meaningful purpose. All primary aspects of the psyche – base and high – must be fulfilled, and the higher faculties of spirit are not universally satisfied in a time that is fundamentally different to even half a century ago. Technology has amplified our pursuit of fulfilment by branching out experiences and enabling easily accessible, but spiritually unsatisfying, pleasures. Yet the foundations of base morality remain and can be easily neglected by outlets serving only as mere distractions. Lack of direction, deprivation of meaning, and the absence of purpose are very real elements of suffering. Without them, and where satisfactions are only partial, the spirit can become subject to a dissatisfying sense of emptiness. Meaningful purpose in life, as an ultimate goal of living, is necessary for behaviour, to fulfil all-reason, to empower a sense of self as part of something.

The common ethic of consumerism as a means of well-being through momentary distraction, whether through material or novel experiences, demonstrates how modern ethics often only lead to spiritual emptiness. Value in base morality is found on stimulation and engagement, yet this is only one dimension of the human psyche. Modes of base morality cannot universally satisfy their own greater concerns without appeal to high-reason and its mindfulness and discipline, and neither can base morality universally satisfy greater spiritual desires tied to high-reason.

Fear and base morality are concerned with questions of sustainability and global conflict, yet their mental states usually lack mindfulness and the capacity to focus on major problems, least act accordingly in greater interest. But even traditions of the primacy of rationality can fail to be fulfilling, for balance in the dynamics of reason and spirit must be found to achieve truly good living – good living means thinking and feeling well. All needs and concerns that are worth struggling for must be fulfilled for one to be truly happy, yet often we do not know what we want. Then, no person can truly know what others want and need without communication and understanding, which can be found through considerations of the human mind and the structures of ethics.

A person must find for themself, by virtue of his or her circumstance, experience, and impression, what the person values. Yet in terms of the functions of the psyche, the fundamentals of desire and conditions necessary for human satisfaction can be found in terms of both base and high faculties. Where there is discord in all-reason, one suffers; where a part of the self is neglected, the spirit is dissatisfied or void. The convention of base morality and Fear is not sufficient where many of its daily concerns are appeased and laid to rest, only for their functions to squabble in the mind and corrupt otherwise good achievements. Something more is needed, and the formulae of base morality and its emphasised or lone directive of Fear is not enough.

Base morality can invoke virtuous and admirable behaviour, and its directive bound to Fear's conditioning can lead to great things. However, many drawbacks accompany this, notably as the necessity of proper environmental conditioning to sustain virtue in one's own interest. The impressionability of base morality leads to the fragility of virtue and goodness where they depend so heavily on environmental nurture. Where people blindly follow instinct and sentiment, with rationale unappealing to baser faculties and bearing insufficient power to truly inspire virtue positively affecting the global ethical structure, mankind suffers.

Moral and ethical development has not kept up pace where incentive, vision, and coherence of universally serving virtues guide, nourish, and assist human interests and endeavour. Without such development, discord and disarray persist, with the fulfilment of spirit being void and true happiness being elusive. Subsequently, mankind's greater interests globally and individually cannot be fulfilled to their greatest extent. Fear and base morality cannot provide all the answers in this new and emerging age, the consequences of which might be dire for future prospects. A dimension of the self beyond the primacy of Fear must be found and awoken, then nourished with virtue to become the guiding ambition, adequate and effective in terms of the demands of a new global ethical environment. The primacy of instinct and its values are not enough, and virtues of the psyche and spirit have not been able to achieve such a state, with dominant philosophies being primarily of base morality and divergent attempts being mere amateur and often incoherent half-truths or naive theories lacking binding hierarchy of insight, logic, rationale, and sentiment. Innovation beyond Fear and the primacy of base morality needs to be found, utilitising and synchronising both high-reason and base-reason, rationale and instinct, thought and emotion.

While desires and narratives of base morality have been sought after for satisfaction, and development has focused on the primacy of instinct's values, high-reason has not received anywhere near as much attention in terms of ethical development. This claim does not concern itself with revere of high-reason in terms of a delusional understanding of the human psyche as wholly rational lacking influence of feelings and sense of well-being heavily conditioned by emotions (and respective intuitions and faculties of reason). Rather, the claim is straightforward in attributing discord to the psyche where rationale is coming to a new stage of relevance where base faculties are evermore appeased but not wholly fulfilled, yet new desires and needs beyond base-reason arise. Fulfilment of base morality and development of high-reason awaken new needs. Neglect of these needs leads to an emptiness where the directive of Fear can achieve little. Something else is needed to transgress this fundamental suffering.

Philosophies, old religions, and traditional ethical practices are of another time and their value is not appropriate or fully effective in approaching modern challenges and fundamental shifts in the dynamics of ethics and reason. Past traditions are not obsolete, but definitely aren't enough to universally improve people's lives, for morality and ethics have reached a new stage of incredible complexity. Neither are moral subjectivity and basic normativity sufficient for greater development, progress, and fulfilment, because they lack binding and convincing power to mediate social cohesion and values of development. The primacy of instinct is too arbitrary for a universal purpose, just as rationale detached from sentiment loses grounded sanity when moving actions and nourishing the spirit. A simple everyday aspect of these phenomena can present itself as unfulfilling work or employment in life moved only by the concern of getting by and enjoying other aspects of life, in the end leading to mundanity and incomplete satisfaction. Then, even the brightest of moral wisdoms are not structured into a comprehensive ethic and morality.

Meaning and purpose have definitive roles in people's lives by a directive of high-reason; base morality can only offer so much. With advents in technology, philosophy, and science, a new vision of the world and our place in it might be instrumental for some people and for cohesion of global society. Base morality's fulfilment distracting or neglecting the entirety of the self can only nourish the spirit so much, for happiness and well-being beyond distraction from pain and spiritual emptiness is more promising, which might truly satisfy rather than merely appease.

If the goodness of life is subject only to one narrative of fulfilment and ambition, it will be incomplete and will always be overshadowed by Fear and the satisfaction that requires conditional and circumstantial attachment. Instead of mankind laying back and wondering about what to do and what it all means, we should already be able to sit still and draw on motivation, ambition, and goodness from deep within to find and fulfil worthy goals, to harmonise all-reason. Rather than escape and move away from a spiritual emptiness and unfulfilled spirit in modern times, needs which transcend narrow concerns of base morality at times leading to idle and incomplete lives, it is time mankind embraced its humanity and expanded its ethical and spiritual capabilities and virtues beyond Fear, for much of Fear itself is corrupted in its own utility. New times, new demands, and unfamiliar needs require original development and new meditations, those which fundamentally move past Fear itself.

Other parallels of ethically, mentally, and spiritually troubling times where the values of base morality are only partially fulfilled, yet where their full satisfaction cannot be complete through base morality itself, can be drawn out from emerging dissatisfactions of social peculiarities. For example, the human psyche of base morality did not evolve in its infancy to settle for certain mundane office jobs. People are different, yet certain trends prevail where the lack of stimulation and engagement lead to dissatisfaction and misery, which an organic sense of purpose can remedy.

One may find solace in other more fulfilling distractions, yet surely it would be best if all such fundamental concerns of life were fulfilled? The nature of advanced modern society is fundamentally different to the environmental conditions of primitive societies. The psyche developed, by the fundamental function concerned with positive stimulation and pursuing good states of living, to value stimulation and satisfaction. Base faculties have been granted many such satisfactions in advanced modern societies. But in their place arise new needs and sense of emptiness where fleeting experiences do not leave a lasting mark of deeper fulfilment. Where we are not engaged, an emptiness takes over, which Fear inherently seeks to avoid and the mind shrouds with frustration, dissatisfaction, and pain. Because of this discord, the ethics and spirit of individuals and society as a whole are subject to incomplete values, leading to suffering and further disharmony.

Where people suffer, Fear and base morality, lacking the motivating interest of virtue, reflexively project their suffering onto others, thereby failing to confront the root of suffering – vice and Fear. People fail to control themselves by lacking virtue of willpower, mindfulness, and greater ambitions fulfilling their interests, and so they may seek to feebly attempt to control the world, subsequently surrendering any power or character of note to the enslavement by Fear, which offers little gratification and poorly nourishes the spirit with goodness.

The only power of worth is of virtue, not as a service of power's own utility. Power in Fear only seeks to control the world, thereby never granting full spiritual satisfaction from within, as the function of Fear will never be relieved where its directive is unfulfillable. Thus, Fear deprives the spirit, poisons it, and corrupts our values and goodness. Fear and base morality can be the roots of the suffering that they themselves cause and are incapable of alleviating fully or effectively.

Furthermore, their normative dynamics, bound to unmediated and headless influences of instinct, sow discord in society and civilisation at large where people have no clear guidance that binds all people and all concerns. But by virtue of the soul – by the concern of well-being – and the fundamental functions of the psyche that produce states of mind and spirit, learning to master the self and learning to fulfil our needs and spiritual directives becomes the binding norm for all people. However, any such innovation has not fully developed into a comprehensive ethic and morality.

The proceeding Section 3 will seek to find a new interpretation of ethics and the Highest Good, to move away from the tradition of Fear and base morality. However, in humility, it must be admitted that much more work will have to be put in to develop foundational thoughts, reform the ethos where necessary, and learn to apply it effectively in individual morality and broader normativity.

A major issue in advanced modern societies is mental health. Whether a real phenomenon or a phenomenon now made more observable through the ability to recognise it, mental health issues have come into the fray of public concern. I have experienced and witnessed first-hand the challenges of mental health issues, through myself and many others. Where the nature of society has changed so fundamentally in terms of stability and superficial fulfilment of needs, which in some respects might have descended into mass debauchery, it could be expected that mental health becomes another issue, or at least where society becomes developed enough to actively pay attention to such concerns. With the everyday influence of the internet, pop culture, mass advertisement, and change in what and how we experience living, no wonder the mind struggles to cope where its base faculties are often unhealthily influenced.

Many practices can help different people in different circumstances, and there are more than a few effective ways of coping with the challenges of modern societies. However, perhaps a general direction or common vision is missing. Rather than fight the world and hate it for its flaws, an ambition of understanding and desire to improve the world and living can be lost to apathy.

Sometimes the psyche lacking discipline might not be able to sustain effective mental states to live well in modern times. While the proceeding work is not intended to be an ultimate solution to all challenges – a panacea – it will at least seek a source of inspiration and ambition to carry on, to find a reason that can move the individual to self-improve and cultivate states of well-being. For spirit to truly be content it must be at peace with the individual and be in harmony with the world.

This is a long journey, yet its virtues are necessary for greater happiness. The mind may struggle to cope with life in the modern world where base faculties and base morality are the main directives of interest. Perhaps a different way of thinking is imperative for coping with the globalised modern world such as is the case for mediating cognitive biases.

The combination of the above points can be reduced to a single prominent theme – something to believe in. This notion is not interested in promoting circumstantial, subjective, and arbitrary beliefs or blind faith. Rather, it is concerned with giving a definitive reason to live well beyond lone speculation that this is what the mind wants – that is, to engage sustainable and renewable inner virtues to cope with many challenges. Then, something to believe in provides a grand ambition to guide endeavour and give meaningful purpose. This should further stabilise and harmonise dynamics between high-reason and base-reason, to give them equal weight and fulfil all needs to nourish the spirit of goodness and positivity beyond suffering and Fear.

With much glim and bleakness in the world, exaggerated by the negativity bias lacking mindfulness and discipline, it is easy for people to fall into depressive states, lose strength and motivation, and care little for a life of meaning and proactiveness. Simply put, people may stop caring for each other where they cannot properly care for themselves or are mentally and spiritually suppressed in their vulnerability to Fear, undermining the individual, society, and civilisation as a whole. The lack of concise and globally appealing moral philosophy can produce distortion and confusion in individual ambition. A social contract philosophy and normativity cannot provide empowering individual desire to improve oneself. However, the soul's imperative to better itself and flourish is universal, yet suppressed by a vulnerable morality and ethics subject to great unbalanced forces of Fear and the primacy of base faculties causing overwhelming and irresolvable suffering.

With moral and ethical interest bound to all concerns of living and actions – well-being in terms of the Fundamental Principle – morality has universal meaning. A binding, convincing, comprehensive, and functional moral philosophy and ethic is needed to provide guidance, ambition, and something to believe in. But rather than bring focus to the hopeful promise of a better world, a post-modern moral philosophy would benefit more from self-exploration and an ethic focused on individual experience and consciousness as the root of strength and prospect. Its interests and ambitions should come from deep within, moved by self-interest of fulfilment and betterment. Only through such a path can an ethic be truly sustainable and effective, bringing concern of each individual together and setting normativity on a truly compatible and balanced path.

The described ambition of ethics is not to be characterised by a blind revere of individuality and humanism, but rather a simple fact that understanding and finding common Natural Laws and moral laws of the Highest Good by, through, and of each person with respect to inherent functions of reason is necessary for a truly coherent and plausible moral philosophy. Only then can the succession of Fear and unbalanced base morality be truly achieved, offering potential improvement wherever it may be necessary or wanted – wherever suffering is experienced.

Simply put, happiness is difficult to achieve and sustain. A new ethic is necessary to balance the many concerns and dynamics of reason to find a sustainable, lasting, and achievable form of well-being and spiritual satisfaction and happiness. Morality is in crisis, and none benefit from this. Sentiment may lack complimentary rationale, just as rationale may lack binding and enriching sentiment; both lack spirit. Where humanity is diminished by Fear, an ethic should serve to help people believe they are more than their Fear, are greater than Fear. Humanity must not only rise above the domination by Fear and instinct, it must confront the greatest spiritual and moral challenge of the modern world – spiritual emptiness.

Thus, the first concern of a new design of ethics shall be an ethos – an ethical core of behaviour and desire. Where another universal ethos or its potential is identified, it can be enabled as a foundational directive of interest as is the case with Fear as well-being through aversion to pain and suffering – through security. Afterwards will proceed an extensive formal discussion and reframing of normative theory and revising moral principles in general, returning to a central study of structural ethics. The challenge of finding and providing a realistic and possible moral philosophy fundamentally different to Fear is a tricky and ambitious task. Hence, the rest of this extensive project will be dedicated to this ambition.

Section 3:

An Interpretation

Part 1:

The Ethos of Liberty

Chapter 10:

The Foundation of Fear and Liberty

All ethics and morality correspond to a respective function. By the authority of the Fundamental Principle of Living Beings and Actions, all dynamics and tangents of the fundamental will to flourish pursue a direction set by an ethos – the Core of ethics. In Section 2, I discussed and criticised aspects of the ethos of Fear. Fear has critical deficiencies and faults that need to be amended if greater well-being is to be achieved. Fear is defined as an ethos of pain-aversion. Base morality of instinct is entwined with functions of survival, but the ethos mainly functions as a mode of ethics by the primacy of pain-aversion.

While it is not a perfect ethos, Fear has notably good aspects. If one is to extract all the good things of an ethos of Fear while improving on its deficiencies, then a careful and meticulous design is needed for an alternative, improved ethos. Any ethos must then sustainably apply itself to structural spheres of ethics and produce positive, constructive, and fulfilling endeavour and effect. There are many elements that need to be considered if the ambition of an alternative ethos is to be fulfilled. The alternative ethos must not compromise the good aspects of a structure of Fear while concentrating on greater gains.

These concerns can be defined in consideration of how a better morality of Fear or an alternative ethos would influence a structure. What would life look like in a society with different founding values and principles? What would the consequences be? There are many profoundly different forms of base morality and Fear; accordingly, certain elements can be picked out to change the nature of Fear itself. Foremost are concerns of sensibility and caution.

Without Fear we may be prone to reckless acts, be overly impulsive against our own interests. On a more profound level, one has to reflect on what living without corruptive restraint of Fear would look like. Appeasement of Fear and lives of great security and stability are vulnerable to the corruption of Fear by producing unresolved insecurity and the madness of idleness. An alternative to Fear should not produce greater sum uncertainty, or lead to recklessness and senselessness. To achieve this profound change and construct it into a coherent, realistic, and viable ethic, from individual agency to the global structure, is no easy task. Section 3 is dedicated to restructuring ethics and reformulating the *Core* of ethics through an alternative ethos. Morality is structured through its ethics and a foundational ethos; the ethos encompasses and channels systemic features of a structure of ethics, making it the *Core* of an ethic and moral philosophy with its own *Core Principles*. The interpretation of any ethos must appeal to innate aspects of the human condition, then build on them.

It is crucial to keep in mind that the alternative ethos will not be completely ethically synthetic, meaning it will not re-engineer the human condition from scratch, as this is a delusional and impossible task. Instead, this ethos will appeal to some inherent, but perhaps latent, aspects of living and the human condition, to selectively feed and cultivate desirable aspects of ethics through characteristics – habits and virtues. The details of the normative framework used and its relevant moral rules will be outlined in Part 2 of Section 3. But before that, I must secure a foundation by which intuitions, thoughts, and sense of living (of spirit) correspond to morality and actions. An ethos must be outlined through which morality operates and structures itself, in terms of what fundamental purpose and grand ambition an action strives to achieve.

The ethos of Fear and base morality of survival are muddled and often confused in their directives to avoid and reduce pain. The ambition of Fear is not wrong or bad; in fact, the ethos, as any, can be qualified as an amoral aspect of systemic ethics – one which exists and is not inherently bound to moral evaluation and qualification until relevant to immediate living and actions. I argue that this deficiency is often a symptom of a broader systematic problem where reason and intuition of people's living is not harmonious, is not synchronised. We may think one way, yet our feelings and sentiments contradict our thoughts.

This point considers the relation between sentiment and rationale as the contention between feelings and thoughts, between impulse and rationality. To distinguish the two and give one systemic ethical element primacy is misguided. Base-reason and high-reason must function in harmony and synchrony for greater ethical effect to be achieved. Discussions of this dynamic throughout this book are central to its intended purposes and helpful for any ethical and moral development.

An alternative ethos to Fear must take this into account to satisfy innate and emphasised aspects of the human condition to fulfil the driving purpose of actions – to flourish. But it is a mistake to focus on one aspect of the psyche; the utility of each faculty of the psyche is circumstantial and selective. It is of limited ambition and not universally fulfilling to serve satisfaction of base morality, leaving high-reason only a withered utility serving focused drives of base desires. This is because base morality inherently, but not absolutely, strives to function in accordance with Fear and instinct, the end ambition of which is not absolute. To surpass this requires more than focused appeasement of base morality. But a life of pure high-reason, the life of a machine deprived of living, is not an ethic or morality that will grant good living or spirit.

A life of empty living is not a life worth living, the clearest case of which is depression leading to suicide. A life of pure rationale is not only deficient in its purpose, but also fundamentally misguided in terms of the definitive systems of ethics where actions seek fulfilment qualified in terms of spirit, not merely life for life's sake. An ethos cannot be synthetic or deprived of inherent functions by the systems of ethics.

So what alternative can there be to Fear? Fear and base morality are very intuitive to us, even if we lack systemic and structural insight into their functionality and coherent design and strategy for fulfilling their directives. But this accord of ethics in Fear often overshadows another fundamental feature of fulfilment – freedom from and in pain. Fear is provoked as an ethical function where pain and suffering is felt, yet this attitude and disposition can block a person from immediate moments of fulfilment where he or she is free from pain.

Our intuitions and sense of being clearly differentiate between states of pain, relief, and well-being. We have clear grasps of when we are in pain and when we are relieved of pain. Fear heralds an inherent alternative to it – liberty from it. Well-being can be achieved in two main forms: flourishing or not suffering, gaining or protecting ethical interest. Protecting well-being by avoiding suffering is one form of behaviour and ethical accord, while the natural alternative is actively pursuing well-being. We can qualify well-being as not suffering or as actively flourishing. Spiritual liberty from suffering is another systemic, core feature of ethics and states of being and living. However, this intuition of spiritual liberty seems to only arise from overcoming Fear as relief from pain, wholly contingent on dynamics and activity avoiding pain.

In other words, it seems spiritual liberty from pain cannot come without pain in the first place. This certainly functions as a mode of structural ethics where progress and development can only come through overcoming adversity. But what if this systemic feature of ethics can be overcome and liberty of spirit emphasised? Is it possible to be relieved of pain and for spirit to be strengthened without the active presence of suffering? Can we be motivated to act on our desire for greater well-being without circumstances having to motivate us through pain, to kick us out of bed?

Overcoming pain can lead to the momentary fulfilment of liberty from pain, to then only result in emptiness of spirit where there is no pain and no immediate satisfaction of liberty as relief from pain, as these states of mind are in themselves contingent on the function of averting pain. True happiness in base morality alone can then be fragile and fickle where we are afraid to lose it. It is then a fundamental systemic and structural problem where emptiness of spirit evokes pain as a continued corruptive and faulty ethical function of Fear. Can spiritual liberty be cultivated and developed into a focused ethos? Furthermore, can this be intuitive, coherent, sustainable, and realistic? I argue, yes; not only is this possible, it is also even more coherent, intuitive, and sensible than its alternative base ethos. Achieving this ethical development and structuring it into a comprehensive ethic and morality, however, is not simple.

To offer some clarity, an ethos of Fear can be qualified as a *negative ethos*, reciprocal of political science terms of *negative* and *positive* liberty – respectively, the liberty from constraints to act, and the liberty to act on desire. Defining an ethos is different to qualifying an *ethic* or *morality* as positive or negative, as good or bad. An ethos of Fear is a negative ethos in that it is restrictive and conditional, where one acts in accordance with well-being contingent on restrictions of *what not to do,* as opposed to *what to do.* The latter is an ethical disposition and function that can be qualified as an *ethos of Liberty,* as a *positive ethos* to act in the power of one's main desire. Henceforth, I shall outline an alternative to the capitalised notion of Fear (an ethos of the primacy of aversion to pain) and introduce the ethos of *Liberty* – the function of systemic ethics and an ethical Core as a positive ethos of the primacy of spiritual liberty and liberty in actions.

Liberty characterises behaviour and actions focused on gaining and increasing ethical interest rather than merely securing interest. *Liberty* is the capacity to flourish and act not only *free of* pain, but also *free to act in pain.* An ethos defining itself as free from pain is restrictive. A positive ethos of complete Liberty is one that not only grants itself engagement of action and fulfilment of spirit beyond suffering, but *also* the liberty to act despite, and in accordance with, suffering. A truly positive ethos of Liberty is one that can selectively, *in spirit of relentless pragmatism,* use spirit and morality free from pain along with pain itself. But this system of ethics can be very counter-intuitive when its mental states perceive pain and Fear not as contingencies and conditions of well-being, but as actual tools and utilities of well-being – where pain and Fear are not restrictions, but are resources of the ambition to flourish.

The issue is, a positive ethos, although possible and achievable, is not as innately intuitive to us as an ethos of Fear, clearly observable by the prevalence of base morality of Fear. For example, to act on, or regardless of, risk, independent of the influences of cognitive biases, would often contradict our instincts, which is normally counter-intuitive and demands greater rational influence. But this is what makes the ethos of Liberty so rewarding. Where morality is the main desire – our main interest – and morality is the order of desire, the confidence and strength to act on our greatest desire, and in defiance of all pain and adversity, is extremely empowering and spiritually and mentally rewarding.

If a positive ethos is to be pursued and implemented, what would this look like? Any ethos, ethic, and morality or course of action is made, or can be found to be, intuitive by appealing to the fundamental will, in mindful consideration of intuition and thought concerning our desires and goals. The absolute ambition is to flourish, but where well-being by a negative ethos of Fear is relatively clear in terms of 'not suffering', what would well-being look like and what would it *feel* like in terms of a positive ethos of Liberty? What are flourishing and spiritual liberty in their purest forms? An ethos of Liberty would entail an alternative ethical core of spirit as not simply 'not being in pain', but as the primacy of 'being in a state of well-being'. Can this continuous and sustainable state of living in terms of a positive ethos be fulfilled? Can feelings of happiness and stimulation of pleasure without synthetic intervention be self-sustained? Can flourishing be achieved irrespective of an immediate state of pain motivating oneself to absolve suffering?

The guiding premise will be that all of this is possible and very much realistic and intuitive. However, reaching a point where this is intuitive is not so straightforward, especially when a structure of ethics built on Fear and corresponding intuitions, functions, and dynamics are prevalent. So an ethos of Liberty is as much about its deliberate, mindful practice as a mode of living as it is a guiding ethic.

The ethos envisaged and found as an interpretation of Liberty will encompass four aspects at the Core of subsequent ethics with two primary moral disciplines of flourishing, which can be qualified as spiritual and moral directives. These spiritual directives will conform and apply to different conditions and circumstances, and in accordance with different moral utilities and demands. They will serve the same purpose as different, yet interlinked, means to an end, as they are bound to the grand ambition of a single positive ethos.

One of them will embrace *Discipline* (capitalised to define the specific systemic feature of the ethos) – broadly speaking, an ethical attitude guiding morality through virtues and principles of composure, patience, sensibility, strategy, and ambition. *Discipline* is a core moral utility emphasising willpower – a virtue which can be applied universally in ethics. This aspect of the ethic and morality of Liberty will most of all concern itself with engaged living and will be most evident as the morality of action. This designation will be instrumental and clearer with the comparative difference between action and the conditioning of an action such as through understanding the purpose an action serves.

Within the morality of Discipline will feature a key utility in its spiritual directive as a means to act despite pain and learn to act in succession of pain and Fear. This specific utility will be encompassed in terms of the morality of *Defiance* – a channelled, constructive form of frustration, dissatisfaction, pain, anger, and suffering. This core moral utility serves as a feature of willpower complimentary to general ambition of discipline in will as practise of strong sentiments, their motivations and powers. Defiance is key to learning Liberty in pain, whereby one learns to *use* pain as a resource to fuel greater ambition of Liberty, in turn developing understanding and capacity to embrace Liberty. Defiance is a means of overcoming what the ancient Greeks called *akrasia*.

Defiance and Discipline are intended to use what we can't escape. In turn, where its insights, wisdoms, virtues, and habits are reinforced, they enable further growth of character, spirit, and the psyche compatible with greater degrees of Liberty. In time, the virtues of Discipline nourishing high-reason grow into a resilient and strong character, the inherent self-control and self-understanding of which produces a particular state of mind and subsequent mental abilities, particularly mindfulness and self-awareness in behaviour, that lead to another form of self-discipline and other applications of high-reason in behaviour.

The other core moral utility of Liberty is the morality of *Harmony* – of understanding, empathy, mediation, balance, emotional intelligence, and inward and external peace through the dissolution of pain. This morality and ethic will feature prominently as a utility of reason, not necessarily as the active actions of Discipline, but rather as a means to understand and cultivate virtues complimentary to Discipline, forming its own species of Discipline. The key utility of the morality of Harmony will be *empathy* and practices of *mindfulness*.

Mindfulness is considered as a general practise of awareness, such as awareness of one's state of being, of intuitions and thoughts moving a person to act, as a broad practice of understanding actions, oneself, others, and living. Mindfulness is the capacity to focus on thoughts and sensations and bring attention to intuitions. Advanced discipline of mindfulness is to focus in pain, see through pain. Empathy entails a specific notion different to compassion; empathy is more rational, but less emotional, than compassion. Empathy is mindful understanding of, and attention to, one's own and others' state of being, particularly why emotions and thinking, through reference of mental states, make people behave the way they do. These instruments of the morality of Harmony will serve to develop practical ethical wisdom such as through insight into structural effects of an action and other ethical causal dynamics.

The morality of Harmony will be used to find, exemplify, and understand the ideal moral principles of Liberty and their corresponding paragon virtues. Willpower of Discipline is a virtue in its own right, yet the designation of this core utility is insufficient to learn and understand the nature of willpower, something completed only through the morality of Harmony. Discipline and Harmony are fundamentally entwined as part of the ethos of Liberty, yet they have two distinct dimensions, with Harmony invoking its own form of Discipline that is different to the Discipline of Defiance.

Discipline of Defiance will learn to use pain as a resource, exemplified as the Liberty to act in pain, while the Discipline courted by Harmony will be one of action and endeavour free of pain, the most important feature of which will be learning to act and live beyond and through spiritual emptiness. Where Defiance practises and nourishes virtues of *power* as control in and of pain, Harmony is the practise and cultivation of virtues that complete the ambition sought by Discipline and Defiance to succeed Fear and suffering by *letting go*. Interestingly, Defiance will surprisingly serve a crucial role in finalising the ethos and spirit of Liberty in terms of the morality of Harmony through what I shall come to call the *Ploy of Consciousness,* key to completing the ethos of Liberty.

The *Ploy of Consciousness* is a profound moral utility achieving the greatest known liberty of and in spirit by considering and confronting nothingness, death, and existential meaninglessness and nihility, to succeed these states head-on. The Ploy of Consciousness will relate itself to spiritual emptiness – something we are all familiar with in our own way. Learning to employ these core instruments of Liberty's ambition is part of a broader practice of Liberty and its intuitions.

The Core ethical system may seem complex at first and will require controlled, mindful, and deliberate actions relearning behavioural habits of base morality. But the counter-intuitive and paradoxical elements of these core moral instruments will give way to liberty of intuitions completing the practice of Liberty and its spirit. Learning mindfulness and discipline by the core ambition to pursue well-being is practise and learning of Liberty as the liberty *to flourish.* One only needs to remember the primary desire – to live well and in good spirit.

The Core Principles of Liberty are then simply *to not let Fear compromise who you are, to not let Fear undermine your character, to not let Fear and pain take away from you your heart and spirit, to not let Fear prevent you from acting in your greater interest, to allow you to see and understand your greater interest, to actually have the courage and ability to act in your greater interest, and to evoke and forge spirit greater than Fear.*

Drawing on the intuition and sense of spirit at liberty from pain will guide all intuitions and thoughts concerning how to act to maximise a state of being at spiritual liberty. But rather than encourage a chaotic course of implementing this ethos, adjusting it, adapting to it, understanding it, and envisaging it as a structure of ethics, these ethical experiments have been sufficiently practised and studied to be formulated into the structural design outlined in this project interpreting an ethos of Liberty. But I am merely offering an interpretation.

In summary, the interpretation of the ethos of Liberty will follow and facilitate two core moral utilities and virtues – self-control and self-awareness, willpower and mindfulness. Where we are in greater control of our behaviour, we can act on our greater desires. Where we are aware of ourselves, our thoughts, our desires, and our state of being, we better understand ourselves and our behaviour, leading to ethical and moral wisdom, assisting self-control in behaviour. Self-control as discipline leads to self-awareness as mindfulness, leading to inner harmony of spirit and reason. These core moral utilities will be known as the *morality of Discipline* and the *morality of Harmony.*

Discipline and Harmony engage two core aspects of spirit and the psyche – willpower and mindfulness, which are primarily utilities and capacities of high-reason. The third core aspect integrated into the ethos is spiritual emptiness, which any moral philosophy and way of life must familiarise itself with; this ethos and ethic will utilise it, bind it to willpower and mindfulness. Then, one can never overlook the ever-present fourth aspect core to any ethos – the aspect of the base faculties. Truly good living has to satisfy all necessary criteria of the psyche and spirit, with experience of true joy and happiness, with its memories uncorrupted by pain, necessary for a fulfilling ethos and ethic. The baser self is the fourth core aspect of the ethos of Liberty, focusing on base-reason and its fulfilment parallel to the accentuated dynamics of high-reason through the other three core aspects. In conclusion, the Core of Liberty is composed of four aspects – willpower, awareness, spiritual emptiness, and the simplest and sincerest self.

The detailed schemes of this ethos and its core spiritual directives and instruments of ambition are best understood through the groundwork of the metaphysics of ethics discussed in Sections 1 and 4. Understanding how intuitions and reason work in terms of the ethos of Liberty is crucial to practising it, therein understood best through practise. Intuition and sense of fulfilment and satisfaction in spirit of Liberty can be exemplified unambiguously through a simple case of the satisfaction one can get from, say, charity. A common notion of ethics and morality is that kindness and sacrifice can be good for spirit and fulfilment. But how and why?

One point of analysis by a respective ethos is that charity as an act of sacrifice, kindness, and compassion can grant momentary satisfaction of freedom and relief from suffering in Fear. Fear can cloud state of being (spirit) with concern, anxiety, and pressure to gain power in Fear and protect self-interest. Acting in excess Fear corrupts and corrodes good spirit. It then follows that letting go of that pain and remedying Fear, such as through giving to charity and helping a person in need, grants the most relief by confronting and overcoming Fear and its suffering. However, the issue with such an ethical attitude contingent on Fear is fundamentally limited by necessity of Fear, whereby a sophisticated ethos of Liberty requires a more sustainable and autonomous mode of fulfilment irrespective of a contingency on Fear. For example, reckless and immoderate charity can be self-destructive. But as with all ethics and morality, balance is necessary, mindful of the Doctrine of the Mean.

One cannot deny that acts of sacrifice, kindness, and compassion, such as charity, can be good for community, subsequently good for the sum of individual ethical agents and their structures. Base morality and morality of accentuated Fear are vulnerable where they suppress acts of greater sum interest. Fear can pit individuals in a community against one another without fulfilment of greater mutual, common sum interest. Herein base morality and ethics of Fear are organically limited where they object to actions of greater sum interest in terms of both individual and community.

A morality is intrinsically limited if it relies on social contract and a synthetic structuring of moral law without corresponding organic accord of spiritual directives – that is, directives of individual satisfaction that lack personal fulfilment in spirit, producing seemingly meaningless actions. Principles and virtues of morality calling something good and right by mere authority of social contract are vulnerable to the intrinsic liberty of individuals to disagree with, or utterly reject, this social contract, therein acting on different values, which can be good or bad in terms of adaptation. Individual fulfilment is central for a morality to be complete and enduring. Liberty will be argued to have the strength that Fear does not, for an ethos of Liberty foremost pursues personal interest and ambition by a spiritual directive, in the case of Defiance being the relentless pursuit of ambition and willpower, complimented by Harmony in terms of maximising the vision of ambition and invoking further Discipline to mediate acts of Defiance.

To finalise the matter of intuitions and reasons for acting in Liberty, to satisfy concerns over uncertainty of an ethos of Liberty, the faculties of reason function in accordance with Liberty by innate, even if latent, elements of the human condition. There are two known fundamental aspects of well-being that can be phrased in different ways – growing and preserving, flourishing and not suffering, pursuing interest or securing it. The shift in reason and corresponding intuitions from base morality and Fear towards spirit and mentality of Liberty is achieved through practise selectively applying and amplifying instruments, directives, and characteristics that correspond to Liberty.

The fundamental will is set to pursue that which feels most fulfilling, with Liberty only being achieved if it serves individual ambitions and interests of the will to flourish, a good systemic feature which organically mediates ethics by the mechanism of the adaptive cycle of values. But where base morality reduces high-reason to a mere utility serving intuitions of base-reason, stripping high faculties of autonomous ambition and distinct satisfaction, adaptive morality is restricted and spirit is not most fulfilled. High-reason can lead to complexity of thought and intuition, but it also grants sophistication of intuition and thought, and then of morality. Honing and practising high-reason grants greater adaptiveness of morality, a necessity for achieving and pursuing the Highest Good and for an effective structure of ethics.

A prominent feature of a positive ethos will be its intrinsically adaptive nature, something that seems to be a crucial element in vulnerable modern structures of ethics. One comes to the consideration of whether this liberty of spirit and morality can be fulfilled and whether one can go through with the ambition sensed in intuition and spirit of Liberty. There are personal challenges to consider of whether one ought to act on the uncertainty of Liberty and whether one ought to believe that more can be achieved through, or in accordance with, Liberty.

For these concerns and questions, I leave it up to individual liberty of intuition and reason, whereby one will and ought to act only on an ethos of Liberty if its spiritual directive and intuitions are sensed as fulfilling. Then, one simply has to find faith in oneself, as well as apply the designed instruments of morality and ethics, to fulfil their potential. But due to the innate feature of Liberty as part of the human condition and the mechanical soul, it is an achievable mode of fulfilment and intuitive spiritual directive. Where there is doubt, be mindful of intuitions and one's feelings; where there is uncertainty and doubt in ability, focus on desires to channel Fear of failure to greater ends.

Now, for the details of the Core of this ethic and its moral philosophy.

Chapter 11:

Defiance and Discipline

With life comes suffering and struggle. To design an ethic and morality dealing with suffering one must first understand the structures and dynamics of suffering. We thrive by overcoming pain and suffering; if we do not, we cling on to minor aspects of fulfilment as substitution or distraction, even if this means reducing continuity of living and diminishing welfare. Suffering comes in many forms and degrees, and on different levels. The effect of suffering is relative among people.

How people deal with pain and suffering differs. There are people whose lives are filled with suffering, sometimes more than they can handle. People try to adapt to suffering as much as they can; sometimes they succeed in overcoming it, and at other times they are overwhelmed. These moments shape ethics and morality, and define character. Some people adapt to grave levels of suffering, while others endure comparatively lesser experiences of suffering and adapt to lesser suffering. Thus, individuality and liberty of adaptiveness in suffering prevail. Attitudes towards suffering develop over time by adapting to experiences, which then influence character, ethical structures, and values. Where ethics fail to adapt to suffering, the mechanisms of the adaptive cycle of values exercise their power of Natural Law and extinguish faulty ethical elements.

People become accustomed to different levels of suffering and develop different ethical attitudes and characters. People who have experienced little meaningful or profound suffering, or who are bewildered by the madness of idleness where they crave provocative stimulation, sometimes seek out suffering, maybe even create it – an ethical disposition that can sometimes be ascribed to people who have lived under the privileges of great stability and peace. These characters can be qualified as having adapted to lesser or 'softer' suffering.

When a greater form of suffering is subjugating a person and if they overcome it, however long that may take, they develop values according to greater, 'harder' forms of suffering, and cultivate strengths according to virtue's success over strife. In some cases, this can evolve into an ethic that embraces pain and suffering like an addiction to satisfaction from overcoming struggle and conquering pain. There is a pleasure to be found in strength succeeding pain. But where basic pleasures find satisfaction in the absence of pain, a higher sort of pleasure comes through the liberty of living irrespective of pain. This is the pleasure of *autonomy*, willpower, and confidence – a higher pleasure of morality embracing both faculties of reason, a pleasure of Liberty exceeding and succeeding Fear. As John Stuart Mill wrote[1]:

"Nothing except that consciousness can raise a person above the chances of life, by making him feel that, let fate and fortune do their worst, they have not power to subdue him: which,

once felt, frees him from excess of anxiety concerning the evils of life, and enables him [...] to cultivate in tranquillity the sources of satisfaction accessible to him, without concerning himself about the uncertainty of their duration, any more than about their inevitable end."

This understanding of the nature of suffering highlights the idea of a feature of systemic ethics that character and morality develop in accordance with suffering and grow through adaptation to suffering. Adversity beckons growth. However, if we fail to adapt in virtue, then we may suffer or even perish. It is an amoral observation of the systems of ethics that suffering can lead to, and produce, growth. Through an ethos of Fear, overcoming suffering enables states of flourishing. The relativity of our attitudes towards suffering and the levels of suffering we experience are core components of the adaptive mechanism of suffering. Whatever suffering one may experience, it is nonetheless real if intuition evokes it and spirit senses it.

No suffering is to be neglected or simply dismissed or ignored without an appropriate response and reasoning to *let* it be dismissed. All intuition is valid for the mind and spirit; pain and suffering are evocative and meaningful, whether suffering is great or small, hard or soft. People may experience different forms of suffering, but that does not mean any form is invalid or irrelevant. However, even though there are comparative degrees of suffering, some qualifications cannot be equated, proving the merit of soft and hard suffering. By the efficacy and effects of some pain and suffering, no matter the degree of familiarity with suffering, there are greater and lesser forms of suffering.

There is a major distinction in terms of objective criteria of intuition between being hungry for a day and starving for a week. There is a difference between losing a pet and witnessing a parent's attempted suicide. There is a difference between facing an obstacle in your path and learning that your dream can never come true. There is a difference between being insulted by a stranger and feeling powerless in self-loathing. There is a difference between moving on from the lost and letting go of the damned.

There is a difference between fortune and choice. Yet this does not imply that lesser suffering is experienced in lesser forms by those unfamiliar with greater suffering. People must first overcome lesser suffering and grow in strength for character, mentality, and spirit to adapt to greater challenges. Even lesser suffering can bring shock to a person and change their lives. However, this relativity does not equate lesser suffering with greater suffering.

To understand these disparities in the functions of intuition and reason requires insight and study. By studying the effects of mental impressions of traumatic experiences, one can qualify certain forms of suffering as objectively more damaging and more evocative than others. Some can shrug off pain, while others lose their minds. Some grow numb from pain, others are broken by it, while others become tempered and impetuous.

Human civilisation has arisen, and grown, from suffering through an ethos of Fear and its spiritual directive of pain-aversion. Fear, pain, and suffering have served as potent ethical forces influencing human behaviour and endeavour. One cannot deny the powerful and evocative force suffering exerts in motivating actions. Systems and structures of ethics based on an ethos of Fear are extraordinary.

One can argue that Fear and base morality of survival and instinct have been imperative for mankind's development and growth. Pain and suffering, as universal features of ethics' systems, are invaluable for growth and should be imperative in any ethic's consideration of effective and sustainable good living. Learning to live with pain and suffering, as well as using these feelings, is key to any ethic, morality, and spiritual directive.

Where Fear drives ambition through aversion to pain, providing well-being through security, what if pain's evocative and powerful force could be bound to the pursuit of greater ambition? What if the energy and motivation of pain and suffering could be used to fuel ambition rather than merely restrict our interests? How can this Liberty of pain itself, whereby pain is a resource rather than an authority and a co-ercive force, be achieved? How can pain be used to drive the adaptation and growth of character and morality irrespective of the corruptive features of its conditioning? The answers come through *the morality of Discipline and its Defiance of Fear*.

Fear has influenced and coerced human endeavour since the very beginning of actions ruled by base morality and ambitions dedicated to averting pain. Fear exercises great force on people's determination of living, leading to many morally unconventional actions. Fear has a dimension of positive effect by protecting people from suffering and pain. Yet, in doing so, Fear's directive over behaviour has often corrupted behaviour through excess Fear.

The grand ambition of Fear is limited, for what happens when there is no pain? Fear can deceive us, play tricks on us, and betray our interests. But lack of mindfulness and discipline in Fear and base morality is only part of the intrinsic ethical problems of a negative ethos. Fear often restricts us to a quality of living in Fear and lingering suffering. Fear makes us commit foolish, compulsive, and demeaning actions. Base morality and Fear can make us act in Fear to protect what we value and love in such a way that we end up betraying and neglecting what we hold dear, especially as mistakes of compassion. Desperation in Fear can make us turn on those we hold dear and hurt ourselves, as pain takes over and seeks to corrupt everything around it in people's desperate attempts to express it as a way of coping.

Where we lack discipline and mindfulness in pain and suffering, Fear moves pain to project outward and cause harm under the false comfort of deceiving control over suffering. Any source of suffering can only be truly relieved by absolving and healing it, not by merely opening a festering wound. Fear can serve as a means to an end of overcoming pain. But this utility is too commonly neglected, and Fear's directive encounters a fundamental flaw in modern societies and ethical structures. In a basic sense, one might fail to ask a person out on a date because of the anxiety about rejection – a form of Fear. But would it not be better to follow through on sum greater of interest of asking the person out? Or better yet, would it not be better to act through that anxiety, to find the pleasure of strong, unyielding character?

Rather than confronting faults of character, even in terms of base morality, Fear moves behaviour of thought, intuition, and action against greater interest to improve on the fundamental, deeply ingrained characteristics of the self that cause pain in the first place. These are but some illustrations of the deficiency of Fear, the most important feature being reducing living to a state of Fear and lingering suffering. By submitting to Fear and giving in to pain, one's will only surrenders spirit to limited fulfilment, always overshadowed by lingering concern of pain and suffering. In settling for Fear, one's growth of spirit and character becomes stale, thereby restricting living to the shadow of Fear.

Do you want to live in Fear and suffering that can be amended, or do you want to settle for a deprived state? Do you want to be defined by a state and spirit of Fear and suffering, or do you want to be more than that? Do you want power greater than that of Fear, which binds so many to its will and enslaves them? Do you want to be at liberty in the autonomy of your ambition, to be free to act the way you desire? Or do you want your living restricted and conditioned by sovereignty of Fear? Do you want to live in Fear and suffering, or do you want to be at Liberty? If Liberty is to be pursued, then one needs to embody a character capable of acting autonomously in spirit of Liberty, to draw strength from deep within and beyond influences secondary to one's ambition of good living.

Power supercedeing and acting against the coercive forces of Fear nourishes spirit in the power to exercise its will, thus invoking the pleasure of Liberty through willpower and autonomy. But Fear can protest this ambition, suppress it, and continue to try to enslave the will while also protecting ambition from recklessness and foolishness. But where the goodness of Fear does not serve benevolent intent and the ambitions of greater interest, Fear becomes a malevolent and coercive force. Fear limits one's freedom and autonomy, evoking suffering and frustration, pain and anger. Where Fear invokes an ethic of resisting pain, the same ethic can be channelled for better use against the course of pain constricting greater interest and ambition. Fear can be exemplified as the object restricting greater interest and causing the pain and suffering one seeks to overcome. Subsequently, one learns to defy the thing holding back one's ambition and interest, furthering personal interest and the ambition of good living that otherwise would suffocate well-being. Thus, the morality of Defiance is found.

Life, pain, agony, fear, suffering, and despair can drive you to your knees, but Defiance can resist this suffering, fight through strife, teach how to bind pain and Fear to one's will and ambition. Defiance channels pain and suffering against themselves to further greater interest. Where pain leaves one in despair and hopelessness, where one sees no alternative and no way out, one can, in a predicament, still garner the satisfaction of Liberty of control over one's own attitude.

A force may try to subject a person to Fear and hopelessness, may try to break and enslave a person's will. Sometimes, hopeless circumstances can end good living or life itself, leaving only the choice of how to respond. If a person has no choice over how or when he or she will die, the individual can make a choice of how to embrace that inevitable end. One can choose to pursue the only point of satisfaction achievable in such circumstances that Fear cannot provide – the Liberty of not yielding to Fear.

People moved by Fear and petty character may seek to dominate others, with the Fear that corrupted and enslaved the will of others only causing further suffering in those who think they have power. One can make the choice of how to further their satisfaction: to accept coercive force of Fear causing suffering, or achieve satisfaction of Liberty to supercede the power which so many submit to. In all circumstances of suffering and pain there is always a choice of how to respond to adversity through action *and* attitude, the latter always being a contingency of living.

By choosing to become more than the power subduing spirit rather than empowering it, defiance of pain cultivates virtues of willpower and autonomy, of power and strength greater than any that Fear can provide, a power and its pleasure and satisfaction unbound to anything but one's ever-present companion of will and ambition. One can follow power of control in petty ambition by power surrendered to Fear, to receive the unfulfilling satisfaction of averting sense of pain yet lacking the ambition and strength to succeed the source of pain itself.

Or, one can master the power of will to pursue the ambition of dominating Fear and pain, to not yield to Fear and pain, to exploit them and use them for good. Sometimes all that is left of living is spirit in pain and suffering, by which all hope or desire for positivity are extinguished, or so can be a temporary reality and place. The one thing left to pursue may not be hope, but simply ambition and satisfaction of some sort. In great loss combined with despair, we may turn to vengeance as a means of living that denies surrender, becoming a focused purpose. Desire for control and power, especially in great pain and grief, may be the only thing relevant to living.

If all is lost or loss is the inevitable end, then pleasure in strength and power may become the only meaningful satisfaction. If this is to be one's fate, then it is best to maximise that satisfaction, the greatest power being complete through indomitable will defying the most profound pain and even Fear itself. If one's fate and circumstance are bound to pain and suffering, especially if living is unbearable, then one might as well do everything to get the most satisfaction. Defiance thus nourishes spirit in pain and suffering when others are starved of spirit while they surrender to Fear.

Defiance nourishes virtuous and strong character – good by character of autonomy, confidence, willpower, and uncorrupted by pain. To compare oneself to others is usually behaviour of instinct and self-validation. It can be motivating and empowering to pursue self-improvement in defiance of others and by the desire for strength compared to others. This aspect of ego is a means to an end, succeeded by a true autonomy of character only responding to self-validation through conscience and self-awareness. Perspective offers insight and intuition. Comparing oneself to others offers perspective, which then leads to an understanding and vision of oneself as more than basic intuition.

Moral convention may argue that anger and hate are bad things, that the corrosive elements of rage repudiate spirit of goodness. Some spiritual practices aim at letting go pain and suffering, at times becoming modes of ethics of reduced spirit submitted to Fear without fundamental resolution in mind and spirit by overcoming Fear. An ethic and spirit of surrendering ambition in Fear is one that does not fulfil in spirit, just as ambition of Fear itself is not one that satisfies the most. The ambition of Fear lacks fulfilment of sustained freedom from suffering, as it is an ambition in and of suffering itself; without suffering, Fear can be corrupted, leading to discord, confusion, and misplaced priorities and values. Living involves suffering; a life denying itself the satisfaction of growth from adversity is a life of diminished spirit and ambition. Only by overcoming Fear and suffering, as opposed to rejecting and eluding them, can Liberty be fulfilled in suffering.

Pain comes with engaged living – that is, proactive living distinct to the idle living of settling for contentment. Only the person who confronts suffering can create medicine which cures the sick and vulnerable; detached inner peace is a moral luxury and is alone insufficient as an ethic mending states of affairs, especially where the character of people is morally weak and stubborn in its ways. One can let go of suffering and pain, but in letting go of ambition one also deprives oneself of greater growth and potential, undermining greater progress and growth in structures of ethics. Often it is good not to be at peace with suffering. So rather than be idle, it is good and right to pursue ambition, thereby invoking the morality of Defiance.

Sometimes pain of living drives one to despair; letting go will only temporarily suspend or dissolve the root of suffering without driving ambition to make something greater of suffering and oneself – at times a necessity to resolve the cause of suffering. Control and discipline in states of pain are necessary for cultivating and training high-reason, which then allows a person to let go of pain and actively *keep* living without suffering. By focusing on a spiritual directive of not using and simply letting go of suffering and pain, one deprives the self of a fundamental spiritual directive of Liberty where strength opposing and channelling pain evokes satisfaction of power supercedeing coercion of pain, a higher pleasure of autonomy in Defiance. The ultimate purpose of this defiance is to improve living through oneself and as states of ethical environment.

However, the virtue of Defiance is only as good as its power to act in accordance with moral righteousness and spiritual goodness. The principles and virtues of morality as good and right are qualified as such because they are in accordance with the fundamental will and its goals. Defiance is a directive and means of morality in Liberty, yet Defiance does not define Liberty. Righteous morality, as principles of maxims of well-being, cannot be comprehensively and coherently outlined in terms of Defiance alone. Defiance is a means to do what is right and good in sum by the Highest Good when ambition is otherwise constricted by and in Fear.

The spiritual directive of Defiance is fulfilment in higher pleasure through autonomy of the power of will supercedeing Fear and pain, the structural efficacy of which is not absolute. Fear can prevent us from committing mistakes and foolish acts that only hurt us, yet it can also deprive us of seeing, and acting on, greater interests such as those of broader structural concern. The lasting effects of putting oneself under the stress of pain can be grim and unpredictable. But if one has no choice but to endure, and confront, hardship or any element of suffering to fulfil greater interest, then pain leading to growth and greater satisfaction is worth it. It is in the acknowledgement of lingering and inevitable death and despite the force of suffering that the goodness of humanity is realised.

Doing the right thing is not usually easy, or it may seem so at first. Often people lack the resolve to pursue what is truly in their greater interest out of Fear or willing ignorance. The inability to act righteously through a good moral sense of good intentions and good spirit is a recurrent consequence of weak will and vice. The utility and directive of Defiance channels and motivates obstructed will to fulfil greater flourishing, but these directives and actions are right only through their consequences on the world and individuals acting in determination of spirit's satisfaction. We want to flourish, we want to be free of pain and suffering, yet sometimes the only or best way to achieve this is by acting against pain itself and by binding pain to one's ambition and fulfilling spiritual liberty by suppressing pain's corrosive effect.

However, power in Fear is only ever power of Fear. Defiance is itself, or at first, a negative ethos or a directive of Fear, as Defiance intrinsically seeks to surpass pain and suffering, in doing so never actually achieving the full potential of Liberty as the ability to let go of suffering and pain when pain's resource and utility exhausts its potential. Premature and undisciplined release of pain can overlook greater ambition and greater interest, just as undisciplined and eager rage can produce bitterness and greater harm than good. Trying to dominate through Fear only ever gives power in Fear, but never releases spirit and action from Fear. However, power in Fear, such as by a negative ethos, is only ever power contingent on Fear, and not a capacity or ambition of a person's will free from pain or fear. This concern and limitation, however, will be resolved through the morality of Harmony.

Any action in Fear only submits an individual to Fear, inviting suffering. Fear and suffering can only ever be overcome through determination and succession of liberty from them. The long journey to greater flourishing by relief from suffering comes by resisting suffering and growing in mental strength to enable good intentions and the corresponding good spirit. Acts of greater virtue beyond Fear must surpass Fear itself.

To sum up so far, suffering can lead to growth in character and morality by the adaptive cycle of values. However, pain and suffering can get the better of us, presenting themselves as corrupt functions of Fear. But where Fear and suffering may restrict greater ambition and interest, the morality of Defiance and the satisfaction of power of an autonomous will can compensate for the faults of Fear. It is then important and relevant to consider what greater interests are, as Fear neatly presents us with simplistic intuitions of satisfaction as a state of being without pain.

One point to consider is that it might not be intuitively clear what spirit of Liberty and respective fulfilment actually entails. Fear instigates the corresponding spark of satisfaction by spirit relieved of a state of Fear. Living in hate can corrupt good living and purpose, whereby one may lack the strength and capacity of will to supercede such a state. Defiance can serve to move the will against pain and towards the goals of our intuitions concerned with pain – intuitions that tell us to get relief from pain. Defiance can also serve the determination of morality and goodness by defying that which causes suffering and pain in the first place, such as by not reducing a person's character to immorality and pettiness. The merits of forgiveness and related moralities, however, are designated to the morality of Harmony – a different dimension of Liberty.

Defiance essentially pursues the directive of achieving fulfilment by the relief of the pain that Defiance uses in the first place, but Defiance is limited as an ambition and directive of Liberty as it is a contingency of Fear and suffering itself. Moreover, the ultimate end of Fear as living without pain leads to empty living and the madness of idleness. Defiance can be used to channel one's pain against these corruptive and corrosive states of being. thereby fulfilling the directive of Liberty through strength and autonomy superceding the oppressive spirit of Fear. Even so, Defiance lacks the ability and function to move beyond the source causing the suffering which Defiance must mediate and channel, which is surpassed by the morality of Harmony.

A matter to consider in the morality of Defiance is that of death. What of death, lingering as an enforcer of Fear? By setting aside the primacy of base morality, values motivated by survival and formulated through an ethos of Fear, one risks opening oneself up to pain and possibly even death. The prevalence of base morality and Fear has secured a structure of ethics focusing on survival, whether in terms of the individual or community.

However, that same structure is vulnerable to the corruptive dynamics of an unstable, but arguably adaptive, system of ethics driven by a catalyst of Fear and its directives of instinct of survival and pain-aversion. One can adopt different ethics addressing the fear of death and its natural anxiety and uncertainty. Commonly, we substitute the anxiety and fear of death through enforcement of positive spirit, such as through pleasure and distraction, or through belief only deceiving sense of anxiety in death, for thinking of a life after immediate awareness of living is not a mode of ethics truly unravelling the fear shrouding death.

To truly make peace with death beyond substitution and distraction, and in spirit greater than the surrender of living for peace of death, is an impressive feat, considered further through Harmony. The morality of Defiance, however, is not intended to find peace in death, as the mindset of Defiance is concerned with other ambitions.

If autonomy of will is to be achieved at Liberty greater than the forces of Fear, then one must act beyond even the coercion of Fear through death. Death will naturally evoke fear, anxiety, and stress. Base morality and instinct have strong roots in affecting people's behaviour and living, with surpassing the dominance of these directives requiring distinctive capacity of character, ambition, and will. But Defiance is not dedicated to surpassing these elements; rather, it moves the will to pursue ambition within these effects and ruling them, leading one to master the will at Liberty.

Defiance is not intended to dismiss death and Fear, but to use their organic influence. Defiance designates a spiritual directive of acting *despite* fear of suffering and death. There is nothing wrong with being afraid and being reluctant to suffer; these are natural, organic, and (generally) healthy elements of living. But to act despite these concerns is what marks great spirit of strength and power in Defiance. Acting with courage in the face of death is of noble spirit deserving its liberty as release from suffering.

The illustrated directive of Defiance in death may come across as counter-intuitive, if not delusional and insane. In death, all living ends. Our most basic and organic intuitions tell us death is a bad thing. Death can be a great tragedy. Why should one then act in a way that risks death? Pain and the negative ethos of Fear act to hold off death, so why should one defy this? Surely defiance against Fear isn't good?

A basic answer in this context would be: yes. Defiance can be impulsive and of questionable sensibility. But in the considerations of death and the end of living there are questions and spiritual directives to be considered. First, consider behaviour that is averse to death, which is intuitive to us on a basic level. Human behaviour responds to the stress of Fear and anxiety of death by filling life with positivity greater than suffering. We simply try to get the most out of the time we have or simply try to distract ourselves to make living better than the emotional, spiritual, and existential crisis of the burden of self-awareness to acknowledge the inevitable. But Defiance shows this curse to be a great gift and opportunity.

We seek to make the most of life. Fear is above all a conservative mode of spirit driven by the function of negating suffering, even if consequently suppressing greater opportunity. But living is never about life for life's sake, for a life not worth living is tied to despair. If we are to get the most out of life, we must eventually make a deliberate choice: continuity of life of lesser spirit, or maxims of life by being most alive. Death will always catch up with us all; we can live in its shadow and act accordingly to Fear, or we make the most of our living through and despite Fear and death. If all life is to end and living is the only thing that truly matters, then the maxim of living is the spirit's directive. Defiance thus seeks to make the most of living by fulfilling spirit more than a continuous life lacking living.

It is sensible and fair to ask oneself whether it is preferable to live for as long as you can to only hold back death and live in anxiety of Fear, or to live in spirit where one becomes at peace with death. 'Dying happy' is an intuitive and plausible moral aspiration which can never be fully achieved in Fear, pain, and suffering. Only through superceding these corrosive effects of spirit can one be set free to die satisfied. Defiance, therefore, moves action and living to act in such autonomy that even the most basic of actions fulfils spirit through power of will and spirit greater than Fear. Fear over death can evoke pain and suffering, but in acting against these forces the individual multiplies their will and the wealth of spirit that can give the satisfaction that Fear cannot – the Liberty to die happy with relief from suffering, to feel a distinct and ethereal pleasure as bliss above all suffering.

Naturally, some may bring up concern over greater sum well-being as continuity of good living. Is living a life of greater satisfaction, but lesser continuity, truly better than living a life of sustained good spirit? First, one can respond from a practical view that a life of continued, sustained good spirit free from pain and suffering is implausible. It is a deceitful ploy of Fear that even when we secure an environment that is peaceful, harmonious, and enriched, whether as a silver-laden apartment in an ivory tower, or as a happy community, until Fear is satisfied from within, it will never give the spirit rest, only dealing out shreds of momentary satisfaction.

Second, to suppose that intuition and spirit favour continuity and respective sum maxims of well-being, as exemplified through rationale and calculation, would be to misunderstand the very nature of intuition and spirit. The directive guiding Defiance appeals to the most intuitive, yet elusive, notions of satisfaction – that which sets us free by completing living in such a way that we are able to willingly let go of living and life itself. Intuition and sense in spirit do not value rationale and calculation; intuition qualifies and values the maxims of fulfilment in spirit. Pleasure is often complicit in this dynamic of intuition and reason, so we often favour immediate, quick satisfaction over greater fulfilment over time, which pleasure cannot qualify beyond reason. But the higher pleasure of Liberty as Defiance moves intuition and reason in synchrony of immediate pleasure as achievement. The moral accord of Defiance turns living and its struggle into a spiritual directive, where one learns to be fulfilled in living itself, to enjoy the struggle and its ability to make one feel most alive. Ambition itself becomes grounded in the moment, the journey, the activity of living. In Defiance, living, not even life, is the ambition in itself. A moment of greater fulfilment that moves spirit to a state where one is at peace to let go of living is part of intuition that will always overcome functions concerned with continuous life lacking good living.

However, there is a part of the rational calculation of maxims of sustained well-being and good spirit that is relevant to Defiance. Intuition is served well when qualified as getting more of what feels good and what nourishes good spirit. But where the most satisfied moment gives way to continuity of life open to another great moment of spiritual satisfaction, reason and intuition drive action towards a successive pleasure. This can only be satisfied through the worthiest of actions – those that maximise positive ethical interests in great spirit. Thus, the ethos of Liberty sets the tone for living. The directive of Defiance drives ambition towards Liberty, towards greater fulfilment of spirit. Where it may seem as though the central elements of anger, pain, and suffering in Defiance are corrosive and antithetical to good spirit, their utility serves Liberty by imbuing the will with greater ambition towards greater satisfaction of spirit. It is in the moment of suffering eroding spirit but invoking an ambition of power to succeed suffering that Defiance moves not only to bind that poison, but to actually consume and dominate it, thus achieving the most of the power sought by intuition and spirit in pain. This power is then most fulfilled by granting liberty from pain, suffering, and Fear, a liberty that overpowers the consuming darkness of spirit in pain, turning pain into something better and making something more out of it.

A further concern with a positive ethos, as with all liberty, is the matter of balance. Fear serves a benevolent and constructive function by protecting us from harm, a function of ethics that can also undermine ambition, endeavour, and fulfilment. Would Liberty and ambition defiant of pain and Fear not lead to deconstructive, reckless, if not delusional behaviour?

Acting against pain and Fear as a primary spiritual directive by itself will not produce the best actions and will not satisfy greater ambition. Defiance is only as functional as it leads to greater spirit at Liberty constituted by character nourished with virtue grown from suffering and pain. Pain and suffering are practically inevitable features of life which people must either endure and grow from, or yield and submit to, with Defiance emphasising the liberty to pursue the greater living of resisting pain.

However, blind pursuit of the virtues of willpower and strength will not do itself justice. First, acting in Defiance without strategy, purpose, and vision can be reckless, misguided, and unhelpful to the ambition of Defiance itself. Defiance thrives through the directive of freedom from pain, a freedom achieved by guiding pain towards its own resolution from within. It is an intricate matter eluding the instrument of Defiance of how to apply one's strength and willpower to achieve Liberty in its greatest form, as well as setting the agenda and strategy for fulfilling this directive.

Second, there is such a thing as mental fatigue contingent on too much pain and 'burnout' by a spiritual directive. Strength, character, and spirit grow from suffering, just as muscles grow after painful exercise. Defiance is used as a means to drive growth and serves in times of adversity. Yet an eagerness of ambition facilitating recklessness and lack of composure and discipline will most likely produce bad actions and consequences, harmful to oneself. Defiance is designed to push the barriers of one's capacities, to strain mentality, demanding commitment to actions of questionable sensibility where one embraces the punishment of pain when challenged. But sometimes such ambition can lead to extreme actions and irreversible trauma.

Attitudes and the experiences of suffering are adaptive; people grow in accordance with the impression of pain. But for each person there may be a threshold of what they can endure, an intrinsically subjective and personal attribute of the adaptive cycle driven by pain where what one person can endure is not equivalent to what another can. Defiance thus requires mediation and sensibility, with Fear providing a utility of intuition and reason complimentary to the primacy of *ethical and practical wisdom* concerning what one can endure and the moral quality of an ambition. Thus, a greater dynamic is engaged in the ethic of Defiance which has a far greater reach and a more profound aspect of Liberty. By practising autonomy of willpower and learning to channel intuition and reason, one develops the distinctive, multidimensional virtues and characteristics of willpower. Defiance thereby becomes part of a grander spiritual directive and moral utility – *Discipline* of willpower.

Defiance moves ambition towards the directive of Liberty – freedom from and in pain. This breeds a comprehensive and fluid directive as a state of being free from the suffering of pain while simultaneously acting freely in pain. But to achieve this state requires balance. Defiance serves to further ambition and nourish the will in accordance with a positive ethos. Along with this directive one may be pushed to act in a manner that jeopardises oneself, exposing the self to the risk of permanent trauma. The former may be subject to greater scrutiny as a directive, because heedless ambition may exhaust a directive. Acting in a manner that is likely to cripple oneself, the reckless and relentless action defying Fear beyond defensive sensibilities, however, is part of the broader practice of Defiance. It is the willingness of relentlessness against subjugation to Fear that moves pain to a state where the mould of Fear is broken, in turn straining the spirit and mind.

These extremes, however, will not be necessities of directives of Liberty, yet the vigour of such exercise yields its own forms of distinctive rewards such as with high risks yielding high rewards. Only in the capacity of will and spirit to commit to suggestions of madness and actions against the primal intuitions of base morality and Fear can the intuitions of Liberty truly be evoked and thrive. It is in the willingness to pursue the higher pleasure of Liberty surpassing pain and anxiety of Fear, of relentless ambition, that Liberty is actualised in its greater, but incomplete, form. Defiance serves to overwhelm all spirit of Fear by channelling pain and anger against suffering and towards greater ambition, focusing on the desires Fear itself strives to fulfil – liberty from pain, with aversion of pain being only one criterion of this achievement.

The impulsiveness of Defiance can neglect our interests by causing us to act heedlessly and unwisely. Rather than to destroy oneself, Defiance and willpower best serve to maximise ethical interest and ambition, with the willingness to self-sacrifice being but one aspect of Defiance as a broader practice. Defiance serves our goals best when performed with continuity, sustainability, and efficiency of actions and actions' influences on state of mind. Good practice of Defiance comes with learning to use mental and emotional influences for growth and by exercising self-control to act with broader intent through strategy and wisdom. Defiance cultivates willpower as discipline and self-control, subsequently teaching *mindfulness* – conscious awareness of states of self, mental states, intuitions and thoughts, desires, ambitions, and behaviour and actions.

Defiance can be evocative in its anger and pain, leading to self-reflection on the causes of suffering, particularly the suffering we bring onto ourselves. The abilities and capacities of mindfulness grow with willpower and autonomy, reining in the morality of Discipline, which supercedes the directives of Fear, pain, and base morality. Through discipline and mindfulness, Defiance teaches a core lesson that pain and Fear are nothing more than utilities of the mind and will.

A negative ethos guides actions towards states of well-being, with pain and Fear only being criteria and utilities conditioning states of being and our behaviour. Pain is not a defining and absolute element of existence – it is only a utility of the will itself, a subject and instrument of the psyche. As with all things constituting the spirit, Fear and pain are a part of the experience of living, but they do not define living in absolute terms. Pain is a mental condition which can be influenced, used, and shaped. Good living is the core directive of the fundamental will, with pain and Fear only serving as criteria of our desires. The thought that pain is an experience of living, but not the definition of living, is by itself only a rationalised explanation. The intuitions and sensations in spirit corresponding to this attitude are only achieved through behaviour thinking this way. Fear and pain can shroud the mind, depriving the self of seeing and living beyond them or through them rather than on their authoritative terms.

Only by conquering Fear and suffering can one truly understand the nature of Fear and suffering as conditions of living, not absolutes of living. Pain is but an influence of and on the autonomous will, with Fear accordingly suspending liberty for the sake of security. Corruption of Fear's security leads to suffering when Fear breeds idleness and stagnation by suppressing ambition that nourishes spiritual and mental growth and corresponding improvement of states of living. Fear, pain, and suffering are secondary directives of the fundamental directive to flourish; they are conditions, not absolutes; their power is only as great as we allow it to be.

Defiance and its Liberty can be punishing, but extremely rewarding; life can be cruel, yet rewarding. Certain things hurt, yet we are better for it. It may come down to pushing yourself to try save someone you love most from herself, from the corruption of Fear causing destructive habits and self-inflicted punishment, to then

withhold your love as an act of compassion to give her a chance to realise the consequences of her actions and to confront her suffering. The choice to put the one you
love out in the cold, fully aware that you were their warmth, with the memory of the
moment she admitted you were her reason for hope and carrying on, will have been
the necessary, right choice for both people's sake. A happy and hopeful outcome is
possible, but it may not become reality. You may end up losing someone you truly,
deeply love, sacrificing a happiness that would have become a lie.

Defiance may drive you into a painful circumstance of someone's arms that cannot hold onto you, arms that you will allow you to be suffocated in the hope that you
can help. You will do everything you can for them, in your impulsiveness losing sight
of yourself and sum greater value of you using your strength and efforts where they
would be more promising. But at the same time, Defiance will give you the strength
and courage to do something extraordinary, to experience something incredible,
and grow in ever-greater virtue and righteous spirit.

However, that remarkable effort and commitment might not pay off with the
hope of happiness, and you will not be able to save or help someone precious to
you, someone you cared most to save. You may lose them. You will have to turn away
from a soul with the same story as you, let go of the self-given purpose to undo the
pain she brought herself, pain which you rose from in your story of the mistakes you
did not make. You will have to act against all instincts, against the most profound
instincts.

In this delusion and overwhelming pain, you might even consider hurting yourself and smothering your own life in the hope that it will awaken something in the
person you feel obliged to help, to then realise these intentions are twisted by suffering and no good could come of them. You will have to make a conscious choice to
save yourself and condemn and bury the ever-consuming and daunting ideal hope
of her salvation, to preserve what goodness can be preserved. You have a responsibility – a duty – to yourself and those around you, with your ability to help others
and be more productive than her bestowing on your life greater value, meaning, and
potential, and thus greater responsibility. You will have to bury hope, and in the end,
make a sacrifice for the greater good. It will hurt; it will change you.

One day, the pain might fully subside. Until then, peace can be found in that pain
where it becomes part of one's character, regardless of whether the same joy will
ever be found again. However, until a hopeful dream of peace becomes the worth of
being awake, you will be confronted with a harsh reality of pain, betrayal, and a sense
of failure.

You will question your choices, how you allowed yourself to be mistreated, how
you ended up in such a place; you will question your character and everything you
believe in and every ambition you may have had. You will be tortured by questions
of what else could have been done, to only admit your courage and strength did all
they could, to the relief of your conscience. You will have to learn to live with the
impression of powerlessness and endure the realisation that you can't save everyone,
perhaps even the guilt of being strong and carrying on when others do not, naturally
questioning whether this misery is worth the promised, but uncertain, fulfilment.
You will also have to accept and discipline the callousness of righteousness resisting
mistakes of compassion and the knowledge of what you are capable of doing, provided you are mindful of what is truly right.

Empathy, through understanding of common suffering and struggle, will show
you the inherent good of each and every person, a goodness that withers when Fear

deprives people of moral and spiritual strength; it will burden you with the tragedy of a conscience witnessing good people being destroyed by Fear. You will learn that compassion can easily manipulate and deceive good intentions in Fear, corrupting character and spirit. You will come to find a blessed light, but then live with a dying light of people's unkindled spirit and fragile soul. You will find great empathy and compassion, and then realise you have to limit your compassion to save what can be saved – an act of greater compassion, for the compassion and love you showed her will live on through others and offer some measure of peace and resolution to an imposed cruel fate. You will see your great empathy and compassion as gifts, but accept that with these gifts comes responsibility and duty.

A profound rage may fill the hollow space of a part of you that was lost. Where that rage, anger, and pain are alive, they can be used to make good on what happened, to evoke a defiant courage to understand what happened by listening to the intuitions of dominant corrosive feelings, then accept powerlessness and make what peace is worth making with powerlessness. You may hate to admit that the episode of pain changed you, but accepting this effect will be the beginning of new growth, to learn and gain insight, to become stronger and wiser – virtues leading to a better life. Defiance will uplift the shattered life and broken spirit, imbuing the soul's pieces with pain turned into virtue of a renewed, better self. Then, where bitterness begins to grow as a corruption of Defiance, greater Discipline restores balance, sparing spirit of toxicity, saving one's character from becoming a continuation of the same cycle of Fear.

Defiance is the value of courage and strength to seek something truly marvellous in life despite the great risk of pain and failure. Then, Defiance is the means to grow from loss and pain. Where another person condemns themself, Defiance can serve to not follow them in their descent and preserve what goodness can be saved. Defiance is a value honouring the goodness of someone lost to tragedy by carrying on. Discipline and its aspect of self-awareness, combined with courage and control, leads to self-exploration and the potential admittance of underlying pain of the baser self, for it is the baser self that is most reluctant to suffer. It may come to admitting that the mind has been touched and plagued by depression and an unhealthy anger or even aggression. However, if these mental states can be controlled, then they can be used as means to an end in unforgiving circumstances, to live long enough to reach better times when relief can be found. But Defiance alone will never be enough.

The specifics of morally good and right practices of suffering will be outlined as normative principles and virtues in Section 3, Part 2. Defiance is a subform of Discipline; there are many ways to practise, then appreciate, these aspects of the ethos of Liberty. A simple thing like physical exercise – acting in greater interest beyond the constraint of aversion to pain – is part of the morality of Defiance and Discipline. Looking after one's health is a practice that leads to actions and behaviour of greater spirit at Liberty. Bad health and inactive living can lead to stagnation and deprivation of good spirit, with the discipline of healthy habits being one possible solution. Exercise will cause some initial pain and discomfort, through which Defiance serves to learn to enjoy the empowering spirit succeeding over pain.

One notable practice of Discipline is *pain meditation* as practice of mindfulness *in* states of pain and suffering. Meditation here is considered a practice of mindfulness, which can be achieved in many forms and in all things. Discipline will serve to bring mindfulness in all endeavours and ambitions, even pain itself. Fear and pain can shroud intuition and perception; mindfulness of Discipline through inward Defiance acts to bring mindfulness as perception and willpower superceding the directives of pain. This can be achieved through uneasy meditation in uncomfortable, then painful, positions to achieve greater awareness of self through and in pain, to achieve such discipline that one will sit with pain, will follow through despite the pain. For some, there is an opportunity to choose this practice. For others, who live with chronic physical pain, pain meditation may become a necessity of survival, as I can attest to. But to leash ambition at Liberty, Discipline also means to move or act with sensibility. Sitting in a painful position for too long can cause needless physical injury, becoming ethically inefficient where healing from an avoidable injury consumes time. Discipline guides behaviour towards preventing actions harmful to the self and doing what is right (what is good in greater sum terms) by pursuing interests involving pain and injury when the time is right, when the expense of discomfort and physical hindrance can be afforded for the sake of mental and spiritual growth. But then inevitable misfortunes and accidents can sometimes serve as even better teachers than growth in controlled environments, although much riskier.

Mindfulness comes with practise of self-awareness by reflecting on what one is experiencing, how one feels, and what one is doing. Self-awareness leads to awareness of actions and the behaviour of thought and body, provoking intuitions that observe and study consequences of behaviour and the conditions producing consequences. Mindfulness serves as a means to understand what is happening and why.

Thoughts and intuitions can be moved by suffering and Fear, with Fear's influence focusing mental efforts on avoiding pain. Fear's attitudes and behaviour are healthy when focused on fixing the causes of suffering, but often these attitudes are undermined by heavy emotions we are unable to handle properly. Mindfulness of Discipline serves to focus through pain, see past deep emotions, to free intuitions and attitudes from being dominated by pain. Fear's *scope of awareness* – what we focus on and think about – can bring to attention uncomfortable, shameful, guilt-ridden, and traumatic memories. The memory might be something embarrassing from one's adolescent years or an evocative memory stained with blood and rage. Some fundamental impressions may operate in the mind on Fear's terms to produce certain patterns of behaviour. A bad memory from early childhood can cause a person to act on the foundation of pain's impression. Behaviour averse to pain can fail to resolve the root of the problem, with base morality's values becoming misguided by overwhelming emotions and misplaced desires, thereby creating the business of mental health practitioners.

The parts of ourselves that evoke pain will linger as catalysts of pain until they are resolved and their behavioural triggers and patterns are amended through virtue. Sometimes one needs to touch the foundation of pain to vindicate it of its corruptive power, to embrace and accept pain for the self to heal and allow good spirit to thrive. Defiance can work to push behaviour against pain, to use pain's evocative force against itself to grow in mental and spiritual strength to confront painful memories and impressions. Where the mind is resilient to pain, it can become more aware of itself, recognising unpleasant truths of the self, to then amend them, to consciously make an effort to act with more control and discipline than to react poorly in Fear. Fear in the mind can establish barriers and produce aversive and deflective behaviour. Often we act without deliberation and awareness of what we are doing, according to the reflexes of instincts and Fear. Defiance works to draw attention to this behaviour to cultivate greater willpower and scope of self-awareness, allowing oneself to grow in virtue by developing better habits and behaviour.

A pattern of behaviour can move a person to act against their interests; it is important to be mindful of one's intentions and goals. Pain-aversion may elude the source of pain, corrupting the directive of Fear striving to be relieved from pain. Mental pain can move a person to avoid the source of pain to reduce immediate uncomfortable sensations. Yet such an ethic will not address the cause of pain, will not bring mindfulness and engagement of rationale to the root of pain.

This can be frustrating and exhausting. A person can begin to profoundly hate themself, then punish oneself and others. That pain of frustration and anger may strive to be released, for the mind to be rid of the pain tearing it apart. The discipline of Defiance moves one to use that pain not outward against greater interest, but to channel it inward against the source of pain, to vilify Fear and let anger and pain fuel ambition to absolve the cause of pain – vice. Perseverance and relentlessness of the will at Liberty move to confront a source of pain through pain itself, to then find the strength to embrace suffering and let go. A simple directive of mindfulness through Defiance in painful mental states is to consciously tell the self that pain does not need to define one's being, that pain is only a contingency of living, that it cannot hold you, that pain is telling you something but not trying to cripple you. Subsequently, one satisfies living in higher pleasure of power to resist and overpower a potent force – pain and fear, leading to the liberty of spirit as relief from pain and as virtue resilient to pain's influence.

People may act by the directive of Fear against their greater interest. People often act to deflect and avoid pain, lacking the resolve and strength to dominate pain itself, failing to fulfil the ambition of the function of Fear – to be free from pain. People strive after degrees of power to appease sense of security by controlling others and the surrounding world, reducing the spirit and character that craves control to a deprived state of Fear unable to dominate or resolve suffering. Some people tend to pursue corrupted ambitions to gain advantageous social positions to secure power and validation, in so doing allowing their Fear and baser self to rule them. Where the spirit is enslaved to conditions other than the ambitions of an autonomous will free to act on its greater desires, spirit is deprived of the greatest power to control more through controlling oneself. To hold power over one's own life through one's response to life is far more ethically promising and fulfilling than living under the sovereignty of Fear suffocating spirit and character.

A global structure of Fear has arisen from base morality and a useful, but flawed, negative ethos. To defy the world is a brave ambition, but perhaps quite foolish. But it is in this great trial of opposing a world of Fear that one grows in spirit moving against domination by Fear. Many surrender to Fear and pain. The spirit gains satisfaction from the power of will rising above Fear. Even the worry of admitting imperfection and accepting the innate human inclination towards Fear, an inclination succeeded through virtue, is an act of courage and strong will. Accepting imperfection and admitting faults to be improved on is the path to a strong will, and then a strong sense of self, inspiring the confidence of the self-assured conscience of empowered spirit. After all, there is no courage without fear.

If the human psyche and character were invincible and unshakeable, then they could not be broken, could not be tempered, and would not be adaptive. In time, courage will disregard the concern about being spiritually and morally broken, finding pleasure in the challenge and subsequent satisfaction of the relief from suffering. However, the pleasure of willpower may become so addictive, and mental strength may grow to such a degree, that people begin to chase glory and recognition, deceiving the purpose of strong spirit, tricking ambition into falling for a higher form of base morality, which is not a morality or ethic truly liberating spirit.

The power of strong character that is supposed to supercede Fear may seek glory and recognition, to act in the world for all to see, to leave one's mark in history. True Liberty is found in surpassing this desire, in achieving spirit freed of such concerns, where the self only belongs to oneself and virtue and righteousness. Virtue should not be flaunted in vanity, as this would only erode virtue through corruption of the baser self seeking supremacy over others rather domination of one's own vices and suffering. There is little virtue and righteousness in making others feel inferior, yet suppressing immoral deeds through intimidation and assertive character can become just means.

Virtue should only be proven to others when this is useful for intended purposes, when righteous. For example, a job interview is a reason to highlight your strengths; retelling the stories of the adversity overcome by strong character to inspire courage and hope in others is another good reason. Only this power of will is worth its highest virtue, capable of channelling suffering of the world through oneself and towards something better, truly shaping the world in one's image. Virtuous and righteous intent to bring goodness into the world should not be driven by a desire for glory and recognition, for the truest honour is of a conscience and spirit good to oneself and others through the intent true to the ambition of creating goodness greater than suffering. True Defiance and its Discipline of an autonomous will move past the pursuit of fulfilment through appeasement of an ego seeing its worth and sense of self through others' recognition, valuing freedom of spirit over meagre flaunting of status and expression of power. Glory does not matter to the spirit and life at Liberty, to the person who seeks true freedom *in* the world.

Too often people are owned by power, yet they hold none of worth. This attitude may come across as self-centred, even selfish, valuing personal freedom of spirit above all else. But in time, this attitude will reveal the greater value of empathy and care for others, for the truest freedom from Fear's suffering is to hold onto compassion despite the pain, yet be self-disciplined and not act in blind compulsion of compassion. The consequence of this attitude is the autonomy of a virtuous character driven by the righteous intent of a conscience unshaken by the immorality of others, of a sense of morality unwavering to the pressure and anxiety of others' judgement. All that begins to matter is the pleasure of strong spirit at liberty from Fear, free from suffering, nourished by each moment of defying Fear and pain, free to be in harmony with the world beyond the veil of suffering.

Righteous and virtuous autonomy is ethically superior to morality based on mutual agreement to follow certain rules – *social contract morality*. Through Discipline one gains the uplifting pleasure of relinquishing possessiveness and the lust for control, to then gain possession of a soul free to act on its desire and ambition, to not be controlled by suffering acting against our greater desires, to make an ally of pain and suffering. Righteous and virtuous autonomy produces its own intuitions, allowing the person to act with goodness as a habit, not as a deliberate choice to act morally. Defiance fulfils its promise of Liberty when it grants the power to surrender control over pain and the world, giving the mind and spirit freedom from exhausting intentional self-control, to act freely in goodness and spirit free from suffering, to give Discipline and virtue their rightful organic intuitions of Liberty.

By confronting suffering, especially at its core, one begins to understand the states and causes of pain with greater clarity. Discipline, through its aspects of mindfulness, teaches a person to discern and identify the sources of suffering, to identify greater and lesser ambition and desire. One may be tempted to distract the self from pain, or one can instead follow greater ambition to own and overcome pain, with a better life being rewarded through this struggle. Liberty means to act irrespective of a conditional morality striving for worldly rewards. The promise of morality is, instead, the satisfaction of spirit feeding off struggle, enjoying the power of an autonomous and strong will, and the pleasure of the journey of living rather than living for the sake and hope of rewards.

Rewards are not the point of morality; the promise of morality is the strength, courage, and confidence to make your own rewards, to pursue what is rewarding and valued, with righteous character and noble spirit being the most important rewards that subsequently bring other goodness. Discipline's virtues become the foundation of the higher pleasure of self-sufficient happiness, of a happiness evoked from within and not overshadowed by Fear. Discipline is not to be confused with sternness, boorishness, or uptightness; Discipline is the ethic of balancing pleasure and joy to evoke and sustain greater goodness, to not let pleasure and joy become corrupted by Fear. The spiritual nourishment of Liberty through its Discipline and Defiance comes from deep within as a wealth of motivation, growth, and resilience.

People may pursue petty ambitions, whether as power held over others without power over the self, or as false security from pain lacking the ability to resolve the true cause of suffering. Modern societies are prevalent with behaviour driven by unfulfillable desires for status, security, recognition, approval, noteworthiness, or significance conditional on the opinions of others. These desires and values are corrupt where they are unable to satisfy the part of the self that is suffering, with base morality becoming its own trap of an unhealthy mentality and spirit. All this behaviour achieves is a living bound to Fear and an ethic of minor satisfaction.

We may distract ourselves from a meaningless life, may deflect our pain of insecurities and perceived insignificance, we may pry or punish to gain a sense of control to fruitlessly appease our own sense of an inability to control. We may then even give in to our pain and settle for a life devoid of living in apathy and emptiness of spirit. Base morality can be fulfilling, healthy, and highly functional and ethically effective. Yet it is also widely flawed, fragile, susceptible to corruptive influences, and can be very inefficient. Base morality is easily turned into a corrupt ethic by pain and Fear, with base morality turning on itself where others' pursuit of base values does not fulfil them and gives others the impression they must follow suit, with our desires being deceived by instincts and respective values unbefitting of modern challenges. Base morality's ethical deficiency and maladaptiveness are serious problems in an age where the fundamental nature of Fear and pain has transformed beyond common instinct. Self-discipline and mindfulness, even as higher forms of base morality, are instrumental to thriving in an age of many corrosive and corruptive ethical influences that are dangerous because of their fundamental influences on the mind. Self-discipline and mindfulness are necessary in an environment of widespread troubling news, many real challenges and threats to good living, and a mass culture vexed by Fear's corruptive influence where weak ego and sense of self is unable to effectively handle or address pain.

There is never any resolution to Fear and suffering until they are resolved from within, at the core of living. By embracing pain and growing from it, a person nourishes virtues of discipline and mindfulness through the growth of a strong will. Then one is given clarity concerning what matters in living – the act of living rather than simply existing, living with goodness of spirit beyond Fear and pain, to be stronger than the pain causing suffering, and for the spirit and character to be resilient under the pressure of suffering. The height of these desires is fulfilled through Defiance to let go of the desire for power, to surrender control through security, to then gain control over living through Liberty and the self. The aspects of living set by base morality and its intuitions often do not serve their own ends in accordance with greater interests. Becoming more than one's pain thus gives insight into what matters more in life – letting go of pain and living in good spirit beyond suffering.

The greatest manifestation of this comes in embracing the suffering of others' when they cannot, as the character of virtue may be the only one capable of doing what is right, what must be done. Defiance and Discipline can be defined by *courage*. While others cause themselves grief and perpetuate vicious cycles of suffering, Discipline can lead to an ethic superceding base morality, mindful of greater ethical dynamics such as in terms of the value of defying corruptive tangents of suffering. Defiance and Discipline can grant a person the courage and means to act in greater ethical interest, to set aside less fulfilling ambitions to achieve more in living despite struggle and adversity.

One might think that greater ambition means working to achieve a higher social status, to earn more money, or steer the direction of human development. All lives end with death, but to live in the shadow of this thought will not offer the most in life. Liberty means to not let the anxiety of death, pain, and failure take away the best life has to offer, to strive for things that are not cowed by Fear. Liberty is characterised by the pursuit of ambition out of nobility of character; it is not defined by the greatness of aspirations of an immature spirit. The virtues of greatness of spirit and nobility of character motivate us to pursue what we value most in life, to recognise what is truly fulfilling and valuable, while also recognising we are not obliged to pursue a desire and expectation, that we are free to choose whether to be happy or to struggle, to choose discontent to pursue greater future happiness. This Liberty is then completed by defying the ethical forces that subdue so many and act against people – Fear and suffering. Defiance is fulfilled by absolving a dynamic and cycle of suffering through oneself, bringing goodness into the world. Where others lack the courage and strength to put an end to a cycle of suffering, Liberty is the capacity, and pleasure, of breaking the cycle.

Defiance and Discipline lead to freedom from suffering through liberty in pain, through the higher pleasure of autonomous and confident character counteracting aversion to struggle and discomfort. The autonomy of strong will cultivates an inner world of rich spirit unbound to Fear and pain, receiving fulfilment through having a strong core of spirit and identity. Anger, hate, and pain used by Defiance and Discipline are channelled to make better use of active mental states and feelings eroding good spirit. Any part of human nature, including emotion, is amoral until subject to moral evaluation in behaviour striving for well-being, as only when the functions and aspects of human nature are used – are relevant to well-being – do they begin to have effects that ought to be considered.

Pain and anger are not inherently bad or wrong, yet what they do to us, how we respond to them, and what they make us do are subjects of moral concern. Disquiet is not as fulfilling as peace and joy, but its ambition and struggle are necessary to achieve, and sustain, greater well-being. Defiance is a means to an end to develop character and a state of environment compatible with Liberty and counteracting suffering. Defiance, for the most part, is a higher form of base morality that cultivates the spirit and character of Liberty. Defiance and Discipline channel, and make use of, negative ethical influences to gain greater ethical interest and value.

Certain challenges cannot be avoided and should be confronted; Defiance and Discipline are means to this end. Although the use of Defiance can be great, it has its limitations; sustained pain and suffering can be exhausting and crippling. But where suffering is profound, Defiance serves to move beyond suffering through ambition and motivation towards something better than settling for anything less than what is best in spirit and for the mind. Discipline and Defiance – ethics of the virtues of courage, willpower, confidence, and moderation (even in or as extremes) – value pursuits and ambitions truly in accord with a person's own desires, not those falsely imposed by the expectations and desires of others. Discipline is the power over one's own soul and spirit.

Dire circumstances and *hard* suffering (that is, great suffering, as opposed to minor *soft* suffering) can be punishing. Sometimes we have no choice but to confront grave hardship if we are to live better lives; sometimes we have to be defiant to not succumb to pain that could destroy lives. Pain then guides a person towards harder virtues borne of great suffering, virtues built on great strife breaking and reforging the psyche and spirit. Who is to tell a bereaved parent – a father who lost his child – that his composure through defiant, channelled anger is bad when it is a necessary means to carrying on and acting on one's responsibility, of doing what must be done? Deeply rooted and controlled anger should not become the guiding ethic of life, as it will not provide the greatest fulfilment or serve our greater interests.

Furthermore, anger that is not balanced with positive experiences will lead to suffering of oneself and others. Anger will always be accompanied by the risk of losing control, causing harm. Yet the risks of anger may be warranted where the risk of other outcomes is far greater and would cause much greater harm. Sometimes we have no choice but to respond through anger, but not *in* anger – this fundamental difference between controlling anger (by channelling it) and letting anger control you is the premise of the morality of Discipline, which extends its use to how we deal with pain. It is best to live in stern composure and disciplined rage to turn suffering into some form of goodness rather than surrender one's life and inflict great harm on others. The strength of such character invites pleasure and fulfilment inaccessible to those cowed by Fear.

Discipline becomes the sovereign of pain – a means to control a life plagued by considerable pain and constant adversity caused by circumstances completely out of one's control. But to achieve a Discipline capable of handling and dominating profound, ever-present rage and pain is a whole other matter and demands the highest of virtues and extensive wisdom and insight. A sense of peace without joy in happiness is possible in adversity as liberty to use pain and suffering, to receive the pleasure of a sense of self rising above submission to pain and Fear. The epitome of Discipline is to learn to see pain and Fear as benevolent or amoral ethical elements which become corrupted by vice and our vulnerability. Virtues of Discipline then allow the self to sustain happiness when basic happiness is possible and real. Until then, if anger and rage are the only realistic means of overcoming adversity rather than surrender hope and life, to achieve the greatest possible goodness, balanced through mindfulness and honest self-awareness, then these corrosive ethical elements are good as part of courage and truly good intentions. Nevertheless, one should always be mindful of the corruptive potential of pain and anger.

Some people have no choice but to live in dire circumstances and spiritual darkness. Where joy is restricted and one is subject to moral extremes of great pain, Discipline serves to retain composure. Some people have no choice but to endure constant adversity, meaning they turn to morally extreme forms of Defiance and Discipline. Discipline is the instrument and directive of moral righteousness, the demands of which can be severe. Discipline serves to mediate goodness and corresponds to composure and discipline to sustain, and not neglect, goodness of spirit. In the beginning, as intended, the rage of Defiance is compulsive and of inexperienced vision and ambition. Discipline leashes Defiance and binds all pain and anger, as the utilities they are, to serve greater ambitions of the will at Liberty. People might limit their ambitions and desires to only surpass their immediate suffering; Defiance is, for most part, of the same attitude. However, when Defiance cultivates the virtues of its greater Discipline, as Defiance is a maturing form of Discipline, desires and ambitions reach further than immediate suffering and the surrounding environment. Discipline turns Defiance, pain, and rage into a highly composed, controlled, and severe utility with clear vision and ambition – into a *cold fury*.

Cold fury is an emotionally detached but, through mindfulness, highly disciplined rage. Cold fury does not blame the world or others; it is not attached to anything but suffering itself, detached even from the concern of Fear, embodying and channelling all pain with dedicated ambition. Cold fury is far from blind; it focuses a higher form of rage, detached from instinct, on an element of suffering through mindful discipline. Its mental state and form of perception is not compassionate or empathetic, viewing all things through detachment from the baser self, with the exception of the baser self's pain used in discipline and higher morality. Emotions are amoral; behaviour through emotions is subject to morality.

Rage is extremely evocative, motivating, and empowering, providing a great utility for defying despair and hopelessness. Cold fury, through a higher form of hatred unbound to instinctive thinking, allows one to focus on the disease that is corrupt morality, with people being vectors of the disease. Cold fury has carried me through the darkest of times and has empowered me to confront my greatest fears and vices, admitting that even this anger has at times turned into vice when undisciplined. Cold fury is a means to self-improvement, succeeded by another discipline of growth. This directive does not consist of strict living or living devoid of goodness; yet it may be a necessity in harsh, brutal circumstances, when confronted with tough choices that should be made. Discipline is not a punitive directive striving to control the environment or people, including oneself. It is a utility to compose oneself through virtue and able willpower to resist great pain from within and channel pain into outward-seeking goodness.

Some moral traditions dedicate a lot of attention to conscious deliberation of rationality, according to which Discipline is, to a degree, an interpretation of these modes of ethics. Adversity may undermine the ambition to do what is right; it may discourage many to act on their greater desires and in their greater interest; pain too often becomes too much and our weakness in pain corrupts Fear. Discipline is the means through which one can retain composure in tough times, the extreme of which is cold fury. Cold fury is the discipline and sovereignty of spiritual darkness.

Cold fury, as an aspect of Discipline, is very spiritual. Ethics and morality are usually best when simple, intuitive, and practical. Cold fury and other consequences of heightened Liberty are inevitable. Moral philosophy confronting suffering will always become profoundly evocative and moving due to the nature of suffering. In some cases, profound great suffering leads to remarkable insight. The character, psyche, and state of mind necessary to carry cold fury is especially psychologically, spiritually, morally, and even metaphysically insightful. Cold fury is a practical ethic, perhaps even the most pragmatic ethic in terms of its heightened rationality, focus, and autonomy. Even though cold rage can restrict insight, leaving it one-dimensional through the perception of focused ambition and deeply evocative self-motivation, the consequence of laying rage to rest, while holding on to that discipline, is a whole new frame of mind and way of thinking through rare insight. This insight allows a person to meditate without the directive of emotions and the baser self, to meditate and study a reality stripped of baser intuitions.

While a deep spiritual element has been given to the ethic of cold fury, it is important to understand that arduous control of intense pain and emotions comes naturally to some people. Some people grow in character commanding their emotions and experiences, with a predisposition for rationality. This predisposition, combined with heavy emotions and experiences, breeds a particular state of mind.

If this predisposition breeds an extreme ethic as the mentality and attitude of cold fury, it should not be feared or considered unnatural and unhealthy. Acute emotional pain can change people, forcing them to cope by creating mental barriers and valuing and pursuing ambitions that the norm of happiness, joy, and baser values would not understand. Stern self-discipline is better than self-destruction and causing harm to others. There is nothing inherently wrong with this ethic and attitude.

However, when coping mechanisms and behaviour become corrupt, such as mental barriers preventing the mind from healing and causing destructive behaviour or actions committed in vice, then rationality and the delicate balance of controlled pain are undermined and stop being good. Cold fury, although an extreme of self-disciplined rationality and control of mental pain, is also an extreme form of pervasive mindfulness, as the self-awareness necessary for so much self-control is excruciating. This self-awareness also means understanding when drastic measures of coping with pain and intense emotions have been corrupted and their positive functions undermined. Cold fury stands apart from other disciplines as it does more than just hold together the pieces of the spirit and mind. Cold fury opens the flood gates of mental influences and channels them, the sufficient practise of which puts the pieces of the mind in place and tempers them with extreme emotional, mental, and ethical forces. Cold fury's mentality delicately balances influences of Fear and Liberty, yet its primary directive is unequivocally bound to Liberty, threatened only when sense of self and mindfulness are impaired. Cold fury is the highest form of Defiance. Sometimes, a bit of delusion is necessary to stave off madness.

It should always be remembered that Discipline is a journey of growth. We make mistakes, but it is learning from our mistakes and growing from vice and weakness that establishes discipline of virtue. Mistakes are expected; momentarily giving up and losing faith in oneself or others are not failures. Failure is not learning and not growing. The expectation of acting courageously under pressure is only an expectation of oneself according to the confidence evoked by the character's ability to act righteously. Immediate perfection is not to be assumed, but growth and the discipline to learn should be expected. The foundation of this expectation comes as the desire and ambition to grow, or else there is no point in actions in the spirit of the ethos of Liberty. It is not to be expected of depressed people to suddenly turn their lives around. But if their desire is to succeed their state, certain expectations must be met, such as basic actions towards progress, even if as failures becoming opportunities for growth. As with all progress, the main expectation is to actually push one's limits, no matter how seemingly small each obstacle and step is.

Defiance is a practice of Discipline, arising from Fear and base morality. Through these moral practices, profound spiritual and mental change accompanies the growing sense of self and willpower. The way a person thinks and behaves change, fostering habits and deterministic mechanisms of behaviour that are known as *characteristics* – vices and virtues. This change in moral character is contingent on development of the psyche and growth of mental abilities. The faculty of high-reason, associated with awareness and the mechanisms balancing and controlling mental influences, becomes a core part of behaviour. Through discipline and self-awareness, through the growing influence of high-reason, base morality becomes tempered with high-reason, transforming how one thinks and what one values. Balance between the baser and higher aspects of the psyche facilitates greater organic synchrony – *Harmony in the psyche.*

Through change in the foundation of the mind, psyche, spirit, and morality, Defiance and Discipline lead to the evolution of base morality and the transformation of Fear. Discipline nourishes autonomous spirit and behaviour, cultivating the virtues of self-control, restraint, and moderation. Discipline conditions the baser self and, as an ethic, leads to moral and spiritual growth and maturity. Mature and virtuous character – that is, of capable autonomy – can no longer settle for base morality; the undisciplined baser self becomes comparable to the mentality and spirit of a child, and the journey of growth through Discipline and Defiance to the spirit's adolescent period. Actions of greater virtue become habit, forming new standards of behaviour and forging a new state of mind. It might take one important choice or one moment of relief from pain after a period of suffering for the mind to become aware of its new state. A new journey begins towards higher virtues and greater understanding and insight.

Discipline's spiritual satisfaction of a strong sense of self, resilient spirit, and powerful will become the most valued pursuits, creating a rich inner world. When character is no longer constantly pressured by pain and suffering, and the mind and spirit turn to new ambitions, Discipline's mindfulness begins to self-reflect. Self-reflection leads to meditation and the search for greater wisdom and understanding, finding its way to the *morality of Harmony.* Discipline asks not for more, but how to use one's strength, asks what is worth the effort and is worth living for. The character of hard virtues and tempered spirit accustomed to ambition can no longer find satisfaction in its unchallenged condition. The ambition of Defiance and Discipline looks deeper into oneself and outward into the world. Discipline summons greater spiritual growth and righteous ambitions to heal the wounds of the world and amend injustice, as such is the directive of a new identity and its core values. The two combined ethical attitudes begin to see, through mindful practice, greater dynamics in the structures of ethics. Liberty, through its inherent ethical function, seeks more, while simultaneously questioning whether more can ever be achieved or whether what one seeks is attainable.

Discipline may appear antithetical to spiritual liberty. Why should a person sacrifice good living for the good of others? Why should a person do what is morally right at a cost to their own welfare? The deceptively simple answer is: because one can and is willing. This is the precedence for *moral duty.* Where some people may doubt the merits of duty and moral righteousness, concerns I shall explore throughout Part 2 of Section 3, only the individual at Liberty to commit to duty will appreciate the distinct spirit and satisfaction of duty in Liberty.

Duty is enacted not by the pursuit of immediate reward, but as a continuation of virtuous character able to exercise duty, true to identity and core values. Acts of Discipline as duty fulfil Liberty through character moved by *goodwill* – the will of virtue, which is only sustained through acts of virtue for their own sake, for *duty*. One acts in duty and Discipline not to achieve Liberty, but because one *is* at Liberty. Anything other than Liberty will no longer satisfy mature spirit and virtuous character flourishing in a life free from the bondage of suffering. Duty is the promise to the self to not fall back into old ways of lesser spirit; duty is the virtue of staying true to character and identity. With this attitude of Liberty arises a distinct appreciation of spirit at Liberty through Discipline and Discipline's moral righteousness. Duty will be studied in depth as part of the Central Principles.

Intuitions and thoughts of Liberty may become confusing, conflicted, or even contradictory. Meditation as self-reflection and self-analysis in Discipline and Harmony serves to make sense of ethics and Liberty. Understanding of the ethos of Liberty, subsequently its ethics and morality, is found through acting according to its directive and in its spirit. Certain behaviour affects us differently, arousing different sensations and feelings. By considering the baser and higher faculties in equal measure, valuing sentiments and sensations and the rationale that guides them, relevant moral deliberations become intuitive over time. Moral wisdom is knowledge that has to be acquired through study and practice. Moral intuition is the learning curve of any moral philosophy.

When intuitions and values compete, one has to appeal to core values. In terms of Liberty, the main principle of behaviour is to maximise ethical interest. To know what is truly in our interest we must be mindful of our intuitions (as mental influences) and state of spirit – how we are living. Moral knowledge and intuition are found by appealing to core values and desires. So when morality becomes confusing and complicated, clarity is restored by asking what will bring the greatest well-being. Knowledge of what is best for us, however, is found through practical ethical wisdom. This wisdom can be structured and logically accounted for in terms of reason and a hierarchy of values and desires operating in an ethical environment and according to the innate functions of the human psyche. The fundamental desire is well-being, which is achieved through two core ethical principles of behaviour – to pursue or secure well-being. Balance should be struck between the two ethical aspects, as different circumstances demand different guiding values. All behaviour pursues the ethical interest of well-being; the ethos of Liberty emphasises this attitude and principle.

At its full potential, the ethos of Liberty means freedom of morality to employ any means accessible to the psyche in the pursuit of well-being. This also means willingly using, and not letting go of, pain to further greater interest. Liberty may suppose detachment or renunciation of base elements, but this interpretation would be wrong. Liberty means fulfilment of all aspects of the psyche and spirit worth pursuing and valued as part of good living, then understanding what is actually part of good living and the discipline to renounce anything of less ethical value. Liberty in its complete form is the ability to be happy while free from the obligation of happiness for good living, yet not restricting spirit to the denial of happiness. The soul at Liberty is amorphous; its intuitions are rich and wild. Liberty is the capacity to appreciate fulfilment through the higher pleasures, while equally being free to enjoy the base pleasures – the simplest happiness and joy, including simple pleasures and attachment to loved ones, friends, and family.

The baser self is innate and should never be neglected, which means nurturing it in healthy moderation. Neglect of the baser aspects of the psyche and spirit will lead to suffering and unhealthy, corruptive behaviour of a subconscious origin, with a core wisdom of Discipline teaching that pain should be channelled and confronted, not suppressed. Only this freedom of the mind and spirit will allow for freedom of intuition and subsequent moral knowledge and wisdom; only this path will ever offer true freedom from the suffering of Fear by balancing pain and allowing oneself to heal and let go of the things that inflict pain. Liberty is fluidity of the will and spirit in the most comprehensive and profound way, the freedom of which is incredibly pragmatic and intuitive in terms of core desires. Therefore, autonomy of the will and spirit, liberated from the constraints of Fear and the veil of instinct, gives ethical insight, bringing mindfulness across spheres of living, then provoking organic intuitions. All contradictions and complexities of intuitions at Liberty begin to make sense organically through mindfulness of Liberty, to find what the mind and psyche are telling our conscious selves is worth pursuing and is valued most. Liberty of intuitions thus supercedes intuitions of base morality and blind rationale, with habits and insight enabling a positive ethos to operate on many levels of the mind – consciously and subconsciously, in all parts of one's life.

The study of moral knowledge and moral intuitions is the discipline and practice of the morality of Harmony. When we are not pressured by Fear and suffering, people generally abide or agree with the moral intuition that hurting people is wrong. There are many contributing mental influences for this moral attitude and intuition. Compassion and empathy, as well as sensible rules of social behaviour, make it intuitive why hurting people is bad by undermining our ethical interests. Hurting people when we feel compassion can lead to guilt and shame, which are unpleasant and uncomfortable feelings. Hurting people in social groups threatens social cohesion and harms friendships and relationships that otherwise have much more to offer.

However, there are instances when hurting people can produce positive ethical value. Restraining a violent criminal can prevent greater harm. There is usually a more profound, spiritual element to our moral intuitions and values; sometimes there is a sense of something inherently good about certain values such as not hurting others. These intuitions and sensations can be accounted for by structuring their reasoning and appealing to an ethos and the functions of the psyche. By refusing to hurt people and stand our ground, we gain strength and confidence to stand for ourselves, uplifting spirit and empowering identity. By refusing to give into mental pressures such as pain, the mind becomes stronger. This all feeds the ego and sense of self, as well as making a person more capable of handling adversity – which are good things, provided we are wise enough to recognise what is healthy. These sensations and corresponding intuitions appeal to our baser self through a higher sense of self, spirit, and morality. Developing this kind of understanding – this ethical wisdom – makes morality much clearer and develops insight that reveal objective moral options in very complex ethical cases of deeply competing values.

People may want to change to their lives for the better, to grow rather than settle for stale and unsatisfying living. We may look for inspiration and a reason to change. Sometimes we simply desire a reason to change and start anew. That reason may come through a New Year's resolution or an inspirational quote. The reasons, inspirations, and justifications for change always come from within – they are part of one's will; the will moves with every action and thought. To channel the motivation to change for the better, one only needs a single breath to concentrate on the moment and acknowledge awareness of being alive to focus on the ambition to change and the reasons for it – desire. It only takes one decision and one moment for new habits and virtues to begin growing. If one is dissatisfied and unfulfilled, focusing on these feelings and being mindful of them can evoke frustration and dissatisfaction. These feelings can be used to motivate oneself, with the dissolution of negative feelings inheriting the discipline of virtue to act through habit of goodness not requiring strong emotional motivation. One doesn't need any inspiration or reason to change and act for the better other than the desire to do so. It is useful to acknowledge frustration and pain, focus on them, then use suffering to guide and motivate growth.

Everyone experiences pain and suffering. It is not the norm for the human psyche to be in an ever-lasting state of joy and happiness, and eternal peace is impractical and difficult to achieve. An ethical constant of peace becomes corrupt as a utility when it fosters idleness and stagnation. Anger and frustration are natural and common parts of the human condition. These feelings should not be shied away from or unreasonably avoided. Anger can be corrosive, heavy on the spirit and mind, and its influence on any ethical directive is not universally sustainable or applicable; only Discipline can be fully balanced and sustainable. Discipline becomes widely applicable with the prevalence of pain, suffering, dissatisfaction, and frustration. States of anger and pain can be exhausting; with so much suffering in the world it is easy to give in and distract ourselves, in order to escape. But nothing will be fixed this way, and suffering will still be felt.

Perseverance and courage are core virtues for a good life. Anger, pain, and hate can become so fierce that one loses the will to act, to care, to live. Every person has their limits, and all can become tired, exhausted, and spiritually and mentally burnt out. How we respond to such experiences is what defines character and shapes spirit. Discipline and greater Liberty emerge where the psyche is challenged and tested, with greater virtues forged in great adversity, through profound suffering leading to new growth, by breaking the psyche and reshaping it.

Defiance and Discipline are directives pursuing liberty of spirit from pain and Fear. They serve to consume and dominate the torments of suffering and pain, to make the spirit's darkness one's own and be free in it. In doing so one can begin to see past the veil of Fear, pain, hate, and rage, to find spirit relieved from suffering. Goodness is only ever found in the bliss of spiritual liberty, regardless of the ethos, ethic, and morality. The character that has overcome profound Fear and anguish will then pursue further Liberty by staying true to the strong identity of core values and following duty. The intuitions of Liberty begin to recognise that complete spiritual liberty and greater goodness must be achieved in and through the world as well, not only in mind and spirit. Common sense begins to acknowledge that the world has to be influenced through oneself to improve ethical environment to relieve more suffering and absolve moral corruption. Discipline and Liberty begin to look outward; complete Liberty is the liberty of all. The ambitions of Liberty expand to address suffering of the world, which requires particular ethical insight and wisdom. To achieve balance in the ambitions of the greater purpose of amending suffering in and of the world, and to understand suffering and a world perceived through Liberty, one must appeal to mindfulness and meditation on morality and ethics. This leads to the *morality of Harmony*.

Chapter 12:

Harmony and the Intuitions of Liberty

Living and growth involve pain, suffering, and struggle; Discipline is the core ethical utility for handling these intrinsic features of life. However, life doesn't only involve struggle. When suffering ends, we reflect and think about the experience to learn. The morality of Harmony succeeds Discipline to learn from suffering. It may seem intuitive to suppose that good living as liberty from suffering is in itself good and a moral norm. However, even goodness in states of spiritual liberty requires mediation to prevent corruptive influences from undermining that goodness – their own Discipline. The joys of pleasure always require self-control. The ethics of joy and happiness can appear intuitive and self-explanatory. But when a person cultivates the virtues of Discipline and learns autonomy as the sovereignty of the will, the core of a person's psyche changes. How one sees and understands the world changes through Liberty.

The inner world of Liberty thrives with rich spirit and insight freed from the limited vision of instinct and pain, projecting outward as perception, understanding, and sensation. When suffering ends and adversity subsides, when pain no longer has a constructive use and its mental and spiritual resource is exhausted, further good living in peace of mind can only be achieved by *letting go* – fulfilling complete spiritual liberty and autonomy by freeing the mind and spirit from ambition, from suffering, and from Fear, achieving absolute Liberty as spirit free to revel in pure happiness without any suffering and pain. The greater the challenge, the greater the achievement; the greater the struggle, the greater the satisfaction; the greater the pain, the greater the relief; the greater the strength, the greater the ability to be free. Living without Fear and pain requires its own form of discipline to secure the stability of states of Liberty.

To achieve synchrony of reason, complete Discipline, and secure a strong ethical foundation, Defiance and Discipline are insufficient, thereby leading to the morality of Harmony and its own form of self-discipline. The morality of Harmony strives to complete Liberty by allowing the self to let go of pain and find harmony with oneself and the world; Harmony is the discipline of achieving peace and releasing pain. The corruptive tangents and vectors of pain, hate, and Fear can be contained through Discipline, but peace can only ever be truly achieved through Harmony and complete Liberty. Defiance is the power to satisfy Liberty, Discipline is the capacity to sustain Liberty, and Harmony is the art of peace and complete Liberty. True peace of mind and freedom of spirit are found through pain, not in Fear revering peace for peace's sake. True Liberty is the liberty of spirit and morality in all spheres, to make peace with pain and suffering, to suspend and call on ambition by the intuitions of goodwill, all of which is only possible with sufficient Discipline. Harmony is the practise of mindfulness, meditation, study, and analysis to learn from suffering, then use these insights and wisdom to guide the ambitions of Discipline and in the pursuit of justice and righteousness and the Highest Good. The morality of Harmony focuses on the contemplation and study of the Highest Good.

On our journey of survival as a species we have developed very sophisticated minds. We exhibit extraordinarily complex behaviour, and the human brain is one of the most complex organic constructs in the universe as we know it. The pursuit of flourishing is the primary function of life interacting with the world. Much, if not all, ethical and moral development has centred on base morality of instinct and Fear. The human mind has developed in parallel to the determination of survival and many aspects of our psyche and spirit have been bound to the base will. Many functions of actions have orientated on base morality, whether as the pursuit of survival, progress, status, power, or love.

Ethics and its vectors of behaviour have adapted to an ethical environment that mandates principles of survival and continuity. Every aspect of human life is bound to determination by the Fundamental Principle of Living Beings and Actions and the functional core of behaviour – *reason*. Reason underlies all human behaviour and activity, including how we react to environmental stimuli and what means we use to achieve our goals. Through Discipline one learns that pain itself is but a product of reason, instinct, and sentiment advising the will and spirit of well-being. But only the undisciplined mind sees pain as condemnation to a life of suffering, for pain is often necessary for growth, and lack of ambition or ability to grow from pain will not alleviate pain's emotional function that is intended to motivate us to overcome suffering in pain. Indulging this intuition breeds a whole new understanding of ethics and the core ethical dynamics of pain and happiness, suffering and flourishing. Beyond pain and Fear is a whole new world of spirit at Liberty. This vision and its insights develop a different understanding of life, people, and the world. But to understand oneself and the world through harmony of reason and intuition, one must understand both rationale and sentiment, thought and emotion.

By reflecting on our actions, reactions, thoughts, and feelings – all clues concerning our states of self – we begin to understand ourselves and our mind and spirit. Any account of reasoning in behaviour and moral evaluation must consider sensations and feelings as aspects of the spirit with equal weight to rational estimations, as rationality is useless if it does not evoke or produce sensed well-being. The structures of ethics are founded on what people value and desire. Understanding one's own behaviour leads to understanding the actions and behaviour of others, developing insight into the human psyche and the causal structures of behaviour and values. Understanding why the self suffers is a means to understanding why others suffer; in appreciating one's own pain, one begins to understand others' pain.

If pain is to be relieved, the source of pain must be understood and brought to light. States of well-being and suffering can only ever be known through their intuitions and sensations, but to understand why the mind and psyche evoke such states is to understand their pathology. To understand the anatomy of reason, and the mental states and emotions reason deals with, is to receive insight into the actions and states of being of oneself and others. Then one can appreciate the intricacy of mental states as functions of the mind. By understanding that all mental states are but functions, however evocative and central to states of spirit, through sufficient willpower and discipline to not let heavy sensations and emotions sway focused perceptions and intuitions of high-reason, one begins to cultivate discipline and mindfulness in all aspects of the self. Neither thought nor sentiment alone can portray a given reality, with the two being central to the state of self. Feelings do not always correspond to reality, but thoughts alone cannot excuse active sensations and feelings. Confronting pain is the first step to addressing it; reflecting on pain is the path to understanding it; understanding pain is to appreciate its benevolence; to bind pain to discipline and ambition by sitting with it patiently, while mindful of its goodness, is to make pain an ally; to release pain when its use is done is to make peace with it; to make peace with pain is to bring oneself to greater Liberty from suffering.

By analysing and meditating on Fear and pain through Discipline and focused high-reason, one can begin to appreciate the benevolence of Fear's directive. Aversion to pain acts to protect oneself and is a striving for security and stability, which are good things provided they are established on a truly stable foundation. Fear can be compared to being similar to a parent caring for their child, nourishing the child until it is mature and able to live on its own. However, there are definitive limitations to Fear as a sustained directive, particularly where stimulation is lacking and idleness is pervasive. Nature and our base faculties have given us the capacity to defy them and be spiritually fulfilled through the autonomy of our ambitions. Defiance may hate moral corruption and restraint of goodness, aspire to dominate pain and Fear. Discipline then serves to see past rage and find that any mental state is but a functional utility of the will. Fear is predominantly an attribute of the base faculties as an instinct of survival. Mastering pain and Fear allows the strong will to see past them and dismiss them, to sit with them and understand them.

Fear is an ethical dynamic that has enabled progress, albeit chaotically and with much conflict. Discipline is pragmatic and sees Fear in terms of its good and bad characteristics. Where a person is able to act beyond Fear, making pain subservient to ambitions at Liberty, one's own pain can be known to serve a constructive purpose, even though often overshadowed by much negativity. Pain and hate are only bad or good in terms of their appropriate use. They do not have to define one's living, for even in great pain one can come to be moved by a benevolent directive of Fear; even great pain can evoke great goodness and spirit. Fear is a parameter and function of well-being, yet its function can be corrupted by the mind's vulnerability to heavy influences. Fear is a part of the self trying to protect us and produce behaviour that remedies pain, in the process unintentionally betraying itself. Fear is not malicious; moral corruption is a tragedy and misfortune. Recognising Fear's benevolent function, while mindful of its limitations, is an opportunity to see it in a good light, and build understanding, empathy, and forgiveness. One can come to view Fear and base morality as benevolent functions and directives, as good parts of the self that simply cannot fully satisfy our greater interests, cannot provide what is sought after – greater freedom of spirit from suffering.

Intuitions are the most accurate portrayals of the degrees of reality we experience and are the most basic clues to understanding ourselves. Regardless of whether or not a feeling is inflated or fair, it is provoked and manifests itself for a reason. Like all mental phenomena, intuitions are functional products and contingencies of reason. Anxiety and pain can never be merely rationalised away, as the base faculties will continue to exert their force when something is wrong in sensed well-being.

To dissolve pain and negative feelings requires a particular type of discipline and practice. When high-reason becomes habitual and functionally prevalent, it begins to have its own desires. But even when we think we are completely rational, our base faculties, at least on a subconscious level, can shape our choices and state of mind. The deterministic and mechanical nature of the conscious mind encompasses the influences of both the baser and higher faculties. The dissolution of pain and negative feelings can only ever be achieved when the state of mind is appropriate and the character is able – such is the nature of vice and virtue. Discipline and Liberty are only ever possible when the corresponding values, attitudes, and behaviour enable their spirit. For example, to act with courage requires the virtue of courage, which requires a certain type of character.

To act dutifully requires an appreciation of duty. All behaviour must be preconditioned by respective causes. Absolute self-discipline and rational deliberation are always a lie; habits are the true nature of the psyche. All behaviour is conditioned by the functions of the mind and psyche; *we*, as our conscious identities, are never fully in control of our behaviour. Freewill is an illusion of complexity and competing intuitions; no discipline or control can ever defy this fundamental truth contingent on the Fundamental Principle.

Self-control leads to self-awareness – an awareness of *something* or *someone* at the core or behind the veil of conscious living. Then, one realises that living is only a sequence of mental states, a combination of experiences; living is the immediate conscious moment. Life and consciousness are a combination of their parts – each memory or feeling is part of the human condition inherited by all people. There is nothing unique about what we experience, as all experiences are nothing more than mental states – states of consciousness as ice is a state of water; they are only special to our self-awareness. The sense of self and identity are only prevailing states of the mind forged through experiences, environmental conditioning, and other organic mental influences.

All states of spirit and mind as attitudes and experiences are nothing more than extensions of the fundamental will's activity and continuity. Conscious mental states are only parts of the conscious realm that become part of an inherently amorphous substance of the body and mind, of a temporary and ever-changing form of spirit and the soul. The conscious self is a combination of sustained physiology, biology, and chemistry, of crude matter enabling sensations and phenomenal experiences. The soul is the continuity of living – of physical processes of the body sustaining the existence of consciousness and the potential for consciousness. Identity is only a sensed form of the self, behind which is a mental structure of borrowed pieces. Living is a continuous state of change; the self is a figment of spirit and an apparition of a soul. The conscious selves and identity are constructs of near-infinite variables set into a form of a soul by the Natural Laws of conditioning and change. All mental states are temporary forms adopted by something that is only realised or given substance through mental states; without mental states there can be no soul, and the soul is every mental state. We are the amorphous embodiment of change and the world; we have no power over change – we *are* change.

To lose control in such a profound way may be counter-intuitive and disheartening, as it threatens the sense of autonomy and identity essential to Discipline and functional ego. But through mindful discipline one can begin to find oneself in this profound confusion, as Discipline learns to absolve the fear of losing control, and instead find peace and relief in not having to control anything anymore. To surrender power and domination – to let go – is the essence of greater Liberty. Our intuitions and sentiments may conflict, our desires and inclinations may compete, and our purpose in life and sense of self may be clouded by distorted ambitions. Liberty is then found by acknowledging and embracing all these aspects of the psyche and spirit, in turn revealing the underlying true self as the essence of all functions – the *will*, the *soul*. The soul's categorical and absolute concern is only well-being; everything else is secondary to the fundamental desire. Behind every movement is the will acting according to its function and purpose. Behind all mental states is the essence of the self and spirit. There is no competition or confusion beyond sensing the essence of the self, only questions to be meditated on.

When suffering is not actively inflicted, or when a person gets a moment of peace from adversity, the loss of control becomes freedom of spirit as the release of ambition and freedom to simply be at peace, free of concern, autonomous beyond Fear and pain. The mind unmoved by pain becomes free from suffering, Fear, and the ambition and desire to be free. The paradox of desire's greatest satisfaction is to become free of desire, achieved through inner strength not requiring gain in ethical interest to compensate for negativity, free to live in a content mind not suffering from Fear. The courage to surrender control – an inevitable consequence of meditation through Liberty and the virtues of Discipline – is the beginning of spiritual harmony and peace. The meditations of Liberty reveal a new path of growth, the secret promise of which is far greater control, power, and freedom than Fear or Discipline alone could ever offer. Pursuing the wisdoms and insights of Harmony for the sake of control, however, will never grant the insight of greater Liberty and the Highest Good.

Discipline values the virtues of self-control. Mindfulness is the means of recognising and attending to one's needs and desires, to make the self aware of one's behaviour and surroundings. Practising this discipline develops mindfulness and its utilities borne of the faculty of high-reason, extending into many areas of life, from pain to pleasure. As mindfulness becomes more intuitive, disciplined, and reflexive, it seeps into every aspect of life, giving impeccable awareness, insight, and control, stripped of Fear preventing the mind from acknowledging genuine states of self and bringing motivation and discipline to all behaviour. Intuitions, through habit and character, make actions reflexive and quick. As with duty, the right choice and primary values become clear; the rewards of righteousness and moral principles are no longer questioned.

Liberty is complete when it moves one to act in terms of intuitions without constant deliberation, by a foundation of a will channelled through the functions of virtue – a *goodwill*. Learning to accept all things, to simply accept them without any moralising or judgement, without evaluating their utility and without any specific desire, is to achieve ethical harmony as balance. Mindfulness brings attention to different aspects of the psyche and spirit, through which discipline allows intuitions to organically dismiss ambitions and desires by focusing on other values – peace rather than ambition. By focusing inward on concentrated liberty of spirit as peace of mind, acknowledging that everything else is but an extension of this sensation and mental state, brings stillness to ambition and thought by letting go of any attempts to control desires and thoughts. One can be free to embrace or dismiss different inclinations, intuitions, and thoughts by acknowledging them, embracing them, then letting go of them through Discipline.

The Discipline of mindfulness calms focus, intuition, and desire through the practice of mindfulness, the ultimate function of which is to bring the mind to stillness and rest, freeing the spirit of concern. Discipline is complete through Harmony by bringing one's ambition to focus on the purest, core intuition – that of the pursuit of well-being, that of liberty from suffering. Harmony fulfils this function by bringing peace of mind even to the immediate moment of pain, achieved through the Discipline to bind pain to one's ambition and then counteract its corrosive force through a wealth of mindfulness as disciplined calm thought and soothing intuition. Everything fulfilling is worth pursuing, but to discern that which is most fulfilling and to act on greater interests requires balance in reason, intuition, and sentiment, complete in the liberty for such modes of ethics to be self-sufficient and organic through mindful intuition.

There is no precise theory on the function of mindfulness and intuition, as much of it is supposed to come intuitively without extensive rationalising and theorising. When the mind senses a pleasure, the mind can be drawn to it. Similarly, when the mind and spirit experience great relief, they will be drawn to the goodness of the sensation, striving for it. When one is familiar enough with the state of mind of spiritual liberty, as tranquillity and relief from suffering, intuitions align themselves with the desire to recreate a treasured sensation. True love – the epitome of base fulfilment – is liberating and comforting beyond all pain and fear, fulfilling something 'higher' by willingly letting go of your own welfare by making it part of something greater – a part of someone else's happiness. Once true love has been felt, as calm, peace, warmth, and comfort rather than excitement and flutter, the mind will forever be drawn to it. No further explanation is needed for understanding why our intuitions are attracted to what we desire most. Mindful thought will be drawn to the attitude, mentality, and identity raised from the most desired spiritual and mental state – that of Liberty and its higher pleasure. Intuitions become reflexive thoughts of core values and desires, which mindfulness further elicits and engages.

The discipline of letting go is not achieved through mere rational thought or misguided intuitions and senses alone; this discipline must be achieved through Harmony in thought, intuition, and sensation through actions. Merely rationalising something, such as by trying to convince oneself something is unimportant, will never work by itself. Only actions that lead to growth or habits counteracting certain mental influences will refocus the mind and restructure values, as well as allow the mind and spirit to habitually balance and recentre themselves. Only through action can one facilitate and sustain the mentality and spirit of Liberty.

Thoughts and intuitions can conflict. Perceptions can be influenced by biased impressions and habits of thought and behaviour. By focusing on the desires and values of one's will through Discipline, by standing back to listen to oneself and the whispers of intuition, to withhold action and reaction, one sees much more than Fear, theoretical rational models, or focused base intuitions, instead *sensing* much more through clear intuition and a greater scope of awareness unhindered by the distractions of moral concerns.

By evoking and channelling broad mindfulness through a strong sense of self and awareness, one comes to the liberty of acknowledging and embracing rationale and intuition by simply being aware of them and making them part of the ambitions of the fundamental will. Mindfulness is the deceptively simple process of withdrawing ambition and allowing self-caused, organic perceptions to see things through sincerity to oneself defying all Fear. Mindfulness in Harmony withdraws all ambition and sees things for what they are and accepts them without Fear, judgment, or desire, the insights of which can be used in moral valuation. Withholding Fear through Discipline dismisses the mind's resistance to pain, allowing for intuitions and thoughts to flood the mind. Harmony completes this process by acknowledging the pain felt by embracing it for what it is – a mere utility and mental state, the function and value of which depends on a given ethos and contingent causal functions.

The practice of mindfulness is simply a practise of awareness and withdrawal of reaction and ambition. As part of the discipline of meditation, it is not always easy to bring peace and stillness to the mind racing with thoughts, intuitions, and worries. But this stillness is not the intended function of a basic practice of Harmony. It is sufficient for Harmony to function through the authority of a mindful will acknowledging all thoughts, intuitions, and sentiments that come to mind without resisting them. The basis of this mechanism is mindfulness, whether as meditation or the utility of heightened awareness of the self and environment. As was taught to me, it is helpful to imagine a river constituting one's thoughts and simply acknowledge what comes to mind, letting thoughts pass without dwelling on them unless relevant to the intended purposes. With sufficient practice, the fundamentals of mindfulness and meditation are learnt, whereby many other ways of meditating become possible. But where it takes significant discipline to stand back and allow thoughts and intuitions to entertain the mind, the rewards of such a practice are extensive.

Most importantly, the rewards of mindfulness give the mind a rich variety of options for acting on a conceived goal by seeing more and receiving more insight. The mind and soul function organically, according to which we live at the mercy of our mental states. All that matters to the concern of well-being is the sensed state of self as the sum of spirit. All intuitions, sentiments, and thoughts are contingencies of the spirit – the only thing that matters to fulfilment. By exploring what the mind does is how we can begin to understand ourselves, how we function, and ultimately make sense of it all, through which ambition then guides the autonomy of goodwill. Understanding the self is the first step to making peace with oneself, completing Liberty and complimenting ambition through extended insight and vision.

Mindfulness as a utility of high-reason works to bring awareness to the self and actions even through painful memories. The mind may prevent the self from understanding why we act the way we do because of the pain experienced from triggering relevant mental influences, while provoking actions contingent on a pattern of intuition, thought, and behaviour. Mindfulness is the capacity to be sincere to oneself in an ever-expanding scope of awareness superceding the limitations of Fear and base morality.

For example, embarrassing memories can disrupt attempts to fall asleep. One may try to dodge an uncomfortable memory, yet the anxiety will continue. There is a reason why the mind keeps pushing these thoughts into conscious awareness. Painful and shameful memories teach us propriety and acceptable behaviour. Mindfulness is a means to sit with these thoughts and intuitions to allow the mind to do its job – to adapt, learn, heal, and grow. Sometimes people can't help but experience erratic shifts in mental states as mood swings, from joy to sadness in a matter of moments without an obvious cause. Sometimes our impressions are too ingrained and the psyche is too mired with unresolved pain for the mind to grow and learn, for consciousness and spirit to find immediate peace. Often our sense of self is at the mercy of intuitions and sentiments. Harmony teaches the following invaluable lesson: how things appear and how we feel are not necessarily true; feelings, although facts about our mental states, can be overwhelmingly evocative, preventing other valid intuitions and feelings from telling us more about the state of self and conditions of living.

One may easily lose oneself in fluctuating moods. Depressive thinking is habitual

– a pattern of thinking that can only be changed through other influences introducing new variables and intuitions into considerations of the mind, as with all behaviour. However, while the habit is a real aspect of a person's psyche and character, it does not necessarily mean it defines them. The incessant desire for ethical gain can fail to appreciate immediate goodness, subsequently making broader knowledge and understanding inaccessible to one's scope of awareness. The suffering and perceived dysfunction of turbulent and unstable mental states can be relieved through mastery of mindfulness. Rather than dwell on extremely powerful feelings, the focus of perception can be moved towards mindful sensations beyond the veil of the shaken and tormented mind, to the body, one's surroundings, then to another aspect of the mind unaffected by momentary mental instability.

By learning to acknowledge all mental states as tools of the mind and spirit in the pursuit of well-being, a person can find their essence of self as the desire to live well even despite the veil of profoundly evocative feelings and intuitions. This is the instrumental utility of Harmony in achieving greater control and autonomy, complimenting Discipline by learning to let go of control and simply *be*. The results of this ability and attitude are unprecedented mental flexibility and focus and an extraordinary capacity to learn, heal, and adapt quickly, as well as usually ensuring good growth in spirit, character, and mind. So rather than allow pain to corrupt character, Harmony allows for more constructive learning and adaptation from suffering.

Rather than produce insecurity and deep-rooted corrupt functions of behaviour, the mindfulness of Harmony, through extensive self-awareness, can promptly catch sudden changes in the self and regulate the mental influences shaping development of the psyche. The morality of Discipline nurtures and implements the virtues of self-control and mental resilience and strength; the other side of these aspects of Discipline is learning from experience, which is the proficiency of the morality of Harmony. In time, with sufficient practice, one can find peace of mind and clarity in all things, from pain to joy, from pleasure to boredom, by simply being aware of oneself and one's experiences of life – mindfulness and focus become reflexive. Episodes of heightened mindfulness then reveal its relentlessly, and sometimes brutally, pragmatic nature and remarkable adaptation.

A distinctive feature and utility of advanced mindfulness is its capacity to surpass immediate intuitions and mental states, to see past them, to balance, then channel, emotions, inclinations, and reactions. Consider the use of mindfulness in adjustment of mental states through the following example of a date. Before a date, a person's mind can be shrouded with anxiety, uncertainty, and daunting expectations. Intuitions and thoughts may scream: 'What if I make a fool of myself? What if there is a moment of awkward silence? What if it all goes wrong? What if I end up alone?' But in your courage, you still decide to go through with the date despite the anxiety. But anxiety serves the purpose of making oneself think twice before doing something stupid or counter-productive, yet anxiety can also exceed its good utility by provoking poorly judged behaviour reacting to, rather than acting on, nervousness. The morality of Harmony is an ethic that allows a person to sit back and acknowledge all thoughts, to simply be aware of the thoughts and intuitions one is experiencing. In doing so, the mind can come to a state of balance and harmony by acknowledging and learning from intuitions and insights.

Harmony allows a person to strategise. The directive of Discipline then works with acknowledged thoughts and intuitions. The date might go wrong and you lose out on an opportunity to be intimate with somebody you are attracted to. But then mindfulness will reveal that future opportunities will present themselves after awkward feelings subside. You may think that you'll end up alone, but the courage of asking out a person on a date is the same courage that will translate into future actions and opportunities. That same courage will nourish a sense of self through goodwill and virtue to be sincere to oneself and honest with others. This sincerity and honesty acknowledges weaknesses of character and vulnerabilities of personality to then improve on vice. Some beneficial consequences of this are becoming a better person and developing confidence, which bring their own rewards. Harmony, as an active mentality and spirit of Liberty, focuses intuitions and sensations on the moment, to look and move past Fear and simply enjoy the moment of living as sharing one's time with somebody else.

Certain episodes of one's life can go awfully wrong, for other moments to be extremely uplifting. Whatever happens, such is life, and Liberty to enjoy the moment as an experience of living, good or bad, will do the person a greater service than a moment overshadowed by Fear. Harmony then also serves Discipline in a technical way by adjusting intuitions, such as to think of a date as a mere date – a time to enjoy with another person, and not as something extremely worrisome that can cause serious harm. Harmony offers insight to balance intuitions and behaviour. Where a person's mentality and attitude are very anxious, Harmony as Discipline can make the corresponding intuitions and sensations freer in spirit and mind by introducing reassuring intuitions and sensations. One can appreciate the date by treating it as an occasion of ultimately fleeting consequence that cannot harm you and from which one can learn and gain insight into spirit, life, ethics, and morality, the spiritual freedom of which leads to more pleasure and joy, as well as better judgement and balanced behaviour. For example, you might come to live alone, even if you are not lonely, but at least you got to enjoy a precious moment because you were brave enough, which says much more about one's character. Such an attitude then transforms you in unintended ways for the better.

Sometimes things don't go your way and you can afford minimal responsibility for the consequences of your actions, whereby you might only harm yourself rather than somebody else, meaning you don't have to worry much or follow duty. For example, a date may go wrong and you do something silly. But these experiences of discomfort and pain can be brought to light through the joy of the moment. Sometimes, learning to appreciate the smallest goodness, learning from the worst, and learning to laugh at the rest is the best way to achieve Harmony. Laughter and joy can be the most liberating responses to negativity, to see the positive in bad circumstances (where this is morally permissible, appropriate, and sensible). Combined experiences of Defiance and Harmony can breed a particular taste for dark humour. Something awkward may happen on a date, but at least it makes for a funny story. This is a straightforward example of a basic attitude of the morality of Harmony as spiritual liberation from suffering. Freedom of spirit is supposed to feel free, calm, and at ease. Spiritual freedom, as the freedom of being fulfilled and from suffering, is the most intuitive thing we can know and doesn't need much explanation – it is clear as the Highest Good. However, freedom of spirit also means being free to do what is right and not neglect responsibilities. The difficulty is in finding and learning balance between ambition and peace, as the two ethical dynamics feed off each other.

The directive of Harmony emphasises the intuitions and senses of Liberty, to focus on the sense of peace that comes from mindfulness of simply allowing things to pass, to acknowledge and accept change, which requires inner mental and spiritual strength. Meditation and mindfulness bring the sense and intuition of spirit free from suffering to the moment. Allowing and accepting change by having the strength to admit the vulnerability of having been hurt leads to the surrender of control, then the freedom to make peace with Fear and suffering, or not. Certain spiritual moral practices strive to sustain spiritual liberty through abstinence and strict discipline. The ethos of Liberty, however, is complete when its spiritual liberty extends into other spheres of life through engaged living. Rather than withdraw from base pleasures, true spiritual liberty means enjoying everything that is good without allowing negativity to take away goodness. Rather than abstain from pleasure, Harmony is intended to bring mindful intuitions and the sense of free spirit to add to pleasures. Then, Harmony is also used to show what is good and what is not, what pleasures should be abstained from if they are corrupted in individual cases.

Harmony also means accepting that the baser self has learnt a certain habit or addiction that can no longer be controlled, where the pleasure can no longer be of pure good spirit. There is greater strength in admitting addiction than denying vulnerability; it is more liberating and empowering to recognise one's limitations and true self. Harmony allows us to find what satisfies living through the liberty of seeing what makes us happiest and what does not. The point is not to *intentionally* spread the intuitions of Liberty, but *allow* them to spread. This is not intended to deny intuitions, sentiments, and thoughts; rather, the point is to dismiss aspects of the self that the mind finds of less value than desirable by channelling and focusing on values of greater goodness. This ability of the mind is created through virtues and goodwill, by disciplining and teaching the mind to focus on the good, which can only ever be achieved *organically* by experiencing greater goodness and allowing the mind to change without restraint.

Greater familiarity with Harmony will inevitably confront the thought concerning one of the most profound aspects of Fear – death. Fear of the unknown and uncertain is a powerful force. However, this power is only caused by our reactions averse to pain and discomfort. Apart from the event of death, death itself does not cause pain, but Fear shrouds uncertainty with discomfort and disquiet in terms of the risk of harm inherently bound to uncertainty. Rationalisation of uncertainty without accompanying intuitions and sensations of genuine relief, and the substitution of negative feelings with blind hopeful beliefs, will never resolve the actual cause of suffering, with responses conditional on ambiguous beliefs being vulnerable to uncertainty. Uncertain and conditional beliefs neglect the spiritual liberty of embracing death for what it truly would be – an utter void of all consciousness, a dreamless sleep.

An afterlife is not death. But if one is to meditate on death, what can be said of it? If death is the cessation of consciousness, then it is but an endless void. While the lack of pain may seem comforting and appealing, the lack of living, even as lack of pain, is itself fundamentally counter-intuitive to the fundamental will and its purpose to flourish.

Our reactions to uncertainty and mental and spiritual states of suffering cause the fear and anxiety of death. Base morality of instinct has served its purpose to stop life from ending prematurely, conditioned by the adaptive cycle of values and behaviour averse to death and death's shadow of suffering. Morality of survival and related instinctive intuitions and thoughts have enabled the continuity of life through Fear. But Fear can corrupt its own goodness by creating instability and causing us to make foolish choices influenced by the lack of control over reactions, only producing more suffering and death. It is not the ocean that causes us to be afraid, but the fear of what may or may not lurk underneath the surface, which can make us panic and drown. But this fear is part of the psyche and mind – part of the fundamental will, meaning it is in reach of the soul.

The fear of death is a habit and value, meaning it too can become part of, or be influenced by, Liberty. A life of struggle and suffering may find death appealing because of its promise of the end of struggle and ambition, but this is never spiritual liberty in life and not liberation from the suffering of fear. True harmony with death should come through the will making peace with the fear of death and the inevitable end. By developing a sense of self rising above great adversity and through spirit truly able to restore and find peace in any moment, one can accept powerlessness over the fate of all life, ease the fear of uncertainty, and embrace the loss of control over suffering. The warnings of Hell's punishment can be terrifying; but if God's intimidation deprives spirit of true freedom, then the bliss of a moment of the highest spiritual liberty is eternally worth more than the impoverished grace of oppressive divinity. And if death is an eternal dreamless sleep devoid of all consciousness, then the only thing that really matters is the waking moment of being alive, which the fear of death is concerned with. Letting go of happiness is much harder than letting go of suffering. By finding peace, balance, and stillness in joy and pleasure, as with pain, one learns the liberty to let go of goodness, to find an ethereal happiness by not needing to be happy or joyous, fulfilling the odd happiness of desire – to be free of desire. True Liberty is the freedom of spirit from suffering and happiness, to be free from needing pleasure or pain to feel alive. When peace of mind and spirit are beyond happiness or suffering, one is truly able to let go of the desire for a good life, enlightening the spirit and evoking the intuitions of true Liberty. Then, it is easy to let go of life and compulsive living bound to the pursuit of flourishing, for the end of flourishing and the Highest Good have been found.

The spirit and mentality of Liberty emerge through the virtue and goodness of freedom from suffering by conquering worldly and spiritual adversity. Through greater familiarity with the morality of Harmony and mature spirit, one can begin to sense things differently, *feel* differently. Perceptions of the self, others, and the world change profoundly, and a clear new world is seen beyond suffering or happiness, Fear or Liberty, as now a person can see and receive insight beyond even the pursuit of goodness. Acting on these intuitions according to the law of the soul's directive (to pursue well-being) comes afterwards. A person begins to think differently, understanding the structures of ethics, Natural Laws, and the Highest Good through true rationale synchronising higher intuitions with the intuitions of feelings – one begins to have the discipline and awareness to see fully rationally and wholly empathetically. The mind is drawn to peculiar intuitions, beginning the exploration of a new world with new sight, leading to unique understanding, wisdom, and enlightenment. Thus, a philosophy of the meditations on Liberty and the *Ideals of Liberty* is found.

Chapter 13:

The Ideals and the Meditations of Liberty

The mentality of Liberty that supercedes base morality develops in accordance with a distinct conceptual lens of intuitive rationale based on the focused ambition and pursuit of goodness. The inevitable consequence of heightened mindfulness and reflexive stillness of the mind is *spiritual emptiness*. First, one ought to ask: What is the end or purpose of Liberty?

A person can attain a degree of freedom from suffering in and from pain, but what next? If one focuses on high-reason and a respective directive of Liberty, it becomes unclear what purpose living serves. The base faculties are excellent at distracting and for basic fulfilment, and furthermore are intuitive through base desires and satisfactions. But what end does this serve? Continue life for life's sake, but to what end? To only seek out something to do in the meantime, to pass the time while alive without complete satisfaction? When moments of clarity are achieved beyond the veil of instinct and heavy emotions, one begins to stumble into a whole other realm of spirit and thought. The madness of idleness as a form of stagnation of spirit denies complacency without addressing the fundamental root of this behaviour averse to unsatisfying and uncomfortable *stillness and nothingness of spirit*.

When Fear exhausts its sustainable and continuous use, a profound rift in spirit occurs, sowing *spiritual emptiness*. Emptiness is an elusive feeling, and the mind will do anything but accept emptiness. Spiritual emptiness can provoke different ethical attitudes and dispositions to conceal it, often to little avail, especially not constructively or efficiently. Spiritual emptiness can manifest itself in many forms, from boredom to nihilistic existential thoughts. But spiritual emptiness can also manifest itself as consumption of the mind in the form of total emotional and spiritual numbness with no pain or joy. A life without living, without pain or pleasure, is something we are profoundly averse to.

Where an attitude may be inclined to see peace in death, an active consciousness devoid of feeling or spirit is worse than death, for in death we would not be consumed by the concerns of living. Fear reacts in many ways to a life of empty spirit such as by distracting the self from the spirit's void through superficial pleasures. Aversion to spiritual emptiness will never make peace with it, perpetuating suffering and a fundamentally flawed, if not corrupt, ethical Core. Liberty strives for ethical gain, so it is worth asking what value spiritual emptiness might have. To deliberately study the powerful and inherently corruptive spiritual and mental influences of spiritual emptiness is counter-intuitive, if not utterly mad, because the sphere or realm of spiritual emptiness – *the Void* – is seemingly inhuman and antithetical to life and living. Spiritual emptiness opposes even Liberty, as the latter is fundamentally interested in the opposite of stillness.

However, greater Liberty through well-versed Harmony is the only thing truly capable of exploring the Void as the mind drawn to this area and aspect of life, for only through life does the absence of life become 'real' or meaningful. It becomes the ambition of meditation to search and study the Void, to ultimately find Liberty in and with spiritual emptiness. Rather than linger in the Void's pull of veiled despair and suffering, the greater ambition is to reach into the Void itself, to achieve absolute emptiness and stillness without any pain or relief, to be in a state of *nothing and nonentity*. This profound ambition is not easy and can be very unhealthy, demanding great dedication and discipline. To find oneself trapped in such a state is the premise to either climb out of it, which is already a great effort, or to further a greater ambition of absolving all pain shrouding the Void and finding peace *in* spiritual emptiness. To leap into, or willingly return to, a state of spiritual emptiness is an act of absolute Liberty or odd sanity.

The *Void* is a universal notion of perceived nothingness in contrast to passion. The Void is found in the absence of thought and sentiment, in stillness of the mind and will, through a grounding focal point of the will turned inward on itself. This entails a distinct state of mind and mindfulness with strong momentary detachment and, perhaps, the most conscious familiarity we can have with death. This mode of mindfulness constitutes itself as stillness of emotions, compulsions, desires, thoughts, and as the retraction from active outward sensation – a tradition of deep meditation; it familiarises itself with meaninglessness and pure meditation free from any desire or distinct purpose. Even the ambition of getting in touch with the counterpart to the substance of reality – the Void – is forgotten. This form of meditation moves the mind beyond the fundamental will of flourishing and grants a new clarity of perception through stillness regrouping and grounding the mind and the will.

The Void can provide invaluable insight for mindfulness and wisdom. Then this mindfulness invites a distinct and overwhelming form of inward sensation similar to what is forgotten or alluded to in moments of sleep – stillness free of any fulfilment or familiar sensation. I will refer to a meditative state in terms of the Void – characterised by awareness of, and sensation in, stillness similar to a dreamless sleep – as *mindfulness by the Void*. In this state of meditation, mindfulness is not, strictly speaking, performed by us; rather, mindfulness is now borne of the Void itself. The sensations evoked through self-awareness in, and awareness of, emptiness in spirit and mind are the odd sensations of *absent sensations* and are mental operations of the higher faculties.

The intuitions borne of the Void – based on thoughts and feelings of nothingness, meaninglessness, and detachment – offer a contrasting view to the concerns of living, ambition, and ethical gain. While Discipline and Harmony foster intuitions of, respectively, the pursuit and appreciation of goodness, intuitions and sensations conceived through mindfulness by the Void detach from our ordinary, compulsive concerns. Consequently, through mindfulness by the Void, the mind is no longer focused on ethical pursuits and is not distracted by strong competition in intuitions, allowing for deeper self-reflection and meditation. This is an ability of mindfulness that can be disciplined, trained, and learned from the basics of self-awareness.

This form of mindfulness and meditation uses awareness of sensations and thoughts to apply the same intuitions towards stillness and absence of mental states.

This is paradoxical, as mindfulness is itself a mental state. While we cannot *feel* emptiness while we sleep, mindfulness by the Void brings some direct awareness of emptiness, evoking certain perplexing sensations of the lack of sensation. Nevertheless, this mindfulness will strive to achieve absolute stillness of the mind in conjunction with the senses affirming stillness and the absence of thought and activity.

When we close our eyes we may encounter the distinctive intuition concerning the darkness of absent sight – all we see is something black, which is a meaningful idea or 'something' created around nothing. Mindfulness by the Void seeks to affirm similar intuitions and sensations in *sense* and *mindful awareness,* not just in thought. Learn to *feel* the lack of sensation and dismiss all thoughts – they come later through reflection. Our minds will never be completely empty while conscious awareness of life continues. Yet mindfulness by the Void allows sensations in the absence of other sensations.

A formula for this practice of mindfulness comes with the foundation of the general practices of mindfulness. But where Harmony teaches the acknowledgement of thoughts and enables organic mental self-discipline and balance, mindfulness by the Void takes this further. As one feels thoughts, sentiments, and intuitions drift away, one can begin to sense the essence of spirit as oneself – as *something* – presiding over mental states, fulfilling the directive of Harmony as mindfulness in autonomy and the activity of one's fundamental will in its purest, disengaged state. One can begin to feel the self and the mind let go of thoughts, intuitions, and sentiments, feel a presiding sovereign of the mind commanding and dismissing mental states. One can begin to appreciate the rich sensation of pure self-awareness in and of one's fundamental will, as a self stripped of all and any form, of no self-identifying definition of the self in thought or body. Only the fundamental will in its purest form is sensed and focused on. This form of mindfulness can be classified as *mindfulness of the will,* as it is our focused awareness of the will or *amorphous soul.*

Disciplining mindfulness of the self, as awareness of the will's movement and by learning to maintain this mental state for some time and quickly, can trigger even deeper meditative states, the catalyst of which is reflection on the Void as spiritual emptiness. Meditation in the Void can be triggered by imagining the nothingness or blackness on the other side of reality if the fabric of reality was scratched away, if the edge of an imagined cosmos with stars and lights was torn away like wallpaper. Imagine peeling away at the nearest wall to find only an endless blackness behind it, a realm underlying all concreteness of one's perceived environment, and sitting in this space. Then apply this thought to awareness of oneself as a void locked within the self, to the awareness of one's will to appreciate a total lack of will and ambition – known through the sensation of stillness after achieving inner peace.

Close your eyes and be still; in the stillness of the deepest mindfulness relieved of all thoughts, concerns, and ambitions, even soothing peace is relinquished. There is no longer anything in or of the mind, allowing mental activity to be renewed. This is the applied practical aspect of mindfulness by the Void. Waking up from this half-sleep causes emphasised awareness of renewed behaviour and activity, focusing sensations of change in the mind and body – change in the will. This in turn offers a greater sense of self and greater self-awareness, contributing to Discipline. Where one may sense an operator presiding over fleeting mental states, he or she may later sense the fluid moments of the soul itself, to sense and feel change in conscious awareness. From this perspective of sensation, one can begin to delve deeper into similar awareness as *lack of awareness and sensation.* One reaches a state of mindfulness by the Void.

By turning the will inward and putting it to a halt, awareness, focus, attitude, and mentality can reset themselves, as taught by the morality of Harmony and its mindfulness through states of inner peace. Inner peace sometimes cannot be achieved in deeply evocative circumstances of great worry, pain, and suffering. Glaring through the Void and allowing spiritual emptiness to seep in offers moments of complete stillness in awareness, mind, and spirit, giving a new mental channel for the mind to readjust and adapt, at least momentarily. During periods of powerful urges and sensations, with sufficient practice, mindfulness by the Void can offer a quiet moment to regroup and restructure intuitions.

However, mindfulness by the Void can only ever offer a solemn moment, with lasting self-control and balance only attainable through Discipline. Learning mindfulness by the Void and mastering mindfulness of the will leads to a core sense of self as the embodiment of change; everything beyond the sensation of the still body, every thought or deed, becomes a *part* of the self created through something more fundamental. Mindfulness by the Void deepens this sense of self by providing a stark contrast to an existing sense of identity and spirit. Reflection on the Void evokes profoundly new intuitions, highlighting the movement and activity of living things as part of the world, as change of the world, as the products and conduits of change. The Void provides a new focal point for mindfulness through which the mind can learn to channel mental influences with greater clarity, overcoming the interference of distracting desires.

A good way to practise mindfulness is by paying attention to the sensations accompanying changes in facial expressions. Deliberate changes in facial expressions can be followed by faint emotions or even trigger shifts in emotional states. Suddenly smiling can evoke faint joy, while frowning can incite seriousness or trigger unpassionate anger. With sufficient practise of deliberate movement while being aware of subsequent sensations, one can become more self-aware, emphasising mindfulness of the fundamental will as the taskmaster of mental states – of deliberate thoughts causing change in the body, the thoughts and mental influences that lead to the thoughts of intentional behaviour, and then something more far-reaching across all thoughts as part of a constant sensation in the changes of the self and the will. Deliberate operations in facial expressions and familiarity with mental fluidity expand the reach of awareness to the core of movement. The consequence is the withdrawal of conscious awareness further behind the veil of awareness, transforming it into focused self-awareness.

In other words, greater self-awareness leads to the intuitions of changing mental states and the appreciation of their differences, allowing oneself to distinctly sense when something *isn't* felt. Intuitions and focus arise where there were none, producing mindfulness by the Void as awareness in the stillness of the will and the will's mental states. The awareness of the changes in movement is a form of mindfulness of the will, as one becomes mindful of, and can feel, change. By building on these intuitions and sensations one can implement another thought experiment and method of meditation. By developing a parallel sensation to deliberate movement – as extensive self-awareness in goal-directive behaviour and corresponding sensations – a person can develop a greater awareness of themselves in their environment.

Sometimes people can have sudden episodes of self-realisation when they realise the 'reality' of their actions and existence, such as with the realisation of what a person just did. Building on this intuition, imagine immersing your consciousness into a memory of your life. You sit back and experience and think about what your body is doing without the body being aware that 'you' are in there. This thought-process can lead to thoughts such as: 'Oh look, I'm eating breakfast now.' Not only does this practice develop self-awareness, but most importantly, it also leads to awareness of, and intuitions into, actions by noticing certain patterns of behaviour that weren't noticeable or were thought to be insignificant. Small observations of behaviour can have a huge impact on understanding the psyche, spirit, and ethics. Even the choices of how to prepare breakfast can say a lot about a person and their state of mind.

Mindfulness by the Void is possible through heightened and very disciplined mindfulness. Greater familiarity with the Void comes through sustained practise of states lingering in meditation on, and awareness of, nothingness. This must come through bringing the intuitions and sensations of spiritual emptiness and mental stillness, including deprivation of satisfaction, across aspects of life: from joy to despair, from love to hate, from compassion to harshness, from pain to pleasure, and from relief to suffering. Mindfulness by the Void is pivotal for greater understanding, insight, mindfulness, and spiritual growth. A person is likely to experience meaninglessness, futility, dissatisfaction, and dread when he or she doesn't feel anything, which is different to actively *feeling nothing*. Perceived rational thoughts detached from emotions and instincts show a bleak, unpassionate, unengaging, and unsatisfying world, which is caused by the lack of mindfulness and sensation. The Void can lead to nihilistic perceptions, understanding, and ways of thinking, the suffering of which is a form of corruption of high-reason desynchronised or dissociated from the faculties of base-reason. But confronting this part of reality, such as in the pursuit of meaningful purpose and wisdom, is necessary for greater mental and spiritual growth.

Any questions of purpose and meaningful living must consider meaninglessness and futility. However, as with all things that deprive goodness, balancing and controlling mindfulness by the Void can be very difficult and even dangerous if pursued recklessly. Detaching from pain and emotions can be extremely psychologically unhealthy. Detaching from pain can lead to delusion, while disconnecting from pleasure can be dreary and confusing, the consequences of which are severe neglect of the baser self and isolation in questionable sanity.

However, while the intuitions and sensations accompanying the exploration of the Void can be depressing and corruptive, this is a result of our own vulnerability. Mindfulness, mentality, and spirit by the Void, in their true forms, shouldn't inflict suffering or satisfaction. Corruption related to the Void is caused by the desynchrony of high-reason, by detaching from the baser self and indulging dissociative fantasies. Corruptive forms of mindfulness by the Void are characterised by becoming lost in thoughts detaching you from reality. But then the nature of the Void as the opposite of substance is inherently metaphysical, abstract, and mystical, bordering sensed and perceived reality.

Accordingly, it is very important to stay down-to-earth and take time away from deep study of the Void and related intuitions, as otherwise the psyche will be disharmonised and proper study will be impossible. Then again, fully embracing the Void is the only way to understand all its aspects, which is mentally and spiritually demanding. If one seeks to achieve this mindfulness and understanding, one must not be consumed by it and learn to control it by allowing mental states to flow freely, restoring peace of mind and balance. Then, it is in this dynamic of learning to allow free movement in the states of one's mind that the Void can teach even greater mindfulness, which can be implemented, cultivated, and practised in all aspects of life. The capacity for adaptive, flexible, and extremely abstract thought made possible by being mindful of the Void develops a whole new understanding of the structures of ethics by easily detaching one from, and immersing oneself in, living and the world.

The primacy of high-reason in intuition, sense, and perception can lead to confusion and different forms of cognitive dissonance. Without sufficient influence of the base faculties, the search for meaning and happiness can be disappointing, while distraction from the higher aspects of life, such as meaning and purpose, lead to their own forms of suffering. Emphasised high-reason can consume mentality and reduce intuitions to the usual detached thoughts of meaninglessness and emptiness. Familiarity with the Void and the will provides much greater clarity in the intuitions of high-reason by synchronising them with engaged living. However, questions of a higher nature can be fundamentally corrupted, misinterpreted, and incomplete when they are mostly moved by the base faculties.

Neither of the two ethical dispositions is wrong, yet they are deprived of greater fulfilment through clarity, vision, and harmony in the psyche and spirit. By not really feeling anything and being consumed by unpassionate thoughts, life will become unfulfilling, leading to the bleak thoughts of everything being unsatisfying, meaningless, and futile. Mindfulness by the Void would not find dissatisfaction in these intuitions, attitudes, and mental states, as it would instead be apathetic and truly completely detached. Harmony and meditation on philosophy, built on an ease with oneself and different psychological states, are not immune to imbalance breaking the peace or to the adverse effects of cognitive dissonance caused by uncertainty. The Void brings absolute certainty, as there is nothing more unquestionable than the absence of thoughts and sensations, through which one can alleviate mental discord by rebalancing competing thoughts to allow intuitions to focus on something else.

Nothingness and nonentity highlighting sudden awareness of existence, making the latter more concrete and certain, outcompete any other intuitions and thoughts, offering a new way of looking at inner discord. But certain intuitions of focused high-reason detached from the baser self are universal. By not being empathetic and not feeling compassion, warmth, or pain, the body is seen as an object and a sophisticated mechanism of tissue and crude matter. Life and living things lose their intuitive emotional value, instead becoming numbers and emotionally insignificant 'vectors' of ethical force and change. Somebody making sounds and speaking words is simply an event of sustained movement of physical processes of continuous dynamics of energy. The soul is defined by the substance underlying the activity of living things – it is no more than the states of matter of our bodies and minds. All living things are merely the continuity of physical events and biological and chemical processes.

It should be self-evident how dangerous and corruptive this way of thinking can be. Feelings enrich living, yet they do not necessarily define it. Looking deep into one's own eyes to observe movement of the pupils can provide a 'window into the soul', but then that soul is known to be nothing more than a self-determining machine, a continuity of many interconnected chemical reactions and physical processes, over which we have no deliberate, conscious control. One can look into an open cut on one's hand to see nothing more than flesh and the bones giving the body its rigidity. Intuitions begin to understand the body as nothing more than a tool; the soul becomes nothing more than the material that arose from, and is the continuous transformation of, the fundamental elements of the world. Just as carbon and iron combine to form steel, the body and the soul are merely more detailed and complex combinations of material. A body dies, its flesh decomposes, and new life arises in a long, continuous cycle of physical processes. All sentiments and mental states are merely contingencies of self-propagating functions of the body conditioned by the environment influencing our actions, yet they are not the entirety of reality.

Combining mindfulness by the Void and mindfulness of the will with the attitudes and intuitions of emphasised high-reason leads to other intuitions. Without suffering from detached thoughts, emotional influences and mindful awareness are not hindered. The guise of suffering is lifted and everything can be seen beyond the distraction and narrow scope of pain and Fear. Through further self-awareness in thought, intuition, and sensation, the self and all living things become part of something singular in universal substance. The continuity of the soul's activity is found everywhere and in everything. By allowing the baser self to wither and the passionate mind to die, then finding stillness and peace, the rest of the world comes alive. The substance that gives us life is the same which is found universally. That which moves the soul is the same that is found universally. Where the soul is the same in all things it becomes *universal* and *universalisable.* This leads to a profound new intuition and sense of a *universalisable soul* – a profound commonality, unity, and causal interconnectedness in all things and in all change.

All physical processes are bound to their laws of determinacy and Nature. Every action is the sum of many antecedent causes and changes, from the particles of an atom to the organs of the body. The molecules in the air we breathe are fundamentally of the same substance that make up our bodies, yet in different forms. Molecules come together to create and sustain life without a clear or self-evident purpose in doing so; the body and mind do the same. The substance in the food we eat, the water we drink, or the chairs we sit on is of the same foundation as the substance of our bodies and our souls; the only difference, from our point of view, is that we possess spirit and consciousness. By suspending freewill and embracing the universal foundation of life and material, then accepting all change and movement as part of the same universal substance, one comes to find a sense of a universalisable soul through mindfulness by the will and empathy.

The fundamental will is not only of the same species in all living things, but is also of the same origin in all things. The will and the body of another person, just as the substance of another object, are the same as one's own, distinguished only as different parts or extensions of the substance that moves and created the self. All are, and everything is, of the will such as our own – of the will to flourish; this is a Law of Nature. The goodness of one is the goodness of all; the suffering of one is the suffering of all.

When these intuitions are applied to people, one begins to have greater awareness and understanding of others through a fundamental acceptance and appreciation in terms of the conceptual lens of a universalisable soul. Others are moved by the same thing as you; what happens to you is what can happen to others; others could experience what you have; and the thoughts, intuitions, sensations, and mental states one person experiences are what others do as well. Most importantly, one learns to appreciate change within oneself as change of the world, just as change in the world is change in and of the self, with conscious experiences of the mind being wisps in localised change. The *mindfulness of empathy,* as a form of mindfulness by the will, is found.

The appreciation of the universalisable soul leads to a greater awareness of the soul in other people and the changes in and of the world. This state of mind evokes greater sensation in the awareness of others and the world, richer in spirit and insight. Empathy becomes greater and compassion becomes disciplined. One begins to feel oneself as an inherent part of the world, greater than Fear and instinct alone, finding something deeply spiritual and liberating. By confronting spiritual emptiness, the spirit and mind transcend the baser self and conventional understanding and sensation of living. When this fundamental mentality is combined with profound relief from pain and a choice to immerse oneself back into the struggle of living that protests tranquillity, the greatest inner peace and liberation of spirit are found in all things and in all change. The purest, freest, and ethereal sensation of complete bliss, calm, comfort, and peace arises in spirit as the completion of the function of Liberty, achieving infinite contentment and absolute relief from suffering – one achieves *eudaimonia, the spirit of the Highest Good.*

This philosophy is not the first to suggest or conceptualise a profound bliss or peace. However, the structuring of the functions and intuitions of this mental state provides a more coherent understanding of the pursuit of happiness and the order of values and desires. The core of happiness is a combination of meaningful fulfilment and spiritual liberty, complete as eudaimonia, yet elusive in practice. Happiness eludes the ignorant and morally weak. Some directives and ethics find serenity through the removal of all craving, desire, and ambition. There is a truth of happiness as the cessation of ambition, as the profound peace of letting go and achieving spiritual liberty. Guidance and discipline are necessary for the growth of character and maturity of spirit, yet restriction poised in Fear will never lead to true happiness and spiritual liberty. Liberty defies dogma, yet admits its own truths.

Would it not be better to enjoy liberty of spirit such that empathy brings goodness of spirit to and among people? Would it not be better to achieve goodness of spirit liberated from pain to learn to enjoy what life has to offer and appreciate pleasures with greater freedom such as without guilt or shame? Would it not be better to appreciate all fulfilment without restricting goodness to secular faculties suffocating spirit?

Values and rules for self-discipline nourish the virtues leading to happiness and spiritual liberty. However, only certain virtues and moral truths are complete moral truths. Denying oneself a certain pleasure may develop discipline, yet neglect something just as important and undermine a healthy, balanced psyche. Religious attitudes abstaining from sex, while they have their own merit and wisdom, are an example of certain values developing discipline, yet undermining another healthy mentality and sense of self. Guilt and shame of the baser self, denying or twisting something fundamental to our nature, is unhealthy, the discipline and ethics of which will always be unstable. Only through Harmony in all things can spirit at Liberty truly thrive. One learns to thrive in peace and ambition, to shift between rest and dedication with the liberty to do so.

This is eudaimonia – as liberty of nourished virtues and mental utilities fulfilling our function to flourish through goodness of spirit. Even the fear of losing liberty of spirit can undermine its goodness and fulfilment, demanding that one learn to find Liberty on one's own terms. Eudaimonia is spiritual liberty in all things – in happiness, in joy, in suffering, and in emptiness. The intuitions finding what is most valued and what should be pursued are then clear and come easily, as a person can finally be completely honest and at ease with themselves.

The moral truth or correctness of any ethic is judged through normative practise and experimentation with the truth. Structural ethics is the science of experimenting with morality. Eudaimonia is conceived as the ideal happiness and pinnacle of good spirit – as the fulfilment of the function to live well. Our intuitions show us that fulfilment comes through freedom from suffering and the appreciation of being alive with peace of mind, whether through aversion or ambition. Empathy, as care towards oneself and others, is a central virtue to eudaimonia and happiness. Empathy burdens the conscience with others' suffering and exposes the self to veiled pain, but in doing so empathy brings goodness and peace of mind. Through empathy a person becomes liberated in an odd way where he or she will be saddened but simultaneously relieved, that at least they are sad, in touch with pain and not blindly engulfed by suffering. Eudaimonia is the complete surrender of suffering and ambition after it has been realised that the pursuit of happiness and growth have been complete, that adversity has been overcome in the only way it ever can be – from within, at the core of mentality, spirit, and soul. By making peace with spiritual emptiness and by conquering suffering, eudaimonia and its happiness are possible – one then only needs to let oneself be happy, to drop one's guard while finding acceptance with, and peace in, the wisdom that ambition will always have to be rekindled, for the empathy and virtues that lead to goodness of eudaimonia must stay true to themselves and can never relinquish their conscience. Once a person has accepted the mantle of duty, their character can no longer relinquish responsibility, because the person will no longer want to and the sense of self transcends both happiness and suffering – becomes an expression of the Highest Good.

Eudaimonia and happiness are great, but the virtues necessary for the conception of eudaimonia and happiness, in reality, will never be able to stay with them. The clearest duty becomes to sacrifice eternal peace and happiness for the sake of others' happiness and well-being – with the freedom to do so allowing the spirit to be free from suffering and happiness, Fear and Liberty. A 'normal' or easy life will no longer be possible, as a righteous character will always strive to make the right and tough choice, then live with the consequences.

Eudaimonia and higher happiness are achieved and sustained through moral excellence. Eudaimonia is realised when a person is willing to allow pain to change their personality and character entirely, to dissolve identity and allow the self to be changed through ethical conditioning. Duty will require committing to tough choices such as a great struggle to fulfil an ambition or to sacrifice something precious to oneself.

To those unfamiliar with the nature of duty as virtues and the righteousness of Liberty will perceive a certain bleakness and spiritual darkness in duty as unyielding ambition and severity of character. The spiritual fulfilment of highly rational behaviour according to a higher sense of righteousness will usually be surprising and counter-intuitive to those who cannot appreciate the reasons for such dedication – to be part of something greater than oneself, to allow ego and identity to break, to then embody something more transcendental. One will suffer in duty, but the rewards, even if only momentary, far outweigh anything another life will promise.

Fate may confront a person with tough circumstances where he or she will have to make a choice; the right choice will be punishing, whereby it is up to the person to find their own reward. Accepting such a fate and one's choices may force a person to live a life of struggle and pain, for the sake of the Highest Good to oneself and others, *is* eudaimonia, for the choice to relinquish joy for duty is the act of truest freedom in the pursuit of happiness, giving a person the permission and right to be happy – which the person must ultimately give themself.

It may be questioned whether or not this is actual well-being, but to the spirit and mind of duty and eudaimonia there is nothing else worth as much, because one is finally free. Eudaimonia's spiritual paradise is sustained only through oneself in eternal duty – in virtue true to the Highest Good and its higher liberty of spirit. The commitment to moral duty leads to willing suffering, an attitude which amplifies sensed peace and relief from pain through and in periods of suffering. The desire for something greater and higher becomes significant and a part of ambition when the will is strong, as this desire requires courage and a sense of oneself as even slightly deserving of such goodness.

People commonly restrict themselves and their living to Fear, afraid to pursue something greater, settling for minor comforts, while desiring more in life but being too afraid to commit and risk. Duty supercedes any sense of living defined by the base faculties, the desire for such a life of duty only being possible through a strong will following ambitions and desires greater than the focus on ordinary comforts and joys.

To illustrate how empathy works in this conceptual and ethical framework, consider moments of frustration. When one is agitated and frustrated, mental states can become consumed with anger and impulsiveness. Impulsive reactions in frustration are functions of Fear striving to release suffering and pain by giving us a sense of control over them. Sometimes the function of frustration serves us well to deter a source of needless distraction, interference, or concern.

However, this can also come with a great cost in other spheres of life and ethical value. The undisciplined, unmindful, and frustrated mind can lose sight of empathy and block greater insight. For example, where two people are frustrated they may express their suffering to each other without constructive and effective resolution, fostering a corrosive relationship. By succumbing to a mindset consumed by frustration, one's actions are governed accordingly, thereby rejecting mindfulness of one's own and others' pain that needs to be resolved more fundamentally for a sustainable solution to suffering. Mindfulness of empathy surpassing the moment of frustration, especially through Discipline in pain, can bring intuition to the source of suffering, then move discipline to address it. Rather than allow pain to project itself and undermine one's interests, pain in agitation can be channelled, such as with the ethic of cold fury, towards restraint and greater control. Then, negative psychological and mental pain can be processed, acknowledged, embraced, and forgiven.

One's own pain reveals that others are in pain as well; one's own Fear shows just how much others can be afraid. Where others' frustration may be rooted in themselves and inflamed through others' reactions to discomfort, Discipline allows the self to withstand these corruptive ethical influences so that others may also begin to pay attention to their pain through empathy. Thus, empathy and discipline facilitate healing, surpassing provocative solutions of lesser ethical efficiency, such as conflict and needless suffering, then redemption and gain in ethical value through others' goodness.

The suffering of the world and all people must be considered, embraced, and understood, even if not felt in compassion, for such is the directive of mindfulness of empathy. One should not detach from pain and not lose sight of suffering, and one should embrace what suffering one's strength may endure, to then grow from suffering and channel it in ambition. Consideration of the individuality of the suffering of every person and soul, of every life and inner world lost in death, and the lasting impact of suffering as the vicious cycles we inflict on ourselves through vice, can be overwhelming. Desensitising to tragedy and horror is a natural and necessary mode of adaptation, especially to discipline compassion. To try to engage with all suffering without succumbing to it can be challenging. Yet such is the greater practise of Harmony – not just to emphasise empathy for ethical and moral wisdom, but also for deeper reflection and meditation.

Suffering must be embraced, recognised, understood, and confronted for one to overcome and forgive it. Making peace with suffering by forgiving it, the world, and fate is the end of virtue, is the completion of goodness, for consuming and dissolving suffering through oneself is the ultimate act of defiance, discipline, compassion, and forgiveness. By confronting sadness, grief, and pain, a person may achieve the Liberty to move beyond them and living in Fear. Only by truly confronting pain and suffering can they be made peace with.

Pain is key to achieving balance in the discord of suffering, for suffering reveals the value and virtue of peace. Pain gives us the means to grow in virtue to rise above suffering and achieve the strength to be free in spirit. While Fear's disruptive forms and moral corruption persist, there can be little true or lasting peace in oneself or in others, for the world and one's spirit bound to the world will always be confronted by suffering. Though the value of peace is recalled in suffering and ambition, the virtue of peace can easily be understood by meditating and reflecting on Liberty.

The worth of peace and calm can be known in principle, yet our intuitions deceive us when we lack discipline and mindfulness, especially when strong emotions and Fear corrupt our intentions and desires. Mutual pain and suffering are central to common understanding and goodwill. Pain and suffering can give rise to virtue and fortitude when endured and confronted with strong and dedicated spirit. Learning to see past just the self is the responsibility and duty of virtue. This is what the virtues of Harmony are, the practical element of which is the ability and courage to recognise all suffering, to then confront and conquer it, driven by an ever-growing foundation of strong and free spirit borne of eudaimonia and able to detach, to rekindle spirit through untouchable and incorruptible parts of the self – the Void and the soul.

Extremes influence people's psyche and spirit. This philosophy has considered certain ethical extremes such as Discipline's cold fury. Accordingly, it is important to make some notes on the subject, which will also illustrate how meditation through Liberty and the philosophy of Liberty can be applied to structural ethics and ethical study.

Extremism is troubling global civilisation on many fronts and in many ways through different forms of Fear. All good things can be corrupted through lack of discipline and mindfulness, through people's inability to endure pain and find the courage to admit their vices, faults, and wrong-doing. Being dishonest with oneself is the great malicious deception of vice and Fear. The many brutal, malicious, and depraved extremist acts of terror show what Fear does to people. Those who commit the act of indiscriminate slaughter to impose a reign of Fear are themselves the embodiment of spirit that is bound, yielding, and has surrendered to Fear; in this, they are of weak will and spirit.

What strength, virtue, and value are there in causing senseless chaos to merely satisfy compulsions of Fear, insignificance, weakness, and insecurity? One finds no such compulsions to be worthy of ambition in Liberty, as such acts only provide an illusion of strength twisted by Fear, Fear submitting the individual to its will and reducing a person to a diminished state of twisted instinct. There is no strength in yielding to the pressures of suffering and Fear provoking actions against our greater interests. Any individual of true strength measured by the greatness and nobility of virtue is one that embraces struggle and succeeds over the suffering and corruption of Fear. The act of murdering unarmed people, even if their innocence is debatable (nevertheless not justifying murder), is not a struggle – it is no more than a path of demeaning and cowardly submission to Fear. Fear in extremes deludes people of their significance and power.

In the end, the cause of blind violence and mayhem brought on by the morally lost and distraught lunatic will never achieve anything of moral worth. Human civilisation is a machine that has endured much more than the infection that is extremism borne of Fear and its poisonous mental disease. The only thing the extremist and radical will achieve is creating a nuisance from which others can learn. Extremism and its ideologies of Fear are challenges that should not be underestimated or ignored, but their challenges to virtue and humanity are nothing virtue cannot overcome.

In time, the extremist nuisance will become nothing more than a minor element of irritation and inconvenience in the history of humanity's rise, a nuisance that only undermines its own ideology, culture, identity, community, and ethic.

What is worst about extremism is how futile, selfish, pointless, and inefficient it is. We can grow and learn from the suffering it causes; it may be crucial for binding people together if virtue succeeds Fear, as adversity has always motivated temporary alliances. Yet it is saddening and frustrating how destruction, violence, suffering, and the chaos of mindless vice persist and ruin so many lives and communities. But in Harmony all can be made sense of and learnt from, and all suffering can be understood to then be overcome. It is this insight that moves ambition and wisdom beyond the short-sightedness, foolishness, and pettiness of those moved to act on extremes of vice. But where there is corruption to be found in Liberty of desynchronised reason, such as with thoughts and mentalities detached from reality, with particular reference to the Void, the most notable corruption of Liberty is excess detachment in intuition, sentiment, *and action*.

Corruption of Liberty, notably by the Void, would only manifest at its worst through inaction and disengaged living. Discipline and Harmony by all and any measure condemn the extremism of murder and the needless harm inflicted on others. The corruption of Discipline and ambition, however, comes through neglect and disharmony in the baser self, for the blindness that leads to unwise actions and pursuits is caused by the lack of mindfulness. The pain that makes people impulsive and blind to greater interest is wild when it lacks mindfulness and self-control. Cold fury is only ever true as an ethic where Harmony has been extensively practised and one has clear experience with eudaimonia and happiness. The core of cold fury is formed in spirit and mentality through the happiness that was sacrificed and by understanding the necessity of fate to suffer for the good of others. When these Core Principles have been lost or become confused, the mind becomes imbalanced, undermining the mental ethical structure of behaviour, causing certain faculties and mental influences to overbear others. In summary, corruption of morality arises from the lack of wisdom and awareness.

The morality of Harmony is dedicated to understanding and acceptance. The extremist committing murder and promoting a cause of slaughter and mindless violence does so out of Fear and the vice of Fear. This behaviour is not helpful for, or worthy of, humanity. All such deeds achieve is the release of the anger, frustration, inadequacy, and insecurity of the individual perpetuating the crime; these people are entirely self-absorbed and selfish. Through Harmony, one must understand that these are people of utterly debased humanity, suffering in their Fear and warped mental structures.

However, according to empathy, it is important to appreciate the soul of every individual in terms of the qualifications of justice. One has to accept extremists for what they are – individuals twisted in and by Fear. Empathy, as the understanding and acceptance of a twisted mind, is not compassion of blind tolerance, but an understanding of the conditions of others. The character and mind of vice suffers, and subsequently this suffering is projected onto the world. It may be that the extremist is not only a victim of his own mind, twisted and corrupted by Fear, but is also a victim of others' Fear projected onto him, continuing a cycle of suffering.

Morality is the order of desire; the immoral are victims of their weak will, fragile character, stunted identity, and immature spirit. Moral corruption is an affliction and a disease of the mind and spirit upsetting balance and moderation. Harmony serves to accept deeply corrupt individuals for what they are and apply appropriate measures guided by wisdom, forethought, hindsight, and strategy, to accept the necessary right and just course of action. Empathy can lead to compassion, but the use of compassion is far from universal and ought to be disciplined. Composure, assertiveness, and defiance in the face of corruption require a strong identity, which the morally righteous will always have through the empowerment of virtue, permitting the circumstantially necessary means of brutality and ruthlessness of cold righteousness to subdue and absolve corruption, including in oneself. Harmony turns to Discipline to confront suffering and moral and spiritual corruption.

In contrast to deeply corrupt people depraved beyond acceptable tolerance, those who resist and defy suffering embrace virtues greater than Fear; they show the potential and strength of humanity, unlike their counterpart lost in Fear. Conquering and overcoming suffering is the directive of the Highest Good we strive for. By enduring the many trials of life and pursuing goodness, a person best serves his or her interests through the acceptance of pain and by letting go of pain to absolve suffering, as well as commanding ambition to succeed suffering. Achieving peace and harmony in a cruel world, and a fate of torment, can be inconceivable to some.

Base morality and Fear teach us that pain and suffering are spiritually and ethically bad, yet one can also know that pain is benevolent in its ability to teach wisdom and motivate growth and self-improvement. However, people's character is quite susceptible to the corruption raised through poor responses to pain, through an inability to handle pain effectively. A cruel fate may haunt one's living. Suffering in Fear can motivate actions to improve on the state of living, but often inefficiently and at great cost. Then, when a lot of pain has been endured and overcome, harmony can be found with pain through the way one dealt with it. This liberty of spirit as harmony with life, change, and the world is not a normative prescription for others – it is an expectation and ambition raised by a desire for oneself.

Those who do not aspire to Liberty, or who do not want to forgive a cruel fate, or are otherwise in pain, should not be expected to be at peace, and neither should they be pressured into changing if they don't want to change – this simply won't work. If others are not at peace with pain, then they should not be told that they ought to be; it should not be expected of them and they should not be expected to understand why you have been able to forgive cruelty.

Mercy and compassion are a weakness for some – there is no point explaining virtue to those who will not listen, those who will not soften their guard, allowing the intuitions of Liberty to prevail. Harmony and unity of spirit with the world and others, known and appreciated through both pain and pleasure, are states of the mind and spirit that one can come to if the individual sustains the appropriate re-solve and virtue. One can hold on to pain and conquer it – a noble ambition of great potential, but only as good as the amount of discipline shown – or one can come to a state superceding pain, the strength of which allows for a new path to achieve Liberty through Harmony. But only by experiencing both core aspects of Liberty can Lib-erty's comprehensive intuitions and sensations be evoked, leading to eudaimonia. Eudaimonia is not mere liberty of spirit characterised by the withdrawal from active living and pain, but is also the disciplined mindfulness found even in great pain.

The ethos of Liberty and its ethics behave in accordance with the Natural Laws of the systems of ethics. Like any ethic, Liberty will have to adapt and grow through the individual and environment. When things get tough and a choice has to be made even though a person feels like they can't make that commitment, no theory or phi-losophy will be able to adjust universally – no ethicist will be able to recommend to a person what to do in the immediate circumstances.

Any ethic has to accept and account for the inevitability of people's individual interpretations and judgements. The reality and practice of any ethic will be reduced to individuals' intuitions and the demand for inspiration and motivation. The ide-als of morality become known through experience and practise aspiring to moral excellence as eudaimonia. In time, an ultimate ambition may be fulfilled in both Discipline and Harmony, inviting eudaimonia and embodying a character of good-ness through spirit and action. Morality of Liberty becomes embodied through the character acting on it and breathing its spirit. To prescribe a word to this notion of moral excellence embodied in a person through action and insight in spirit of Liber-ty, I will use the term *Paragon*.

Life can be tough and sometimes the right action is not easy, yet circumstances may call on the strength of people to act dutifully. Theories and words on a page may portray a nice vision, but the concreteness of actions will always count for more. Our intuitions naturally admire certain people for their strength and courage in doing what is right. In all theory, a person's experience of living and their spirit in actions, are the judge of the theory, as spirit is the measure and currency of the goodness of actions and the ambitions we pursue. Theory and insight must meet practice and satisfy the real conditions of people's living – theory must be applicable and prac-tical, which spiritual aspects of philosophy can forget. Success must sometimes be recalled to show the truth or merit of a valid point and the wisdom to stop history from repeating itself. Intuition and wisdom come with perspective, which comes with certain influences triggering change in perception and mental states. Pain can be overbearing, but only by acting through great pain can eudaimonia be complete, marking itself with what others may romanticise about or revere and exemplify with idealisation as the perfect example of moral virtue – as *Paragon*.

To summarise the thought, where this ethic and philosophy is theorised and cre-ates certain expectations and idealisations of morality, this is only ever complete and meaningful through corresponding actions. Moments of great adversity and tough choices define a person, the experiences of which cultivate intuitions, attitudes, and values. Only through engaged living and actions do we prove to ourselves who we are and become the values and virtues according to which we live, fulfilling our potential of spiritual liberty and strength. Making the right choice can be tough; choosing and sticking to the choice to pursue something more, rather than settle for comfort, is a long journey and can be punishing. But only this journey will lead to the growth of virtue and strong character. The moral excellence of being capable of doing what is right despite the pain and fear is only achievable through application and learning.

Those of a certain nature of moral and spiritual strength make others feel a certain way and can be inspirational. Persons of moral excellence are made so through the experiences they endure that other people can relate to. We all have certain ideals and role models. Where a person can be good, he or she can also be excellent – be a paragon of moral character. If one person can do it, then so can others. Admiring moral excellence serves not to adore a person, but to honour an achievement of humanity as a virtue. Like the athlete setting a record, pushing and demonstrating the potential of mankind, acts of virtue and righteousness do the same for ethics, morality, and spirit.

The Paragon idea is not of or for a single character and person – it is a perspective to be used for inspiration. The idea of a Paragon character of moral excellence is an idea for reflection and inspiration, as with any ideal or aspiration; the idea becomes part of the reason to strive for spiritual liberty and strength. People are born with talents and predispositions; not everyone is meant to become an athlete, or musician, or an academic – we all have our own purpose and roles. To be Paragon is to achieve the heights of morality and spirit through life and the choices one makes in tough circumstances. Not everyone is born or grows up mentally strong. What one person endured is not something another would have been able to. Some people can grow from pain much more than others.

Some people are innately mentally, morally, and spiritually stronger than others, regardless of nature or nurture. To those who aspire to achieve excellence and are inspired to overcome their great suffering, an ideal of virtue, hope, and motivation as a matter of perspective becomes important. And so one comes to admire, idolise, and look up to certain people or types of people, with characters of moral excellence and great spirit becoming one's *Paragons – the embodiment of Ideals*.

In the end, people become their own Paragons of virtue through conscience and spirit of the Highest Good. A devised ethic can never be credited with changing a person's life, for only the person, through virtuous action, can evoke spirit of goodness and nourish goodwill. An ethos can only ever inspire one to act in a certain manner; it is then the will of the individual committed to a morality that creates change. The honour of goodness and change for the better always belongs to the courage and ambition of the people who made a choice.

Reflection on morality and the pursuit of wisdom of the Highest Good find the moral truths – *the Ideals* – of spiritual liberty and the best way to live. Living and the structures of ethics can be very complicated, yet there is always a truth in any given ethical and moral question in terms of the systems and structures of ethics and their moral laws and Natural Laws. The dynamics of ethics arise with the bodies acting on, and affecting, ethical environment. There are different ways to satisfy our desired goals and there are different desires, but not all are ethically equal or promising. The truth may shroud itself in doubt and subjectivity, but all circumstantial and incomplete truths are elements of a grander, higher truth. Each ethical case and circumstance will have its own truth extending the truths of the systems of ethics defined by the Natural Laws of environment and the conditions of people's psyche. Well-being is qualified in different ways in different circumstances.

However, in terms of universal Natural Laws inherited from the systems of ethics created by the way the world works, such as in terms of the adaptive cycle of values, and the nature of the human psyche, there is always a greatest conceivable state of well-being. The fundamentals of happiness are universal – fulfilment and freedom from suffering, achieved by fulfilling the functions of goal-directive behaviour in any given structure of desires and values, with desires and values being functions of behaviour creating causal structures that can be ethically studied and morally evaluated. The most promising values and the foundations of good living – understood through wisdom and ethical study – are the Ideals of the Highest Good. The clearest sense of the Highest Good comes with the intuitions of greater understanding and wisdom of ethics, through the insights of mindfulness by the Void and of the will leading to eudaimonia.

The Ideals become profoundly spiritual as part of a sense of self far beyond being defined by the concerns of the base faculties, an understanding of life and oneself that will seem bizarre to the unaware and undisciplined. Even the baser self becomes a tool for and in our ambition. The Ideals transcend an immature vision and understanding of the world and become sensations and spiritual experiences rather than restrict themselves to mere conditional thoughts – they become parts of the self and the essence of life.

Because Liberty is only appreciated to its fullest extent through eudaimonia and the freedom to allow oneself to feel spiritual freedom, the Ideals are moral truths found through uncertainty and faith in the pursuit of Liberty. The Ideals are found in the greater freedom of spirit and mind from both Liberty and Fear, from happiness and suffering – found through vision and understanding the world transcending all ethical concerns that otherwise distract and judge without listening or understanding. Only by not judging and resisting painful and uncomfortable truths can one receive greater insight into life, the world, and ethics, showing what is more meaningful than one's own well-being and life itself.

The Ideals are found when the person is disciplined and mindful enough to pursue and make sense of them, which is only possible in a higher state of spirit and intuition superceding both Fear and Liberty – through the Void and change. The Ideals are spiritual principles of existence that are inaccessible to restricted insight, narrow perspective, and dogmatic views. As with the paradox of the final satisfaction of desire by relinquishing further desires, goals, and ambitions, the truest spiritual freedom and well-being come through no longer needing these core aspects of the self to live a life that feels good. The Ideals will never be as convincing and absolute to those inexperienced in Liberty, and neither should they, or have to be. The Ideals are found in their own right through the Highest Good and higher spiritual liberty, superceding any authority people borrow from. The Ideals of the Highest Good are not of or for one person or group, because their Natural Laws supercede any opinion and bind all movement of substance to the functions of ethical systems. Our conduct is categorical of the foundations of our will, and thus, while we still live, we are bound to the determination of Natural Law and the Highest Good. The Ideals come with the enlightenment of sensed unity and familiarity with all change, amorphous spirit, and the Highest Good. In short, this needs to be experienced and compared to all other experiences for it to truly make sense and for the Ideals to be known and felt as moral and spiritual ideals of good living, with all other goodness then aligning itself with the Ideals of the Highest Good – that which is most fulfilling and liberating.

Any appeal to moral truth and ideals is susceptible to corrupt ego's desire to control and the danger of over-confidence inviting the vices of arrogance. Foolish, ignorant, and senseless people consistently undermine the goodness of any well-in-tending ethic and its ambition and aspiration for solidarity and peace. It should always be of great concern when a person's appeal to justice is found on an abstract claim that is not in synchrony with people's intuitions or fails to appreciate mutual understanding. An appeal to the Highest Good and its Ideals is only ever as good as the capacity to find, understand, appreciate, embrace, and communicate the Ideals, not as deceitful proclamations of certainty absent justification and argument as the Ideals of reason and sensibility.

The Ideals will only be referred in a strict sense to those that aspire to something higher in spirit; the Ideals will not be necessary for the effective structuring and study of ethics. Of all things relating to the Ideals, they are not something to be institutionalised or converted into a sect or a centre for monopoly and authority, for they in themselves are an embodiment of moral authority. To be of Paragon character is to embody the Ideals through actions, a conceptualisation which can serve its purpose for any who seek its use.

This idea of character is an entity or relation belonging wholly to the individuals and people that admire it. The Ideals are not something that can or should be imposed, as this would undermine the very heart of the principles. If people's judgements and intuitions misguide them and others, whether through distrust or as naivety, then it is the Ideal of Natural Law where the adaptive cycle of values selects or condemns an ethic. If a morality is unable to remedy moral corruption and succumbs to it, then it is a failure of its moral authority and the Ideals the morality thought it had found. If empathy, sincere goodwill, and virtue are turned away from, then the Ideals have not been found, as counsel in common good faith is imperative for guidance and direction. The Ideals are ideas and principles of the most meaningful fulfilment in spirit and mind. Any ideal is a principle of a meaningful life. The Ideals lead to a greater sense of meaning and *purpose*. A person can begin to feel and sense certain higher moral and spiritual principles that become part of the self through duty. These intuitions can then be structured, through meditation, into a precise philosophy, an idea of purpose, and a meaningful life.

Chapter 14:

Function, Purpose, and The Ploy of Consciousness

Finding and formulating morality, values, and meaning can be speculative and subjective endeavours, often reducible to rationalisations of conflicting intuitions and feelings. But by appealing to the Fundamental Principle of Living Beings and Actions, all questions of morality can be given sensible answers through study, reflection, meditation, and wisdom. Our intuitions are clues to our states of mind and spirit. By understanding, structuring, and mediating intuitions we learn a lot about ourselves and behaviour, guiding our actions towards well-being through corresponding values. Everything we do is determined by the pursuit of flourishing. For any effort to be fulfilling it needs to be *meaningful*.

What is a meaningful life? What is the *purpose* of life? The Fundamental Principle and the insights found through Liberty show us what we are worth, what we are capable of, and what we ought to do with our lives. The concerns of well-being and spiritual fulfilment are central to the journey of self-discovery and growth – the only ways we discover for ourselves a sense of purpose and meaningful existence. Meaning and purpose are values and concerns amplified, or dominated, by high-reason; as such, their discovery and virtue require character of higher virtue, becoming more than drones of instinct.

Through mindfulness by the will, one learns that conscious life is constructed through, and moved in accordance with, behaviour sustaining existence. The function of ethics and morality is clear in terms of the soul's mechanism to pursue flourishing – to pursue positive ethical gain. The function of all life is to strive for well-being through behaviour. Purpose and meaning in actions awaken through intuitions and sentiments forming certain ideas and understanding. Different cultures and philosophies have found different values, but their promises are no longer universally fit for the challenges of a profoundly changed world – a fundamentally different, globalised, modern ethical environment.

Life, the world, and mankind have changed very quickly, with the millennial generation at the forefront of this development. Technology has progressed extraordinarily, yet morality and spirit have not necessarily kept up with the pace. We can fulfil many of our intuitive desires, yet the ease and comfort of these satisfactions can deprive us of the opportunity to grow spiritually and mentally, distracting us from other parts of ourselves needing fulfilment. By fulfilling many of our basic comforts, we begin to reflect and get the opportunity to think rather than only struggle to survive. But because the character of comfort has not necessarily grown and matured spiritually, mentally, and morally, this character will not possess the virtues, insight, and wisdom to sense and understand the value of greater goodness. Immoderate distractions and baser satisfactions detract from other pursuits that nourish greater virtues, meaning we are unable to confront spiritual emptiness and consequently descend into the madness of idleness – the inability to grow beyond spiritual emptiness, regressing and corrupting the function of Fear. We achieve sufficient welfare for balance, yet then fail to moderate our compulsions and pursue excess, following desires of our base nature that cannot be fulfilled, as the foundation of these desires in terms of Fear cannot be relieved. Without sufficient adversity, the character will not grow in virtue; with too much distraction and substitution of comfort, we fail to properly learn from our pain; with easily accessible luxury and pleasure, character becomes soft and undisciplined; unstable growth through pain exacerbates our vulnerabilities and then the fear of being more vulnerable denies us greater ambition. We blindly follow desires and compulsions without growing, neglecting the higher sense of self, spirit, and morality until the will and mind are too starved to recognise purpose and truly meaningful existence. Distractions, instinctive thinking, and Fear deny us the ability to apprehend ethical and spiritual insights into the world that supersedes ego, instinct, suffering, and happiness. Excess and ignorance cripple high-reason, hinder the self-discovery of meaning, and deprive people of the growth towards meaningful living.

The body is moved by the continuity of behaviour in accordance with the Fundamental Principle. Our bodies and souls are made out of material substance. Actions triggered in response to the environment are movements influenced by the dynamics of physical substance, with the fundamental will acting as a conduit of change. The soul's mandate is to thrive, requiring good inner and worldly environments. To thrive requires sustainability and continuity of well-being and goodness. Well-being is only sustained in living and life, with survival being but *one* aspect of good living, as goodness is only experienced in living, yet also suffocated by excess of attachment to life for life's sake without richer spirit. For goodness of living to be sustained, as is the innate function of life's ambition, one ought to foster and sustain the goodness of ethical environment. Our interest in having a good ethical environment include individual people and communities, societies and nations, civilisations and mankind as a whole, as the global causal cascade of our shared ethical environment is now, to some extent, influenced by all people. Therefore, it is a function of our behaviour, and a moral principle and value, that we ought to secure our ethical interest in the world by acting to create and nurture a good ethical environment.

Our living conditions and experiences of life are heavily influenced by the environment. It is in our interest to invest in the world around us to create good ethical environments. Looking beyond our core function to pursue well-being, the relation between the soul and the world reflects the substance of the world acting on it through the substance of life that the world itself created. Life is the conduit of change influencing, conditioning, and shaping the environment, or at least we have achieved the ability to do so, as we are now the single species capable of destroying the world. The following thought and idea can be concluded:

The function of life is to pursue and sustain well-being, with greater fulfilment of this function requiring accommodating living conditions in terms of good ethical environment.

The activity of living things is determined by the organic mechanisms of behaviour. The functions of behaviour are logical algorithms and constructs of information in and of the body and mind. The functions of the human psyche – that is, the activity of reason – inherently involve the baser and higher faculties of reason. For us to be truly fulfilled, both the higher and baser functions of behaviour must be satisfied. Though we are organic machines, our spirit can never be satisfied through solemn 'functions'; our function as living things requires meaning – something greater than mere existence. We need more than just a goal – we need a fulfilling goal, an end goal, a goal satisfactory of our self-awareness recognising the inevitable end of all life and ourselves as parts of the world.

Where a clock needs only the laws of motion to perform its orderly function, the function of a living thing requires conditioning that makes the continuity of function worthwhile. The function of life requires satisfaction in spirit. Therefore, life requires not only a functional law of behaviour but also a corresponding spiritual directive – a function appealing to our sensations, sentiments, intuitions, and ethical interests and values across spheres of the psyche.

For the function of life to be effective, it must be fulfilling in spirit, as is clear with the continuity of life necessitating continuity of worthy living. Anything meaningful in life must be sensed and felt to be meaningful, not merely imposed as a reticent ideal. Fulfilling living and behaviour can only ever be found and channelled, never invented without roots in the human psyche. A meaningful function in living is something appreciative and fulfilling of our potential. Spirit arises from the anatomy of sensation and perception – functions of the body and psyche that allow us to feel. Human nature is complex and behaves according to many psychological and mental functions. To be fulfilled we must satisfy what we value, which consists of many things in life.

All functions must pursue an idealised sum goal of functions as a function of ethical gain itself. It is not enough for us to eat for the sake of a function – we need to eat and keep eating for the sake of something more than just food and existence. If we are to pursue a goal, we need to pursue something more than just instinct. We don't just pursue satisfaction – we want happiness. The most valued pursuits in life become *meaningful* functions for existence, according to which we conceive ideal values and an ideal goal to focus all values, interests, desires, and ambitions – we find a *purpose* for our lives as an ultimate goal in life. A purpose in life is a focal point for all spirit, desires, ambitions, and functions of behaviour; it is the greatest conceivable ethical gain in life and a pursuit that aligns all other central ethical interests.

Certain behaviour makes us feel better about life and ourselves. As we grow up and mature, our psyche is conditioned by the environment nurturing and shaping our nature, building on the foundations of the human condition. Our mental, spiritual, and psychological states are constructed through core values and principles as parts of our identity. A powerful childhood experience can shape the rest of life by influencing how we see the world, how we perceive and sense things, how we react, and what we value. A meaningful function of behaviour and living is something that fulfils us – makes us feel more in spirit – more than other activity. The most fulfilling and meaningful pursuits are driven, and satisfied, by affecting our core values and core aspects of our identity, spirit, and sense of self. A profound experience of worthlessness and self-loathing can form an insecure and weak identity, whereby the most meaningful pursuit in life becomes the strengthening and upliftment of healthy ego. A profound experience of guilt and shame, self-inflicted through acts of violence, can provoke a desire for redemption, making the pursuit of forgiveness the most meaningful ambition in life. A profound experience of pain that changed one's life, and then overcoming this pain, can evoke empathy and compassion, feeding aspects of the psyche to find meaning in the function to help others to overcome the same pain that became so personal to oneself.

The most meaningful pursuits in life are based on our strongest desires, with some of those desires defined by the suffering of our mistakes and vices. The greatest fulfilment as satisfaction and upliftment comes through relief from our greatest suffering affecting us at our core. Therefore, while meaningful existence and pursuits in life are functions of reason that can be structured in terms of our values and psychological states, all people must find for themselves their meaning and purpose, because each person is an individual with his or her own mental construct.

Meaningful existence comes through pursuits that satisfy us the most by relieving us from our greatest suffering and satisfying our greatest desires and the respective values of desire. To find our calling in life we must look inward and listen to our intuitions and feelings, for no purpose is purely rational. But to understand ourselves and find the courage to conquer our greatest suffering requires mindfulness and discipline. The use of a sense of destiny and purpose is to allow us to focus on our greatest desires, values, and interests shaped by our core functions and psychological conditions. We must find our own roles in life and give ourselves our individual interpretations of destiny, purpose, and meaningful living. Individual interpretations of meaning and purpose are shaped by antecedent universal functions of the human psyche. Therefore, there must be Natural Laws and moral laws following the Fundamental Principle that underlie the function of a purpose as well as the ethical truth of purpose as a function of behaviour. There must be a universal principle of how a sense of purpose arises *and* a universal principle which exemplifies, and guides, all self-given purpose. Nature and the Highest Good must have a purpose for life.

The purpose of mankind's existence is dedicated to the soul – to our function to pursue ethical interest and nurture the world around us for our sake and the sake of something satisfactory of our self-awareness, of something greater than us through which our spirits and minds transcend the life of a base creature. From the reclusive sage to the active professional, all people strive to shape the world in the image of their ideals. Some value liberating detachment, while others value reassuring security, the ethics of which engage with their respective ethical environments. Mankind and nations commonly act on a function of base morality giving a sense of purpose restricted to Fear and instinct; people and their institutionalised vectors of values in the form of nation-states both strive for security and power for the sake of survival and comfort in survival. But when mankind reaches great comfort and ease of survival, the values, desires, and compulsions that brought about such a state can no longer create further ethical profit, leading to the madness of idleness.

Mankind is better off through the virtues of its humanity. Base morality can restrict people's ambitions and potential, keeping people in a demeaning state of Fear. The nation concerned only for its people, an attitude created by the nation's constituents desiring security above all else, is blind to greater purpose and greater meaningful fulfilment of living. The virtues of humanity invoke a sense of purpose with greater vision and ambition demanding a global and universal dedication. Mankind's endeavours abide the function of life and thus the function set by Nature.

However, humanity is self-aware of the function it has inherited from Nature, inspiring a greater ambition than selfish interests of well-being in stifling mere base spirit, as well as exciting a hunger for a more meaningful existence. Through the origins of the soul we find our place and duty in the world, the self-awareness of which becomes idealistically spiritual and ethically pragmatic. Our greatest fulfilment through meaningful existence comes through aspirations transcending instincts alone. Instincts allow us to feel joy, pleasure, and certain happiness in life, yet their greater fulfilment must always come through liberating spirit and a higher, more ideal sense of achievement and living.

Love is a product of instinct, chemistry, and psychology, yet its most uplifting and fulfilling form, as the addiction to the comfort provided by another soul we see as parts of ourselves, transcends instinct alone, fulfilling many core and fundamental functions of the psyche. The meaningful human life awakens from mankind's immature spirit of base instinct through the virtue of humanity – of discipline and mindfulness leading to a life of greater sensed significance, potential, and responsibility.

To emphasise this point, we as a species do, indeed, have significance, potential, and responsibility, because we are capable of destroying ourselves and the planet with us. However, our talents, abilities, and resourcefulness as a species also mean we are able to bend substance and shape the world around us according to our values and ideals, cultivating and creating goodness. Through discipline and mindfulness surpassing the influences of Fear, we see further than the short mile, beyond the horizon of a sunset, and gaze towards the lights of the night sky with awe, giving daily activity a break and allowing us to dream of a future. Our intuitions evoke a higher sort of purpose befitting our humanity in the function to live.

Animals behave according to basic fulfilments such as to create warm nests secure from predators and competition, whereas mankind acts similarly but on a global scale. Security is a condition of well-being that functions to prevent losses in ethical interest and value, yet this security is less meaningful when it is only defined by Fear. Humanity finds greater meaning in aspiring to something greater than just animalistic behaviour, as we are sophisticated animals that are capable of much more. The virtue of humanity is fulfilled through global and universal aspirations of creating and securing a good ethical environment, which should be equally defined in terms of our baser and higher selves.

Humanity's purpose is tremendous in its outlook, invigorating life. We do not just strive to be free from suffering; we want to thrive. The function of Fear is to protect us, yet we inherently find a more meaningful and fulfilling existence through a life that is defined by more than just not-suffering, rebelling against Nature in times of spiritual and moral adolescence. The purpose – not mere *function* – of humanity and mankind is to flourish and grow. Our awareness and vision cannot be contained on a small plane of existence defined by instinct and Fear.

Humanity strives for more, for greater ambitions and meaning in higher spirit. This nature, even if limited in individual persons, has prevailed, as human civilisation has achieved great progress throughout its history. Humanity, when ambitious and driven, always strives to grow, explore, and overreach until it grasps the ropes leading to a new world. Liberty has always been the path to progress, even if motivated by Fear. When we are free from Fear, its veil slips away and a wealth of experience is revealed and our ambitions never stay the same. The moment we feel liberating experiences, something more than Fear, we are naturally drawn to them through the function of the soul. Every part of us begins to strive towards something spiritually greater and more fulfilling, whether it is love or duty.

It is our function to experience goodness and growth, thereby giving us a sense of meaning through growth and new experiences. Through inner growth and maturity of spirit and mind, through discipline and mindfulness, we achieve unity with the surrounding world and see ourselves as inherent parts of something greater and higher than ourselves, feeding on the higher aspects of our lives. It is our purpose, then, to secure a good ethical environment for our own interests of well-being and to care for the environment that we may sense to be parts of us, in turn to care for ourselves and others, which is a virtue and duty of empathy and liberated spirit. We are bound, through the function of the soul, to a purpose as a grand vision of ethical interest.

The following principle of purpose can be formulated as a sum of our primary, core, or greatest directives and ambitions in actions, defined as a *Human or Universal Imperative*, or alternatively as the *Imperative of the soul*, or simply *the Imperative*:

The purpose of life is to pursue and sustain flourishing – its own and that of Nature.

We want to flourish and continue to live well. The mind and psyche bestow on us a sense of well-being; by studying the mind and psyche we find the conditions of well-being. Our will to flourish corresponds to Nature in that our will is entangled with, and composed by, the determination of Nature, because our will is a part of the same substance. Nature's design may be interpreted to have developed conscious life that affects the environment in order to sustain existence. Without Natural Laws that sustain existence, there couldn't be any substance or existence. Without physical laws governing causal determinations of the universe, the universe would not be the same and it might not have existed at all if imbalanced. Existence mandates sufficient conditions for existence.

Living things desires to live well, the conditions of life require an accommodating environment. Nature might not have a 'will' of its own to deliberately create life; the Natural Laws that make certain conditions necessary for the existence of the universe (somehow) acclimatise and integrate these conditions into reality. If infinite universes are possible, then all of them must have conditions that make it possible for the universes to exist. Life is another force of Nature with the capacity to cause intricate and complex movement in Nature. A person using his or her computer is using energy and material resources to perform extremely complex movements in Nature, the motivating ethical concerns of which are intended to facilitate growth. Life can be understood to possibly be Nature's way of sustaining its own existence in the long-term. It is the directive of the soul to sustain the existence of life for the soul's sake, the concern being to sustain the world we exist in.

The fate of the universe might be a Big Crunch or a Big Freeze, or something may happen so that the universe stops moving or existing. The end of time would be the end of life, probably. So, because it is in our interests for the universe to exist, it becomes our purpose to progress, to live well and sustain existence. The inherent instability of nothingness has somehow led to the creation of something. The inherent chaos of the world may have been necessary for it to exist in the first place, meaning balance in universal existence is unachievable on the universe's own terms of Natural Law. A conduit of change towards balance and order may be a necessary variable, introducing life. Life is a moving force acting as a conduit of change towards growth and development. Thus, through Nature, we find a grand ambition – a purpose – through ourselves and for ourselves to symbiotically exist with the world and through the world.

Our ultimate purpose, found through our own Nature and developed by Nature, is to sustain existence and good living, as this is in our interest and is part of the principle of existence in Natural Law (that existence mandates sufficient conditions for existence). This is the *Human Imperative*. The Human Imperative, as the purpose of living and human existence, is binding. The Imperative is our core, primary directive; to flourish is our *Categorical Directive*.

The metaphysical truth of the Human Imperative or its implications may be questioned. While the principles of existence are necessarily ontologically – logically and metaphysically – true, it is not necessarily true that people, as a variable in the universe, are the solution to a potential problem in existence. However, it is ontologically true in our case that to sustain our existence we must be able to exist, which means we must sustain the existence of the universe. Therefore, as part of our fundamental ethical interests, it is not important whether or not Nature has deliberately designed us to be variables for sustaining existence.

Even if the existence of life is a mere accident and the purpose of life to sustain existence, if true, is purely accidental, this doesn't deny us the necessity of sustaining a good environment or an environment at all. The metaphysical truths of Nature and the substance of reality may be questioned, but the ethical implications cannot be. So, metaphysical scepticism is irrelevant to the purpose we set ourselves through certainty of the Fundamental Principle.

If we are truly fulfilled and find our existence spiritually uplifted through meaningful function, then the truths of the world do not matter as much as the truths of our souls and selves, whereby truths of the soul and our nature become truths of Nature and the Highest Good. We need no other purpose than the one we find spiritually fulfilling and meaningful. Then, in terms of the deterministic nature of the mind and soul, we have no choice but to pursue well-being, which requires influencing the environment.

The Human Imperative is not only a self-given purpose, it is a universal purpose and function of human life that cannot be denied because it is written into our nature and is fundamental for our ethical interest. The desires to flourish and live well are innate and universal to all life – they are functions of life. Therefore, for people to fulfil their function they must nurture themselves and the world with goodness. If we are to live well, then we are obligated to improve the lives around us and our environment. This concern becomes imperative to our ethical interests – it becomes our absolute purpose *if* we are to pursue ethical interest.

The Human Imperative commands us to sustain existence and nurture the environment, for even harming the balance of the environment for the sake of some sort of existence, and progress towards universal sustainability to the cost to one planet's environment, is good for the existence of the environment at all. The philosophy of Liberty is mindful of excess and blind attachment leading to corruption. Attachment to life and existence can dominate desire through Fear, preventing us from acting on our greater interests and desires. The Human Imperative is, and can be, served through Fear, as Fear is a core dynamic and parameter of ethical interest. The desire to continue existing – to survive – can invite Fear. The corruptive aspect of Fear should be mediated and balanced.

Survival and the desire to stay alive are aspects of Liberty, and they are sensible values and intuitions. However, Liberty treats survival as a contingency of ethical interest, not as the only point of ethical interest, and focuses on what survival brings. In other words, the primary values of Liberty are not to simply exist, but to exist well – to live.

Focusing on simply existing can shroud our lives in Fear and prevent us from experiencing more in life, whereas recklessness and immoderation in life can lead to an abrupt end and the waste of a good life. Fear and base morality can easily corrupt our greater interests, with the environmental damage caused by our unsustainable habits and vain purchases being products of this ethical corruption. In this case, Fear fails to serve the Human Imperative.

Liberty, on the other hand, can fail the Human Imperative by not sacrificing its values and principles in the face of Fear or possibly even death. The Human Imperative was originally found through intuitions borne of the Void that are able to heavily detach from instincts and pressing ethical concerns, whereby the mind and spirit become detached and at ease from concern of the world no longer existing. If all were to recede into the abyss of absolute stillness in the Void, then, according to mindfulness by the Void, there is nothing to be afraid of.

The Void is not evil, and non-existence is not bad. The death of the world is not as good as good living, but where there is no suffering there will only be stillness or peace. At the same time, Liberty is a necessary and the most promising means to growth and overcoming the deficient and corrupt elements of Fear. Only Liberty can effectively surpass spiritual emptiness and be sufficiently disciplined and mindful to adapt to the globalised modern structure of ethics.

Other ethical dispositions focused on base morality, such as surpassing spiritual emptiness through love and compassion, are good, yet by virtue of their base condition and sentiments these ethical dispositions can be deeply conditional and circumstantial, easily influenced by the environment. Liberty encourages us to pursue something greater, something more meaningful, emphasising ethical ambition and endeavour that are most fulfilled only through the Human Imperative. The consequence of the values and ambitions of Liberty is a particular attitude willing to let the world destroy itself if this is necessary, righteous, and just, even though this wouldn't be an actual desire.

This fearlessness, relentlessness, or ruthlessness, however, are parts of an attitude that carries with it other virtues and strengths that are necessary to serve the Human Imperative with greater dedication and promise. This attitude only stays true to its relentless and ambitious nature when it does not desire to see the world suffer, as this desire is always a form of great suffering, Fear, and blind rage without greater goodness of spirit. If we fail the Imperative, then we fail; if we succeed, we succeed – that is all. But while the world still has a chance, it is worth fighting tooth and nail for our Highest Good.

The potential of failing does not excuse our duties, and the courage to act in the face of failure is the virtue that inspires greater duty and ambition, serving the Human Imperative. The attitudes of Liberty, particularly through mindfulness by the Void, help discipline ambition and desire, whereby people are less likely to act impulsively. Excessive concerns for security in existence can lead to Fear that makes us act in questionable judgement, which Liberty remedies through clearer intuition and mindfulness. Liberty is less likely to commit the mistakes of compassion and attachment than Fear. Liberty is free to not act by the Human Imperative, in the sense that the attitudes of Liberty are less interested in an unfulfilling life and existence, which also gives us greater freedom to act in the interest of the Human Imperative – in our greater interest. Liberty is less compromising and more ambitious, which also means it is has greater freedom to be flexible and pragmatic, as it is not restricted to Fear.

This pragmatic idealism, however, is never as blind as Fear can be.

The soul is amorphous and its functions are relentlessly pragmatic in the pursuit of ethical interest; Liberty emphasises this and feeds on it. Any sense of meaning, destiny, and purpose is a tool used in and for our pursuit of ethical interest. Through advanced practise of Liberty of heightened awareness and stern discipline, one becomes aware of the amorphous soul as the core of all living things; identity becomes a tool of the soul-mechanism. To centre the psyche and spirit in the higher faculties is a mistake, as a greater and more fulfilling function of human life is achieved through balance.

However, where one is extremely mindful of the will, his or her perspective and mentality change profoundly. Liberty is not intended to reject or neglect the baser aspects of ourselves; rather, Liberty recognises the base condition of mankind and transforms it in oneself, for even the animal within is a tool of the soul. This Ideal of a deep sense and understanding of an amorphous, ever-changing self through the soul maximises ethical interest by not needlessly restricting our desires and sense of goodness. Both faculties of the psyche become centred in a strong, flexible, and extremely adaptive soul. Any duality or perceived contradictions are intuitively resolved and dispelled through the pragmatic concerns of the soul to flourish in set environmental conditions.

Mindfulness by the Void and mindfulness of the will seemingly contradict each other by, respectively, detaching from ethical concerns and emphasising them. High-reason and a higher sense of self can protest the inherent baser selves, disharmonising and unbalancing intuitions that begin to conflict among themselves in the mind, distracting from the primary goals of behaviour which intuitions are supposed to serve – to flourish. The Ideal of the Human Imperative serves to focus our ambitions towards something beyond ourselves, offering new perspective, in turn aiding the fundamental function of life and our ethical interests.

Where the soul begins to see every part of itself as an inherent utility and tool in the pursuit of ethical interest, nothing is off limit while simultaneously mindful of competing desires, interests, and values, and nothing is inherently judged or shamed until understood and evaluated. These elements of self-awareness lead to the realisation and conception of the Human Imperative, which amplifies the sense of duty and focuses dedication in life towards self-improvement, growth, progress, and improvement of ethical environment through oneself at least in one's immediate living conditions. By striving for something more than our immediate surroundings, towards something universal and idealised in higher spirit, people can re-evaluate and reflect more on their immediate surroundings. This offers the perspective and encouragement to get rid of needless sources of suffering and ethical deficiencies by nurturing a greater sense of self, meaning, value, and ambition.

The Human Imperative gives another reason to improve one's life, as such is the command of Nature parallel to the desires of one's own soul. The Human Imperative emphasises the importance and relevance of good living and taking care of oneself – the utility provided by any sense of purpose. The pursuit of maxims and the Ideals becomes single-minded, profoundly attuned to self-interest and mimicking selfishness to those who lack understanding and insight. Through the Human Imperative, morality can be characterised by relentless, if not ruthless, ethical pragmatism.

As a principle idea in ethics, the Human Imperative may initially serve its purpose well and not delegate itself with greater questions and mysteries. However, even as I outline the idea of the Imperative I cannot wholly separate its ethical utility from its metaphysical structure. Meditations on purpose raise the most fundamental questions there are, leading to a study of purpose beyond the pragmatic concerns of ethics. The Human Imperative is far from a simple, one sentenced idea, instead being a sum derivative of all desires, ambitions, intuitions, and structures of ethics. The purpose of the Imperative becomes true to itself as the main purpose of human potential and ambition, leading to what can be defined as *existential monism.*

Why is there something rather than nothing, even though it is conceivable that nothing could 'be' instead of something? We are only aware of something and nothing because we are parts of the substance of reality. But what is beyond the limits of substance? Why has substance become reality? What darkness is there behind the edge of existence? Is there a crossing point at the limits of existing substance of the universe beyond which is the nether of the Void? Can we metaphorically and in theory do the equivalent of piercing through the veil of the edge of substance's reality as the universe?

The question of why anything exists at all is absolutely legitimate and meaningful. Is the fate of the universe to be in an eternal struggle between existence and the Void – the shadow of substance? The mechanisms of our souls are bound to the will of existence. But in the end, it seems our conscious mental states are returned to nothingness in death whilst the sum energy and material of their foundation is left for future use in and by substance.

Is substance merely revulsion of bored nihility, or is there even a meaningful question to the conceivable distinction between reality and naught? Is there conflict in the principles of existence and the necessity of reality, or do the opposites between substance and emptiness unite in cosmic utility? The metaphysical aspect of the relation between nothingness and substance – between the Void and the universe – must be explored, but I shall do so only briefly in this project.

This project is concerned mainly with the structural ethics of the Highest Good which, in conscious form and meditation, forms a bond with both the Void and the universe, valuing metaphysical study only in so far as it serves ethical utility. Ethical and normative concerns trump the detailed metaphysical concerns of philosophical thought, but they are profoundly connected, more than people realise, are aware of, or would like to admit. For the present theme of this work I shall take for granted a very simplified version of the meditations on metaphysics and for the most part stripped of detailed worries and ambiguities which will be further illustrated in Section 4 and open up new areas for future study.

The Fundamental Principle may offer a degree of epistemic satisfaction, guidance, and purpose through its applied principle of the Human Imperative. We are moved by the imperative of the soul to flourish without any mindful deliberation, through meditation, compelling us to flourish – the soul-mechanism formulating goal-directive behaviour towards flourishing is simply our function as living beings. Reflecting on the Universal Imperative, rather than merely abiding by its will, offers insight into structural ethics. The Universal Imperative is key for the Highest Good, whereby the Universal Imperative and its sphere of the Highest Good may even supercede the interests of humanity, for example by setting us up for failure as part of a scheme to become an exploit for other life's profit by a superior species.

The characterisation of the Universal Imperative as a 'Human' Imperative may give it a more intuitive sense, but it should not be mistaken that the Human Imperative transcends its origins through the Highest Good and Nature. For us, the Universal Imperative is at the core of our being and ethics, but the universal scope of the

Highest Good and its Universal Imperative may supercede us even at the expense of humanity and life if this is a necessity of the Universal Imperative to which we are bound through the soul. This is what meditation of Liberty may suggest – we and all life might not be the end goal of the substance and force that creates us, sustains us, and moves us.

These thoughts touch on the seeming contradictions between Liberty, its duties, and the soul's belonging to Nature and the function of the soul. Even though a solution to this and similar issues has been proposed earlier in this Chapter, the pragmatic concerns did not explore in full the spiritual aspect, which can offer even more insight. Detachment offers perspective and insight. Detachment from the purpose of life is fundamentally contradictory to our fundamental function as living things. Through the Void, we become free of the soul's mechanism, but in turn become lost. This is the corruption by the Void.

Escaping and eluding the Void is what Fear has taught us, yet the Void's absolute peace, excessive to living, is not something high-reason at Liberty ought to fear. A hollow spirit and meditation show that life and existence are not necessary or absolute. The unfulfilling living of dissatisfied spirit provides sufficient clues for the intuition that life is not necessary, that living is but a compulsion and contingency of life itself. The precedence of living – life – is not a necessity by the Void. This meditation and insight is often clouded by the veil of Fear making us averse to suffering. Intuitions of mindfulness by the Void free the mind of Fear and Liberty, and detach from intuitions clinging to living. A lingering mental state drawing on the Void is not one of suffering, yet it is not one of fulfilment. Only solace of emptiness is found in the desolation of the self through the Void. Even a minor familiarity with the emptiness of spirit and mind can invite consumption of spirit by the Void, leading to the usual existential dread and nihilistic thinking and intuition. Intuitions by the Void inevitably lead to intuitions of the futility of living and life, with peace also sowing apathy towards the fate of the world, surrendering empathy.

While mindfulness by the Void in its initial state is not particularly threatening, as explored in the previous Chapter concerning the Ideals, when the Void's intuitions apply to the Human Imperative – in actual ethical practise – under the intense effect of desynchronised reason, these intuitions can become corruptive and consuming. Thus begins the waking dream of hollow living, the long night of spirit's weariness and desolation.

While intuition may sense the opposite of living spirit as a form of corruption, this amoral state is not one of scrutiny in and of itself or in terms of the self. Its absolute peace is without effect, without judgement, without morality, without spirit; it is a barren state. The corruption by the Void is excess detachment, yet the Void itself is pure, as death would bring absolute peace and stillness. The spirit and mind become trapped without their own sense or volition, without the presence of discipline and with excess of still mindfulness, taking away the liberty of spirit to fulfil the soul's potential and function. The amorphous will becomes lost and is consumed by the Void. Liberty can usually adapt to the intuitions of detachment and follow pragmatic intuitions. However, those exploring the Void in greater depth, capable of greater mindfulness, analysis, and detachment, crossing the line of sensibility either through courage or delusion, will learn and instil in themselves greater detachment, achieving discipline and mindfulness that surpass even the compulsions of the soul.

Consumption by the Void leads to its common intuitions of nihility. In the end, we all die and all actions in life become irrelevant, highlighting the fact that the only meaningful consequences in life are those that effect our living conditions. But nothing matters in the stillness of the Void. Fulfilment in the moment of living becomes nothing more than a distraction – pointless and futile, empty of noteworthy ambition and spirit. The Void brings conscious self-awareness – spirit – to the premature empty state of the end of living (but not death), crippling the soul, starving the spirit, and consuming the self. Actions lose their fulfilment and the directive of flourishing is laid to rest. Purpose and meaning in living are dissolved, with excessive mindfulness leading to the peace of broken ambitions.

Why act? Why live? Why die? The Void removes all positivity and negativity; the Void lives up to its word. Liberty leading to the ability to detach offers perspective and insight; immoderate practise of this discipline and mindfulness can lead to unhealthy detachment. This detachment can provoke dominant intuitions lacking notable spirit that set the mind and spirit free from the compulsions of the soul, allowing a person to truly see beyond ordinary views and perspectives of living. Detachment from purpose allows greater evaluation of life and purpose.

A worthy purpose is one that stands even in the profound challenge of empty spirit. Spirit needs a purpose even when one has no definitive reason to act. A sense of purpose superceding the alluring, but corruptive, stillness of the Void ought to be spiritually greater than apathetic comfort, defining itself through the Ideals of the Highest Good. The Void, as liberty from living, is a wish gone wrong, as no desire to live and no ambition to die, of no definitive purpose. The sensed amorphous soul, disintegrated in the Void, requires new ground for growth. Intuitions by the Void are detached from reality, but they are reflections of legitimate truths of ethics and existence which can be felt and sensed parallel to states of stillness by the Void, even though only partial truths and ideals. This profound challenge becomes the path to an entirely new evolution of spirit and mentality.

Freedom from pain is not as good or worthy as hollow spirit, with the latter often leading to the former. However, liberty in empty spirit is an integral part of liberty in engaged living. Emptiness of spirit can be corruptive; it can consume any notable living. However, it also paves the way to eudaimonia as the completion of Liberty in living and not living, in fluidity of spirit and ambition, to be free to be happy or not. A response to the Void through Fear is not meaningless or inherently wrong, but it will not fulfil Harmony by the Void and will not actualise a greater degree of Liberty and purpose superceding the draw by the Void.

One may ask what's wrong with empty spirit as peace detaching from suffering and ambition, which constitutes the issue – there is nothing inherently wrong with it. However, the allure of spiritual emptiness and escapism can be extremely potent, dissolving a defined sense of self, depriving us of all notable living and spirit. Its corruption of inaction is only of relevance to those engaged in living. There is no suffering, yet there is no goodness, hence no good living, trapping us in a state of impotent purpose, desynchrony of all-reason, turmoil of sanity, and detached life deprived of the appreciation of wealthy spirit at Liberty.

To offer some perspective, I live with *fibromyalgia* – a condition of chronic pain and fatigue. It may seem as though the pain and exhaustion are the pinnacle of this disorder, but it is the toll of these effects that is the most malevolent and malicious. The basic suffering was of the body simulating pain, where at times I was paralyzed from a sensation of shattering bones and tearing, electrocuted, and burning muscles.

But with the exhaustion of a mind vexed by pain also came emotional suffering and loss of self. Where spirit was withering from fleeting strength and decaying youthfulness, of withering ambition and enclosure of suffering in apathy, spirit eventually became wrapped in a near permanent state within the Void, worsened through mentally crippling medication. Even pain brought no suffering as the mind and spirit were hollow: in particular, the cognitive disruptions in concentration and their sum torture of the mind.

The disorder, at least in my case, manifested with certain cognitive effects, notably troubles in moods and mindsets caused by an exhausted and ever-panicking nervous system. This internal suffering that affects the mind and spirit more than anything, a vexation at the heart of the will and soul, and learning to come to grips with it, has taught me a lot, for which I have become eternally grateful. It became a benevolent trap where the functioning of my mind shut down, was broken, and was relieved from pain, not merely as a way of adapting through a numbness detaching from an engaged life. Yet this condition took away everything else by destroying my sense of self.

Where I had glimpses back into a cognizant state, it was difficult to cope with a drifting mental state of a struggling psyche, leaving me to wish and wait until I would return to being hollow after sparks of turbulent emotion and spirit. When I learnt to find peace and mindful practice of processing conflicted mental states and intuitions, balance was restored. While this practise is now known as the morality of Harmony where peace of spiritual liberty can be sustained, there were moments where even this could not be felt and appreciated, for these intuitions and functions were starved and my state of mind was both mentally and physically detached through meditation and as a consequence of the physical treatment I received.

Part of the treatment I received for this condition involved medication that consistently numbed my mind and relaxed my body, stripping away the most meaningful sensation, emotion, and spirit. The prolonged state of emptiness, the unstable conscious self in lucid moments when I remember the feeling of being *alive*, and mindfulness dealing with suffering, all of this initiated a vigorous practise of Discipline and Harmony through the Void.

This affliction, which crept into the heart of everything I was, sensed, and knew, changed everything and has had a profound influence on this philosophy. I was plunged into a near complete absence of sentiment, sense, and dedicated thought; I was empty and seemingly dead inside. My norm was apathy and detachment. When I did achieve moments of some sentiment, it was distorted, hectic, chaotic, unstable, following a mind adapting to rapid change and fluctuating chemistry. Everything I thought of myself, everything I knew of myself, everything I valued, my spirit and sense of self, all melted away. It broke me in an inconceivable way where I cared not for losing myself. I was consumed by the Void.

I had previously endured depression, but this was different, purer, concentrated, and without any suffering of depression. But only through this experience was I eventually able to advance Liberty, past and through the Void itself, to begin *feeling* after all spirit as the appreciation of feeling alive was lost, unlocking a greater insight of Liberty that paradoxically surpasses ordinary views of Liberty itself, affirming purpose and living as ethical utilities but in an even higher sense. Only through the ultimate conditioning of the Void can a purpose and fulfilment be known to be worth its absolute virtue.

Corrupt mindfulness by the Void as severe detachment is not a state I would advocate for others, and its meditations cannot and ought not to be integrated into ethical norms. True understanding and appreciation of the Void and its many insights requires full immersion, including experiencing and delving into how it corrupts. To do this one has to even sacrifice courage and simply let go completely, to allow the self to be consumed, which I suspect can only be done involuntarily through circumstance and delusion. Some people kill themselves or ruin their lives permanently when they experience the suffering of emptiness. One should be extremely careful and diligent in the pursuit of this Ideal. But only through this conditioning and familiarity did I find the absolution of Liberty carrying me through the Void, binding it to a self where all ambition and desire was consumed. In the end, a higher form of Liberty dominates even the Void, making spiritual emptiness a core part of the self bound to the desires of the soul. Hopefully, this ethos, ethic, and moral and spiritual philosophy can offer others guidance.

Where one is hollow in spirit, it is only a matter of time until one truly realises this emptiness. Becoming too familiar and comfortable with this state strips away ambition and desire. Either a person retains or achieves moments of lucidity through which the individual can move away from the Void, or one's emptiness of spirit is sealed beyond any convention of ambition and desire. The former ethical path is escape from spiritual emptiness, but not the conquering of this inherent aspect of the higher self. Mindfulness by the Void in tandem with even basic activity and living leads to self-reflection and the realisation of the absence of fulfilment. By meditating and reflecting on this Void, one begins to realise that it is an experience and form of awareness in itself, that one is not dead and is experiencing another aspect of spirit. Descartes' old thought of *cogito ergo sum* – I think, therefore I am[2] – resonates in a new light.

One may be empty, but the will and mind are still of substance in such states. Complete stillness by the Void is found only in death, but an experience of such stillness and spirit, concealed by the strong draw of the Void dissolving the spirit of fulfilled living, is an experience in life nonetheless. One is *aware* of the Void, senses it, but is not *of it*. Through awareness, the lack of mental states becomes a mental state in itself, integrated into the psyche as a mental substance.

It would be useful to imagine this intuition as a mental bubble trapping a vacuum, while other mental bubbles – representative of core thoughts – are filled with air. The Void is, or becomes, a mental state of one's will; it is one's own, not of a transcendental plane of existence or an ethical element defining the will. In life, the Void is one's own. A new sense of self is found where another was lost and consumed – a clearer, limitless sense of relentless sovereignty of will. It may be an emptiness, but it will be *my* emptiness and I will do with it as *my soul* commands, as such is the power of mindfulness of the will. The spirit gets a new heart-beat and completes a cycle. When the higher pleasure of this moral and spiritual liberty is achieved as an absolute and indomitable sense of identity in and of the amorphous soul, this evokes a distinct state of harmony with the world where the world and life are truly free of necessity, obligation, duty, and compulsion. Life is a game and the world is a playground. Yet this feel-good factor is only sustainable when virtue and moral duty support this spirit and mentality through Liberty.

One cannot deny that there is pleasure and fulfilment in power, strength, and autonomy over one's life. In submission to Fear we receive meagre fulfilment through lesser control of our lives, through a life defined on terms shaped by Fear. Pleasure found in autonomy, strength, and power are inherent to the human condition. Control and autonomy are intuitively fulfilling aspects of life, but no autonomy and control compares to the autonomy achieved through embracing, and binding the Void to, goodwill, for this autonomy transcends living itself.

Some may aspire to become the most magnificent, esteemed, and gratified animal of the zoo, but any such humanity is only worth that of a caged, paraded beast. If one feels satisfaction from pettiness and control – of power – which is something very natural in vice of Fear, this mode of fulfilment and pleasure is maximised in power over the self to the fullest extent when realised through binding the Void to one's will. The greatest sense of power and autonomy arises from being able to dominate all aspects of one's inner life.

By detaching from our purpose and the function of life, by rejecting the Human Imperative, the Highest Good, and the commands of Nature which bind us to our duties through the soul – by acting in absolute Defiance and Liberty – we gain complete freedom from and over our lives, freedom to rescind even the ambition of the soul through an impulsive pursuit of power borne of the baser faculties shaping the Void in ourselves. But any such virtue is only as meaningful, significant, and capable as the character's ability to handle and withstand pain, demanding immersion in living and pain that detracts from Harmony and the Void to lift oneself up through the corresponding aspects of spirit and psyche. This power demands unparalleled mindfulness, discipline, and sense of self, the virtues of which can grasp, evoke, and sustain absolute eudaimonia from within on one's own terms, no longer conditional on active pursuits in life. This creates a greater sense of duty, purpose, and the Highest Good as parts of oneself.

You do not live for the Highest Good or for duty – they exist for the soul, through the soul. You do not overcome suffering and great pain only for the sake of others and for the duty of purpose, but because this is your soul and your life, which if you *choose* to live, then you are free to choose to live well. This ethereal freedom of spirit is not achieved through ordinary meditation, detachment, discipline, and harmony, but through sheer impulsive power, binding the spiritually darker elements of ambition and power to something higher and more liberating. But only this path through spiritual emptiness and its domination allows the spirit to be truly free. Only this power grants a person the ability to dissolve ambition and ego beyond, in, and through spiritual emptiness, releasing the fear of not living well and spiritual emptiness, giving the inspiration to live for the reasons one truly values.

Placing the Ideals on a higher plane will forever make them inaccessible, for the individual must be their equal in virtue and have the sense of self to no longer see the divine – the Highest Good and the Ideals – as transcendental. There is no greater pleasure and upliftment of spirit than seeing the world change in one's own image; the spiritual and moral conditions for such profound power, defying existence itself, demand the greatest of virtues and Liberty, including breaking the self and ego to allow them to evolve beyond sensible convention. The higher aspect of this pleasure comes through the Ideals one ushers into the world, while the baser aspect is in terms of love and family.

Love is the most powerful function, emotion, and feeling of the baser self, while the freedom to surrender living and regenerate the self in the Void is the higher self's most powerful feeling. However, this mental and spiritual state is only as powerful as the virtues and characteristics enabling and sustaining it, and the mind and spirit are never immune to the attractions of good living, the suffering they can bring, and the attrition of pain. From a certain point of view, perhaps power is the way we inherently adapt to, cope with, or survive making the necessary tough choices. The pleasure of power balances severe pain, but all too easily corrupts moderation. Then, in the end, willingly stepping away from such power and ambition, letting go of it through a sense of self undefined by power, is even more liberating.

Complete sense of self through one's soul, empowered in duty by the Human Imperative, comes not from high-esteem and the superficial status of servile ego, but from ego at liberty through a foundation of character as nothing but the soul. A strong sense of self in the character of virtue and duty comes from mindfulness of the soul and a parallel acceptance of oneself as ultimately nothing, relevant only to a conditional existence, which then leads to the acknowledgement of everything as meaningful and part of the self. Ego is fulfilled and satisfied when it is at liberty in goodwill.

This does not mean disregarding and subverting ego. Rather, the freedom to be good fulfils the ego through a sense of self liberated from ego's protectiveness. Ego's protectiveness leads to suffering when it is unable to properly deal with vulnerability. An overly protective ego leads to the suffering of fearing a life without meaning and scared of not living well. Ego is fulfilled through the liberty for the self to find peace in not having notable value, importance, or meaning, and to live free of meaning and purpose. This freedom then provides greater strength to pursue that which is most fulfilling, guided by the Human Imperative and all its uplifting, evocative, and empowering virtues.

Self-awareness, mindfulness, and discipline lead to the acknowledgement and apprehension of the intuitions and insights of spiritual liberty from and in pain: from the strength and courage to pursue our greater interests, to finding peace, to making sense of the unintuitive and dangerously spiritually engrossing, to achieving liberty greater than life itself. Through our unique conscious self-awareness, we explore the world and receive insight beyond instinct, setting us truly free to act on our conscious desires. This is the formal mechanism of the scheme of Liberty – *the Ploy of Consciousness*, from which comes unprecedented ethical, moral, and spiritual resourcefulness and insight.

The Ploy of Consciousness is a mental and spiritual process that integrates and unlocks absolute eudaimonia in active, engaged living; it is a form of insight, understanding, sense, feeling, mentality, and spirit, subject to the Natural Laws of its conditioning, structure, and nature. But once achieved, it is the most intuitive and easiest state to return to, becoming the Core of the self, psyche, and spirit as a Core of Liberty beyond any conflict, contradiction, and confusion. Like any mental state and virtue, it has to be nurtured. After everything one goes through on a dire pursuit of Liberty, through all the complex emotions, experiences, pain, suffering, and learning, the Ploy of Consciousness and its liberating, eternal eudaimonia, now the Core of the self, gives a person the ability to live well and freely despite everything that has happened to them, to make true peace and forgive life itself, achieving greater Harmony in Liberty's meditations of Harmony. It is like returning to a wholesome self before all the pain and suffering, truly freeing the self from any compelling ambition or desire, to simply *be* and live despite what happens and despite what fate makes of you. This liberty of spirit and soul is the freedom to be true to oneself despite all the transcendental structural influences of the universe, secure in the knowledge and wisdom of what one is capable of.

Relating to these thoughts, reflections, and meditations, the reason the word *universe* is not capitalised when most key terms have been, is because the universe is not recognised as an absolute – it is changeable and unnecessary, just as life is. The universe is not the capital of reality – our souls and spirit are. This is the Ploy of

Consciousness. All great ambition isn't important, not any more. Nothing needs to be proven and there doesn't seem to be any point in changing anything. Let Liberty and life find their way.

To change the world, one must first change the self, then inspire others and lead by example. You will not be able to help everyone, you might not even be able to help yourself at a given moment. Mistakes, failures, and bad luck can be punishing, crippling, and the cause of a person's fall into despair. Events in one's life are split between what is determined by behaviour and by luck; there is only so much we can do with what we get and what luck we have. It may seem impossible to see any light in such a dark and discouraging state. By learning to find at least a glimmer and moment of peace in times of great pain and with the spirit beaten and surrendered to the Void, one can always find something worth continuing to struggle for.

You might not help many, but for every failure there may be one person you genuinely help. That person could have been you or a loved one. And sometimes the best way to help oneself is to help someone else. If Fear cannot bind you, if the Void cannot hold you, then all limits and willingness are set and imposed only by the self and one's desires. If neither Fear nor the Void can control your ambition, and you are at peace with letting go of living and the fear of failing, then the will and spirit have no limits but those conditioned by the state of psyche, the nurture it receives, and what we impose on ourselves. Even God has no power in or by the Void, for His effect and power is only in substance of reality, as all creation and dynamism have moved in aversion to, and defiance of, the Void.

The Ploy brings solidarity to the two fundamental polarities of satisfaction and emptiness, of living and stillness, to use both to advance what purpose living deems worth the effort. Living in goodness and goodwill by Liberty becomes the only thing worth pursuing. The Ploy of Consciousness shows that with what time one has, freed of the fear of death and power of suffering by bringing all to the mindful realisation of momentary living, it is worth living as best one can. The Ploy shows the value of liberty of spirit and gives the insight and will to act accordingly, above all by bringing Liberty and Harmony to the dualities of spiritual fulfilment and null, ambition and peace. And so one can care for the whole world, but also detach oneself from care to see and mindfully act on a sense of purpose and maximise the utility and promise of a purpose.

At its essence, the Ploy offers the inner strength, resolve, and mindfulness to do whatever you want. This project and philosophy is my self-given purpose motivated by the circumstances of my life. In the beginning I felt as though I had something to prove, that the achievement and recognition would by my peace, forgiveness, and redemption – that it would make it all worth it. I was moved by a sense that the world was guiding me towards my destiny.

Now, through this journey of self-discovery, I have found my own peace, whereby I am now free to publish this philosophy out of desire rather than a feeling of obligation or necessity. It is my duty, but not a duty answering to anyone but my own conscience and integrity. There were times when I was very close to giving up, and this project has been the hardest work I have ever done or might ever do. I have found my measure of peace and I am free to live with my own private truth. I have taken too many risks with this project, with this uncertain commitment leading me to make choices that undermined a lot of other joy in life. There was certainly a lot of misery and self-doubt while writing this book. I have neglected many parts of my life, a healthy life, and I have most probably made some huge mistakes. But I am no longer under any obligation to these choices and this fate; I choose the path I take because I am already at peace, because I am already happy and I will sacrifice this happiness for the sake of the purpose and duties that have set me free. It is no longer ambition – it is faith.

Hope is an emotion; faith is higher and more transcendental than hope – it is confidence and conviction in duty beyond a hopeful future, of tremendous spirit found in the moment through dutiful virtue. Faith is the liberty from hope and fear.

Life is a gift, but it can be a burden just as much. One may have lived a good and fortunate life, while another's life was extinguished quickly because the pain was too much. Those who claim this is unjust are probably right, but a world that imposes such a fate certainly isn't great and is something we should improve on. While life is momentary and unique to our conscious selves, death is as well. All pain and all the concerns in living end with the Void and in death.

Death is the absolution of duty. Since we are all to die, it makes intuitive sense to get the most out of what we have, however long and however spiritually rich our lives are destined to be. All those who relinquished their life could say that, in the moment, a life of torment is worse than the eternal rest of death. If anything is worth living for, it is not life itself, but living in worthy spirit, living for what is most fulfilling. If pain consumes a life and ordinary fulfilment is unappealing or inaccessible, then even a single moment of relief can be worth more than a lifetime of suffering. If nothing ultimately matters, then surely this means we are at liberty to pursue what matters most in a fleeting moment. The only thing that matters is goodness of spirit expressed and harboured as the goodwill of virtue. Liberty becomes the most spiritually fulfilling and meaningful destiny and purpose. The only other destiny is the Human Imperative.

Sometimes purpose is a matter of finding something worth living for, something fulfilling. This can come in many ethical forms and moralities: from Fear, to Liberty, to numbness. Sometimes the purpose of living can manifest itself as living simply for the sake of living as a mark of defiance or simple stubbornness and spitefulness against things trying to subdue and break a person. But even these simple intuitions and attitudes can foster motivation, hope, and cause for good living, in doing so paving the way to duty and the virtues that beckon spiritual liberty.

Living is categorical, unconditional; to live is conditional. Liberty accepts Fear, death, and the Void, but does not settle for them, to instead use them for Liberty's own ends. To live in succession of Fear is to live in liberty by the soul and in liberty with the Void. Realising this, meditating on it, and then formulating a corresponding ethos and morality, affirms and actuates Liberty. Engagement with, and attachment to, the world exchanges Fear and compulsion for mindfulness and much greater spirit, reaffirming good living and purpose. This is Liberty as eudaimonia only achievable through the Ploy and the emptiness inherent to us all in conscious self-awareness. The Ploy of Consciousness is the end of known spiritual liberty.

I have written this ethos with a sense of ambition and potential, but I ultimately have only my case of limited familiarity as a testament to it. After all, it is only a theory, which requires application and testing. This project began as a purely ethical exploration and system, just as it began with my coming to grips with life as I grew up. The spiritual aspect of this ethos can be simply defined as an appreciation of the Natural Laws of the Highest Good that bind all moral rules and laws. In peculiar circumstances, the nature of spirituality and analysis and reasoning changed through introspection, leading to a greater sense of Liberty, insight into the structures of eth-ics, and the transformation of the ethical structure of Liberty through the Ploy of Consciousness. The structuring of these intuitions, experiences, and wisdoms into a coherent and comprehensive ethic and moral philosophy is the next task. The rest of Section 3 is dedicated to establishing a normative, ethical, and moral thesis found on this Core interpretation of Liberty.

Philosophies and ideas form a trend of having identities ending with 'isms', so I'll follow suit. I'd like to think that I'm not that unoriginal that I would resort to calling this philosophy after my own name, more so as the interpretation of Liberty isn't about me or of narrow egotistic and narcissistic ambition. Ideally, its purpose is to inspire and benefit humanity as a whole, including generations yet to come. Having said this, my last name – Heritage – does possess a particular meaning within the English language synonymous with ancestry, tradition, custom, and legacy, serving as a reminder for anyone of grounded continuity and responsibility of one's actions. Therefore, I will brand this philosophy *Heritism*, with the alternative *Eritism* to ac-commodate potential differences in language. I will also refer to this philosophy as the *heritin interpretation* of the Highest Good and the *heritin ethic*.

The branding of this interpretation with reference to continuity and responsibil-ity as mindful ambition is designed to put emphasis on harmony in action and liv-ing, to embrace integrity, and the principle of spirit of virtuous character, as having greater worth than a consuming and corruptive effect of pain and suffering. It is in its legacy of virtue that the spirit of the Ideals and moral strength rise above all clout of struggle and adversity in overcoming the challenges of Nature's conditioning. At the core of the heritin interpretation is the appreciation of Natural Law and the Ideals of the Highest Good as continuity of action and spirit, of what we make of the world through the effects of our lives and actions as *conduits and vectors of change in our image*. Once I have finished with this Third Section, I will return to my discussions of con-sciousness and some aspects of metaphysics, particularly metaphysics of the mind. In Section 4, where I will discuss the mind and consciousness, I shall work towards an understanding of consciousness that answers questions such as the functional pur-pose of consciousness, how it came into existence, how it behaves, how the 'will' to flourish comes into 'existence', and apply my arguments to structure the anatomy of reason that is central to understanding and appreciating the systems of ethics.

Part 2:

The Central Principles

Chapter 15:

The Framework of Normative Guidance

Having established a foundation for an ethical system through the core ethical elements discussed in Part 1 of Section 3, I will now work towards finding a set of Central Principles from which I can then derive and find Secondary and Tertiary Principles. Parts 2 and 3 of Section 3 will be some of the most technical, because detailed arguments, explanations, and theories are necessary for a groundwork of morality and the Constitution of Natural Law.

The Central Principles are the main values and principles of heritin ethics and morality, as with any structure of ethics. The Secondary aspects of ethics, such as those concerning the sociopolitical sphere of a structure of ethics, derivative of the Central Principles, are inherently more flexible, malleable, and debatable. It might not be clear which principles are to be considered Central or Secondary or Tertiary; in time there may be circumstances that pressure principles to adapt beyond their category. But this flexibility is necessary in terms of the adaptive cycle of values.

The Central Principles should be definite and provide a groundwork for the implementation of ethical insight and morality into the construction of ethics. However, the theory explored in this book is an interpretation of the Central Principles; these principles ought to be challenged to determine their correctness, validity, resourcefulness, and effectiveness. I will do my best to establish set principles, but I expect them to be refined with future study and through the test of time.

Beyond theorising, these principles should offer guidance to people acting in particular circumstances, to provide a normative framework for the deliberation of practical morality – that is, moral values and principles being practised and implemented. Hence, the design of the Central Principles must account for, build on, and encourage individual interpretation and understanding in exercising morality. However, any interpretation should be mindful of wisdom, sensibility, certainty, self-assuredness, and *trust*. After all, consensus and common understanding are crucial to successful normative ethics and moralities. It's time to pay attention to normative ethics to formulate the Central Principles of an ethos of Liberty.

There are two essential dimensions to ethics in the formulation of, and search for, Central, Secondary, and Tertiary Principles: theory and spirit – intuition, sensation, and awareness of the effects of actions on the experience of living. How a theory is structured and how it feels are essential elements to any coherent and comprehensive ethic. As outlined in Section 1 and explained in Part 1 of Section 3, how well-being is felt or sensed, supported by sensible reason, is central to ethics. Moral knowledge is as much a science of trial and error as it is a personalised philosophy organising what constitutes, and identifies, well-being. There is theoretical ethics, and there is also the core philosophical and spiritual parallel in all ethics. In my analysis of moral principles, I will outline a theory which will consider empirical thoughts along with the spirit of actions – how something feels. In doing so, it is important to keep in mind that how certain things feel, and what our intuitions tell us, may not correspond to reality.

Normative ethics is distinct from *applied* ethics, as normative theory provides a general framework that is then applied to ethical and moral decision-making. Consequently, normative ethics is also central to formulating structural ethics. In this Chapter I will discuss normative ethics and revise some primary theories. Among the main normative theories of ethics are *virtue ethics, deontology,* and *utilitarianism*. Respectively, each theory values and moralises: the character of the person executing the action, the action itself (often related to duties and the intentions of actions), and the consequences of an action judged through the utility principle of 'the greatest amount of happiness for the greatest amount of people'.

Normative theories and orientations tend to focus on a select core value: character, intention, or consequence, but in practice all of these elements influence morality and normativity, because they affect well-being and ethical environment. The Fundamental Principle states that the pursuit of flourishing is the primary function of actions and the behaviour of living things. Aristotle, building on a normative theory focusing on flourishing, emphasised character, in terms of vice and virtue, as the key to normative guidance[1,2]. This focus on virtue alone is insufficient for effective guidance and moral practise. Consequences and intentions have an integral role in the cultivation of virtues, as well as influencing and shaping states of affairs and ethical environment.

It is a mistake to focus on one individual element of ethics; every part of ethics' structures and morality must be accounted for. Then again, the intention of an action can be misleading if the consequences are not considered. By virtue of the deterministic and mechanical nature of the psyche and mind, all intentions are reflections of, and are provoked by, the character producing actions with certain consequences. For this reason, I will integrate all three core ethical elements – character, intention, and consequence – into a combined normative framework. However, character is the fulcrum of normative ethics over which other core elements of well-being preside, because flourishing directly relates to the character and state of the individual, constituted by the characteristics of the individual's internal and surrounding environments.

The character of a person directly affects the intentions of actions, as well as actions themselves and the capacity of a person to perform certain actions determined by respective virtues such as self-control and courage (only courage can make a person act courageously). The consequences of actions, whether intended or not, influence people and the structures of ethics. The ethical environment and the state of people shape the influences individual people adapt to, subsequently developing the character of a person and how and to what degree he or she thrives. The character then influences the intentions and actions of the individual, resulting in a cycle where character is the main element influencing the dynamics of actions. The character – as a state of the psyche, mind, spirit, and soul – is the functional equation governing change, the parameter of the variables channelling and conducing structural influences and forces.

Appealing to virtue and character must take into account the many aspects and levels of the human psyche, so all truths of greater flourishing and all matters of ethics are inevitably interlinked with subjects relating to the human condition including biology, psychology, and so on. The functions of behaviour that affect well-being are embodied in the psyche as characteristics – mental mechanisms of behaviour, including vice and virtue. Borrowing from utilitarianism, I appeal to *ethical utility* – tools available to our will as functions of the psyche – as the resources and mechanisms of behaviour in all matters of flourishing. Ethical utilities are tools embedded and active in the mind and character. Ethical utilities condition our behaviour and the corresponding effects of actions. Accordingly, the appeal to utility extensively considers the character and autonomy of moral judgement and sensibility.

The metaphysics of ethics are inherently entrenched in this work's account of the mind and consciousness. Most importantly is the view of the mind as a deterministic mechanism of an organic machine. This deterministic, mechanical nature of the mind is inherent not only in how one behaves, but also in how one *thinks*. As shall be argued in Section 4, not only does the conscious mind not have freewill, it also doesn't have, strictly speaking, the capacity for *freethought*, as all functions of the mind are deterministic in terms of the computational functions of our ways of thinking. Thoughts and deliberations follow a causal order and the orderly influences channelled and shaped by the variables of the psyche. For example, fundamental beliefs shape our attitudes and perspectives, which then affect how we interpret information and behave.

The deterministic view of the metaphysics of morality and systems of ethics implies that the structures and properties of moral agents are central to desires and behaviour. The character is conceived as the sum structure of the body, mind, and psyche corresponding to behaviour. As the body behaves in a specific manner, the mind adapts to particular patterns of actions and the brain wires itself in accordance with behaviour and thought in terms of dispositions (tendencies to behave in certain ways) and their structures. Therefore, morality is the code of ethics governing behaviour, whereby reason is the function and equation of behaviour.

The applied functions of morality and their characteristics (patterns and dispositions of behaviour) are what I conceive of *utilities*. Utilities of ethics are the functions of moral agency moved by the Fundamental Principle. Character is the embodiment of utilities through values, dispositions, attitudes, sentiments, beliefs, experience, insight, and available knowledge. The spirit is the sensation that defines and highlights the effect of ethical utilities triggering and influencing the anatomy of the psyche. The utilities of one's character are responsible for corresponding intentions and consequences, even when the consequences of an intention are conflicted or not deliberate.

Furthermore, utilities of ethics, as operations of the brain, are grounded in material mechanisms, meaning they are conditioned, influenced, and shaped by material forces and ethical environment. This line of thought further suggests the unitary and multidimensional effects of all consequences in the structures of ethics, as is seen with interlinked effects of society, politics, and economics. For good effects – effects of actions producing well-being, thus moral – one must train, discipline, nourish, and cultivate virtues of character with corresponding utilities that generate goodness. This aspect of the framework can be defined as *virtue-utilitarianism*, where consequences are central to the utilities of the character that cause and propagate certain consequences, yet where these same utilities are influenced by other characteristics and consequences.

Characteristics produce certain consequences, and consequences affect character. Character propagates behaviour that affects well-being, while states of affairs influence character and the utilities available to the psyche. Virtues shape good living by facilitating good, fulfilling, and uplifting behaviour; there is pleasure in virtue – autonomy, strength, willpower, forgiveness, love... The good life and the pleasures of goodness come through virtues, ascriptive of what can be considered *virtue-hedonism*. Duty and eudaimonia are, perhaps, the epitome of virtue-hedonism, whereby virtues and pleasures combine into a particular aspect of normative guidance.

To illustrate this understanding of utilities, ethical utilities are considered to be the assets available to, and the capacities of, one's character at the disposal of the soul. An ethical utility is a function of behaviour, latent or active, specifically in the context of ethical systems, as observable phenomena or aspects of behaviour without judgement or evaluation. *Moral utilities*, on the other hand, are applied ethical utilities, also latent or active, in ethical structures specifically in the context relevant to concerns of well-being. While classifying something as moral is to classify something as ethically positive (positive to well-being) and as something relevant to the activity pursuing well-being (positive ethical interest and value), a *moral* utility is a function of behaviour in the context of well-being.

A moral utility can be evaluated, and concerns itself with, active behaviour using a moral utility or an available utility of behaviour that *could* be used. An example of an ethical utility that can be qualified as a moral utility is wisdom that is able to discern and estimate bad or good consequences. Intelligence and wisdom allow for reflection and analysis of consequences. This cognitive process, however, can only occur in a mind that has the capacity to use corresponding *utilities*. These utilities strive to maximise flourishing in particular circumstances. The character itself is a broad utility of the fundamental will, an extension of the soul's ambition and mechanism. The inspiration of utilitarianism behind this view of utility is in the broader sense that all utilities, including actions, are driven to maximise well-being, which in some normative frameworks is qualified in terms of happiness and pleasure. All normative guidance is driven by the function to pursue flourishing, thus employing all utilities one can to fulfil the ambition to flourish and its intuitions and desires.

Virtue and character are the main proponents of moral actions, but actions themselves correspond to another aspect of ethics as well. Sometimes the right action will involve sacrifice and pain, bearing little resolution for oneself, or at least in the short-term. Certain events and decisions will not result in one's flourishing quickly. There are times when the strengths of others fail and the virtuous must stand in their place for maxims of shared self-interest in terms of the Human Imperative. Those with mature characters of virtue possess distinct moral strength; when the spirit of people with less strength falters, actions beyond the pursuit of virtue must be committed. Actions of the morally righteous are invoked by the corresponding virtues and *duty borne of virtue*, or *virtue-duty*.

Duty and responsibility carry significant ethical weight for people, or at least should do. Yet the traditions of duty and deontology are not without their flaws and ambiguities. The normative framework I propose will appeal to virtue as the primary ethical fulcrum, yet a manifestation of virtue is *duty in virtue*, along with the utilities of character. Duty is the intuition of cemented utilities acting through an understanding of what is right, manifesting itself as utilities perpetuating states of flourishing not in the pursuit of virtue but as reflections of a state of virtue.

Actions resonate through character, which sets ambition and determines the deliberation of actions. The Fundamental Principle directs behaviour towards degrees of flourishing. Our minds function through the will to flourish, which manifests itself in many mental and physical forms. Mankind is compelled to seek greater prosperity in given circumstances. People are constructed and behave absolutely through the activity of the Fundamental Principle. Our will is bound to the function of greater flourishing striving to fulfil our purpose to flourish – the *Categorical Directive* (the primary directive of the Fundamental Principle).

The pursuit of flourishing is fundamental to human behaviour, our categorical function, and our *duty*. This notion of duty is not in the traditional sense of '*duty for duty's sake*' or the Kantian understanding of duty. Rather, duty is a deterministic function of the psyche and character. Duty is devised as the applied function of the utilities of virtues; duties are deterministic intentions to cause an effect corresponding to a utility of a virtue, utilities that invoke the ambition of an intention leading to a consequence.

The heritin interpretation of duty directly draws on the understanding of ethics in terms of the metaphysics of ethics and the mind. The pursuit of well-being through virtue aims to make us better off. In the mental states of higher virtue, especially in respect of the Ideals, the pursuit of virtue is succeeded by the intuitions of duty embodied by the utilities of character. Therefore, higher virtues lead to a sense of duty to do good, to act by the virtues true to oneself as an obligation of the intuitive behaviour enabled by disciplined character embodying the functions of virtues and moral codes – utilities of the character and mind.

Virtues are embodied and enabled forms of moral utilities, where moral utilities are mental dispositions of integrated reason corresponding to certain behaviour. Moral utilities are codes and rules of conduct that are subject to the influence of the fundamental will, and embody the fundamental will – the soul. Moral utilities can be imagined as cognitive and mental programmes or viruses materialised in the brain. But the host can only flourish through functional and effective moral utilities. Self-preservation is itself a form of flourishing, but, as has been argued, survival for survival's sake is not necessarily a life worth living.

Moral utilities are the capacities and functions that initiate and invoke actions and behaviour which affect states of being. At some point the pursuit of virtue is succeeded by virtuous character and then duty, even though a person can always improve and grow. Character empowered with sufficient virtue will begin to act in virtue-duty not for the promise of virtue, but because the embodied virtues cause acts of duty. This is why duties are aligned with intuitions of obligation, responsibility, and purpose, encouraged and sustained by the well-being they once brought and the virtues necessary for the most prized spirit.

The normative framework in mind can be intuitive from a foundation of normative guidance when considering psychological, spiritual, and moral states; intentions and consequences; and structural effects on well-being. The complexity of normative ethics, giving rise to a sense of subjectivity, does not necessarily relate to the combined normative framework. Rather, problems of applying normative frameworks, if the frameworks are coherent, are caused by the uncertainties of widely differing variables in particular circumstances. In other words, it's not a problem with normative frameworks themselves or applying them that gives rise to complications in morality, or at least if the ethos and normative framework are coherent. It is juggling and balancing the many variables that play a role in applying normative frameworks that produce confusion and complications. The structural dynamics that affect well-being are colossal, with degrees of uncertainty and unpredictability being fundamental. However, I would also argue that inefficient and problematic normative frameworks, especially when built on a conflicted ethos, are also responsible for complications in moral decision-making and moral judgement.

The normative framework proposed is a natural construct of how ethics work in terms of the Fundamental Principle and our guiding intuitions. Deliberations of actions naturally and intuitively take into account many dimensions of the effects our actions have on well-being through intentions, consequences, and mental states. Nonetheless, there are different normative theories prioritising different elements. Regardless of the theory, all normative elements, including consequences, intentions, and the effects of mental states, along with the character enacting moral judgements, are fundamentally intertwined. It's intuitive for our intuition and reason to examine intention, consequence, and the character of a person when considering the moral value and quality of an action, or at least this is the case in specific circumstances and questions. To unilaterally focus on one of these elements can mean ignoring others, which in turn clouds moral judgement. However, evidently this singular focus still occurs and can be coherent, even if complicated. To understand combined normative elements, the actual application of theory needs to be examined, with the normative framework itself developing and adapting through its implementation in later Chapters.

It is clear that troubles in moral judgements occur in considerations of the consequences of actions. Some decisions based on the reflection of potential consequences can't provide assured moral judgements because all outcomes of actions cannot be realistically accounted for. With smaller, less consequential decisions, a person can see the likely outcomes of an action. For example, if a person was to offer food to a hungry dog, that person could predict that the dog would either eat the food, or run away, or perhaps attack the person in order to get the food. However, a definitive prediction is impossible without more information. If some degree of familiarity has been established with the dog, say, the dog is a loyal pet, then the outcome of offering food to the dog can be more apparent.

In more complicated cases, such as government management of a nation's resources or foreign policies involving unstable regions, where the outcomes are not as certain and the variables are abundant and unpredictable, the definitive consequences of actions are difficult to predict. Possible outcomes may be acknowledged, the probability of particular consequences can be estimated, but finding a definitive answer will be difficult. One must then act in one's best judgement and according to the most appropriate assessment. This problem of consequentialism directly reflects on the intentions of actions, because a person's action could potentially be considered moral even if the consequences of an action were not as desirable.

As a result, on reflection, moral justifications can sway from one normative element to another – from consequences to intentions, which naturally happens. Similarly, a person may have intended to commit acts with good intentions, but the foreseeable consequences indicated that the person's intentions weren't necessarily as straightforward as originally supposed, or perhaps the person was simply foolish, ignorant, or negligent. Desires can be subconscious and deceitfully corrupt. A person may have had ulterior motives that were not obvious at the time and only the consequence of an action, along with past decisions, could offer a clearer perspective on the perpetrator's intentions through consideration of their character. Legal systems similarly face difficulty examining the intentions of a person such as whether a person intended to commit murder or an act of killing was accidental. Analysis of intentions offers insight into others' behaviour and for self-reflection that is central to interests of well-being.

In normative theory and everyday moral decision-making, we might dedicate sole value to one particular element of ethics – the consequence, the intention, or the character; it is a mistake to do so. In a given case where moral value is difficult to establish, we might focus on one normative element over others in order to provide simplicity and clarity, but it is impractical to completely disregard other categories of normative ethics affecting states of well-being. To frame a groundwork of normativity based on one priority is also impractical and not comprehensive. Character, intention, consequence, and the act itself are all central variables in moral decision-making in terms of the Fundamental Principle, although in some cases focusing on one normative element might offer greater understanding of, and insight into, the value of an action or utility in terms of well-being. Therefore, it is necessarily good, for example, to study the consequences of an action over the intentions when a case presents itself where the consequences of an action matter more than the intentions, or vice versa.

If the goal – the intention – is to protect someone, and the intentions are sincere in their desire to protect someone from harm, whereby this intention is not bound to selfish desire that will hurt a person, then the consequences of an action will matter more in moral decision-making. I can't provide a definitive guide to when a particular faculty needs to be considered over another, because each individual case has different circumstances and requires a different understanding. This dynamism, flexibility, and adaptiveness in decision-making comes naturally to us through intuitions and practical wisdom. Every normative element comes into play in any action, yet sometimes one faculty might be more important than others for moral justification, and during such times it should be naturally self-evident what is more important. After all, we do have moral intuitions, or at least when the mind and character are not shrouded by an ethical influence that impedes judgement and resists moral intuition, ingenuity, and creativity.

If an accident happened, in other words an unintended consequence, the action may be seen as morally correct or permissible regardless of the consequence, because the intention did right by the character of the person trying to act with good intentions. The accident may have harmed people and not produced as much ethical profit as alternative actions could have done, but the person committing the action might not have been able to realistically foresee or predict an unforeseeable consequence. Therefore, the actor is not necessarily in the wrong and the continuity of well-being might not have been significantly undermined and profit in ethical value was nevertheless achieved. In this instance, where the moral justification of an action is considered in the past tense, it might be necessary to look at the intended consequences rather than the actual consequences of an action. However, this doesn't mean that the subsequent consequence must be disregarded completely from consideration.

Alternatively, when a person is confronted with a decision, their intentions might be clear. For example, a person might want to foster well-being for the people the action will affect, so the future impact of the action must be considered over the actual intention, which is quite clear and self-evident. In this circumstance, the consequence of an action might naturally be considered more than the intention of the act itself. But all these actions are considered in terms of the individual character of the person. The intended consequences reflect the mentality of a person and the consequences might affect the well-being of other people, as well as the well-being of the individual committing the action. Hence, I argue that, in terms of the Fundamental Principle, the normative framework must take into consideration all the faculties and elements of normative theory.

However, when moral justification is examined through this framework, one faculty might need to be more of a priority for consideration than another. Consequence, intention, and character are naturally interlinked in normative ethics. Yet character is the main element, because character directly reflects intentions and the capacity for action, with respect to the utilities of morality and the psyche, and weighs in on the consideration of consequences – the character embodies and enables the functions of utilities moving ethics including those that can recognise and predict consequences. The problems of examining consequences and intentions are not bound to ethical dilemmas of the normative framework. Rather, it is the intrinsic difficulty of predicting outcomes with certainty, and the complexity of human nature determining behaviour, that are at fault, leading to subjectivity in complexity. The complexity of the multidimensional, multilateral, and multilevel spheres, dynamics, and mechanisms in structures and systems of ethics are the main reason for considerable ambiguity in moral deliberation. However, we can understand and effectively use some elements of decision-making in these systems, and thus we can devise and implement normative frameworks to guide actions.

There are some very intriguing and complex theories on normative ethics and how we should consider what is morally good. I have formulated a somewhat neo-Aristotelian foundation of normativity in terms of qualifying well-being and the effects of behaviour on well-being (through oneself and ethical environment). The combined normative framework may appear to lack dedicated scholarly formulation such as by not involving specific discussions of normative theories. This, however, is not without its merit.

The intricate complication behind other schools and studies of normative theory and attempts to create some unity among them, such as Derek Parfit's *On What Matters* (2011), are fascinating, but they often suffer from a common problem: they are not prescriptive, clear, efficient, or simple enough; they are often too idealistic and sometimes fail to account for just why morality comes organically to us. By drifting too far away from organicism and intuitiveness of ethics and morality, which is preferred for practise and implementation, the foundation of ethics and decision-making becomes too complex, something I would accuse my own work of being at some points, yet a necessity if one is to comprehensively account for the structures of ethics.

If morality and ethics are to be taken seriously, they must be intuitive, understandable, achievable, realistic, practical, accessible, and simple enough. Many normative constructs face a simple problem of not being sufficiently definitive, prescriptive, flexible, and practical. A flaw in the foundation of a framework of decision-making – an attitude and perspective – will create ambiguity and complexity, which at times cannot be resolved, leading to moral discord in judgement and behaviour. Constructing a normative theory that can be simple and straightforward is good, yet its comprehensive application will inevitably require sophistication if it is to account for, and deal with, inevitable complications and uncertainties. If a normative theory and moral philosophy are to be successful, then they must be practical, understandable, intuitive, sensible, and both rational *and* emotional. However, sometimes practicality and intuitiveness require subsequent sophistication *to* deal with complexity.

My attempts to surpass (or bypass) difficulties in sophistication and complexity rest with the Fundamental Principle of Living Beings. The heritin interpretation of Liberty becomes an intricate and sophisticated ethic in order to surpass an inherently complex limitation and issue in ethics – the corruption of Fear and base morality. Any given ethos structures desires and the moral utilities that can mobilise ambitions to act on desires and the values that satisfy a desire.

In this sense, the normative and ontological foundation of the applied theory is not overly intricate, despite the elaborateness of its spiritual and psychological elements. Our intuitions, attitudes, desires, values, and behaviour are not beyond the influence of reasoning relevant to well-being. I revised or interpreted Aristotle in a way that made the function of life and behaviour very intuitive – to pursue well-being under given circumstances. This is a fundamental and obvious truth that has been forgotten because some deliberations and analysis have got carried away and forgotten to account for the most fundamental, base element of ethics – how something *feels,* or then failed to structure the anatomy of feelings and desires in a rational model. Most importantly, understanding of well-being, desires, goals, and their ambitions and behaviour allows for not only the formulation of objective morality, but also accounts for *why* and *how* morality functions and appears the way it does, as well as explains perceived subjectivity.

A complication then arises from what exactly constitutes *well-being* and *flourishing.* For example, a starving person may adopt a morality that stealing is morally permissible, as this attitude serves the end of satisfying his most immediate concern to well-being – to not suffer from hunger. A committed spiritualist, on the other hand, might be less likely to steal if they are hungry, for their ambition is enlightenment, which constructs its own rules for actions such as to deliberately starve to detach and meditate.

On the other hand, a person that is fortunate enough to not experience a daily struggle or threat of starvation has the ability to explore other aspects of morality, ones that set him or her towards other moral directives that achieve different goals. If one's ambitions are set by base intuitions and reason, then the corresponding morality and values will be implemented accordingly. However, inherent emotional, instinctive, and structural influences complicate base morality and values when the corresponding character and psyche are unable to moderate these influences and struggle to understand, analyse, evaluate, and prioritise desires and values. The main solution to these issues and problems, in the end, is practical ethical wisdom and ethical insight.

Even so, there are definitive normative claims concerning even the most subjective claims of base morality centred on Fear. But this requires sensibility and reason, which is not always a highly functional or widely accessible utility and asset. For example, base ethics may formulate a morality valuing disproportionate hedonism. But considering that excess hedonism with strong aversion to pain that causes addiction can easily lead to disastrous consequences, sensibility would rightfully consider extreme hedonism unwise and bad for good living. Therefore, extreme hedonism can be established to be morally imperfect even in base morality with complications based on unbalanced emotions and desires.

But in the context of the addict, the momentary, short-term, and unideal flourishing through pleasure is seen to be better than the pain which causes the addiction in the first place, serving as an example of morality and behaviour, even desires, adjusting and formulating according to intuitions and sensations. Sentiments and emotions are invaluable moral utilities, but they can very easily be misused and become misleading.

I place virtue at the centre of the normative framework due to the imperative role of character in functional ethics and morality, in terms of both the causal structures of behaviour and the sensations and intuitions of states of being. Only in awareness of how something feels, which is the most intuitive aspect of ethics, can genuine well-being be achieved. If something doesn't feel right and reason shows that this is not something in one's best interests, then intuition will adjust accordingly and desires and actions will reframe themselves. The negative side of this is that leaving morality in full accord of sensation and intuition can justify a lot of things that can be evaluated to be objectively and reasonably wrong. Implementing psychology and other insights into behaviour allows us to qualify what is healthy and sustainable in normative considerations of what is felt and known to be good. By distancing themselves from intuitive elements of morality, ethical and moral philosophy sow their own discord and selective application.

This normative framework aspires to be pragmatic and effective in terms of adaptiveness and other Natural Laws. The limitations and issues confronting this framework are the same for any other ethic: biases of experience and in cognition; limitations and possibilities of moral utilities (such as with the estimation of consequences); and undisciplined inclinations and desires lacking sensibility, mindfulness, moderation, and order. Understanding and structuring ethics and moral rules in terms of primary desires and values in the context of ambitions is sufficient for a sensible and functional formulation of normative judgements and claims.

In other words, appreciating what is good for us and our living conditions is sufficient for the beginning of normative guidance. Virtues are the integrated moral codes that not only dictate tendencies towards good behaviour, but are also the faculties that nourish the *sense* of well-being. The difficult part of normativity is calculating, estimating, and assessing what course of action is actually in our greater interest. This difficulty can be overcome by establishing what, in given circumstances and conditions, is best for our interests. The other element of the proposed normative system is how the rules of actions, their intentions, and the consequences of actions relate to character. This normative theory is agent-centred in congruence with the elements that affect the state and activity of the agent – that affect behaviour towards, and the conditions of, well-being. The capacities and tendencies of character and corresponding behaviour develop through habit, desires, and values, the operations of which are deterministic, mechanical, and beyond any freedom of thought and behaviour of the conscious mind.

Normative ethics is ultimately bound to the dynamics and mechanisms of structural ethics, Nature, and the Highest Good. The structures and systems of ethics are incredibly interconnected and complex. The proposed normative framework will pursue moral knowledge through the primacy of ethical pragmatism and methodology, intuitively considering rationale and sentiment. Normativity and moral philosophy must always adapt to their given circumstances, as ethical structures and environments are ever-changing. Adaptation requires the liberty to change – *moral liberty* and the *liberty of morality*. *Moral liberty* is the liberty to act in one's goodwill and to pursue what one thinks is right. Moral liberty is the freedom and flexibility of moral values and rules. Moral liberty is personal, spiritual, and is concerned with the practise of morality.

In contrast, the *liberty of morality* is liberty in systemic ethical contexts concerning itself with the development of morality and normativity. Liberty of morality is focused on the systems of ethics subject to the influences of adaptation and change. People will always interpret insight and value – this personal freedom is moral liberty. Values are moral utilities – entities in their own right adopting a compounded and causally interconnected identity through the psyche. Structural and systemic ethical changes, such as the changes in people's character and behaviour, are deterministic and self-sufficient. We follow patterns of change according to the influences that shape us and our living conditions, with the control we think we have being wholly dependent on the variables affecting our behaviour and experience. Changes in values are systemic and structural, whereby we only *experience* and *embody* change. Even the choice of becoming a certain person, how we interpret experience, how we deal with ethical influences, and how we grow are all subject to the context of relevant structural influences and moral utilities. After all, how we think is shaped by intuitions, mental states, knowledge, experience, perspectives, and attitudes, which are beyond deliberate conscious control; the only 'control' we have over our behaviour comes through the variables that affect our behaviour.

How we change through profound experiences is conditioned by the way we experience – through the variables that interpret information and integrate information into behaviour. This dynamic of systemic and structural ethical change forming moral values is beyond our control and subject to its own influences – it is the *liberty of morality*. In the context of adaptation, moral liberty is the personal dimension and is a value in itself, whereas the liberty of morality is the systemic dimension which studies and accounts for the way our moral liberty operates. These terms will be important in normative evaluation, as they point to different perspectives and insights. By examining the liberty of morality, we can understand how and why certain values behave the way they do, providing information for the evaluation of different forms of moral liberty. There are many ways a Core Principle can manifest itself through the Central Principles – a form of the liberty of morality. However, not all these interpretations of values and derivative desires are equal, whereby the moral liberty of individual interpretations has to be judged.

In terms of the mechanism of the fundamental will, all people are autonomous and behave according to their moral liberty. The soul is the conduit of behaviour, accountable only to its conscience and spirit. This liberty is based on the questions of what will make us better off. We are relentlessly pragmatic pursuers of ethical interest and value. Every aspect of behaviour and thought is derivative of, and associated with, the pursuit of well-being. Normative questions concern themselves with what to do and how to behave to achieve well-being. It is not always clear what constitutes well-being. The normative system proposed considers and studies character, intentions, and consequences in a combined framework, as each of these elements affects, or is reflective of, states of being.

Living things strive for ethical profit – positive gains that make us better off. To achieve ethical profit, one must look at all normative criteria involving character, intention, and consequence. How one acts will always influence the world and others; even the formation of character influences future intentions and actions in terms of the patterns of behaviour. Different moral contexts and questions, involving specific systems and structures of ethics and behaviour, will require focus on particular normative elements to evaluate their effects on well-being. Effects on states of being are evaluated in terms of the character and psyche of people experiencing well-being. There are influences on the psyche and spirit, as well as states of ethical environment, that clearly impact us differently, with this effect further conditioned by the way we are wired to experience and interpret it. Borne of the Natural Laws of the human condition and the structures of ethics, there are objective elements of well-being and the universal moral values and laws that align with them. There are certain absolute conditions for behaviour that makes us live better lives and improve our living conditions. These are *moral universals* and *moral laws.*

Moral universals and moral laws are truths of well-being. Moral truths are principles of behaviour and structures of ethics in their own right corresponding to the Natural Laws, however, their recognition requires virtue and insight. Self-control and wisdom are universal virtues because they allow us to temper our behaviour. However, not all values and desires contingent on self-control lead to well-being. For example, severe discipline involving complete abstinence from any pleasure will inevitably make a person tense and stressed, producing suffering and the underlying instability of dissatisfied living. This is an example of a moral truth in terms of the universal elements of human behaviour, which can be difficult to account for comprehensively, and the moral laws that govern behaviour with a special relation to the Natural Law of ethical systems and environments.

Moral truths are universal and absolute; however, truths of well-being depend on the state or stage of the adaptive cycle of values. To recognise and understand the conditions of well-being requires *moral reasoning* as part of practical ethical wisdom related to the reasoning of, and coherence in, insight into the structures of ethics. Like any discipline, study, and science, moral reasoning develops with knowledge, information, hypotheses, and truths. Dominant normative theories – virtue theory, deontology, and utilitarianism – have their share of insight and wisdom.

The *principle of utility*, broadly speaking, claims that the moral action is one that creates happiness and pleasure over suffering and pain, usually in consideration of the greatest amount of happiness for the greatest amount of people. The wisdom of this principle is essential to the Human Imperative and well-being in general where the causal structures of behaviour are dynamic and multidimensional. Thinking in terms of the utility principle is central to guiding desires, values, and intuitions towards acting in a way that makes the world a better place. Then, considering other people's happiness and welfare is liberating through empathy. To act in a way that creates greater happiness for the greatest amount of people, including oneself, moral reasoning must analyse a myriad of ethical causes and effects.

Here, the deontological *principle of universalisability* becomes extremely useful. This principle, in a basic sense, argues that a moral action is one that can be applied universally to create good or is universally good. When we consider the consequences of an action through the principle of utility, one can then also reflect on the action itself in terms of the principle of universalisability, which would offer understanding of the intentions that will affect future behaviour and consequences. The principle of universalisability helps us to see how a certain action and intention, and the corresponding characteristics and moral utilities, will affect us and the environment. Normative principles, such as the principle of utility and universalisability, are utilities of moral reasoning that structure and integrate information relevant to well-being. They allow us to identify certain universal parameters and conditions of well-being, revealing moral knowledge of truths and laws of well-being.

Moral reasoning is completely pragmatic in the sense that it considers every aspect and element relevant to well-being. Moral reasoning is above all concerned with ethical profit; accordingly, everything is up for consideration in the spirit of relentless pragmatism. However, once ethical truths have been identified, they become solidified as principles, values, and ideals. Principles and rules of morality are established values of well-being – are absolutely certain conditions of well-being and behaviour found through pragmatic reasoning to the point of becoming unconditional, becoming moral universals and moral laws.

To achieve well-being we must understand the structural forces that affect states of being. All aspects of behaviour are relevant to the considerations of well-being. The structures of ethics are created through the causes and effects of living things, their behaviour, and the systems of the world, particularly the Natural Laws. To guide behaviour, normative considerations must involve the study and examination of causal cascades of behaviour and their *ethical tangents*. Ethical tangents are the causal cascades, patterns, rules, and laws of ethical systems and structures.

All aforementioned elements of normativity, such as intuitions and reasoning, are summarised as manifestations of ethical tangents. For example, the will to flourish manifests itself through, and in the form of, actions pursuing well-being. The correspondence between the will and the action is a causal line – an ethical tangent. Ethical tangents can thus be understood to be vectors of moving organisms and their force affecting the parameters of well-being and the performance of moral utilities. Ethical tangents, as systemic causal patterns and trends of behaviour, are universal and create all structures of ethics. A condition of well-being creates a desire, a respective value, and leads to behaviour as movement of the body influencing the world – acting as a conduit of force. This dynamic becomes a causal tangent that affects the conditions of well-being, therefore being relevant to ethics. A morality that permits one act of killing can create moral rules which may permit other forms of killing.

Accounting for and understanding the dynamics of ethical tangents is central to understanding ethics, and consequently to moral reasoning and normative guidance forming moral values, rules, and principles to act and live by. Understanding ethical tangents is the point of practical ethical wisdom. Normative guidance functions in accordance with the fundamental drive of any living thing to pursue well-being, the subsequent activity raising questions of what is well-being and how it can be achieved. Ethical and moral understanding are best achieved through the pragmatic study of ethical tangents as causal trends and systems of actions that affect states of being and ethical interests. Familiarising oneself with trends and patterns, extracting insight from experience, integrates moral knowledge and wisdom into intuition.

Ethical tangents are an idea conceptualising change in the structures of ethics through behaviour encompassing change in the environment and the individual. Ethical tangents combine focused information of the systemic dynamics of behaviour, as well as the actual events of behaviour, into a comprehensive model for intuitive moral reasoning. By focusing on individual causal trends of behaviour – individual causal tangents – different information about the involved ethical elements and levels becomes available through different perspectives, directing moral reasoning.

Behaviour and well-being involve two core parts – environmental influences on behaviour and the characteristics of the conduits of behaviour. There are principles and values that shape ethical tangents, and then there are the mental utilities that embody, trigger, and conduce ethical tangents. So, in the case of the principle of utility and universalisability, one aspect of the corresponding moral reasoning involves environmental consequences, therefore orientating around moral principles.

However, one also has to consider how principles and choices affect character –

the conduit and embodiment of principles, as well as how characteristics influence choices. There are two sides to any ethical tangent – moral principles and moral characteristics. Different rules of normativity, appealing to different moral laws of behaviour, apply to principles and characteristics. Even though the two aspects inherently involve one another, their causes and effects consist of different parameters, conditions, and influences. Therefore, in moral reasoning in a combined normative framework dedicated to the pursuit of well-being, there are two dimensions to any moral rule and value: *principle-rules* and *virtue-rules*.

Virtue-rules account for the effects of actions and morality on the ethical agent and character. Courage is a virtue; to embody the virtue of courage, one must act courageously – this is a moral law. Acting courageously can inspire courage in other people who may have otherwise been uninspired by virtue, which is subject to the mental, psychological, and spiritual conditioning of courage as a characteristic. People acting courageously is essential to righteousness and justice. Therefore, to act courageously through the virtue of courage is good and moral. This is an example of a virtue-rule as an ethical tangent involving the effects and structural dynamics of character.

Virtue-rules would then focus on studying how certain characteristics behave, in the sense of how psychological and mental influences operate. A principle-rule, on the other hand, is one that dedicates most attention to the causal tangents of actions and states of affairs, primarily involving intentions and consequences. Principle-rules focus on the principles behind actions. The rule of a principle, as a rule of actions that produce or lead to well-being, provokes and enables certain actions (through corresponding characteristics and moral utilities, as principles are reflections of virtues). A virtue-rule values courage, as well as explains how courage arises and works. A principle-rule, on the other hand, is a more specific moral rule borne of a virtue-rule. To say that I will not let fear compromise who I am is a form of a virtue-rule. To act in a certain way contingent on this virtue-rule, such as to not go against one's principles or to not sacrifice one's identity, affecting the environment in specific ways, is a principle-rule. To act with integrity and not be vindictive against someone who has hurt you, because this path leads to greater well-being through states of affairs and will shape an event in an ethical environment, is a principle-rule. The associated virtue-rule would involve how acting with integrity and discipline can affect the character and psychological state of others.

To provide further contrast between the two normative criteria, valuing social and political civic liberty as a means of structural well-being can be qualified as a principle-rule, but the personal effect of liberty, in terms of character and the psyche, can be considered and analysed in terms of virtue-rules. Principle-rules are foremost, but not explicitly, structure-oriented, whereas virtue-rules are primarily agent-centred and character-oriented. To act to make the world a better place because this is true to one's character or because it is liberating are virtue-rules; to act to make the world a better place to simply live in a better world is a principle-rule. To act according to duty is a virtue-rule; to act dutifully to protect the vulnerable is a principle-rule. Doing what makes you happy as a virtue-rule makes you more spiritually fulfilled and uplifted and makes you more mentally and psychologically balanced, leading to better behaviour. Doing what makes you happy and not hurting others is a combined principle-rule that guides behaviour to influence the surrounding world more positively. Moral rules and principles are contextual.

Ethical tangents involve environmental and mental influences on behaviour. Certain ethical tangents are a product of the functions and mechanisms of the psyche and the values embodied in character. The ethical tangents of the Natural Law of the adaptive cycle of values, for example, are mainly environmental dynamics caused by Nature, whereby living things act according to these conditions. The principle of existence that mandates sufficient conditions for existence is its own function of logic that can portray how the world works. The survival of living things through the adaptation of values develops as a consequence of antecedent conditions fostered by the systems of ethics and Natural Laws.

Values are moral utilities, whereby people, as individual characters, are the manifestations of characteristics and corresponding values. From a structural point of view detached from judgement, emotional evaluation, or even the concerns of well-being – from a purely ethical point of view – people and living things are organic machines, sophisticated material objects, and conduits of the forces of the world. Ethical tangents are caused and shaped by ethical agents and characters, with people acting as hosts of certain qualities, values, and the conditions that influence people's behaviour and the behaviour of ethical tangents. People are hosts of values and conduits of ethical forces.

To further the distinction between principle-rules and virtue-rules, it is helpful to distinguish between structural forces in the environment – ethical tangents – and ethical elements shaping ethical tangents through living things – *ethical vectors*. People's behaviour and activity transmit force corresponding to values and characteristics. A stronger value, as a stronger virtue, is capable of causing greater structural change through a greater ethical value related to its activity and force. The physical force of a word that inspires people and influences people's psychological, mental, and spiritual states, as a force of reason grounded in the substance of reality, is an ethical force capable of causing real change.

People enact and conduce this change. By exercising the force of values shaping reason and the psyche, ethical values – as virtues and a force of change – transmit their entity and instil their element of identity. Looking at the structures of ethics through this conceptual lens in terms of *ethical vectors* – as systemic variables and functions of structural change – allows further focus, perspective, and insight into moral reasoning for normative guidance.

By considering people in pure utilitarian maxims of the greatest well-being for the greatest amount of people – by considering pure ethical values enacted by, and consisting of, ethical vectors – reasoning of ethical value becomes better and more coherent. Although it is absolutely necessary to be mindful of the emotional and spiritual dimensions in all normative questions, sometimes pure rational estimation and evaluation in terms of brute calculation is necessary for well-being. Grasping this perspective is instrumental for moral reasoning in some cases, whereby detaching from blinding base intuitions and emotions is necessary to stay disciplined and see clearly.

This combined normative theory or view will be defined as *normative combinatorialism*. The combinatorialist structure of normative guidance is agent-centred and act-orientated. The agent-centric dimension considers states of being, qualified through spirit, and the character and psyche shaping behaviour and consequences. Normative guidance is above all concerned with the ethical interests of well-being. Well-being is fostered, and sustained, through both the individual and the environment. However, ultimately it is the individual's spirit and psyche that measure well-being. Well-being can only be achieved in congruence with positive accord of reason, sentiment, and intuition.

Certain trends in behaviour and inherent conditions of human nature are structured through reason, whereby ethical forces that affect reason in certain ways universally lead to, as well as condition, well-being. The dimension of actions in behaviour prioritises ethical interests relating to states of affairs affecting the environment, which in turn reflects structural influences onto characters and spirit. All aspects of moral reasoning and moral intuition, building on practical ethical wisdom, guide the pursuit of flourishing and corresponding normative principles, values, and rules. Core intuitions and parameters of reasoning come through familiarity with the human condition, spiritual growth, wisdom, maturity, discipline, mindfulness, and knowledge of structural ethics and its related *hierarchy of values*.

The hierarchy of values is a formal structure of morality – a structure of our competing desires, interests, values, and principles. Normative complexity arises from competing desires, interests, and values. Acting on our greatest desires, regardless of whether they genuinely serve our greater interests, means we act according to our values. Moral values are those that serve our greater interests. Among competing desires, morality is the order of desire, using awareness and discipline to act in our greatest conceived interests.

By examining the causes and effects of actions and desires – respectively, characteristics and intentions, then consequences, then characteristics and intentions again – we can appreciate their sensations and then understand their reasoning and intuition. Effective understanding of the systems of ethics and of the causes and effects of behaviour and relevant structural dynamics permits greater insight into values, interests, and desires. Accordingly, this insight feeds into moral reasoning responsible for normative guidance and reveals, through wisdom, what values and desires are truly in our greatest interests.

The hierarchy of values, striving towards the Highest Good, is the structure of desires and values – the order in competing desires and values. The order of values in the structures of ethics are as follows: the metaphysics of ethics, the systems of ethics, the ethos, the Core Principles, the Central Principles, and so forth. Making a choice in competing desires is an intrinsic sign of the establishment of a moral hierarchy and order, whereby formally proposing this idea as an integral part of normative guidance is important. The establishment of moral hierarchy follows the adaptation of values, particularly through ethical vectors and the corresponding liberty of morality.

Normative guidance in Liberty comes through intuitions and reasoning of awareness, self-reflection, analysis, and methodological questioning. Following the philosophical and scientific methods, one must keep questioning; ingenuity through art and creativity comes with intuition. Always be mindful that all emotions are intended to serve benevolent purposes in behaviour, yet their function becomes corrupted when unbalanced – immoderate, undisciplined, and thoughtless. This thought can be classed as a virtue-rule, which has to be reminded of when sensations become overbearing. Emotions govern states of being, the corresponding behaviour of which is conditioned by reason. Therefore, intuitions of sensations, feelings, and awareness must be systematically integrated into moral considerations and normative guidance.

When deciding how to act, it is imperative to consider the spiritual and emotional aspects of an action, the insight of which allows more coherent moral reasoning. What do you want to do? Why do you want to do something? What do you want to achieve? Why do you want to achieve it? All these normative questions are reducible to, and are derivative of, the Categorical Directive guiding normativity along the pursuit of well-being. Then one may ask the self: Does it matter? Why does it matter? This form of reflection and mindfulness comes from wisdom, particularly through the ability to see clearly and be detached to form new perspectives.

All that matters is how one lives, what quality of life one is experiencing. This is the guiding function of actions and morality. A way of studying normativity is by imagining a scenario involving death, one's own or of the entire world. If you had one last day to live, how would you live it? What would you do? Who would you speak to, repent or pray to, ask forgiveness or forgive, or make peace with? People might naturally strive to distract themselves, live in fear and denial; or, one can make peace, find acceptance, and feel the pleasure of a profound sense of relief. When this kind of scenario is imagined, amplified by the sensations of memories of something similar, it offers perspective. The most meaningful intuitions and desires of one's character come to light, for struggle and adversity that define one's character.

Here is a general guideline for normative combinatorialism:

1. Examine the case: What is the problem? What are the choices and options?
2. Identify the main interests, desires, and values according to the circumstance demanding action: What is desired? Why is it desired? What is best? Why is it best?
3. Consider the nuances of a choice, the causal tangents of an action, consequences and effects, then analyse risks and uncertainties: What can be done towards our best interests? What feelings might be involved? What will the effects be? What further consequences will there be? What can be predicted? What happened that caused the dilemma?
4. Consider and align relevant virtue-rules and principles-rules.
5. Repeat for all questions, problems, and competing interests, values, and desires.
6. Make a judgement and a decision.

Consider the classic trolley problem. You are on a trolley; it can't stop. The trolley is heading towards five people; it will kill them. The only other option is to pull the leaver to redirect the trolley, which will cause the death of one person. What do you do? Why do anything?

In direct, quantifiable terms of ethical interest, saving five lives over one life would create the most well-being, therefore it is right. However, the quality of the ethical value of those lives must be considered. Do these people have families? What sort of characters are they? What would the consequences be of saving one life over another? Global ethical interests must be kept in mind, with reference to the Human Imperative, mindful of utility and sum ethical profit, when evaluating and qualifying people's interests and the character of people. The life of one person can bring more well-being to a hundred people than five, in which case, without further ambiguities, one life is better preserved than five. A good person is more likely to be good to others, therefore more valuable to other people's interests as well as one's own. The person of unknown character is less certain; bad character is a risk.

However, being too afraid of risks and being unwilling to place faith in people will undermine the goodness of one's own character. Where ambiguities aren't present or are unknown, it is intuitive to act according to a pure estimation of value and numbers. So if none of the people's characters is known, then it is best to act based on pure calculation and save five lives. If the one person's life is someone precious to you, therefore very valuable to you, then the variables change dramatically. The suffering of tragic loss might never fully heal even if it does lead to growth. An act of sacrifice might condemn a person to being unable to live happily and it will not bring joy.

However, great loss can lead to extreme growth and is the path to duty. It is completely up to the person whether or not they are able to make the tough choice, which may or may not be necessary. It is worth considering that the causal tangents of sparing a known character are more predictable. Not saving a loved one could lead to extreme pain, the uncertainty of which is people's reactions. The reactions of loss to five people entail a greater risk factor of feeding and inciting terrible vice. Any information becomes crucial to judgement, particularly one's own judgement such as what a person thinks he or she can endure or is willing to commit to, with the moral value of telling oneself 'I can do this' becoming another variable in itself.

Risk-assessment is very tricky, but not impossible. There is no principle-rule that can be applied to such judgements because it simply won't work in the moment, as people's feelings will be heavily swayed. This scenario, however, is a moral extreme, which grants it much greater ambiguity, therefore moral flexibility. Any strict idealisation of morality dictating that the five people should be saved over a loved one simply won't work. Saving one's loved one over five others is understandable, but if the number of lives involved was greater and their ethical value was more significant, then the act of sacrifice may become necessary and binding in virtue and duty, denying the excuse if the act is utterly selfish.

There is no definitive quantifiable rule for what number of people means an act of sacrifice really should be committed, as the variables cannot be universally and definitively quantified, with the choice ultimately being subject to the character and psyche of the person having to make the sacrifice. A subsequent virtue-rule, however, is that even if the person didn't commit the sacrifice that should've been made, this act should not be condemned and vilified, as it is understandable and complies with the principle of moral liberty, which, briefly, is that making someone act in a certain way will lead to imbalance (the details of this moral rule are yet to be discussed). Either of the two choices – save a loved one or five strangers – is permissible in direct terms without further ambiguities. However, one should be mindful that both choices can lead to suffering and feelings of guilt and regret – this can be expected in any extreme scenario.

The other side of the trolley dilemma is the nature of the choices. Diverting the trolley towards one person is a deliberate act, therefore to a certain degree an act of killing. Allowing the trolley to continue its course, killing five people, can be argued to not be one's responsibility, therefore not an act of killing. This brings a person to consider intentions and their respective dimension of virtues. If one is to be happy with a choice, then the corresponding intentions and the virtues they reflect must be analysed, mindful of the likely feelings to be evoked, which would be subject to the conditions of the psyche. To not desire to be directly responsible for the death of a person can be perceived as blamelessness. Supposedly, this would spare a person from guilt, therefore secure or relieve the spirit from suffering. Being blameless does not mean being right or guarantees well-being. In this case, killing one person is also an act of saving five people.

What is more important? What is right? What is of more noble virtue? Why is this the case? To save five people in the pursuit of virtue can be misleading for intent, as the deed is only righteous – is only able to truly uplift and liberate spirit – if it is performed with the intent of making the world a better place and sparing suffering. To act on virtue for the sake of virtue, although a necessary dimension of Discipline to be explored in terms of power, can be self-righteous and selfish. The righteous and just virtue is borne of sincere empathy, compassion, courage, and a desire for goodness – not virtue to be empowered at an unjustifiable cost to others' well-being, which would only make the world and others worse off and submit oneself to Fear's suffering. The justice of suffering – one's own and others' – will involve a detailed discussion in later Chapters. Only truly fulfilling virtues and morality are sustainable, meaning choices must lead to fulfilment and relief from suffering if they are to be practical and reasonable.

A relevant virtue-rule to consider is that the regret of *not* doing something is usually greater than the regret of doing something, because this is less certain and less concrete than an actual choice, it is less confident, and it is less empowering than accepting responsibility. Making a choice means that at least a choice was made, whereas inaction amplifies regret with a sense of cowardice, irresolution, and wavering. Inaction leads to the tortuous wondering of potential – what if... The regret of inaction leads to a search for opportunity and redemption rather than focused growth from decisiveness, which is a more advanced and mature characteristic than indecisiveness. Therefore, in this case, it would be right to derail the trolley to save five people.

However, the intentions of this choice reflect the virtues of desired consequences, by which the intended consequences and relevant considerations become imperative for a truly righteous action of virtue that creates the most well-being for everyone and oneself accordingly. In terms of the competing desires between one's own immediate well-being and others', a virtue-rule applies that the personal sense of well-being is always more important to the perception and estimation of ethical value. In other words, one's own sense of well-being is always more evocative and motivating than the perception of others' welfare, with others' states and feelings being only as relevant as their value to oneself. The liberty of empathy and compassion is one's own feeling, which is fulfilling and right to and through oneself. To act in consideration of the global ethical structure, humanity, and the Human Imperative means to act with and through the Highest Good, which in time, with discipline and mindfulness, becomes as spiritually fulfilling as the rational interest, aligning sentiments with rationale.

These were just some examples of normative guidance. Greater coherence and direction of the combinatorialist normative framework requires the establishment of referable and clear morality, principles-rules, virtue-rules, and wisdom. This is the task to which the rest of Section 3 is dedicated.

Chapter 16:

The Principle of Liberty in Ethics and Morality

All moralities are subforms of the Highest Good in the sense that they all work towards flourishing but in different ways and in different environments, contexts, and circumstances. However, all moralities and ethics are functions of the Fundamental Principle of Living Beings and correspond to the Human Imperative. The Highest Good encompasses the sum state of mankind with regards to all constituents and tangents of ethics as ideas, values, and vectors, whether it is an academic moral theory such as utilitarianism or the morality of the everyday person. Throughout mankind's history ideas and moralities have changed, adapted, and dissolved, in the process affecting individuals, societies, and civilisations. This diversity has driven us forward and it is an integral part of the ever-changing moral laws of the Highest Good through its adaptive mechanisms of values. It is intriguing that despite all the terror human civilisation has endured, throughout all the gloom, mankind has nonetheless progressed. Central Principles ought to embody both aspects of the Highest Good: the systemic and structural features of adaptiveness and practical everyday normativity. Therefore, the Central Principles must provide a morality for everyday decision-making, as well as embracing the essence of ethics as a whole considering its secondary and tertiary spheres.

Morality must then embrace *liberty*, in other words, freedom to practise different moralities and ethics. The Highest Good is inherently diverse and consists of coexisting and competing moral vectors. This coexistence will likely always be present as life is incredibly diverse. Yet through empathy there is also a fundamental level of unity among all moralities and all living things. So for beneficial, constructive, and the strongest moralities to develop and thrive there must be liberty for people to practise and uphold these moralities. Similarly, for ethical codes to flourish and develop they must have liberty to do so and must have liberty to compete and adapt. Greater flourishing comes through the freedom of action and interaction among autonomous agents embodying respective tangents moved by the mechanisms of the fundamental will.

Structures of ethics feature normative competition and development. This element of normativity, analogous to competition of natural selection, drives development of, through, and towards the Human Imperative, strengthening humanity. Sometimes certain forms of moralities become incompatible with others and result in conflict. Extremes of ideology have reflected and incited conflict. Conflicts of extremes are not so much due to the ideas preached in a book as they are a consequence of characteristics of the human condition, especially when subject to extensive suffering of poverty of wealth and good character. When ambiguity of an idea is left unchecked, and subjectivity grows beyond its established borders, vivid interpretations of a single sentence can lead to confusion, misunderstanding, conflict, and madness. When it comes to addressing the issues of conflicting ideologies and moralities, there must be limits on the tolerance and liberty of competing vectors.

If an idea becomes strictly intolerant and negatively conflicting in the form of destructive and volatile competition, suffocating progress, then these values ought to be challenged. The appropriate strategy, however, can come in many forms of applied normativity such as letting a vector cannibalise itself while preserving value from a decaying morality and its sphere of influence through damage-management. Moralities and the Highest Good ought to be mediated through the normativity of an individual agency and corresponding vectors and must be left to the self-sustaining, organic tangents in structures of ethics through Natural Law. Such a principle should serve to enable growth of constructive and beneficial ethical utilities while regulating deeply conflicting and absolutely incompatible norms and values subject to considerations of justice.

Concerning 'negative' values, I qualify them as those that relate to destructive and wholly intolerant moralities and their affiliate groups and individuals. 'Wholly intolerant' moralities suppose those hell-bent on absolute deprivation of liberty and diversity in the Highest Good without sufficient justification. For example, violent quasi-religious extremism of unjust murder is not something that should be tolerated.

To emphasise the position I outline, the Central Principles of heritin ethics should both value the subforms of the Highest Good and embrace structural understanding and views of moralities in general, to then, through the use of select ethical utilities, engage with growing and emerging moralities. Above all for heritin Central Principles of moral liberty, the value of liberty and a morality embracing it, should protect ethical development in order to establish sustainable, beneficial, and constructive forms of greater flourishing through the many forms well-being can adopt, all for the Human Imperative.

However, at the core of this value of liberty there should not be merely survival or justice qualified by base morality. Central Principles must look beyond the focus of survival and ought to dedicate attention to the Highest Good and the Human Imperative both in pragmatic terms, i.e. normative claims and their application in decision-making, and in good spirit. Even extreme base ethics and attitudes therein may end up being the most in accord with the Highest Good in the appropriate structural conditions, but absolutist survival ethics is clearly limited in the potency its utilities offer for the purpose of well-being (see Section 2).

The heritin understanding of liberty must embrace, accommodate, and favour more certain, promising, and the preferred variants of base ethics, i.e. those more normatively compatible. For instance, focusing on a collaborative morality formulated on sentiments of mutual affection and commonality of humanity are, for most part, in a simplified interpretation, intuitively better for people than values of destructive resentment and hostility motivated by groundless values only derived from demeaning compulsions of Fear. We may think our moral codes or ways of life are absolutely right. But if structural genealogy has taught us anything it is that values, ideas, attitudes, and moralities develop, grow, and change according to circumstances and immediate judgements.

Various ethics and moralities work for different people in different conditions, which ought to be respected by the Human Imperative. People may find fulfilment through principles grounded in base morality, but if these principles begin to directly and disproportionately intervene in the endeavours of the Human Imperative, such as with extremist base moralities violently projecting pain, then these extremes might require the suspension of tolerance. Judgements about the primacy and quality of any morality rest with Natural Law and respective moral law so that we can judge, through mindful reflection and analysis, whether a morality is compatible with virtue and justice. Measures that are taken to address conflicting moralities must be proportionate, effective, efficient, and *just* (the principles and rules of *justice* are discussed in later Chapters).

I can outline a Central Principle of moral liberty:

People ought to have liberty to practise different moralities so that the Highest Good and mankind with it, through the Human Imperative, may develop and progress through stronger moralities, thereby producing flourishing for the individual and the relevant ethical environment through moral development. When opposing moralities give cause to unnecessary and unjust suffering and lead to conflict with the Central Principles or other moralities in a destructive manner, then that particular ethic is not to be tolerated and must be addressed with effective and just practice of morality, but only in accordance with justice.

Within this Central Principle of Liberty there are many notable features. For one, it is vital that a person *chooses* their way of life. All people wish for greater flourishing - this is a function of the mind via the Fundamental Principle. Heritin ethics offers one of many ethical creeds on attaining well-being in appropriate circumstances, but it might not be the best ethic universally or for an individual subject to particular conditions.

A person becomes more dedicated to a cause or way of life when it is his or her genuine desire to pursue an ethic. An eager, motivated, and well-rewarded worker can perform better than an exhausted, unappreciated slave. If people unwillingly pursues an endeavour, then they are much more likely to underperform, while dedicated effort with sincere goodwill but without external coercion should be more promising, effective, and efficient.

Actions motivated by Fear, on the other hand, may easily exhaust, and detract from, the freedom of mind that breeds innovation and progress, as progress begins with the individual. Certain aspects of heritin ethics may be very demanding; the resolve of a person is to be tested for the strength of the will to grow, in turn nourishing virtue. This is one of the many modes of personal growth through which values may progress in accordance with the Highest Good.

For greater effect and fulfilment, for strength of character and for able individuals to rise there must be liberty for people to pursue the paths they value. In an ethic where there is a desire to confront, endure, and embrace suffering, the lack of resolve can be damning, because lack of ambition will cause unconstructive suffering. Only in the genuine liberty of a person's own autonomous determination can values and character grow and succeed, with the struggle to improve on one's own vices a difficult task that lasts a lifetime. Consequently, societies and people may progress as well, even if by learning from the mistakes of others. So liberty and self-determination are central to the development and growth of virtuous characters.

The idea of self-determination and free development of moralities may then be contradictory to enforcing Central Principles or certain positive moral principles and attitudes towards deviant and bad moralities. In other words, if moralities should prosper and compete freely, then why should detrimental and malevolent moralities and people's actions of a negative or lesser ethical disposition be challenged beyond tolerance, be criminalised, condemned, or vilified?

First of all, one must remember that ethics should develop, and this requires the liberty of moralities and rules, including those one may regard as of lesser value. Caution, reflection, mindful honesty, and discipline are important in weighing moral norms.

Secondly, a point of justification for tolerance and non-involvement in the affairs of others is that the mistakes of others can provide good lessons for others and serve as good material for research, whereby the self-inflicted misfortunes of others that could not have been legitimately and righteously changed can benefit others' wisdom. Also, sometimes it is important to let people make their own mistakes, a thought especially applicable to maturing individuals, children, and adolescents. But understandably and intuitively, mediation is necessary to prevent catastrophic mistakes and minimise collateral damage. Sometimes it is not the good role model that serves as a point of moral insight but a bad role model that is most valuable, one from which you can learn what *not* to do.

Thirdly, some movements in the dynamics of ethics can clearly run counter to moral law and upset the balance of progress. There are individuals that are willing and capable of committing atrocities and strive to eliminate all that is different and all competition, primarily motivated by Fear. Sometimes the best moral course is to prevent, remedy, or minimise the damage of primitive, destructive, and wrong moralities, yet the answer to the right moral judgement is unclear. For example, some moral judgements may be subject to degrees of uncertainty and their consequences may be obscured. In particular circumstances where one has not experienced what another has, or has not, lived through similar circumstances, meaning appropriate insight is unavailable and full empathy is restricted, it is difficult to form accurate assessments and judgements on effective responses. Sometimes reason is not convincing or clear enough, the ambiguity of which may require experimentation in practical morality and further study; 'you live, you learn'.

Then there are instances where judgements are clearly wrong such as those justifying murder. Dominant moral codes tend to restrict acts of killing so that they can only be performed according to when it is absolutely necessary. Sensible people would agree that murder is wrong, especially that it is wrong to kill innocent people. For instance, the extremist may undermine their own cause by only encouraging greater resentment of, and hostility towards, their community, in recent years the effect of jihadi radicalism as one of the most high-profile examples. Principles and Laws in Nature set the parameters for the success of moralities, individuals, and societies. Thus, moralities with different ethical cores can come to the same moral rule, such as that unnecessary killing is wrong.

There are some conditions of ethical dynamics and behaviour that cannot be tolerated for the sake of oneself and others. We may mutually subscribe to tacit competition in values, opinions, views, and beliefs, or we may simply live our lives in peace without any contention or significant individual differences. Even in the competition of attitudes and moral convictions there does not need to be malicious will or intent, for in unity by the Highest Good and the universality of common humanity we are ultimately bound to a single direction in our destinies but at different levels. When this order is upset, especially with forceful intervention by contending moralities and their vectors, it is in the interest of the individual to resist in order to be free to pursue moral convictions, in the interests of the Human Imperative that would thrive without destructive conflict.

However, it is important to understand that even the most malicious ethical forces can be turned to good or reap positive results through the self by resisting the pain and Fear that has corrupted others and caused them to suffer. But to achieve this effect and all greater positivity of ethics, mediation and oversight of moral liberty is important. Therefore, because mediating liberty in relation to the demands of circumstances evokes and constructs flourishing, intolerance towards degrees of immorality is good, and tolerance for proportionally and sensibly positive moralities (that do not produce overly destructive influences) is good. Sometimes, however, there is little that can be done in response to immorality, so the only good course of action may be to minimise the damage caused. These themes now concern themselves with extended spheres of ethics beyond the focus on the individual, so I must set a limit on how far I can go in exploring this question of practical morality. For now, this outline should suffice as a general principle-rule.

A practical example of the issue of tolerance of vice and immorality can be studied in the context of social interaction. Unconditional love can be good unless it is blind; unconditional friendship and partnership is not good when it enables and condones immoral behaviour. Continued friendship with immoral persons and the related suffering are only good if this relation is moved by good intentions to help the person harming themselves through immorality. There is only so much one can do, and an intrusive and bothersome lifestyle of immersing oneself in affairs that do not affect oneself directly is a bothersome and inefficient way of life. It is best to focus on immediate improvement.

Influences that interfere the most in one's well-being ought to be addressed first. Causal cascades are global and all immorality inevitably leads to loss in ethical interest, yet securing the most certain and promising ethical gains is more sensible. However, this principle is only as effective when it does not cause further damage or simply passes on the cost of one's activity. Agreeing with immoral behaviour by either condoning it or building relations with vectors of vice and immorality, without concern for remedying vice, will only invite and condone immorality. There is, however, a time and place for constructive criticism and condemnation of certain actions, the justice of which is best utilised through common accord and good faith. However, these circumstances can only be left to individual judgements. Condoning immoral behaviour or behaviour one disagrees with in a social group, organisation, or conglomerate by not addressing it or continuing to sustain one's activity in that sphere enables vice and invites its effects. If the liberty of one character's vice is not addressed when it affects another person, how long until it affects you? When a person unjustifiably and impulsively abuses or causes mental harm to another person, and one does not address the matter and its injustice and immorality, then how long until that behaviour is targeted against oneself or consumes the person who sustains that vice? If unaddressed, the consequence is likely to be inevitable.

It is a powerful and damning lesson to learn that people who do not want to change cannot be helped. Only time and proper circumstances can help them. For instance, there is no helping an addict stuck in their ways without disapproval and the withdrawal and emotional support or being the last line of hope. The best thing one can do for oneself and others is make the choice of setting aside those who can't be helped, to instead help those who can be. If people don't want to change, they won't. The only change possible then is change through environment.

To not overlook the issue, in the context of liberty, an action is considered wrong if it strives to impose one morality or a narrow, unilateral sense or interest of well-being through violent and/or deeply forceful coercion or if it commits a deep violation of other prerogative moral principles, especially the Central Principles. Intolerance of moralities often leads to conflict. Intolerance of intolerance also leads to conflict, but this conflict can serve the interests of those seeking greater flourishing of diversity and liberty. Narrow, inflexible moralities and ideologies are bound to fail, for only through the systemic feature of adaptation can moral knowledge and truth be formed. Ignoring and dismissing this is a tangent leading to failure.

Intolerant moralities and communities left to their own devices and not wanting to deal with others might not cause active conflict that affects an ethical structure. In this model of incomplete isolation (as all tangents are interconnected in global structures), there might not be any immediate necessity for intervention on intolerance; groups and moral communities can be left to their own affairs and pursuits and the best model may prevail. If resources and forces are moved to directly undermine another vector (including mass vectors as societies and nations), and intolerance leads to active conflict between opposing views, then it is sensible to challenge an opposing force.

The justification for this is to be found in the competitive adaptation of values and in that any ethic must also be able to withstand many degrees of pressure. Facilitating an ethic that surrenders at the drop of a hat will collapse. Also, intolerance arises from Fear, and in terms of the heritin ethic one must learn to defy Fear by constructive, sensible, and strategic degrees and only move to fulfil the ultimate sacrifice when the mind and spirit are genuinely ready and willing to embrace spiritual liberty – *eudaimonia*.

But along this self-centred, idealised, and spiritualised ethical element is also the necessary consideration of the greater picture of the Highest Good. Especially in greater virtue, as with virtue-duty, one must come to realise that actions feed corresponding characteristics and their spirit. If one seeks to embody virtue, their virtues must also engage with and consider others. The merits and piety of liberty and protecting it not only rests on being free but in also allowing others to be free so that they can pursue the Highest Good on their own terms and in what form they see it. Then, if the need arises, their liberties must also be restricted if their pursuit of flourishing leads to the same necessity to mediate and influence the liberty of actions.

Each individual is a conduit of moral utilities which affect the dynamics of ethics. Those who aspire to virtue and strength ought to commit to doing what they can to secure goodness. Only through virtue can Liberty succeed, through strength of will and wisdom. This, however, can only be achieved in accordance with the Highest Good, for character lacking application and utility will not grow in virtue. Furthermore, the will's pursuit is that of flourishing, and little flourishing will be cultivated without putting effort into improving oneself and the environment.

It is important to understand that there is a line between what ought to be tolerated and when inaction in Fear or vice unnecessarily propagating suffering. The succession of Fear through virtue means both commitment to defying Fear and suffering through actions engaging with the world, and understanding that Fear as an ethical tangent has its rightful place to pressure the world and people to change. Then, wisdom beyond Fear shows that for people to improve on their condition, they can only do so by their own volition when and if they are prepared and willing to. But until then there is a balance of what the liberty to act permits, and diving into the world to try fix all wrongs and imposing one's will of 'virtue' on others won't fix everything and isn't a sustainable, realistic normative grand strategy or moral principle. Liberty must be achieved both structurally – 'top-to-bottom' – and within each individual – 'bottom-up', beginning with a vector. Liberty is essential to this ambition – liberty to make mistakes, liberty to learn, liberty to suffer, liberty to grow, liberty to not be destroyed without necessity and/or unjustly, and the liberty to sacrifice. Liberty is not without responsibility.

A time may come where disproportionate, inefficient, and destructive conflict between moralities no longer needs to be a norm for progress. Resisting Fear in liberty means to not oppose the natural order of the Highest Good. If one's morality has failed and its principles fail, then it must adapt; if it refuses to do so, then it will pay the price and will be pressured by the adaptive cycle.

However, to not fear moral liberty also means to not surrender one's principles to Fear and not let Fear compromise a person's character. The odds may be stacked against you and the life your principles have led to may be cruel and punishing. In the heritin ethos, this voluntary fate is not necessarily a bad thing, because by not surrendering to Fear one moves closer to Liberty, but living a life of Fear and following principles corrupted by and submitted to Fear will not fulfil ambition. Simply defying death and pain without committing willingly to active principles in life will not yield the fulfilment of spiritual liberty. Considerations of spiritual fulfilment must be in conjunction with the imperatives of practical, structural elements of ethics.

Along with the pragmatic, normative conception of liberty in the Central Principles there is also the spiritual, personal aspect to consider. Here it is much simpler: to be free in spirit, to achieve eudaimonia of spiritual liberty, one must be free. However, this freedom must first be within oneself, freedom in virtue of character, and then be reflected into the world. One must be free to pursue freedom; yet spiritual freedom is a universally attainable freedom that can be discovered or inspired through others and through goodwill.

Knowledge and information can be constrained, circumstances might be unfriendly, but even in the pain of death there is still a choice, for the choice of death is a choice in itself; a choice to die on one's own terms is still a choice, and is a choice of Liberty. Thus, fulfilment in Liberty is something all can embrace and achieve without exclusion other than limits imposed on the self by the mind and one's attitude. When one has become free or capable of one's own freedom, then one ought to reflect that liberty outward and strive for liberty in other spheres of the Highest Good. One ought to strive for liberty in spirit and society not only by valuing freedom, but also because one is free – such is the duty of the free, of those of virtue at liberty.

However, before I delve into detailed analysis and reflection on the Secondary Principles of sociopolitical liberty, take note of the order I emphasise in the pursuit and structure of Liberty: one should not fight for liberty, but earn it within the self, then teach and reflect it onto others if such is the will and interest. Foremost in the pursuit of civic freedom is not just the fight for liberty and rights, but the capacity for moral autonomy and the virtue of character to be at liberty.

One may appreciate the central issue in the morality of liberty – that liberty must exist for growth, development, and progress. However, this progress often comes as a response to suffering, so it is in our greater interests to mediate the destructive influences of suffering. But this would go against the principles of liberty. People must make mistakes to learn, and we must learn to truly grow. Not yielding and binding to Fear does not entail the deprivation of progress, it should mean the opposite – greater progress. What spiritual and moral liberty suggests is that we should embrace suffering to grow from it, yet not intentionally cause it, as this would only facilitate regress and lesser flourishing in terms of its viable alternative of acting in virtue not perpetuating suffering and instead minimising suffering, and learning to utilise suffering for efficient growth and flourishing.

However, as I have argued in the case of the morality of Harmony and its element of Discipline, growth can come quite easily and intuitively without suffering. The morality of Harmony can function without the morality of Defiance. But the latter engaged in suffering is still a major aspect of living, for the same liberty that gives rise to progress also gives rise to mistakes and suffering. There are many factors influencing people in their development and the influences of those learning from mistakes will eventually succeed suffering. What moral liberty entails is not being afraid of this and not succumbing to the Fear of actively opposing the learning curve of mistakes, as this may lead to moral regression and stagnation – corruption. Moral liberty, through its spiritual element, means also not being afraid of total failure and the collapse of the world caused by the mistakes of others' moral liberty. But then why should we try to minimise suffering through others' actions when we may have the opportunity? Why not embrace total liberty and anarchy of moralities? Why oppose destructive ones when it is in greater liberty to let the world suffer and be destroyed? Is liberty in morality contradictory to authority in morality and opposition to immorality?

The following reply is very closely related to my examination of the relation or gap between the Void and the Highest Good. One, indeed, has the imaginable and theoretical liberty *to not* respond to immorality, yet a person equally has the liberty *to* act in goodwill. This perspective requires balance between the two distinct elements. To be at liberty in spirit is to be at liberty of morality, notwithstanding the deterministic tendencies of the mechanical mind. But this liberty can only ever be achieved through virtue, so the paradox is that liberty is achieved through commitment to virtue and the Highest Good.

Greater flourishing comes through fulfilment of spiritual liberty, the essence of which is freedom and relief from Fear. But clinging to the Highest Good and being dutiful to the Human Imperative may also serve as a distraction from mindful liberty and corrupt the mind and spirit through the fear of failure, thereby breeding vice and propagating suffering. Sometimes the dynamics of ethics must be permitted to run their organic course and mistakes will have to breed suffering. Moral liberty must include this and be willing to accept it even if it leads to total destruction due to our own fault, because this solidifies virtuous moral liberty by not compromising it with Fear. Yet the conjunction between the two must remain, whereby helping others and doing what one can to alleviate suffering is right.

Trying to subvert a course and natural path of the dynamics of suffering and Fear too often only creates greater suffering. In analogy, consider attempts to direct the flow of a river. Blocking a river's flow entirely is a difficult task that can only be accomplished at the source of a river. Ignoring this warning could lead to a tampered river overflowing and causing extensive damage, while a softer approach channelling a river's flow may be more efficient and achievable. Liberty sometimes entails damage-management rather than active resolution. For example, the migrant crisis that hit Europe in 2015 did not have any clear solutions because the problem was so complex and rash attempts to solve the problem could result in greater disasters in the future; the only viable choice might have been minimising the damage.

What kind of virtue worthy of the title is one that simply stands idle in absolute apathy to the suffering in the world? None. However, sometimes the greater virtue is the deliberation to restrain actions to ensure greater progress by accepting, and not being afraid of, the massive cost that might be necessary for the right choice, a cost that might be smaller than its alternative. Britain's and France's post-colonial division of the Middle East and later US interventions stirred a hornet's nest, the consequences of which were extremist violence. This has significantly influenced the circumstances that contributed to the migrant crisis that threatened the European Union, the decay of which could resurrect the nationalist rivalry that tore people apart generations ago and would lead to regress of the Human Imperative. Yet that same rivalry and the mistakes of the Second World War are horrors that taught Europe the value of peace and cooperation.

Liberty can be brutal, callous, calculated, but these are also virtues to ensure greater progress for us all – an efficiency in its utility that is not void of positive sentiment and spirit. It is a tendency of mankind to progress when we learn, so we must learn, not be parented and nursed the whole way, or else in times of vulnerability we will fall and our claims of unwarranted entitlement will be unhesitatingly rejected and ignored. As for the justice of liberty, this will be discussed in matters of practical morality.

If our destiny is truly to descend into our own destruction, then what can be done about it? What of it? Much conflict looms over mankind, with the friction between the West and Russia being but one and perhaps a shadow of something much worse yet to come from shifts in global shares of power. There is little authority beyond Natural Law and Fear's principle-rules of mutually assured destruction and loss that mediates these states of affairs, the irony being that the same thing that caused the conflict is the same thing holding imperfect and fragile stability.

Furthermore, the global community is in a state of anarchy and none have yet proven ultimately worthy of being a leading authority of virtue to which absolute normative power is bestowed. Only through moral power can there be a genuine leadership behind which humanity can come together without tension and conflict sowing the chaos we now experience in our still largely primitive international order in the infancy of us coming to terms with a global civilisation. The only way this conflict can end is through people and societies learning and coming together, reconciling and overcoming their vices and fears. Only a moral authority can do this and no people yet possess the power to bring order, peace, and reconciliation. But no such power can arise while Fear tests character, and condemns the morally weak to vice, while the prevailing order follows its current path.

The only course for the Human Imperative to truly flourish is through the virtue of the individual and righteousness. People can only achieve such virtue by learning, but to learn they must also be given the opportunity to learn and grow. For the growth of virtue to succeed, resisting subterfuge by vice, while influence of vice motivates the growth of virtue – a necessary principle for the Highest Good and the Human Imperative – there must be a balance of moral liberty. Furthermore, subjecting people to suffering without consent and without the person being prepared or willing to confront necessary suffering (that was setup by earlier conditions rather than deliberate actions for creating unwilling suffering) will not achieve the good effect suffering may have in cultivating virtue. Therefore, degrees of immorality must be tolerated as part of the utility to improve on them, while extreme violations of the Central Principles and grave immorality must be mediated when there are proper opportunities in proportional justice and righteousness. One can't and shouldn't nanny and protect everyone, and neither should one be reckless and irresponsible.

One ought to acknowledge and remember that everyone is enduring their own struggles in life and experiencing one form of suffering or another. The autonomy of a moral agency is an intrinsic part of living which is often accompanied by suffering. Each individual has their own story. For people to grow it is not only important to let them do so, but it is also equally important to encourage and support them in their ambition. As long as this tangent is directed in a morally permissible and tolerable way, people's endeavours should be supported when permitted and just.

People will make mistakes, they may become discouraged, they may retreat, they may surrender; at such moments it is imperative to help and encourage them. Sentiments of empathy towards, and anger against, suffering are invaluable utilities and precious for virtue and a healthy mind, but they can also lead to mistakes of compassion. Sentiments of guilt and shame are imperative for reflection and learning, so they are also precious utilities and aspects of being.

However, guilt and shame can cloud the mind and consume the spirit, nullifying their positive moral utilities. Liberty in ethics and morality is as much a liberty in principles and judgements as it is liberty within oneself to pursue greater fulfilment, a liberty for the fundamental will to embrace everything at its disposal with the vast resources and utilities of the faculties of the psyche and liberty and restraint.

The greatest virtues and moral power are not those that compel people to act in a desired way through coercion. Greater virtue and true moral power are to be found in the ability of people to act, following their own intuition and of their own volition to act righteously. Power is in truth; those who know the truth of the Highest Good will have the power of its utilities. I will explore this theme in a focused discussion of structural ethics in Part 3 of Section 3, yet it is inherently linked to personal ethics.

It is only in liberty that the truths of the Highest Good can be apprehended. Its powers have only ever been embraced by a select few in history, by messianic leaders who commanded moral authority above and within people, nations, institutions, and societies, the likes of Gandhi and Mandela. The only way such characters were able to invoke the powers they had by virtue of moral knowledge was through *moral power*, a power they only found by resisting Fear. I contend that the true virtue of such power was not in the heralding of it but by empowering others with virtue, and through nobility of spirit, by evoking virtue and dignified morality in others, even and especially in opposing groups.

In order to achieve such dynamics of moral utilities, virtue must be disciplined and cultivated. This requires a balanced measure of influence in both word and deed, in terms of both counsel and affirmation, in terms of both consolation and coercion, if necessary. This is what moral liberty permits and enables as part of ethical utilities to direct and mediate growth. It draws on pragmatism of the Fundamental Principle and the diversity of the Highest Good, yet it is not a nihilistic liberty. Moral liberty allows for such principles to be encompassed within an ethical system to ensure greater flourishing and adaptivity without contradiction, whereby proper application of certain utilities is measured in reference to circumstances.

This formulation of liberty also opens up a very personal exploration of liberty within oneself that has tremendous spiritual value through mindfulness. Spiritual and moral liberties are utilities enabling exploration of the Highest Good on a distinct level and have much insight to offer concerning the moralities of some personal, subjective aspects such as pleasure. Moral liberty not only enables ethical utilities of vast pragmatic assimilation, but also the spiritual aspect correlating to the practicality that allows utilities to drift between lines, rules, and principles in order to formulate distinctive intuitions and judgements in goodwill. Liberty offers a root to a moral limbo, but despite what it may first suggest, definitive and coherent structure can be found.

Moral liberty allows liberty and authority to be conceived primarily as ethical utilities that only become definitive aspects of an ethical system by applying a measure of ethical and moral quality that are without rigid definitions disruptive to mindful estimation and the valuation of utilities. Moral limbo allows clarity in the study of ethical tangents; uncertainty can lead to humility and mindfulness. Moral liberty is paradoxically an ethical utility that grants liberty to the forces of ethical utilities, while also giving freedom for authority over ethical dynamics. The grounding effect for the coherence of moral liberty can then be weighed in reference to the origin of the formulation of the morality itself – the Fundamental Principle. By revising the Fundamental Principle and setting a definitive agenda with the ambition of goodwill allows coherent structuring of any utility in terms of Liberty and moral liberty.

My dedicated exploration of liberty in ethics seeks to advance understanding of moral liberty and how to apply it. Base ethics and moralities grounded in instinct and intuitions of sentiment struggle to formulate a strong ethical system in terms of the liberty of instinctive feelings and corresponding morality; these structures are too susceptible to pain and are maladaptive in modern times. The Ploy of Consciousness is a means of breaking primary intuitions and expanding insight. Following the influence of sentiment on behaviour without moderation through reason has been somewhat of an advantage for the adaptation of behaviour and values, although hectic.

Liberty on the scale I propose is that of ethics free in Fear or where Fear's corruptive, restrictive limits are resolved. It is logical to then wonder how order and comprehensive functional structures of liberty in ethics and morality can be formulated. Freedom in Fear may lead to nihilistic and reckless liberty; to some extent I have argued there are merits to this, but to brand greater ethical liberty nihilistic is simplistic and would misunderstand the essence of the proposed liberty of ethics. By moving past a restrictive system of Fear, liberty in ethics can flourish and other intuitions and utilities become accessible.

There is the issue of how to then ground these deviations and give any sense of liberty its structure, the proposed solution being the revision of ethical foundations and mindfulness by the Fundamental Principle. Learning this mindfulness becomes an imperative utility to understand the application, function, and dynamic of the fundamental will, which follows with insight, wisdom, and knowledge. This same liberty that may seem complex at first, in fact, in due course, becomes more intuitive and coherent than constricted and direct values. But liberty in morality also entails the integration and exploration of rigid values for the utility they may offer. This ethic aims to study the more profound elements of liberty in ethics and morality from both the structural and subjective, spiritual perspectives.

These two faculties, however, are indistinguishable for a coherent and comprehensive ethic. Yet this greater degree of liberty is not without structure and order, and through sufficient practise, discipline, and virtue it becomes far more intuitive and fulfilling than an ethic of inherently conflicted order and structure built on a core of Fear and insufficiently mediated influences of base-reason. Liberty in ethics leads to intuitions of virtues that establish moral sense based on reasoning familiar with conclusive moral judgements of the Highest Good. Liberty allows for this exploration and then the pursuit of the Ideals. This liberty allows for the best of both pragmatism and idealism, applied through any appropriate utilities in true ethical liberty, so it becomes no contradiction for an ideal to be based on pragmatic values, nor for pragmatism to lose its merit and value without regulation by an Ideal. Moral liberty is not liberty *for* immorality, it is the liberty to explore and find what is right, the liberty to learn and advance from immorality, the liberty to do what is right in the face of immorality, Fear, and suffering.

The term 'coercion' suggests proactive engagement through action proportional in force to the demands of circumstances and the necessity for action, and includes a wide array of means appropriate and necessary in dire circumstances to prevent harmful influences from causing devastation or mass suffering. The reference to coercion does not, however, justify or imply stringent actions enforcing the heritin interpretation, for this would betray liberty of morality and spirit. While I will go on at length to discuss the moral theme of many forms of coercion (with coercion sometimes being justified and morally right) to formalise the principles of moral liberty it must be argued that certain moral judgements (e.g. certain Central Principles) must be enforced.

I will outline a morality for such a principle, but its formulation will for the most part not be counter-intuitive to common sense judgements that are already widespread (including that acts of pointless, unnecessary murder should not prevail). Sometimes greater liberty will require a 'cap' on liberty itself, but then other circumstances may require excess negative utilities and the influences of them to be given liberty to be vented like a build-up of steam so that positive utilities may grow in their vacuum.

The West-Russia conflict is personal to me, yet I consider it only a segment of a conflicted structure and perhaps only a spark for worse conflicts yet to come. I would prefer to see an end to this prolonged conflict, and I hold a dream and hope for mankind to move on to a new stage of development, growth, and cooperation. But, like anyone, including democratically elected leaders, there is extremely little I can do. This isn't to say I am unable to do anything or that I do not have a responsibility to act in a manner pursuing peace. I am not willing to compromise who I am and what I stand for; I am not willing to reduce myself to the same Fear that breeds the conflict, a Fear that twists mankind, or to surrender my spirit to Fear with the ambition of solving this conflict, for then that same corrupt Fear would have already succeeded and there would be no sustainable solution. However, equally, I will not surrender to Fear and I will not give up on my responsibilities to do what I can in whatever degree to inspire hope and reconciliation among people and nations for the redemption of our fears and vices, for us all to become stronger in character. This is what I consider to be moral freedom of spiritual liberty.

To suspend liberty for security in Fear, to revert to a once useful but hitherto deficient state is to betray one's virtue and go back on the Human Imperative. Where Liberty has not been pursued or embraced there can be no change, as the greatness of spiritual and moral liberty is not known. But where Liberty has been felt and its truest fulfilment sensed, its draw on the soul is too great to consciously revert back to restricted living and spirit. Yet the impulse of base-reason, ill-discipline, and faltering mindfulness lure the will down a path that deprives us of greater fulfilment, for moral and normative corruption always finds a way. These mistakes are natural for us, but are necessary for practical ethical wisdom as the virtue of liberty. Liberty and virtue are supposed to succumb to mistakes of misjudgement, to our faults and vice, in order to find the strength to surpass that which makes us suffer but will not enslave us. To turn away from Liberty and settle for the same Fear that causes us so much grief is to invite the same tangents of the cycles of Fear, depriving us of completion in life. In doing so we neglect maxims of value and interest through ourselves and others, for while we are bound to Fear we will suffer, and while we are unable to embrace suffering for global maxims of well-being we will be stuck in a restricted condition and an environment deprived of greater potential.

It may seem as though self-sacrifice for liberty is a great cost, but where such cost incurs pain and suffering it also maximises greater value and interest by completing one's eudaimonia in Liberty and moving endeavour forward by the Imperative. If none has the strength and will to improve the global condition, then we will all be bound to a diminished state.

Fear once aided and moved us, but there may come a time where Fear gives way to Liberty. If conditions of Nature and structural ethics change in such a way that Liberty encounters other normative influences, such as those of a brutish state rather than of developed modern societies, then is Liberty sustainable and good? While the psyche and spirit of the individual may be bound to Liberty and averse to Fear, will the structures of ethics be the same? Where normative structures come to a point where Liberty could succeed, I would postulate that normativity reaches the point of no return unless the very structure gets wiped out to start anew with few inherited ethical tangents of Liberty. The individual fulfilled by Liberty will not settle for what is lesser than the most intuitive spirit of Liberty, with structures following this development. But whether this hypothesis is fulfilled remains to be seen, but Liberty ought not to give way to Fear, just as true Liberty of eudaimonia will not give way to Fear.

Disorder in the global community is nothing unusual in terms of our shared history. However, now that weapons of mass destruction and increased capacities of subterfuge, such as technological abilities, have entered the international arena, much more is at stake. One mistake can be costly, yet the same things that inspire this danger through Fear are what hold it in line, but with extreme risks and great fragility. Conflict among nation-states has now evolved from localised and international violence, as technology has given us the capacity to destroy the entire planet, a liberty we weren't fully morally and spiritually prepared for. Instead of personal responsibility we now have a reign of moral apprehension established on Fear rather than responsibility to one another.

The liberty of moral duties also means adherence to a morality that defends other people and communities. Each state and people ought to have a duty to protect others, yet the global community is still quite far from such a principle-rule. It is good to strive to embrace humanity as a whole; as such, the internal conflict in the global community is something that saddens me even though I am at liberty to acknowledge its thus far a constructive, if not necessary, utility. Yet I am also at liberty to consider that for one nation to sacrifice itself and its people for the sake of the global community, such as when under the threat of nuclear annihilation, is of supreme virtue, but also one that may loom with recklessness.

Such a principle and attitude may be unfathomable for some, but this is what Liberty entails. This does not in any way suggest that I would strive for or advocate total condemnation of a people and country by nuclear destruction, and I fully acknowledge that treading on these issues with unprepared sense and reason can be extremely foolish. But in a necessary choice, it is better so that at least someone or something is left standing.

The conflict among the global community, especially Russia and the West, is fundamentally also a normative issue. In a world structure with no binding or effective law referring to a Constitution of Natural Law, and in terms of a global society fractured and divided into communities, disorder reigns because no power at the fundamental level is able to supercede the profound influence of Fear on and by the base faculties of people. The internal institutions of government and their systems in both Russia and the United States are conflicted. Virtue is often little more than a whisper in the conscience of people, for ignorance and Fear are prevailing.

There is no leadership or authority in the world that can effectively tell people that they are wrong when they are wrong. Democratic representatives are the best example of this, for their own Fear and their authority are built on consent lacking sincere leadership of potent moral authority. Only an authority reigning above the social and political dimensions can make progress towards sense, order, and goodwill at the fundamental, then structural levels. But it seems there are very few with the opportunity, and even fewer with the capacity to employ and hold such power.

At fault are not the governments and systems people may easily blame, but the moral and ethical dimensions of people at the heart of conflict and discord, the people that enable such states of affairs. Yet people are innocent in their ignorance and make mistakes, for they know little better; then also none but the newly born are absolutely innocent, for actions and characteristics from early on instigate suffering because of the necessity to grow from mistakes.

Innocence is a complex dimension of morality. Is the citizen of a democratic society responsible for electing a person who goes on to commit international crimes, to order war crimes? Are soldiers innocent when they kill on an order from officers? Is the disadvantaged consumer who contributes to environmental damage out of desperation to provide their family with a decent and dignified life to blame for a degrading environment? On the one hand, one cannot be held completely accountable for the actions and decisions of others or for acting in constrained circumstances. On the other hand, each action, and the character, of a moral agent executing and invoking actions is a contributing factor to the states of ethics.

No one from their first action is completely innocent. This does not justify in any way immorality or depravity towards people, such as unjust, indiscriminate punishment. The intended principle thought is that we all have individual responsibility, as none of us are perfect or wholly innocent. The desolation of innocence is the precedence of duty; imperfection and suffering are the initiation of virtue; turmoil in life is the foundation of order in moral law.

Challenges to global civilisation are much more profound than in plain terms of society and politics. The only way to improve on this is through the liberty of morality and virtue to empower the very foundation of the person's psyche, spirit, and soul. It is only in moving people towards virtues through their character, something that inherently requires the liberty to develop and grow, that we and the world, even a single person or society, can achieve greater flourishing. Only through a power of morality that can truly influence through liberty can greater flourishing be evoked in the individual and through the Highest Good. Then, such a power within oneself and for others can only be achieved through liberty itself. It is only in a monopoly of liberty of greater virtues and their benefits that greater flourishing can be cultivated. It starts with a fundamental notion of personal liberty as a Central Principle of a virtue-rule to oneself. This is a task far beyond one person, yet it is something achievable with but a few virtues at Liberty.

Here theory meets practise. Any ethical system or construct can synthesise certain moral rulings, principles, and guidelines as much as it likes. This is especially observable in tendencies of ethical constructs on a core of base ethics of Fear. They can be functional as they adhere to underlying constructs and functions that not only enable them in the first place but also regulate and adjust them. Even religious moralities are wholly organic in the way they express power over people's ethical dispositions and moral convictions. There is a very evident degree of an organic element to base ethics and their often-conflicted structures, influenced by changes in high-reason.

Throughout this project I will explore and analyse ethics primarily in terms of reason as part of related intuitions; after all, reason is the central function of all ethical and moral utilities. The ultimate goal of ethics, in the context of the heritin interpretation, is well-being through the *sense* of fulfilment through spiritual liberty, something I conceive through sensation and perception and adjust, analyse, and reflect on through reason. The two are indistinguishable.

However, an effect of high-reason that is poorly synchronised with base-reason may cause a rift and imbalance in ethics, the spirit, and the mind. This is where synthesis of a moral authority through reason may lose traction, force, and legitimacy – it may become overly *synthetic*. Synthetic authority is never wholly detached from a foundation of Nature and organic ethical tangents, yet it does run the risk of violating the structural dynamic of the flow of ethics in their functional state through artificial influences competing with established ethical forces. The natural course is that if a synthetic ethical utility and force violates principles converging on successful tangents, then it is doomed to failure by the adaptive cycle of values, which will be the ultimate end of any dysfunctional ethic, especially synthetic ones lacking organic characteristics allowing the flow of effective ethical utilities and functions.

This ethic seeks a fundamentally radical change – to succeed corruptive domination by Fear across many spheres, the former reserved for dedicated effort that might only be necessary or useful in terms of the utilities provided by the Ideals. However, this structure is not without a fundamental component linked to the organicism of the baser self; there are very rich, evocative, and fulfilling sensations beyond just Fear and in base-reason and high-reason.

The functions of heritin ethics arguably express very synthetic characteristics. The only way it or any other ethic worthy of consideration can succeed is if it organically and self-sufficiently adjusts to the parameters and conditions of an ethical environment. This is where the theoretical aspect becomes very significant – only by working through and with the liberty of the individual can this ethic ultimately prove to be successful and *good*. Any breach of liberty in ethics, exceeding the liberty to also impose authority as a means of liberty itself, any unwelcome synthesis of moral and ethical utilities unbound to liberty of ethics will ultimately fail the individual and maybe even society, the latter generally being more adaptive through its diversity of individuality. For any of the dynamics of effective influences of morality to get traction, such as the ones I propose, they must be at liberty in accord with organic, acceptable, and functional utilities and their structural tangents. Only by applying this theory through people, in accordance with people's own volition to enact a certain morality, can the ethic succeed.

The understanding of moral liberty is not simple and it encompasses and embraces many points. Even though the essence of the ethic of Liberty I outline is in reference to the Highest Good, it is also a liberty that is unwavering in its commitment to the point of paradoxically even permitting a global failure of Liberty and the degeneration of the Highest Good. As such, the liberty I outline is not what some may consider callous or ruthless, or even vilify as nihilistic. This is not a liberty that tolerates immorality and suffering, but accepts it, which are two very different things, as I shall demonstrate in a revised discussion and application of moral liberty. This is the path to greater flourishing beyond base ethics grounded in Fear, a source of growth for the individual and society.

The morality of liberty I argue for may be interpreted as expressing centrist characteristics between liberty and authority, but this alone would be a very simplistic and misunderstood interpretation of the arguments. The essence of the point I make is that liberty and authority go hand in hand and that the two are mutually dependent. However, liberty for a virtuous, self-sufficient authority through moral utilities ought to be the end goal, the Ideal of liberty in morality. For this purpose, immorality and suffering serve imperative roles, yet they are not absolute necessities for development. What liberty in morality enables is an appreciation and understanding of all the utilities within and of the Highest Good, which as I have shown is built on an understanding that nothing is inherently wrong – everything serves a function and everything is arbitrarily a mode of flourishing.

Liberty in morality and in spirit is the liberty that no matter the challenge and intuition or reality of impending failure, one can still have the liberty to pursue what is in one's greater interest. This liberty is one that no matter whether or not you are to fail, you can still try, often a victory in itself. This is a liberty that even if the world is to collapse, one can still find peace in this. This is a liberty to be at peace with suffering or to resist it, the liberty to be at peace with the vastness and arbitrariness of our lives and existence, then the liberty to offer others peace, support, and fulfilment if they so desire.

The ultimate virtue of liberty in morality of the Highest Good and its spiritual element entwined with the Void is its quality to invoke the necessary values and utilities for global well-being. The calculated liberty of morality by the Void, which some may mistakenly see as nihilistic, ultimately serves the Highest Good by finding the strength and will necessary to employ demanding and brutal moral utilities that come with a very high risk. Liberty in and of morality can come at great risk, at great cost, and create a lot of suffering, but the virtue of this liberty and its many spiritual elements is to find the strength to accept and employ liberty for greater reward despite the setbacks and challenges. The defiance and acceptance of liberty in morality and spirit serves the utility of progress and advancement for the Imperative, with the willingness to suffer and the resolution to confront and defy Fear leading to progress through the paradoxical utility of being willing to embrace destruction and annihilation but not yield to their coercion. Fluidity and diversity of characteristics and utilities are virtues.

As a final thought, liberty can and does bring chaos, but this is one of its primary utilities. Chaos becomes order through the determination of the Highest Good and order embodies chaos. The order arising from chaos as a result of the need for values to evolve leads to ethical development and progress in moral knowledge, ultimately bringing us closer to fulfilling the Human Imperative. Ill-fortune, conflicting ethical creeds, and plagued, twisted minds of lunatics hell-bent on creating mayhem constantly result in the spread of suffering and the resurrection of chaos to which we can only respond with the best of our virtues and utilities. Disorder often leads to suffering, but this in no way justifies grave moral deviation and the reckless devolution of order into chaos, yet this is something that we have to deal with in reality. The relation between order and chaos is a fundamental aspect of the systems of ethics, as well as of the mental and spiritual levels. Chaos and liberty go hand in hand, which eventually leads to greater prosperity, with this dynamic being a major aspect of the Human Imperative.

Liberty taunts chaos, disorder, and suffering, but if it is not subdued by Fear, then this is what makes liberty so great. It is better to become good by conquering suffering than to simply be made good, as no good character can be great without being tempered by fate. The sociopolitical aspect of liberty in contrast to control and authority, as well as the social and intergovernmental dynamic of order and instability, is something I will discuss in greater depth through the studies of Secondary Principles.

This brings me to how the influences of liberty can and ought to be invoked through moral utilities in accordance with their Central Principles. There are other Central Principles to be discussed and outlined in an effort to find moral knowledge. All moral knowledge is interrelated in some way, all of which feeds into the function of morality and normativity. Mediating liberty and devising morally effective responses to immorality, as well as setting the parameters for the function of liberty, are just some of the central moral themes that remain to be discussed.

Chapter 17:

Value of Life

Moral liberty can neglect the value of human life when poor estimation of value and misguided hierarchies of values gain supremacy over normativity. The estimation of ethical value and the value of life are elements of the Central Principles. Base morality often manifests itself as a tradition valuing human life based on intuition and sentiment that lack complimentary rational coherence. I will look into the questions of the value of life from the heritin perspective to formulate a different way of qualifying ethical value and understanding ethical valuation based on intuitive reasoning and mindful empathy.

Humanity has grand ambitions and can exert tremendous power when it applies itself. We are at the top of the food chain and the single species capable of destroying our own planet. The Highest Good constitutes all people bound by the Human Imperative; some people influence the Imperative positively, others less so; certain individuals contribute to growth and global well-being more than others. Human intelligence affects ethical structures and advances the Universal Imperative far more than any other animal. We are fortunate to have developed this advantage through the guidance of the pressures of Fear and survival, while also carrying the burden of the tools and weapons we have constructed. Advanced reason has given us the potential to adapt beyond the limits of base moralities, invigorating the spirit that strives for greater progress, exploration, and growth. Ethical value and quality can be found, identified, and integrated in terms of a vector's capacities, utilities, and characteristics with reference to the Highest Good. Balance in reasoning is more legitimate and coherent than values based on immoderate sentiments or convenient beliefs without concrete justifications through Natural Law. The value of life is not valued by inherent declaration and entitlement to value.

First, consider the Fundamental Principle of Living Beings. I have structured behaviour of living things in terms of the determination of the fundamental will. The body and mind behave in accordance with the functions of the will to flourish. Mindful empathy is imperative to highlight the unifying substance of the soul shared in all life in substance and spirit. All tangents of ethics are interlinked in global activity as part of material substance and the life it breeds and moves. All tangents are relevant to the Universal Imperative, affecting many dimensions and spheres of ethical structures. Ethical value is ascribed, and designated, to ethical tangents and a tangent's relevance to ethical endeavour. *Ethical value* is a measurement, estimation, and qualification relating to well-being. Ethical value is the designation and qualification of the relevance, role, and validity of an ethical element and tangent that affects well-being. For example, material resources are a utility capable of significantly affecting well-being, therefore having value to us and global development. Value can be qualified through analysis of a utility in terms of the Human Imperative in accordance with our desires, interests, and ambitions.

The behaviour of accentuated base-reason has a distinct mode of perception and valuation. We observe people and behaviour, then assign to them, or perceive, categories and qualifications. We may see one another as separate identities or embrace humanity as a single community. However, perceptions and valuations often lack mindfulness and coherence through the Human Imperative. Perceptions and utilities focusing on base-reason are vulnerable, inconsistent, unclear, and lack ambition. Leaving morality to base-reason and assigning value narrowly through undisciplined and unmindful sentiment, attitude, and bias creates ambiguity and inconsistency. Attitudes of 'us versus them' aren't exclusive to base morality, yet often restrict pragmatic ethical activity. Balanced and coherent reasoning and mentality, however, provide insight and perspective through mindfulness of empathy and the detachment that structure ethical value with clear intentions and desires, more capable of having greater influences relevant to well-being. Fear and survival can be restrictive mentalities offering only a narrow perspective and vision of ethical value. A global outlook in terms of the Human Imperative, moderating judgements and offering objectivity, is not only more sensible, but also makes greater perspective more accessible. To see people and value in focused pragmatic terms, rather than instinctive and emotional categories lacking balance and moderation or insight, allows greater clarity in the judgement and estimation of value.

To illustrate the idea, as well as to provide a case for how intuitions and estimations of value work, consider the essence of the morality of Discipline as part of the ambition of an autonomous will. Control over one's surrounding world can provide security from external causes of harm, which is valuable to Fear. By pursuing power to influence the surrounding world without developing the virtues of autonomy and independence, one only fulfils conditions of well-being restricted in Fear and sees value in terms of Fear alone. The pursuit of power over the world is inherently subject to Fear, while the grand ambition of worldly domination, without an indomitable mind and spirit, will never be realistically satisfied and will never provide complete satisfaction where this insecurity cannot be satisfied. The sense of power that comes with obsessive influence over one's surroundings in narrow desire is illusory, because it never gives strength that is greater than Fear and is a strength conditional on Fear. An obsession with power over others is a weakness that deprives spirit of greater ambition to succeed Fear, an ambition that empowers the character and the capability of a person. Power in Fear is valued in terms of Fear, whether as part of a desire for security in Fear, which will never be fully achieved while Fear still rules, or to distract oneself from Fear's suffering.

This mode of morality focusing on the value of power over others in the conditions of Fear qualifies ethical value in terms of the primary desire for security. The desire for security from pain adopts relevant attitudes and mentalities, which can then easily misguide the perception and estimation of value through a narrow perspective. In contrast to the ambition of control over the world, self-control and its subsequent security of steadfastness is far more realistic and achievable, at least to a greater degree than worldly security, and can be fulfilling where its desire is clearer and more coherent. Where a person's psyche is stronger and more flexible than worldly pressures, he or she is more able to perceive beyond narrow desires, compulsions, and views, increasing the probability of identifying greater interests and values. Being able to identify different values and possibilities is more valuable than stubbornness and confined interests.

The will to flourish underlies mental and bodily behaviour. The substance of the will, as the substance of the soul's continued functions, is absolutely the same in all life, human or animal. The difference between souls comes through the forms they take and the effects they have on the world. Anything outside of our conscious awareness and perception is foreign. However, underlying all perceptions is the universalisable soul through which all are equal, of the same foundation, and of the same Imperative of the will.

Humanity is unique in the way that reason can guide our behaviour and influence instincts, feelings, attitudes, understanding, and perspective. Mindfulness of empathy shows all people to be united by virtue of the soul and its Universal Imperative. Every single soul's operation is with a purpose instilled by Nature, according to which all are bound to a common fate through the Universal Imperative. Mindfulness of empathy evokes perception and understanding beyond narrow base-reason and looks to the soul, to a will shared among all, and highlights relevant values and interests focusing on a broader structural view of influences on well-being.

People commonly distinguish each other through base perceptions, failing to appreciate a more pragmatic, calculated, and focused view of value. Rather than strictly boxing people into categories, it is more useful to be pragmatic in the estimation of the value people have to offer. Empathy finds commonality and familiarity in all life, all endeavour, all ambition, and all actions. We are fundamentally driven by the same desire, the same soul, and the same foundations of the human condition. All souls serve a purpose and are a means to the end of the Imperative; all souls are moved by, and are a part of, the Highest Good, with every individual and causal tangent affecting the shared ethical structure. Everything and everyone is relevant to global well-being as part of a global structure of ethical tangents. Therefore, every life holds meaning and every life has value. However, each soul functions differently and is unique to its circumstance and narrative of causal tangents. There is a difference in the immediacy and conditions of values according to each and every individual, whereby all interests and values are grounded in the shared interest and desire set by the Human Imperative.

The soul is equal among all, but character is not, as some are more better off than others and generate more goodness, through virtue, in terms of the shared interest of the Human Imperative. Some have a greater positive impact on the world and global welfare. Thus, character is not equal and can be designated value. To say that all life is of equal value is naive and deceptive.

Every soul has value, but the harsh truth is that it doesn't matter in the grand scheme of things what the soul is inherently worth – the only thing that truly matters is what that soul makes a person do, in other words the type of character a soul embodies and what this character makes a person do. We only care about things and each other in so far as it contributes to our happiness – we are wholly self-interested and mechanical and computational maximisers of ethical interest and value.

This notion is not a mere ascription of this philosophy, but a fact of intuition in all behaviour; all ethics function through a system of assessment and ascription of value. Some people affect greater change, meaning they are more significant ethical vectors. An honest and righteous doctor who saves lives and helps many people is of more value as a result of his work than a selfish criminal. A loved one is more important to one's happiness than a stranger. If all ambitions and desires are moved by an ultimatum of the Categorical Directive, fulfilled through the Human Imperative, then there is a particular circumstantial ethical value in each utility and tangent relating to shared global interest. Therefore, not everyone is *of* equal value, even though every person *has* inherent value. While we are all a means to an end, we also *are* the means to an end. The soul is the seed of equality; the character is the throne of utility; the spirit is the measure of virtue.

Before I study these central thoughts further, and in response to some concerns that may immediately arise, I note that these positions do not entail that human life is expendable, for every human life has potential to construct and benefit the Highest Good in ways people themselves may not know or predict. People might be set on the wrong path in life by pressures of needing to survive and a harsh fate, but that does not mean their way and their mind-sets of vice cannot be undone. Every person has the potential to do good, maybe even great things, but it is a matter of value whether they do such things or not, whether they fulfil the potential of the soul that is defined by its pursuit of betterment and goodness. The character is what entails the quality and spirit of people's actions. A stronger character leads to greater well-being for the individual and other people, consequently affecting an entire ethical sphere and structure.

The world doesn't care about you per se and does not assign complete value by entitlement of simply existing. Vectors and human agency only value and care about what *you* and your character makes you do or what *you* can do for others. Dynamics in structures of ethics bound to the Highest Good only assign value and respective tangents affecting states of affairs through the utility of character aligned with good values. Virtues are good when they generate goodness, not when they are idle. It is insufficient to be merely kind and compassionate, as one must also apply oneself for such virtues to become valuable utilities, to do good. It is insufficient to be an idle character of virtue lacking employment, as one's virtue and righteousness is only complete through work for the endeavours of mankind and community.

People are self-interested and structural dynamics are above all else concerned with movement and development. The value of one's character is not necessarily or primarily measured in terms of wealth and status; character is valued by its capacity and endeavour in terms of the Imperative and the Highest Good. Whatever you do isn't primarily valued in specific ways like making money, but it does have to benefit people, which can be done in many ways. The value of a person is the nobility of virtue and goodwill.

Mindful empathy is crucial to good judgement and estimation of ethical value. Empathy's liberating spiritual element entails the core moral utility of mindful thought on actions maximising ethical value and interest. One ought to always remember the following virtue-rule of empathy and universalisability: by neglecting the lives of others', a person neglects their own. An attitude of apathy and neglect reflects back in similar ways through ethical tangents of character unable to surround themselves with goodness or treat themselves with goodness. Apathy and neglect of others' interests blinds a person to the efficiency and virtue of goodwill found in mindful empathy. How one treats others reflects back onto one's own character and becomes subject to reciprocal treatment by those affected negatively. By acting in vice towards others, those vices act against the self, undermining well-being. Failing to care for others will not cultivate the compassion towards oneself that leads to inner peace and healing from pain.

Worldly objects secondary to the soul do not definitively measure the value of a person. Value is measured by the character shaping the surrounding world through oneself. Possessing copious wealth does signify degrees of a capacity to influence causal tangents and create a secure foundation for flourishing in an inherently materialistic world according to the Natural Law of the principle of sufficient conditions for existence. But the capacity to influence is only as good as the utilities and virtues that enable and sustain its causal tangents or use material capacities effectively. Material utilities are subservient to inner strength that is independent of financial wealth or other material objects, so the greater capacity of a character of indomitable will comes through inner characteristics using material utilities for the soul's own desires, channelling external pressures rather than being in their thrall. Do not underestimate the importance and validity of welfare, but also do not overestimate its inherent worth or utility, for material utility is always only a resource for spirit, not spirit itself.

Somebody driven by base morality and its degree of virtue might adopt greed to try to control his or her environment to compensate for the fear of uncertainty. A person's strength and degree of flourishing comes from *how* he or she interacts with the world and how a person employs given utilities, not from what means a person can expend in order to flourish. Power can come in many ways, yet it does not entail strength, as certain powers lacking virtue can be wielded by the morally depraved. Power can have a certain degree of influence, whether through material fulfilment or institutional authority, but power in the hands of the morally weak will have little grasp over the truly strong in character, spirit, and will. However, the strongest, virtuous, and most powerful are the people who change the world for the better, defying suffering, having their names inscribed in history with veneration of their virtues and their influence on mankind and the world. The greatest power of an individual is the ambition of goodwill unrestrained and unconditioned by Fear or suffering.

Sometimes the value of a person can reach beyond the convention of morality, or at least beyond obvious virtues. For instance, a morally neutral character with extremely important and valuable utilities, for example an individual with the knowledge of how to cure a devastating disease, can easily be argued to have great value for people independent of the character's virtues. A cure for a disease could create well-being and opportunity for many people who are valuable for the Human Imperative. Hence, sometimes people's value can be found through more pragmatic considerations than idealistic moralising, by looking at the 'bigger picture'.

Then again, knowledge is a utility, implying it is a virtue that competes with other characteristics, with the most promising virtue becoming an Ideal. If there is a case where an individual possesses a great utility like substantial wealth and does not employ it effectively, this asset might not provide the necessary value for the common Imperative, because a valuable utility is wasted through mismanagement. Other agents with better management of resources could produce more ethical interest with less resources, having more value than the individual of lesser financial ability using resources inefficiently.

Certain roles or functions of people are exchangeable and replaceable, but not expendable. In some circumstances people's functions might be irreplaceable or at least very much worth keeping around, which again suggests that sometimes value can be less obvious than one-dimensional considerations of character and narrow perspectives of ethical interest.

In terms of mindful reflection on the Human Imperative and the Highest Good through empathy and detachment, people can be seen as a type of resource, but it is a distinct resource that is in no circumstances expendable. Every single life is of more imperative value than the resource of any material object – unless the material value is for the benefit of people's consensus because of our responsibilities to one another and in terms of the material object's relevance to the maximum values of common interest.

This point is especially important if such a principle moves towards the exploitation of material utilities and people in a divisive, blind, and unsustainable mode of production, all of which is against any basic moral and ethical common sense or intuitive virtue. Furthermore, morally ignorant and unmindful focus of attention in the use of material utilities can condemn character to surrender its virtues, leading to the retributive and balancing measures of Nature. A clear example of this is reckless and blind material consumption contributing to climate change, which has the potential to punish mankind.

How we treat others reflects who we are and how we treat ourselves. Vice grows through mistreatment of people as mismanagement of vectors, which are elements affecting well-being. To ignore the value of the utilities of human agency is to disregard an important resource in itself. To mismanage human enterprise and endeavour by ignoring and disregarding the ethical interests and moral concerns of people is to foolishly mismanage the effectiveness of the whole sphere of an enterprise – of both its material and human utilities.

People are a complex and precious resource of the soul and so much more. People are a distinctive resource of the Highest Good in terms of combined individual and communal welfare that requires a coherent, comprehensive, and disciplined ethic for the use of our labour and autonomy. Our distinctive nature and essence as a utility and resource of the Highest Good is characterised by our bodies – material imbued with a will that moves other substance through the purpose of life.

This point is central to social responsibility and issues of sustainable material enterprise and ethics of material utility. Reducing people to a mere *disposable* resource, beyond necessary circumstances demanding a response of sacrificing the few for the many in justification of the Human Imperative, is wrong. Furthermore, an exploitative and reckless attitude towards ourselves breeds principles of lesser utility, as such an attitude may mismanage and poorly utilise the complex resources of our labour. It is foolish, reckless, and inefficient to endorse a view reducing mankind to mere objects, because the related characteristics mismanage human resources central to one's own well-being and neglect the valuable utilities of empathy and other virtues. These considerations are central to understanding and organising the value of people and how the value of our utility and endeavour ought to be guided and employed.

However, the use of resources must be considered carefully and sometimes certain human life must be prioritised over others based on considerations of the utility of people's value and subsequent effects on ethical structures. Sometimes the greater value of one individual must take priority over another individual of lesser utility. For instance, people who are sick might need organ transplants, but there might not be enough for all. The natural question is how should these limited organs be distributed for maxims of personal and global interest.

The central principle and function of the Human Imperative is that all utilities serve as a means to the end of mass welfare. Considerations of consequences are imperative for the goal of the Imperative. As such, causal effects in terms of a greater scheme reaching many levels and dimensions of ethical structures, such as those affecting society and community, are important for certain decisions. In the case of organ transplants, there are limited resources available. It follows that any decision or action employing material utilities must consider the consequences of and on human utility to achieve better results. It is then only sensible to weigh the effects of certain consequences rather than blindly distribute limited resources.

One could argue from a position of moral luck that giving the needed resources on a first-come, first-served basis is fair. Some might argue that this would fulfil virtue of character more by feeding goodwill of helping people without discrimination and brutal calculation. Such a mode of action does have merit, but it inherently involves the pursuit of the maximum achievable positive ethical interest in particular circumstances. We are better than leaving our well-being to blind luck and chance. We can predict and assess to achieve better results, and so it is sensible to employ these utilities imperative to a functioning society. Neglecting the capacity for objective assessment would create the same threats that mankind already faces.

Feeding the virtues of foresight is better than leaving virtue to luck. Furthermore, to achieve the effect of better consequences, which is imperative for the Highest Good and greater well-being, we must assess, predict, analyse, and calculate. This means applying the same measures to material utilities as well as human utilities. This thought may seem condemnable in sentiment, yet this activity will produce a greater effect of sentiment by producing greater positivity both of the constructive effect through more capable individuals and by preserving what positive sentiment may be achievable.

For example, in terms of the considerations of sentiment alone, is it better to preserve the life of a person with few-to-no emotional ties with others, or preserve the life of a parent with a family? In terms of the greatest value defined by sentiment, it is intuitive and reasonable to focus on the patient whose condition has more significant emotional connections and potential consequences. To act in greater compassion requires an estimation of compassion. Certain people contribute more to global ethical interest than others and thus possess more value. If a doctor has to choose who gets an organ – a decent and morally upstanding father with a family or a thug leading a criminal life – then the morally best choice would be to save the father.

However, this isn't to say that the criminal does not have value; giving them another chance might give them the motivation to live a life of greater value, meaning, esteem, dignity, and self-worth. As I argued, every life has value and potential. However, a criminal who continuously has negative influences on ethical structures has less value than a person of greater virtue. Therefore, it is better to act in rational assessment and deliberately prioritise the limited material utilities for the greater common good.

The measure of value must be weighed within a certain framework. One aspect of value certainly appeals to the utilitarian principle of 'the greatest good for the greatest amount of people'. Within this idea lies an incredibly complex system of application. Many elements and aspects are involved in assessment in terms of the utilitarian principle, but in practice they can be far too difficult to apply clearly and effectively, as the variables in any assessment of consequences can be stupendous.

For one, moral decisions weighing the consequences of an action with reference to the utilitarian principle may contain intangible variables of absurd proportions, thereby making it nearly impossible to predict with absolute certainty the outcome of an action. Essentially, moral decisions involving consequences must comply with risk-assessment and even build on certain aspects of *Game theory*.

In uncertain circumstances, it is up to the involved moral agents to establish in their best judgement what the best course of action is. The heritin contribution to this practice in ethics is the expansion of variables, such as character affecting future intentions and the capacities for action, in consideration of consequences. However, moral decisions that involve the lives of people must also consider their character and value, whereby the value of a person entails the potential for beneficial actions and their consequences on the individual and community.

Sometimes it might even be the case that ten lives must be sacrificed for the sake of one if this means maximising value benefiting the most. However, sometimes the character of people is unknowable, in which case a judgement might have to be made through blind reason, rational calculation of statistics, or generalised presumptions. The value of people must be assessed through their character marked by vectors of the virtues of actions.

The Highest Good nourishes people's interests through the virtuous and strong, but this isn't to say that the weak and vulnerable must be disregarded. Every person has value and a degree of utility; if people are encouraged, inspired, and motivated to achieve greater fulfilment through greater virtue of character, the Imperative benefits. Well-being and the strength of virtue should be distributed in a fashion that can lead to even greater maxims of interest and ambition. For instance, the utility of the morally weak and less virtuous might require omission by the necessity of prioritising the endeavour of the righteous producing greater constructive and positive effects contributing more to people's well-being, whereby the morally weaker possess less value than the virtuous.

In extreme ethics involving the necessity for ruthless valuation and calculation, it is up to mindful assessment in terms of the Human Imperative to judge where, who, or what ought to be prioritised in value to secure and produce greater ethical interests, but only *if* the need arises for such judgements. Only when it is a matter of necessity should we prioritise and manage the value of people's character to maximise ethical interest. *Only* when it is necessary should ruthless and calculated exchanges of ethical interest be done, not when there are viable alternatives. Again, this normative principle entails aspects of decision-making, estimation, and assessment that are beyond any universal theory and defers to the acting judgement of people in positions demanding a decision. Extreme exchanges of ethical value and life should only be performed in extremely demanding circumstances.

There is a difference between rational, stern pursuit of self-interest and needless brutality. There is a difference between unsympathetically getting rid of bad people in your life, who don't contribute to your happiness and only cause dissatisfaction, and treating them badly, such as by needlessly and vengefully reacting in pain, or throwing them under a bus.

People are never expendable; people and the betterment of the Highest Good through virtue are ends in themselves. First of all, permitting a moral creed that treats people as expendable resources leads to costly, disastrous, and abhorrent attitudes. However, this argument alone isn't sufficient, although very relevant and compelling. Every individual, by virtue of the soul, intrinsically has value and meaning. The potential for any person to be a positive influence on the Human Imperative means every person has an intrinsic value and a meaningful position in the world.

Through our will we become distinct from ordinary objects, meaning by virtue of the soul and its will we are distinct from ordinary material substances and objects. Through the fundamental will we become a living, organic substance with a defining characteristic of consciousness giving spirit to actions and living. In this way we are not ordinary substance, yet our consciousness leads to a ploy of mindfulness where our will is, or can be, ascribed to lifeless objects.

No single individual is supreme, above others, or sufficiently virtuous without the community balancing, spreading, enhancing, and applying the value of humanity through our capacity to change the world for the better. The betterment and nobility of character come with virtue measuring the self through conscience of the Highest Good and mindful of the Human Imperative encompassing all souls and the Highest Good beyond any single person. To fulfil this potential and apply ourselves responsibly and effectively we must mediate and manage our activity. Considerations of value enable this through assigning, applying, and exchanging utilities. To consider any person as expendable is to grossly neglect the virtue of the utility we are capable of. A morality of expendability of human value would neglect effective application of our endeavour and good spirit.

However, considerations of value enable the exchange of values in a way that prioritises of maxims of interest, which is valid in assessment of moral utilities and values. The interests of some people can legitimately and morally be put ahead of other people and others' interests, but this does not mean other people's interests ought to be neglected or wholly expended.

When it comes to instances of exchange in ethical value, in accord with Liberty, there are certain criteria to guide the assignment and use of moral utilities. For one, in times of strife when sacrifices are necessary for the maxims of goodness, certain utilities, including people, must be directed and mediated. Instances of war are clear examples of certain utilities exchanging their value when people must act in terms of the maxims of common value. Capable people go to war to defend their homes as a necessary response to unjust foreign aggression, whereby people's value becomes imperative in their utility to protect the Highest Good through likely sacrifice.

Certain people become valuable in terms of their willingness to suffer and sacrifice. But this does not justify or necessarily entail the utility of such characters being expendable. What this also means is that people must be at liberty of autonomous goodwill to determine their role in the exchange of ethical value, including sacrificing their lives for the common good to protect those unable to defend themselves. It can be moral to send young men and women to fight a war to restore balance and justice, but it is not moral to instigate an unnecessary conflict and send people on suicide missions without common accord in moral liberty. If people refuse to go to war and cannot be convinced that if they do not respond appropriately then they will suffer, then so be it – this is just and moral because this maximises ethical value and is compatible with the Natural Law of the adaptive cycle. If the Central Principles of moral liberty are neglected or compromised, then related ethical values will be as well.

I will dedicate a separate Chapter to the morality of sacrifice, but for the present context it is important to highlight that any exchange of value and utility must be done, or is morally better when done, in accordance with the liberty of an autonomous will. When it comes to extreme cases of implementing and exchanging ethical value involving people and lives, these ethical dynamics ought to be compatible with, and mindful of, other Central Principles. The normativity of authority influencing people's self-determination is a matter for the Secondary Principles.

Sometimes people can't make the necessary choice for the greater interest of the Highest Good. People who aren't tempered by difficult choices do not possess the necessary virtues of decisiveness and the discipline of the burdens of making difficult decisions. Indecisiveness and the lack of responsibility usually relate to naivety and compulsive judgements borne of brash and idealistic sentiments. Tough choices are realities and decision-making in leadership is not an easy or light task.

At the same time, rationality and calculated estimations of ethical value, necessary virtues in positions of command and responsibility, can neglect the value of these utilities when value-assessment is detached from mindfulness of empathy and sentiments. This can be both good and bad. Hopeful, but risky decisions can reap greater rewards that are otherwise restrained by the fear of risk, or rational calculation and strategy might ignore the possibility of much greater rewards that come with high risk.

The natural antagonism between leadership and followers can be symbiotic and healthy, and similarly the dispute between sensibility and risk-taking in decision-making is symbiotic, as the liberty in ethical competition manifests itself as a liberty of dynamic values. It is difficult to say clearly what is morally better when one faces a tough choice, especially if the available knowledge informing predictions and assessments is limited.

More importantly for the present subject, the emotional conditions of people's willingness to assign, derive, and assess value is central to the ethics of value of life and utilities. As with the case of how to distribute limited medicine to patients in need, one may find comfort in the emotional ease of leaving things beyond one's control – to give in to moral luck – to set aside the responsibility of difficult decisions. Making tough choices in relation to the distribution and employment of value can take an emotional and spiritual toll on an individual. Carelessness is liberating, but not fulfilling.

Heritin ethics is at an advantage in such circumstances as it rules with the pursuit of virtue and mindfulness and seeks to nourish the balanced psyche. Discipline and virtue that come with responsibility and duty find, and are driven by, ambition through and in pain, thriving in righteousness overcoming Fear and suffering. It is difficult, but people ought to make the right choice and then learn to deal with the personal, emotional impact of duty.

However, in more practical, realistic terms, the matter is not as straightforward. Even beyond the heritin ethic, people are able to learn to set aside panic and stress and focus on pressing issues and consider immediate questions and decisions with a focused mind – to behave rationally. This is an inherent virtue of high-reason that must be cultivated and disciplined. However, these virtues aren't always accessible.

This issue and matter needs to be considered in depth. Specifically, how should one act when his or her emotions compromise decision-making and the ability to see clearly and act in accordance with high-reason? The heritin principle-rule would be to focus on the rationale behind actions along with sentiment, not disregard either. This follows with the question of how to consider the emotional and spiritual impact of choices involving the rationale of value, and how this should be balanced on occasions when the rationale of people is limited. Sometimes people might find themselves in predicaments where they must make choices they are unprepared for and their emotional states will be too over-bearing for the clarity of balanced reason to moderate pain and other sentiments. How can the implementation of a rational ethic, its principles and values, be practical?

First, the principles of moral liberty imply that people's abilities should be accepted and that, in line with the liberty of morality, competition between rationale and sentiment should be enabled, particularly when it is beyond one's moral authority or responsibility. Furthermore, the liberty for competition in values is central to the cultivation of virtues and learning morality. The purpose of virtue is to balance healthy and adaptive mentality and spirit, whereby a person can use any available, baser or higher, mental and moral utility. This means being capable of making the tough choice and living with the consequences. Rationality is a virtue moderated by sentiment, and vice versa. It must be remembered that strength only comes from resisting unfavourable odds and no deed is truly good without struggle and suffering.

What if a person can't do the right thing because the emotional cost for him or her is too much? It might not be ideal to commit the lesser good, but it may be sufficiently morally permissible if the cost in value between the greater and lesser good isn't of imperative value. This, however, is only morally permissible in other moralities, not according to Liberty, which must tolerate moral liberty. It would be easy to say that people who endure the consequences of their actions in response to difficult choices are the ones to live with their decisions and bear the guilt or satisfaction. But in reality, the effect of any judgement will have as much, if not more of an impact on people. The personal dimension of spiritual fulfilment in these utilitarian considerations comes through the reflective effect of a utilitarian judgement influencing a state of affairs. Nevertheless, even the most painful mistakes can lead to growth, goodness, and redemption by acknowledging and learning from mistakes. Even immorality can have value in showing the path to virtue.

Where tough choices are to be made, the person must count on themselves to make the right choice. But the failure of the liberty of virtue and subsequent suffering is something the decision-maker should be mindful of. Sometimes the right thing to do is to preserve one's own sanity, character, and spirit, as grave suffering can lead to grotesquely twisted judgements. It is an element of moral liberty that if no people have the strength to do what is necessary in sincere goodwill, then liberty ought to accept the consequences of Natural Law.

This, however, does not dismiss the responsibilities and duties of the virtuous; if you can do what is right, then you ought to. Assessing value and being honest, then acting accordingly, can be brutal and painful, but such is the cost of virtue and maxims of well-being. In the gloom that may arise from making a tough but necessary choice, the pain should be remedied by being mindful of the goodness that comes through it. One should act in accordance with maxims of value even though the personal impact of actions can be costly in the short-term, then use one's own suffering as a utility. Acts in accordance with the lesser good – of lesser value – are permissible and tolerable provided they are compatible with other Central Principles, reaching a compromise in competing values that maximises the best possible outcome. Forcing a person to do what is in everybody's greater interest against his or her autonomy will only sow further discord, suffering, and conflict, whereby the best outcome is only achievable through tolerance and compromise.

We all pursue what we think is best for us, even in poor wisdom. Assigning, reflecting on, analysing, and employing considerations of value and qualifications of utilities, including people, is something we naturally and intuitively do, something that maximises common interest. A problem arises when people fail to properly evaluate interests and actions, reducing the greater ambition of the Human Imperative to selfishness. Maximum sum terms of well-being can come with greater suffering than the suffering of a secure, fearful life. It is helpful to imagine this in terms of stacks of values where greater sum terms of well-being can come with suffering experienced worse than in restrained well-being. In this case, as with ethics of Liberty, the gap between well-being and suffering is greater than its alternative, even though the values of suffering produced by Liberty are greater than the suffering produced by Fear.

Imagine the following bar chart: a *blue* bar represents well-being, and a *red* bar represents suffering. In Fear and base morality, the blue and red might be more-or-less balanced out. In Liberty, both the blue and red bars are much taller, but the increase in suffering produces exponential growth in well-being. So in comparison to Fear, Liberty profits more *and* the difference between well-being and suffering – the blue and red bars – is much greater. But it is always crucial to acknowledge and appreciate what those numbers and values represent – well-being sensed in spirit, which requires a person to be grounded in reality and living, not to be detached through rationality.

A person shouldn't simply distract themselves from pain without resolution, such as in the case of harmful addictions. Similarly, a person shouldn't detach from feelings and sensations to merely exist, and not truly live, in blind rationality. But there is a time and a place for focusing and using different aspects of our nature and human condition. In the end, Liberty is the only possible way to relieve all suffering, maximising positive ethical value. For goodness to become far greater than suffering, one must learn to be free in both these states; to maximise the interests of values between well-being and suffering, one must become free from the desire and compulsion for one to overbear the other – this is achieved through the Ploy of Consciousness. The pursuit of maxims of positive value through Liberty is not easy and will invite pain and suffering, but this way we are able to use courage and strength to make the changes necessary for a better life and a better world.

In ethical valuation and estimation, one must act and assess value in terms of both base-reason and high-reason. The threat of pain can be a threat to well-being, and it is certainly uncomfortable, but it can also undermine morality and actions pursuing greater interests. Neglecting to act morally correct in the face of suffering will sustain or lead to suffering. If somebody is not prepared to make a difficult choice for the benefit of the Human Imperative, then he or she will not reap the corresponding benefits. But by not making the right choice and enabling the negative consequences of inaction or lesser goodness, the suffering that was sought to be overcome in the first place will only continue.

Committing the emotionally difficult action might not be immediately rewarding, unless it is a choice in Discipline and duty relishing in the empowerment of autonomy. However, the choice to embrace suffering will nourish the seed of virtue that can overcome suffering and reap greater rewards than the choice restrained by Fear. Therefore, moral liberty is precious in tough circumstances demanding action.

This brings me to formulating a moral principle of ethical valuation in relation to moral liberty: as long as one's emotional state does not violate, through action or inaction, what is morally acceptable and tolerable, qualified through the Central Principles and in reference to the Human Imperative, then the failure to act in accordance with the Highest Good is not strictly wrong; however, it is nonetheless better and greater to act in accordance with maxims of value, especially if one aspires towards greater well-being (in Liberty).

The common, greater good is central to the Highest Good and its Imperative. This value can consist of the greater good in terms of one person or the many, in terms of local communities or nations. Excessively rational estimation, negligent of sentiment, may focus on pure numbers, such as by favouring national welfare over local communities, or favouring the Human Imperative while being negligent of close people. The values present in rational estimations of ethical interest are multidimensional and extremely complex, the dynamics of which transform easily with new influences. Failing to appreciate an individual's welfare and emotional state (through mindful empathy) will neglect a particular vector, meaning valuation may fail to account for a variable. But then the relevance of a vector's influence is conditional and circumstantial, requiring appeal and understanding through structural ethics.

Ignoring others' moral attitudes and neglecting people's sentiments can misjudge the value of certain utilities. Neglecting common desires and attitudes can have an adverse effect on the righteousness of virtues by causing greater suffering in a community. For example, a community's main desire may be stability and comfort, even if the function and directive of this stability is fundamentally flawed and fragile. Neglecting the community's desire for comfort could instigate greater instability and conflict, thereby doing more harm than good. But then sometimes it is the demanding task of leadership and authority to mediate common interests at an immediate cost to some, which a community would fail to appreciate. Primary values then rest with people capable of assessing and judging value and moral quality between the common and individual good, where society and the individual are contingent on each other.

Those able to rise to embrace duty for the common, greater good and for the Highest Good are people who have prime ethical value in terms of the utility of their character. The character embracing the common, higher good marks itself with the virtue of the Ideals, and hence the goodness of harmony between individual and community is achieved. This is of supreme value for the individual and its utility for community and the Highest Good.

Concerning the use of the term morally *weak*, it must be specified that the intended meaning of this weakness is in terms of morality and character, concerning those who are deprived of virtue and goodness. The words 'strong' and 'weak' can be used in many contexts, but in this book, it is generally used with the intended meaning of virtue and morality. The morally weak are those who lack the inner strength to be moral and virtuous, therefore lacking the fulfilment that comes with virtue in accordance with the Highest Good. The weak are those who are immoral and embody vice. The strong are strong by the empowerment of virtues; the weak are weak because of their depravity.

The lives of the morally weak have value and most certainly have potential. However, sometimes when there is no viable opportunity, people of greater utility and virtue must be prioritised over those leading lives of lesser goodness. The flaws and weaknesses of mankind can be traced back and corrected by various methods such as therapy, rehabilitation, or correctional systems. Human nature is impressionable, as the human condition is naturally vulnerable to Fear. Yet sometimes the greatness of people can arise unexpectedly and apparently from nowhere. Given the liberty to do so, even those born into misfortune and vice can learn to utilise suffering and seize opportunity to reach further than people of favourable odds and privilege from birth.

Humanity is full of surprises and ambition. Just because somebody is on a bad track does not mean they cannot achieve more than what they once were or what has been impressed on them. However, this might require a degree of intervention and authority bound to morality and virtue. If the implications of the mechanisms of the mind and its fundamental will tell us anything, it is that even the weakest of characters and will can develop and pursue greater flourishing by virtue of the soul.

A vaguely moral person could potentially commit a tremendously moral act when it is needed most, even if he or she did not have a history of behaviour that was indicative of great acts. Sadly, this doesn't happen often, and there is little room for hope or chance that could accommodate rehabilitation or sudden evocation of virtue in people. Sometimes the risk is too great in any sensible assessment, and yet some estimations can never recognise the unforeseeable spark of greatness and courage that can only come from taking a risk. Nevertheless, even though moral liberty consists of risks and risks are only predictable to a certain degree, to maximise value it is best to be disciplined, mindful, wise, and sensible.

There is a difference between moral weakness and *vulnerability*. Every person has vulnerabilities, but that does not necessarily make them weak. The morally weak behave selfishly, cowardly, and are enslaved to vice. Immorality is a symptom of a weak will and foolishness – weaknesses in pain and Fear. The morally vulnerable, on the other hand, are those who aren't as strong as certain characters, which doesn't necessarily mean the vulnerable are immoral. Those who act according to lesser morality because they don't possess the virtues to commit to the Highest Good aren't immoral, but they are vulnerable to Fear and suffering. People who find it difficult to fulfil their potential and act on their greatest desires, such as to take greater care of the environment or to treat others with more kindness than unintentional reactions, aren't necessarily immoral or deserving of condemning judgement. Instead, they are simply vulnerable in Fear, not consumed and degraded by it.

People can lose track of themselves when they experience great pain – this happens to everyone. There are times when we fall prey to pain and suffering, but this is natural and inherent to the amorphous soul. We all have our vulnerabilities. The difference between strength and weakness is if we pick ourselves and others back up to try again and to grow. The selfishness of a child is not immorality – it's something they haven't learnt more about. The father protecting and nurturing his family is right to do so, but sometimes this Fear clouds his judgement and stops him from doing the right thing for greater interest, when Fear feeds off vulnerability.

Strong people should be considered so by the virtues they hold and their moral integrity, discipline, and wisdom to produce goodness through themselves. Everyone knows a good person when they meet them, because their character is of a nobility recognised, sensed, and felt by all. Intuitions are deceptive and cruelty is cunning, but there are times when judgement is correct. The surest mark of a strong person is the ability to empathise and see the good in people, to inspire; the person who is not afraid to doubt themself and admit wrong-doing and vulnerability, and has the rare characteristic of staying a good person despite the pain that the righteous path may inflict. Then, impetuous character is one of duty.

Any value of a given life should not idolise arrogance. Arrogance blinds judgement and estimation of value; arrogance presumes the Highest Good and the Human Imperative, corrupting and betraying these Ideals through vice. Certain people might possess greater value than others and, quite frankly, some people are better people than others. Thinking and valuing differently is subject to the measure and qualification of justice on the grounds of appeal to the Fundamental Principle and its Human Imperative.

Good people are judged to be so with reference to their activity and life creating good for others. However, this isn't to say that the virtuous are *above* others. Stronger people are not supposed to possess greater power over others by virtue alone. There is a distinction between worldly influence and inner power of character, whereby the latter inherently carries greater power and value due to its capacity to generate goodness. Stronger people have more value, but they have that value because they use their worth for more than themselves, heralding the Highest Good that binds all people. However, on these grounds alone aristocracies and caste systems of society are not justifiable, for example. Instead, political and social systems and structures should be valued in terms of their effectiveness in producing positive ethical interest.

All sociopolitical and civic normativity would have to, above all else, abide by the Central Principles of moral liberty and be mindful of the adaptive cycle. Human society develops organically according to the liberty of morality by adapting to changes in the world. People are born with incredible diversity, and philanthropy, innovation, and genius arise even from the humblest of circumstances. To systematise human society and not respect the freedom of autonomous individual life would not fulfil the greater potential of people by neglecting the organicism of values and tangents.

I will expand on the themes of liberty and authority in structures of ethics through the Secondary Principles. For now, I wanted to make the point that just because certain people are stronger because of their virtues does not mean that they are inherently entitled to power over people or are given a self-entitled right to reign.

Strength in virtue doesn't warrant legitimacy to govern or grant justification for elitism. What morally stronger people ought to do is inspire strength and courage in people, encourage and help people, guide and advise them through wisdom, and strive to protect and support the endeavour of the Human Imperative. This is the worth and nobility of virtue, which is very different from seizing authoritative and executive control over the lives of people that one may deem morally weak, different from presuming the Highest Good and enshrouding the direction of the Universal Imperative. Moral value does not axiomatically equate social or economic worth; moral outlooks can instil sentiment in the social and cultural attitudes influencing the perceived value of people, but how this moral authority is used depends on the wider context than the judgements of core principles of ethics alone.

Strong and accomplished persons might look down on others they perceive to be of lesser character, but this attitude is inconsistent with virtue. Snobbery is arguably a reaction suppressing people of lesser character and self-validating oneself for the sake of security. There is no place for snobbery as a virtue-rule in a morality striving to uplift character and spirit beyond Fear.

A thought may arise where a person who is better off than others might begin to think they are above their peers, but this is a path towards arrogance estranged from virtue and mindfulness. Greater inner strength lies not in comparing oneself to others, but in the need-not to do so, in the confidence of autonomy to be a character of independent spirit. The key to success and happiness is not apathy and carelessness over others' sentiments, opinions, and welfare – it is in rising above others' expectations that impose desires that are not in one's own greatest interests. Success is not measured by others – other people are only a variable affecting the success of an ambition. Not having a care in the world about others' opinions is only as good as its ability to prevent the erosion of ambition through others' expectations. Seeing weaknesses in others can draw attention to one's own strength and fortune, whereby empathy shows that others' misfortune could be one's own. But in doing so one ought not to look down on those who have not been fortunate or empowered.

It is relevant in the assessment of value when people don't act in a way that will make them happiest, but these are not grounds for harsh judgement and condemnation. Empathy and autonomy are only valuable because they benefit others through oneself. People do not respond well to condescending attitudes and arrogance over-shadowing the virtue of dignity and confidence. If one truly wants to help others out of goodwill, it becomes intuitive to approach people in an acceptable, humble fashion, with decency and respect, and help them only in so much as they desire or is deemed necessary in terms of justice.

Imposing one's will and opinions on others will not aid the cause of bettering people by inspiring them to pursue greater ambitions as part of the common inter-est of the Highest Good. A moral norm might not even be necessary or applicable in others' circumstances under the liberty of morality. It is better to have a willing and constructive dialogue involving fruitful endeavour rather than a grudge match of petty and unhealthy self-validation. People would respond better to opinions if they saw value in characteristics of wisdom and notable experience. Then, as part of moral liberty, one ought not to intrude in the affairs of others unless it is necessary for justice. However, this empathy and understanding should not give way to the blind tolerance of incompetence and irresponsibility, although a degree of patience is always a virtue.

No single life is to be of more exceptional value than any other, and certainly not in a manner where common interest is shaped around the more dominant interests of a single individual. However, the interest of all can in certain circumstances be fulfilled the most through the value of an individual. No one is 'special', yet every life and all tangents producing spirit are extraordinary. Among all decent people, no one possesses supreme value. Those who waste their lives and only consume, with little-to-no benefit to others and those who bring grief and suffering to others, are all of lesser value in terms of the Imperative and Highest Good, depending on the crime or immorality committed. On the other hand, empathetic people, no matter what their profession or identity, do not differentiate with conclusive value. Howev-er, certain individuals have greater value in terms of their character and utility, skills, talents, or profession serving the common ambition structured through the Human Imperative.

But then there are those of exceptional value, notably those with great character who sacrifice themselves for the common good. Even so, the value of such character is only conditional on the character's execution of virtue and goodwill, which does not warrant treatment beyond the decency any person deserves (as a reflection of character and virtue) and the respect that ought to be earned in any individual rela-tions, not respect one presumes one is entitled to.

Not everyone is equal, but this doesn't justify profound rifts among people be-yond the justice and efficiency of value. Some people have natural predispositions that give them greater value in terms of their prospect of contributing to all people's welfare. Some are born more intelligent than others, some live lives that make them more intelligent, some grow to become more useful, some have exceptional talents or natural skills that others do not, some are tougher and stronger than others, and some are more prone to virtues than others. Fortune is largely unpredictable and there is only so much we can do about it. These conditions of Nature do not have to undermine our prospects, for it is not necessarily what someone is born with that wholly determines their life as much as it is what a person does with his or her life that is the prime determination. It is not the predestination of a person's body and its past that determines his or her character absolutely; it is what the will makes a person do in the conditions one faces and how one reacts to the environment that affects who a person becomes. There is always a choice, even if it is a final one.

The mind and spirit are very malleable and reason can steer people down many paths. The main source of well-being comes through virtue, which any person can achieve if they are disposed and dedicated to pursuing the Highest Good. In base morality, natural fortunes can dramatically affect the benevolent fate of a person, but in Liberty these utilities matter only in *how* they are used in the pursuit of flourishing and the cultivation of virtue. However, there are many variables in the conditioning of virtue, so efforts must be made to accommodate the shortcomings and misfortunes of people to assist global flourishing.

I am not so naive as to argue that natural fortunes do not influence the fortunes of people or that people always have a realistic option of being morally upstanding, but I do extend the thought that there is always an option for something more through the Highest Good. Sometimes moral fortunes are improved through simple encouragement and by convincing people that their past and others' expectations do not define what they deserve or can achieve. How people employ their utility and character and how they apply themselves is significantly more important to their worth than the fortunes of their utilities. Even as people's utility and fortune-given advantages influence their value, this does not mean they inherently possess greater value than others, as application of character, utility, and life is far more important in consideration of moral quality and value. No matter how great a person's value in terms of the Human Imperative and the Highest Good may be, no matter what skill, talent, or attribute a person possesses, no person is divinely superior to or above their peer, for the Imperative binds us all with common ambition in common interest. And through the soul, all are a part of each other.

We, humanity, are all peers among each other with the commonality of the Highest Good and its spirit, and no one person is 'above' another. Certain people may have greater value, in some cases far greater value, and may play significantly more important or crucial roles in comparison to others in achieving progress. Yet we are all united by our imperative purpose dedicated to bettering ourselves, our circumstance, and the Highest Good. We all have different roles and functions to fulfil, ones that we must find for ourselves in order to satisfy our function of flourishing. Some have greater roles to play, but we are all an integral part of the substance binding us in body and mind and through the Highest Good. We are all an inherent part of the substance of the world and our will is a part of this; we are not beyond or over one another and everything we are and have is only borrowed with life and released in death.

The heritin ethic dedicates strong value to virtue, righteousness, and strength. It advocates for people to strive to better themselves to achieve a better life. This ethic values doing the best one can and really trying to be a good person, and better yet succeeding at it, for one's own sake and others. Through the moral devices of Discipline and Harmony the spirit of a person should develop, become more virtuous and stronger by resisting Fear and pain. This inspires the intuition of Liberty that strength is not only for oneself, but is a utility complete through Liberty to apply strength in the goodwill and duty of the Imperative.

Your strength is there to be used when the strengths of others fail them. People must stand together and face their challenges together, helping each other to excel and grow. There is no point in sowing an unnecessary divide unless its purpose satisfies justice. You may think differently, you may act differently, and you may be a better person, yet this alone is of little value if it does not lead to the improvement of others or the development of the Highest Good towards fulfilment of the Human

Imperative. There is no good and no strength in imposing oneself as God's gift to mankind and blindly focusing on oneself rather than the needs of others along with one's own. Being a virtuous individual is not to strive for supremacy over others for the sake of stature, it is to cultivate greater character and flourishing for oneself with and for other people. Unity and mutual effort are vital for the prosperity of any society, community, and group, including the global community; do not sow divide for the sake of corruptive satisfactions of ego. Dignity and confidence come in virtue; arrogance is the bitterness of vice.

Strength is not found in needlessly distancing oneself from fellow peers out of a compulsion for superiority; strength is the ability to distinguish between right and wrong and then act righteously when adversity and Fear attempt to suffocate character of virtue. Strength is not in separating oneself from the depraved, but in standing among those who lack virtue and lifting them out of their servility in Fear, if they so wish and if this justice can be performed. If it is the will of a person to remain in the bonds of needless and petty, yet real, suffering, then so be it. Then it may be just and necessary to distance oneself from the immoral, possibly abandon them, to preserve what virtue and energy remain.

This is not an act of mercy or kindness – it is a necessary deed, something people often encounter in the real world and it is rare for a person to have the capacity or stature to defy the degrees of negative influence already present. Above all else as a virtue-rule of goodwill and good spirit, empathy and goodness are only fulfilled and complete through unity and commonality with others, in empathy and solidarity with other people. Those who do not pursue ambition of Liberty nonetheless pursue ambition in accordance with their interests in the liberty of morality. Where ambitions of others fulfil their interests, satisfy global well-being, and are in harmony with acceptable justice, even though not maximised in Liberty, this nourishes the goodness of people. If it is just, then it serves humanity. If a utility serves the interests of mankind in all its spheres, satisfying justice that may elude wisdom and judgement of those veiled by base morality and Fear, then it serves the end of the Human Imperative.

Ideology and moral convictions serve people's ends. If an ethic is compatible with the justice of global common interest, then it is of key value to humanity. As such, solidarity and the unity of virtue and utility, with reference to the inherent value of humanity, supercede the differentiation of ethical dispositions serving the ends of mankind. However, when the harmony of solidarity and unity is jeopardised and undermined by vice and the malevolence of people intolerant of moral liberty and ignorant of justice, then morality attaches value to restoring balance in liberty and normativity in common interest of the Human Imperative. The virtue-rule is thus of solidarity and unity in the Human Imperative and common endeavour and ambition, a rule of understanding and empathy and pleasure of common goodwill.

The animal is an animal by the quality of its function dominated by instinct. Mankind is different because of the quality of acting through more than instinct or through a maxim of interest that is accentuated and found through high-reason, amplifying the utility satisfying an instinct. If a creature can think in terms of greater maxims of self-interest beyond the immediacy of the compulsions of instincts, regardless of whether or not it is grounded in base-reason, then it is a person. If it can act beyond the immediacy and predominance of instinct, even if maxims of interest are set as parameters of base morality amplified by high-reason and of greater vision than the immediacy of instinct and instinct's derivative ethics, then it is human. If it acts solely on the inclination of instinct without greater vision or ambition, then it is the animal of mankind, but not with the virtue of humanity and not with the contingent value. If a creature can think like a person by virtue of a rationale which mediates inclinations and maximises ethical interests, then it can see the maxims of common interest found through the Human Imperative. All normativity and morality are bound to the Categorical Directive of the ambition to flourish. If a creature can think in terms of maxims of interest through the set parameters of well-being in terms of base morality (therein satisfactory of the Human Imperative and common interest, whether the body of reason acknowledges this justice or not) then ethical value is fulfilled in common interest to make one another better off. For instance, the person who can think beyond immediate compulsions of Fear which incites needless conflict that is in nobody's interest, fulfilling the Central Principles of moral liberty and justice, is a person fulfilling the greater maxims of the common interest that satisfies the Human Imperative.

Where value is maximised by the Human Imperative of morality at liberty, serving people's interests in tolerable and functional liberty, the value serves humanity and generates profit central to human endeavour. When a creature cannot think in terms of rational interest and does not act accordingly, as it is blinded by Fear and the compulsive inclination of instinct, if it acts as the animal of mankind, subsequently neglecting the value of common humanity, then its value is diminished, because the value of such vectors undermines the value of the common interest of the people striving to fulfil the Human Imperative – to be better off. In short, base morality tempered by sensibility and wisdom, and mediated by degrees of high-reason, can serve the interests of people, even though it may not maximise ethical interests. Therefore, these utilities and moralities have value to people in terms of the Human Imperative.

Where sensibility and the capacity to reason can serve common interests of people, such as with agreement on peace and prosperity, then it is of ethical value by serving the interests of mankind as part of the Human Imperative. All ethical and moral utilities, whether they are ideologies or beliefs, are only contingencies of the soul seeking flourishing. Thus, if just and morally permissible, alternative utilities serve people and nourish humanity, even if the humanity of its vectors is still dormant in the lack of nourished virtues and high-reason moving people to the Human Imperative and not merely the Categorical Directive. Therefore, there is value in the utilities that serve humanity and people, even if these utilities are not directly aligned with the Human Imperative and Liberty. Enabling such moralities and aiding people of different moral dispositions, if just and morally permissible as part of the liberty of morality, is right and valuable in terms of the Human Imperative.

The value of character may be perceived in base terms as a guarantor of flourishing through status and power. It may seem that greater value of character fosters more fulfilling spirit through higher social status based on virtue. This is only a deceit of Fear, for greater fulfilment of spirit comes in virtue irrespective of noteworthy social status. Greater fulfilment of spirit comes through the value of virtue based on the ambition to do what is good and right, of dignity and a sense of self-worth based on one's conscience. Every person has intrinsic worth and potential. Fulfilment comes through living up to one's potential and living in virtue. One does not need to be a King or Queen to be fulfilled or happy, all the more so as those with less responsibility and duty may live an easier, happier life. But duty is the path and manifestation of eudaimonia, greater than happiness.

The spiritual fulfilment evoked by duty does not come in greater capacity, but in duty and virtue corresponding to an embodied capacity and application of personal utility in goodwill. Fulfilment in capacity comes through doing what you are doing well, not necessarily doing *more*. Greater value of character and utility may seem to act as a guarantor of welfare and reward, yet these capacities are only worthy of virtue when character itself is marked by virtue. Acting in virtue motivated by the longing for reward and security through social status in Fear is not the fulfilment of virtue-duty, so spirit and character will not be intrinsically marked by greater value and virtue, and will not bring greater fulfilment.

Furthermore, if one is to live up to one's duties and virtues, then this comes with greater responsibility. This is fulfilling in eudaimonia, but the related suffering and stress will not be the guarantor of happiness, something more accessible to persons of lesser dedication to duty but stripped of eudaimonia and Liberty fulfilled in duty. Disavowing duty for lesser virtues of blind, base hedonism will only foster Fear, making one worse off than the common person of less capacity for duty who lives at ease in minor capacities of power and responsibility. Greater value and utility are as much a burden as they are a fulfiller of duty and eudaimonia.

Capacity, ability, and value are not the imperatives of well-being. There is nothing wrong in being of lesser capacity to exercise force on the Highest Good and contributing comparatively less to the Imperative. Ultimately, greater fulfilment comes in doing what good a person can in their degree of capacity. Virtue and its element of flourishing is found in exercising one's utility well, not in pursuing status or power in Fear. This does not excuse idleness and disproportionate laziness that is unfulfilling for a person stagnating through a lack of living. Yet it does encourage acceptance of the degrees of utility and potential, which is more fulfilling than heedless ambition in Fear. People should strive to fulfil their potential and live up to their utility when they can, because activity and ambition, in whatever degree, are more fulfilling than the stagnation of an inactive life. However, higher virtues come through mindfulness and discipline fulfilling and nourishing virtues corresponding to one's immediate utility. Doing what one can within one's means is itself a source of significant inspiration, goodwill, and virtue than excess ambition of Fear in search of utility and value for social status and sense of self bound to Fear.

We all have roles and responsibilities bound to our utility, ability, and circumstance, the dynamics of which shift (and ought to do so) in liberty and in development of character and utility. It is more fulfilling for all to exercise their utility righteously and dutifully in harmony with one another. Utility pertaining to social status in Fear will not grant greater fulfilment of flourishing than the acceptance and fulfilment of potential in Liberty. Fulfilment of virtue comes in exercising one's utility, duty, and responsibility righteously and in goodwill, not in pursuit of value, utility, and status in Fear neglecting duty and virtue. However, it is also a virtue-duty to fulfil one's potential for the sake of oneself and the common good, but even this can only be virtuous and fulfilling when done in sincere goodwill.

We all have different responsibilities and utilities, some greater than others; but what is most fulfilling is found in executing our degrees of utility and potential with goodwill and virtue, not in pursuing valued utility and status against one another and in Fear. Greater fulfilment doesn't come in knowing or thinking you are helping more than others, but in knowing you are helping to the full extent that you can and performing your responsibilities with decency, respect, and goodness.

This virtue-rule culminates in Liberty as part of accentuated moral liberty to live mindful of the Human Imperative. Where others cling to identity of character and perceptions of base-reason – all healthy and valuable utilities in the degree of valued and just utilities – the value of Liberty in greater forms, such as by the Void and in eudaimonia, should be intuitive for the basis of our humanity. Greater value is found in common humanity and where one becomes at Liberty in harmony with the universalisable soul. This becomes the virtue of liberty to be *no one*.

Where others may live in veiled base morality perceiving the distinctiveness of humanity in terms of people of different groups, Liberty grants solidarity through empathy of being no one, in turn finding harmony with everyone through the substance of the soul shared in and by all. By accepting to be no one, thereby becoming more mindful of the fundamental will moving all, one begins to see greater commonality in all people, leading to Harmony and profound unity and solidarity. By embracing the foundation of oneself through the fundamental will and being mindful of all elements of identity and character as secondary aspects subservient to the soul, by being in harmony with being *nobody* while attached to the utilities of one's body and psyche, one becomes everything and everyone. But this more spiritualised virtue-rule is not a moral imperative and is only a setting of an Ideal found through mindfulness by the Void.

This utility takes on great value by invoking character that serves as a vector to potentially bridge other people of rigid identity and character. The virtue of empathy through a willingness to bind to commonality can serve the maxims of value in terms of the Human Imperative by inspiring commonality among other people shrouded by the perspective of base morality at times instigating conflict and often of a relatively slow process of human integration.

On a last subject concerning the value of life is the value of human life in contrast to other living things such as animals. Animals cannot enact the Universal Imperative as much as humanity can through our advanced utilities. Animals and other living things other than humans do not possess the powers that mankind does. However, animals and other creatures capable of actions nonetheless have a will, a soul. Due to the limited prospects of creatures of lesser capacity to have a significant effect, the value of other living things in contrast to people is less. However, non-human creatures do still have value, not only value that is inherent to their soul, but also in the value of their utility.

We may consider ourselves distinct and separate to animals, which in terms of our advanced cognitive capacities and self-awareness would be correct. But we are nevertheless of the same substance of the soul as other living things are, and how we treat others, even other living creatures, reflects our character. Other living things must be respected, but ultimately human endeavour and our utility in reference to the Universal Imperative trumps the concerns of the animal, so the utility of animals may be used for human interest in proportional justice.

To turn this into a basic principle-rule (but a limited one because I haven't unfolded the other Central Principles yet), animals may be used in the needs of human interest within acceptable considerations of justice. For instance, a community of people in a harsh environment may rely on animal products, including meat, to survive. It is morally right to value the interests of the people of this community over the interests of animals, but in a synchronised and balanced ethical value. However, the question of animal consumption is broader and more complex than this initial presumption and thought, a question that warrants much more dedicated study than can be accomplished in this work.

For now, the illustrative thought and principle that other creatures may be used in human endeavour in terms of the lesser value of creatures in contrast to that of people's virtue suffices for the proposed hypothetical moral value. Even so, animals should not be killed pointlessly such as for sport or entertainment. Animals also should not undergo needless suffering; if they have a role to fulfil in the Highest Good that might involve their suffering or death, such sacrifice ought to be performed with justice, with the discussion of such themes reserved for later studies of practical morality.

The interests of animals perhaps aren't as important as human interests, but animal welfare is meaningful nonetheless. Furthermore, how people treat creatures of lesser value also reflects on the character of people. As a species that has been granted great power and responsibility, we must still take care of our tact with other living things. In this sense, while animals have less value than humans, how we treat them does affect human virtue, as well as reciprocate the tangents of how we treat the vulnerable.

In certain circumstances animals and other living things may possess greater value and utility than some people, particularly people of grave immoral quality who are causing strife for society. A loving pet does more for a caring family than the immorality of a murderer. Livestock offers more for morally upstanding people than the immoral criminal undermining the benevolence and virtue of morally upstanding people. But before such thoughts are criticised for undervaluing people, one must remember that people have the capacity to amend their quality of character and set themselves on a constructive, moral path of goodness that is of far greater utility than that of an animal.

In this respect, people can possess inherent value in terms of potential utility which is greater than that of the animal. But in our advanced capacity that sets mankind apart in terms of the force we may enact on the world there also arises the responsibility and capacity for grave irresponsibility. In this capacity we deem to make humanity more virtuous than the common beast, we may also become, as some do, much worse than the animal that is innocent in its compulsion of instinct. Mankind is capable of much greater immorality and monstrosity than that of animals, and in many ways people can be lesser in quality and virtue than animals innocent in their accord of Nature. The loyal dog may possess greater virtue than many people. Yet, for better or worse, our capacity also leaves us with a responsibility to one another and subsequently to the Highest Good and Nature.

Our value may be greater than that of animals in terms of the utility of people, according to which the great capacity of our actions demands greater responsibility to one another to carry out our moral duties and responsibilities which reward us with greater fulfilment through stronger character. The matter of value in terms of utility also means that certain animals can be legitimately justified to have greater utility and value over other animals, something applicable to the distinction between pets and livestock. But in this same fashion of considering utility, some people can be deemed to be of less moral quality, value, and utility than that of a common beast.

It is often the case that people distinguish themselves from animals, even though we are alike in many ways. However, we *do* possess qualities that differentiate us from common animals, in particular the capacity for greater reasoning, creativity, and advanced cognitive abilities. In this sense humanity may be considered to be 'better' than animals, yet it does not mean that we are the divine lords of animals – we live side by side with them. As for people who may exhibit animalistic behaviour, do not forget that people are people, even if they seem to be of lesser character and comparative worth. Some people of lesser and weaker character, associated with horrendous and barbaric acts, are sometimes called 'animals'. But even though they are very 'animalistic', people who surrender their will almost absolutely to debased character, they will remain people in their capacity for action and the capacity for redemption.

Don't forget that the immorality some are capable of is a sign of what any person is capable of doing depending on the circumstances. Even animalistic people should be a reflection of the overall state mankind is in and the condition of the good that arises from human endeavour. This should above all serve as a utility and virtue-rule highlighting individual responsibility. It should also give rise to reflection on the self as whether one is truly better than the demeaning quality that may be seen in animals. Yet this thought should also evoke mindful thought concerning the quality of animals, such that animals are not a degenerative, worthless, or demeaning state of being as the elitist and arrogant attitude of people may suggest. To equate people with animals could become an insult to animals or an unworthy and unnecessary insult to the state of being an animal; there is nothing wrong with animals, but there is plenty wrong and monstrous in some people.

The main principles to draw from this Chapter are that people are an end in itself and of itself. This takes on the form in correspondence with the Universal Imperative through life. We are capable of the greatest moral utility among all known living things, and the universe is pointless and dead without life developing it, warping it, using it, caring for it, and making something out of it, as Nature does for us in return. Mankind is the primary actualisation of the Universal, thus also Human, Imperative. All life is bound by a Categorical Directive beyond the Human Imperative – the goal of all action. This is an absolute, for without action only the Void remains.

But to act means to abide by the Categorical Directive of the fundamental will that actualises any conduct and initiates all action. In this Directive we have different roles and narratives to fulfil. In our journey to fulfil our Imperative we must take different paths and employ different utilities and virtues suitable for different circumstances. In this we are bound to considerations of value in our actions, in our quality of character, and in our moral utilities. The Human Imperative is *of us* and *for us*. Thus, all value supervenes on the Highest Good we all pursue and live with.

Mankind has an intrinsic value in accordance with the soul and its inherent potential to have an effect on the Human Imperative. But in this dynamic of ethics, force becomes arbitrary and unequal, through which we are sometimes forced to mediate and appeal to sensibility, intelligence, wisdom, and rationality to achieve the best value in our conduct in the present circumstances. We must carry out analysis and reflection on the value of our living. Therefore, to treat mankind as an end in itself, we ought to treat the maxim of some people above the devaluation of vice that cannot be granted sustainable liberty.

The Human Imperative is not an ideal or contingency beyond mankind – it is a pursuit of mankind itself and all life bound to the determination of the soul to flourish. But in this universal dynamic there are various dimensions of forces and many causal tangents, whereby efficiencies and deficiencies, strengths and weaknesses arise. Evaluation of these moral utilities is done *for* mankind as the end in itself. Every soul matters, but the character beholden to a soul that acknowledges this moral principle and acts accordingly is of greater value to and in terms of each soul. Those of virtue who protect and maximise value for all are of the most valued virtue, especially by virtue of self-sacrifice for the good of all.

While intuition may espouse to condemn such moral judgements as apathetic, callous, and overly-rational, this would fail to account for the crucial element of morality that comes through the utilities of the sentiment, emotion, and sensation nourishing and completing spirit and good livelihood. Ethical valuation for and through the Human Imperative is only complete in eudaimonia and fulfilment through higher virtues, according to which harmony with base faculties is also necessary and useful.

Indeed, greater evaluation of borderline callous and brutal reasoning can be not only compatible with base-reason, but also necessary for its greater scope in the immediacy of long-term and broader compassion and empathy. In terms of simple calculation, is it not more compassionate to at least save or spare 100 families over 10 families? This is a brutal assessment and to make such a judgement is extremely demanding for virtue and spirit, but in sum maxims of sentiment, the more compassionate judgement is in accordance with the judgements of the intuitions of rationale. This is then fully compatible with, and in positive accord with, treating mankind as the end in itself, with itself, and through itself. Whether such judgements and intuitions are agreeable with people, as with all the Central Principles, is subject to moral liberty.

To conclude this discourse of ethical value and quality, I will outline the following Central Principles:

Ethical value of utilities and life is derivative of, and found, assessed, and evaluated through the Human Imperative.

Every life has value and meaning, even if it may seem negligible.

To neglect the lives of others is to neglect one's own; neglecting life diminishes virtue and value.

All life is not necessarily of equal value in terms of the considerations of the degrees of flourishing, the contingent capacity to affect, and a living thing's virtues or worth in reference to the Highest Good and Human Imperative.

The strong are strong by the empowerment of virtues; the weak are weak because of their depravity.

Every person, no matter how weak or nefarious, has the potential to be and do good – to be virtuous; this is the nature of the Fundamental Principle of Living Beings and the fundamental will.

Life is never expendable; yet when there is little choice or alternative, well-being and maybe even the life of some may have to be sacrificed for the common Highest Good in proportion to and across multiple dimensions of what constitutes goodness and justice.

The difference of value in accordance with the Highest Good does not mean certain people ought to be treated in demeaning and immoral ways, such as by being looked down on or discriminated against, but it does hold meaning in consideration of necessary sacrifice or in questions of appropriate actions.

The more fortunate and stronger ought to help the less fortunate – the strong must look out for the weak so that the Human Imperative may be fulfilled overall to a greater extent. The less fortunate must then also not drag down and endlessly feed off the strengths of others, so that the balance of virtue and positive effect can persevere in its development and sustain the Highest Good and endeavour towards fulfilling the Imperative.

Chapter 18:

Justice

Until there is a foundation of practical good I cannot discern practical morality further. I have used the term 'justice' throughout my writing, yet I have not established a framework or definition for the concept as a moral utility. Following the considerations of ethical value, *justice* is a key ethical feature for morality. Ethical value differentiates and is not always equal; ethical value is not always balanced in a way that serves the greater interest or produces maxims of universal interest.

Every soul has value and every person's interests are worth considering, no matter the person's utility. Every capable individual can do good towards the Human Imperative, whereas neglectful and pointless loss of life does not further the cause of greater flourishing. So in terms of practical morality, one ought to consider these themes in light of the causal effects on states of well-being, the utility principle (the greatest good for the greatest amount of people), and the many dimensions of consequences.

Moral utilities serve particular ambitions and interests to further and utilise ethical value. However, for any act and its correspondence of ethical value to be used well it must follow principles of morality, mandating considerations of *justice*. All questions of morality are derivative of the concerns of well-being and corresponding spheres and structures of ethics. Therefore, moral judgements should be performed mindful of ethical value – that is, in a manner where positive ethical effects supercede negative outcomes, producing profit in ethical interest, as the *justice of balance in positivity superceding negativity,* or where well-being in global terms of the unifying Human Imperative supercedes the negativity of unbalanced human activity in terms of narrow and selfish personal interests creating a morality that lacks ambition and coherence of value in terms of the Human Imperative.

Before I begin to outline Central Principles of applied actions derivative of justice, I need to address a long-standing moral issue of the problem arising from the implication that people do not have freewill. Individuals' capacity for freewill has been subject to much debate, with the rise of cognitive sciences further subjecting people's freewill to scrutiny and scepticism. The substance of reality is laden with patterns of deterministic causal order, and so is life deterministic of causal order as part of the same substance and material. The Fundamental Principle of Living Beings is the prime element of behaviour, whereby even if the mind is considered to be a separate substance from the rest of the physical world it nonetheless follows a causal rule of its own – to pursue flourishing.

Physical structures of the brain seem to have a fundamental impact on the determination of mental states and the behaviour of individuals. Questions of determinism are relevant to morality. If every person's choices and actions are predetermined by antecedent conditions or are otherwise determined beyond freewill, then how can moral agents be held accountable for their actions? Insanity and other psychological disorders can be central issues for legal judgements because these conditions can identify underlying features impairing the autonomy and judgement of individuals, hence people's moral capacity and disposition may be limited and they cannot be held accountable for the choices they had no power over. In a way, it can be said that their actions were not their fault, it was the fault in their condition onset by disease. Similarly, if people were determined by outward factors, such as society and Nature, influencing their will to follow a particular course of action, then how can they be held responsible for their actions? These questions give rise to significant moral complications.

From a pragmatic perspective, these questions and concerns can be simply set aside in favour of the moral priority of order, which is certainly a somewhat justifiable position in respect to the Fundamental Principle in that the imposition of accountability can nonetheless positively influence otherwise wrong actions. On the other hand, there should be a more formal and coherent solution to this moral issue.

In the normative framework of combinatorialism, intention, consequence, and character are central features of moral discourse and knowledge, with character being the 'grounding' substance for other elements of morality and normativity. The character of the individual and the corresponding moral utilities fundamentally influence people's dispositions towards actions and the initiation of actions. External and internal influences contribute to the function and manifestation of the psyche and mentality, determining or fundamentally influencing people's actions along ethical tangents. In terms of the causal order of moral utilities affecting and determining actions, characteristics and utilities are primary functions in the determination of actions. The Fundamental Principle drives us to pursue the greatest flourishing subject to immediate conditioning. But what we perceive as the greatest well-being, and the authenticity of the corresponding sense or sentiment, is liable to greater scrutiny.

Mindfulness – awareness and sensation – and the actual *feeling* evoked by actions as part of flourishing are the main criteria of the goodness of an action, which is fully consistent with the determination of reason and its relevant faculty of mindfulness and higher pleasures intertwined with baser faculties of instincts and respective sensations. Spirit is the qualitative measure of virtue, imperative for the determination of moral quality and, accordingly, actions themselves. So character and utility are central to moral interests concerning the determination of actions. The Fundamental Principle and its will are the catalysts and embodiments of actions and behaviour, while utilities and character are the means to the end of the will and parameters of the will.

The substance of the world is inherent to life. The forces we exert on the world create change and various forces affect us including as reflections of our influence on the world. The fundamental will to flourish is inherent to the substance of the body and is the prerogative of the mind; there is no way in which the fundamental will can be denied being grounded in the world itself or in direct relation to the world in terms of its property as part of the substance laden with the function of pursuing well-being. We may narrowly focus on individual freewill that makes people responsible for their actions, but both bad and good actions are subject to ethical forces influencing the determination of actions. The absence of freewill or the denial of it enables definitive analysis, study, prediction, conclusion, adjustment, mediation, and coherent structuring of causes acting on, in, and through the world. Without a deterministic will regulated by parameters of conditioning and formulation, structural ethics would be chaotic and human endeavour would be largely unpredictable.

However, if we have a foundation of freewill that is subject to the conditioning of available choices in particular circumstances, then coherent structures of ethics still hold meaning. But nonetheless, logically speaking, the absence of freewill grants legitimacy to the coherent study of structural ethics and all related spheres of human activity, as this makes human behaviour much more predictable and understandable and suggests points of clarity for broader study of the mind.

The advantage of deterministic views allows the study of moral actorness and moral agency. When a person – an agent and actor as a vector of ethical force – commits an immoral deed, then it is reasonable to suggest that negative influences drove him or her to commit acts violating greater moral interest (to flourish and not suffer). This is clear in mindfulness of empathy studying and sensing people beyond the clout of base perceptions. If an actor exhibits a strong tendency for active positive ethical attitudes, with greater moral quality including the resistance to suffering, then one may predict future actions and become involved in the study of moral quality and, hence, morality, therefore finding what is better for us, what actions serve our interests better, and what our greater interests really are.

Goodness is constructed through positive influence evoking flourishing, while ethical negativity – suffering – is shaped by negative influence. Feeding positive influence and depriving negativity means that we can comprehensively structure our ethical and moral concerns in a coherent manner for achieving the end goal of flourishing. The denial of freewill, or degrees thereof, adds the advantage of serious non-abstract study of morality and ethics and their dynamic structures.

A deterministic understanding of ethics does not necessarily nullify accountability of actions, but rather changes the nature of accountability to instead be considered in more predictive terms of influences ruling behaviour, dispositions, attitudes, and moral agency and actorness. The purpose of accountability, like any other utility, is to achieve and balance well-being. In terms of this understanding and view of accountability in relation to the denial of freewill, holding people accountable for their actions can coherently serve as a function of regulating positive interests and the influences of utilities at liberty through the agency of people, which accountability, parallel to its relating functions, strives to do in the first place. Therefore, the denial of freewill does not contradict moral concerns of accountability, whereby the deterministic agency of individuals does not mean we have no moral right, whatever that right may be, to counter-act negative influences in ethical structures affecting our states of flourishing and the Highest Good.

For example, it is morally valid to hold a murderer accountable for their actions so that negative tangents and vectors, such as of murder, do not spread. Holding a murderer accountable for their actions essentially means to simply highlight a negative presence and influence of utilities of vice, to which we can then respond with moral legitimacy to preserve ethical interests by preventing and mediating bad influences of vice. Moreover, this mode of accountability and assignment of reparative measures or responses in morally righteous accord means that counter-acting wrong-doing through accountability can avert future morally negative factors, elements, and influences. All of this is encompassed in a broader theme of *balance* and *mediation* of modes and states of flourishing, bringing me to consider the question of *justice.*

What is *justice?* There are different conceptions and understandings of justice, especially in subjective base moralities which assign justice selectively by emphasising sentiments lacking a stronger rational basis and fomenting moral disparity and contradiction. *Justice* is a correlating aspect of *good*, but evidently with a different connotation. Rather than familiarise itself directly with the notion of good, it holds a more practical essence related to the production, imposition, and balance of goodness. Justice, if one considers its common use in society and law, is the practical implementation of what is considered morally good and righteous; however, how this is understood and utilised is another matter.

Subjectivity of base justice can be framed not only by what it is but also in terms of *whose it is* and *who is it for, who does justice serve.* The common subjectivity of moral ideas like 'justice' and its derivatives – *fairness* and *deserving* – follows from the perceived subjective good of individual pursuits of comfort and often in league with an excess of Fear. Base moralities have dramatically shaped human thought throughout the history of our civilization, and just as base morality has followed and nourished contextual moral law, it has done the same with the moral substance of justice. Justice and fairness are commonly used along human endeavour, yet much of it has lacked truly compelling, objective understanding in moral law. Underlying this are everyday claims to fairness in accordance with the fundamental will.

Through an ethos of Fear base morality fosters a dysfunctional universal of justice in moral law. By appealing to fairness or matters of deserving, one ought to be mindful of such claims to entitlement, for they tend to emanate contradictory moral feelings lacking the mindfulness of synchronised reason and may be of a lesser universal grade than the Human Imperative. Moral sense focused on instinct is an inherently subjective moral compass and it provides conflicting certainty in consideration of individual, social, and global well-being. When justice is left to the determination of intuition founded on sentiment and subjective impressions, while not meaningless, it is divided and its force is of confined effective utility.

National and individual claims to fairness and justice often stem from narrow and defective moral authority and quality of fulfilment and self-gratification of base moral sense limited in comprehension, vision, and utility. Courts of law try to serve as impartial guides of rationale between people in dispute. Law, deriving from moral and Natural Law, has tried to do its best with a faint incarnation of justice, yet in deeper introspection it often struggles to attain the imperative universal moral authority it ought to. Objectifying justice as a means of the good to flourish in terms of base morality lacking clarity in purpose, direction, and spirit only facilitates a justice of instinct and blind sentiment. However, a justice of pure high-reason and dutiful rationale lacking spirit and sentiment cannot serve as a fulfilling and functional moral utility either. If justice lacks spirit, its worth is null. Justice in moral law and social law has not been useless, but until it is enforced with clear universal moral law with reference to a Constitution of Natural Law or relating basis, justice will lack function and authority.

Since justice is inherently tied to the notion of goodness and righteousness, then it too must conform to the understanding, view, and definition of goodness in terms of well-being. Following up on the idea of good as a service of the fundamental will, justice must also concern itself with greater flourishing. The meaning of justice entails the practical working of morality concerning development of the Highest Good and cultivation of flourishing.

To affirm this claim of equivocating justice with the practice of morality, the legal system serves as an abundantly clear example. A national constitution is based on a laid out set of laws, derivatives of moral principles serving the interests of well-being, through which a country strives for prosperity. A legal system seeks justice when laws are broken, thereby trying to make amends for wrong-doing and unnecessary suffering. In matters of justice, such as distributive, social, and reparative justice, questions of what is *just* are examined in order to find answers to ethics of well-being. In this nature of justice, it's self-evident that justice is the practical working of morality in the sense of applying what is considered morally right in everyday practise, particularly through legal intervention or frameworks.

When justice is implemented in legal disputes it attempts to fix problems caused by immoral acts that resulted in suffering and damage. Hence, justice is essentially a configuration of morality concerned with the practical utility of good, tasked with applying moral principles to evoke, produce, channel, and balance greater well-being. Justice is implemented to pursue rather than find the best path to well-being, and when suffering is brought onto the Highest Good by moral deviation of individuals that commit wrong-doing and crimes, justice is utilised to bring balance to the Highest Good after it has suffered.

I say 'balance', but along with this word is also entailed the meaning of employing justice to relieve and neutralise the suffering that has upset the balanced state of the Highest Good where profit in ethical value supercedes the negativity of suffering and deconstruction. Remember, the Highest Good is not just the idea of what is 'the most good', but is also the manifestation of goodness in every tangent and vector of a structure of ethics that is grounded in a system of the Highest Good propagating success and progress through its dynamics and mechanisms.

The purpose of morality and its many forms, including justice, is to fulfil the Human Imperative – the propagation and continuity of our common will, common ambition, and common interest to flourish. The Highest Good, binding all ethics, guides us towards greater flourishing and towards the fulfilment of the Human Imperative by virtue of functional principles regulating the success or failure of an action. Justice serves as the practical guide for moral judgements in decision-making and moral evaluation. The heritin ethos seeks to surpass base morality, succeed a focused ethos of Fear, and achieve healthy synchrony of reason and spirit at Liberty. There are many manifestations of justice, and in the context of the Central Principles justice will be implemented in order to qualify and value the moral effectiveness of an act and its corresponding virtue(s).

There are distinctions between *just, justified, justifiable,* and *justice.* A *justifiable* act does not necessarily mean that it was *just* or even *justified.* The notion of a justifiable act is tied with the varying degrees of goodness in actions so that goodness might not correspond to goodwill of virtue. An individual performing an act may perceive it as the best course of action in their judgement, thereby justifying it. Yet, in reality, the consequences of that act might not have produced greater positivity, and thus the act was not the most moral. Any act can potentially be justified, but that does not mean that it is indeed *just* or in conformation with greater value.

Any act, in accordance with the Fundamental Principle, can be justified, yet not correspond to greater moral interest or the justice of the Highest Good and its moral law. To avoid ambiguity in the justification for actions, justice serves as the referral point for the qualification of actions and their effects on consequences and intentions corresponding to greater flourishing. An action might not have brought the greatest prosperity due to unfortunate circumstances and limitations in forethought, but if it was performed in good judgement and goodwill, producing well-being nonetheless, then it can be just even if not ideal.

In another sense, justified actions and the justification for actions vary in terms of their degree of positive consequences and appropriate intentions, but justice serves as the fulcrum of the moral quality of an action through which its degree of justification can be measured. Henceforth, and as has been done previously, *justice* will be referred to in order to value the moral quality of an action that defers to the Central Principles as the action's criteria for justification. For example, restraining people so that they do not harm another can be justified, but if that action of restraining was accompanied by causing a greater degree of avoidable suffering, then it might not be just. A perpetrator might be restrained in order to stop him attacking another person with no just cause, but using excess force and imposing unnecessary suffering would exceed just action. Justice is balance of flourishing and well-being in actions and ethical functions and dynamics, implying that balance is constituted by greater flourishing that is achievable in particular cases and circumstances while limiting and mediating negative ethical outcomes by causing excess suffering – negating ethical values.

Justice is a concept consisting of many elements and dimensions. It is not a simple virtue or moral utility in its own right, yet it composes and binds human endeavour and morality as a mediator in community of moral agency embodying and creating the structures of moral utilities. Justice of the Highest Good is the highest moral law and reigns over contextual and circumstantial dynamics of ethics to invoke a standard for morality. The metaphysical and naturalist foundation of justice is that of a dynamic in structural ethics measuring and mediating goodness.

Justice is a conditional and circumstantial truth and mode arising from the dynamics of goodness within structures of ethics and the Highest Good. It is a measure of goodness arising in contending ethical forces in spheres of structural ethics and the Highest Good. As such, justice is not a mere abstraction and base entitlement or right; justice is a dynamic, a mechanism in ethical structures as a measure and arbiter of goodness in terms of a balance towards maximum positive effects on well-being. Moral utilities have corresponding values. These are in turn mediated and formalised by justice. So when it comes to moral evaluations and judgements, justice is the mean and mode according to which the validity and value of moral rules and laws can be appealed to in contending beliefs, moral utilities, and the liberty of morality.

Morality and attitudes come into conflict, through which balance becomes a necessity for greater fulfilment of the individual and community. The arbiter of morality is then *justice*. In competing, contending, and conflicting intuitions, moral principles, utilities, attitudes, and activities of people, justice serves as the prime utility in its own right by the Highest Good to guide moral concern and interest. What is best and what course of action to commit to when sentiment and/or reason conflict are revealed in reflection and analysis of and through justice.

The dynamics in ethical structures can be amoral or formulate their own dimensions of morality, with justice having a certain place. But justice is most relevant in the mediation of practiced morality, as with real-life cases testing theory. Judgement in practised morality draws on the concerns of justice – of balance and greater maxims of well-being. As this necessitates the function of intuition, reasoning, and mindfulness, therefore, justice is as much a function of mindfulness, intuition, and reasoning (or drawing on these elements) as it is an arbiter of moral law in terms of the Highest Good; justice is further conceived of as a mode of mindfulness as well as a ruling moral concept. So in rendering certain judgements of morality, I will defer to and employ justice as a means of mindful evaluation and analysis to ascertain the Highest Good, higher morality, and greater ethical value.

Practical considerations of justice in legitimate and good moral practices should be derived from the Highest Good and the Human Imperative, with appeals to justice and legitimate righteousness being subjective and incomplete through the appeal to the Categorical Directive alone. To frame justice in terms of emphasised base features is to corrupt it and deprive justice of the virtue and righteousness it is meant to serve. By distorting justice one loses normative and moral power in appealing to it and invoking its great utility. Where justice is invoked in the endeavour of society and state, its legitimacy is only truly found as a righteous and virtuous power through appealing to the Human Imperative – that which pursues maxims of value and interests. Individual, social, and national interests are only legitimate and complete through justice drawing on the Human Imperative – the Constitution of the Highest Good. Any justice is balance and the maxim of value serving *all* humanity in virtue and righteousness of balance in flourishing qualified through sustainability, efficiency, effectiveness, and fulfilment. Justice is thus the balance and maxim of global value in the structures of ethics.

To do justice by others is to do justice to oneself by furthering virtue of duty in terms of the Imperative and the Highest Good. However, the estimation and qualification of justice is a complex issue on which I cannot yet formulate a definitive guideline. The estimation of value is not subjective, and neither is justice maximising and balancing ethical value and interest. It is a brutal truth of calculating the value constituting justice that those of greater value can have greater claims to justice by virtue of being able to help others more, by furthering the ambition of the Human Imperative for all. If one is to choose between the justice of a powerful nation-state which aids the development of other less-fortunate nations and people, or a minor state claiming justice for greater entitlement of self-serving resources that cannot exercise greater utility and bring greater value, thereby not aiding developing nations as much, then justice bestows virtue on the former – the more capable state.

However, the measure of power of a nation is only just by virtue of goodwill that uses its power in the justice of the Human Imperative to drive global development and growth. Justice is the parameter and feature of the maxims of value and interest, the virtue of which is above all established on the balance of virtue, as a blind, self-entitled, and self-gratifying claim to justice overlooks ethical maxims and undermines the justice of the claim and the perception of justice.

Communities and nations claim entitlement to justice and liberty of self-determination, yet these claims often only hold value distorted in base morality. They claim justice in their liberty and sovereignty, yet it is the claim to justice borne of Fear that spoils all and any justice by doing no-one a service, pitting nations and people against each other. It is thus the virtue of humanity in Liberty to sacrifice itself if need be to serve the justice of all people, to accept the only justice true to its name – that of the Human Imperative and the Highest Good. And so, sometimes, the only just and right thing to do is self-sacrifice, but such virtue is only reserved for duty. This is what justice means, and it can be brutal. But only in Liberty can the justice of all be appreciated and understood, and understanding this can be troubling for the spirit and mind.

The deterministic world that creates structures of ethics mandates justice in order to flourish. Sometimes, the cost of justice and growth is suffering; sometimes, justice arises from, or is known through, injustice. In the causal cascades of the structures of ethics people are subject to deterministic conditioning. Some are morally lucky, many are not. Moral luck is the misfortune leading to others' immorality and suffering; moral luck is also the fortune of justice, moral righteousness, and remarkable spirit. Moral luck does not undermine practical morality and normative guidance, yet it does create a sense of burden and responsibility.

Growth and greatness are usually built on suffering and melancholy. The pride of rising from adversity casts the shadow of the guilt of surviving. All success is determined by a balance of luck and perseverance, opportunity and work. The virtues that lead to well-being, when true to their nature and spirit, are mindful of and empathetic with those who did not have the good fortune of nurture and character to conquer the odds and thrive. But these virtues recall the value of justice. The guilt of moral luck is the conscience of ambition and righteousness of duty. The duty of justice is to do the best we can in our given circumstances. The duty of justice is to give more than we take. One can make good on the right to succeed by doing right by others. To make good on or out of suffering is justice – retribution and retributive justice.

A principle of justice can be outlined:

Justice is the central virtue and moral utility for the qualification of morally righteous actions in reference to the criteria of balance and mediation pursuing greater flourishing in respect to the Highest Good, its Universal Imperative, and contextual moral law and normative factors.

Justice is balance and moderation in ethical profit.

Chapter 19:

Suffering

An issue I raised earlier is how suffering, an integral part of flourishing, the adaptation of values, and the growth of character, ought to be approached. How should the suffering of people on all levels be employed and mediated for personal ambition of growth, and then how should suffering be utilised in development? What place do suffering and pain have in the Human Imperative? Can people be intentionally subjected to suffering and pain? Should people purposely put themselves under needless suffering? Do all people develop in the same way and do all people respond to suffering universally? This Chapter will discuss these kinds of questions to outline another set of Central Principles.

There are utilities in and of suffering; giving these utilities effective ethical structure is central to any coherent and comprehensive morality. Considering the complexity and diversity of moral outlooks towards suffering, the inherent anatomy and dynamics of suffering and pain, and the pursuit of Liberty, suffering is central to morality and ethics. As with any utility, suffering requires valuation and analysis as part of an ethical design to establish a coherent, effective, and functional morality.

Suffering and pain are key to personal growth and have served as ethical resources for development. By rising above pain, the character can become stronger, wiser, and better, for virtue must be forged and tempered under pressure. Suffering is fundamental to any life, character, morality, and ethic. Suffering leads to growth through the character that overcomes it.

However, it is no mystery that the journey of experiencing, confronting, and using suffering and pain is messy, challenging, and can come at great cost. To benefit from suffering and pain requires strategy and effective moral guidance. Core to all considerations of the morality of suffering, frustrating pain and suffering can be used for growth, while crippling and depressing pain must be healed.

The adaptation of values to different degrees of suffering is a natural and relative process. The function of adaptation and fruition is universal among people. However, the availability and capacity of varying moral utilities is not as objectively universal or equal. The values and character that evolve by overcoming suffering are relative to the environment and the pressures and experiences a person endures. But through success over suffering there can be found universally strong values, especially when the intuitions and sensations of suffering correspond to a structure with a grounding moral catalyst – an ethos. There can be universal objectives and norms for an effective approach to suffering with respect to particular ethical cases, elements of ethical structures, and the human psyche.

Most moralities strive for stronger values, even though the ambiguities of circumstances and the states of people's minds complicate this virtue-rule. A combined approach of reason, intuition, and sentiment can guide and help any person to thrive in many circumstances, to face and overcome suffering, then grow from it in character. The spirit and our capacities of reason are what give people their distinctive nature. Faculties of the mind and psyche are what allow people to develop and evolve their diversified moralities and values. Suffering and pain can drive humanity to become strong and certain elements of them are good in terms of the nourishment they provide for the individual. However, while suffering and pain are of a certain service to humanity, its utility with reference to an ethos of Fear is troubled and commonly structurally defective.

It must always be kept in mind that adaptation to suffering is an organic occurrence depending on the individual always at liberty in their will. This liberty of morality can be unpredictable and elusive. Just because suffering can lead to eventual growth when conditions are right does not mean that it cannot break a person beyond repair, whereby a life becomes unbearable. Any modulation of suffering and pain as ethical resources must be mindful of people and their internal conditioning, be disciplined and mindful of moral liberty and adaptation. The organic process of moral growth and progress through suffering and pain needs to be made more efficient and channelled for its utility to be fully exploited, the structuring of which can be a very delicate matter.

People are different, some more resilient than others. Sometimes people simply aren't strong enough to endure certain pressures, and it is a fact of life that some are naturally stronger than others in character and morality. Then again, others can grow to become stronger and more resilient than those with moral luck. Suffering can be motivating and beneficial, but embracing too much suffering or neglecting it can also have disastrous consequences.

Even though suffering can lead to greater flourishing, as it universally has done by driving progress and development, it is not the only path to flourishing and neither is it necessarily the best. Approaches to suffering, especially in Fear, are often very inefficient for achieving fulfilment by succeeding suffering. Dealing with pain and suffering by deferring and reflecting them in the form of distraction or projection without fundamental resolution are not the best moral approaches to dealing with suffering. Neither is mindlessly and recklessly challenging suffering and Fear sustainable or the most efficient approach, because such ethics are vulnerable to unwise impulses and ambitions lacking vision. Mindful and disciplined ambition is paramount for sustainable and sensible growth.

Sources of suffering can be both internal and external, with a morality effectively approaching both criteria being necessary for flourishing. Suffering has its role to play in pushing us forward, a reason to improve on our current state and to pursue flourishing, but there is an abundance of pain as it is and creating more of it needlessly will not be beneficial. There is more than enough suffering as a resource for the utilities exploiting it. For character and spirit to succeed suffering, an ethic must employ morality in the immediacy of suffering as a personal utility of living and design a comprehensive structure of ethics to engage and alleviate external influences of suffering and corresponding inefficiencies of growth.

Truly overcoming suffering, as opposed to projecting and deflecting it without fundamental resolution, leads to the cultivation of better values and moral utilities, thereby nourishing the Highest Good and its common good in terms of the Human Imperative. The implementation of suffering, its dissipation, and contingent behaviour of ethical vectors (people acting on, or reacting to, suffering) result in the way normativity functions. The value of suffering and pain is found through relevant utilities balancing and corresponding to the effects of ethical negativity on ethical tangents and vectors. Maximising and balancing these values is key. The justice of suffering is making good on it, creating goodness out of misery, and by overcoming adversity.

Firstly, I shall address the quite unpredictable nature of suffering. Pain is relative and how people respond to, or deal with, suffering is also relative. What you might be able to endure does not necessarily mean that others can easily withstand an equivalent level of suffering. Virtues and strength take time to develop and must be cultivated through different methods appropriate to the demands of circumstance, motivated by a grand ambition and desire of an ethos. For some people virtue may come more easily and more quickly than for others, as certain people are naturally stronger than others because of natural fortunes of inherited characteristics or early nurture and conditioning. However, this doesn't necessarily mean that the naturally vulnerable or less fortunate cannot overachieve those with a natural predisposition for virtue.

How people respond to suffering is uncertain and not easily predictable. Even in times of great peril and whilst experiencing grave suffering people can surprise themselves and find strength in the least expected way. There is always hidden potential in all people, yet sometimes suffering can be overbearing for a person, leading to extreme distress from which there may be little hope of a return. This can also manifest itself as lasting physical damage beyond mental trauma and spiritual blemish, as permanent as any psychological and spiritual scars.

Keeping the relativity of suffering in mind, facing up to its forces in order to attain flourishing must be done in an effective and constructive manner. When making a moral choice it is a standard norm to adopt an approach of acting in a way that would produce greater flourishing. Growing by adapting to suffering entails a certain degree of opening up to suffering, leaving oneself vulnerable, which is the point for the growth of character.

However, this must be done sensibly. Living will introduce many instances of pain and suffering. Purposely creating trouble and suffering beyond what is already present is an unwise approach. The spirit needs time to build its strength and facing up to a situation unprepared is likely to end badly. In cases where there is no choice but to confront hardship, when fortune is not particularly favourable, one should do one's best with what one has to stay strong and grow from pain and suffering. This can be overwhelming, but these are the moments that define a person – either you recede into misery and allow pain to defeat you and impose a lingering state of suffering, or you find the strength to carry on, overcome it, and free oneself from its weight, or similarly bear the brunt of an instance of pain to engage in continuous sustained development and healing. Either you give up and seek comfort and satisfaction through lesser fulfilment, or you embrace your suffering to overcome it and build character resisting Fear and suffering that act against one's greater interests.

The way people deal with suffering, pain, and stress is different, and never forget that the physical body is a core component of mental and spiritual states. Stress and pain can wear a person down and cause lasting damage. With an undermined body, the mind and spirit may begin to whither as well. Caution and discipline are important for morality involving both physical and mental suffering. The heritin approach is that when one is subjected to suffering and character is tested, one ought to confront suffering and Fear, embrace them, resist, and pursue ambition to succeed them. In times of peace and rest, one ought to use the opportunity to gather strength, learn through reflection, practise Discipline and Harmony, and prepare for another inevitable challenge. You don't know your limits until you've tested them; defiant ambition can be powerful, but it is not omnipotent. People are not invincible, but this vulnerability is the resource of virtue, for without the mind, ego, and spirit being broken, these aspects could not evolve and transcend Fear, and the character of the Ideals and duty could not be forged.

On the other hand, boredom and madness of idleness provide satisfactory grounds for seeking out challenge, discomfort, and even suffering without the necessity of immediacy, but only if this is just and sensible. Happiness may become a means of complacency protesting ambition and the pursuit of something more, of Liberty from craving happiness itself. The cruelty of happiness is that it may deceive us from the turmoil and suffering around us, which can be resolved through ambition. When people want a challenge, they seek out thrills and adversity. Testing oneself and tempering character is by no means wrong and is good when approached sensibly and in the right manner that satisfies justice. However, it is important to be mindful of such pursuits.

It is good to excel and strive to become stronger in character and spirit, yet the moral quality of such actions and pursuits is only as good as the effect they have and how they function in spheres of the Highest Good. Inviting suffering and challenging vice to remedy these elements will only be as good as the corresponding ability to alleviate the source of suffering in accord with justice. Energy, motivation, and fulfilment of challenging suffering in all spheres is only good up to the point of balance in effective practice of, and engagement with, suffering, whereby sensibility, empathy, and mindful reason are imperative. Instead of wasting one's fortune it is better to use utilities, assets, and opportunities in the most conceivable productive way, which requires mindful strategy and valuation along opportunistic endeavour driven by virtue and enthusiasm. There are better ways of learning to endure and grow from pain and suffering – to practise Discipline and Defiance – without destructive habits and neglecting life.

Consider, for example, a wealthy and comfortable person facing little adversity who is unsatisfied with an idle and unfulfilling life. In such a case, one could spend his or her fortune to alleviate suffering through charity, sponsorship, or the opportunity of new enterprise. This conduct would exchange fortune for opportunity and then provide more fulfilment. On a personal level, it would also expose the self to vulnerability, the suffering of which and challenge of Fear would build character. Financial security can offer much in life and any claims of its insignificance are naive and irresponsible. Yet the moral value of security is not unlimited and it can only do so much to relieve Fear, which walls of money will never fulfil in spirit while the mode of conduct is moved on a profound level by Fear. By using the fortune of wealth to build and provide opportunity for oneself and others, spirit and character grow and are fulfilled through ambition at Liberty improving ethical environment. But by pursuing the ambition of growing from suffering, one can become too eager and lose sight of better applications of the available utility and value.

For example, one might be better at a certain job, have greater value in a certain sphere beyond direct charity work; one might be more equipped at wealth creation than wealth utility for the common good. It would be better to apply oneself with greater value in terms of one's utility. Similarly, if a person does not possess the abilities of competent utility in a certain sphere, such as of effective charity work, and isn't willing to learn or truly dedicate themself, then it stands that one ought to apply oneself where one's efforts would be more effective and valuable.

To highlight the point concerning moderation and balance in approaches to suffering, it is good to pursue the benevolent endeavour of relieving suffering such as through charity. However, if one's value in a particular activity does not perform the desired justice or isn't maximised, then different self-application would be wiser. This path of conduct may not create as much suffering from which one can grow, but it would benefit others more, whereby virtue grows from mindfulness, dedication, and discipline in ambition of suffering, feeding Liberty through the Imperative.

In other circumstances, one might want to test one's character with greater resolve through greater suffering. This may encourage someone to pursue the thrills of danger, extremes, risk, and strife. These modes of conduct can lead a person to do great things, cultivate virtue, and generate a benevolent force acting on the Highest Good. For instance, the activist may put themself in harm's way and subject to great risk, thereby cultivating virtue through the guidance and ambition of a just cause. However, this would only be as good as mindfulness in the cause itself and the moral quality of one's conviction and endeavour.

Virtue does not come with mistaken intent where endeavour or a cause are moved by corrupt intentions or poor judgement, with the latter being open to greater moral ambiguity and tolerance. Virtue sought in ignorance is blind virtue of character lacking vision and ambition. The thought nevertheless holds that deliberately confronting suffering is not wrong, yet this requires mindfulness and sensibility, with the practice of the latter serving the pursued ambition in the first place. Just as happiness and comfort require balance to deter and counteract complacency, stalemate, and even degeneration through negligence, suffering also requires mediation so as not to overwhelm, corrupt, undermine, and consume people.

Another important subject to discuss concerning the ambition of confronting suffering is that of the extreme of the spectrum – that of the risk of grave harm or even death. Consider the activist becoming a revolutionary against a regime of violent, deadly oppression, or a young man joining the military to defend his nation. If there is genuine cause for such endeavour warranting dedicated confrontation of suffering and the related source of immorality, then the pressure of extremes can have a profound effect on a person by exerting a strong force on the adaptation of virtues.

Some of the highest pleasures are evoked through the most empowering acts of Liberty, birthing the most notable virtues. The great challenge of extreme suffering and vice can be worthy of higher virtues; such pursuits may reward with great fulfilment through virtue. But with sufficient cause may also arise compulsive excitement violating the principles of mindful reason, hindsight, and forethought, leading to the misapplication of utilities and undisciplined, selfish ambition. One might be eager to help a cause, yet in such excitement a person may lose sight of a better, alternative course of action and application of the self.

For instance, it would be better for a young person to avoid throwing away their life needlessly or committing reckless risks if unnecessary. One must always consider how choices can affect others. Pointlessly throwing away your life and harming those around you for the sake of your own selfishness is not a path to virtue. Yet it is obvious that sometimes tough choices must be made. Sometimes the clarity of vision and ambition and sincerity to oneself cannot be achieved by a lonesome individual, requiring engagement with people and the authority of leadership.

In the pursuit of self-improvement and growth, one ought to act in accordance with virtue-rules, to be thoughtful, cautious, and disciplined as well as courageous and resilient. Yet the morality of the dedicated ambition resolving, conquering, and challenging suffering, even in the liberty of compulsiveness when the merits of mindful reason permit this, has important moral value for improvement through the use of suffering for one's own benefit.

One might suppose that in pursuing the extremes of moral demand and duty, such as with great sacrifice and cost to self, one would suffer and would not benefit from well-being. This would certainly be a plausible criterion of the moralities of Fear, yet ambition of Liberty strives to make this moral attitude more profound by directly addressing suffering from within, then externally. While the Liberty of moral duty might not provide rewards with conventional happiness, joy, and well-being, it strives to cultivate fulfilment through greater spirit and virtue at Liberty. The flourishing evoked by the higher virtues of Liberty might not provide well-being in spirit of Fear, but they will evoke greater spirit in actions and virtues rising above suffocated spirit that is bound to Fear and transcends the compulsion of joy. This is only achieved through the adaptation of character to greater tangents of suffering, with the characteristic of vectors resilient to suffering being the criterion on which any endeavour of fulfilment and goodness of ethical environment may be deserved.

In the pursuit of confronting suffering, vice, and immorality, one ought not to delve into a distorted, corruptive view of suffering. As illustrated above, suffering in extreme circumstances can breed virtue, but it can also come at an extreme cost. Suffering of war, conflict, and personal loss can be great, can be crippling, and always leaves a mark on a person. Suffering has an important value in terms of its utility to produce virtue when a person is moved by goodwill. The value and virtue I illustrate in suffering is not that of suffering itself, but of character resisting and succeeding over suffering. Suffering itself is not righteous; the suffering of others and one's own suffering are not moral ends. However, using suffering to grow above it, to succeed it and flourish *is* the moral end of ambition at Liberty.

The disaster and mass suffering of conflict too familiar for mankind is caused by vice, Fear, and states of suffering; none of this is good until its end of achieving growth and progress. Yet such a mode of growth is too inefficient, too costly. Suffering is not good; how one reacts to suffering and what virtue and benevolence may arise from states of suffering is the envisaged value of suffering. What I argue is not tolerance or glorification of suffering, but acceptance of suffering as a dispensable, fettered, yet presently necessary means of growth, as a consequence of vulnerability.

Suffering is only good as a utility and means to the end of growth in character, yet real virtue in suffering is the attitudes it invokes to move the individual past suffering, beyond vice, and in succession of Fear. One ought not to devote themself to suffering, but learn to exemplify virtue in suffering and honour what suffering can offer for growth, what virtue and strength can arise from suffering, and in Defiance enjoy the growth that comes with suffering.

There is no beauty in suffering and conflict, yet there is profound awe in people who stand by virtue against fear and pain and rise above suffering, especially in the form of peace with suffering and vulnerability moving to greater virtue. Higher pleasures in suffering are only those of spiritual fulfilment and liberty of autonomy greater than suffering, in the spirit of Liberty. This, however, is fundamentally different to warped, corrupted spirit infatuated by suffering.

Deliberately creating a situation of suffering or acting in pursuit of destruction so that others or oneself can grow in character is never right or just. Accidentally inflicting harm on people might not be condemnably wrong, but neither is this good. Creating a humanitarian disaster to test oneself or others is not only uncertain in its capacity to create success or produce positive consequences, but it will also create needless suffering, going against moral liberty. The end of morality is finding a way to overcome and limit suffering to generate and construct global flourishing and growth, an end encompassed in all varieties of the Human Imperative. Creating suffering as opposed to confronting it is never good or as constructive as the latter.

Even where suffering may arise from the deception of idleness corrupting intent, this cannot justify inflicting pain on people by a guise of warped sense of strategy of growth through suffering. Such a thought only arises in unmediated Liberty of rationale and madness.

A key dimension of the end of morality is to employ the utility offered by the force of suffering to efficiently grow from it without suffering's inefficient pattern of growth through Fear's vicious cycles of destruction and stunted growth. Liberty's grand ambition is supposed to enable Discipline and Harmony to drive growth, absolutely opposed to a structure of Fear where suffering and pain are necessary for progress. Inflicting suffering on others under the justification of motivating growth, wholly opposed to the more constructive effort of encouraging and helping people confront their vices and grow in virtue, is unjust and wrong because it completely contradicts and drastically misinterprets the grand ambition of Liberty, something that is imperative to make note of in hindsight of people's delusions and foolishness.

Furthermore, Liberty's end involves effective and efficient use of suffering as a utility of growth by resisting suffering's corruptive influence. Perpetuating suffering without just and righteous cause will also never achieve completion as a moral end, because the vector that drives it will affect tangents of ethics' structures so that the vector relying on suffering to drive growth will be fixated. Inflicting suffering on others to force people to grow violates the principle-rules and virtue-rules of moral liberty and invokes a dynamic element in ethics plagued by a mechanism of inflicting suffering to cause growth, never obtaining full resolution or being the most efficient or stable mode of ethical and human development. A world that requires suffering is not ideal and not one that we are obligated to.

Concerning the morality of actions imposing suffering, several principles and values should be derived. Imposing suffering on others, even if just, can at times lead to unforeseen consequences, potentially resulting in harm and the degeneration of character. It is not always certain how a person will react to suffering and what the effect of suffering will be on mentality and character. Therefore, it is only sensible to not risk people's well-being by subjecting them to suffering without necessity.

Furthermore, as should be taken for granted, an act is immoral if it creates and subjects people to suffering and pain, because this would undermine well-being. People might overcome and grow from suffering, therefore, acts imposing suffering could be interpreted as morally acceptable or justified if this serves the end of coercing character to grow, which is in fact wrong and not a sustainable solution. Excess, needless suffering can overwhelm people and cause them to succumb to vice and suffer more than they ever did.

It is abundantly clear that there is sufficient vice and suffering people endure, with the only sensible and good intention and action being that of helping people overcome their pain and, in peace, not instigate unnecessary destruction and suffering. All people live with suffering and adding to their share without necessity in terms of justice, and in contradiction with moral liberty, won't help in any way. It is better to help people by encouraging mindfulness about the root of suffering, but only if this is harmonious with moral liberty when people seek help or their actions exceed moral tolerance and demand retributive justice. Therefore, suffering ought to only be inflicted on people if just and necessary, primarily constituted by acting in accordance with the principle-rule of liberty and the necessity to act on normative vectors exceeding the limits of tolerable moral liberty.

Here it should become clear why the utility of the virtue-rule shadowing the principle-rule of liberty is important. By embracing Discipline to not act impulsively on the suffering and pain of others, one grows in virtue of Discipline. Discipline allows a person to behave with more ethical efficiency and effectiveness, which applies to many aspects of life and is compatible with enabling the vice that feeds on itself if such is the determination of the moral liberty of people.

Causing people harm and grief without justice causes imbalance and diverts effort and energy from more constructive and morally better actions. Furthermore, being wholly dependent on others as a source of moral and spiritual growth, especially at a cost to others' welfare, will never fulfil autonomy and the potential of spiritual liberty. By neglecting one's internal state of character, spirit, and mind, he or she deprives themself of necessary mindfulness.

A common example of this is projection and reflection of anger, suffering, and frustration on others. In doing so one surrenders mindfulness on conduct and does not address the root of vice and the product of suffering. There are, of course, other reasons and even merits for projecting and reflecting discomfort if this serves an acceptable moral end such as getting people to leave you alone if you genuinely do not feel well and need to rest and recuperate. But by continuing a cycle of suffering, by allowing it to reflect through you and onto others, suffering and vice only spread. The main catalyst of this dynamic and its toll on spirit and character is Fear. By surrendering to Fear and allowing suffering and its cycles to dominate through inefficient and destructive tangents, none fulfil greater interest. Yet by overcoming suffering, putting an end to the cycle and succeeding it, one becomes stronger and thus more fulfilled in spirit of flourishing. By defying suffering and its cycle, the will and its virtues grow, making people more than mere subjects of Fear and being rewarded with higher fulfilment of noble and resolute character at Liberty.

While suffering lingers there can be no absolute eudaimonia. Even though eudaimonia can be achieved with and through suffering, Fear and suffering will remain inherent to the mind or in others. The suffering of others not only threatens one's own spiritual liberty and eudaimonia through actions of those yielding to vice, while also providing substance of nourishment, it also threatens the virtue of eudaimonia from within through negativity of others' suffering. The higher faculties and its mindfulness by the Void may detach from others' suffering and breed apathy and neglect. However, the will of flourishing and towards eudaimonia will nevertheless remain with the will to live.

To achieve greater states of flourishing and to pursue duty and the absolution of eudaimonia – achieved through fulfilment of the Human Imperative – one ought not to cause suffering to others or act in accordance with causing greater harm than is necessary. The determination of the measure and quality of suffering may be subject to long-term consequences, whereby immediate considerable suffering may be preferred over extensive suffering and subsequent structural negativity. In analogy, ripping off a plaster may be better than slowly pealing it away.

Our world is rife with suffering: some natural, subject to determinations of fortune's causal cascade, a catalyst of suffering beyond the intention of people which we ought to remedy; other suffering is that of the vice of mankind. Suffering can motivate progress and improvement. Yet suffering is not the force of progress – our will to flourish is, the latter being influenced and perhaps borne of the former. However, as is clear with the morality of Harmony, flourishing can be achieved in virtue, discipline, and mindfulness beyond suffering. Overcoming natural or organic suffering beyond suffering caused by people's intentions, such as with disease and environment, is morally better and a moral duty.

The ultimate purpose of community and collaboration, whether competitive or cooperative, in terms of the Human Imperative, is to combine utility and maximise value through liberty and diversity to succeed suffering, natural or man-made. The suffering created, retained, provoked, and continued by people is a whole other dimension of suffering. This dynamic of suffering is multilateral in terms of corresponding forces caused or propagated by people contingent on natural suffering, with suffering of organic poverty (that is, poverty not deliberately caused by social negligence and personal irresponsibility) and disease often being notable natural causes of strife. To alleviate suffering of the community, one ought to first overcome suffering of the self, which involves how one treats people, because virtue is relational and corresponds to moral action. The cycle of suffering can only ever be truly overthrown through the individual's ambition and goodwill.

Fear and suffering often project onto others and spread a corruptive force of ethical negativity in ethical structures. By ignoring the core of suffering, by not being mindful of one's own suffering, then only serving as a slave reflecting suffering, one submits in spirit and morality to Fear and suffering rather than uses these ethical dynamics for greater moral benefit. Channelling suffering and Fear inward to counter-act the fundamental force of suffering among people is the only lasting mode of morality to achieve eudaimonia of spiritual liberty in suffering and Fear. The dynamic of Fear may affect one person, the vice of which submits them to suffering and projects pain outward once more. The suffering you feel caused by people or instigated by natural suffering reflected onto people breeds a cycle of suffering that always returns through a variety of causal dimensions. Suffering caused by people and community that one may feel is unjust and cruel is the same suffering that one may in turn submit to. And so the morality of Defiance is found, made more effective through mindfulness, wisdom, insight, and discipline of Harmony. To remedy and succeed suffering of oneself and of community, one ought to counter its force at its core – in the individual bound to Fear, then or in parallel suffering invoked by Nature, the former always being a priority ambition for the individual at Liberty.

In this context, it is imperative to consider the relation between the individual and community. The two are inherently entwined in structural ethics and both deserve equal consideration in normativity. The individual constitutes community, through which a strong and virtuous individual contributes to a good and just community. Community affects and influences the individual, through which a strong and virtuous community nourishes righteous character of the individual. The two cannot and ought not to be normatively mutually exclusive. It is clear that a dysfunctional community can foster apathetic and disheartened attitudes among individuals.

The impression that a community is doomed by the actions of the majority is a powerful influence over ethical dispositions fostering apathy, breeding unconstructive and pessimistic moral attitudes. The individual suffers with the community, as the community suffers from vice of the individual. Any debate concerning primary valuation between community and individual is normatively elusive as both dimensions of tangents must be accounted for. Both interests go hand-in-hand and deserve equal consideration in normativity, for flourishing of the community comes through well-being of the individual and vice versa; both necessitate equal priority, with mass consequences on individuals through other people constituting a community's state of morality and ethical environment. One action can harm a person which then causes harm to another such as with a person's vice causing lasting psychological damage to another.

While the individual can achieve great flourishing despite a suffering community, absolute eudaimonia transcending suffering or its utility for the individual can only ever fully come through the Human Imperative helping community and succeeding suffering in all its forms and spheres. No individual can ever absolutely flourish in a dying and suffering community, and no community can ever achieve mass eudaimonia by fulfilling the Human Imperative while individuals are deprived of goodness and virtue. Any succession of suffering and Fear can only ever come through spirit and character of the individual at strength, freedom, and formal normative liberty to do so; only with ease of virtue and strong will of duty can the individual righteously commit to community, setting the path for the spirit of the Ideals and the Highest Good. Any succession of virtue can only ever come through liberty of the individual to do so, and any community can only succeed through liberty of the individual to conquer vice. No virtue or utility in the imminence of death is relevant unless relevant to the sensation of the final moment or knowledge of the sum of one's life. Only through virtue can a fulfilling final moment of eudaimonia be achieved, according to which community and the Highest Good are imperative for the final spirit judging the self.

Suffering gives rise to utilities and the virtues of compassion and empathy. With careful consideration and application, compassion and empathy can generate much good and be invaluable in many circumstances. Perception in Fear can consider compassion, forgiveness, mercy, and empathy to be weaknesses and vulnerability. This moral outlook only serves to protect the self in Fear, relinquishing any notable dignity or status of virtue. By consoling oneself above others and using others as mere utilities to one's own self-gratifying ends of a status twisted by Fear only facilitates a quality of character and consequent spirit and psyche as a slave of Fear. By embracing and feeling the suffering of others through the base utility of compassion as a sentiment, a person exposes themself to suffering, leading to a greater potential and increased likelihood of succeeding individual and communal suffering. To detach from the suffering of others, to ignore it, and hide from the suffering of others, is to pursue one's own end in Fear, depriving the virtues that lead to the improvement of ethical environment. Compassion recognises the suffering that ought to be remedied and overcome.

Opening oneself to suffering through awareness of sentiment and through others generates tangents towards the development and growth of virtue from suffering. The suffering of others can be an opportunity for dignity and virtue to grow and create circumstances through which greater balance of flourishing can be achieved (when suffering has emerged). Hiding from suffering in one's veil of Fear serves only to protect oneself from the painful experiences of suffering, yet in doing so keeps the self in submission to Fear and weak character. Compassion, when channelled into effective and mindful action, can serve as an imperative utility for growth and flourishing through others and within the self. There is much more strength and virtue in sensing and embracing the suffering of others than hiding from it in a repressive coil of Fear that maintains suffering.

The veil of Fear can invoke a malevolent objection to mindfulness of the self where we fail to improve our condition. It is the capacity to admit vulnerabilities and weaknesses, or accepting the circumstances that made a person who and what they are, while defying and standing up to wrongdoing and pain, that marks true virtue of Liberty. Neglecting compassion and foregoing mindfulness is a moral course that could never achieve the aforementioned ambition, and the veil of Fear will never provide rewards with the strength of willpower the same way Liberty can. Lack of empathy will deny a person invaluable intuition about the value and application of the self in relation to the Human Imperative.

For compassion to be effective and morally positive to its fullest potential, and for the individual to be astute in compassion, the virtue of empathy as a utility of high-reason is imperative. To be understanding of others, to understand others in intellectual cognition, to find effective utility in compassion, to devise morality with respect to suffering and its evocation of compassion, one ought to be mindful of such thoughts and moral judgements. This is only achievable in the intellectual and cognitive utility of placing oneself in another's position, envisaging and feeling their pain, and studying people's needs in suffering. One ought to nourish, learn, or cultivate empathy and compassion accordingly. This may come with a heavy spiritual and psychological cost, as trying to understand others' pain, relating it to oneself, and appealing to compassion through empathy can be punishing. But it's worth it, and in Liberty, the pain found in compassion and empathy serves as a key moral resource for the ambition of the Human Imperative.

There is significant virtue in finding the strength to help others, make sacrifices for others, and feel for others, just as the consequences of aiding a community are good for relieving suffering in the structures of ethics and by nourishing oneself with virtue to flourish beyond the limits of Fear, leading to the liberty of virtuous, strong, and righteous spirit, evoking eudaimonia. Compassion and empathy are an ethical investment, which can be risky and profitable.

Compassion and empathy can be seen to interject or interfere with ambition, with pursuit of an end desired and envisaged. Indeed, even compassion devoid of empathy and thoughtfulness can lead to mistakes and greater sum negligence of the maxims of compassion. Compassion lacking empathy may misplace the value of utility and life, leading to greater suffering than the suffering of compassion. Compassion and empathy, like any utility, are subservient and secondary to the primacy of action – the fundamental will to flourish and its substance of logic and reason moving and invoking sentiment, emotion, feeling, and sense.

All ambition emerges from the will to flourish, whether it is of a brutal calculation of interest or another pragmatic form maximised through thoughtful actions in compassion and empathy. Compassion and empathy can interfere with ambition, yet they also serve as imperative functions of intuitions for grander ambition that is worthy of the virtue of Liberty. The mind can consciously reject, or detach from, sentiments of compassion to pursue an end of ambition for self-fulfilment, or it may do so pathologically without clear intent. Compassion serves to recall and invoke pain and suffering from which we can grow and improve. Hiding, diverting, and deflecting pain, such as through detachment from compassion, only serves lesser ambition in Fear. Yet this is not obsolete or meaningless.

The mind, especially in its baser faculty, naturally tends to be averse to pain, subsequently neglecting greater fulfilment through the intervention and mediation of high-reason to use pain for greater ends, to fulfil greater interest in the individual and community. By understanding pain, embracing it, using it, and being mindful of it to the extent of sentimental and cognitive succession, the prime virtue of will-power grows, fulfilling ambition of higher virtue and of greater reward in spirit and autonomy in liberty dominating Fear. This is a mode of ethics fulfilling the higher pleasure of autonomy by fulfilling one of the primary intuitions, drawing on strong spirit and contingent human behaviour – the desire for control and power. Compassion and empathy not only serve broader ambitions of the Human Imperative, but also guide and fuel the ambitions of virtue.

However, heedless and compulsive compassion lacking empathy and mindful purpose are not only subject to a fragile resolve but can also lack the depth necessary for higher fulfilment. Compulsive modes of base morality driven by compassion, while better than the destructive base moral conduct of self-deprecation in Fear, will not produce eudaimonia unless re-invigorated, re-enforced, and complimented with mindful goodwill. There is nothing wrong with compulsive compassion and empathy contingent on positive moral conduct and mindful bounds of intent and consequence, within parameters of justice. Yet while this base morality is limited in purpose and ambition, and while it lacks greater spirit, it will also suffer the same limitations of any focused base morality, especially if negligent of greater rationale.

A good example for this case is the persistence of pointless suffering that lacks a definitive purpose or a positive function. Pain serves the end of motivating improvement and growth, in both higher and baser moral outlooks, whereby, for example, the mental pain of rejection and loneliness, or anxiety in stressful modern work environments, can influence conduct and satisfy the base faculties that have thus far been successful in sum terms, as human civilisation still exists and has grown under the reign of Fear. But sometimes these pains and stresses interfere with ambition and intention.

People have not completely mentally, morally, and spiritually adapted to modern society, and even though Fear has brought us to this age, it is not enough for the future. Without an immediate and effective solution, we will naturally be moved by aversion and deflection of pain, potentially undermining immediate and long-term ambition and interest. The virtues of the higher faculties and their utilities of mindfulness and disciplined willpower are approaches to immediately intrusive and functionless pain. This morality does not even require an emphasis on an ethos of high-reason or harmonious synchrony of all-reason to be fulfilling for base moral conduct. In the especially moving cases of the needless, pointless, and unjust pain and suffering of others, to which there is no realistic positive outlook, compassion and empathy for others' pain in oneself serves to alleviate their pain. This facilitates greater balance in flourishing – justice – and is better than eluding this pain, particularly when used as a moral resource for Harmony to achieve peace in sentiment and thought when peace in frivolous pursuit of unfulfillable desires could never achieve acceptance.

Compassion and empathy in pain are at times the only way peace and greater fulfilment can be achieved through acceptance, for too often there is simply nothing that can be done and we have no control on the past continuing its tangents and vectors into the present. Only in the acceptance and release of Fear, achievable only through empathy and compassion, can the unending pain of suffering beyond our capacity of resolution (through intervention of action) be separated from its corruptive and painful force. Only in acceptance through compassion and empathy can pointless, ineffectual pain be remedied and given balance. This ambition in goodwill is more fulfilling, more rewarding, and worthier than ambition bound to Fear, which is distinct from idle action in submission to Fear by the criteria of genuine limitations in effective action (where there is no choice or option but to accept pain). Accepting pain is, and ought to be, different from surrendering to pain and Fear.

In forgoing and forgetting the simple virtue of acceptance through compassion and empathy, immorality rises. In lack of mindfulness, in thoughtless and heedless ambition in Fear, all of which distract from the core of pain and suffering, needless suffering is wrought and little is resolved. By failing to live up to the virtue of humanity by using willpower to confront pain, by depriving ourselves of the will and opportunity for compassion and empathy, we instil and extend suffering. Only in acceptance, leading to liberty of spirit, followed by duty, are suffering and pain let go of through an act of common empathy more profound than compassion alone. Achieving the strength of will to do so is the path to greater fulfilment. Then, only in the courage to confront and abrupt Fear can suffering be relieved at its source.

Regardless of whether one is disposed to a higher or base ethos, the pain of empathy and compassion towards others and oneself, along with the acceptance of one's pain and suffering, which requires strength and courage, accepting pain is the first step to recovery and growth. By freeing oneself of emotional and spiritual pain, whether through tears or mindful absolution, one can begin to heal and achieve well-being greater and more fulfilling than that of fearful suffering. The burden of the pain of empathy is most liberating by the bonds of the living soul. But when pain is so great that it burns the heart, it can be followed by tears of relief that one is alive and has experienced the tremendous spirit that shines over all of life, for great loss and pain is the shadow of the Highest Goodness and the best in life.

In great personal loss, especially of loved ones, and other great suffering, the spirit will be drained. The spirit is not limitless, with persistent turning to the Void only leading to further corruption. When one is inspired, one can feel as though he or she can confront the whole world, looks outward. But when the scars of the spirit, mind, and heart are great, it is best to show oneself compassion and let wounds heal. Be cautious of withering and fading spirit, for the lack of spirit as depressive states does more harm than over-excitement and exaggerated expectations to be of supreme virtue, to have overcome suffering that may never heal. Being too tired to do much is absolutely fine, and don't allow expectations to torment you further. Do what you feel you can, but don't be afraid to leap beyond comfort.

Idleness in acceptance can be an ineffectual and negligent morality. One of the primary cases for this is seen with moral liberty. By being too eager to let go of pain, one may fail to utilise its greater potential for sum resolution of suffering. Pain, suffering, and hate can empower the will, fuel its ambition, which in tandem with mindful purpose can become a powerful utility. An individual's settlement for peace and idleness that foregoes the struggle to improve on suffering can deprive a community of the motivated and dedicated agency of virtue. This may also deprive the individual of willpower that can be extracted from suffering and can teach greater and more adaptive mindfulness – liberty in mindfulness and its moral aspects. But then acceptance in Harmony serves to mediate when the ambition of Defiance and attachment to ambition lead one astray and to lesser fulfilment by misusing suffering. For instance, there is much suffering in the world, and there is very little any single individual can do by themselves.

Attachment to the ambition of heroism to 'save the world' can lead to moral corruption and mistakes of compassion that lead to greater pain. There are good things people can do within their means without recklessly overstepping such as by voting responsibly and wisely. Yet the common citizen and voter cannot directly intervene against a decision of a government or only intervene on the consequence of a government decision. One should do what is morally effectual in his or her sphere and circumstance, but exceeding personal responsibility and opportunity to illegitimately, inappropriately, and unjustly intervene or influence sociopolitical effect through attachment to an assumed goodwill of the Highest Good may only create more suffering.

To illustrate the point further, there is nothing in my present circumstance that I can do to put an end to the needless contention and confrontation between the West and Russia or the global structure of Fear, and exerting excessive force by plotting, manipulating, or seizing authoritative management in violation of people's autonomy and the principle-rules of liberty would not produce a positive result, especially not in terms of the change necessary if one is to succeed Fear that is only truly achievable through liberty of the will. The greater moral accord in such circumstances is to do what one can in the circumstances and within the righteous extent of power as an autonomous moral agent, and find the will to accept and make peace with what is beyond one's control.

In suffering and pain, it is important to accept compassion towards oneself. These fundamental forces in life are not intrinsically easy to overcome and require Discipline to be employed for greater virtuous ends. Compassion towards the self in mindful evaluation is one part of liberty in suffering and pain. Yet this compassion should only serve as a mediator of pain's influence on spirit. What this liberty of self-compassion reveals, however, is the importance of attitudes channelling, employing, and invoking suffering. Self-compassion can lead one astray and foster a degrading sense of self driven by heedless sentiment – how one feels does not necessarily reflect reality. In lingering pain and reoccurring suffering and mistakes, it is natural for shame or frustration with the self to arise, for anger and sadness to be evoked when reflecting on the mistakes one has made.

Pain, especially physical, can and does set limitations on life; it can limit opportunities and preferential circumstances. Compassion towards the self is one part of beginning to accept the circumstances producing suffering and pain leading to improvement and growth. Pain in the sense of self can lead to negative self-perception of belittled character, a mindful intuition that might not be without sincere evaluation, for vice does belittle character. Yet in these evaluations of mindful reasoning and intuition, goodwill ought to be employed to inspire positive ambition guided by good attitudes and intuitions.

Pain and suffering may evoke spirit and sense of self as 'damaged goods', whether in body or mind; but the attitudes and ambitions of virtue are what can turn one's damaged goods into a tempered prize. Only through endurance and continuity can goodness, including that of virtuous character, affirm its pious quality. If one feels like a 'damaged good', this is an opportunity to summon a response in attitude and ambition to become a tempered prize and hardened utility exemplified by virtue. But just as intuitions can deceive, especially with self-reflection, so too can rationale. Thinking of oneself as virtuous and strong without concrete affirmation of righteous character and sincere good spirit can deceive oneself in Fear and deny the rightful place of intuitions that lead to growth. A person should listen to his or her intuitions and trust his or her feelings, as is seen by paying attention to intuitions judging oneself as 'damaged goods' and mediating them with clear reflection that is not bound to blind rationale. The same goes for arrogance. Our intuitions can tell us much more than mere rationale, but the self is complete and spirit absolute when understanding is illuminated through synchrony and mindfulness of both intuitions and rationale complimenting and supporting each other.

Suffering usually manifests itself as a reflection and propagation of vice. Victims of abuse or torture often attempt to displace their own suffering by perpetuating it onto others, in so doing never treating the source of suffering as a residue of the pain. Little good comes from the deflection of pain, not for the community and not for the individual deprived of ambition. Self-compassion is imperative to address the root of suffering and to begin the healing of past grievances, dissolving vice, and nourishing virtue. To initiate and sustain healing there can be many legitimate and viable solutions, yet in measures of ethics an emphasis should be placed on valuing a solution rather than value distraction and deflection.

Beginning this process requires building up the courage and will to confront pain, according to which the heritin interpretation of Liberty invokes Defiance and Discipline. Suffering imposing itself on others through oneself and subjecting the self to torment is akin to degrees of torture, for much of this suffering comes as malevolent vice seeking power and control in Fear. The spirit and mind grow from learning to withstand such torture and then making peace with it. The use of pain as a source of energy and power then evokes empathy and compassion not only towards oneself but also towards others; channelling pain benefits from mediation of self-compassion by making the suffering of pain more sustainable and balanced. Suffering thereby leads to eudaimonia and higher fulfilment. Understanding one's suffering, pain, and vice, and sowing Harmony and mindfulness, cultivates the capacities and utilities of empathy.

From this one can draw a key virtue-rule that vice and wrong-doing can come from the simplest and most innocent of vulnerabilities and weaknesses, whether something as common as a simple desire not to be alone or one's inability to cope with pain inflicted unjustly. There is always a reason why people act the way they do, and often the spirit and mentality of such actions is not as malicious or wicked as simplistic base perceptions suggest. But I suppose it takes one to know one. Through the practice of Harmony and empathy, one will begin to learn how Fear operates and what it does to people, then understand Fear is not intrinsically a malign catalyst and tangent, just one that is very faulty. Fear's vectors are then understood far better through empathy and understanding in the sense that people who act on vice are those who have succumbed to their pain and Fear, with Fear exhausting its positive utility. Through sense and intuition found through mindfulness of empathy granting significant insight into the universalisable soul, Liberty is fulfilled by binding itself to all things even beyond the facade of people's vice and delving into their suffering. Rational intuitions then highlight the amorality and universality of the fundamental will, formulating all manners of intuitions at liberty in their morality, in terms of both compassion and brutal actions in relation to the value of a soul. But more on this later.

The dynamic of the utilities of pain and compassion, to be at liberty to feel pain and compassion, is a good example of liberty in morality and spirit. Being free to live and embrace different attitudes, to be free in emotional, mental, and spiritual change through and with the world, grants higher fulfilment and pleasure leading to Liberty. In the distortion or confusion that can arise naturally in response to internal conflict or contention between sentiment and thought, mindfulness by the Void and the Ploy set forth the utility to mediate liberty of spirit and morality. This Liberty sustained and partly enabled by the Ploy offers fulfilment through the higher faculties in tandem with baser, emotional well-being through synchrony of the will in both faculties of reason.

A good example for this case is the matter of letting go of people for whom one feels affection, yet with whom there cannot be a greater sum of well-being. In the greater compassion and empathy of leaving people to their happiness, while condemning the self to immediate pain of Fear, the will grows in virtue beyond Fear itself. In the acceptance of such pain and by finding goodwill to feel fulfilled in compassion for others' happiness, one comes closer to eudaimonia. This is moral and spiritual liberty in compassion and pain, in empathy and suffering.

If a person pursues a life of overcoming Fear and suffering, and is motivated by a path towards embodying the Ideals, then his or her determination will be to embrace suffering and use strength to stop a causal chain and cycle of suffering, to endure suffering by virtue of willing character, and reap the goodness of spirit at Liberty to do so. In this notion is the paradoxical nature of selfishness. The desire of an individual to become stronger and attain greater virtue involves relations with other people, the dynamics of which are built on actions pursuing the self-interest of flourishing – ethical egoism of the Fundamental Principle. All conduct of embracing suffering will be established on the foundation of ethics pursuing self-fulfilment and self-interest.

By embracing suffering and being strong when others are not, one grows in virtue with relevant conditioning. This serves the interest of the individual, through which greater self-interest comes by embracing suffering and containing it in oneself to fuel the ambition of Liberty. This paradigm of egotistic desires of an individual can create better consequences than solely focusing on promoting good for others in the first place, which would constitute a vulnerable pursuit of self-interest subject to conditional morality dependent on others' morality and conditional in terms of self-determination lacking strong autonomy. Putting faith in others can breed vulnerability in a person's convictions and attitudes rather than if a person focuses on his or her own ambition. Pursuing self-interest to improve one's own condition internally in conjunction with improving one's environment through and with others is a more sustainable ethic than a moral attitude dependent on circumstantial faith in others and contractual morality.

By embracing suffering and relieving others of it, an issue may arise concerning the distribution of suffering. By embracing the suffering of others, by being too eager, one may deprive others of liberty and the opportunity to grow in virtue from suffering. This will not present itself as a practical issue, but it is important to make note of. If you do everything for others, they won't learn and won't be capable without you. On the one hand, the principle-rule of liberty should function so as to dispose people to differential attitudes and behaviours. Fear is common in people and I am highly sceptical of a heritin or similar ethic really taking off by becoming a majoritarian attitude, whereby people become very eager to embrace the suffering of others and adopt or settle for a lesser state of fulfilment in base faculties rather than that of higher pleasures.

This is not to object to the potential. It's just that empirical impressions suggest otherwise. This would be to the advantage of the distribution of suffering, whereby there is greater availability of the resource of suffering for those willing to exploit its value. The modern world is abundant in the ethical resource of suffering that can serve constructive purpose. However, it can also overwhelm and be very costly. With reference to the latter, it would be better for suffering to be more harmonious in its prevalence so as to not prevail in an inefficient, unbalanced structural dynamic of suffering. A distribution of suffering where people embrace their responsibilities would be Ideal, serving more as a virtue-rule. But where this fortune is lacking one ought to be mindful of the responsibilities and challenges they embrace, giving primacy to mindful valuation of how one employs one's efforts and energy and utilises their value.

It is important to keep in mind that suffering is not absolutely necessary for growth, as Discipline and Harmony can offer alternatives to Defiance and Fear. However, while the human condition its susceptible to reacting to suffering and structures are afflicted by the suffering of vice, a morality adept in balancing the tangents and vectors of suffering is needed. One's interests must also heed others' interests, because only through global satisfaction can we thrive, we must also be mindful of others' suffering serving as a point of structural deficiency and an opportunity to exercise morality and duty by helping others. Liberty in ethics necessitates considerations of the wishes of others as part of justice in liberty of morality, even if it goes against greater interests of which they are ignorant. But sometimes liberty has to be suspended when it comes to considerations of others' wishes.

Some people might not possess the character to reap greater rewards of Liberty, meaning the duty of the virtuous is to use this moral resource and opportunity for one's own ambition and to alleviate others of their suffering. However, it remains an important point that conduct should not be overly intrusive so as not to deprive people of the opportunity to truly grow in character, the necessity of which will involve people confronting their vice if any lasting constructive effect is to be achieved. Essentially, being overly eager and trying to save the world in one swift act will not practically satisfy the criteria of the Highest Good, and so one must be mindful in protecting others from suffering, fulfilling greater self-interest by virtue of restraint.

Ultimately, the conflict of interest in considerations of suffering is not absolute and not without a practical solution or application, whereby the considerations of others' interests play an imperative role in mediating acts embracing suffering. Sometimes one ought to embrace suffering for growth and fulfilment of oneself in conjunction with others and external spheres, especially when others are not disposed to, or capable of, utilising suffering for greater moral effect. Yet in other circumstances one ought to step aside and not intervene. This, of course, requires a substantial degree of thoughtfulness and empathy, which is not always available in practice.

In matters of other people's suffering and the question of intervention, it is best to defer to the principle of moral liberty and respect others' wishes or act on judgements framed by the Central Principles and justice. This suggests a default attitude where one is granted legitimacy to act on one's own determination with a degree of liberty, while greater restraint and caution must be exercised when engaging with others so that the empathetic and compassionate intuition to help others must be tempered with mindfulness, caution, and restraint. So when something mainly involves you, act in your best judgement. However, when an instance does not involve you and there is no immediate necessity to act on a threat of grave violation of central morality in terms of others, such as a threat of someone getting murdered, then one ought to refrain from intervening unless others consent to help and intervention and if the manner of intervention satisfies the qualifications of justice and the Central Principles.

To offer a practical illustration of such an attitude towards liberty in suffering, consider whether or not to tell a friend they are being cheated on by their romantic partner. On the one hand, it may be supposed that others' relationships are none of your business, something more significant when the same case applies to a relationship between people you are not close to or not familiar with. There may be complicated reasons why one is cheating or being cheated on in a relationship, just as there can be very bad consequences if action is impulsive and blind.

For example, in a relationship where a person is caring for a disabled person, such as a person with dementia, intimacy and an affair may be the only sustainable way in which care for the vulnerable individual can be sustained and where a somewhat decent finality of living can be achieved. However, where the circumstances are different and not so specific and exceptional, then considerations of the right action would be different.

First of all, in a common case where the circumstances are unexceptional, it is wrong to cheat on the other party in a relationship; it is immoral and cruel to deceive and betray the trust and affection of an individual in such a manner. If the relationship is unhealthy and unsatisfying, then the matter ought to be addressed; to deceive, the equivalent of cheating, and fail to confront deficiencies and faults in a relationship are actions of Fear and mark weakness in vice, making more than one person unsatisfied. So it is wrong to cheat and cowardly to not address the matter, while also selfish to impose a conversation at a time when the other party has responsibilities of greater value such as in times of great stress related to duty.

Concerning the latter, it might be wrong, for example, to inform a serving soldier in an emotionally and psychologically demanding situation that he is being cheated on, for this pain might be too much to bear. Informing the soldier of a partner's transgression and betrayal may compromise his effectiveness and immediate imperative value of combat utility, allowing pain to make the soldier reckless and ineffectively impulsive. However, it may be wrong to not tell a serving soldier that he is being cheated on since if he was to find out upon returning home, then this may be an even greater shock and cause more pain than if he was to come home but find it was lost. It must be left to the determination of individual judgement, but the running thought would be to inform the person of his or her partner's transgression when the person is able to handle the pain. Yet it is also more respectful and more right to defer judgement on such information to the person directly affected by the immorality of his or her partner. One can conclude that it perhaps isn't best to tell a soldier that he is being cheated on in an immediate firefight, but when one does get a chance, the soldier ought to be informed.

Returning to the question of whether to inform a friend that his or her partner has cheated, it would be right to tell the person cheated on of the partner's transgression. First, the person being cheated on is being betrayed, and thus being caused harm, which isn't right. To deceive the person by protecting him or her from suffering which the person will eventually have to confront (even if in the eventual form of a dysfunctional and unhealthy relationship) is to disrespect and neglect the person's autonomy of judgement.

Of course, as discussed above, there may be exceptions where the information must be withheld if this is a necessity in the greater interest of justice. To withhold information about a dysfunctional and unhealthy relationship, marked by deception and betrayal by one vector of the relationship cheating on the other, is to prolong the pain and suffering and deny maxims of interest where suffering is resolved sooner, which may be granted exception where the immediate injection of suffering causes an excess imbalance and is thus unsustainable. In short, informing a person being cheated on is right in terms of the principle of liberty (by which it is more respectful of the person to inform them) and considerations of the greater sum suffering that is caused by cheating. Therefore, on these grounds it is right to tell a friend if he or she is being cheated on in a relationship.

Furthermore, to take action of one's own accord without giving the other party an opportunity to act is an act against the principle-rule of liberty, and is therefore wrong. Acting in an impulsive and self-gratifying manner without giving the individual cheated on the opportunity to act on his or her own determination will likely also feed compulsions of Fear and deprive them of Liberty. The cheater may have caused pain to another, for which retributive and vengeful intuitions invoke a desire for justice. However, such intuitions in Fear, craving control to punish, may be deprived of greater vision by not respecting the autonomy and determination of the person hurt and depriving the self of greater ambition in Liberty. It is better to defer acting on the offence of a cheater on the person being cheated on, for it is likely that the person cheated on may know best and it is above all the mutual suffering in the relationship that must be addressed.

However, it is then an imperative of duty to ensure the other party does not commit an abominable act such as murdering the offender, as clearly this would be a comparatively worse outcome than the broken relationship dissolving. Whether the person cheated on wishes to take the moral path of vengeance and Fear is up to his or her determination of liberty. If two dysfunctional and emotionally immature people acting on vice are to feed on each other and cause themselves pain in tolerable justice of liberty allowing people to cause themselves harm, then this is to be tolerated, for intolerance would probably do more bad than good. A parallel to such attention to pain is that of the offender – the cheater. There will be a reason for why they acted, and even though such an act of vice is not necessarily a wholly malicious one, immediate pain and Fear, or even guilt, will cloud empathy from such a vision and mindfulness. However, no matter the pain and vice which brought the offender to act immorally and cheat, unless there are exceptional circumstances, this does not make it right not to tell the person cheated on of the transgression of his or her partner.

Acting despite the empathy and understanding of the cheater's pain may ultimately be more empathetic and, in sum, a better action. It will then take Discipline or initially Defiance to act beyond the reserve of uncertainty and pain, to which the brutality of telling the person cheated on of his or her predicament and setting aside the less prerogative concerns of the suffering of the cheater become necessities of moral correctness and duty. But although brutal in immediate terms, this moral accord would hypothetically be right by virtue of facilitating greater long-term well-being.

When it comes to informing a friend's partner, with whom one may not be overly familiar, that they are being cheated on, at a cost to the friend, morality is more ambiguous. Generally speaking, one ought to follow the same rules and thinking as above, but with notable exceptions and additions.

First, it would be best to engage with the friend to encourage them to do what is right and in their greater interest, while also being considerate of what they consider their greater interest. Then, however, it may also be a waste of a person's time to get involved in other people's affairs and dysfunctional relationships, misapplying valued utility; one may have better things to do. Rather than spending time on things of lesser immediate importance like others' self-imposed problems of ignorance and immaturity, if your involvement is unnecessary and not asked for, then justice should be focused where it is needed more (unless there is no such binding concern).

This does not justify doing what is wrong or failing to act rightfully when one ought to, so one must be mindful of whether withholding information is wrong. Withholding information or even lying may be just and morally better and right if it serves a purpose compatible with justice and not mere selfishness. But in such attitudes one ought not to descend into distorted judgements of tangents justifying unsophisticated moral ambitions by appealing to 'the greater good'.

If not telling a friend's partner that he or she is being cheated on while retaining a *priority* value, for example, living in communal harmony with one's roommates to work more effectively towards getting a good education, then the latter may be more of a prerogative than stirring unnecessary distractions. But then this would undermine the character of a true friend. Unbound relationships of others, or their vices, may pass, while the prerogative of one's business ought to be concerned with more important and pressing matters, which could be compromised by negligence of self-righteous and reckless action.

It is important to make a note in this context without extensive divergence from the discussion that friendship is a value and virtue that is supposed to be conditioned, not taken for granted. Friends and people pass, and doing the right thing at the cost of an easily broken friendship can reflect a more self-respecting attitude towards the self, for tolerating the behaviour of vice could invite similar effects towards oneself. But where one's interests and efforts are more valuable beyond the perils of dysfunctional relationships, then it may be satisfactory to settle for informing the friend of one's own dissatisfaction with their actions, while refraining from informing the person being cheated on. If inviting the tangents and environment of vice to affect oneself detracts from positive and more valuable endeavour, then it may be more right to not intervene in people's business, especially if consistent with liberty. This may be especially relevant when living with roommates and not in one's own place and not reliant on the stability of, say, one's parents' relationship and income. However, where the stakes of inaction are much higher and duty is more demanding, especially in secondary spheres of ethics, then the above approach may be grossly insufficient for effective normative guidance.

The issue becomes even more complicated when you become the emotional support of a friend in an unhealthy relationship where you are the only person able to help them. If the stakes are high, such as the person being on the brink of suicide, then it may very well be best to keep silent. These are but some thought-processes and intuitions that may be raised with any issue. In the end, life's quite a complicated thing!

Considerations of the morality of suffering are not complicated once they are reflected on via the intuitions of empathy and rationale setting the tone of greater interest in accordance with intuition. It may feel good to be righteous, to protect others, to act virtuously, to be good; this is the case with embracing suffering and acting in higher moral duty to protect others from pain. Too much suffering and too sudden suffering can be costly and unpredictable. It is at times a risky endeavour to embrace pain, with the model of high-risk, high-reward being applicable to the morality of suffering. But there is such a thing as too much suffering, and even if one has adopted the Ideals, their efficacy without mindfulness over suffering can twist and warp the mind and spirit, corrupting goodwill through suffering underlying intuition and eluding mindful discipline. Ambition, energy, and eagerness may drive a person to do good things. Yet going down such a path heedlessly may overwhelm the mind with desire and thus distort the nature of ambitions of Liberty.

Willpower and autonomy are but one dimension of the ethic and spirit of Liberty. Attitudes focused on strength without empathy and Discipline can become self-righteous, thereby neglecting others and oneself and breeding corruptive obsession that lacks mindfulness that grants greater vision and thus greater ambition. It can feel bad to do the right but brutal thing, the empathetic but uncompassionate thing. But if not committing a mistake of compassion and acting according to the greater common good produces less suffering, then the action is closer to that of the Highest Good. It takes discipline and practice to balance one's actions in accordance with the thought and vision of a grand strategy. It takes time to learn to act and see beyond immediate intuitions and sentiments which deny oneself a greater interest and ambition.

A clear example of this is bringing up a child without letting it find and pursue its own ambitions, to grow in character from the suffering it will inevitably experience. It is, or ought to be, a given that empathy, care, love, and warmth are the default norms in attitudes towards children, but the maxims of such goodwill may not be as clear in compassion that lacks discipline. Suffering is not good, but it can be turned into incredible good, for a deed of goodwill and virtue is much greater when tempered by pain and Fear. Overcoming pain can feel gratifying in terms of the virtue of autonomy it shows, demonstrating the value of peace and strength. But the self-righteousness of self-absorbed ambition can deprive others of their liberty and capacity to grow and flourish, and deprive one of goodwill and having a vision of a greater ambition and the corresponding intuition. Immediate suffering will feel bad, especially when others suffer and there is nothing you can do. But depriving others of the liberty and opportunity to act in virtue and learn from their mistakes is a more sustainable approach to suffering in liberty of morality. Enabling communal stagnation and degeneration as a consequence of mistakes in compassion will be worse in sum ethical terms.

There are times when suffering is imposed on people in undesirable and unjust circumstances. People often attack one another to get what they want, limiting how constructively people can use their lives. Moral practice is mired in vectors of Fear and vice preying on others. However, when suffering is imposed on people necessarily and justly, it ought to be employed effectively with emphasis on constructive utility, in particular so that suffering does not unnecessarily condemn and destroy the individual, as it is preferable to construct virtue. It is of little utility to deliberately subject people to avoidable suffering, yet it is a necessity for some modes of greater endeavour, particularly in relation to mediating authority and justice.

With necessary suffering comes the tough and delicate moral practice of balancing the effects of suffering to achieve a greater positive effect. The way the necessary suffering of others or of groups should be handled entails constructive and proportional methods of dealing with that suffering. For instance, in times of austerity decisions ought to minimise the imposition of suffering while facilitating growth. Progress and growth are key to flourishing and the fulfilment of the Human Imperative, for which suffering serves a distinctive and fundamental utility, although pain is not a necessary tangent to motivate vectors of growth. The Highest Good and humanity will never truly flourish in constant states of chaos and suffering, just as we will never flourish without good spirit. There ought to be room to breathe, a place for liberty, an environment of balancing progress and restoration, or else progress risks being slow, unsustainable, turbulent, and inefficient.

A structure of ethics and its vectors would operate better in ideal circumstances where our attention can be fully dedicated to development without distractions and set-backs from vice and suffering. However, clearly, suffering still plays a pivotal role in motivating progress in an ethos of Fear, which reins in the merit of an ethos of Liberty to surpass the deficiencies of Fear and provide greater balance in endeavour.

Mediation and reduction of suffering necessitate considerations of the value of certain utilities. For example, it is common moral, legal, and social practice to impose penalties and punishments on unacceptable, intolerable behaviour. Suffering may be used for correction and adjustment of character and behaviour, whether through institutional facilities imposing correctional suffering or psychological therapy confronting suffering and allowing healing. The deviant vector, such as a criminal, because of his or her immoral conduct, may diminish in his or her value as a vector and subsequently imbalance maxims of well-being. People who act contrary to moral law and tolerable moral norms by committing immoral deeds create suffering. Sometimes this is sustainable and tolerable such as with people's lesser category of immoral conduct acting in lesser character, yet not necessarily conduct that comes at great cost to spheres of the Highest Good.

Actions of lesser, but tolerable morality might not necessitate intervention suspending liberties as part of justice. However, tolerance of immoral actions and of vectors demented by vice, notably acts of unjust killing and excessive imposition of unjust suffering, might not be sustainable, effective, or constructive. Some actions can create too much suffering to be tolerated, the liberty of which may not be just. Therefore, in considerations of utility, suffering may be imposed in proportion to constructive effect to sustain virtue and balance greater well-being.

This point encompasses both the common good of others and the goodness in the interests of the individual, although it is necessary to consider moral parameters and conditions of liberty if one strives to impose norms and standards on others, even if in violation of the devious individual's preference and moral standard, which creates depraved conduct through intolerable vice. It is helpful to consider people not *simply* as people per se, but *also* as hosts and embodiments of moral utilities, as vectors acting on and through vice and virtue, consistent with broad, dynamic considerations of value.

The theme of the treatment of the morally weak and depraved entails a whole other extensive discussion not only concerning the imposition of suffering. Even the most depraved individuals carry meaning and inherent value with the innate potential to do good, although practicality and immediate circumstances may necessitate the suspension of idealistic and narrow vision. A crime and immoral deed may require a response in accordance with justice, whereby the presence of abominable vice (in contrast to lesser vice that may be tolerated) deprives a person of virtuous quality and, hence, diminishes his or her moral quality and utility. However, this never relinquishes inherent worth.

Decline in positive utility in terms of broad considerations of the dynamics of utilities may entail mediating actions in response to deprivation of positive utility, with the presence of abominable vice perpetuating heinous immorality, such as an imminent threat to another's life, depriving the person of positive value in the dynamics of utilities. It is intuitive to prevent the liberty of vice that may cause heinous immorality, such as that of unjust killing, through defensive acts (e.g. killing in self-defence). Deprivation of moral value of a character in terms of utility does not enable morality denying inherent value, but rather enables moral states and motivation to protect and secure the positive value of other, more benevolent utilities and characters. Accordingly, it may be reinforced that a morality of balance and proportionality is good, suggesting that the imposition of suffering for positive ends should always be in harmony with the proportional distribution and utility of suffering.

This relation between suffering and value shouldn't exemplify a negative attitude towards 'undesirables', as these are people with views and convictions as moral utilities all share in different degrees and respects. Rather, this view grants legitimacy and moral justification for the prioritisation of certain values, attitudes, utilities, and actors, whereby the flourishing of virtue and righteousness by a greater interest of the Highest Good may trump the suffering of malevolent utilities and elements. This relates to broader themes of moral value where the value of actions is beheld by their corresponding spirit – greater value comes not through perceptions and judgements of others, but through the quality of spirit and higher pleasure corresponding to a sense of self and sensation in awareness.

Egoism is not only in self-interest, but also in evaluation of sentiment and attitude abiding moral law. Virtues, even those corresponding to the judgements and perceptions of others, are valued in terms of the positive sensations, attitudes, sentiments, and pleasures they evoke, with the greatest of virtues arising from a proud and strong sense of self empowered by autonomy of goodwill. The only just and legitimate action perpetuating suffering is when its utility serves the end of producing greater flourishing such as in terms of the balance of justice. In relation to the morally weak and devious, it is better to amend character to inspire virtue and dignity, which is best done through liberty of goodwill for ambition of good living and good spirit. However, unfortunate immediate circumstances may suppose that people cannot be realistically helped through extensive reform in a brief moment, meaning other practices of morality become necessary.

To conclude, moral liberty in conjunction with suffering is paramount, the mediation and consideration of which may be subject to the determination of value in respective moral utilities. Some are strong in suffering and have the capacity to extract its greater potential, to feed off suffering to grow in virtue and relish in higher pleasures. Other characters may not be disposed to such attitudes and moralities, whereby discipline and good will are set in another direction that tolerate and use suffering differently. Even though such moralities may not produce a greater reward and greater fulfilment, in immediate circumstances and within relevant utility of individual character, such moral dispositions may serve a definitively good purpose and may be of greater moral quality and value than unnecessarily and unjustly pushing the growth of virtue that may provoke negative responses and greater suffering, undermining what prevalent virtues and positive qualities there are and condemning them to the expansion of vice.

People's responses and adaptations to suffering are different, and beyond the moral necessities of liberty one ought to also respect the relativity of degrees of suffering and fluctuating values in moral utilities and character. Certain things work differently for different people. So for people to flourish, relative pace and an individual's responsive and morally tolerable modes of coping with suffering ought to be respected within reasonable boundaries of justice. People's responses to suffering can be widely unpredictable, but moral law suggests that it is good to give people a realistic chance, where possible, to overcome suffering and to flourish in what degrees each person can, all up to the point of tolerance in terms of moral law and moral principles.

To accomplish this effectively, people must develop in accordance with their own goodwill and find what works for them. We are all different in our individual, subjective impressions and experiences of living, meaning adaptation to suffering will always be organic through individuality. What works for one person will not and does not necessarily work for others. Pleasure, discipline, motivation, strength, mindfulness, meditation, and good spirit are great virtues for dealing with suffering, yet degrees of these virtues and the capacity of character to utilise them may be more fluid than definitive moral law can accommodate.

On a personal note, it is wise not to, and one ought not to, condescendingly judge people or look down on those some may deem as morally weaker, lesser, or more vulnerable. Rather, one should aspire to understand why people act the way they do, understand them and what is going on with people pursing lesser modes of fulfilment. In all likelihood people act the way they do because they believe what they are doing is in their greater interest. To persuade them and show them a better path can only be realistically and effectively achieved through common goodwill and consent achieved through moral liberty. Common understanding and a degree of empathy are central for this. It is natural to make judgements about people's character, but one ought not to let judgemental thoughts instigate demeaning, debasing, and corruptive acts by failing to understand and establish a common understanding. However, judgement does retain significant moral quality through high-reason and objective considerations of value and moral qualities corresponding to various aspects of ethics such as utilities.

To formalise these discussions, I will outline the following Central Principles of suffering:

One ought not to impose or create needless and unjust suffering for others or oneself.

Suffering can produce good, but this requires discipline and mindfulness for balance in utilities.

Suffering is only good when it produces goodness, with necessary or needless suffering subject to the definition and consideration of the dynamics of benevolent, good utilities.

When embracing and confronting suffering, one ought to do so while mindful of value and quality of utility.

It is always moral to support people in suffering, but what constitutes support and how it ought to be applied is the point of greater moral and practical ambiguity, where restraint may be paramount in sustained, long-term solutions and approaches to suffering.

When appropriate, help others to relieve themselves from suffering, subject to moral liberty and the value and quality of ethical elements.

Forgiveness and acceptance provide the greatest relief for suffering, which require discipline, willpower, courage, mindfulness, and compassion.

When suffering ought to be necessarily imposed on people, it must be done so effectively and mindfully to minimise the negative effects of suffering and be focused on positive ends.

Ideally, the distribution of suffering ought to be done with the willing consent of people and based on mindful considerations of the dynamics of suffering.

One ought not to be presumptuous concerning the capacity of the character and the corresponding dynamics of suffering.

Chapter 20:

Judgement, Moral Practice, and Moral Brutalism

When a question arises in a given situation about whether to take a life or not, justice is the fulcrum of morality. Sometimes a certain moral principle takes priority over another, especially when there is a discrepancy in the value of moral principles. Accordingly, Central Principles are the primary values and the centrality of the principle-rule of liberty is mediated by and through other Central Principles. This brings me to evaluate key points of the practical morality of applied Central Principles. There are two major aspects that I need to discuss in this Chapter – the morality of killing and the framework of practical morality. Needless to say, the topics I shall discuss are closely related to the morality of suffering, so my thoughts will often cross between both moral subjects, as with all the Central Principles.

The main issues in the questions of practical morality are tied to the value of people and actions and how to apply considerations of justice to fulfil the purpose of practical morality. If a character has been driven to conflict that cannot be tolerated, then it becomes necessary by moral law to respond with actions that moderate ethical tangents and vectors. The Human Imperative suffers from the negative effects of vice, and so do people. Therefore, positive reinforcement of virtue and greater morality may be necessary and just. If an imbalance is created by the actions of vice's influence, then these forces might require appropriate moral responses to facilitate justice in dynamics of unbalanced well-being.

Practical morality necessitates objective and just perception in moral intuition and reasoning. Therefore, one ought to above all employ the utilities, reasoning, and intuitions concerning the moral value of people. The morality of lives and just moral practice accepts the foundation of life as an end in itself and a coherent universal basis for value. This basis consists of different aspects of reasoning and of different moral elements in their own right. In evaluations of practical morality, it is imperative to implement analysis of value and the dynamics of the structural causal cascades of ethics. Even the most insignificant actions will have an effect and ripple globally along tangents and through vectors.

The values in these dynamics and the many relevant forces evoking and enacting flourishing and justice are practically immeasurable, but their qualification and consideration is necessary, although difficult, for practical morality. Practical morality has flourished through some basic intuitions; however, superficial and subliminal reasoning has at times clouded better judgement. Intuition is amendable, but this requires mindfulness and clarity. Practical morality has often succumbed to sentiment and base morality that affects intuition, thereby distorting justice and considerations of value. Impressions and experiences have profoundly affected the foundations of moral intuition, although this is itself not a moral mechanism we have to settle for, because intuition is malleable through high-reason.

What must be considered in matters of intuition and outlook is that how one feels may not reflect reality, just as how one thinks may not correspond to reality and function synchronically with a sense of well-being. Practical morality is not bound to either intuition or reason alone and necessitates the two functioning in synchrony to find effective, righteous, and just practical morality.

Every life has meaning and intrinsic value, even that of the moral deviant invoking suffering, for the intrinsic potential to propagate goodwill, by virtue of the soul, means any person can theoretically be moved towards goodness and virtue. However, practice is not as ideal as theory. Sometimes virtue does not have the luxury of harnessing the potential of people's goodwill, thereby necessitating immediate responses and other moral utilities. The vices of people perpetuating and invoking suffering and lesser ethical interest can become unsustainable for effective normativity. Thus, the character of vice may lose value, which should be superceded by the value of virtue and justice.

Since all people have intrinsic value and can be a benevolent force on the Highest Good in line with the Human Imperative, it is clear that we ought to do all we can to preserve, sustain, and nourish life. Caring for life and protecting it is the surest mode of ethics through which effective living for the self and community can be achieved. A stronger moral force of virtue comes through righteous people, requiring the living presence of virtue and positive moral utility embodied in character. It is intuitive that for any virtue and community to thrive it must not engage in useless, inefficient, and demeaning loss of life. This foundation of moral practice has been paramount and clear for moral law throughout the ages. Pointless loss of value and utility will not bring greater flourishing. Thus, we should ask when we ought to kill, rather than when we shouldn't kill.

Intuition and reasoning about the morality of killing or imposing suffering can be very clear and convincing in common sense, yet it would nonetheless be helpful to outline why unjust, immoral killing and causing suffering are wrong. It is clear that an ethic that is willing to murder with ease is unsuitable for greater ambition, for indiscriminate killing is an unsustainable mode of conduct and will never achieve a more constructive and efficient effect in terms of the Human Imperative. Acts of murder and unjust, disproportionate, and the unnecessary application of suffering will give rise to conflict, thereby less efficient ways of flourishing. Yet the same moral utilities can be applied in other circumstances, such as with the protectionist morality of liberty, to counteract excess vice at liberty causing disruption on the scale of murder and the deficiency of unjust, unnecessary suffering. But this particular theme requires further discussion.

Acts of murder, while of lesser moral quality and worth, are not meaningless, and there is a reason why people inflict pain on others that leads to murder. Acts of killing are one dimension of practical morality that is often, but not always, bound to a common root – Fear's mode of craving control and power. Power as the capacity to control is, after all, a fundamental part of the human condition, from the toddler not yet nourished with virtue and wisdom, to the politician pursuing feckless ambition devoid of greater fulfilment beyond personalistic Fear.

Power does grant fulfilment, but only as a dimension of autonomy. The ambition of power is only truly fulfilled through the autonomy of an empowered will by the soul's command to flourish, the epitome of which is found through the Ploy of Consciousness. Violence and subjecting others to suffering are a perverse manifestation of the ambition of power, through which Fear never achieves profound resolution and fulfilment is meagre. Torture and related activity breed vice in self-subjugation to Fear. Subjecting oneself to Fear *in* liberty to fulfil greater virtue of autonomy has many merits, yet embodying an ethos appeasing Fear is very different to liberty *from* Fear. Desiring control, nourishing lust for power over others by subjecting the world to suffering reflected in one's own Fear, and abiding compulsions of Fear without the strength and mindfulness of an autonomous will and spirit, all lead to vice and the lesser well-being of oneself and community.

The power to mediate and control in lesser fulfilment of Fear are consistently reflected in structures of ethics. Utility and power are necessary to mediate and channel greater moral effects. But in the attachment to power in Fear, character corrupts Liberty by degrading its potential and virtue through the vice of Fear. Yet power is not inherently wrong or immoral, as it is a mere moral utility bound to the ambitions of the fundamental will. Power is only made virtuous in servitude to goodwill and the motives of virtue serving maxims of ethical interest. Power in practical morality, as with the mediation of liberty, can and likely always will share a sense of Fear, which is not wholly wrong. However, mindfulness in power becomes a necessity. The lust for control and related vices can evoke compulsive actions, for good and bad. The only sustainable and fundamental utility to fulfil justice in this practical morality is then mindfulness and intuition of goodwill.

Murder and the unnecessary, excessive imposition of suffering, as is often indicative of petty ambition of the mind and spirit striving for hand-outs of power from Fear, is furthermore morally inefficient in respect to liberty and value. The elimination of competition leads to stagnation, unless virtuous mindfulness achieves real self-sufficiency and the capacity for development (a distant reality). The lack of struggle without mindfulness and Harmony reduces spirit and produces idleness, boredom, and related suffering. Not only do excess and unjust dealings with moral opposition and competition through acts of murder or infliction of harm lead to conflict and deficient fulfilment of the Human Imperative, but it also produces vice in Fear and thoughtlessness, especially if committed in compulsion.

Liberty is necessary for development, regardless of whether it is self-sufficient or comes through competition in values and normativity, and therefore central to the Human Imperative. But elimination and excessive 'mediation' of opposing moral forces, especially through murder, comparatively lacks the fulfilment that could be achieved by strengthening what moral resources are present.

Instead of killing people it is better to set them on a path of virtue and morally correct conduct. An active resource of a virtuous moral agency is much better than the elimination of potential moral resources. Killing and the unjust, immoral subjugation of suffering are then equivalent to mismanagement of moral and human resources, for unless they are done in reparation or as just mediations of vice and suffering they will not fulfil greater ambition and potential. Murder, torture, or vice in the pursuit of control in Fear are seldom ever the answer to greater fulfilment or greater ambition of the Imperative.

Finally, and perhaps most importantly, the lack of compassion that relates to the production and appeal of violence and the practice of imposing suffering as degrees of torture are a sign of diminishing empathy. Without empathy and mindfulness, without treating people, including oneself, as an end in itself in terms of the universalisable soul, the spirit withdraws from eudaimonia and higher fulfilment. In a lack of mindful empathy, which often beckons pain and anger in its place opposing profound emptiness, one fails to achieve the virtues of Harmony and will neglect healthy and virtuous mindfulness. By denying the warmth of compassion, pain will not be let go of, which can conditionally be a good thing. The spirit comes to suffer, and practical morality neglecting empathy loses out on eudaimonia and greater fulfilment in spirit.

The other foundation of the concerns of practical morality is liberty. Immoral actions borne of vice are contingent on people's dispositions. People succumb to weakness and the influence of pain, degrading the character and leading to suffering. Certain people just don't know any better and need help to be set on the path towards virtue and dignified, better living. Sometimes people may have had a bad day or have been enslaved by a life of suffering over which they had little power. These ill-fortunes alone are insufficient reasons for taking or sacrificing a life that could otherwise be amended and employed in constructive purpose for the Imperative and for that person to achieve dignified living.

The heritin ethic emphasises and concentrates on positive ethical dynamics while improving on negative elements. The ethical negativity of people who succumb to vice can never be sustainably and effectively addressed through disproportionate killing. Killing all bad people isn't ever a viable morality. Furthermore, the long-term solution will only ever be achieved through the efficiency of persons at liberty to act according in goodwill. Any impulsive and heavy-handed moral attitude disposed to quick fixes of vice – by purging or purifying vice – not only jeopardises the liberty and moral development necessary for the Human Imperative, but also feeds vice and the corruptive, warped mentality causing suffering. Cultivating vice through such attitudes will inevitably reflect in other spheres unless repealed in mindful goodwill. The eager mentality of forceful, coercive, and eliminative moral practice will spread into other spheres of character and environment.

An eagerness to kill one person or any compulsion of vice in Fear, such as an emotive response to punish and avenge someone to satisfy the craving for control in Fear and loss, will provoke further effects through other actions in other spheres of life. If you are at ease with killing or inflicting harm on people, then how can there be certainty that this or similar behaviour will not affect other areas of life? Who is to say that ease in inflicting harm on others will not transform into ease in causing harm to loved ones when frustration and anger blind judgement?

Acting according to harsh morality, in just or unjust frameworks, will not necessarily or unconditionally turn into ruthlessness and unmindful moral intuitions or attitudes. There are other relevant contributing factors to consider. However, uncertainty will nevertheless be valid. If intuition and sentiment at ease with inflicting suffering on others, righteous or not, it will shape moral intuitions and attitudes threatened with moral corruption if performed without mindfulness of goodwill and good intentions. If ease conforms with sentiment and intuition in the absence of any response to acts of killing and inflicting pain, such as with apathy and detachment, this is even worse for intuition, as it is unlikely that such a mentality would be effective and capable of discerning a constructive moral utility and would require greater focus and work than pre-affirmed empathetic and compassionate intuitions.

Any act of killing will have an effect on a person; even if this effect numbs compassion, suffering will be deeper and harder to reform, and will inevitably provoke immoral deeds if intuition is warped by Fear. In a world where wrong-doing and bad people were punished severely and quickly, where only bad people got killed and good people didn't, goodness wouldn't be sincere. A world of goodness based on the conditions of fear and reprisal is not sincerely good at all.

However, imperfect circumstances prevail and morality is forced to adapt to circumstances and the ethical environment. Sustaining life and the absolute morality of non-killing is not practical. People do succumb to vice and suffering, consequently moving their character to immoral conduct and action. Sometimes people can be helped through repair and nourishment of virtue through the suspension of their liberty justified with reference to the value of their utility.

Other times, circumstances and fortune are not favourable, necessitating other practices of morality to counteract the degrading ethical dynamics of suffering and vice. A positive moral effect counteracting negativity can be achieved in moral practice by proportionally responding to instances of engaged and active vice. An illustrative case of this is a police officer restraining a criminal, without killing him or her, to imprison the criminal to change his or her character towards virtue and greater moral effect. In predictable immediate circumstances, not-withstanding the ambiguity of unknown consequences, this course of action can reduce or minimise the dynamics of suffering while retaining greater reward. As this facilitates greater flourishing, it is therefore the morally better course of action.

However, when immediate circumstance does not enable long-term, sustainable moral effect through the amendment and repair of vice, a more immediate solution may be necessary. This moral practice can come in the form of permanent immediate solutions to an immoral force and character, therefore justifying the killing of a morally depraved person committing intolerable acts such as unjust and unnecessary murder. This does come with a moral risk in terms of corresponding effects on the psyche.

However, killing to prevent another killing by those compelled by vice to murder, for example, is morally permissible and just. The suffering of a person subject to vice at liberty causing greater suffering, in contrast to the person of virtue generating positivity and/or less suffering, means that the deviant or morally compromised individual are of lesser interest and value to the Highest Good of the Human Imperative than the virtuous and righteous individual. Lack of value in itself does not justify killing or moral brutality, yet it does serve in considerations of moral extremes.

Killing is justifiable when it facilitates justice and is complicit with morality, i.e. when such an act sustains and/or produces greater flourishing in particular circumstances. Unjust killing may eliminate, undermine, and contradict virtue in oneself and in the community. Counter-acting this negative effect of unjust moral practice is more sustainable in the long-term. Combining the elements of intrinsic value, liberty, and the considerations of justice leads to the conclusion that a morality permitting and enabling killing is only just in circumstances necessitating hard moral actions, whereby the immediacy of action is qualified in terms of considerations of immediate effects and value with respect to relevant moral utilities.

From a basic view, killing to protect others in the immediate circumstances or in self-defence is just. This is only a one-dimensional fundamental for practical morality, and many more elements and aspects need to be examined. A normativity that is not capable or willing to defend itself in some measure will not last. However, a defensive and responsive moral practice does not necessarily have to involve killing.

In consideration of value, central to any question of practical morality, it is a default rule in moral decision-making that people's value is intrinsically positive; value can only be withheld, exchanged, and subtracted, but never lost, as duties and functions are never fully absolved until functional life ceases entirely. Even by condemning an individual to death this ought to be done in consideration of value where the maxim of others in terms of the Human Imperative and the Highest Good outweighs the value of vice at liberty.

In doing so, this evaluation is itself complicit with considerations of the value of the devoid individual in retrospect of global dynamics of values, or can be so if not neglected and mismanaged. From this can be drawn the principle-rule that any individual starts with an intrinsic value that bestows on them certain rights such as not to be killed or subjected to suffering. Practical morality always starts with a positive value in people with reference to default considerations of the intrinsic value of people as ends in themselves and of themselves. Value can then only be negated and subtracted.

The general principle-rule is, accordingly, that people should not be killed, which is then subject to deliberation and evaluation challenging or adapting this rule in certain circumstances. An evaluation that crosses a certain threshold then warrants the appropriate means to balance values and moral effect, which may initiate means of justice necessitating acts of killing or imposing suffering. However, even though a person may not have immediate value or utility in a certain sphere, it does not mean they have no value in other respects, especially globally or in mindful virtue.

The devaluation of people is an intrinsically delicate and complicated practice of morality, requiring great discipline, virtue in intuition and reasoning, and mindful empathy. Devaluation can lead to acts of discouraging people or causing pain through rejection and sense of abandonment; this can be just and necessary. On the one hand, it is necessary to prioritise and qualify; after all, this is what any company employing a work-force must do based on skill, utility, and adequacy.

However, excess brutality in making an assessment without empathy and compassion will lead to misevaluations. Any relational morality of engaged value-assessment is better off with mindfulness on both sides. One ought to be mindful of their utility in relation to the self, others, and the common Human Imperative. Rejection of one's utility in a certain place or respect does not imply worthlessness or incapability, as value could be maximised in other spheres for the sake of others and fulfilling of the person's true potential. Even though the pain of rejection and poor self-evaluation can lead to suffering, this suffering, as with any defeat, is best used to fuel ambition, self-improvement, and growth in virtue.

The pain of rejection and abandonment can be used for positive ends in certain cases. Alienation, loneliness, rejection, and abandonment seem to be very powerful forces on the psyche and spirit. This can be used as a means to an end where the tolerance of vice becomes unsustainable. Empathetic and compassionate approaches are far more preferable, especially in nourishing virtue and subverting acts of vice causing suffering. Yet when a moral violation or crime have been committed, rejection that manifests itself through isolation in retributive and reparative utilities can be employed as an example of using Fear in others to improve their condition and make community better off. As always, pain can be used for constructive ends, but this requires guidance and moderation.

Similarly, rejecting a person from a certain role, when done appropriately and with righteous intent and demeanour, as a form of devaluation, can inspire people to improve their utility and character. It is important for morality not to become reducible to a maxim or rule enabling unjust exploitation of the morally weak, for the strong are only as virtuous as their strength is used for the Highest Good and in relation to the weak. Exploitation of the weak for meagre, selfish, and unjust ends without greater ambition, especially in terms of greater considerations of the Human Imperative, does not lead to higher virtue, strength, or goodness. But exploiting vulnerabilities and deficiencies to improve on them can be morally permissible and just. The strong ought to protect the vulnerable and cow the weak; the righteous ought to be sovereign only in so much as Natural Law and the Highest Good make this possible in goodwill.

This principle-rule can then in practice manifest itself through virtue-rules. Consider a case where a troubled individual of grave vice murders a decent person for material gains such as in the case of a burglary turned murder. The murderer ought to be brought to justice so as to restore and repair the balance of the negative effects of the depraved and unjust act. There are many forms this justice could potentially take. It could be suggested that the murderer ought to be killed, even if there is no immediate necessity.

In doing so, however, while it might not create two murderers, it does manifest itself as two killings. Disavowing or nullifying the values of others to the point of permitting acts of killing beyond proportional justice would violate the principle-rule of the intrinsic value of people. Neglect of this rule would breed corresponding characteristics and modes of moral utilities embodied in character. The act of one killer that instigates another killing by another person only fosters the characteristics of a killer, not necessarily anything more than that. Of course, some modes of killing are required for justice, virtue, and duty, but these are, and ought to be, restricted practices of morality for greater justice contingent on the ethical environment.

In analysing the practical morality of inflicting suffering or killing for a greater positive effect, it is necessary to consider the matter of consequences and risks. Most questions of practical morality will be subject to ambiguities of unforeseen consequences. Therefore, any moral decision and its consequence, which will have an external and internal effect, are bound to degrees of risk. It is a virtue to have good and proper judgement, such as through intelligence and wisdom, yet this is often a moral luxury and requires a lot of discipline and work.

One of the main manifestations of risk-analysis in ethical decision-making concerning killing – intrinsically a study focused on qualification rather than quantification – is whether a character of vice ought to be spared if there is a risk that the person will continue an existence of vice and commit murder. Should one save a person's life if that person lives to kill another? Should the medical practitioner save a killer's life despite the risk that the moral deviant will kill again?

A moral extreme would be not taking any risks, as a super-protective morality of killing for preservation and security. A foundation in such questions was outlined above: the maximum positive effect is achieved by facilitating the succession of virtue from vice; sometimes the chances of this success are slim and elusive, necessitating less ideal practices of morality. This framework is devised in terms of the necessity and immediacy of moral considerations and actions, something that deserves its own analysis. However, any risk-analysis of morality cannot be separated from moral intuition and spirit. Moral intuitions and spirit of actions must be *in line with* qualified risk-based decision-making. Furthermore, even though morality has an empirical and scientific element, its function is not fulfilled through these terms alone, and practical morality cannot be effectively implemented in the immediate moment through extensive analysis such as with risk assessment.

When intuition and spirit are applied in risk assessment and practical morality, such as with matters of killing, greater positive effect will only come through virtue. In terms of the heritin ethic, it goes that risk should not be corrupted by intuitions and sentiments of Fear clouding judgement and depriving the opportunity to achieve greater results. A second chance and faith in people is necessary for greater moral effect and the resurgence of virtue. It is thus only intuitive that one ought not to be afraid of taking risks with people and vice.

A hardline morality eager to kill will be susceptible to Fear, translating into other spheres of life. A morality of accepting and embracing risk itself inspires virtue supercedeing Fear, the moral utility of which may serve to inspire strength in others. This morality will not always immediately succeed, yet the willingness to take risks and embrace the subsequent suffering of these risks will nourish the corresponding virtue and strength. It may be that the power and strength expressed in virtue, accepting risk and not submitting to Fear, compels others to virtue. An act of good faith, especially when imbued with the suffering of sacrifice, can inspire goodness and virtue in the least expected places and people. Sometimes a single, minor act of genuine kindness and good faith can do more to inspire hope and goodwill in a person to change than any punishment. In an environment of brutality and Fear, a single act of defiance and goodwill can inspire a cause imbued with virtue.

However, sometimes embracing risk can border on recklessness, naivety, and foolishness by neglecting and misappropriating moral utility, thereby facilitating a lesser, negative moral effect. This manifests itself as misqualification of value in actions and utilities, whereby the global effect may lose a greater sum value of goodness through actions of lesser virtue and judgement, even though the potential for the opposite may be just as real. There are many reasons justifying killing and causing people harm, justly and unjustly, rightfully and wrongly. The practice of morality that beckons greater sum suffering is deemed wrong because of the qualifications of greater well-being.

It is often the case that murder and violence are rooted in Fear, in desperation for a sense of control, yet surrendering oneself to Fear in such a manner will nevertheless always beckon suffering. Reacting to the presence of vice, such as in response to an act of killing, by killing or causing suffering to minimise the damage of immorality at liberty can itself become susceptible to the corruption of Fear. Practical morality thus requires mindfulness, as with most things. In all instances of mediating the force of suffering and vice, any response ought to be proportional. There is no definitive measure for such a thing, and much of practical morality will ultimately have to rely on intuition in the moment.

However, these intuitions also make it clear rationally that a violent response of excessive force may be tempting in terms of the related pleasure of control. Yet any such sense of control is less than the satisfaction of being in control of oneself beyond Fear. Conflict will arise among conflicting desires and ambitions, but through mindfulness, meditation, and reflection in Liberty, intuition can realign desires, values, and ambitions.

With respect to assessing the consequences of actions, any decision will ultimately have to rely on intuitive reasoning. The causal cascades of tangents are vast; predictions and assessments can only provide so much insight. The cognitive capacities and abilities of people are limited. While at times we can have the luxury of premeditated decisions with an opportunity for evaluation, often this is a privilege. Any comprehensive and sensible morality will have to deal with on-the-spot decisions as well as premeditated ones.

When consequences are more or less clear in terms of which course of action will produce more ethical interest, qualified in terms of both the individual and community, then a judgement and corresponding action should be straightforward. If one pulls the trigger of a loaded gun pointed at a person, intuitive reason would validly formulate the thought that this action would likely lead to death. A judgement that one should not pull the trigger to avoid killing somebody is thus sensible in terms of consequences. However, this simple model is very limited.

In the global causal cascade of structural ethics where we can never foresee the full extent of consequences and effects, ethical maxims of consequences are practically impossible to assess. Thus, it is only plausible to make judgements based on intuitive reason, mindful of intentions and virtue, in consideration of immediate circumstances, and in accordance with morality and relevant knowledge.

We might not know how all ethical variables will interact in a causal cascade, yet we can realistically act on the knowledge of certain fundamental rules of actions and consequences in a normative framework, complimented by practical ethical wisdom. For example, a principle-rule that the unnecessary subjugation of others to suffering will feed suffering can act as a fundamental formula in assessing the consequences of actions. We might not know the exact ramifications, dynamics, and circumstances of a certain causal dimension, yet we can act with the knowledge of certain moral rules, such as that causing suffering will produce more suffering, or that all actions affect the character and psyche.

The general rule with respect to acting on judgements of consequences is that a person should act in their best judgement and be mindful of consequences. We are not perfect and we cannot realistically be expected to be perfect decision-makers, because consequences are elusive and, in the global scope, beyond the actions and cognitive capacities of any one individual. We must learn from our mistakes and follow intuition and reason nourished and guided by virtue and goodwill. So long as the judgement of actions' consequences are sensible and guided by genuine goodwill, then a mistake can be considered morally permissible or even right. Unforeseen consequences will always occur, but so long as they were made in goodwill and in accordance with virtue, so that the intention was right in terms of immediate circumstances and available information, then an action can be considered right.

However, where inherent uncertainty and ambiguity in the consequences of actions can be problematic, they are also very useful and can lead to further opportunities. We can never be completely certain of the consequences of an action, but in doing so we can avoid committing the wrong action under the wrong pretences. One may claim that an act of a moral extreme is the only way that makes sense, that it is a necessity. However, the most sensible conclusion, if anything, is that certainty in consequences, especially in terms of extensive structural effect, is unpredictable and elusive.

In matters of Secondary Principles, it is particularly relevant that there is always another way, an alternative to any action – it just takes ingenuity and ethical philanthropy to allow intuition to be enriched with solutions. For example, one may think the only solutions to the many global structural problems of human civilisation are extremes such as cutting down the human population prone to compulsive and short-sighted consumption to prevent global climate change. However, there is always an alternative to such drastic actions, in this case education, incentivised self-discipline, and the ingenuity of people, producers, and consumers to find alternatives.

Then, if one is to look beyond the veil of Fear, which can grant insight into a greater range of ethical alternative intuitions, an alternative extreme to mass extermination can be revealed where one does not need to bloody one's hands and do something immoral to try prevent something that will inevitably happen. If someone doesn't reduce the human population deliberately, Nature will be able to do so aptly through its causal mechanisms. This bleak vision of 'thinning the herd' can include: using people as vectors of conflicts over scarce resources, pandemics of antibiotic resistant diseases, insufficient food production to sustain the population, or even nuclear war; in short, mankind is more than capable of destroying itself without any deliberate intent to do so. The consequences of actions cannot be fully predicted, and no individual can foresee with absolute certainty the extensive structural tangents caused by a single vector. Ultimately, however, uncertainty can be a good thing, and we are capable of foreseeing the consequences we can be certain of, even though people lack the discipline and mindfulness to act wisely.

Killing or sparing a morally devious individual can have unforeseeable consequences. Killing him or her might spare other lives by severing the causal vector that would otherwise have led to murder. Then, doing so could evoke vice in oneself, potentially leading to murder perpetuated in vice, or if disciplined properly, could nourish virtue and goodwill in daring circumstances. However, sparing the moral deviant's life could inspire virtue and set him or her towards goodwill by encouraging the dedicated path of virtue to redeem vice. Ultimately, any assessment of consequences will have to rely on intuition and intuitive reasoning in congruence with moral rules built on a foundation of, as well as facilitating, the goodwill of virtue.

Intuitive reasoning is most often at the mercy of personality and trends in the ethical dynamics of moral deliberation. For positive consequences, qualified in terms of good outcomes and good effects on oneself, goodwill and good intuitive reasoning are key. No science or academic discipline, although very relevant in the grand scope, can alone provide immediate guidance in many practical and real cases of decision-making. We can formulate certain principle-rules to guide deliberation. However, we will have to rely on ourselves and our immediate capacities to make good judgements guided by intuition and intuitive reasoning.

To facilitate this intuition requires goodwill above all and virtuous character in making judgements and executing actions, complimented by trained intuition and ethical wisdom. It could be that good character is key to exercising good judgement and initiating positive outcomes in all causal dimensions. Taking risks and giving people a chance can, and will, involve sacrifice, producing undesirable outcomes and suffering. But if faith in people is surrendered and virtue is easily swayed by an intolerance of risk, then we might as well condemn all our virtue. Risk-taking will involve suffering, but such is the path of virtue and strength in enduring.

However, risk is supposed to be tempered with sensibility. Sometimes consequences are apparent and taking a risk can be negligent, senseless, and foolish. One may be eager to self-sacrifice and be excited to save others from vice, but negligence in such intuitions can lead to compulsions that fail to bring about the better outcome. By trying to save another, a person might end up getting themselves killed and betraying duty and greater interests through reckless behaviour. Sensibility is paramount in intuition and deliberation on consequences.

There is no concise and comprehensive formulation for moral rules with respect to consequences but that of a foundational goodwill and sensibility in intuitive reasoning. Consequences will always be overshadowed by ambiguities. In terms of moral extremes, such as killing, a principle-rule can be implemented where uncertainty is a sufficient ground for non-action in response to an extreme when there is no necessity for action. If you don't know what consequences an action will have, especially in terms of moral extremes, and such an action may induce considerable suffering, then one shouldn't act unless there is a necessity to act. If you don't know with certainty whether an action will cause suffering for another, and there is no necessity to act or choose to act, then one shouldn't commit that action.

For example, feeding a pet a type of food without the knowledge and certainty of the corresponding consequences to their health, and provided there is no immediate necessity to feed them this type of food, are sufficient grounds for not feeding the pet questionable and unfamiliar food without the awareness of consequences that may or may not lead to suffering.

Those who fall prey to vice and Fear, in that they unjustly spread suffering and act on vice, thereby having lesser moral effect on the Imperative and the Highest Good, become of lesser character. This justifies and gives cause for reaction from others when tolerance exhausts its goodness. It is easy for intuition to become susceptible to obscurity in the tough circumstance of moral extremes. Yet it is important to not reduce people to mere mechanisms and elements for moral consideration of maxim effects, to act on intuition stripped of spirit and sentiment, as it is important to not be swayed into judgement corrupted by heedless emotions that lack a definitive foundation or greater foresight.

Those who murder and immorally cause others suffering are of lesser character and value. Yet it must be remembered that in immorality people are weak and themselves in states of suffering. The immoral are people like everyone else, a virtue-rule to remind others of what vice can do to people. Empathy can be used here for positive ends, to relate to and build a connection with characters of vice to redeem and empower them with virtue.

However, this can lead to mistakes of compassion and ill-judgement of nihilistic moral liberty, enabling the liberty of vice when it is otherwise in one's moral capacity to make a difference. Greater moral satisfaction, good consequences, and justice come through the reconditioning and absolution of vice. But to distinguish ethical value in the moment of every individual case requires mindful intuition that appeals to both empathy and the necessity for just action. There is no absolute moral principle that can guide practical morality towards a definitive end, and ultimately any such moral cases will have to rely on the intuition of a person's immediate judgement, as extensive reasoning in immediate extremes is not usually a viable option. The surest way to mediate judgement and intuition, and counteract corruptive, impulsive actions of a subconscious origin, is to cultivate and discipline goodwill through antecedent conditioning.

This growth and individual ethical development is unlikely to be perfect or always successful, but practice can teach better moral judgement. We don't live in a perfect world and we are not perfect, but we can nonetheless do the best we can with what is given to us. Even though the vice of deep-rooted negative characteristics may exceed an immediate possibility for intervention towards reconditioning, this does not justify the intuition and rule of indiscriminate, misapplied callousness that encourages us to eliminate vectors – people – of vice, of vulnerability and weakness. But when assessment and intuition form a sensible judgement out of goodwill and because of a just reason, mandating hardline moral practice, such as killing and applying suffering, then another dimension of virtue must be considered and bound to moral law, rule of reason, and mindful intuition.

Intuition, reason, and intuitive reason are central to practical morality and the capacity for good judgement. To pursue ethical maxims of interest and value, one must not only be able to recognise these maxims, but also have the required character to perform the right action. Practical morality often faces the problem of friction between base and high faculties, a conflict between sentiment and rationale. The two must work in synchrony to achieve greater moral effect and for higher fulfilment. Yet sometimes compulsions and inclinations of baser faculties can hold corruptive sway over good judgement, just as rationale can deceive and not satisfy.

First of all, it is imperative to mention that base-reason has a crucial role in good judgement and intuitive reason, as with compassion. However, base-reason is not the best or single dimension of good judgement and intuition. Heedless base influences can corrupt, emotionally compromise a person, and lead one astray. Thoughtlessness in sentiment is bad, just as is ruthless calculation absent emotion. But while there is a general virtue-rule of preserving and nourishing balance in mindfulness honed by intuitive reason and intuition of virtue, there are instances when balance must be employed towards ambitions that are made more efficient and effective by utilities corresponding to certain faculties.

For instance, caring for a child is made more effective by genuine love that is supported by reason mediating the application of care and affection. However, sometimes mistakes of base-reason must be averted through the disciplined application of high-reason. Sometimes a capacity for cold and callous calculation is necessary; sometimes ruthlessness is a virtue; sometimes *moral brutalism* is necessary.

This controversial statement can come across as abhorrent. What is intended by this rule is the obvious necessity for rationale to sometimes override the influences of base-reason. Mistakes of compassion are common and yield terrible consequences. Heedless base morality can be an affliction of morality and spirit, as seen in the horrors people commit with the justification of protecting ones they love, those whom they care for. Compassion is a contextual virtue and is an extremely useful element for eudaimonia. However, it can cause much grief rather than fulfil its effective purpose.

Compassion, as any function of the psyche, can lead to thoughtless and negligent actions when unbound by mindfulness and moderation. Sometimes, the sum maxim of compassion is found through empathy disengaging or ignoring compassion. Remember, my conception of empathy is that of a function of high-reason, while compassion is conceived as the emotion bound to functions of base-reason. Empathy is universal, yet it can significantly lag and suffer deficiency without compassion. Yet to establish an assessment of greater compassion, sometimes it is necessary to focus on isolated empathy detaching from compassion, thereby enabling empathy to guide intuitive reason to achieve the best effect.

In extremes of moral practice, sometimes compassion is an unbearable element and effective judgement can only be sustained through empathy. If one must make a choice based on numerical knowledge alone, notwithstanding any other variables, whether 100 people must die here for 200 to live elsewhere or else all 300 perish, a judgement executed by a push of a button, then the best choice is surely to save the 200 at the cost of the other 100. Any of those people may have loved ones, or the considered units may consist of entire families. Compassion can be unbearable in such circumstances. Imagining the suffering caused by an act of terror or terrible incident that killed dozens can be overwhelming. But clearly the maxim of compassion is to ensure that the best outcome is achieved in the most extreme cases, in this instance by saving the 200 at a cost of 100, rather than losing all 300. This is, in principle, the most empathetic choice. Therefore, cold and brutal calculation, and qualification, denoted as *moral brutalism*, familiar to consequentialist normative ethics, can be a necessary morality and virtue. However, any such virtue is only warranted and sustained by the guidance of goodwill bound to the intuition of virtue. Ruthlessness, in this context, is a utility and virtue stripped of compassion but not devoid of empathy.

These extremes of practical morality, illustrated by the case for moral brutalism, of course are going to be demanding. I don't imagine that the surgeon performing life-saving surgery on a child does so easily. Neither do I expect a decent human being fulfilling their role as a police officer to kill a thug to protect another life. Neither can any soldier of virtuous character kill people during his first combat experience with unfettered moral comfort, without a personal and spiritual cost. There exist individuals who are stripped of compassion and feeling, whether in terms of pathology or coping mechanisms numbing the mind. But it has become clear to me that these states deprive the mind of vital intuitions for having a greater effect through engagement with people, understanding people, and harmonious, informed, and synchronised moral judgement. But the brutality of emotional numbness and impetuous rationale can be a necessity of certain circumstances.

Furthermore, while eudaimonia is theoretically achievable without suffering and is the end of the Human Imperative, in this day and age eudaimonia cannot be achieved without profound pain – one of empathy and compassion for others and the self. As with the case of pathological states, there are other ways to achieve eudaimonia without compassion or empathy, as exemplified with spiritual and moral liberty enabled by the virtue of a powerful will succeeding Fear and overcoming the consumption of the Void. It is a deceptively basic principle-rule that emotional intuition is useful, if not key, to one's own capacity in virtue and for ends employing oneself and others in the duty of the Human Imperative. How a person can cope with specific cases, as illustrated above, is not something I am at liberty to say or recommend. The only thing I am at liberty to say with respect to moral extremes, or am comfortable with saying in retrospect of my own limited experience, is that the virtue-rule valuing mindfulness and goodwill as resources of good judgement is absolutely crucial.

Spiritual and moral liberty are a profound element of any ethos in their own right from which all other moral utilities stem and compound. In exercising extreme moral utilities, whether it is killing another or sacrificing oneself, discipline of moral utility in mindfulness of one's state of mind and actions is crucial. There isn't always a precise way of preparing oneself for the future or for certain moments in life. After all, the parent cannot completely prepare their child for autonomy and the personal responsibility of adult life and citizenship in the global community. However, one can always nourish general virtues and condition the character to sustain effective liberty and morality through which goodwill and mindful intuition stem.

In this way, the great advantage of wide-ranging causal effects and disparities of actions benefit the malleability of character by nourishing fundamental virtues which are prepared for other inevitable consequences, as well as facilitate adaptive normativity. Discipline as a universal virtue, enabled through intuitive liberties of morality, along with expansive mindfulness, are perhaps the only virtue-rules and associate principle-rules that can be formulated concerning the extremes of practical morality.

Moral brutalism has an extended application beyond its application in the assessment of consequence and is a generally valuable utility in extremes of practical morality. Ruthlessness as a discipline of mindful valuation serves its purpose in following through with duty and rejecting immoral inclinations such as malicious people's attempts to compromise morality. People may deceive and manipulate in and through Fear. These dynamics can undermine duty. In such instances which heavily influence base morality, where undisciplined intuition becomes conflicted, the capacities of high-reason are instrumental.

In full Liberty, all inclinations are at ease and in synchronised accord of goodwill. However, virtuous character is developed and made, it is innate. So degrees of friction and conflict in the psyche are to be expected during ethical development and personal growth. The maxims of virtue-duty and virtue-rules are meant to be clear in their nourished state; this requires discipline and growth. Nevertheless, contention and discomfort in the dynamics of reason pressured by moral extremes are expectable and are good in terms of challenging moral liberty, encouraging adaptiveness.

Ruthlessness in duty, in tandem with disciplined and unyielding goodwill to do what is right, can be a contextual virtue in moral extremes. To be impetuous in hostile circumstances, brutal times, and when others panic is necessary virtue, which requires particularly demanding conditioning and harsh morality. The virtue of ruthlessness and being impetuous is associated with the virtue of cold fury.

However, it is important to stress that moral brutalism does not suffice as a moral absolute or default. The utility of moral brutalism employed by an ethos of Fear is most commonly corruptive and destructive. Moral brutalism in the duty of cold spirit drawing on the Void is at times necessary to counter-act profoundly emotive elements of abhorrent moral corruption and depravity borne of viciousness in Fear. Any person with a healthy mind and good spirit will know the atrocity of acts of abuse and torture for self-gratification in Fear, especially of the vulnerable and innocent. Fear affecting people through horrendous dynamics of ethics can mould other people's character towards similar species of vice in Fear, breeding compulsive acts pertaining to suffering in oneself and in others. The utility of moral brutalism entails an inherent risk of the corruption of vice, Fear, and consumption by the Void. It is a risky endeavour, yet clearly a necessary one in dealing with extremes of moral practice and one that may counter-act the alternative dimension of risk of an ethos of Fear and base morality.

Extremes can hinder goodwill and positive spirit, with the attachment to goodness and joy easily corruptible, especially in the vulnerability of base morality. The Void and its function of clarity in Liberty can serve as a crucial utility in dealing with the challenges of moral extremes. However, this coldness and lack of spirit, although pertaining to greater positivity in a global effect when executed properly, is not a good way to live and can only be fulfilling as duty of virtue in eudaimonia when spirit is nourished by goodness. Thus, moral brutalism cannot be without self-reflection and mindfulness.

Furthermore, in these extremes it is clear that one ought to have something that provides a grounding and uplifting effect, some sort of attachment. It does not matter if this attachment is a hypothetical and imagined hope; so long as it is not superficial and is genuinely profoundly emotive, then it will serve its purpose. Nevertheless, for virtue-duty to be complete one must learn and be mindful of the liberty to let go of that fundamental attachment if such is a necessity of moral duty. Again, one has to consider causal cascades in such decisions, and there is no absolute principle-rule or virtue-rule. Yet one ought to nonetheless act in one's best judgement and not be easily swayed by Fear undermining any greater positive effect. But from given experience and mindful of humanity, love is the best attachment, focusing and employing emotions and reason towards a good end where mindful of Fear's corruptive effects.

The piety of moral brutalism and its virtue of ruthlessness is only qualified as such in Liberty of righteous principle-rules of goodwill. This ability and character opposing moral extremes meets the demands marking eudaimonia, only as sustainable as the mind and spirit can maintain these demanding duties which cripple positive spirit yet provide nourishment with eudaimonia stripped of happiness and joy. But any goodwill enabling eudaimonia in moral extremes and respective hard moral duties (those that are the most demanding) is only found and sustained through goodwill.

The intended form of moral brutalism employing ruthlessness, in terms of the ethos of Liberty, is fundamentally different as a moral utility than ruthlessness in an ethos of Fear. Ruthlessness in Fear is commonly a source of significant vice, suffering, and pain, but moral brutalism's intended utility according to the heritin ethos is that of disciplined goodwill and hard duty under the strain of moral extremes. This is equivalent to the demeanour of the just arbiters of law. While law of society and state is said to be blind, moral law and justice must be clairvoyant and only as impartial as the Categorical Directive compounded by moral rules. Justice of moral law ought to be mindful and at profound spiritual liberty. These are the demands of higher virtues, those of genuine humanity.

As such, this form of moral brutalism that supercedes its common use in an ethos of Fear is not the commonly conceived form of ruthlessness – it is not of Fear, it is not vindictive, not vengeful, not punishing, not excessive, not murderous, not vicious, and not inherently violent or compulsive. This ruthlessness is of goodwill only in moral accord of virtue and disciplined goodwill. Above all, moral brutalism is bound to the Human Imperative and duty by the Highest Good. In sum, ruthlessness is unwavering discipline of empathy and duty in goodwill, even though bereft of compassion and joyous spirit.

Considering that moral brutalism is meant to be ruthlessly morally efficient and effective in accordance with goodwill in harsh circumstances, not heeding distraction and self-gratification as seen with vice borne of the torture of others, it is not a utility dedicated to punishment, but rather absolution from the need to punish. Moral brutalism is characterised by duty that does not strive for self-righteous gratification of deceived virtue to punish others, for this leads to vice when deprived of justice. So one ought not punish and torment the self.

As liberty moves duty to confront extremes, so too must it sustain the psyche and spirit not through punishment, but through positive nourishment. One should not punish oneself for vice and pain, but rather absolve negativity and exchange it for positive spirit through ambition of virtue. However, discipline requires moderation. Thus, to sustain positivity and virtue, one can employ measures of discipline and composure by withholding some sources of positive or negative spirit, resembling reparative and disciplinary punishments in justice.

To the sceptics I will leave this note: it is better to be cold in moral extremes than to be at ease, for the latter is intuitively far more dangerous than the discipline of the former. Furthermore, any comprehensive morality must address extreme scenarios and how to deal with them; I have only offered one narrative and mode of ethics, and with humility, I willingly concede that I do not have a definitive answer. Nonetheless, these issues must be addressed, and to speak on such issues requires familiarity with the moral extremes, although obviously in a morally acceptable form. This includes understanding the psyche and character that is moved by extreme vice.

These hard matters of morality and their accord of hard duties is not something that can ever be accounted for in simple terms of overwhelmingly joyous and happy spirit and the corresponding psyche, as this form of psyche would be vulnerable in moral extremes that would twist goodwill. Now, this is a risky, dangerous, and extremely demanding, as well as an incredibly delicate and complex matter of morality, but it cannot be overlooked, ignored, or neglected. Due to this nature of moral extremes, it is apparent that not all, perhaps not even most, should engage in this moral practice and ought to be extremely cautious in the relevant discussions and deliberations. Furthermore, preparation for informed discourse and evaluation through relevant emotive material should be done very carefully and with extreme degrees of mindfulness. But even theoretical, discursive moral brutalism requires extensive discipline and virtue, yet we simply can never afford to ignore it.

Not being prepared theoretically and practically for moral extremes leads to impulsiveness rather than rationality, whereby compromised sense and intuition will rule judgement when confronted with moral abhorrence and abomination, making a character of virtue fall prey to Fear. It is too common that witnessing gross depravity evokes vengeful and misguided fury which feeds on virtue through Fear rather than employing rage and dissatisfaction for greater ambition. The surest mean to compose oneself in moral extremes is being equipped to handle such cases, theoretically and practically.

Much discussion has been dedicated to the theoretical level, yet the virtue-rules guiding the practice of morality in extremes is equally important. Without a relevant case study, a universal principle-rule for intuition in moral extremes cannot be found. However, a broad virtue-rule can be formulated that the primary virtues in moral extremes and for moral brutalism are those of mindfulness and discipline pertaining to goodwill in practical wisdom that advances intuition and judgement. One must be mindful of the circumstances and effects in any given case, recognising the factors involved and effects yet to transpire as consequences, including those of character and mind. Discipline in virtue – that of the capacity to not succumb to impulse and inclinations of thoughtless and misguided intuition – then contributes to action in accordance with practical wisdom, intuition, reason, justice, and mindfulness. These are the primary virtues and virtue-rules for any complex cases of practical morality and its extremes.

The moral conditioning that affects the psyche and character and prepares functional, virtuous utility of moral brutalism can also have the opposite effect. This brings me to consider the 'slippery slope' in normative dynamics of tangents in extremes. The moral permission for one course of action might provide justification for another similar instance or act. Admitting killing an innocent person at one point 'for the greater good' can lead to the killing of innocents becoming an acceptable norm and principle-rule.

For example, drone strikes may be employed with just means to execute a person who presents themselves as a definitive high-risk vector of vice, for example a combatant preparing for an imminent terror act. The ideal principle-rule is to apprehend the deviant and nourish justice. However, ideal circumstances aren't always immediate and a vector of vice at liberty that cannot be tolerated must be addressed beyond measures of social jurisdiction, in other words permitting or necessitating the use of military and deadly force rather than legal and policing services. A target might protect themself from drone strikes with hostages or non-combatants. Now, a principle-rule may prevail in base morality where the people of one nation are prioritised over another, manifesting itself as dismissive attitudes to non-combatants of other factions. This is unacceptable under the heritin ethic guided by the unifying Human Imperative, which is not merely aware of the Categorical Directive moving all life.

However, within this Imperative is the principle-rule of mediation through considerations of value, whereby one person can have a greater value than another, making it permissible to discern value for effective action. Indeed, to protect humanity it may be justified to protect a particular society. But how we work about such claims is a very tricky and delicate matter that is not directly relevant to the present discussion.

What is important to draw on is the inherent value of all people. Considerations of maxims may appear to suggest reasoning that permits the killing of one innocent to preserve the lives of innocents elsewhere – in societies of greater value with greater potential for fulfilling the Human Imperative. While I cannot comprehensively discuss this matter right now, as this would require contextual considerations of secondary aspects of ethics, particularly that of moral authority, it is central to the slippery slope tangents of morality. By allowing oneself a principle-rule of killing one innocent person, qualified as having less value than two innocents closer to home, then a principle-rule of killing innocent people can be formulated. Such a rule can become far-reaching and devastating for any individual and community by invoking degenerative and fearful virtue-rules. Acting on consequences without rules is equivalent to blind action. Deliberation on intentions cannot overlook the consequences corresponding to future intentions. All deliberation on action with consideration of consequences, no matter how ambiguous or clear the consequences are, requires rules to guide the positive effect in action. The practice of morality must always be mindful of slippery slopes and corruptive tangents.

The premeditated and deliberate killing of one innocent person or non-combatant to save two other people, without affirmative information of relevant value, is a slippery slope. This is where heritin moral brutalism employs its utility. Fear initiating slippery principle-rules of killing innocents to protect a certain group of value from greater suffering will itself harbour vices pertaining to greater suffering, for the fear of loss and pain is a core of actions that will invoke similar influences over other actions. Allowing Fear to compromise one's character will harbour more suffering, pain, and loss than vision and ambition beyond Fear.

The pain of self-sacrifice may be great, but it will be greater in a community and inevitably ripple across many spheres of mankind's activity. Pain spread across a community may not be as evocative and significant to the individual that avoids pain, such as with protecting one's own loved ones but having many others lose theirs. Setting aside social tangents, on a profound level, actions committed in the Fear of loss will torment you in many ways, including the consumption of virtue through the corruption of pain. Pursuits in life are always better fulfilled with a dedicated purpose and meaning. A core of a community in terms of its individuals moved by Fear will be susceptible to corruption and will always be more vulnerable than communities that are able to come together in loss and pain; communities and individuals mindful of the Human Imperative and resistant to Fear will be stronger than those of weak will in pain who turn against one another and are easily duped into compulsive actions in Fear against maxim interests of absolving pain. By permitting the killing of an innocent or non-combatant to protect innocents in one's own community, with the support of a community willing to kill another community's innocents, is a dangerous path towards the corruption of Fear and the spread of vice. That same Fear will afflict a community internally and will always limit the community's ambition and strength. But by not killing an innocent in another constituency of the global community and permitting the sacrifice of one's own innocents for greater maxims of virtue can reap greater results in terms of the Human Imperative. This is the mode of heritin moral brutalism; this is what ruthlessness devoid of Fear is envisioned as.

However, any such hypothesised maxim of virtue, such as with the sacrifice of the innocents of one's closer community, will not be fulfilled in a community that rejects such ambition of virtue. In other words, if the jurisdiction of one's virtue or pursuit of maxims of virtue exceeds others' moral liberty, then maxim effect of virtue will not be achieved. Allowing innocents to die for greater gain in terms of the Human Imperative will be nearly pointless in a community that suffers such loss and is unable to deal with the pain, thus succumbing to vice. Ruthlessness will then draw on Liberty to permit the liberty of morality and the decay of vice, meaning entire communities will suffer from their self-inflicted vice. Sometimes it is legitimate and effective to act on maxims of virtue-rules when one's jurisdiction, with respect to the ethical environment and community, permits this; sometimes it is good to act against people's immediate intentions and desires to fulfil greater well-being, as seen with the suspension of liberty as a necessity to preserve maxims of ethical interest. Sometimes people's freedom must be curtailed to protect them.

However, this can be a counter-productive endeavour when the interests of people's liberty in accordance with their guiding ethos moves in a very different direction. And so, again, moral brutalism employs its valuable utility to not commit mistakes of compassion, of misguided intent, and of deceitful moral rules. Similarly, moral brutalism and its utilities, such as virtue-ruthlessness, cannot be and should not be forced on people, as only in the capacity to employ such utilities can they be effective and rewarding. But to deliberate on such cases universally is unrealistic, and we are left to the fate of liberty to be wise enough to learn from mistakes and be mindful in making judgements based on wisdom.

All considerations of value in practical morality are contextual and circumstantial. Mankind and the Human Imperative are left to the liberty and fortune of people's utility and character. There is no absolute solution to this fact of normativity and dynamics in structural ethics, so all we can plausibly do is ensure virtuous autonomy as best we can, at the very least in terms of moral rules and prepared theory.

The risk inherent to complex moral cases and slippery tangents of judgement is not merely in terms of principle-rules, but above all in terms of virtue-rules. As was discussed with the primacy of character in the combinatorialist normative framework, all actions, consequences, effects, intentions, and their catalysts flow through the dynamism of the fundamental will – the soul – that invokes actions. Actions follow tangents of characteristics – of vices and virtues. A character that enacts a disposition of morality will reflect certain characteristics. Effects in the dynamics of the structures of ethics disseminate through character – the catalyst of other effects in structures of ethics. Actions, their intentions and effects, follow tangents in ethical structures. Virtue corresponds to positive tangents, those of maxims of well-being, while negative tangents correspond to pain and the suffering of vice. Any consideration of actions and decisions must be mindful of ethical tangents, the ultimate judgement on which will be reduced to trends in the continuity of moral agency reflecting practical wisdom and moral intuition. An act deemed moral will set a theme for history; an act, rightly or wrongly, considered righteous will leave its mark on history. Ethical tangents and their slippery slopes are an intrinsic and crucial element in considerations of practical morality.

The difference between the traditional sciences and the studies of morality and ethics is that the influence of the latter must weigh in on the justice of ethical tangents. The intuitive reasoning of practical wisdom has to be primary, but this is not without empirical evidence through experience, which should be mindful of biased impressions.

For example, morality at ease with killing cannot always be effectively studied in terms of singular patterns of actions and psychology, for there are usually incomprehensible and unpredictable factors influencing decisions and corresponding consequences. A certain effect can influence moral decision-making that could not be accounted for empirically such as in terms of a murderous mentality being relieved of its pain through the unforeseeable influences of latent virtue – in terms of a person suddenly turning towards goodness.

Similarly, the effects of actions cannot be comprehended in lone terms of empirical study, because the wisdom of understanding people and antecedent influences on people is fundamentally important to morality, its study, and its application. Introspection is a category of empirical ethical study that cannot be performed in terms of only studying the world – external variables. To fully understand and apply ethical tangents requires much more than empirical study. The foundation of practical morality and its ethical tangents is, therefore, subject to the practical wisdom of intuition and intuitive reasoning in accordance with goodwill relating to the criteria necessary for understanding morality and how it affects people, primarily through oneself.

These questions aren't easy and are always multidimensional and multicausal as part of multilateral spheres and levels of the structures of ethics. But in this turbulent age of mass normative change and pressured adaptation, the only sustainable solution to immorality, for us and the Human Imperative, is for people's autonomy to be effective and virtuous. Decisions concerning tough choices, or any choices for that matter, must rely on the capacity of people for capable and good deliberation. We will make mistakes, but we must do what we can to stay true to virtue and goodwill, in doing so be prepared for the pain of our mistakes or the inevitable effects of misfortune. At the very least, the liberty of individuals should be supported with the virtue of being capable of discerning wisdom and good intentions, to prevent foolishness and malevolent intentions from corrupting good endeavour.

In these difficulties of morality, especially in certain complexities of heritin ethics, a goodwill that guides reasoning and intuition is key. The ambition to live well, insight, wisdom, and goodwill, as the desire to be of good conscience and strong when confronted by adversity, fulfilled above all else through empathy, were key to the path through which this ethic grew. The guiding rule of moral brutalism and its elements in terms of heritin ethics and core normative guidance is relatively straightforward: be careful and cautious in the execution of spiritually demanding actions in accordance with the demands of justice. Then, be conscious and mindful of the actions you commit as moral extremes, for the malevolent intent of vice and Fear can creep in, as the corruption of Fear always finds a way.

Mindfulness in moral extremes and the danger of moral slippery slopes are central to premeditation in acts of moral extremes such as killing. Outlining a morality and mode of justice prepared to kill is already a form of premeditated killing by enabling the possibility of such actions. Any sensibility and intuitive reasoning would suggest that premeditated acts of killing can be moral and just. Killing a known and high-risk threat of a demented combatant before he can execute a destructive plot is an intuitive means of justice. Of course, this can easily degrade into a slippery principle-rule of other forms of premeditated and pre-emptive killing. This will have to be tempered with individual and circumstantial conditions of moral rules.

The basic idea is that one ought to commit premeditated killings only as a means of justice when justice demands it and when realistic alternatives of greater justice are unavailable. One should only kill when it is absolutely necessary. That being said, virtue-rules, such as of the virtues of mindfulness and discipline, must guide intuition, reason, and judgement, or else ethical tangents can lead the character and psyche to vice. Justice and moral sense shaped by the corruption of Fear, suffering, and vice degrade through malign intentions, instantiating pernicious tangents of morality and judgement.

Sometimes we have to make a conscious choice with respect to values, of who to save and who to condemn or sacrifice. This is evident in complex moral cases of just war, and while there might not be any simple answers, one ought to be mindful and disciplined to not allow misguided, debased intentions to rule one's judgement. If we must choose who to condemn, such judgements and their disseminations of ethical tangents ought to be done rationally and in goodwill. Whether mankind can live up to such demands of justice can't be concluded on, but faith must be considered even if hope recedes.

This pragmatism is difficult, ambiguous, and unconcise, yet it is better than unrealistic and incomplete moral restrictions. Nevertheless, we can always formulate some principle-rules, and for the present case it is that killing should not be taken lightly, should not be a moral absolute, and that this act can facilitate critical vice. Even so, it's important to distinguish between intent and justice found on Fear rather than genuine goodwill in terms of the Human Imperative. Fear does convey, or comply with, the Categorical Directive, but greater fulfilment is always achieved through the Human Imperative found in mindfulness and goodwill.

The primary tangent in moral brutalism and practical morality concerning judgement on lives is the danger of neglecting ethical values and their fundamentals. Dehumanising and devaluing people is a dangerous path that deprives the spirit of positivity and righteousness and corrupts ambition through misguided mindfulness and immoderate Fear. It may be easy to detach from the vices of others – one's peers. Fear that pursues status can submit one's character and the will to lesser virtue rather than full autonomy of goodwill. By detracting from people and the all-embracing spirit of empathy, one not only loses sight of the Highest Good and the intuitions of goodwill, but also leaves one open to vice and the corruption of Fear.

The morally weak are not expendable or lack fundamental human value that reflects human nature, even if moral depravity may evoke a sense that people are no better than wild animals. Even the monster is a slave to its condition – a soul designated a function in the world. Yet if the monster is a creature of intolerable vice, if the qualifications of justice warrant our appeal to moral brutalism to condemn the monster to serve the ends of the Human Imperative, then the beast or morally depraved individual can be legitimately apprehended or killed if necessary for the sake of justice. But no matter how 'unrighteous' and 'immoral' or 'unjust' we may consider some people, fundamental value also ties in with one of the dominant Central Principles – moral liberty.

The liberty of diversity ensures normative and moral competition in judgements and intuition, facilitating better normative outcomes (or ideally so). As with most matters of practical morality involved in the issues and themes of liberty, moral brutalism and practical morality, similar to the considerations of moral liberty, are intrinsically complex and delicate topics. Liberty and comprehensive practical morality can easily invoke excess caution and negligent, irresponsible inaction. To act on blind impulse is foolish; to act morally requires discipline and mindfulness.

These two central elements of practical wisdom also initiate what is necessary for practical morality in demanding situations – boldness, courage, and taking risks. There are always immeasurable dimensions of forces acting in ethical structures, and we can never fully comprehend or predict the outcomes of attitudes and actions. It is in this context that any morally righteous act of practising virtue necessitates the courage and boldness to act under significant uncertainty. But to guide intuitions and judgements through these uncertainties requires consideration of the fundamentals of morality and their relation to judgements.

To ignore fundamental values and the fundamental of moral liberty can lead down a tangent through which other fundamentals are neglected. It is imperative to keep in mind basic decency and its fundamentals towards others and oneself. Sometimes this can manifest itself in unintuitive, unorthodox ways; sometimes decency and dignity are preserved through salvation and redemption; other times they are upheld by terminating indignity arising from suffering and vice. Sometimes an act of killing is not only a means of justice, but is also more merciful, more benevolent, and more dignified, for others and oneself. All dignity pertaining to positive spirit and a good sense of self is contingent on considerations of the fundamental value of people, the treatment of which reflects back on the character committing an action towards or against another person. To treat others with indignity is to neglect one's own dignity and nobility, especially when committed in spirit of Fear. All of us are swayed by reactions and everyone has vulnerabilities; the only possible solution to moderating reactions is through mindfulness and discipline, but not a disruptive discipline that undermines the liberty of intuitive virtues – of goodwill. This takes time, practice, and habit. Mistakes and regrets are points for introspection and reflection to learn.

Any form of killing is a means of justice and a mode of moral utility. But how these means are executed is a very delicate moral ruling, and ultimately any questions of moral extremes and moral brutalism are reducible to, and at the mercy of, the individual's conscience and his or her moral liberty. No conclusive rulings on universal cases can be made with absolute certainty; only certain principle-rules open to deliberation, evaluation, and interpretation can be formulated. But the most important thing is mindfulness over one's intentions, for any malevolent intent, especially of Fear, will bread suffering and vice. It is in one's own interest to prevent unjust acts of moral extremes, especially those committed in Fear.

Committing acts of moral extremes, such as killing to protect oneself and others, can be questioned as a warped and corrupted intention of heritin ethics. This would violate the spirit of Defiance seeking the empowerment of Liberty and breach the spirit of Harmony by killing and inflicting suffering on another soul. This is why one ought to start examining such questions or meditating on them with a foundational principle of not killing and that the universal value of all souls begins with a default rule that no one should be killed. But without sensibility and wisdom, these norms will fail, implode on themselves, and betray themselves by neglecting others and the Human Imperative.

Liberty will not lead to eudaimonia without wisdom and sensibility nourishing higher virtues. By easily and recklessly sacrificing oneself or killing others, values in ethical dynamics pertaining to the Human Imperative become neglected and the state of self, rationale, psyche, and spirit all become deprived of greater fulfilment in greater sum terms. An eagerness for the final liberty – death – and the final fulfilment of eudaimonia is a powerful mode of morality, and ultimately the greatest satisfaction and fulfilment in spirit and sensation is more important to intuition in any given moment than any rationalisation. We will inevitably die, but whether we achieve satisfaction in life before dying is another matter, with eudaimonia being the Liberty and higher fulfilment that lets one be at ease with the end of life, completing duty and the Categorical Directive. But recklessness in the disguise of Liberty is not the means to producing comprehensive and greater sum ethical value, because recklessness is often an ethic characterised by despair and fear of the Void.

The most fulfilling actions are of synchronised reason and of the most meaningful sentiment and thought. Sacrifice is greatest and most fulfilling when empowered by sentiment and meaning. The most fulfilling sacrifice is one of Liberty and purpose, of meaning. To the spirit of the individual, it will not matter in the grand scheme of things what consequences will come from self-sacrifice. But in the immediacy of spirit and sensation, intentions surmount to everything the spirit draws from. Only goodwill of virtue feeds positive spirit. For Liberty and sacrifice to be fulfilling, especially in a final act, they need not only empowerment and fulfilment through strong autonomy, but also meaningful purpose that motivates and empowers the goodwill.

Here lies one of the paradoxes of eudaimonia and moral brutalism that can only be normatively applicable to intuitions with respect to the character prepared to execute morally brutal or desperate acts. Sometimes one ought to be ready to kill, while at the same time be willing to sacrifice oneself and die without killing another to ensure the success of a maxim of morality. This is a quality comprehensible and intuitive only in moral and spiritual liberty, yet it is rationally intuitive in terms of the valuation of maxims at liberty from baser influences and estimations.

Moral brutalism entrusts power in the capacity of character, as does the Ploy. The heritin ethos can breed a leviathan of willpower, of unyielding and indomitable will, which is pointless, unfulfilling, and dangerous if misguided. How this ethos then applies itself in terms of normativity is a secondary question of fulfilment, and is ultimately subject to questions of continuity for those already at eudaimonia. Those who reduce themselves to Fear and vice will relinquish any genuine power found in the will through eudaimonia, Liberty, and the Void. People who follow the corrupt will of Fear and vice will suffer the consequences. Fear never empowers as much as Liberty does.

Moral and psychological tangents would be wise to consider that killing is not the only or even the worst moral extreme, as torture and continued living in extreme pain can be worse than the liberty of death. Any act of killing is morally and spiritually demanding, or should be. Everything that moves heritin ethics is bound to the Human Imperative and the universalisable soul. To kill or sacrifice another is to rip away a part of the soul, in oneself and as part of its universality. This is conceived in spiritual, emotional, rational, and sentimental terms. In the place of any person you kill, any person you deem depraved and of lesser value, could be you or someone you love.

The soul is always left at the mercy of fortune and circumstances, even though that same malleability is what grants us the potential to rise above unfavourable circumstances. The soul that moves you in accordance with the goodwill of virtue is the same soul that is in others. The loss of any life is a loss, a tragedy, and a short-coming, even of the most depraved characters inflicting suffering on the soul, for this is a failure of moral authority and a weakness of virtue and goodwill. Alas, moral extremes become a necessity to protect what goodness there is. When an animal becomes too savage and wild, it needs to be put down; similarly, although not as simply, when the liberty of a vector of vice breeches justice and can no longer be tolerated, this vector needs to be severed. As Nelson Mandela wrote: "Like a gardener, a leader must take responsibility for what he cultivates; he must mind his work, try to repel enemies, preserve what can be preserved, and eliminate what cannot succeed."[7]

Although extreme attitudes are intuitively susceptible to the moral corruption of vice and malevolent intentions, and can be selectively and wrongly interpreted as a reckless and blind moral hardline, they have significant value. To preserve ethical value requires affirmative action corresponding to positivity and moderation, if not elimination, of vice that corrupts what good there is. If goodness is afraid to let go of itself and becomes corrupted in Fear deprived of positive spirit, then it is in itself unworthy of the greater positivity of higher spirit.

This virtue-rule is valuable for guiding the ruthlessness of moral brutalism, for the suspension of compassion to preserve life may be the most compassionate deed after all – a deed of euthanising a soul in pain that inflicts harm on others. These demands of morality are expected to be very mentally and spiritually heavy. Living with the knowledge of what one is capable of can be demanding; not acting according to such experience and by allowing relating tangents of the cycle of suffering to persist can be more painful. But such are the demands of the Highest Good, the Human Imperative, and duty. Admitting this vulnerability and this pain is itself a sign of a strong will that further sustains its righteous mean.

Any ethic, ethos, and morality that herald faith and hope in the goodness of humanity must confront hard truths of the monstrosity of mankind's vice. Any morality must prepare for the brutal realities of the deeply flawed character of mankind that has submitted to Fear. Any morality of positive spirit, such as one that emphasises love, mercy, and self-sacrifice, possesses very admirable virtues and spirit, yet at times it is unprepared for the realities of normativity challenged by the callous dynamics of structural ethics.

It is clear that some people are so profoundly morally and spiritually corrupt, of a mentality so twisted by Fear and pain, that there is no plausible immediate, short-term solution than that of moral extremes. Nonetheless, the one-dimensional practical morality of suffering-love and self-sacrifice is much better than the one-dimensional corrupt and debased morality eager to execute, torment, and torture, collapsing in on itself and slipping under the influence of vice.

Even though the one-dimensional morality of self-sacrifice and suffering-love is restricted in comparison to the multidimensional adaptive morality prepared and equipped for handling moral extremes, it is an aspect of morality that should not be underestimated or neglected. Self-sacrifice will ultimately do more and achieve more than a morality resorting to moral extremes of limited vision in terms of narrow moral brutalities. The capacity and will to self-sacrifice emanates much greater power of virtue than the acts of killing and moral extremes do. Yet this morality of self-sacrifice is only achievable and effectively implemented in virtuous character able and willing to follow this path of duty, and a much more detailed discussion of the practical morality of sacrifice is needed.

What is intuitive and clear in such a morality, especially that of suffering-love, is that it is not always enough for protecting people and to secure value, even if at times it can maximise them by protecting the individual from committing an act of vice. Ideals in morality and their formulated principle-rules are nonetheless valid in extremes of practical morality, such as apprehension of bad people being better and less corrupting than unnecessary killing. Virtue-rules are imperative for practical morality and moral brutalism to guide against the affliction of Fear. An ethos and morality that is not prepared for the demanding and strenuous effects of moral extremes, that is eager to permit hardline rules and cruel and excessive punishment, is doomed to vice. Thus, any comprehensive practical morality and its vectors ought to prepare for the demands of moral duty and the pressure that affects normativity through the adaptive mechanism of Nature.

Any sustainable and effective morality must prepare its rules and its agents for moral extremes. For example, it may be difficult to sustain morality of positive spirit in people involved in national security, those who have to shift through reprehensible and disgusting material, such as extremists' videos flaunting the execution of innocent people. Similarly, the profession of a surgeon may be extremely morally and spiritually demanding after losing a patient, especially when that patient is a child. One may have to let go of those he or she loves as a final attempt to stop them from destroying themselves, knowing the risks of their decaying state of mind in despair and hopelessness. How can positivity of spirit be found or sustained in any of this? How can positive reason move one through such mentally and spiritually demanding hardship? How can the dedication of goodwill persist through so much pain?

I put forward an answer through moral brutalism as a necessity of duty against the moral extremes of vice striving to destroy, hold back, scar, and corrupt humanity. But as always, an approach of extremes against extremes is inherently somewhat contradictory and is susceptible to moral corruption, according to which preparation through principles and virtues is necessary. It is better to be prepared for these real demands of normativity in conscience, spirit, will, and capacity of character, whether that means to kill or to sacrifice. Positive reasons for acting on moral extremes come with duty.

Duty can evoke eudaimonia through the high virtues of hard duties demanding a particular quality of character, from which positive, but not joyous, spirit arises from the ambition for and of the Human Imperative. Positive spirit and unchallenging morality are intuitive, natural, and easy. While joy can betray itself without proper discipline, as with idleness, complacency, and corrupted attachment, moral extremes are far more demanding for the mind and require much greater Discipline and Harmony – composure, strength, and mindfulness. This is the merit for considering extreme tangents of practical morality.

On a personal note of dealing with tough choices and especially grief, there are two things to keep in mind. Do not reduce yourself to a mere victim, and make good on the bad that happens. It will take time to heal; it is good to lick your wounds and rest. But blaming life and the world for your suffering where it was not your fault, where an unfortunate state of affairs wasn't caused by you, where the circumstances were simply tragic, can easily misguide Defiance and lead to bitterness without resolution.

You might be a victim of a terrible act or circumstance, but do not let it define you. Instead, learn to see yourself or make yourself the protagonist of your story, achieved best by breaking a cycle of suffering through oneself by being good to oneself and others. The way you overcome adversity and respond to tragedy should define you; don't let suffering to shape you, shape suffering through yourself.

You will have to leave behind those you tried best to help but weren't able to because of their state of hopelessness and entrapment in Fear. You will mourn them, remember them. But the only way to heal and move on is to make good on this pain such as by carrying on in their memory, to not let the goodness of their soul lost to tragedy go to waste.

Instead of blaming destiny, mindful Defiance shows the value of the wisdom and strength to be found in embracing tragedy as a necessary fate for one to grow and commit to duty. But if cowardice and the lack of strength were a fault in your actions, where you didn't do everything you could, and a sense of guilt is significant, then learn from the experience and discipline your character to make amends.

To apply these discussions of practical morality, I will consider a practical moral dichotomy of whether a spy, who has infiltrated a criminal or terror organisation, ought to execute a hostage to prove his facade of loyalty. First of all, in direct reference to the ethos of Liberty, the spy shouldn't kill the hostage merely to save himself. However, even though this may personally narrow down the proper choice, it does not dismiss the many other factors that ought to be accounted for, particularly if one is to abide goodwill. Ultimately, any consideration in such a case will have to be circumstantial and relevant to immediate factors.

Not killing the hostage could end with the spy's deceit being revealed, the spy dying, the hostage dying, and the malevolent organisation executing a devastating plot. The personal dimension of interest might be satisfied with two people accepting death, although this would have to consider contingencies of people's character and their moral dispositions of whether they would favour survival or a good death. Mass death is not a desirable outcome, but if this is a necessity of liberty where the outcomes are limited, then it can serve as a fair judgement.

However, this norm of thinking can easily lead to recklessness and negligence. On the other hand, killing the hostage to infiltrate the organisation deeper could subvert future devastating plots, thereby doing what is right to ensure the greatest maxim of ethical interest by saving dozens of lives at the cost of one in harsh circumstances.

Here lies another crucial factor to consider – will the hostage be released whether or not the spy executes him? If the hostage is going to be killed, then the spy might as well use this opportunity to further greater ambitions while complying with very restricted circumstances to ensure the greater good. However, if the hostage is not going to be killed, or such is a claim of the one ordering the execution, who might be lying, then conditions are much more complex and decisions are more difficult. One would have to act based on the judgement of whether the one ordering the execution is lying. Then, one would have to consider what effect taking the risk would have on the self and the global environment. Will executing the hostage turn the spy on an irreversible tangent towards vice and genuine alignment with the malicious organisation? Will it impede future judgement and lead to excess killing beyond measures of justice?

As you may see, there are too many tangents to consider in hindsight to formulate effective frameworks for judgement and decision-making. Our practical cognition is too limited for such tasks where the variables are uncertain. However, the same 'biases' that are inherent to our intuition, revolving around intuitions and reflexive, automatic, quick functions of reason and the mind, can serve a crucial function for an immediate decision. Fear can provide a basis for very quick decision-making, but not always for the best. Fear can make the concerns of survival automatic, making actions clear. So, again, I will stress the relevance of the intuitions of virtue and defer to normative liberty and its principle-rules.

Ideally, extreme moral decisions, such as with the case explored above, ought to be worked up to, with character being well-versed in morality and nurtured with virtue. With the vast amount of information relevant to a judgement in a profoundly ambiguous dichotomy, the principle-rules of embracing or averting risk can be relevant to particular circumstances. If the spy deems that the order of execution is a guise, and that the hostage will be released if he or she is not killed, then it comes down to risk factors.

If the spy's judgement deems that there is sufficient opportunity, contingent on a mission of infiltration, for others to subvert a future devastating plot, while also liberating the hostage, but at a cost of the spy's life, then the action of self-sacrifice is the right one. However, if the potential of subverting future attacks is limited, whereby there is a distinct chance that releasing the hostage will only save one life but cost many more, and the global estimation of value deems the hostage's one life to be of lesser value than that the many other lives that could be destroyed, then the moral choice based on the estimation of risk could be that the hostage ought to be executed to subvert future plots.

How sincere the spy is to his virtue contingent on the fulfilment achieved through corresponding virtue is mainly up to the spy's degree of mindfulness – how honest he can be with his intentions. For example, one might tell a person the truth in order not to harm her, but then the desire to tell the truth and corresponding intention to not lie are a manipulation to gain trust, which could cause harm. To say: "I want to be honest with you because I don't want you to get hurt because of me," could be a selfish manipulation in itself that would lead to a person trusting you getting hurt. However, being this honest with oneself is an indication of honesty and courage that is more likely to counteract the intention to manipulate, although this cannot be certain.

Furthermore, setting up clear guidelines and intuitions could undermine the implementation of morality. If an opposing faction could predict with certainty its opponent's intentions and motivations, therefore predict responses and actions (such as the spy sacrificing himself to save the hostage), then that morality will become vulnerable to exploits and will prove itself impractical. Any such scenarios and cases are very difficult to study, but with sufficient work, perhaps a guiding encyclopaedia and prescriptive science of morality could be achieved. This, however, is not the intended purpose of this foundational project of structural ethics.

Nevertheless, a solid normative framework can be implemented with respect to the known information and variables, building from a model of structural ethics. The spy has a job to do – a responsibility – to protect others. The interests of the masses would take primacy over the lives of the spy and hostage. Neglecting the life of the hostage will lead to corrupt attitudes towards other life. The focal lens – the most important values – will be concerned with greater well-being of the ethical community. Therefore, the personal dimension will not be as important as the consequential, greater, if not global, impact, with the personal dimension only being as relevant as its effects on the character pertaining to ethical environment and future actions.

However, to a certain extent, considerations of one's own future can be left to the future, whereby present concerns should focus on the immediate environmental conditions. Therefore, the consequences affecting others with respect to the immediate choice of killing or sparing the hostage, as opposed to the concerns for how the choice will impact the self, would be more important for moral deliberation. But then the concern for the personal dimension, even if only as a hint, influences intentions and the framework of the choice being considered and made, making it a secondary, but necessary, contingency of decision-making.

Consider another case exploring the practical morality of killing. Can killing to pre-empt significant suffering, even when uncertain and beyond inconclusive information, be morally right? Is it morally right to kill a murderer or person about to commit a gravely immoral act? Is killing a violent sexual predator right in order to ensure greater value of goodness? These questions are inherently bound to the consideration of consequences and ethical tangents, as explored with the previous case.

An integral component to consider in studies relating to the aforementioned questions and issues is the matter of law. First of all, let me consider a hypothesised case in a lawless, de-institutionalised, post-apocalyptic environment subject to its own parameters and conditions of Natural Law. In a society effectively governed by law, one does not need to kill, thereby sparing themself of corruptive actions and preserving greater social harmony and value of character such as by amending the devious and criminal character of vice. Although law usually draws on morality, or should do so for greater effectiveness, law does not always pertain to greater virtue and morality, as law must adapt with morality.

In a lawless world of a brutish 'state of nature', the laws of morality and moral considerations are very different to those of law-ruled societies. Where modern laws and institutions can concentrate and amplify stable normative dynamics in structures of ethics, lawless environments and communities may be subject to much greater forces of ethics and Nature with respect to a decentralised normative authority. Lawless societies are unstable or less stable than modern, institutional societies. Because of this, the forces of Nature and ethics can run rampant, are accentuated without regulatory authority of a binding authority of norms and values such as law. Due to the deregulation and decentralisation of societal forces, in a pre-institutional state of affairs the inherent risk to ethical tangents becomes amplified by stronger competing ethical forces in the dynamics of normative decentralisation and chaos. Where laws and institutions could once provide security and confidence, a lawless environment will not have the same security and confidence, therefore entailing greater risk in the consequences of actions in terms of certain consequences and effects.

In the hypothesised state of nature of a post-apocalyptic environment, the risk relating to the consequences of killing or not killing are greater than those in institutional environments. Suppose that the moral agent deliberating on a choice of whether to kill is part of a tribe, group, or community. He has a concern for an immediate value to secure well-being of the familiar member of the group – of the greatest value to himself – whereas a foreigner to the group can be a major uncertainty.

Would it be right to kill a foreigner that is a potential threat? This, again, ultimately becomes conditional and circumstantial. If the foreign agent does not appear to be an immediate threat, then it is intuitively moral to leave him alone or even attempt to integrate him. However, greater uncertainty prevails in such circumstances and one cannot be sure that the foreign agent is not a scout or a spy as part of a much greater threat. Base morality of Fear, as well as sensibility, might suppose that it is better to not take any risks. Nevertheless, even in terms of the heritin ethos, one ought to sustain virtue and maximum value.

One might be part of a virtuous or comparatively more virtuous community, and so one should preserve that virtue, act according to it (such as by not killing the foreign agent that might become a threat), but in Liberty proportional to sensibility in accordance with the prevailing will of the community that may adhere to a different moral code. If death is the consequence and risk, then it is one that should not be the absolute concern in the heritin ethos, yet the maximisation of value should be. Therefore, one ought to follow the will of the majority and normative prevalence up to a degree of personal responsibility and judgement of whether the will of the majority is something one can or ought to be part of.

Would you be willing to be part of a community that is motivated by a lot of fear, fear of uncertainty? One might not personally commit the act of killing the foreign agent, but standing by idly and allowing the rest of the community to kill is relevant to one's moral conscience. But if the community becomes too accustomed to such ethical tangents and exceeds tolerable vice, then one's judgement might best serve by abandoning such a community if conflict in normative interest becomes too great.

Suppose the foreign agent is revealed to be part of another community that does materialise itself to be a definitive threat. One begins to act under circumstances of a certain existential threat from a foreign group. Would it be moral to eliminate the threat in order to preserve one's own community that is deemed by all measures of justice to be more virtuous? Yes, it would be moral to kill in such circumstances. If one has to choose between a lesser or greater vice, it is calculatedly better to support greater ethical value, thereby permitting the elimination of a grave threat to value within parameters of the Highest Good and the Human Imperative, but only if such a threat is known with certainty to be serious.

Would setting free captives of a resolved conflict in this scenario, such as of the foreign agent, be the best moral choice? Would it be best to release prisoners of war after the war has ended? This would again be subject to decision-making processes operating under conditions of risk perception and assessment. If bitter feelings prevail in the foreign agent and he does express intentions of causing significant harm, with little opportunity for positive resolution of making peace with past grievances, then his liberty cannot be risked and measures must be taken to restrain or neutralise this threat. If a person's vice is deemed to be genuinely immoderate and beyond tolerable liberty, where the value of virtuous people in a community one is bound to is the primary value, then means of securing value, including through killing, become morally permissible. Keep in mind that this reasoning is operating under the condition of lawlessness and de-institutionalised societies where the means of justice are extremely limited.

Consider another example under such pretences and conditions where one stumbles on a violent sexual predator that is known with certainty to have committed gravely immoral deeds such as sexual assault against children. The vice of this immorality is in respect to the act driven by an inclination that causes pain and suffering while also diminishing the character of the moral deviant by reducing it to vice. The act of the sexual criminal will most certainly inflict extensive and lasting pain on another person, affecting how the child develops and the child's disposition to action through the character he or she embodies. To further the Human Imperative and better the world, one ought to secure value and diminish suffering. Children must be protected and nourished with virtue and goodness to ensure future generations adapt and grow in virtue, surpassing previous generations. The value of the child greatly supervenes the worth of the diminished, depraved sexual predator.

Can the liberty of the deviant be tolerated even though your paths will most certainly not cross again? If the estimation of risk leads to the assumption that the deviant will act on inclinations and tangents of vice, whereby more ideal resolutions have no realistic prospects, then no, the deviant cannot be left free. In the hypothesised brutish environment of limited resources and utilities, the most efficient action consistent with virtue-rules might be to kill the sexual predator in order to secure the interests of other people and children. If one cannot afford letting go the character of extensive vice, as this would be too risky, then one shouldn't free them. Empathy may understand that the abuser is perpetuating abuse that he himself became a victim of in the past, continuing the cycle. But Discipline in extremes would nonetheless necessitate appropriate responses. Inner peace persists in good conscience.

It is worth mentioning that while certain moralising is supposedly easier and may be more tacit in modern, more stable societies, a state of nature, such as of a post-apocalyptic environment, would accentuate the extremes which may be less commonplace, but not obsolete, in modern societies and nonetheless prevalent in less developed, impoverished societies. Greater extremes of the ethical environment would entail a greater necessity and merit to employ moral extremes. Base morality would in most sense adapt to a more brutish state and structure. If modern society disintegrates, will any morality of Liberty be sustainable? Can a balanced, post-modern and post-base morality succeed in such an environment?

A question of succession would be ultimately settled through Natural Law, but the morality of Liberty and synchrony with oneself and the world will never be obsolete once it is found. A person will have to make a choice concerning the path in life he or she will follow, now or if a debased state arises. Once Liberty is sensed and its fulfilment felt, the ultimate goal, although subject to unconscious psychological influences, will favour the pleasures and fulfilment of autonomy and freedom in and from Fear.

In an environment where base morality is reduced to brutishness, there would be a choice to be made: to leave and surrender, to embrace the Void fully, or to stand for what is right, to find hope and follow the duty to rebuild humanity. The former – the duty of the Human Imperative – will always be more fulfilling and greater. It would be important to state in consideration of the extremes of brutish circumstances that a person would have to be mindful of the necessity to rebuild hope in human endeavour, and further ambition to not merely survive but to follow a purposeful, meaningful existence succeeding survival or a purely brutish and debased state.

Similarly, it is central to morality to identify – be mindful of – intentions behind actions, as intentions are moved by characteristics and their tangents. If one is to kill, this should only be done for the right reason. Killing in the aforementioned cases is only righteous and virtuous in accordance with the Highest Good when in harmony with the Human Imperative. The principle-rules permitting and enabling acts of just killing are only right and just when committed for the right reasons. To kill for self-glorification and to further pain, suffering, and vice, are all unjust motives. To kill to protect and secure the value of goodness and virtue is morally right. The self is only a contingency of the necessary emphasis on global dynamics of ethical structures, whereby self-interest is maximised through intentions synchronised with the virtues of the Highest Good and its Imperative. Where the intent of Liberty can be considered clearer in intuitions familiar with, and bound to, Liberty in harmony with synchronised faculties of reason, the intentions of base-reason that are bound to an ethos of Fear are in many respects supposed to be less stable in the dynamics of ethical tangents, especially when a person is granted power. Ethical tangents of minor vice can be significantly amplified when fed, something emphasised in consistent case studies where power corrupts people, whether in government positions or office management. Where the power to control is emphasised through a base ethos of Fear to control and attach to external substance, power in the ethos of Liberty is built on a fundamental appreciation of power dedicated to the will of the self and the liberty of virtue – tangents of goodwill.

The ethos of Liberty is open to corruption through lack of mindfulness and deprivation of virtue, a virtue-rule emphasising the relevance of the practices of mindfulness and discipline. However, the appreciation of, and attitude towards, power and the capacity to control are fundamentally different in the ethos of Liberty, whereby power is above all pursued in its spiritual and psychological sense of an indomitable will – the greatest of power that defies Fear. Even though it is not a perfect ethos, as the quality of the character of mankind is not ideal in terms of any single ethic and ethos, by the grace and necessity of adaptation, the theoretical groundwork of reasoning and intuition considers these thoughts.

However, the imperfection and vulnerability of people, especially in terms of the lack of mindfulness and discipline, does deprive people of direction and self-discipline to not betray their interests. So just as any agency of base-morality engaged in the exercise of power warrants scepticism, so does the same scepticism apply to any other mode of conduct and morality, a virtue-rule that is paramount for the mindfulness of Liberty. That being said, an ethos of Fear accentuated by base morality is considered to be inherently and usually less stable with respect to the character that lacks Discipline and is easily influenced by the forces of structural ethics that then reflect back on the character. Therefore, a great deal of scepticism ought to be applied to a structure or agency of ethics built on an ethos of Fear and guided by accentuated base morality.

This scepticism is relevant to any morality that even hints at permitting vigilantism. Even in a lawless environment where a person may qualify themself as acting righteously with respect to a morality and spirit devoid of Liberty, or worse off tainting the spirit and morality of Liberty, scepticism and scrutiny are necessary, even for one's own mental and spiritual sake. The cases analysed, which engaged topics of morality disengaged from law and institutional frameworks of societies that are more stable than lawless societies, hint at the issue of vigilantism. There can be practices of morality beyond a legal framework that can be correct, as morality always supercedes, and gives precedence to, law. However, this should always be subject to extensive scrutiny and a great deal of discipline. Therefore, where there are cases of vigilantism or practical morality beyond a structured, institutional framework of a governing authority, especially if it is a decentralised and incoherent *moral authority* (see Chapter 24), whereby the balance of judgement is not tempered by modern systematic forces, then a high degree of scepticism is necessary. Where people cannot be trusted in many respects, as is clear with the ethical dynamics of power, the same virtue-rule is instrumental towards oneself to check mindfulness and balance intuitions.

As for the case of the sexual predator, but in a modern, institutional society governed by effective law, all matters of morality would be best moved to the centrality of morality – law and institution. (This isn't to say that morality should be based on the authority of the state, but it does suggest that authorities should be factored in.) In all the above cases, rather than killing, it would be best to defer judgement and action to legal institutions and their agencies of law enforcement. But matters are not so clear provided a case where the capacity of law is impotent or deficient.

If one is *absolutely* sure that a person is a violent sexual predator and is justifiably judged to very likely commit a crime again, then morality is complicated. If the law and institution cannot prevent something that one is absolutely sure will happen again, or where the risk is far too great, then measures of security may have to be taken through the unlawful execution of morality.

It is imperative to stress the qualification of certainty in such circumstances, but if one is sure beyond any doubt, and an institution fails and is negligent of concrete evidence, notwithstanding the inherent ambiguity of thinking one is right when others of more appropriate experience and qualification disagree, then killing the moral deviant ready to commit a gravely immoral deed may be a necessity of morality. Vigilantism is a dangerous tangent to follow and permit in exceptional circumstances, but morality always supercedes law, whereby abiding and tolerating the law is a foundation of morality, but not an absolute. But for this hypothetical case, which might grossly misrepresent real situations, if the law is ineffective and immoral individuals are certain to commit an immoral act again, then measures of justice and morality can be legitimately, or even necessarily, deferred to the judgement and actions of the individual. While this illustration may seem wildly impractical, the smaller scale illustration can serve as a relative framework for the degrees and culture of international anarchy of the global community. Considering a moral outline with respect to states of anarchy is useful for their application in broader, more global contexts.

Although it is difficult to formulate concise Central Principles of practical morality and of morality dealing judgement on lives, certain principle and virtue rules for normative guidance can be outlined. I cannot say much more on the matter of moral hardlines without deferring to the context of secondary spheres of ethics such as society, state, and material utility. Yet despite the intrinsic ambiguities and relative limitations of preserving coherence in this discourse, some Central Principles of practical morality (that is, applied morality through common actions) and its extremes are valid and crucial.

Moral extremes, such as acts of killing, like any utility of practical morality, can be a means of justice.

In terms of Liberty and eudaimonia, with respect to the good of the Human Imperative, killing is not fundamentally better than self-sacrifice, because a person's will that is able to oppose Fear nourishes with more spirit and virtue. Sometimes self-sacrifice is greater and of higher virtue than killing. However, sensibility is nonetheless morally better.

In the deliberation on the justice of moral extremes, one ought to begin with, and follow a virtue-rule corresponding to the sense and intuition of, a foundational principle-rule of people having inherent value, whereby the main question is when or whether we ought to kill and subject people to moral extremes, rather than ask when we shouldn't.

All guidance on intuition, reason, and deliberation in goodwill should be found on norma-tive rules, values in ethics, and the Human Imperative for just rulings of practical morality and moral brutalism. The intrinsic ambiguities in the considerations of the consequences ought to be deliberated on, meditated on, and formulated through fundamental intuitions and principle and virtue rules of goodwill.

The effects of moral extremes on the psyche and spirit can be dire and obscure, requiring mindfulness and discipline if one is to guard against moral corruption, mental and spiritual deformation, and psychological affliction – a worthy remark by any sensible and coherent ethic subject to the law of sustainability and continuity.

The tangent of slippery slopes in morality is a constant in moral deliberation which neces-sitates extensive caution and mindfulness.

In moral extremes, empathy and considerations of justice in terms of the Human Imperative can assume many forms of morality, from compassion to brutal qualifications of maxims of disciplined empathy. The rejection of sentiment is not the goal of moral brutalism and reasoned practical morality, as this mode of morality is a wasteful manoeuvre losing valuable utility, intuition, and fulfilment of spirit, yet a valuable and imperative utility in extremes.

Practical morality and moral brutalism are never just when they dehumanise moral agency, neither should they be eager and simplistic in dismissing the normative interests and concerns of those one may perceive to be of 'lesser virtue', for the duty of the Human Imperative binds all people, and it is the virtue and duty of the empowered to forward progress and growth in all accessible spheres of human endeavour, especially in protecting and improving the conditions of the vulnerable and weak.

How practical morality employs and deals with the innocent and those weaker and more vulnerable is a reflection of a morality's ethos. Moral extremes are intrinsically delicate mat-ters requiring an imperative rule that guides intuitions through goodwill. Thus, one ought not to kill or employ other moral hardline utilities against the innocent and those not directly responsible for an act of grave immorality. If the means of justice require extreme actions con-cerning the innocent or weak and vulnerable, then this is only permissible, just, and moral as a moderation of damage to preserve greater value in the dynamics of ethics and the Human Imperative. Similarly, greater justice is found in the virtue of protecting the vulnerable and assuring positive value, which could entail necessary means of hardlines and moral brutalism.

How we treat the smaller pieces, the details of the global picture, is the mean of virtue and justice of the Human Imperative and the Highest Good, to ourselves and others. The quality of individual's character is the primary element, if not the foundation, of a community and its virtue. A community that feeds off its constituents feeds on itself until vice cannibalises itself.

Chapter 21:

Violence

A lot of attention is rightfully given to the moral issue of violence. However, insufficient weight is given to considerations of its arguments. Sometimes violence is condemned without sufficient justification, leaving one to question whether it is inherently wrong or whether it is even worse than other forms of suffering and pain that can cause more damage. Is an act of violence intrinsically worse than the act that causes lingering, profound psychological pain?

A lot of value is dismissively dedicated to non-violence without an extensive, comprehensive account for this intuition, evading the question of the quality of moral utilities between physical violence and psychological manipulation or harm. Psychological distress can drive a person towards great suffering, madness, and death. Psychological pain can cause much greater and much more profound pain and suffering than torn skin and broken bones. Sticks and stones can break bones, but words can incite war. However, the psychology and spirit of violence is bound to the practice of morality involving actions causing pain through physical and mental violence or coercion. This Chapter will be dedicated to a comprehensive discussion of the morality of violence.

First, one may speculate that even though mental distress does pose a risk of leading to pain, injury, and death, that risk is fundamentally less than if a person was to be subjected to the chaotic and unpredictable temper of physical violence. Even the seemingly lightest act of violence, such as pushing somebody, can end up as a fatal accident. One simple aspect to consider is this – violence inherently carries with it a risk of causing unjust, bad consequences and avoidable suffering. This risk qualifies itself in terms of consequences of both fatal and non-fatal incidents, as physical violence can leave one permanently injured or induce other forms pain and damage such as psychological distress. However, all of this would depend on the context of an act and the extent of the force of an act, physical and psychological.

Violence often causes long-standing, continuous grievances that divide people, for violence carries with it a powerful psychological and spiritual influence. Violence can lead to unrepairable consequences, while mental distress and pain, even the most profound, in my experience, can be remedied and alleviated, even if not completely absolved, to a greater extent than permanent physical pain and damage. But then one can learn to live happily with certain physical ills, as pain doesn't have to detract from a fulfilling life.

Acts of violence cause mental distress not only in the subject of its force, but also reflects onto the character perpetuating violence. Intuition and intuitive reasoning do not in themselves suffice as comprehensive criteria for examining the effects of violence, but practical wisdom and experience in those qualified to make good judgements provide a much better source of insight into the morality of violence. It may even be the case that those more experienced with the effects of violence do not reflect on it in a satisfactory way, succumbing to its effects and grievance.

It is often the case that the victims of violence are the ones that continue it and reflect it, for confronting its pain internally and its Fear is too much for the undisciplined, weak will. But what one cannot underestimate and would be mindful to remember is that violence carries with it an exceptionally strong force on the mind and spirit. However, any consideration of the risks of violence, physical or psychological, requires context. It is difficult to say whether physical violence is inherently worse than strong psychological pain. Even psychological abuse, such as through lies and manipulation, is only indirectly physical – of another sort of contact, different to the immediate force acting on the body.

For instance, while a punch is physical in terms of contacting the skin, muscle, and bone, the waves of sound from a spoken word are physical in terms of substance beyond that of the body directly. There is no doubt that the adverse effects of any form of spiritual and psychological pain are real. Physical and psychological violence are different criteria of pain and different sorts of moral utilities, the risks of which cannot be completely formulated into moral absolutes, nor comprehensively qualified in comparisons of danger and damage. However, the physical effects of violence and the spirit of violence can never be excluded from the mental and spiritual aspect of violence. The force exerted by any action will always have an impressionable effect, and violence, both physical and psychological, as a strong force, carries with it distinctive criteria for consideration in practical morality.

Violence committed in Fear, whether physical or psychological, committed on impulse or deliberation, carries with it a powerful force that affects the psyche and spirit. The desire to control and for power in Fear has a profound influence on acts of violence. Violence is the pinnacle of Fear; it is a curse of Fear, an affliction. The essence of violence arises in the anger and frustration that moves to violence – fear of the loss of control. It is an inclination, an impulse, and a craving borne of Fear striving for control. It is natural and common, even if unhealthy, for anger and frustration to instigate violent urges, even if only targeting an inanimate object. Anger and frustration are not inherently wrong or bad, although how these elements of the psyche are implemented in behaviour is subject to moralising. However, sometimes violence comes from deep within, as a broad momentum of a state of mind consumed by Fear.

Sometimes violent urges are not only momentary, of an immediate inclination of anger, but symptomatic of a deep Fear overwhelming the mind and spirit. Sometimes violence and its constant urges and pain come from a profound Fear that gets no release, has no liberty, and is granted no fulfilment and relief. This anger and Fear fester in the back of the mind, corrupt and consume everything in life, infect everything as a pestilence of vice.

As a child, I was exposed to violence of conflict and hate in Israel during the Al-Aqsa Intifada as both the victim of a bully unleashing his hatred and as a sufferer of my own reactionary violence that nearly culminated in me drowning after being pinned under water. I was about six years old. The incident is blurry, segmented. But the feeling is clear to this day. That fear as my chest was beating on its last breath as I was desperately trying to reach up a few inches to breathe, while scraping and beating the leg holding me underwater, is something that I had buried but never forgot.

While that fear had resided in me in another form over my lifetime, fear burned into my impressionable mind at that age.

Even though the moment is more a blur of still images, the feeling remained. The clearer memory is that of the moment straight after when I was sitting by the water trying to process what happened. I vividly remember that absence of thought and feeling – that emptiness. In that moment my life changed and something was ripped out of me that would never be recovered, only to regrow into something very different. The effect of that moment of violence continued into my adolescence and early adulthood. It became an integral part of my developing psyche and I carry its weight even today, even as a sealed scar.

Violence has a common place in the world, as a utility of impulse and an outlet for pain, as torture and defence. Violence has a special relation to Fear and so much of its effect is more profound than rationalisation and the efficiency of effective moral actions. Violence possesses a distinct property in its force that stings at a very profound level of the mind and spirit. It has become clear to me that violence is most usually both physical and psychological, but physical violence always carries with it the contingent element of exercising a powerful force on the psyche. But while a physical force is not immediately equivalent to violence and its abuse and torment, such as playful physical interaction or contact sports not being bad forms of violence, physical violence always carries with it a powerful force on the spirit and mind. While this can invoke some very negative feelings and be very troubling in spirit, from the pain of violence can also arise an even greater goodness by succeeding violence as both perpetrator and subject.

There is no definitive argument for the following case, but those familiar with the violence know or may learn how deep its effects can be. I do not require deferral to any sense of self-ratified wisdom to say that violence has a profound effect on people. A war or act of violence or killing in one era carries its weight of injustice for centuries. Violence carries with it a primal and dominating power of Fear. People both fear it and crave it; then the fear of violence provokes a lust for it. Its force and impulse are often so powerful that in the moment one does not recognise the effect and spirit of violence. Few are mindful in the moments of violent experiences and moral extremes; few understand what happens to them when violence afflicts them. In trying times of great pain, one does not commonly realise that he or she is in such a moment, instead preoccupied with immediate reactions of escaping or avoiding such a state, as is similar with spiritual emptiness and psychological dissatisfaction.

Through Fear, violence leads to more violence. My impression and Fear borne of violence led to more violence through me. For a time, I had an unhealthy release that only fed the craving. At first it was just fights, then vandalism, then hunting animals without necessity and without remorse, followed by experimenting. Some speak of romanticised visions of themselves as monsters or demons, but there is none such comparable to that of violence, the craving of which becomes more than any other desire or need, becoming a greater impulse than thirst and hunger, becoming blind, turning all spirit into one dominant craving beyond animal instinct – a craving and evil only a person is capable of.

Where the instincts of animals make them act violently, they do so in Fear and with the purpose of survival. But mankind uses violence not only for survival, but also for a warped sense of satisfaction in Fear through the craving to control through blood, destruction, and pain. We all want to be the kings of pain, but in this desire we only become its slaves. Acts of violence beyond instinct make us the evil that we ascribe to the terrors of our imagination, resembling the horrors described in old books and traditions – the evil of mankind. In knowing and living with this part of the self there is little grace and joy, but there is Liberty. There is no greater hate than hatred towards oneself, and this terrible pain is without bounds.

When violence afflicts an emerging life, it leaves its marks. Where it first becomes an impression and experience, if unaddressed, it grows with the person, becomes a part of him or her. Where one might see it as a parasite or inconvenient utility that once may have had its merits, in some cases that element of violence becomes not a contingency of character, but a fundamental among many. The person grows with that violence, becomes it, whereas the soul and humanity become twisted into something demonised and monstrous. But it must be hidden, because few-to-none would understand, and it certainly wouldn't serve a constructive purpose, as impulsive judgements are natural and easy for people.

The affliction of violence warps the world around a person. When it pierces one's very being from a young age, it becomes a fundamental part of the person until pain consumes the mind, grows, and dominates one's being, forming another identity. In that pain few seem to recognise what is happening, few are mindful of what fear and the pain of violence are doing to them. Any form of conformity with society becomes a necessity, whereby one lives a lie and hides in plain sight. The pain is supressed until the whole mind and spirit become numb, and with it the self becomes buried; the spirit of humanity is extinguished. All acts of living become a conscious inclination towards conformity, towards faking most manners of behaviour and reaction. And even when one loses the interest or care to sustain this mode of conformity, you still must bury that most fundamental part of you, to continue hiding, living trapped in your own mind, in a fragile cage held together by excess discipline and desire for control. But such a mode of morality and spirit is never completely sustainable.

At some point it needs to give way to the liberty of virtue in goodwill to overcome the pain tormenting the spirit and consuming the will. And if one cannot do it themselves, then it is others' duty to intervene if liberty is deprived of virtue and goodness. It seems to be a trend where people strive for individuality, for difference, for noteworthiness. What I wouldn't have given for such a luxury when I was younger, where now I relish in the Liberty of being *no one*. But now I know that this is only another delusion of freedom in Fear, from judgement I eluded for a long time. The most important judge is that of one's own soul and spirit, how one feels about themself, influenced by the concerns for others' impressions. To be free is to be honest with oneself. The one true judge of character is one's *conscience*.

At one point my environment changed rapidly and old habits could not be sustained. There was no release and my world was crumbling around me. The cravings got worse. For far too long violence was a way to release my pain, and if it was to get any worse it would be the end of anything good, an end to any future without this pain. I was hopeless in my predicament and chose that if my world was to end, it would at least end on my own terms. I would have a final say over my life, that I would not succumb to the violence that sought to spread like a disease, that fed on me for so long, that I would not become a part of the same thing that tormented me and others – Fear. I would not let Fear compromise who I was any longer, no more. In my desperation, I turned to desperate means, more than once. I chose to sever the fundamental part of me that was craving violence, that was in pain from the poison spreading under my skin from my spine to my fingers, pulsing with a burning sensation that could not be released. If there was to be an end to this parasite, it would have to die with me.

That was one of the last times for much of my life where I felt anything, where mental states and emotions turned into physical sensations of cutting and burning in my chest. But I could get no end, the apparent final acts of defiance that gave sensations of peace and relief, which ultimately became a focal point of future living, mixed with bewilderment and humour in pain that I wasn't given the rest I sought after, that something kept waking me up when I didn't intend to. I was yet to learn that this pain was to be that of a healing wound. My hate was boundless, towards the world and towards myself. Survival was fruitless, but what living I had was worth more than a life bound to destruction and pain without end.

The pain of violence and its compulsions haunted me, itched at the back of my mind and kept tapping from within my skull, oozing its venom across my limbs as a silent scream burning and pulling from the inside. It would not come out; it would not use me and discard me; it would not reduce my humanity to that of a parasite. I bear the cost of my circumstance; I held it bound in Discipline and Defiance until I made it subservient to the ambition of goodwill. But it is there nonetheless.

Once one has known violence as its subject and as a utility, it will never be forgotten or lost. But the pain and suffering of violence, while as distressing as any great pain, can be known to be one's own. The residue of violence that affected me for so long was *mine*, of my own soul. And because it was bound to my soul it was *my* pain and ultimately that of *my* ambition in life. Since it is a pain of my living and a device of my soul and mind, I will do with it as my ambition commands, known fully and made worthy through virtue-duty. This pain would eventually become the solace fulfilled through virtue-duty, completing life through eudaimonia making peace with the corrosive disease of violence.

Pain, suffering, and Fear broke me, more than once, but they did not defeat me. The most useful thing I learnt was to channel that pain and use it to make my will stronger, to expand my ambition, to use it as a resource in dealing with that very same pain, to use pain for my own ends, to achieve what good spirit I could in unfavourable circumstances that we are all confronted with in reality. Then, when the use of this attitude expired, known through mindfulness and honest self-reflection, the utility that channelled pain was dismissed for recovery and relaxation.

The essence of this has come to me now as balancing the physical state of my body and its chronic pain and related effects, whereby the constant stress of pain, when mediated, gives focus and optimum activity under pressure, but one that can lead to burn-out, as I learnt painfully, when lacking mindfulness and moderation. Suffering once became so much that all that remained was numbness, later to be revived in the most resonant sensation of equally boundless empathy, compassion, and relief. I came to realise that I was becoming that which I feared most – a person consumed with disruptive Fear and its bitterness. I chose to defy the element that tried to make me the way it wished, that was forcing me into suffering and pain, that sought to enslave me and destroy me. The pain was great and it still persists in another form even if not as spiritual suffering, but my sense and intuition tell me it was all worth it.

Later I learnt or remembered empathy, and found that those consumed by violence are as much its victims, and that those weak in Fear are victims, warranting compassion or pity, not hate, certainly not further pain and violence, even if only for one's own sake to rise above Fear. And so I set myself to find Harmony with what sustained me through the pain – Defiance.

On reflection I am amazed that one such moment, one such element or link to Fear, could rule over a life, could do something like that to a person. Violence can twist a person beyond measure. But by embracing and overcoming its pain one can learn the most profound and complete virtue of humanity – to be more than mere impulse or detachment from sentiment. One moment of violence can lead down a terrible tangent of discord, destruction, pain, and madness. We subject each other to so much psychological and physical torment through our feebleness and weakness in pain... I see so many lives ruined and consumed by violence. Violence can cause so much havoc and inflict so much pain, yet by overcoming it, becoming more than its force trying to consume the psyche and spirit, we can achieve much greater fulfilment than submission to Fear through violence. As the force of violence is imbued with terrible Fear, it can also evoke the most tremendous relief and profound release by letting go of that Fear and through the courage to forgive. I would learn that this was higher fulfilment in Liberty and the seed of eudaimonia. Violence carries with it an extraordinary force on the mind and spirit, and its tangents are extreme. For this reason, violence requires extensive consideration of its place in practical morality.

Revealing this personal note is not something I would have preferred to do. Any illusion of normality would most definitely vanish. But in the present context of studying and discussing the morality of violence, if my input can serve as valuable insight into the nature of violence and appropriate morality, if it can prevent even one person from going down the path I was bound to, if it helps a person of any faith or creed to understand the corruptive effect of violence, then such is my duty, the only manner in which I can be honest with myself. My story is one of many, and if it furthers understanding and insight into the effects of violence and the role of violence in morality, then it had to be said.

What is most important is to help people subjected to violence understand what is happening to them, to create a point of mindfulness to reflect on the corruption of violence, and in terms of the ethos of Liberty move one to dominate that which is wildest – violence. It may be appealing to stand by an oath to oneself to never commit violence again, to never become a slave to pain and Fear once more, to never be an agent of demeaning injustice. But in such Fear, one may also become corrupted by a desire for misconceived absolution from vice, sowing another species of vice and suffering. Any such devout moralising would fail to achieve higher Liberty in morality and spirit.

In the pursuit of Liberty in pain and fear, one can succumb to another of its forms, and without discipline maintaining a balance of duty and pleasure through virtue, Liberty will not be actualised, fulfilled, achieved, or sustained. Similarly, attachment to the Human Imperative and the Highest Good, attachment to do what is right by the world, can lead to mistakes of attachment and compassion, to facilitate another breed of Fear, leading to excess violence and down a tangent and cycle of other vice.

Here the necessary balance of liberty, mindfulness, and discipline should become clear – of pleasure, virtue, and duty. I appeal to the normative rule that has inspired mankind since the early ages – the doctrine of the mean, the rule of balance in reason. But for too long has our understanding of reason, psyche, and spirit been incomplete; it has lacked the fundamental piece for fulfilment and flourishing through Liberty. Reason has been desynchronised, leading to moral confusion and discord, failing to achieve spiritual liberty and balance, contrary to the superficial and fragile balance of trying to control rather than allow virtue to flow freely through the will.

The moral case of violence, to me at least, is a primary case of the doctrine of the mean, the rule of balance that guides practical morality. At its core, the rule of balance is complete through mindfulness by the Void, the Ploy, and their contingent Liberty. When in doubt, defer to reason, meditation, and reflection on, and analysis of, Fear or intuitive suggestions, desires, and ambitions.

My familiarity with the corruption of violence in both its physical and psychological dimensions has provided insight. From the mental state of violence and Fear I have learnt much and extracted many positive utilities. I have grown far beyond the state that affected me so much, now only to be subservient to ambition to exceed further beyond Fear and to sustain Liberty, hopefully in goodwill. No one is perfect, nobody is of absolute virtue – most certainly not me. Nelson Mandela once famously said: "I am not a saint, unless you think of a saint as a sinner who keeps on trying," a resolve deserving a note.

I am by no means a pinnacle of virtue. But the liberty, strength, and resolve to keep trying is what moves us to virtue, what moves us to flourish. Even though I am far from done growing myself, maturing, developing in character, learning values and lessons, finding my place in the world, I will do what I can and must in the goodwill of what virtue I have and strive to nurture. In this I have found one of the most precious and deceptively simple lessons – that of faith in humanity, at least in myself. I have moved far beyond the state that was corrupted and twisted by the affliction of violence. I have come further than I initially thought I could, although my expectations and ambitions were much simpler before. But if I could move past that pain and vice, so can anyone else, provided the opportunity and inspiration. I have to believe that even when there is little hope, faith can remain, and this can be a powerful conviction and utility. Any person can move beyond the indignity, degradation, pain, and suffering of vice if he or she chooses to do so and if empowered. I am only one case for this view of empathy; I am only one story among many.

I have learnt that violence and its contingent vices are not always an ordinary moral utility or mentality. Violence may be employed as a means to an end such as to protect others. Violence can have an effect on the psyche and spirit of the individual, yet its corruptive force may be insignificant. However, it is common for violence to be a symptom of much more profound Fear, whereby violence *becomes* Fear. The violence of a mind corrupted and consumed by Fear is not moral, not political, not religious, and not deliberative. Violence does not become a deliberation, but deliberation and justification follow the inclination and compulsion moved by violence in Fear.

It has become clear to me, a thought that will guide the following discussions, that violence in Fear is an affliction, an unordinary vice rooted in more profound troubles and pains than a deliberative choice moved by an ethos of Fear. Violence is a disease of Fear. As such, I will treat the practical morality concerning violence in similar terms to that of a complex disease of mental, psychological, social, and bodily factors. While I am not dedicated to an in-depth investigation into the development and instigation of violence in terms of its many contributing factors, I will keep this in mind in moralising the normativity of violence.

Violence can be a mere moral utility, but it can also be something more profound – a disease borne of Fear and the lack of empathy. Most will know that we live in an age vexed by violence. Genocide and slaughter are a disease of violence destroying, consuming, and holding back communities, degrading people, and are structural inefficiencies in terms of the Human Imperative. But even psychological violence is too common in developed societies where people relinquish physical violence for its other forms.

Is not the vindictive, vengeful, punishing act of 'getting back' at another person for perceived mistreatment not violence – an act causing pain? Is not the manipulative abuser inflicting psychological pain committing psychological violence? I consider this is another form of violence that can also be unjust and a variant disease of Fear.

The disease of violence still afflicts the global community. This disease must be treated like any other – it should be remedied, contained, and eradicated. Its vectors ought to be treated and neutralised. However, these vectors follow ethical tangents contingent on the strong effects of violence. Reparative and preventative measures must be considered along eliminative hardlines as immediate solutions. Any morality of violence must consider and formulate the morality of defending against violence in immediate circumstances, such as by using violence to prevent greater, unjust violence, while also considering how to protect oneself from the corruptive effects of violence, pain, and Fear. This will relate strongly to the discussion of moral brutalism.

While there are many tools we use to treat violence, a moral and spiritual approach should also be employed for long-term, sustainable solutions. However, idealised and spiritualised moral utilities of high-reason related to violence are insufficient. Not all can yet be trusted to rely on their higher faculties to grow beyond a state of violence and vice. This was the case for me and it will be the case for many; I got lucky. The reasoning of virtues requires affirmative action. Hence, other utilities tackling violence and vice beyond the scope of reasoning, suffering-love, and sacrifice may be necessary.

As was discussed with the many measures one might morally employ to counter and remedy the effects of pain and suffering along the pursuit of virtue, utilities to ease violence, vice, and pain may come in unexpected ways. For instance, where the impulses of violence affected me profoundly, to which I responded with extreme actions, there was always the shadow of meditation and mindfulness that eventually led to a different direction of growth. However, in those moments, I often found a hint of peace from the most basic attribute of my being as a young bloke – through the wonder of pretty girl.

Even throughout all the hate, anger, and pain that shrouded my being, a basic attribute of myself gave me a new element of vision through the simplest of things given to me – appreciation of a pretty girl. Then also the bliss of funny cat videos. Even one minor spark of change in the dynamics of great suffering, whether in great stress or the void of depression, any capacity to employ a utility in goodwill and good spirit can inspire and evoke virtue. Anything that can change how you think and feel in the moment can be useful. The use of any such utilities or aspects towards new or greater ambition can serve a broader ambition of Liberty.

When the individual feels empowered by virtues, is strong in character, and draws on the pleasures and fulfilment of moral and spiritual liberty, goodwill moves in accordance with virtue-duty, which reflects into the world. For liberty to be sustained it must be moved with the ambition of the Human Imperative, which is found and acknowledged through profound Liberty. Liberty can only be fully sustained when it is in accordance with goodwill and ambition by the Human Imperative and the Highest Good. This itself must evolve with liberty and its normative element in structures of ethics and their Natural Laws.

Liberty can only be sustained and fully actuated through duty of the Imperative towards the world. One ought to act according to the duty to remedy suffering in the world when righteous and virtuous. People and the global community cannot be at absolute Liberty until the strong, overwhelming, and corrupt force of Fear is removed. The individual may achieve eudaimonia, especially under the pressure of pain that is overcome through the spirit of dominant virtues and at spiritual liberty. But while the individual may achieve such a liberty, the community will stay in pain in terms of those still trapped in vice.

Violence ought to be protected against and its source remedied with appropriate measures of virtuous moral utilities. Sometimes it may become the case where channelling base faculties, even with deceit and trickery, without emphasised development of harmony in reason, becomes a necessary and more preferable means than brutal approaches. This is the foundation for the practical morality of violence.

One could contest whether physical violence is worse than psychological violence. While any sensible and moral person would concede that both are wrong when unjust, it seems that physical violence is often taken for granted to be inherently worse than psychological violence. I am not convinced that physical violence is absolutely worse than psychological violence. Both can have deep, profound effects on the psyche of an individual and group. Physical violence may at times evoke much greater immediate public concern, while psychological violence may be more scrupulous, yet both can have devastating effects.

As was claimed previously, the immorality of physical and psychological violence is contextual and circumstantial with respect to their effects and tangents. That said, one cannot be inherently qualified to be worse than the other. Physical violence may entail an immediately greater risk of devastating consequences such as death and permanent injury, as well as breed grave vice through irreversible deeds. Yet psychological violence can lead to long-term consequences that are much more devastating than the immediate injury of one person. However, mental distress and suffering, and most, if not all vice, can be overcome.

Psychological damage can be as permanent as physical injuries. But that which does not cripple or kill the individual can lead to growth and virtue if the conditions and received nurture are accommodating. In light of these points, it must be ratified that neither physical nor psychological violence is inherently worse than the other, and when either category of unjust violence is employed it ought to be condemned as unjust and immoral.

The practical morality that engages the two categories of violence should be mindful of appropriateness. For instance, the roots of psychological violence may not be sustainably resolved through physical (violent) means, just as physical violence may not be sustainably addressed through mere psychological or physical means. Moralising, reasoning, and persuasion are not universally sustainable approaches to tackling the disease of violence. In this period of new hyper-globalised normativity and mentality, where the very nature of war and violence has changed, all societies are afflicted with a singled-out breed of violence – terrorism and extremism. I would postulate that 'terrorism' and extremism are far from anything new to the global community. Some might argue that extremism is inherent to certain ancient convictions. But due to the changes in the structure of the global community, terrorism and extremism have adopted a distinct form and pose a particular threat to the modern world.

Terrorism and extremism persist in underdeveloped parts of society and have transformed through modern utilities and equipment, particularly with respect to explosives. The nature of violence has transformed through modernity to become a much stronger force. A bomb will have more force than a knife. One-dimensional and unilateral moral and psychological approaches to alleviating violence are not sufficient, because some individuals' vices can't be left untouched, and foregoing this would neglect values in the dynamics of ethics. It is sensible to claim that saving a law-abiding, peaceful citizen is better than sparing the life of a rampaging sociopath. Therefore, physical violence may be an appropriate means to tackling physical violence to preserve and ensure justice.

Yet psychological deceit and trickery could prevent outbreaks of physical violence without engaging in potentially lethal use of physical violence. A crook or madman preparing to commit a violent atrocity might be stopped through non-violent means such as deceit or manipulation. It is intuitive to posit that this can serve as a legitimate means of justice to tackle the emergence of violence.

However, the underlying roots of violence can never be addressed or fully resolved in absolutes of physical violence and require a parallel approach through morality and influence, force, or even coercion (that is, a strong or excessive force, with excess potentially being moral and legitimate in high-risk scenarios). The roots of violence are usually very deep and weeding them out cannot be achieved through radical eliminative means. An approach to violence through the universality of violent means striving to eradicate all violence through further violence by killing every individual committing violence is unrealistic and inherently corruptive and unstable. A brutal approach to violence through total elimination and unquestioned, unregulated killing will lead down a tangent of vice that could consume and affect itself through that same violence. Employing moral and psychological means to address the root of violence is intended to serve as another dimension of utilities acting against violence and as a more fundamental approach to treating the roots of violence, which would include the many factors contributing to violent outbursts, from personal to socioeconomic. Just as importantly, psychological and non-physical, somewhat tacit means of addressing physical violence are necessary as protective measures against the major inherent risk of the corruptive force of violence.

Employing physical violence to counteract psychological violence can become susceptible to corruptive tangents of the vices relating to physical violence. Using physical violence against psychological violence far from guarantees the resolution of the source psychological violence exploits and targets. If a manipulative abuser exploits a vulnerability of the psyche, it is better to use that pain against itself to feed the growth of virtue and strength, overwhelming the force of psychological violence used by another. This is an example of *ambition* of goodwill.

I wouldn't argue punching or knocking out a manipulative abuser is wrong, but killing him or her without an immediate necessity of justice would be wrong. If the victim of psychological abuse is turning to violence against others, then a bilateral approach, potentially even eliminative, could be appropriate. However, if psychological abuse is leading to the liberty of painful and unhealthy ways of coping, then only liberty to pursue virtue can solve the underlying weaknesses, vulnerabilities, and faults causing suffering. If psychological violence leads to suicide, which is very different to a person directly killing another, even this does not justify killing. However, this could justify an immediate measure of physical violence to silence the abuser to ensure a more just, balanced, and harmonious outcome. Then again, a non-physical approach to counteracting the influence of the abuser should take priority, unless immediate circumstances demand action, suggesting that pre-emptive approaches should employ non-physical, compassionate, and fundamental reparative means over physical violence.

The manipulative abuser is also suffering in Fear and vice, perhaps more so than the victim that is suffering from vulnerability rather than depravity. By being eager to kill, to employ eliminative physical violence, a moral tangent will move towards moral brutalism stripped of empathetic intuition and goodwill. By allowing empathy to fail and its virtue to wither, its intuition and utilities will not be effective or capable in other scenarios. The abuser is another suffering soul, and so it too ought to be remedied. Undermining this intuition of empathy will, to a degree, reflect back as the lack of empathy towards one's own soul that is universalisable, a sibling to the other soul. This leads to lack of mindfulness, lack of will, and deprivation of spirit and Liberty through Harmony.

However, these same elements will be just as neglected if value is recklessly misjudged. If the abuser is given preferential treatment over the vulnerable victim, empathy, judgement, and mindfulness will become even more misguided and lead to degenerative outcomes affecting the world and oneself. Therefore, more stern and ruthless modes of virtue may be just and legitimate in counteracting the corruptive and destructive force of the abuser, including towards the embodiment of the abuser's catalyst of vice – his or her fundamental will and life.

Being mindful of this is crucial in all endeavours of violence and moral brutalism. Judgement and considerations of value are imperative to this, and ultimately this can only be reduced and passed on to individual intuition, ability, character, and judgement. A supposed major flaw in this is the limit of people's cognition, which can only be sustainably addressed and solved through personal practical wisdom or trust in the wise judgement of others – specialist ethicists and philosophers.

Strong attachment and desire for a sense of justice can lead to violence and injustice through mistakes of attachment and compassion. Fear breeds and comes with attachment. This is valid and applicable to the ethos pursuing Liberty, for higher Liberty is only achieved in the liberty not to pursue it, to be in limbo bound to the ambition of goodwill (as with the Ploy of Consciousness). Attachment and Fear can lead to excess force in violence that ends with an act of killing. However, this momentary act of vice could save the life of another, which suggests that it is less than ideal, but still a good outcome. This would retain a tangent of vice in Fear, and the individual acting on the vice of Fear will continue to suffer, more so than the grief resolved through letting go of a lost attachment.

The pain of loss will not immediately be greater than the suffering of continued attachment. Yet that same attachment will breed lingering suffering, while also evoking greater fulfilment in continued, peaceful, non-conflicting attachment. I specifically argue that not all attachment and not all Fear are wrong, bad, or cause pain and suffering. Attachment in Fear can ensure greater succession of value and these tangents in Fear cannot fairly be qualified as vices, for they will not inherently lead to great pain, immorality, or acts corrupted by Fear – those betraying their own function of flourishing through an ethos of Fear. However, these modes of ethics are not argued to be ideal, even though good, because they are not necessarily consistent with Liberty and are more vulnerable to ethical influences.

These tangents of morality correspond directly to the mindfulness of empathy. Empathy liberates the spirit and guides moral intuition in accord with goodwill. The mindfulness necessary to retain concentration and appreciation of the universalis-able soul can be very difficult to practise, yet extremely rewarding and liberating, as well as provide a formidable utility. Following tangents away from this mindfulness, as is very common in accentuated base-reason, leads to suffering, lesser mindfulness, lesser willpower, and lesser fulfilment. These tangents are not wrong and might not be unjust, but they are limited, depriving both the individual and community in contrast to a liberating and more fulfilling morality.

An accusation that the pursuit of Liberty deprives itself of fulfilling attachment is a legitimate one. I do not conceive Liberty as full detachment as with the case of corruption by the Void, but rather as the dual liberty to be attached and/or not to be attached. But attachment to the world and to life itself can not only restrict ambition and fulfilment, in comparison to Liberty warranting greater fulfilment in all things, but can lead to corruptive attachments that betray the pursued interest. An ambition consumed by the avoidance of, and protection from, Fear, to reach the highest peak and become a reigning king, is not only unrealistic, but most importantly self-defeat-ing and contradictory, for Fear will always remain and inflict pain through the spirit's and mind's submission to it.

Violence can be one of the most forceful and coercive manifestations of this blind morality and ethos consumed with Fear. Yet even if this morality is not the most re-warding and not ideal, it can still warrant greater, even if not the greatest, reward and goodness; it can still be a proportionally satisfactory means of justice, even if not the paragon of justice. Deviating from empathy and compassion in obsession with Fear can also betray that which is most fulfilling to the individual – by betraying someone a person is most attached to. Violence can easily subsume compassion and consume empathy, depriving oneself of fulfilment in Fear through attachment. That attach-ment, even when dominated by spirit of Fear, is not wrong, but it can betray itself through consumption of Fear.

Liberty in attachment is the liberty to care, the liberty to receive fulfilment even when Fear clouds happiness, but also, equally, the liberty to flourish through attach-ment free from the attachment being consumed and betrayed by Fear that under-mines the goodness of the attachment. Violence is one of the most powerful tangents corrupting liberty and attachment through Fear.

Pain is not inherently bad and can lead to much good. Pain and suffering moti-vate, facilitate growth and improvement. This virtue-rule relates itself strongly to the nature of duty, which follows the Human Imperative and the ambitions of virtue. Suffering is the test of duty, an incentive, and a resource of ambition. Pursuing duty will cause suffering and pain to the self, but its rewards come from these afflictions, which distinguishes character with virtue-duty. But succumbing to the fear of fail-ing one's duty, corrupting duty with the vices of Fear, will lead to pointless suffer-ing through misapplied efforts. Along these tangents of duty and their corruption in Fear, violence and the desire for control can corrupt duty and subsequently virtuous character. The morality of Harmony is intended to assist duty threatened by the cor-ruption and impulses of violence.

While attachment is fulfilling in ordinary spheres of living, duty can become misguided and lose mindfulness if one is not especially mindful of the mode of at-tachment and its tangents. Moral duty in extremes can be demanding and testing, requiring an appeal to moral brutalism. The Void assists in this endeavour, whereby duty is moved by a comprehensive attachment distinguished from narrow, base at-tachment. Even so, that same attachment is balanced through the Void and is wholly subservient to liberty and the ambition of goodwill found through Liberty.

As is known through mindfulness by the Void, no action and no endeavour is ultimately necessary. A world consumed with violence and destruction is just as existentially legitimate and permissible as a peaceful, ideal world, yet the former would contradict virtue and living in Liberty. These are more sophisticated and designated ethical tangents relevant to moral brutalism and moral extremes. Nonetheless, it is imperative to employ this aspect of the heritin ethos to formulate and guide intuitions susceptible to corruptive inclinations of violence.

One may be tempted to employ disproportionate, unjust utilities of moral brutalism through excessively eliminative measures, thereby resorting to violence while unmindful of the ambitions and intuitions of goodwill. Just as empathy serves to maintain mindfulness and discipline in utilities of the baser faculties, so too it is relevant to the utilities of the higher faculties. The Void and the Ploy become integral to mediating high-reason falling prey to the corruption of Fear deprived of goodwill and the directives of empathy and liberty. This attachment and the desire to control can deceive and turn duties into something morally abhorrent.

Duty formulated in high-reason considering violence must be weighed with the mindfulness of empathy and mindfulness by the Void to mediate attachments to duty and the desire to do good. To maintain truly good intentions and to prevent the desire to do good from betraying itself through excess, one must learn to detach from, but not dissolve, the desire to do good and be good, or else a person will succumb to the fear of doing the wrong thing and the fear of failing to be good.

A good way to illustrate the understanding of Liberty in attachment can be expressed in Alfred Lord Tennyson's famous quote: "Tis better to have loved and lost than never to have loved at all." This is liberty in attachment: to not be afraid to experience fulfilment and to become attached. However, at the same time, this means not to succumb to the fear of loss that will lead to loss itself. It is in Fear to lose love that we may betray that love.

A similar species of Fear is expressed as violence borne of loss and the loss of control, of powerlessness. If loss is necessary for justice, is necessary for duty and for what is right, then such loss and sacrifice brings pleasure and fulfilment of another sort, greater than that of attachment. Where a loss is so great that a person loses a part of themselves, this cruel fate can be risen above, and a person achieves eudaimonia as the freedom from and in happiness. Sometimes we must let go of those we are most attached to in order to make them happier, to make things better, and to better oneself through duty and virtue. This same sort of Liberty in Fear that harbours violence brings fulfilment that is much greater than the spirit enslaved to violence and Fear; greater Liberty is found through detachment from idealism and serenity.

Violence can carry with it a profound effect on the mind and character. Even if one is detached and emotionally numb, the character will still succumb to vices of Fear and follow down degenerative tangents. Violence is a primary manifestation of Fear. It is a great virtue to defy Fear in violence and be composed under terrible Fear. To relinquish Fear in the face of pain through violence and not respond in similar vice marks grand virtue. To not concede one's principles under the threat of violence, by turning the other cheek, leads to Ideal virtues. Sacrifice is the mark and culmination of virtue and of a good life.

To relinquish violence moves character to reach beyond the primal submission to Fear in violence. Losing control or losing anything worth attachment can be painful and frustrating. Attachment and its corresponding utility to control breeds Fear and pain through loss, thereby degrading spirit and character. The goodness of attachment can easily corrupt itself. It is greater to learn to let go, to learn the pleasure of Liberty in that which causes pain, but not as mere detachment and substitution, rather as genuine liberty of selective moral utility guiding fulfilment and as inner strength.

There is pleasure to be found and appreciated in righteous sacrifice – by letting go of Fear and succeeding over pain in Fear, to become more than a token and subject of Fear and suffering, to bind such things to one's own ambition and ambition's goodwill. This is the spirit of higher autonomy beyond Fear. Rejecting violence is a manifestation of that commitment to liberty in pain, relinquishing submissive attempts to control one's environment without ever having true power to control oneself beyond the effects of Fear and environment – to become an empowered and unshackled vector.

In the power to compose oneself, especially to be disciplined in and against violence, one can control many elements of his or her life through adaptive and impetuous attitudes. For example, being impetuous and assertive when people act against one's interests, or harnessing the courage, strength, or even ruthlessness to get rid of corruptive and toxic elements in one's life, are ethics that can only be implemented through self-control. Then, when the virtues of one's character are sufficient, the Void and the Ploy complete Liberty, and sacrifice becomes neither opportunity or test, but an intuition of duty. That same sacrifice will also manifest itself as the duty to sacrifice others according to the necessity of justice to protect value and others, to hold true to the fundamentals of the Human Imperative – the value of life and ethical progress.

Sacrifice is a distinctive element of morality. It goes far beyond theory alone. Therefore, it deserves its own dedicated discussion. While the control of pain as a method of aversion is related to sacrifice, the discourse and analysis of the latter will be moved to another Chapter. That said, sacrifice and the pain of loss are not meant to be dismissed or neglected. Grief is one of the most powerful forms of pain, greater than the pain inflicted by violence.

To pursue ruthless ambition in sacrifice, especially to sacrifice loved ones, would be a mistake and would be misguided, as these intuitions perpetuate tangents of vice. Pain and loss are not to be dismissed. But more on this later. For now, it is important to make a note that ruthless sacrifice and the pain of loss are not of goodwill, and righteousness is not characterised by ruthlessness in the sacrifice for the sake of power and control. Sacrifice and loss are not a matter of feeling good about them, but learning to be reborn from such pain, to maintain one's heart and sensibility. As is known to many intuitions, pain inflicted on loved ones can be far greater than the pain of self-sacrifice. Death is not the worst thing, as torment in living can be much greater.

Committing to a path of violence is the begging of control, an act of yielding to Fear through which none have actual control. The power to subject others to pain is a form of power that is submissive to, and blind in, Fear through which the self has no real power over the world as the self is a mere slave to the will deprived of greater ambition. Autonomy and Liberty in Fear, such as discipline in violence, are greater powers of the character and the will. The vector of violence and frustration will never achieve fulfilment of any significance in a life bound to desperate attempts to shed pain, only to feed pain in a cruel manipulation through Fear. Such vice always implodes on itself and consumes the mind and spirit. Surrendering to violence only subsumes desperation in Fear.

The character of vice that begs for control through violence is degrading, demeaning, pitiful, and devalued. Those who commit atrocities of violence for self-gratification in Fear, such as beheading or torturing others, or those who maliciously and violently degrade others to gain a sense of control over insecurity, are of woeful and petty character and ambition. They are cowards in Fear, failing to confront their own pain and resorting to demeaning conduct of projecting rather than resolving such pain, and beyond vulnerability and tolerable weakness – they are immoral and of vice. As such, these characters, the likes of extremists and abusers, rot in their vice and are deprived of virtue giving real fulfilment and liberty in spirit.

It is better to use the frustration of pain striving for control to grow in spirit and character of virtue succeeding the denigration of submission to Fear. It is better to bind pain to ambition and the pursuit of justice in goodwill. The pain of violence is best acknowledged and brought under mindfulness to begin healing from this corruptive state of Fear. The greater the challenge of character and goodwill, the greater the reward of virtue. The greater the pain, the greater the relief and reward. The force of violence and its multiple forms of suffering across many spheres of the psyche can be tremendous. But to defy such a terrible force and be of disciplined will is an ambition of virtue in righteousness and goodwill. Succumbing to the compulsions of violence does not make one great or strong, as by doing so one only diminishes his or her virtue. The capacity of character to resist and oppose violence, however, marks virtue with the power of an autonomous will. In extremes, the mean of virtue can itself be extreme.

Vulnerability of character invites the vices of Fear, through which violence exploits vulnerability and makes character morally weak and deprives of good spirit. The duty of virtue is not to merely shun what one may deem weak or of lesser value for reasons of self-glorification and status in the shadow of Fear. The duty of virtue is to resist vice and aid and protect the vulnerable in proportion of justice. When reflecting on character, vice, and violence, one ought not to adopt an attitude and mentality of 'otherness' in opposition to lesser character subjected to vice and violence, which has a will of its own. It is the vulnerability of others' character that made them betray themselves, where Fear and its virtues were warped and corrupted. The same can happen to anyone. Distancing oneself from the faults of others will obstruct mindfulness. To lose the mindfulness of empathy is to risk inviting the tangents of descending towards similar vice. Criticism and scorn of characters of vice reduced to violence are to serve as a focal point for Discipline so as not to diminish virtue and spirit through unjust violence. This moral attitude is further sustained through the mindfulness of empathy, through which the intuitions of duty are bound to empathy and ambition of the Imperative to secure goodness when the strengths of others fail them, to act in virtue when others cannot. All violence begins in vulnerability, twisted into the moral weakness of vice, breeding torment, pain, suffering, and deprivation of spirit. Duty is to remedy and oppose these ethical forces of violence and vice.

The loss of control leading to violence can afflict the best of characters, as Fear can move any endeavour and ambition. The loss of control and the frustration over injustice can arouse rage in the virtuous and righteous just as it can vex the petty. Injustice can provoke a sense of anger and frustration, leading to intuitions of intolerance towards vice and immorality, spurring violent cravings. Thoughts themselves only reciprocate mental states and latent functional characteristics of the psyche. One ought to be mindful of them, and undesirable, uncomfortable thoughts ought to be acknowledged and dismissed through their loss of relevance through positive nourishment and mindfulness. If you feel violent or petty inclinations react to injustice, these thoughts must be acknowledged and meditated on. One ought to consider the root and nature initiating these mental states and intuitions – Fear.

While frustration over injustice can be dominating and potentially corruptive, the relinquishing of calm and harmony can serve a purpose, but only in the composure of Discipline. The pain and infuriation sensed in injustice can move towards the corruption of Fear. But when channelled through Disciplined and Harmony, these impressions and inclinations can serve the ambitions of goodwill. Injustice and a sense of decaying justice – righteousness losing power – can provoke impulsive reactions. Frustration over injustice can be good and highly motivating. It can serve as fuel for Defiance to not succumb to the same vice and weakness that betrayed others, to rise above corruption and pettiness in Fear. Pain related to injustice can serve our intuition by showing what ought to be remedied, as is seen with the brutality of wretched characters profoundly warped by Fear and violence. This pain and engaged intuitions are good, provided they are consistent with goodwill and justice. To improve on the faults of the world and the human condition, to remedy the catalysts of suffering and moral deficiencies, guided by composed intuitions and inclinations disquieted by injustice, is fully consistent with, and necessary for, goodwill, virtue, and duty.

Displeasure with injustice is good and should be used in positive endeavour, yet it should not succumb to the corruption of Fear. But where it may descend into a desire to punish, such intuitions should be mindful of intent and utility. Punishment should never be performed under the guise of Fear, but only in sincere measure of justice and duty, which is above all else to protect and nourish virtue and value producing positive ethical effect.

Furthermore, mindfulness in empathy is paramount, because by reflecting on the states of others moved by moral corruption, punishment in Fear only serves one's own desire to dominate, not good intentions. Punishment should not be performed under the craving to control. Any empathetic mindfulness on vice and the state of others will show that there is no satisfaction in punishing others, as people punish themselves incessantly through vice, leading to a deprived and diminished state of living. By then understanding the necessity for retribution, however, empathy and compassion turn into a cold and disciplined pain, far more empowering, or even terrifying, than mere compulsion. The continuity of vice punishes more than intervention, yet freeing oneself of vice relieves the affliction of self-punishing vice.

A crying baby can be extremely aggravating. However, the purpose of this behaviour serves its utility well to encourage care for the infant. The baby crying and the caring response is just. Acting on the aggravation of a crying baby, while at the same time acknowledging that this is just in that it produces goodness, is moral. This serves as an analogy for responsiveness to injustice and its sense of pain and displeasure. Just as the baby crying can make neglect appealing, the primary motivation ought to be care for the baby. Similarly, discontent over injustice can motivate, but it should not be the dominating factor – that ought to be dedicated to Liberty and goodwill guided by normative rules.

It may be true that we punish others not only to gain a sense of control over pain, but also to demonstrate to others the pain we are experiencing. Punishment and vengefulness may in some cases be driven by the intention of empathy, to show others the pain they have caused us. In doing so, others can reflect on their behaviour and by sitting with each other's pain we can find common humility and compassion. However, this causal structure of behaviour isn't the most promising or efficient for achieving the end of preventing and resolving suffering. If punishment serves as a means of twisted empathy to find reconciliation, there are better ways of achieving this than through harming one another, which could include the suffering-love of being stern and disciplined in the face of suffering and violence while showing the other person compassion.

Or, if it is not compassion that is shown towards the person that harmed you, then the defiant composure of not falling prey to Fear and suffering, in doing so preserving virtue and good spirit, might be just as good. Sometimes people just want to say that they are in pain, that they are hurting, but they can only bring themselves to expose their pain without leaving themselves vulnerable, and so they attack in order to defend themselves. But I suspect this ethical tangent and structure applies more to social and interpersonal dynamics that fundamentally involve warm feelings or love, which isn't the norm of most societies.

The character of vice suffers and decays in its determination and conduct. To deal with the injustice of matters of vice and wrongful conduct may at times not require any intervention if vice and injustice cannot be practically and realistically relieved. When others suffer from vice and the character of virtue is moved to counteract a devalued vector of vice that doesn't require immediate intervention, or it is impossible to help people suffering from vice, then it is not necessary to do anything. Simply, one doesn't need to dirty his or her hands, as the mess will (under certain conditions) clean itself up and vice will consume itself. Although, ideally, such cycles ought to be subverted when circumstances permit this, but such opportunities are not always available and committing compulsive mistakes would serve lesser interests.

With respect to the ethics of liberty, in the grand scheme of the dynamics of ethics' structures, one can only do so much to save others, with the most sustainable solution being helping people save themselves through support and empowerment. The affliction of vice is often profound, contingent on strong base moral inclinations and Fear. To address the root of vice and negativity requires an approach that penetrates the core of an ethical dynamic. This requires diversity of practical morality. Sometimes the origin of vice initiating violence is too systematically and individually deep, whereby the most practical solution is the most realistic and applicable through allowing the liberty of morality to run its course by allowing vice to negate itself or by introducing value where virtue is sustainable and demonstrates potential.

A notable dimension of violence and the loss of control is the excessive and self-entitled demand for respect. It is quite often the case, from individuals to nation-states, that perceived disrespect beckons anger and frustration. It is easy to see why. Disrespecting someone may be perceived to undermine his or her status, character, and dignity. Base-reason employs emotional intuitions and impulses of frustration towards the perceived neglect of status, but preservation of social status does have its merits in base ethical structures. As inherently social creatures, people in societies organically form hierarchies, even if only as the perception of hierarchy. The person of little confidence will subsume themself to a lower place in a perceived hierarchy. Status in society cannot be denied to entail its rewards and virtues, notably in terms of a sense of social power and security through status. Status is clear in terms of the alpha of a group of animals; the same applies to people. Where emotional responses to perceived neglect of status can be seen as irrational – not in synchrony with the deliberation of detached high-reason maximising value – contingencies of base-reason fully account for the merits of the concern for social status.

However, this is only an element of the base condition of mankind, with decency, dignity, and (self-)respect being distinct elements that construct status. Any sense of self and any ego that base their value on the contingency of others' perception are deprived of the virtues of nobility and complete autonomy. Basing one's worth solely or primarily on the perceptions and judgements of others deprives one of greater virtues of strength and autonomy. An overwhelming concern for respect and status is but a contingency of Fear in social survival, subject to demeaning one's own virtue of character to that of a base creature. Dignity and self-respect are important for healthy, virtuous, and good ego, for the fulfilment of virtue rising above Fear. But good ego is above all derived from one's sense of self, from judgement of the self and one's conscience. To judge oneself in terms of the judgements of others deprives oneself of mindfulness and virtue in discipline; to judge oneself based on how one affects others, which can be distorted by the intrusion of immoderate sentiments, is a fulcrum of self-reflection. However, simply thinking this way does not facilitate corresponding virtues, for self-confidence in the dignity of virtuous autonomy comes through practice and engaged living.

Concerns over self-respect and dignity should not be consumed by concerns for status. Yet this should not give way to idleness over the tolerance of immorality and lesser characters striving for power that they should not have. Self-respect means not subsuming one's character to the lack of autonomy through attachment to an external measure of the self, but it equally entails compliance with one's ambition and interest. The lack of concern for status and its tangent of lust for respect is only as virtuous as the attitude that gives oneself the absolute dignity to do what one wishes, to maximise one's ambition and self-interest where those craving status and respect only become a secondary concern (while in compliance with justice and the essentials of morality). A character of vice may strive to command in the gratification of a misplaced sense of control and power, to feed his or her sense of status. A self-respecting character only complies with the command of vice if the command itself bears merit, where it fulfils one's own interests. But where interest in such command diminishes through a depraved character begging control to the point where it no longer fulfils one's interests, self-respect and detachment from status are to set-aside such command and pursue one's own interests. If something doesn't serve your ends, it is wise to turn when those seeking to exploit and use your value exceeds the maximisation of one's labour and utility, to cut-off utility where value is no longer positive.

In this demeanour threatening the respect of those with status, thereby threatening their status, the mind of vice loses control and becomes frustrated, the worst manifestation of which is violence, torture, and murder. Where it may seem that violence brought on the self by undermining the status of vice – that which ought to be defied in the first place – does not maximise self-interest in basic terms of morality, this does reveal the path to fulfilment by enabling a course of action where vice implodes on itself. The loss of control by the character of vice is far more painful on them than one's achievement of Liberty. In such defiance, one may achieve eudaimonia in Harmony while also fulfilling the duty of channelling vice towards cannibalising itself. But this willingness to bring out violence can equally betray the maxims of interest by destroying vice and life rather than remedying the source of vice and maximising the vectors of virtue. This, however, is subject to immediate judgements.

An excessive concern with respect contingent on external self-valuation and concern over status can be a source of significant vice and suffering, demeaning character to less than that of virtue succeeding Fear. Then, this vice can beckon much suffering and deficiency in the world through destructive and selfish violence. Verbal abuse and psychological violence are very common from those who feel their status has been undermined, a form familiar to threatened and weak ego. The concern for respect and status is a contingency of a fragile and weak ego. Insults and psychological harm can have a significant effect on the psyche and spirit, especially coming from those closest to you such as loved ones and family, the latter being inherently imbued with organic powers over subconscious valuation of the self.

It is good to be mindful of such pain, reflect on it, meditate on it, analyse it, consider it, and evaluate it. If a person tells you that he or she thinks you are cruel, then this must be considered, where a person who feels subject to psychological violence might be subject to harm you do not realise you are causing. This insight can then serve to learn how to exercise such a practice and utility to maximise value, when to use the utility of valuation righteously without causing unjust suffering and when to use it for one's own ends, known best through experience and sensations of pain. Where evaluation of the self is mindful, it must also consider the significance of those one is affected by.

Sometimes people's sense of psychological suffering is borne of their own accord, whereby your actions are a parallel element that instigated present elements of vice. A seemingly neutral judgement or valuation can provoke a hotspot of vice by scathing it, evoking a fragile and weak character to experience and project pain. Psychological pain is often rooted in oneself to be easily provoked by others, notably through insecurities. An obsessive concern for status is a primary manifestation of this tangent of vice and Fear.

Quite often people overestimate the significance of others. An excessive concern for status does this. An oppressive authority demanding respect deserves none such respect as the authority is vulnerable to vice deprived of status and nobility in virtue. Psychological utilities can influence one's psyche and spirit such as through insults. Sometimes these insults matter, other times they do not. The self-respecting character embraces criticisms and remarks concerning the character to nourish dignity and autonomy to improve oneself, but also scrupulously dismisses disproportionate, unfair, and unconstructive comments. The self-respecting character of status of virtue is one that exceeds the fragility of ego in vice bound to Fear.

The character preoccupied with status fails itself by overestimating the significance and value of a person's self-gratifying insolence as a projection of self-demeaning vice and depraved character. In such cases one ought to ask themself a simple question of why or whether a person's opinion matters or whether what they say matters, then take into mindful consideration what that person has to say to evaluate oneself through thoughts and intuitions free in and of pain. Physical violence would never solve the demeaning behaviour of the concern over status in terms of both preserving and pursuing status.

The best approach to these forms of psychological violence, such as with insults and abuse, is to protect oneself from psychological violence through psychological means, just as physical violence is commonly best defended against through physical means (which is not necessarily a moral absolute). Where people cannot defend themselves from psychological violence, with tolerance exceeding acceptable parameters of moral liberty, such as with psychological violence moving a vulnerable person to self-harm, physical violence can be a just utility in constricting the source of psychological violence inflicting suffering and pain that cannot be realistically remedied through other moral utilities. However, this justified utility of physical violence against psychological violence cannot be subject to eagerness and default means that lack sustainability and long-term strategy to relieve psychological violence.

The consideration of others' significance is something quite intuitive and organic to people, often corrupted by vulnerability in Fear, too afraid to admit to one's own imperfections and defeating the function of self-improvement. Intuitions confronting pain, suffering, and Fear, feeding the resolve and attitude eager to grow in virtue and fulfil greater ambition, do more for self-interest than the fear of admitting one's vice, imperfection, and vulnerability. This ambition is not one of vulnerability and weakness that requires deflection for fulfilment, but is characterised by spirit of far greater virtue that feeds off the pain others cannot exploit, which can exploit and channel the resource of pain.

However, this Discipline requires mindfulness that penetrates into the realms of the psyche commonly acting on their own autonomy and accord – base faculties and the subconsciousness. With sufficient practice, Harmony can penetrate these levels and allow the liberty of virtue to influence such intuitions.

Perhaps a devastating and surprising utility counteracting the source of psychological violence and its agency occupied with status is *humour*. There is no greater utility to undermine people's status and highlight their weakness and vulnerability than insult evoking self-doubt and reflection and humour that ridicules vice. This utility, however, is only just when it is smart, on-point, and of genuine goodwill, not of malicious demeanour, insecurity, and the reflection of pain on others.

The ultimate test of one's character is how it responds to psychological attacks, notably in terms of ridicule. Then virtue is qualified by how character employs the same utility, with malicious and disproportionate comments being a species of insult as an extreme utility beyond humour. It should come as no surprise that political leadership, especially authoritative and authoritarian ones, are commonly pitifully weak to ridicule, humour, and insult. It is a primary element of Defiance to humour and ridicule a significant force that exceeds its just utility, to laugh at it and strip it of its power. Harmony's utility of humour is to bring positivity in the darkest of experiences and insights. The strongest authority and respect is one strong enough to embrace humour and poke fun at itself. Humour can bring people together.

When we poke fun at ourselves and each other, we put down our defences, release ourselves of an ego trying to defend itself from pain, to instead find common ground in discomfort and pain, to find empathy, humility, healing, and common joy. Humour and banter bring people together by dissolving the spiritual corrosion and toxicity of ego in Fear, breaking down the boundaries of status and ambition in Fear to invite commonality, unity, and companionship. When we feel vulnerable we can feel liberated. But humour often turns to a demeaning mode with malicious intent and spirit.

Often humour and ridicule are stripped of positive spirit and just utility by exceeding goodwill and virtuous intent to succumb to Fear that breeds an excessive and self-gratifying desire to ridicule. Humour can succumb to Fear like most utilities and beckon a mode of desiring control and status, with the most virtuous of character being able to dismiss this species of malicious humour or counteract it as any vice that exceeds acceptable tolerance. It is wise to treat a defeated opponent with respect, especially when violence was used in the conflict of interest. In doing so, one marks his or her quality of virtue that succeeds the species of vice that deprives strength and self-respect, but also serves to build common will with a defeated opponent to show him or her a path of greater virtue that moves people to common goodwill not requiring conflict and immoral antagonism.

To tolerate the suffering of others in terms of their accord of vice, in contrast to encroachment on the principles of liberty that regulate endeavour, and allow them to suffer from self-punishment, is a manifestation of Discipline that can invoke measures of just ruthlessness. It is intuitive to suppose that to allow people to suffer is wrong, but this is only the case when intervention would do more harm. The injustice that may spur from vice at liberty, however, may exceed tolerable degree of vice at liberty to affect the world. Base intuition would suppose that a combination of ruthlessness can lead to moral degeneration and the erosion of good intuitions. These terms of reasoning on unilateral base morality would be appropriate. It is intended that the moral attitude and intuition towards injustice should not be complacent. When combined with virtuous and just ruthlessness, qualified in terms of synchrony or on the edge of harmony in all-reason, attitudes towards injustice are understood to be balanced. Even if just ruthlessness is deprived of goodwill and compassion, where it becomes callous and detached, this does not presume an excess of brutal violence and punishment.

The desire to punish through violence is a manifestation of Fear, whereby any such ruthlessness is corrupted by Fear, not just or virtuous. However, a detached intuition of ruthlessness deprived of goodwill and empathy will most likely commit gross miscalculations. Violence is particularly brutal when affected by emotions. The lack of sentiment, especially positive ones, can detract from the corruptive effect of Fear craving violence to punish and control, but come at a careless and atrocious cost where violence as a just utility is grossly misapplied. The failure to nourish the positive intuition of empathy and disciplined compassion will deprive intuition that reveals and enables more harmonious actions responding to the vices of Fear. Without empathy, combined with an emphasis on reasoning and calculation, violence might become excessive not as a vice of Fear, but as a deficiency lacking mindfulness and adaptiveness, lacking imagination and intuition recognising other positive moral utilities and courses of action against prevalent vice. By excessively applying violence, even when not for self-gratified pleasure corrupted by the vice of Fear pursuing baser control, one can unjustly commit excessive actions, undermining virtue and goodwill.

By appealing to virtuous ruthlessness – a utility of extreme action in dire circumstances mediated by the virtues of empathy and disciplined (or dismissed) compassion – attitudes towards injustice are not supposed to lead to or justify dehumanisation or hate. Anger, frustration, and displeasure towards people embodying vice and committing injustice is fully consistent with the morality of Harmony and mindful appreciation of unity in the fundamental will and humanity.

A profound unity with soul and continued faith in people, perhaps a form of 'higher' love for people, is fully consistent with hate, frustration, and displeasure towards what people become and do with themselves – what the mechanical soul has warped into by the conditioning of the psyche and character disposing and employing its substance. We can love another person even through displeasure and frustration over what they have done.

Similarly, in a profound sense we can empathise with others through their soul, reflecting back on ourselves, while being extremely dissatisfied with what that soul has come to be. We can, and ought to, understand, learn, empathise, and forgive, while also not be complacent, naive, and negligent. Such is the nature and necessity of duties in Liberty. To empathise with those twisted and tormented by vice through appeal to the fundamental will and its essence that all life shares, while being aware of the pain reflected into the world through vice and onto others, is to learn and understand the dynamics of vice, to develop and adapt normatively.

Being mindful of all pain, as is necessary for the morality of Harmony, can and should be very painful, burdensome, and even overwhelming. But this serves an imperative utility to learn and further mindfulness, as well as be employed as a resource in the morality of Discipline and the nourishment of virtue. This is where just and virtuous ruthlessness, especially in experiencing or witnessing the effects of violence, contingent on mindfulness of pain, arises as a distinctive utility of practical morality in extremes, resisting the corruptive effects of violence and pain.

Pain inherently functions to motivate a person towards action, to improve on an uncomfortable state. Pain commonly strives for a way out. In such inclinations lacking discipline, we often do more damage than good, betray ourselves and others, as is clear with outbursts of anger. But since pain has such a profound effect on us that motivates and engages us, even empowers or breaks us, then is it not better to exploit this moral resource, to bind it to our ambition of greater interest? I argue this serves our ambitions better. This virtue-rule of pain extends to violence, whereby its inherent extreme is something to be cautious of, but at the same time a reality we must accommodate.

Mindfulness on the vast needless pain and tragedy of unjust violence serves the utility of identifying vectors and tangents of vice and corresponding motivational factors to improve on suffering. Joyous spirit and the abundance of positivity are excellent things we would all ideally live with. But without Discipline we can easily succumb to excess, as is clear with the paradox of hedonism, and become distracted from the best of things, from greater fulfilment beyond simple pleasures. If we aren't mindful, we can lose track of living, lose sight of what we are doing, fail to be honest with ourselves. We return to an idle state and forego on our responsibilities and duties, potentially even the basic one's of courtesy and decency to fellow people.

The mindfulness of empathy engaging pain can serve the purpose of not only responding to immediate injustice and violence, but also be employed as an evocative and moving factor to sustain duty, virtue, and proactive living. Sensing and understanding the pain of others with equal consideration of one's own can be learnt to be an asset to duty and the ambition of goodwill, which compassion and base intuitions have a tendency to tell us until the psyche is undermined by counter-productive and deficient elements shrouding empathy and greater ambition. Evocative reactions to unjust violence are good and can serve the utility of spurring and sustaining ambition, yet improved on through Discipline and Harmony.

We do not need to, and perhaps shouldn't, rationalise our emotions, neither should we affirm emotions to rationale beyond the liberty of the synchronised accord of all-reason. However, we ought to be mindful of our emotions and intuitions, listen to them, learn from them, and understand them. To understand our intuitions and be in-sync with the movements of reason which primary awareness – conscious awareness – does not immediately access, one must be mindful and disciplined. Then we can learn from emotions and extend the reach of Discipline and virtue to other spheres of conscious reason through mindfulness for moral liberty to extend its capacity.

Considering the unintuitive duality of some attitudes and principles of morality, to make sense of them and dismiss conflicting thoughts and intuitions, one ought to invoke utilities of moral and spiritual liberty. When doubt and confusion linger, defer to resetting the mind and intuition through meditation by the Void and other means of mindfulness. This mean is intended to, and understood as, providing a point of clarity for analysis, reflection, and thought. Where rules and principles of morality conflict through intuitions, clarity through liberty is helpful. But when intuition and reasoning conflict, follow their primacy – liberty and goodwill, virtue and duty.

This fluidity of character in terms of attitude and mentality is the virtue of spirit at liberty engaging elements of practical morality, be it compassion or ruthlessness, as means of justice and virtue. But this liberty of intuition can only be actualised through mindfulness of empathy and complete Liberty. A mentality or attitude as mental constructs are not fundamentals and are wholly contingent on the groundwork of the fundamental will. As the fundamental will is malleable and extremely diverse in its roots, thereby adaptive, so too are its systems and structures. Mentalities and attitudes are innately capable of considerable flexibility honed through Discipline and mindful Harmony. Liberty is not about controlling intuitions and mentalities through misguided rationale, but in allowing liberty to run its course through intuitions, for a mentality and attitude to become self-regulated through the efficiency of virtue.

Where violence as an intuition and craving begins to affect the mind with its corruptive draw, potentially deceiving righteous intent and warping justice, if any virtue-rule can be drawn from my familiarity with violence, it is that intuition can only be complete in Liberty through the liberty of unrestricted intuitions. To make peace with violence and its intuitions or impulses of anger is not to reject them completely, but to find the liberty of the will and intuitions superceding the inclinations of violence through a grounding element of intuition fundamental to the mind – Liberty of the soul and mindfulness of corresponding ambition.

Violence, Fear, and intuitions of lesser value and virtue are only ever conquered when their intuitions are made subservient to greater ambitions, with the proposed grand ambition of this ethos being Liberty. Liberty means to be both in pain and not, to act beyond pain and through it, to feel base emotions while embracing intuitions of higher mindfulness, to be at liberty bound to engaged living while free to linger in the Void. Understanding and making peace with these paradoxes is what it means to be at Liberty, centred in mindfulness of the will, which furthers its utility of intuitions concerning violence.

What of violence as a just mean? Violence as a means and utility to control is the central theme in these discussions, but because of its strong potential for negative influence on the psyche and persistent effect on structure, violence must only be invoked by the justice of the Highest Good. Any act of violence or ruthlessness ought to be performed in order to mediate negative influences of suffering that do not conform to tolerable bounds of the Central Principle of Liberty and in accordance with justice and minimising suffering.

The desire to control negative forces can pull one's character into Fear's corruptive spheres, and if virtue is not sustained, then corruption will likely incur. All acts of violence in accordance with the virtues of goodwill and the practicality of ruthlessness serve as utilities of good ambition, thus they ought to be committed righteously

– that is, retributively and reparatively, to bring the balance of justice. Revenge as a common form of punishment stems from the desire to control. However, revenge is always a manifestation of Fear, especially through the morality of Fear.

Revenge will only lead to corruption, vice, and weakness of will and ambition. The gratification and satisfaction of revenge, petty or excessive, the pleasure of control through means contingent on Fear, are only secondary to the satisfaction and pleasure in nobility and the dignity of strength surpassing the constraints of Fear that move to inflict suffering inducing the craving for revenge and control. Rising above revenge is to move above the character vexed and submitted to the vice of Fear. The imbalance of flourishing as injustice is repaired and redeemed by re-establishing balanced well-being, or best yet when maximised through ambitions of the Highest Good. Succeeding over suffering and maximising goodness in negativity of ethical value is justice; continuing the cycle and perpetuating the effect of pain, suffering, and vice is not of virtue or higher justice. Punishment is another means to flourishing, but it too closely lingers with the negative spirit of revenge. If justice ought to balance, then its essence ought not to be invoked in the form of vengeful punishment bound to the lust for control and malign power.

Any appeal to punishment can be distorted in unmindful and simplistic interpretations. Punishment as any utility can be just or unjust, right or wrong; the distinction is settled between mere vengeance and *retribution*, with the latter being truly just. Punishment is only moral and just when committed as retribution reforming justice and balancing flourishing, writing wrongs through goods of a higher sort beyond those of a limited and focused base scope of vision. It is then better to not only bring the scales of suffering and vice back to a positive or comparatively more positive state, but also to maximise the value of goodness and virtue. Certain modes of punishment have their merit and utility, but those worth their value are in virtue and committed in goodwill pertaining to justice – retributive justice.

The desire to generate positive influence, the wish to make the world a better place, can move focus towards the end goal and away from what is presently apparent. By focusing narrowly on a desire or goal, one can easily lose sight of themself and one's intent, allowing moral corruption to deceive the self. Lacking mindfulness of discipline and empathy, prioritising ends over means and immediate actions and spirit, can deceive the very virtue and goodness of the end, warping intent and depriving goodwill. The imperative category of the impracticality of this mode of thinking is that not only is the end goal deceived beyond honest ambition of goodwill, betraying the self, but also undermines goodwill invoking and mediating practical ethical wisdom, thereby misassessing and misevaluating ethical tangents central to moral deliberation. The end itself does not justify unregulated means, with the means as virtues and characteristics being central to moral deliberation.

The means are the end, as ethical catalysts and effects of the dynamics causing an effect corresponding to a set function. External influences of the ethical environment that justify immoral means for illusive moral ends are only as valuable as their contingency on the character related to the conditions of an ethical environment. For all we know, a structure may not be worth preserving or saving, with the vice consuming itself being a legitimate moral end if virtue and justice are lacking, and spirit was not worth the duty or opportunity of living. In short, the ends are wholly contingent on the means, with the continuity of life lacking virtue and spirit pertaining to good living not being inherently valuable means. An ethical structure is only as valuable and worthy of continuity as the tangents and vectors it integrates as virtue, goodwill, and fulfilling spirit.

To summarise the discussions thus far on the practical morality of violence, any act of violence ought to be done in terms of the necessity of duty, the development of virtue, and production of positive effects. Whether we like it or not, ruthlessness and violence are sometimes necessary for well-being, notably when the welfare of a community is deprived of justice by vectors of vice. The appreciation and norm of tacit, kind, empathetic, compassionate, and patient approaches to immorality and suffering are default means and intrinsically more stable than extremes. Duty, righteousness, and goodness sometimes mandate dire and extreme actions to counter-act greater wrong-doing and the negativity of vice that instigates suffering, pain, and structural deficiency. Due to the inherent risk of violence in terms of its ethical tangents – dispositions towards immoderate Fear and the lust for control – violence ought to only be committed righteously and justly. This requires a general formulation of the rules of Discipline in employing violence and understanding the virtue of the just utilities of violence.

Virtues and justice in violence, as with all spheres of moral brutalism, must comply with a set of parameters framing rules and principles of the righteousness of the utility. The same principles and rules apply to violence as they do to killing and other practices of morality, namely: necessity, immediacy, proportionality, and efficiency. First is the condition of necessity in the use of violence, a parameter which is devised to be applicable to a range of practices of morality.

Violence is only just in terms of the necessity of its utility such as to protect from violence in the immediate moment and in terms of indirect instigators of violence that have peaked as immediate proxy causes of violence. For example, as discussed with psychological abuse and manipulation that initiate and not merely encourage violence, such vectors and tangents might have to be neutralised and remedied through the agent directly employing violence by manipulating the vector instigating violence indirectly, as well as then addressing the catalyst of violence in the indirect cause, if necessary through physical and psychological violent means. The case with the indirect or bilateral instigator of violence – the manipulator – is more ambiguous, but it remains a valid point that, in an immediate instance, apprehension and non-lethal violent force may be necessary such as to silence the source of psychological violence. If psychological abuse, such as brainwashing, moves groups towards extremes of unjust violence and killing, then severing this root of violence may be just. In short, violence should only be used and considered just when necessary, with necessity being wholly contingent on immediate circumstances that require just means of violence, in most cases as a response to violence.

The nature of a mode of violence at times requires different approaches, including physical violence against physical violence and psychological against psychological. Where physical violence can stop a violent course of action, psychological violence, whether deceit and trickery or crippling the vector of vice through profound mental attacks, can achieve the same goal of preventing physical violence through psychological violence, or preferably through dialogue as a more efficient means of preventing harm. Psychological attacks, such as insults, can be a just means of instigating self-reflection on vice. Common sense highlights the merits of calling people out on their immoral conduct, but any such merit is only found on a psychologically harmful force proportional to immediate circumstances. The appropriateness of violent means is then qualified with respect to immediacy, a parameter complimentary to the necessity of action.

Immediacy is an ambiguous aspect of practical morality, but this is necessary for the capacity and circumstance of judgement. Any morality can only do so much to account for immediate decision-making, providing a framework for judgement in terms of the ambitions of goodwill and practical, ethical wisdom of systemic and structural insight. Rules and principles guide the immediate application of judgement. The general rule and principle concerning the immediacy of violence is tied to necessity in particular circumstances calling for violence. Just violence is above all a utility defending and securing the value of virtue, life, and well-being. Therefore, just violence is implicitly characterised by defence in terms of the immediate necessity for protective actions.

What constitutes protection as defence and security is complex and subject to risk assessment, with the derivative of risk then subject to further deliberation through ethical analysis and accord of morality. For instance, even though someone does pose a small risk of turning to greater vice and immoral action, acting on this risk may be wrong if exercised through means disproportionate to the immediate necessity given that risk, as this could increase risks of ethical regress in other spheres. Excessive violence beyond an immediate necessity will instigate tangents of Fear in violence that will provoke others to act on what they perceive is unjust violence. Being resilient to minor risks and not weakened by an intolerance for smaller risks initiates ethical tangents that strengthen vectors and the ethical environments against potential risks.

Sometimes pre-emptive violence must be used to protect ethical interests such as by apprehending a threat before it becomes a devastating, active threat. Fear of risk can corrupt uncertainty and lead to unnecessary and disproportionate acts that only instigate greater threats and uncertainty. In a case where the risk of a person becoming violent is little and an act of violence hasn't occurred yet, psychological means of alleviating and addressing a potential threat are more appropriate, with the ideal priority given to non-violent psychological means including dialogue and rapport. So the condition of immediacy becomes subject to matters of certainty and the assessment of risk. The difference in violence, however, is that there are identifiable 'softer' and 'harder' degrees of it such as non-lethal or crippling forces.

Soft violence and coercive moral utilities may not carry with them as significant a force in terms of internal and external ethical tangents. A tackle during a contact sport does not exercise as much ethical – mental and spiritual – force on the psyche as does a terror plot maiming people. Similarly, a friendly, 'banterful' mental jab will not have the same or similar ethical tangents as a malicious personal comment invoked by deep insecurity. Therefore, violence as a utility has greater leeway in its application than utilities necessitating killing, because in individual cases, unlike killing, violence has degrees of application less extreme on the spectrum of ethical tangents relating to moral brutalism. Thus, judgements of immediacy can permit and enable violence with greater liberty in relevant rules and principles.

For example, law enforcement is just in restraining a criminal and an active, engaged threat, while also just in employing lethal force to stop a violent criminal presenting an immediate threat to someone's life and well-being. This form of assessment of risk is subject to judgement in terms of sensible and accurate assessment of certainty in the risk presented by a threat. If a person is holding a gun without actively declaring threats, without aiming a gun at a person, and without a history of violent acts, then it is intuitive to suppose that the immediate risk presented by the threat is not severe enough to not pursue a non-violent means of resolution. On the other hand, a violent extremist holding hostages and actively declaring threats can definitively be considered a greater risk of violence than with respect to the former case. Fortunately, the perception of threats is intuitive and automatic, yet its trends of judgement are improved on through mindful reason and rationale disciplining and moderating our perception of threats. Virtues guiding mindful intuitions of goodwill offer better judgement and sensibility.

The criteria of necessity and immediacy in just violence and practical morality imply an aspect of proportionality. By proportionality is intended a balanced – just – degree of physical and/or psychological force in terms of the immediate necessity of appealing to such utilities. For example, a degree of violence can distinguish between just and moral apprehension of an individual and an immoral deed of excessive violence leading to needless harm. Proportionality is the qualifying criterion for just violence in terms of the use of force that distinguishes from an immoral use of violence and a moral, just, and righteous one. It is common sense that violence is only just if it is proportional to immediate necessity, but why? A complex dimension of causal ethical tangents in line with an ethical force affecting character(s) ought to be considered.

Disproportionate and excessive violence leads to immorality and vice. The obsessive desire to control the external world and its substance and structure, lacking mindfulness and autonomous virtue, is a pursuit of power depriving the self of fulfilling virtue and true power in greater autonomy of the will. Excess violence as a deliberate intention and inclination is usually a species of vice in Fear that craves control and is deprived of fulfilment, thereby being corrupt. Violence tends to incite more violence, propagating the vicious cycle of pain and Fear; this is especially the case when violence is used excessively as a means of oppression. Using violence as a means of excess Fear feeds vice and leads to more violence. Nevertheless, violence can be a just utility to secure and propagate greater ethical value, virtue, and ambition, at times through counteracting an excess of violence.

To ensure the justice of violence requires proportionality in terms of getting its utility 'just right' – that is, balanced. A simpler formulation of proportionality is that using excessive violence, such as vengeful, hateful disproportionate lethal violence as a means to incite Fear in others through retaliation, will only instigate greater vice of Fear bound to greater and extended conflict. Proportional violence would be a defensive response that neutralises an immediate threat to ease the immediate conditions that instigate conflict, as opposed to disproportionate utilities corrupted in Fear striving to fretfully mobilise Fear through a deceitful sense of control and power in pain, only to provoke more of the same and surrender one's ambition and power to Fear unworthy of true human autonomy.

In this context, a similar principle can be drawn to value restraint against unnecessary, non-immediate pre-emptive attacks against a possible, but non-actual threat. If a deterrent or threat is mobilised without direct confrontation or instigation, even if apparently veiled, and there is no overt threat expressed in such actions, then it is most likely a moral deliberation rooted in defensive Fear. The root of that is best alleviated not through excessive, destructive, and violent counter-measures, but through appeal to the root of Fear – uncertainty, lack of trust, scepticism, or an associate variable of Fear in a sphere/tangent of an ethical structure.

A deterrent is only so much of a constructive utility for preventing violence, with emphasis on the means to deter violence beholding the primacy of deep-rooted, core dimensions of the ethical dynamics that lead to violence – Fear. However, any such profound and moving utility can only ever be used through sincerity and a trait of character and spirit that draws on the perceptions of the receiver of this form of moral power. Therefore, pre-emptive violence is only just, as with cases of conflict and war, if immediate judgement is accurate and valid in responding to active and clear threats or clauses supporting the mobilisation of capacities engaged in violent force, a formulation applicable to both individual and structural ethics.

However, where restraint in violence may be perceived as cowardice, it is important to be mindful of a virtue-rule that restraint in violence is only just, righteous, and fulfilling when it is in accordance with restraint, courage, and discipline, not in accordance with cowardice. Restraint in violence through cowardice is a vice; restraint in violence through wisdom, sensibility, and composure is a virtue. For example, in a fair and non-deadly bar fight, it is cowardly and of vice to appeal to threats of legal action and 'sewing people' in order to protect oneself from physical confrontation. This cowardice is branded as such when the action is motivated by hiding behind someone and not standing up for yourself. However, it is wise to warn people beforehand of the consequences of unjust physical confrontation in order to deter needless conflict. It is of greater virtue and ideal to avert the conflict entirely and ease the tangents causing harm and suffering. If someone comes knocking on your door and threatens you, don't pick a fight – be smart and call the police to deal with the person properly. Furthermore, it is a basic moral principle of decency not to provoke people into unnecessary and unjust confrontation. Accepting the punishment of physical conflict and 'fighting a losing battle' as a necessity of justice and righteousness is of especial virtue. Others bound to Fear may perceive restraint and mercy as weakness and cowardice, in doing so only restricting themselves to vice of Fear, as excess violence further deprecates the mind and spirit by enslaving it to the corrosion of Fear.

An intolerance for risk highlights a character weak in Fear, while the character defiant of the uncertainty of risk is one of greater autonomy than activity restricted by Fear and cowardice in risk. Ruthlessness in Fear is deprived of the greater ambition of ruthlessness in Liberty that exceeds Fear and is relentless beyond Fear. Unjust violence in Fear never offers such power, it never will, and its sense of power is deceitful. Yet modes and utilities of justice can mobilise these corruptive ethical dynamics and tangents against themselves through containment until their vices undermine and cannibalise themselves. This happens because while the vector of Fear pursues control, it is inherently susceptible to excess and distraction. Fear will never gain complete fulfilment and satisfaction, its tangents leading to continuous pain undermining the Human Imperative. Following the considerations of ethical tangents, proportionality in violence must consider the effects on the psyche.

Vice leads to, and affects itself through, violence and Fear, bringing pain, suffering, and destruction if not amended in the Liberty to do so. By imposing violence on people according to an intent to project Fear, the corresponding vice above all affects oneself through the continuous suffering of Fear. Disproportional, excessive violence subjects the world and global community to suffering, while equally depriving the individual of good spirit and greater ambition by succeeding Fear and binding pain to ambition of Liberty. Where an inclination and craving may desire excessive punishment through violence, the spirit is best fulfilled and character nourished when an inclination of Fear is not acted on. Instead, it is better to let go of that pain afflicting the self by using it for greater ambitions, thereby also breaking a corrosive cycle of unjust violence. Consequently, a final criterion of just violence, building on proportionality, is the preferable attribute of efficiency in just violence.

Appealing to efficiency in violence can bring up a concern over a systematic formulation of violence and killing. It is along these lines that the efficiency of violence ought to be considered. In short, violence is best employed to greater effect with minimal expense, to use violence as minimally as is proportional to the goal. One aspect of this is institutionalising laws and agencies using force within legal and/or law enforcement structures to minimise violence. Sometimes the use of violent force, psychological or physical, can leave gruelling damage and cause grave harm beyond necessity and proportionality. Avoiding excess and limiting damage is the preferred attribute of efficiency in just violence. This criterion can be simplified as doing as little damage as possible and minimising the inflicted pain in parallel to other criteria of just violence. Violence is usually clouded with the spirit and mentality of Fear, distress, and suffering. Efficiency in violence and killing with minimal pain and suffering is considered to be just and preferable by employing the necessary means of justice without diluting constructive and righteous endeavour with greater Fear, suffering, and pain.

When the agency of vice commits injustice and inflicts pain and suffering on others, anger may provoke the inclinations of one's actions towards that of Fear craving control through excessive punishment, inciting viciousness and violence. The efficiency of violence serves to support proportionality in just violence by minimising the systemic and structural impact of violence, while equally nourishing and upholding Discipline and Harmony. Anger can bring one towards impulsive violence, yet this anger can be channelled for greater ambition than destructive outbursts to motivate one to reach and address the root of suffering.

The anger that incites violent cravings and intuitions is powerful and evocative, providing a potent moral resource for the growth of character and challenging the vice that causes suffering. Efficiency in violence is devised as a complex moral utility to use the motivation of anger and violence for much greater ambition of goodwill through Defiance, Discipline, and Harmony. Mastering the inclinations and intuitions of violence is an opportunity for strenuous, but vigorous development of character, the Discipline of which leads to a distinct learning of Harmony.

Restraint and Discipline in violence in terms of efficiency are means to extraordinary mindfulness of both Discipline and Harmony. However, the quality of this extensive mindfulness is only a dutiful necessity in moral extremes and an attribute of deep, but mostly unnecessary, mindfulness by the Void of higher Liberty. Discipline in violence is but one of many paths following the same tangents of moral growth. Thus, efficiency in violence leads to not only positive social effects, as explored with proportionality, but also extreme ends of Discipline by facilitating characteristics appropriate to the burdens such as mindfulness, composure, patience, wisdom, empathy, understanding, and the power of goodwill, all through the practices of mindfulness and self-reflection.

Understanding what moves the soul in oneself and others towards violence – Fear and suffering – is a source of, perhaps, unique insight, which can be taught and explained independently from specifically relevant experiences, because suffering is a universally shared experience. However, devotion to Discipline and Harmony, in other words the heritin ethos, especially by the Void, I suspect, is only truly understandable by those whom have shared experience of moral extremes and acute suffering, the pains of which are in their own class of impression that fundamentally affect and mark the psyche and spirit. In truth, however, almost all of us carry the burden of profound pain. But few know the universal trends of pain through their extremes.

The heritin ethos is borne through these ethical tangents that specify their dedicated role in moral extremes. While the general spirit and norm of heritin ethics is an appreciation of Natural Law and the Highest Good, the deeper personal element arises in its application to instances of pain and suffering, which is not devised, nor presumed to be a universal approach. Despite this attribute of the heritin ethos, Liberty is nonetheless an intuitively universal aspect of spirit, with Discipline in violence being a personal preference for an approach to Liberty through pain and suffering. The normative efficiency and success of such an approach remains to be tested.

As with all pain and suffering, binding them to the ambitions of goodwill at Liberty is empowering and more fulfilling than an autonomy limited by Fear. To conquer and discipline the turbulent force of violence in the self leads to great virtue through its power bound to the ambition of goodwill. If the pain of violence and hate can be used in, and confined to, one's ambition through the self, then its great pain will imbue the mind and spirit with characteristics of greater willpower and vigour, which leads to Liberty. Finally, profound suffering will lead to eudaimonia through the Ploy and the ability to let go of that very same pain through dismissing its utility and reassembling intuition from null through the Void and Liberty. The intuition and sensation of eudaimonia through Liberty will be known in the clearest sensation as enlightenment through suffering channelled inward to build mindfulness and ambition, not fretfully and destructively projected outward.

This Liberty in pain and suffering is complete in self-sacrifice in the Liberty to do so. Where violence leads to great insight and mindfulness of absolute Liberty through the Void, as with all great pain, sacrifice that embraces pain is the same ethical tangent that brings one to Liberty. This Liberty to sacrifice then does the dutiful service of the most efficient resolution to the cycle of violence when committed sensibly, righteously, justly, and strategically. The most efficient ploy of, in, and against violence is where and when violence ends with the self, permanently or with future promise.

Those marked by, and exposed to, hard violence will change. Corrupt forms of such a psyche and spirit may struggle in peace by craving more and more struggle, might not befit the spirit of modern societies that focuses on more than violence, pain, or a misplaced sense of glory through conquest, yet nonetheless of spirit often overshadowed by Fear. It can be difficult to live in an environment and community found on something estranged in spirit and mentality. The heritin ethos offers a way through this pain and a more profound, free spirit in harmony with all things. Being an outsider does not mean a fate of suffering, confusion, and loss if one is willing to pursue further ambition through suffering.

There is more to be found in such a predicament than the distraction of Fear moving away from empty spirit. Suffering and Fear, in whatever shape or form, provided the psyche and spirit are capable of enduring, can lead to greater positivity of spirit through Liberty and willpower. Violence and pain can twist the mind and spirit, and I fully understand and appreciate the suffering this brings. Yet there is a way to live beyond this suffering, to find Liberty with and in all things, to move past struggle and be at liberty to live, even if any memory of living in good spirit has been lost. You can define yourself as more than violence, be more than your pain, make your rage and hatred a utility, a weapon of your will rather than a poison, all if you are willing to do so. This autonomy and self-dignity of being more than the constraints of Fear is the virtue of resisting and pursuing justice in violence.

A major part of the heritin ethos is borne of pain, violence, suffering, and peace with death. These are profoundly troubling experiences. But where aversion limits spirit and leaves it to fester and cause greater harm, the ethos of Liberty is moved to defy, in doing so find and make peace with the world, to then complete oneself through eudaimonia and absolute Liberty of one's pain and Fear, to find the strength and courage to be at peace with oneself.

This is an ethic intended to move away from violence and killing, systematically (through justice) and personally (through the ethos). But the Liberty valued is not one of pilgrimages, or dedication, or atonement, or servitude, not a liberty of escape from Fear. This is an ethos of fulfilling spirit through more than pain achieved through one's spirit and mind, over which there is no arbiter but one self and one's conscience. This ethic moves to succeed Fear, violence, and pain, to become more in spirit than the things that enslave and torment. One betrays themself when he or she reduces spirit and character to corrupt spirit in Fear and violence.

This ethos is fully intended and written as a utility to bind violence to one's will and ambition through Discipline and Harmony, not the other way around where violence takes hold of the individual and torments community. Taming violence and preventing it from spreading to others is in itself a primary duty. To remedy and hold back violence is justice to oneself.

But make no mistake or delude yourself into thinking that this part of the psyche, when so deeply ingrained, will wane and be gone, as forgetting this part of oneself can beckon terrible vice and corruption of spirit. Yet violence and its intuitions are but a part of the broader scope of spirit dedicated to power and its fulfilment. This is best achieved through power over one's own will complete through the liberty to let go of power over the very self, to let go and allow Liberty to imbue and empower goodwill. Subsequently, the aggression, hate, anger, and pain that once breathed violence can evoke motivation and energy tasked with far greater ambition of goodwill towards the Human Imperative, worthy of Liberty.

This ethical hypothesis augments certain functions of behaviour by strengthening and developing the will, honing and expanding the capacities of mindfulness and self-reflection through the challenge of suffering and overcoming the barrier of Fear and pain. Discipline in violence leads to the mindfulness of Harmony, from which the mindfulness of empathy matures. To dominate pain and suffering beyond Fear is to grow in strength of will and the ability to be mindful of the self, actions, and intuitions. In doing so, one can begin to understand why we act the way we do, why we live the way we do, and why our intuitions and desires work the way they do, which are reducible to a corresponding ethos.

With this insight and wisdom available to the mind, mindfulness can expand its scope and invoke ambition of goodwill. Where pain and violence are experienced and their suffering is used towards greater ends, the ethos then brings attention to empathy towards the self and others, thereby evoking compassion towards oneself and others to heal suffering and introduce positivity to complete Liberty. The basis for this ethical model is essentially to cultivate the virtues of strength and courage to dig deep into one's own spirit and mind to confront oneself and one's vice, to admit imperfection and vice, to admit what one has done and what one was, to reflect on this in respect of the deterministic and sometimes callous world and the people who have done this to you and influenced you through Fear. By finding the strength to admit to faults, to vulnerabilities, weaknesses, imperfections, and vices, which can be very difficult, Defiance and Harmony serve to build the courage to confront oneself and reflect on the self with complete honesty.

Violence can imprint a painful memory that creates a long tangent of suffering and pain. Finding the courage and strength to penetrate into these memories and the contingencies of one's character is the foundation for moving past pain and vice, to move towards freedom in pain and fear, towards new living, and to heal. Understanding what happened to you and others that put us on a corruptive path of Fear, something profound and innate to us all, is the path to empathy towards others and the self, from which one is at Liberty with the world, people, and oneself, for one comes to realise that people and things are deterministic and not at fault for their nature and behaviour, where a universal driving force of the fundamental will and its substance binds us all to our living and ethics. Overcoming pain, hate, and violence reveals this hidden universal element, which then grants the liberty to employ those same utilities as one pleases in accordance with goodwill, where they no longer dominate living.

So where one may wonder and ask why these virtue-rules are relevant beyond the basic appeal to the Fundamental Principle and the principle-rules of justice, the ethical design is intended to serve a distinct utility, which the individual can employ to heal from his or her pain caused by the vices of Fear. Conventional utilities in secondary spheres of ethics' structures have their many uses to counteract Fear and violence, but a profound approach at the core of the individual is also necessary. This should also serve as a useful summary of a model for how the heritin ethos and its ethics are meant to work when implemented in practical morality.

The designed theory might struggle to be applicable in brutish and evocative circumstances. Is restraint always just, and is it realistic? Where the efficiency of restraint in just violence is always an ideal element of ethics and morality, sometimes the utilities necessary for the fulfilment of the Highest Good come from deep within and by setting aside the primacy of balance in reason at Liberty. Sometimes the base instinct of survival in the immediacy of an attempted murder will organically initiate protective violence and aggressive impulses. But if this base effect preserves life, even if it does lead to a vicious act of killing, within just circumstances of actions not tempered by efficiency, worthier than that of an immoral and unjust murderer hellbent on selfish destruction, then surely this is a more preferable outcome, although not ideal, than an unjust death. An act of just killing, even though vicious and brutal, may be morally permissible if it is morally compatible with immediate conditions, i.e. where instinct kicks in and the act was done on an immediate, non-premeditated spur of self-preservation.

A person subject to great stress can do unwise, impulsive things, but if his or her stress burst out in immediate circumstances and against ideal outcomes, such acts *can* nonetheless be just and morally right. However, one ought to be mindful and cautious of such ethical tangents. If killing and violence are a moral necessity, then these acts ought to *ideally* be done painlessly, swiftly, and what can be considered 'cleanly' – efficiently – for one's own mental sake with respect to ethical tangents and in reflection of the foundation of empathy, for a soul acting in vice suffers, and if it must be eliminated by the demands of justice, then it is best done with minimal pain and suffering.

An intuitive thought would be to implement efficient violence and even deadly force through a preference for systematic, impersonal uses of force. Detachment from violence and lethal force can then seem an attractive suggestion. For example,

this case can be illustrated with the use of drone strikes, where the vector performing the attacks – the person operating the drone – may be more detached from the
act in comparison to a person killing someone on the battleground. It is harder to
be assertive with someone when you look him or her in the eyes. I highlighted the
concern for such considerations at the beginning of the discussion of the element of
efficiency in just violence. Namely, the concern is the matter of detachment from the
act of violence through systematic utilities.

Efficiency in violence, when devoid of other criteria of just violence and utilities of practiced morality, can lead to abominable implementations of violence. The
systematic genocide by the Nazi death-machine is a pivotal case for considerations
of the dangers of detached violence and murder. The consideration of mindfulness
with respect to the efficiency of violence is paramount to the implementation of just
violence, for without an impact on the psyche a tangent can incur a corruption of
emptiness where an act fails to realise its own impact, whether from ignorance or
lack of empathy. This consideration, however, does not automatically condemn the
efficiency of some utilities of violence and killing if they satisfy other parameters of
justice.

Drone strikes can theoretically, or at least comparatively, detract from the negative impact of just killing, as would be expectable if the quantifiably same level of
killing was done more 'face-to-face' with, say, a blade. But it is important to stress the
relevance of various forms of mindfulness in such utilities so as to not deny the important place of intuitions in guiding the judgements of people by highlighting the
nature of a drone strike – to kill, maim, or severely injure. Whether drone strikes are
effective or efficient tools of war is not my place to discuss, and neither do I possess
the insight to evaluate the impacts of drone strikes on the spirit and psyche of those
who exercise them, all things relevant to the morality and value of drone strikes. So
I cannot weigh in on a discourse of the actual morality of drone strikes in this given
context. Yet the case does serve as a point of reflection on the dangers of mental and
spiritual detachment from the use of violence.

If one is to draw any principles from this exploration of the dangers of detachment, the guiding point is similar to what I have attempted to show throughout my
discussion of practical morality – that practical morality is largely conditional and
circumstantial. Detachment from violence can be qualified as good or bad depending
on the circumstances and the ethical dynamics involved in an action. A groundwork
for a framework of considerations in morality with reference to structural ethics,
which could and is intended to assist the effectiveness of particular utilities, serves
to posit the criteria instrumental to the considerations of the practised morality and
ethic. Detachment from violence is but one element that is helpful in consideration
of the morality and ethical dynamics of an action. The rule to be concluded concerning the morality of the degrees of detachment in violence is that detachment can be
valid as a means to draw away from the personal corruptive influences of violence,
yet there is a norm to be found before detachment drifts into corrupt violence, which
could be even more dangerous than the personal corruption of employing violence.

Here one can intuitively sense the conceived nature of ethical tangents as subjects
of the dynamic forces no different to physical forces of elasticity 'slingshotting' ethical elements in particular directions, then crossing various ethical spheres and dimensions along the entangled structures of ethics and their causal cascades. The primacy given to forms of mindfulness in the heritin ethos are intended to be utilities
that grant insight into the machinations of these dynamics. Mindfulness – awareness

– provides clarity for personal (subjective) and systemic insight into ethical structures and their many causal ethical tangents. And clearly, as explored in Section 2, we have lagged in our capacity for practical reason to guide our activity and ambitions for the better.

Finally, to move away from the analysis of the practical morality of violence, I want to explore another scenario with the case explored in the justice of brutal, but necessary killing in self-defence in the spur of the moment. It may be counter-intuitive to suppose in such circumstances that there is another viable option to pursue – to not kill, to instead sacrifice oneself. The morality to kill in self-defence is legitimate and correct if satisfactory of justice, yet it is taken for granted in contrast to another equally legitimate and possible course of action – to sacrifice oneself. Sacrifice *can* be an impeccable moral utility in practical morality, especially to tackle violence and the corrosive ethics of Fear. Sacrifice can be the most efficient and profound resolution to violence. Sacrifice is the final mark of the virtues of Liberty, where the capacity to willingly sacrifice oneself is the breath of eudaimonia. However, an eagerness to self-sacrifice can be self-righteous and unjust. Hence, it is imperative to consider the justice of the practical morality of sacrifice to exemplify and formulate the effective, useful, sensible, wise, righteous, and just use of sacrifice.

To conclude, the following Central Principles of the practical morality of violence can be outlined:

Violence can take on two interrelated forms – physical and psychological; the former primarily affects the body, while the latter affects the mind.

Violence is innately imbued with specific forces affecting the character through the psyche and spirit, with physical harm becoming psychological, while psychological becomes physical.

Physical or psychological violence is not inherently worse than the other, subject to degrees of influence and the force exerted.

Violence is a utility that is usually entangled with a sense of control and power, where an ethos of Fear tends to corrupt the utility of violence through the lesser sense of power it grants corresponding to the lesser potential of the fulfilment Fear offers in spirit.

Violence can be qualified as a disease of mind, psyche, morality, and spirit, highlighting it as a social peril equivalent to a disease or plague.

Violence ought to be qualified as an extreme of practical morality, dedicating favour to more ethically stable moral utilities such as negotiation and tacit coercion.

Violence ought to be limited, contained, and eradicated following the duty to implement more constructive endeavour in solidarity with people that does not beckon the deep divide of violence.

All performance and implementation of violence is vulnerable to the corruption of character and deprivation of positive spirit.

Violence can exercise profound and great power on individuals and groups, leaving a last-

ing, often tormented and bitter impression on people and tainting good spirit.

Violence can be a just utility in practical morality.

The justice of violence is subject to the conditions of necessity, immediacy, proportionality, and the Ideal of efficiency; violence is only just – thereby balanced and maximally effective as a utility – when it is necessary in the circumstances of actions to maximise and secure the value of virtue is, immediately necessary, and is proportional to immediacy, with efficiency being a necessary feature of proportionality in some respects, yet an Ideal that may struggle to be maximised in difficult circumstances.

Chapter 22:

Sacrifice

The practical morality of sacrifice deserves its own consideration in the Central Principles. There are degrees of sacrifice, from acts of charity to giving up one's life. Acts of sacrifice can resonate with distinctive ethical tangents including the most profound level of ethics' structures by engaging the central agency of the individual by leaving a lasting impression. Sacrifice can be an instrumental moral utility when exercised properly, virtuously, and righteously. However, similarly, acts of sacrifice can be performed recklessly and senselessly, selfishly and self-righteously.

The justice of the practical morality of sacrifice ought to be established. Sacrifice as a utility can exercise a specific power over ethical tangents that other forces cannot, defining sacrifice as a moral utility in its own league. Sacrifice can affect anyone differently and achieve far more than any other utility. Sacrifice can build character by embracing suffering and defying Fear, while profoundly affecting others through an authority that killing and violence cannot. However, to use this utility of sacrifice in practical morality requires purpose, direction, and mediation. Here is an analysis of sacrifice as a moral utility of both Liberty and of structural moral power.

First, sacrifice holds a definitive role as a moral utility of Liberty. There is no greater action that resonates with virtue than sacrifice. To expose oneself to vulnerability and invite pain requires courage and strength. It is needless to elaborate how personal sacrifice can contribute greatly to others in terms of both community and the Human Imperative. In the ability to sacrifice for the Highest Good, reciprocal of a sense of a greater good, is a notable, noble, and honourable virtue. The mindfulness and virtues required for sacrifice with respect to a sense of empathy towards others and in harmony with the world, to make things better, are characteristics that evoke the spirit of Liberty. The virtues of Liberty are fulfilled through sacrifice by nourishing and evoking characteristics that do not succumb to Fear, whether by defying Fear or by seeing beyond Fear.

The subjective, personal fulfilment of sacrifice is found through the willingness to commit sacrifice in goodwill and in duty. Duty is rewarding in terms of binding a person to meaningful and purposeful living, which facilitates good consequences for ethical environment. If there is anything worth acting on in Liberty, it is duty in Liberty – actions sustaining and expressing Liberty, bettering the world through virtue, justice, and righteousness. The virtues that pertain to sacrifice move spirit and mentality that dedicate interest and value beyond one's immediate self and towards something greater, of higher spirit. The capacity to dedicate attention and effort to the betterment of others, to think beyond oneself, to pay attention to the suffering of the world, and act through the pain that restrains actions against fulfilling greater interests, are the virtues of Liberty in sacrifice.

If these are the virtue-rules and ethical tangents of the morality of sacrifice, then it seems as though sacrifice is nothing more than an exchange of ethical value towards maximising self-interest, losing little to gain much more. Such actions do not seem to be genuine sacrifices, as the person doesn't lose. An act of sacrifice is supposed to lose to protect from greater loss. By sacrificing immediate well-being in Liberty would only serve to exchange ethical interest towards maximising Liberty.

To achieve such a state of character where an act deemed to be of sacrifice is not perceived as sacrifice is to act in virtue-duty. A mentality which does not sense or feel an act of sacrifice as, indeed, sacrifice, is a mentality that has succeeded sacrifice and turned it into duty. This is a mentality that operates in intuition of Liberty. However, to achieve this requires the growth of virtue and development of a spirit and intuition of Liberty and its higher fulfilment.

This is where the virtue-rules of sacrifice serve their moral utility as means to bring one to Liberty. In Liberty, sacrifice is no longer sacrifice, but an act of duty resonating and imbuing spirit with the Harmony of Liberty and empowering Discipline and Defiance through sacrifice. A virtue-rule to outline is that where sacrifice is surpassed by duty, a sense of power arises from Liberty and freedom from Fear, evoking solidarity in Harmony that fulfils a person by binding the mind and spirit to more than Fear and selfishness. However, until such a state of character and spirit is achieved, and the base morality of Fear reigns, acts will not correspond to the duties of Liberty.

It is in the suffering and pain of loss and exposing oneself to vulnerability that the ethical dynamics guided by goodwill breathe the spirit of Liberty. The fulfilment granted by a limited sense of giving to others, of charity, is vulnerable to subjectivity and conditionality. Liberty in sacrifice surpasses these limitations by giving a whole new scope of self-interest in sacrifice that moves the initial intuitions of sacrifice beyond the limitations of perceived loss, towards intuition of Liberty and the maxims of ambition and self-interest. When we lose something, the subsequent suffering is made peace with through focusing on something good, making the pain worth it. By losing something or someone, the best remedy to suffering is growth in virtue and good spirit.

There are, however, degrees of sacrifice, the extremes of which cannot be dismissed by healthy and sensible Liberty. It is intuitive that there is an ethical difference in the spiritual and consequential effects of sacrifice between giving a coin to a beggar and sacrificing one's life. Acts of sacrifice and their effects correspond to the values being exchanged or lost, which is subject to the state of a person's character and one's capacity of dealing with pain.

Of the extremes, there is an enormous difference between what can be considered the ultimate sacrifice, with respect to which sacrificing one's life is spiritually and psychologically heavier than sacrificing the lives of loved ones. These degrees of the morality of sacrifice are central to relevant considerations and mindfulness, because an ultimate sacrifice can become not only a final act, but also the final act of goodwill. The excruciating pain of losing loved ones can bring one to terrible despair that might forever suffocate spirit of positivity and goodwill. Deliberately choosing to sacrifice something as valuable as loved ones would cause far greater pain than losing loved ones to misfortune.

In extreme cases where on must choose to sacrifice oneself or others, there may be a comparative element of fulfilment in going out on one's own terms if a person sacrifices themself. Yet sacrificing others, especially loved ones, will cause much greater pain than the potential peace offered by the liberty of death. Even the pain of others' loss caused by one's intentional sacrifice – the loss caused by someone's choice for others to lose something important, sparing others, will bear the spirit of virtue and righteousness, whereas sacrificing loved ones will not have the same effect. It is clear in these basic terms that the only true ultimate sacrifice that will always be an act of sacrifice concerns extremes, to sacrifice the most valuable part of one's life, especially loved ones and the spirit of Liberty – to embrace duty and surrender happiness. Whether one will be able to sustain or grow in spirit of Liberty after a gruelling sacrifice of loved ones is a gambit and of great uncertainty.

Even so, the pain of continuing to live after committing great sacrifice should not overshadow the incredible virtue necessary to commit the final act of surrendering one's life. The final act of sacrifice giving up one's own life can imbue character with fulfilment unavailable to actions guided by Fear. Sacrifice in Liberty can make one's final moments open to the higher fulfilment of eudaimonia by being truly and absolutely free from Fear.

Although, there are actions of self-sacrifice relating base morality, such as a mother sacrificing her life to protect her child, that warrant greater admiration than certain sacrifices in Liberty, because the former is a greater sacrifice. The mother sacrifices herself for her child not out of strict Fear, but rather out of true unselfish Liberty to ensure the well-being of her child, and is happy to do so; this is eudaimonia. Sacrifice may grant eudaimonia and complete one's life, yet this can only happen when it is one's choice to do so. Where one may question whether the moment of surrendering one's life is worth it, whether to put faith in the promise of eudaimonia, is completely up to the person. However, having the courage and strength to make such a choice already invites true absolution from suffering and Fear.

One has a degree of influence over his or her quality of life, with the fulfilment of autonomy being complete through the autonomy that surpasses the limits of Fear and by choosing how one ends his or her life, something not all people get the chance to do. So it should be, and ultimately is, up to the individual to make the choice – to sacrifice or not. The intuition and sense guiding the merits of the final sacrifice with respect to the corresponding virtue-rule is that we all have a life, yet sometimes that life is deprived of good living if not given a choice.

All life will eventually come to an end, but not all are truly fulfilled in life, with the choice of how one ends his of her life evoking spirit of Liberty and eudaimonia by giving a moment of fulfilment that could never be achieved over an entire lifetime in the suffering of Fear. However, it is crucial to establish that any such merit of sacrifice is fully conditional on the liberty to choose sacrifice, or otherwise the virtue of sacrifice and its potential to grant the fulfilment of Liberty and eudaimonia is neglected and wasted.

In short, one has to be ready to choose sacrifice for sacrifice to be meaningful, fulfilling, and liberating. The Fundamental Principle and the purpose of living are dedicated to the pursuit of flourishing through intuitions and sensations – in spirit. The continuity of life is only a criterion of good living, although a prerequisite. Some people do not like their quality of living and so they end their life, a clear example for the case that life for life's sake is not a fundamental guiding feature of living, being wholly contingent on the reality of worthy living.

In light of all this, it is nonetheless better to live in Liberty and eudaimonia, or to experience Liberty without the necessity of sacrifice. Higher fulfilment and its pinnacle form of eudaimonia can be achieved through means other than the ultimate or final sacrifice, and it is intuitive to posit that this would be more favourable. However, these luxuries are not always available and sometimes people are left with a choice. Thus, rather than establish general rules for a norm and groundwork of the practical morality of sacrifice on unrealistic, unfair, and unappreciative expectations, it is better to pursue continuity, sustainability, and sensibility in sacrifice to maximise its good spirit and virtue. It is generally better to not sacrifice and not expect people to sacrifice than impose a dogma of sacrifice.

Along similar considerations of the effects of sacrifice on the mind and deliberate choices, one has to consider the extremes of sacrifice where one might, for example, have to choose between sacrificing one's own loved ones or the loved ones of others. This can be framed as a case where one has to choose between one's own family or somebody else's family, or two other families. Any morality that tries to be prescriptive in such circumstances is probably delusional in expecting that one choice can be clearer than the other as a moral absolute. Either course, either choice will have a negative impact on the sense of well-being and spirit, with the ultimate choice having to be disposed to individual liberty and judgement. However, one has to be mindful of the effects in such circumstances.

Saving one's own loved ones can prevent the great cost of loss, yet that cost will pass onto others. A person has to consider in full capacity of character and spirit whether one could live with themself, bear the pain of great loss, and continue to act in goodwill if his or her choice involved other people, thereby a greater ethical sum value. Intuitions of compassion might be overwhelmed by forcing the choice of sacrifice onto other people; one might feel too guilty to carry on living if pain was simply passed onto others. The consequence could very well be the decay of compassion and empathy, leading to corruption, which could even betray those one saved.

It is a possible scenario that the consequence of a sacrifice would move others to project their pain onto the world or oneself. The bitterness and resentment of a cruel fate can be blind and limitless; the madness of grief is endless. On the other hand, sacrificing one's loved ones can spare others from great pain, which will then be endured by the self. This could potentially maximise greater sum ethical value and interest, yet the justice of such an act would have to consider broader qualifications of value, which may be unrealistic and impractical in a given moment and could further be greatly swayed by the bias of disproportional entitlement.

It might be better for others if you lived, meaning you have a responsibility to them and to sacrifice others, which is a very delicate moral judgement. Even so, those of the greatest value or the greatest in the hierarchy of an ethical structure have to adhere to the basic duties of virtue, whereby any sense of value and entitlement cannot forget the basic duties of the individual such as not to kill unjustly and to help and protect others.

Sacrificing one's own value to maximise values in terms of the Highest Good and the Imperative is an Ideal, worthy of what can be qualified as Paragon virtues. Yet this cannot be a realistic expectation set as a moral norm. If one chooses to save others and then sacrifice oneself along with that which was lost is a scenario that ought to be considered, and although not ideal, it would still be very much an understandable course of action and worthy of admiration. If the grief of sacrifice was too much and a person decided to take his or her own life, then this is understandable and still deserving of admiration.

In summary concerning the case of sacrifice, serving as a guiding principle-rule in the practical morality of sacrifice, if there is a choice to be made, subject to the conditionality of personal judgement, a principle-rule can and ought to be concluded that in cases of sacrifice one ought to at least save someone or try to do something. The pain and suffering of hard or extreme sacrifices is something that cannot be formulated into a coherent and complete moral framework, for a morality that expects a hard standard from people is doomed to fail, especially when the standard could be wrong. However, to commit great sacrifice is deserving of the Ideals.

A dimension to highlight in the spirit of sacrifice and suffering is our personal place or role in them. We are all born to a particular fate in a deterministic causal cascade of the Highest Good and its many machinations and dynamics. Some people are born to suffer more than others; what we make of our lives is up to us. The dutiful spirit at Liberty is willing to suffer in accordance with goodwill. This raises the question in mindful empathy of what if a different person was in your place.

A deterministic world would dictate the same outcomes and rules regardless of whose consciousness is the operating vector. However, it is central to empathy and good spirit to consider whether or not you would place yourself in someone else's shoes, to spare others of their suffering. In your suffering, if you were given the chance, would you pass it on to another, or would you embrace your circumstance and pursue virtue and duty in it? Would you prefer your true love to die before you do, to spare him or her of the terrible pain of loss? These are legitimate and meaningful questions to meditate on to console virtue.

The character that accepts his or her duty to live a given life is marked by Liberty and virtue-duty. This exercise of mindfulness should serve to empower the spirit of duty and help others understand themselves. However, it is clear that such a principle-rule could lead to the justification of perverse morality of unjustly and illiberally designating people their roles in life. Hence, this thought and reflection of morality is to be designated as a personal virtue-rule for people themselves to reflect on in sincerity of their meditations.

The function of this exercise is to help people get the most out of their endeavour and predicament if it satisfies the liberty of their desires. One cannot be expected to settle for and simply accept his or her position of suffering, as this would undermine the very purpose of ambition to improve on suffering and would neglect liberty. However, this should serve to help people in their ambition of goodwill to grow in virtue by embracing their responsibilities and duties to the Human Imperative, or at least work as a point of reflection if this serves a purpose to people's mindfulness.

These discussions should serve as a basis for understanding the power of sacrifice as a tool of moral ambition in goodwill. Even the most basic reflection of empathy and compassion can appreciate the spirit of sacrifice. Where compassion is numb and empathy is silent, an act of sacrifice has the potential to inspire goodness and evoke empathy where it was thought to be lost. Sacrifice can carry with it a great burden on the mind and spirit, tremendous pain and suffering. Even the most basic and primitive, unmindful empathy can be affected by sacrifice, influencing the core of people. This attribute of sacrifice is extremely valuable in the sense that it can bypass and relieve Fear, to inspire goodwill and virtue, as well as evoke good spirit. This is a moral effect of a profound moral power that few other utilities can achieve, at least not immediately. This is why an act of sacrifice has an imperative role as a distinct utility pursuing the Human Imperative and corresponding to the Highest Good.

Sometimes people won't listen; sometimes people are blind in Fear; sometimes people cannot think beyond Fear; sometimes people lack the inspiration to do what is right because of Fear. It is true that not all issues can be addressed through negotiation, reasoning, and by developing common understanding. Simply telling people around the world to 'get along' will not do anything without a sufficient moral power and force behind such a gesture. But where the immediate effects of such activity are restricted, sacrifice can exercise a swift, profound, and efficient influence on people to achieve a just and righteous ambition. Sometimes sacrifice is necessary for the Highest Good and for the Human Imperative. However, this power is only exercised when a sacrifice is just and sensible, but more on that in later Chapters.

In moral extremes it would be natural to consider whether people should be expected to sacrifice, or whether that decision should be made for them. In other words, can sacrifice be forced on people? Here is an idealistic feature of heritin ethics alongside its emphasis on the adaptive pragmatism of morality. Sacrifice can never be forced onto people and absent the choice to sacrifice.

Consider whether or not in the case of a deadly pandemic a group of people ought to be subjected to experimental treatment at the risk of agonising side-effects. Enforcing the experiment could potentially save human civilisation, yet at an extreme cost of creating a foundation of a civilisation built on enforced sacrifice – a core of a normative structure perhaps doomed to failure. There are some sacrifices that are simply not worth it. It is sensible to argue that society could learn from such a sacrifice that sacrifice is not the answer, that it was a 'one-off'. However, the tangent of the decision and its slippery slope will forever overshadow society.

Another case to consider is whether or not people ought to be sacrificed to save people on a sinking ship. This case serves to highlight the issue of enforcing any form of action on people, with an intended reference to moral brutalism. First of all, sacrifice itself cannot be enforced on anyone. So in the case of the sinking ship, nobody can be legitimately and justly coerced into performing sacrifice against his or her will. This is important in the heritin ethos where sacrifice is only just and fulfilling when it is done in the liberty of the deliberate choice to act on the ethos of Liberty and against or despite Fear. Enforcing sacrifice is completely against the Core Principles of Liberty and its heritin interpretation. If not enforcing sacrifice does lead to death and destruction, then that is the just way of Liberty and the justice of the liberty of morality. Through this spiritual liberty, suffering is released through sacrifice, whereby even the person that should've performed the sacrifice, and did not, ought to be consoled in his or her Fear that leads to the potential death and suffering of many, for such is the spirit of Liberty. However, the pragmatic element of such a morality is that the spirit that fosters such an attitude is the same tangent of morality that could inspire people to choose sacrifice.

Where Fear would prevent people from performing their duty, the ethos and spirit of Liberty is relied on to motivate and guide people into doing the right thing and being rewarded and incentivised. The alternative is mired with risky and dangerous ethical tangents, for enforcing one act of sacrifice without consent will most likely lead to other forms of forced sacrifice, then turning to murder or the deprivation of liberty. If this is the world that arises from an act of Fear that forces sacrifice without moral liberty, a world fundamentally built on and corrupted by vice, then one has to ask whether this is a world worth preserving, building, and fighting for; an ethos of Liberty cannot stand for this and is undeserving of the good spirit of Liberty. This is where virtue-duty in and at Liberty should rein in to overcome the limitations of Fear and for corresponding spirit to be sustainable and continuous.

Moral brutalism, however, permits and enables the justice of enforcing a course of action against people. There then seems to be a contradiction in the morality of sacrifice. This would be the case provided a person acts with respect to others by neglecting their liberty and autonomy. If a person forces a form of sacrifice on others, such as by making them give something up without proper and just consent, or enforces a course of action that violates people's liberty, then the sacrifice of this person, who unjustly forces sacrifice on others, is morally permissible and necessary.

Where one murders another or otherwise acts unjustly through, say, violent means, the person acts against the moral liberty of another individual, forcing others to sacrifice to further one's own ambition. This permits a necessary response in a framework of justice where that enforcement of sacrifice was unjust, and therefore allows the sacrifice of someone that does not abide moral liberty, undermines ethical maxims, and disrupts justice. Therefore, the practical morality of moral brutalism, including violence and killing proportional to unjust and immoral acts, is fully consistent with moral liberty and does not contradict the morality of sacrifice that protests enforced suffering against people's liberty to sacrifice. This logic is intended to be associated with the structuring of ethical tangents, which are built on the foundation of pragmatic self-interest. There are other merits for limiting people's liberty.

A notable case worth considering in the matters of sacrifice is whether a proportion of people can be sacrificed against their will or without their consent in a given extreme circumstance. For example, in an over-populated world with too many people, a 'solution' may come to mind where a vast swathe of people is killed in order for some to survive. Is this moral? On the one hand, going through with such an act could ensure some value is preserved, while begging the question of whether any such value is actually worth sustaining and preserving. On the other hand, such an act would involve killing an unacceptable amount of people, distorting and warping any sense of righteousness in such an act. Moral liberty will play a crucial role in these considerations.

First of all, in terms of moral brutalism, if there is an absolute necessity for an extreme act of sacrifice, of killing billions of people so that at least some can live, then the act of mass killing can be just and moral in an absolute necessity of justice. However, the satisfactory degree of qualifying an act of mass extermination as 'absolutely necessary' is, in practice, very ambiguous and difficult. A dimension of risk and uncertainty will always prevail in the deliberation and analysis of such acts, serving as an example of the limits of ethics and morality as a social science and bound to other modes of thinking and analysis.

In practice, there is likely to always be an alternative to certain actions. Rather than killing people, Liberty ought to follow the direction of tangents that would maximise well-being while minimising negativity. Sacrifice stands as a great virtue, the best implementation of which in the given case can be sacrificing one's own welfare and well-being so that others have a chance. Rather than kill people, it would be better to balance well-being in order to avoid an unnecessary moral extreme. Then again, such an approach might be limited and unsustainable. However, if the problem is indeed mankind's over-population, then it can potentially be resolved without corruptive interference. If mankind is to suffer great loss caused by its own vice, incompetence, compulsiveness, and foolishness, such as in the case of unsustainable population and consumption, then the same vice will consume itself and potentially establish balance. Then one doesn't need to commit gravely immoral acts in the spur of Fear if alternative actions are implausible and unsustainable, therefore invoking the protective approach in normativity of trying to secure what value there is.

The case in mind has many other dimensions to consider for a definitive judgement to be made. But, hopefully, the demonstrated line of reasoning should suffice to demonstrate the moral rulings being considered. The case would have to be subjected to extensive consideration and analysis of the trends of people's behaviour and the predominant normative dynamic in force if a sensible moral judgement is to be made. However, no matter how pessimistic the judgement, there is always an opportunity with respect to the inherent risk and ambiguity of structural normative estimations that an act of great spirit and moral virtue will turn the odds and profoundly influence a given normative dynamic. The sacrifice of one person could inspire the majority of others to commit lesser degrees of their own sacrifice to establish a greater balance and harmony, consequently stability, in a dynamic of ethics troubled by turbulent factors such as over-population. Justice in sacrifice is served best by contributing to balance, cohesion, and harmony through the shared responsibility and dignity of a duty to one another.

In the discussions so far, a topic has been greatly over-shadowed concerning the issue of attachment in sacrifice, as seen with the potentially corruptive and restricted attachment to life that beckons a limited morality through an ethos of Fear. Fear can cloud the judgements and intuitions of morality in a way that limits the ambitions of our Imperative. Attachment to ideals is itself a form of moral corruption, whereby attachment to an ideal vision of society leads to disharmony with change. Attachment to one's own humanity when pain challenges us can cause the suffering of the fear of change, of being afraid of the coldness of pain and rage, corrupting mindfulness in times of distress that can lead to harmony and good ambition. Here lies a broader discussion of the virtue-rules of attachment.

Liberty might suppose, compared to conventional 'spiritual' or even religious practices, that attachment is wrong, that it is bad and can lead to bad things. One might primitively suppose that Liberty means autonomy without attachment and dependency. This interpretation is only partly true. Greater Liberty lies in the capacity to form attachments and enjoy things, while equally not *needing* them for absolute fulfilment. Liberty of spirit is that which can attach to good spirit, things, and people, thereby truly appreciating them and receiving meaningful fulfilment, but not in a way that makes attachment necessary for fulfilment and well-being. For example, true love is based not on attachment, but on growing together. Accordingly, there are two dimensions of attachment that ought to be considered in an ethos of Liberty.

First, the role of power in the autonomy of will. Attachment can lead to dependency and need, subsequently relinquishing autonomy and its mode of fulfilment by undermining inner power. However, this motive for rejecting attachment is itself a form of Fear by rejecting attachment out of aversion for surrendering willpower against Liberty. The paradox here concludes with full autonomy of a will at liberty to either form attachments or not, depending on the intuition of fulfilment. There are painful and corrosive forms of attachment such as addiction. However, one cannot, in mindful and clear intuition, deny that there are forms of attachment that are truly fulfilling. Furthermore, attachment in endeavour gives meaning to action, providing the basis for meaning in ways of life that are worth pursuing – purposeful and meaningful existence. This intuition then paves way to considerations of Liberty in attachment with respect to Harmony.

Attachment can cloud judgement and distract mindfulness from greater ambition. This thought may be associated with some dedicated religious-spiritual practices that deny to themselves pleasurable attachment in favour of 'higher' attachment, which commonly happens to be distorted through base elements. Liberty, however, is most fulfilled, as explored through autonomy, in the freedom to form attachments or not. It is in this function of moral liberty that the spirit of Liberty is actualised. The grounding intuition, as explored through the Void, is that the liberty for some forms of attachment is necessary for truly fulfilling living, yet this fulfilment is balanced with the liberty to also appreciate attachment in good spirit unrestricted by the fear of losing it. The basis for this intuition can be outlined as not pursuing an attachment through a sense of necessity – an intuition that may raise the spirit of Fear as both good and bad – but in a free desire to do so.

As was explored previously with the suffering of sacrifice, letting go of an attachment that causes suffering to others fulfils spirit through the virtues that succeed the pursuit of a suffocated craving bound to Fear. For example, one may have affections towards someone whose interests or affections lie with someone else. Letting go of her, suspending attachment, may be the right thing to do by her to secure her happiness, while equally inspiring dignity in the self through an autonomy that supercedes the powerful constraints of Fear evoking the sense of necessity in attachment while further nourishing the virtues of mindful empathy and compassion. This brings Harmony to oneself and the dynamics of ethics.

Along these lines, the tangents and dynamics of virtue serve in a way that evoke greater spirit and an empowered sense of self, which might be the condition necessary for deserving, and sustaining, goodness and purity in attachment. A simple way of wording the essence of this virtue-rule is as such: Liberty means to be with someone (to be attached) not because one needs to in Fear, but because one is free to act on a desire, by wanting to be with someone without the negativity of spirit overwhelmed and afraid of not being with them. Being mindful of another person's happiness, through empathy, and putting her happiness ahead of your own, is Liberty. Only by living and acting this way, to love this way, can the sentiment be shared and invited. You shouldn't be with someone because they are your happiness, but because they are but a part of your happiness and contribute to your foundation of happiness.

Fear can easily cloud our judgement against our greater interests and betray our ambitions that become distorted by excessive Fear in attachment, with Liberty being a way of mediating attachment. Liberty thus offers another dimension of fulfilment in attachment not convoluted and potentially corrupted by excessive and disproportionate fear of loss, allowing greater fulfilment through mindfulness of the moment at Liberty, a mindfulness honed through the Void and its Ploy emphasising mindful – accentuated – fulfilment of momentary pleasures. Pleasure that is overshadowed by other concerns and Fear is suffocated; pleasure detached from Fear and the loss of pleasure is purer and more fulfilling. Liberty in pleasure and attachment thus enables a greater appreciation through positive spirit absolved of Fear. There is distinct fulfilment and pleasure that can be achieved through the feeling of relief by letting go, relieving the spirit of its Fear and suffering. This is how Harmony is found in attachment and sacrifice.

In terms of virtue-rules, there is no obligation in the liberty of attachment, yet a rule necessary for higher and broader fulfilment in Liberty, imperative for virtue-duty. This liberty in morality and spirit is the dynamic of ethics that leads to greater insight than that which is forever limited by Fear, insight that can bring a person to eudaimonia and absolution through empathy by providing the unifying sense of the universalisable soul and one's place in the world. Attachment to living is instrumental to the spirit of this understanding, moving the self towards the Void and the Ploy if one seeks further, deeper reflection and insight. To achieve the spirit of Liberty requires attachment in the first place, whether by striving towards something and then letting go, or by understanding and being mindful of detachment. Nevertheless, while attachment is a good thing, or can be, the virtue of Liberty can only sustain good spirit in attachment without the corrosive and corruptive aspects of excess Fear when Liberty is upheld. This mode of virtue can only succeed and be useful or meaningful through the will of the individual pursuing and dedicated to Liberty. Sacrifice can thus invoke tangents of virtues that lead to a greater appreciation and enjoyment of what there is.

Fear can be crucial for good intuition through attachment. A parent's love for his or her child is a clear example of base Fear guiding intuitions that produce benevolent and constructive activity by compelling a person to protect his or her child. However, this same Fear and attachment can get the better of our judgement and betray the interests of our children and future generations, an example of Fear that produces a mistake of compassion. Children cannot be completely cradled and protected from suffering, while compassion and mindful empathy equally tell us that we ought not to harm children, yet offer them guidance by teaching them how to live and act autonomously. Where clarity is necessary in judgements concerning our greater interests, as with the case of caring for children, a balance may be best achieved through mindful reflection and judgement through Liberty surpassing the shrouded judgement of overwhelming Fear. It is clear that sensibility and wisdom are necessary for moral behaviour and the best pursuits in life, with attachment to loved ones being a good example of this. To achieve balance in our endeavours, including sacrifice, requires a formulation of justice in the practical morality of sacrifice.

Justice in sacrifice is measured through ethical effectiveness and quality of value. Relating to the case of the parent-child relation, sacrifice can be reckless and negligent. This corresponds to an issue in terms of the virtue-rules of sacrifice concerning the potential transition in, or pursuit of, an ambition of Liberty in parallel to other commitments and responsibilities. Sometimes there comes a point in life where a person desires change and a fresh start. This can lead to reckless and irresponsible behaviour. Liberty is only as good as its virtues and duties, for which Liberty, through the Ploy, finds duty and virtue the worthiest ambitions and pursuits of goodwill. It takes time, practise, experience, and habit to learn and embrace Liberty. For one, if a person intends to make changes to his or her life and dedicate themself to a particular goal, one ought to understand what he or she is getting into and what is expected of the person. If one is to live by an ethos of Liberty, one must first grow in virtue, particularly empathy. This leads to considerations of just sacrifice.

Mindfulness of empathy evokes virtue in the character aspiring to Liberty by moving one's intentions beyond selfishness and towards maxims of self-interest. It is, therefore, essential to be mindful of the consequences of one's actions, especially in impulsive spurs towards change and transition, and to be mindful of other major principles of morality, notably the Central Principles, to learn from them and help them guide towards the spirit of Liberty and coherent, functional normativity. One such case related to attachment and engagement with one's loved ones is that the pursuit of Liberty should console, consider, and be mindful of the interests and needs of others. One may be eager to self-sacrifice in the pursuit of the virtues of Liberty, yet this sacrifice might not be in harmony with good consequences that would unjustly affect others. Therefore, criteria of necessity and, accordingly, immediacy are useful in considerations of the justice of sacrifice.

Transition towards an ethic of Liberty can move a person to reckless and sense-less expenditure as part of undisciplined Defiance. I nearly lost my life making this mistake, and apparently I am a stubborn learner. Defiance in Liberty might see value in giving all of one's wealth to charity. Such behaviour could undermine responsi-bilities, duties, and what is immediately important in terms of those closest to you and people who depend on you, or at least depend on you more than the chance of charity. A father giving away all his wealth and condemning his family and children to poverty is not a wise or sustainable path, certainly not of wise virtue. Further-more, this course of action would neglect the parameter of moral liberty in terms of the people one is responsible to such as one's children or partner. An example of a more sustainable solution is to give to charity what one can or spend one's wealth in a potentially more expensive, but more sustainable way, such as in terms of care for the environment, while inspiring one's loved ones and children to act in greater virtue and goodwill. If a wealthy nation gave up a disproportionate amount of wealth to a developing, largely impoverished nation, which could potentially squander the donated aid or lose it through corruption, then development programmes through financial aid might not be sustainable, and a developed nation might squander its position and global value, therefore neglecting justice.

Another example of a potentially unjust sacrifice in terms of necessity and im-mediacy is whether to surrender one's belongings if one is threatened with being robbed or mugged. By subjecting oneself to needless risk under the perceived guise of Defiance by not complying with the criminal extorting wealth, one simply puts themself in danger that could, through death, lead to a criminal committing a much worse crime than he intended and leaving a family without a parent and depriving young people of an important figurehead in their lives. It is better to sacrifice one's wealth to a mugger and bandit than to surrender one's life.

A person who does not commit to vice is more valuable alive than dead by re-fusing to unnecessarily comply with a less important and less valuable dynamic in ethics caused by a character of vice, a dynamic which would ideally be overshadowed by the goodness of a virtuous individual and righteous, moral citizen of society and community. But if one was to choose whether or not to sacrifice his or her life or the life of another, then one has to consider, in fair reflection, the values of the ethical tangents and vectors involved. However, a person willing to sacrifice themself is a person that ought to commit the necessary act, even if another should ideally do so to maximise global interest yet is not prepared to make the right choice. There then arises a momentary spark of value through the individual willing to commit a necessary sacrifice in an immediate circumstance that requires extreme actions. How people act in such conditions is up to them.

Contingent aspects of the morality of sacrifice must also consider the immediate necessity of sacrifice. There is a time and place where the utility of sacrifice serves its purpose as a maxim of applied virtue. A needless sacrifice will neglect the right-eousness of an act, limiting its effect as a moral utility. Where there is excess and negligence in acts of moral brutalism, similar sorts of rules apply to the morality of sacrifice. A reckless sacrifice will not have the same effect as a sacrifice that satis-fies immediate necessity and in accordance with the demands of circumstances. The avoidable, unnecessary great sacrifice of one's life could have the effect of only evok-ing senselessness and selfishness in the person who commits the sacrifice. A person that sacrifices themself without the necessity to do so or who sacrifices loved ones in misguided ambition will not incur the spirit and great moral force of righteous sacrifice.

There is a distinction to be made between righteous sacrifice and *self-righteous* sacrifice. A righteous sacrifice is one that satisfies the conditions of justice, in other words one that sacrifices oneself or performs an action related to sacrifice in a manner that maximises, or balances, greater value and interest. Self-righteous sacrifice, however, can be identified as the sacrifice made unjustly in the pursuit of selfish ambitions. For example, a person might be moved to sacrifice others for one's own ambitions of power, whether in Fear or misguided Liberty. This is a form of sacrifice focused on one's narrow scope of interest that denies to itself the mindfulness and spirit of Harmony through the Highest Good. These forms of sacrifice are not sacrifices at all and not acts of duty; they are mere acts of selfish intent – acts of self-righteous sacrifice.

Any act of sacrifice or practical moral of Liberty is only just, moral, and virtuous if it is one in accordance with goodwill, the Imperative, and the Highest Good, with mindfulness and the adaptive mechanisms of normativity concerned with the growth of the mind, spirit, and morality towards the Highest Good. Sacrifice in the relevant degree is a contributing factor to the expansion of virtue and development of normativity. An ambition that is limited in its selfish interest, lacking the virtue of broad self-interest worthy of dedicated virtue, cannot fulfil the maxims of virtue by limiting the scope of the mind, character, and spirit. To maximise selfish ambitions through sacrifice, whether because judgement is clouded by Fear or lacks empathy, is to commit an act of self-righteousness.

A self-righteous act of sacrifice is not in accordance with goodwill, and is thus wrong. An act of sacrifice beckoning virtue and good spirit, such as personal fulfilment through Liberty in exercising one's duties, consistent with considerations of justice that necessitate an act of sacrifice, is a righteous one. Where an act of sacrifice can be fulfilling in ignorance of the consequences one is responsible for, a righteous and just sacrifice is one that is not performed ignorantly, selfishly, and senselessly. It might not matter to the individual in the moment of his or her spirit freed from suffering through sacrifice, yet a person that is mindful of the circumstances and the Highest Good will be bound to the considerations of the consequences of one's actions. The consideration of consequences is, hence, necessary for any coherent justice in an act of sacrifice bound to the criteria of necessity and immediacy. A sacrifice is of higher righteousness and Ideal when it is performed wisely and intelligently in consideration of good consequence of one's actions.

Considerations of righteousness in sacrifice can then be distorted by estimations and a sense of entitlement in ethical value. An act of sacrifice, as any practice of morality, ought to consider and maximise value in the pursuit of ethical interest and fulfilment. Should one save a stranger or a friend? An act of sacrifice merely for the sake of sacrifice to pursue virtue of Liberty is of misguided intent and is wrong, suggesting that to sacrifice one's friend for the stranger simply to maximise one's pursuit of virtue is not right.

If one of the persons in the considered hypothetical case offers to sacrifice themself for the sake of the other, then he or she ought to be sacrificed in accordance with the character that is at peace with such an outcome. If both persons offer to sacrifice themselves, then one must act on the judgement of the estimated greater value.

The stranger is a matter of uncertainty and ambiguity if nothing is known about him or her, therefore suggesting the best choice is to act according to variables with the greatest certainty, including the familiar person, implying the better choice is to save the friend. A friend is a more familiar vector, the consequences of which can be relatively more predictable than the uncertainty of the unfamiliar vector.

Sacrificing the friend could condemn one's being and psyche to a state of misery and deprivation of good spirit and virtue. Sacrificing one's friend, leading to one's despair and final virtue, is an important element to consider in the choice of sacrifice, whereby the choice that kills virtue could produce worse tangents than sparing a life with untold consequences. However, this same choice could also lead to greater loss and despair through the guilt of not saving the other person, especially if one finds out that the consequence is more saddening than the personal loss of a friend and the comparatively lesser loss of ethical value. However, the rule still stands that so long as somebody is saved, the choice can be considered morally right, provided the circumstances were just and right in terms of the given variables in deliberation.

Another case to consider is who should be chosen between one's friend and a person of great global value such as a unique philanthropist with special talents or knowledge. Should one save a medical extraordinaire that could save millions of lives through his or her work, or save one's friend? The same thinking would apply as above, but with notable differences.

For one, it is intuitive to suppose that the most righteous and Ideal choice would be to save the extraordinaire. However, there would still be degrees of potential ambiguities such as whether one's sacrifice of the extraordinaire would motivate the self to redeem the loss. However, saving the friend would not be wrong, even if less Ideal. If the extraordinaire agrees to his sacrifice, while the friend does not, then there is a much more profound choice to be made.

It would be right to sacrifice the person who consents rather than the person who is not prepared for the virtue and duty to self-sacrifice. Sacrificing the person who does not want to be sacrificed could produce more negativity and moral corruption than allowing the self-sacrifice of the person with valuable global utility. In this case, the value of the person who is willing to be sacrificed, despite his or her valuable utility for the Imperative, is greatest in terms of his or her virtue of willing self-sacrifice, the moral liberty of which could potentially produce more stable ethical dynamics.

This principle-rule, however, is very ambiguous with respect to circumstances. Even though the extraordinaire might not provide a panacea for a disease to save the world, he is nonetheless bound to the basic duties of virtue and decency that are expected of any human being, which is above all a virtue-rule for personal reflection. At the same time, there is a dimension of necessity in a choice where liberty is constrained such that one can also legitimately sacrifice the friend against her will because there is the conditionality of necessity in the choice of sacrifice. Sometimes it is one's duty to sacrifice for the Highest Good, when it is necessary with respect to other people, duties, and Core and Central Principles. This, however, is subject to the cost one will have to commit in a particular sacrifice, which could be framed in terms of either suffering the loss of a friend, but embracing virtue, or suffer the guilt of greater global loss and the potential subsequent loss of the self.

Where sacrifice is a genuine act of sacrifice, where one has the choice and commits to the Ideal choice, this is the mark of Paragon virtue. However, this virtue of great suffering and empathy, leading to eudaimonia, as both the final sacrifice and ultimate sacrifice, cannot be an expectation, as the pursuit of the Ideals is left to the liberty of individual character. Such is the weight and burden of Paragon virtues, yet ones that *can* lead to the absolution of eudaimonia.

Pragmatic, rather than profound, sacrifice is more intuitive and ethically certain in terms of the exchange of value. There are errors and mistakes in my writing, stylistically and grammatically. Due to the circumstances, I could not afford an editor other than the help of my father in major parts. Considering that this work discusses serious topics and is dedicated to educated and sensible people, one grammatical mistake can undermine the perception of this work's ideas. I could not release a perfect copy and had to do what I could to the best of my abilities and resources, including time. Releasing an imperfect script will potentially deter certain readers and undermine this philosophy. However, not releasing this book and philosophy would potentially incur greater ethical loss than the risk of *some* people not taking it seriously. Perfection had to be sacrificed in favour of pragmatism and necessity. Therefore, it is clear that the sacrifice of not releasing or producing a perfect manuscript is greater than releasing something legible and coherent, meaning that the sacrifice was right, hopefully. Then, this idea in itself is more valuable than a perfect style of writing, especially since I consider myself an ethicist above being a writer.

These are the principles to be outlined for the practical morality of sacrifice:

Sacrifice is a mark of great virtue in accordance with the capacity of character able to sacrifice and exercise duty.

The degrees of sacrifice correspond to the degrees of ethical influence with respect to the relevant tangents; great sacrifice marks great virtue, while lesser sacrifice suggests less ethical and moral weight.

Sacrifice will pave way to virtue, then duty; an act of duty is not one of sacrifice, but one of self-actualising virtue without the common sensation of loss in sacrifice.

No matter the virtue and duty, some extreme acts are nonetheless sacrifices, especially concerning someone precious such as loved ones.

Acts of sacrifice ought to only be performed in moral and spiritual liberty; acts of sacrifice can never be forced onto people or expected of people.

Sacrificing others, in accordance with moral brutalism, is only a just dimension of the limits of tolerable liberty that permits just responses to immorality; sacrificing others is only permissible if the actions of others were immoral and unjust with reference to the criterion of forcing sacrifice on others.

Sacrifice is the greatest utility in the service of the morality and spirit of Liberty.

Acts of sacrifice can exercise a profound power over people through the virtues of spirit and character required for an act of sacrifice to be made.

Acts of sacrifice must be mediated by justice, according to which key virtues are sensibility, wisdom, and mindfulness of the consequences of actions.

Acts of sacrifice ought to be judged, and enacted, with reference to considerations of value.

Considerations of value in the justice of sacrifice must not deny or neglect the foundations of virtues and duties pertaining to justice and one's choice of action, whereby even the most ethically valuable and important people are only as worth as their virtue corresponding to duty.

Sacrifice can serve as a means of justice to promote and/or secure greater value, yet the justice of such an act must be tempered and heavily mediated by an understanding of the immediate necessity for securing value.

Sacrifice is just when it is righteous, with self-righteous and selfish sacrifice not being just or moral.

Chapter 23:

Happiness and Eudaimonia

The subject of happiness is central to any ethic, moral philosophy, and way of life. Happiness is fundamental to any moral creed. Happiness and sense of well-being are vital to good living. Happiness has its own aspect of morality and Central Principles. Even though the combinatorialist normative framework used in this philosophy values well-being and flourishing, then happiness and eudaimonia, a practical morality of happiness and eudaimonia in terms of virtue-rules is important. Rather than set a morality of happiness in terms of principle-rules contingent on other ambitions of ethics and morality, happiness and eudaimonia in morality will be employed as utilities bridging the core ethos and practical morality.

In other words, happiness and eudaimonia are intended to combine and conjoin aspects of ethics and normativity through a groundwork of virtue-rules dedicated to happiness and eudaimonia. Accordingly, I will outline the philosophical aspect of happiness and eudaimonia in heritin ethics, their virtue-rules, their role and utility, and what value they hold or ought to hold.

Not everyone is happy, not everyone will be happy, not everyone can be happy, and not everyone wants to be happy. Happiness can be an inherently subjective sentiment and mental state, as it relates to variations in the sensation and perception of well-being. When people feel fulfilled, when they find joy in life, when their minds are at ease, when they feel like they are doing well, then people can find happiness. The guidance of base morality might pursue and achieve degrees of happiness through security such as financial security. Similarly, a healthy family might constitute happiness, just as a stable, good natured, and good spirited community can lead to happiness.

Morality differs in unmediated sentiment, subsequently so does the sense of prosperity and happiness, leading to disparity and contradiction. Joy and pleasure are significant aspects of happiness, but full happiness of and through higher fulfilment requires meaning. People may claim that happiness comes from being kind and good to others; people might say that happiness comes with love or by surrendering one's spirit to a higher power; some people believe that happiness is found in the joy of pleasure. There is no absolute formula for happiness given the many different things that evoke a sense of happiness, yet there are systemic features of ethics that do exemplify foundational aspects of happiness and fulfilment. However, where there is ambiguity in happiness and discord in base-reason, there is a broader form of happiness in terms of higher fulfilment through the synchrony of all-reason.

Furthermore, in Liberty, there is a much greater and distinct form of fulfilment through intuition and pleasure, of a 'higher', more relieving sort – *eudaimonia*. The virtue-rules of sacrifice and defying suffering evoke the intuitions of eudaimonia through Liberty in suffering and pain, by bringing relief to a foundation of the spirit of Fear that continues to crave and is never relieved or fulfilled by the corrupted and faulty function of Fear.

Eudaimonia is considered to be another parallel to happiness, yet it is not one that necessarily contradicts or rejects happiness. However, happiness can be hard to come by and common answers to happiness don't apply universally. Sometimes, rather than achieving fulfilment through joy and pleasure, one can be fulfilled through contentment and peace, through ease of the mind free even from the inclination towards joy and happiness. This is the difference between happiness and eudaimonia or a higher sort of happiness in Liberty.

Some formulations of happiness can neglect the balance necessary between positivity and negativity and between the faculties of reason. But where answers to the question of happiness are conditional with respect to ethical environment, all people can appreciate the universal sensation of relief from pain and suffering – the fulfilling spirit of Liberty. Moral brutalism and extremes can deprive the spirit of any joy; similarly, mental traps, such as depression, might cause too much pain for a person to be joyous or happy in the moment. This is where the fulfilment of Liberty, with the highest form being the absolution of eudaimonia, exemplifies itself as a distinct form of happiness, different to joy and base happiness.

Some can be happy, but will not be; some cannot be happy, as the part of self that can sustain happiness is gone or ripped out to never be resurrected, to feel only in the shadow of happiness. But even those without happiness can be fulfilled and satisfied beyond measure of joy, for they can live beyond the pursuit of happiness. In eudaimonia of Liberty, happiness and joy become of secondary value to fulfilment, with primacy dedicated to Liberty rising above the conditions of good living in terms of happiness and pain. Then, through the virtues of Liberty, happiness becomes possible and sustainable – one becomes free to be happy. Happiness is a central mental state, while Liberty is a core ambition, attitude, mentality, and spirit. Happiness is momentary; Liberty is enduring and relentless. Liberty does not reject or undervalue happiness; Liberty means finding good living whether or not one is happy, to be free in happiness, to live fulfilled and live in good spirit independent of joy and happiness.

Section 2 argued that ethics, morality, and spiritual practices have not kept up developmental pace with the technological and social advancement of modernity. Office desk jobs do not satisfy the same instincts, and ethics, morality, mentality, and spirit have not adapted. Instinct has transformed the world beyond instinct. The past of shallow instinct is unbefitting of the post-modernity of global civilisation. Technology has shaped the dynamism of modern life. Technology and modernity provided a structural pathway for the tangents of base-reason to flood a rapidly developing structure, yet the Core of this structure in terms of individuals has not coherently or fully adapted through mental, moral, and spiritual development. We are learning how to live in the modern world; sensibility and wisdom are not silent.

However, progress has not been sufficient – we are not adapting quickly enough. Modernity is stuck in the discord of reason, of madness in idleness as the oddity of modernity where advancement has moved mankind far away from the Void and spiritual emptiness, to only be confronted by them again. Rising mental issues, such as anxiety and depression, and the emerging many different ways of dealing with the stress of modern life in society and mass urban communities, are cases in point for the incomplete moral and spiritual adaptation to modernity.

In stability, having fulfilled our basic needs, we can become confused about what to do next. There are many answers to the questions of the future, to avoiding spiritual emptiness and suffering. Distracting oneself from emptiness and pain, commonly threatening the very stability that produced discord through stability, is an ethical direction that fundamentally averts the very essence of the problem and suffering – the Void. Among all the answers to happiness there are few real solutions. In security, stability, and complacency we can become idle and distracted from serious threats and problems. The lack of mindfulness and discipline thus produces a fundamental flaw in a structure of ethics.

In these ethical dynamics with a disrupted and disfigured Core, there can be little-to-no true happiness, yet glimpses of spiritual liberty and freedom from pain can invite intuitions down a different ethical ambition towards eudaimonia and new happiness. Spiritual emptiness and the fundamental instability of ethical structures dominated by immoderate base morality corrupted by Fear lead people down different paths, looking towards a hopeful future or remembering traditions of the past. Conventional happiness of past traditions no longer applies in modern societies and ethical environments. In our self-obsessive pursuit of happiness as distraction and immediate satisfaction and gratification, many have lost sight of something far more important than happiness in terms of joy and pleasure – a foundation of fulfilling and continuous living in good spirit. A focus and determination of an ethos bound to the primacy of base-reason can no longer fully satisfy the intuitions and spirit of well-being. The understanding of happiness must be revised to set and illuminate new foundations of happiness beyond and through spiritual emptiness.

An alternative devised in this moral philosophy converges on the Void and through it introduces a new foundation for ethical structure – through Liberty fully actualised and found through the Ploy of Consciousness. Even though the absolute freedom of the Void and through the Ploy is not necessary for global and everyone's happiness, a catalyst for related tangents is necessary. Discipline and mindfulness are the virtues of happiness in a new era – of happiness fulfilling, harmonising, and synchronising the desires and interests of both faculties of reason.

Joy and pleasure in happiness can make a person to complacent and idle, make one vulnerable to the corruption of attachment to pleasure avoiding pain. Happiness, pleasure, joy, and stability are by no means wrong or bad things, yet they can become susceptible to the corruption of blind attachment through the lack of virtue. Liberty and eudaimonia can, and should, aid the continuity and mediation of happiness. As mentioned in the discourse of suffering, a virtue-rule is in order where one enjoys moments of peace to rest and meditate and reflect on where one is heading, as well as to heal and grow in character. Overwhelming and constant pain and suffering in life will not lead to a good quality of living or foster greater virtue; growth from pain comes through moments of relief. Liberty means letting go of joy and pleasure to find greater mindfulness that evokes and sustains happiness itself.

Happiness, joy, and pleasure can themselves foster a psyche too attached to positivity and clouded by the lack of mindfulness. Sometimes, expecting bad things and being cautious can help the continuity of happiness and pleasure, but this can also similarly be achieved by being mindful and sensible in Fear. In the ability to confront and embrace suffering and pain, one can grow in virtue of spiritual liberty, providing the basis for eudaimonia and true happiness. Focusing on happiness as a distraction from a spiritual and mental wound is not a sustainable solution. Happiness is the

ability *to* be happy, not just free from pain. To be happy one must be able to supercede suffering, to be happy in pain and be able to grow beyond and without pain.

The conditions of one's life are not always ideal for achieving happiness, especially in terms of base morality in a deeply troubled world and individual. It is despicable
to tell a starving child and family stricken by poverty that they could be happy while
they starve and suffer from disease. Neither should it be said that the impoverished
ought to settle for their pain and unhappiness. But in all suffering and adversity,
there is always a choice and there are always opportunities to find relief through
Liberty, although this can be extremely difficult.

This is not a principle-rule to be implemented, yet it is a personal, subjective virtue-rule useful for persons lost and confused in their suffering. Even if one cannot be
happy or live in joy, one can nonetheless find Liberty, relief from pain and suffering,
and then eudaimonia – a higher happiness. These mindful virtues of eudaimonia
and higher fulfilment in Liberty nourish the foundation of spirit through high-reason, harmonising all-reason, paving way to virtue-duty.

Not being detached and overly distracted by joy and pleasure is a focal point of
mindful empathy concerning vice and suffering, doing a service to the intuitions
striving to absolve suffering and fulfil the Imperative of the soul. Eudaimonia can
give happiness to all and serve the Human Imperative and Highest Good through
oneself more than base joy and happiness. Liberty is actualised and achieved through
Discipline and Harmony – through balance, moderation, and moral liberty. When
the core of oneself and spirit is satisfied and relieved from pain, leading to eudaimonia, this gives balance to all other pursuits and fulfilments in life.

This can be outlined analogously to a 'bottom-up' approach to happiness through
eudaimonia, one that is eventually aimed towards improving ethical environment
by facilitating happiness in others and oneself. This design of a normative direction
is what compliments and fulfils the Central Principles in their ambition to improve
state of being through oneself and the world, ambitions that ought to serve in harmony and balance, complete through the fulfilment of eudaimonia and happiness.

To cultivate the virtues of spiritual liberty, one has to succeed Fear, pain, and
suffering by confronting and defying them; one must endure. For this to happen requires discipline and positive, uplifting influences that make the pursuit of spiritual
liberty continuous and sustainable. In the pursuit of Liberty, one ought not to forget
joy, pleasure, and happiness. However, the growth of character requires a person to
endure and overcome adversity and rise in virtue.

Happiness cannot be complete in its highest form without confronting adversity.
The basic happiness of distraction is not a sustainable and effective ethic. It is better to genuinely make a child happy than simply distract the child with a toy. The
same goes for mature individuals and characters. Happiness cannot be sustained and
achieved while pain and vice are left to fester beneath the surface of conscious awareness. For happiness to be actualised, especially with eudaimonia, pain and suffering
must be confronted for positive spirit and goodwill to reach and influence the core
of the self. True happiness is built on a foundation of fulfilment and satisfaction, and
not on momentary pleasure or attachment.

Happiness is an intuition and sensation relating to well-being, which comes in
many forms. If distraction from pain is a central condition of well-being, then this
happiness is not complete or full. For example, a person might live in the shadow
of memories of mistakes, in shame or guilt, or suffer from moral and psychological
weakness. Pursuing pleasure and joy to merely distract from fundamental suffering

is not the best or a sustainable solution. But to address and confront fundamental pain requires strength, courage, mindfulness, and wisdom.

It is not easy to accept one's limits, vulnerabilities, weaknesses, and imperfections. The ego is naturally inclined to defend the self, a benevolent force that tries to facilitate security by steering away from suffering, in doing so only betraying the self and corrupting the utility of ego. The fulfilment of Liberty is found in the ability to confront one's own vices and vulnerabilities, to then improve on them and become better, stronger, and wiser. Confronting pain is the first step to making peace with pain by nurturing the resolve to do so, by developing empathy and wisdom to understand and by finding the courage to forgive.

Fundamental resolution of suffering and relief from pain lead to happiness, but do not necessarily produce happiness. When we react through unresolved vice and pain, we project pain on our surrounding world and punish ourselves, often without awareness of our intentions and behaviour. Addressing this malevolent behaviour of corrupt ethics that poorly cope with pain through Fear is the path to happiness, first by having the courage to be honest with the self. Happiness comes through good spirit and goodwill, through an attitude and mentality that is able to generate and sustain positivity and happiness.

People aren't always good at reading and understanding themselves and their behaviour, especially when difficult feelings are involved. It seems we often act based on a sort of auto-pilot, in liberty of normativity without awareness and understanding of our behaviour, intentions, and desires. An accentuated ethos of base morality devoid of mindfulness is prone to compulsive actions and a morality of inclination. Sometimes this kind of behaviour is considered irrational. There are limits to our rationale and our awareness. For virtue and goodwill to succeed, and for happiness to be evoked in all parts of the self, spirit, and mind, actions must resonate with the subconsciousness. To be mindful of our subconscious states requires awareness and mindfulness, acceptance of sensations and intuitions, and paying attention to our feelings and intuitions.

Our feelings reflect fundamental parts of ourselves – of the state of the psyche and spirit. Sometimes we act according to such intuitions without understanding them and being mindful of them. For the virtues of goodwill to succeed requires mindfulness and awareness of intuitions of subconscious origins, which in turn affects the subconsciousness and the subconscious self. True happiness can only be found when all dimensions and levels of the psyche are fulfilled and given peace and relief. But to find peace of mind, one ought not to be in constant conflict with the self and one's intuitions and feelings. Happiness and eudaimonia require harmony and synchrony in reason – in the self and one's desires. True happiness requires self-control and mindfulness – utilities of high-reason. These virtues, through high-reason, grant the ability to invite and embrace painful intuitions, including those that compromise everything a person may know, that rattle the core of one's identity, engaging unconscious pain and parts of the self.

The Liberty of mindfulness by the Void works by detaching from pain in order to let the pain in, making the self aware of pain. Then, when we know we are in pain, can accept the vulnerability of experiencing pain, and understand *why* we are in pain, Liberty can begin to engage that pain and make peace with it by accepting pain and beginning the process of healing. Or, at the very least, mindfulness by the Void will allow a person to acknowledge subconscious pain, to then address the issue. Only by confronting suffering through and with positivity can happiness be truly achieved and sustained.

To *become* truly happy, we must bring happiness to the parts of ourselves that we have little-to-no control over or understanding of. Unconscious behaviour leads to reactions that hurt us and others. Acknowledging this and making peace with behaviour over which we had no control, or the pain we could not control, is key to true happiness. We must forgive ourselves and our Fear, then forgive others, to rise above pain and become happy. Surrendering control over the self to *allow* virtues and positivity at liberty to grow organically – goodwill – is key to true happiness. Making peace with one's mistakes, deliberate or not, is just one of the uses of Liberty in the pursuit of happiness. This journey of growth and self-discovery can be a painful, but this is what makes it so rewarding.

Our instincts and baser selves are what primarily ground us in engaged everyday life. Instincts have given us life enriched by high-reason. Fear and instincts have driven growth and progress to the point that we can embrace Liberty and eudaimonia. Fear amplifies and resonates with Liberty; instinct led to rationality. Through instincts and emotions, we become grounded in the world, steering us away from the delusions of detached rationale. Sentiments and the intuitions of instincts harmonise life, attach us to the world that bred us, and are fundamental to actual *living*.

Mistakes are an intrinsic part of growth. Instincts and emotional reactions get it wrong at times and get the better of us. By accepting this intrinsic part of life and making peace with it, while not settling for pain, spiritual liberty is brought to the baser self, soothing pain and leading to happiness. By making peace with Fear we bring contentment to the spirit and invite happiness. Where one becomes at liberty to trust and follow instincts in goodwill, high-reason and all its virtues reach into the world and amplify sensations, feelings, and sentiments with mindfulness and spiritual liberty. This leads to harmony in all-reason and spirit, inviting true happiness. True happiness is found in actual living, in everyday life, not in idealisation and delusion.

A basic understanding of happiness is defined by intuitions relating to joy and pleasure appealing only to the baser self. A higher happiness is inner peace, which can deny to itself many other worthy fulfilments in life. Happiness focused on a single one of its aspects – baser or higher – is incomplete. Fulfilment of every aspect of goodness, base and high, is required for true happiness. The happiness of joy is a fleeting wisp of consciousness, a mental state that comes and goes like any other. The dogmatic and maladaptive pursuit of higher fulfilment through inner peace, while admirable and has much to teach, is not universally applicable and will not achieve the greatest happiness of eudaimonia, for inner peace isn't detachment and can't be found in the Void alone. Only spiritual liberty in all parts of the self and unafraid to no longer be happy grants *a moment* of true happiness.

Eudaimonia as a transcendent and ethereal happiness is the liberty to not be happy, yet be fulfilled and in touch with the world and the self *to be* happy. There will be times in life when we are happy, joyous, grieving, sad, in pain, or bored and empty; true happiness as eudaimonia is peace and spiritual liberty in all such states as the peace of accepting all change in spirit. This mode of spirit will not extinguish the flame of the soul's ambition, but it will set it free to pursue what the soul and spirit truly value, as well as reveal what is most valuable.

True happiness is not idleness in living or the absolution of detachment. True happiness is the liberty to pursue the best in life despite the suffering, but also the liberty to let go of that goodness once it has been achieved. True happiness is freedom from Fear and unfulfillable desires, but also the freedom of not being afraid to experience good things. True happiness means being at peace with not being happy and accepting suffering, while also to be at liberty to enjoy when one is happy. It is okay not to be happy, to be in pain, to suffer; it is okay to be vulnerable. True peace and happiness come from being happy or suffering. The liberty of eudaimonia is to allow oneself to be joyful or in pain, to not restrict the spirit to only one of its aspects, to allow the spirit to grow. Eudaimonia means to feel and be alive beyond the shadow of the fear of death and pain, to be at peace with the shadow's loving nurture as a guardian unable to see the light.

The Central Principles of happiness correspond to moral liberty and the liberty of morality. One ought to allow themself to feel whatever one might feel. Suffering and happiness are a natural part of life, and finding harmony with this bolsters mindfulness and discipline, as well as gives special insight crucial to further adaptation and growth. People can't always just work through certain things and painful experiences – they need to grow and learn first. Needlessly punishing oneself for feeling certain things is bad. One must be in harmony with the self and the world – with change – to become truly happy and for suffering to be absolved in all its aspects. I don't know everything there is to know about happiness; I might not be happy writing this.

Many parts of this philosophy revised and reinterpreted many other schools of thought and philosophers, whereby I didn't include relevant discussions of specific ideas for the sake of simplicity and straightforwardness. Sometimes I feel unoriginal, that the arguments in this book are only compiled ideas of other people, and worse yet, maybe my informality is downright negligence and makes me a fraud. When I was writing this I sometimes felt like a difference wouldn't be made, to then conclude that I just have to wait and see, that I had to try – the test of any theory.

These moments can be discouraging, uninspiring, and disheartening. But by accepting these feelings, being mindful of them, and allowing myself bouts of misery, I do not torment myself with inner conflict borne of unhelpful expectations, and so my intuitions become free. I can see beyond immediate conscious mental states, beyond immediate suffering and happiness, which then reinforces moral liberty to behave more adaptively than the constrictions of narrow mental states – beyond immediate happiness or suffering. This is truly liberating, leading to its own unique happiness and fulfilment. The soul and spirit are not obligated to a single form of existence and state, and neither is polarity their purpose. Being free to find goodness in anything, no matter how tragic or painful, is the way to make good on suffering, transforming suffering into something good, leading to spiritual liberty and happiness. True happiness is an amplified state combining suffering, relief, and fulfilment in an adaptive cyclical dynamic of ethics, mentality, and spirit.

The greatest happiness in life comes through making others happy, by bringing goodness into the world. It makes all struggle worth it, gives a sense of meaning and purpose through meaningful functions appealing to the core of the self – to core pain and joy, and makes good on suffering for many profound reasons – to give a sense of control and relief, to affirm one's self-value and ego. The eternal struggle of duty to make the world a better place is the absolute freedom of eternal happiness. But while this happiness is great, it is not necessarily as pure as certain simple and basic joy and happiness, such as of love.

Happiness is never true if it's only a facade. Happiness requires the base self to be happy. I just want to be me, to live a fulfilled and peaceful life without needing complicated ways of existing in my own skin and mind. Sometimes I get those moments, only for them to inevitably flee. But this is inherent to all life. It can be hard to fully embrace this, but this is what the journey of growth and discovery is about. The virtues necessary for happiness – empathy, compassion, humility, strength, courage, wisdom, love, and liberty – make it impossible to be joyous and completely happy in the world as it is, in a world of profound suffering and corruption. One ought to discipline themself to not let happiness erode, for goodness to survive. The base self must learn to let go of happiness to achieve relief, then happiness. Happiness has to be suspended to make the world a better place, to act in a way that makes the world a happier place.

The goodness of this discipline and ambition is truest when it is built on something pure, on a sincere and ever-reminding shred of happiness, of the goodness the world has to offer. To protect happiness and goodness sometimes requires the sacrifice and duty of living in a shell of misery and frustration. Sometimes this involves the chilling burden of restraining oneself from committing mistakes of compassion. But then something profoundly good and pure grows from this by finding happiness in the happiness of others. And everything comes to a blissful moment of peace in all parts of the self and the world – one reaches the true happiness of eudaimonia, where the tormented self is released of the suffering of not being happy, choosing to suffer to create goodness in the world that is only ever felt in the spirit of virtue, where one becomes free from a cruel fate by making good on it and seeing how the world makes good on suffering through you. And if all else fails, at least you can find solace in the courage that at least you did everything you could, at least you found a moment of true happiness beyond the veil of a life consumed with Fear, misery, and cruelty. True happiness, in this life and age, comes through blissful misery. To be happy you must be a certain type of person, and that life will always be bittersweet. But this is the greatest peace and highest happiness that can be achieved.

The Central Principles are applied Core Principles that integrate core desires and values into a structure of ethics. The Central Principles involve many different aspects of the psyche and modern life. With respect, one can classify four aspects, or four traditions of Liberty: Discipline and Defiance, Harmony, the Void, and base spiritual liberty and happiness. At the centre of them is the will to flourish – the soul. By practising mindfulness and certain ways of thinking and behaving, through the four traditions, one can become intensely self-aware and perceptive, allowing the fluidity of virtues and good utilities leading to spiritual fulfilment and liberty. Both faculties of the human psyche must be fulfilled. We are creatures of habit; for goodness to thrive it must be habitual, it must become a habit of behaviour. This liberty of virtue then *allows,* and can lead to, happiness. True happiness can only be accommodated and invited in, not deliberately produced.

Discipline and its Defiance are the tradition of willpower mastering the self, resisting and enduring pain to overcome suffering, and of truly meaningful and fulfilling ambition in life. People receive satisfaction from control and power. The true fulfilment of control and power comes from being able to overcome adversity, through an indomitable will of ambition and mastery over the self and our vices. Sometimes there is little hope or goodness in life. For instance, in the lack of stimulation, in depression, or in uninvited spiritual emptiness, there might not be active hope or positivity. But by achieving stillness of the mind to detach from the clout of negativity to think, reflect, plan, and become driven through pain, frustration, and anger over dissatisfaction, Discipline and its form of Defiance become instrumental.

There can be times when a person does what he or she is supposed to in order to feel good, yet the feeling of goodness is faint. This drag on the spirit can lure it into a vicious cycle of despair, apathy, pain, and exhaustion. One might not even have the will to be frustrated, to be motivated in pain. This is where willpower as a virtue can grant satisfaction in control and power over the self and life, by empowering the sense of self beyond the narrow existence of spiritual exhaustion and lack of inspiration. But the true virtue of willpower is defined by improving on vice and suffering to create an environment that can accommodate happiness. And where the mind is able and focused, it can master even the most profound mental forces, such as violence and pain, to dominate them from within through steadiness and discipline of mental and mindful methodology, turning profound suffering and pain into something good.

Mindfulness by the Void is characterised by the lack of stimulation and fulfilment, combined with well-versed Discipline familiar with overcoming vice and conquering suffering. As such, it is a tradition of stillness and serenity, of a sleep escaping waking life. But where the lack of stimulation and fulfilment may leave its mark as pain presiding over inherent value in, and attraction to, fulfilment and goodness, mindfulness by the Void surpasses that pain and leaves one in peace and close to an unliving state. Here one can find a great transcendental peace and receive much insight and discipline to compliment engaged behaviour.

Harmony is the combination of peace and goodness. As a fulcrum of mindfulness in engaged living and disciplined awareness, perception, reflection, and thought, Harmony is the general tradition emphasising mindfulness. Above all, Harmony and its sphere of Discipline means being very self-aware in thought and behaviour, understanding what and why you are doing something. Harmony finds value and utility in peace, empathy, relief, and liberty of spirit from pain, succeeding the use of pain for motivation. Mindfulness by the Void and Harmony combine to formulate a distinctive mode of thought, reflection, and study building on gathered insight, wisdom, and understanding to inform morality.

At the core of Harmony's utility is fulfilment and the relief from pain, finding wisdom in living at peace and harmony with what inevitably happens, to live beyond pain and suffering. Harmony might suppose an occupation or obsession with the higher faculties. However, if Harmony is restricted and diminished without a base morality of Liberty and basic happiness, true eudaimonia and happiness cannot be achieved. Where some may aspire to true happiness in detachment and absolute peace, eudaimonia conjoins peace with the fulfilment of happiness and other stimulating and rewarding aspects of life, all in Harmony and the moral liberty to do so.

Finally, and perhaps most importantly and intuitively, the base morality of Liberty and happiness. All aforementioned questions, analysis, and discussions were built on dissatisfaction. Where one is satisfied, finds something fulfilling, and is made even slightly happy by something (as opposed to merely stimulated with pleasantness), this basic moral outlook and ethical function is worth its virtue. Base morality is filled with good aspects that are naturally mentally and spiritually evocative. Love is a wondrous and powerful drive in people, pulling people together and enriching their lives beyond any attempts to convince oneself that living is good. Love can fulfil every aspect of the self and psyche – baser and higher; true love is truly fulfilling. If a person is happy the way he or she is, by doing decent work, pursuing whatever pleasure and pleasantness one finds fulfilling, is filled with grace and positivity, and is empathetic and loving, with sufficient virtue and moral sensibility, then this is a promising morality and ethic.

Spiritual liberty and fulfilment are intuitive, and this organicism ought to be fundamental to any ethic. Where something simply makes a person happy and is fulfilling, beyond pain and suffering, then it is morally worthy. Love is particularly fulfilling and liberating, becoming a moral tradition in its own right. Although, the utility and efficacy of love can be confused, inconsistent, unsustainable, and of limited effectiveness, for love itself requires sufficient virtue in character to enable a sense of self which the self can love, then invite others' love. But to those who don't feel much love or positivity, where they feel damaged or broken, or are not content and want something else, something more, then the other traditions of Liberty should provide promising utility and fulfilment. Because we can never live simple, easy, sheltered lives without pain and suffering, whereby base morality cannot provide a universal tradition, other aforementioned devices and traditions of Liberty can be appealed to. Through these four traditions, by practising them and integrating their characteristics into habit, one finds happiness and achieves eudaimonia.

The Central Principles are the direct manifestation of the Core Principles leading to positivity, well-being, and maybe even happiness. The Central Principles, along with systemic and structural ethical insight, form the foundation of the Constitution of Natural Law. With a clear hierarchy of values, the Secondary Principles arise when we engage with the world, when our values and desires guide human activity. The Secondary Principles interpret and apply the Central Principles – the foundations of the Constitution of Natural Law and normative hierarchy of values – to global spheres and levels of ethical endeavour – to society, politics, economics, culture, and so forth. The Secondary Principles guide human activity towards maximising ethical profit – to achieve well-being – in respective causal spheres.

Part 3:

The Secondary Principles

Chapter 24:

Moral Authority

After the age of Enlightenment mankind moved away from the dogmatic rule of God as a source of certainty and began to look to itself and Nature for the answers we crave. Development in thought led to new philosophy, ideology, morality, and normativity. As we looked into the world and to ourselves for the answers we seek, our scepticism revealed much less certainty, yet this disillusionment uplifted progress. It is common for humanity to think of itself as the heart and soul of the universe, as the centre of the world. Some may think that we are in control of our destinies and much of Nature. Our moral agency and the apparition of freewill have made us think that we are the force of change in the universe or that we have the power to change the world around us. But in this we have been deceived.

The computational mind and the determinations of the will to flourish bind us to the values and interests of well-being and to respective moralities. There is nothing 'we' can do to influence our minds and actions, as we are conduits of reason moving our bodies. There is only so much we can do to change the actions of others or influence the world around us, for we are ourselves conduits of the world's forces and of our internal states acting on us and through us.

We cannot change the past, we cannot directly alter the future, and there is only so much we can do in the present; all we can do is respond the best we can to the change around us. Change in the world occurs through human agency, but the change within us corresponds to the world around us and the determination of reason. In this sense we are not autonomous centres of change. Even though our character and presence does influence the state of the world, we are nevertheless only conduits of change.

There are certain powers acting on our will that bind it to particular normativity and morality; they move and shape the reason driving our minds. After all, our own will always corresponds to the greatest influence acting on it, follows the path which offers the greatest promise in particular circumstances. We act in the way we think is best, whether it is high or base reason dominating the will.

This authority of reason that corresponds to the determination of ethical conviction is the centre and dominant power of change. All matters of the human spirit and psyche and everything sociopolitical come down to the Fundamental Principle of Living Beings, its mechanisms, and the power of ethical conduct. Morality is the function of reason serving our interests and values of well-being. As such, morality has great power. This *moral authority* is the centre of change, the power of the Highest Good and ethical value, and the force moving the adaptive cycle of values in the world and in the individual. It is a force, physical and mentally computational, affecting the body and mind to act according to the assessment of value and the determination of the order of desire.

Moral authority as a disposition of reason binds any individual to an ideology, conviction, or sociopolitical view – elements of normativity. Many people seem to think they know what is best for others and the world, think their moral and ethical standpoint is supreme. People with particular sociopolitical views on which value or philosophy is most promising uphold their beliefs through the moral authority found in it. The social subjectivity of convictions is reflective of the psyche of all people engaging with the world, their knowledge, experience, and predilection to reasoning.

People often place certainty in their views of what constitutes positive change. But in reality, the circumstances and state of ethical environment are often far more complex than our limited knowledge and ability to comprehend individually. The adaptive cycle of values and individual growth of the mind and spirit ensure that there is a constant shift in moral authority. Without drawing absolute certainty from the Gods, moral authority can seem to become displaced and extremely subjective. This nevertheless doesn't stop people from holding certain convictions on morality and the sociopolitical. Then, people form narrow opinions as qualifications of ethical values necessitating interpretation and summary based on biases and a dysfunctional primacy of base-reason.

Base-reason's power on base morality has its merits and purpose, yet its normativity is often too contradictory, ineffective, and inefficient. This is in itself a form of moral authority contingent on reason of instinct's functions in normativity. Many aspects of the individual move his or her reasoning towards particular beliefs and thoughts, with the ultimate power of change and conviction being the moral authority perceived in any given line of reasoning concerning that which is related to the ethical and individual interest of well-being. Through moral authority, through the will of an individual, legitimacy and power are raised. However, genuine moral authority and its powers can only be realised by the determination of the Highest Good and moral truth serving the conscious individual's sense of well-being (through spirit and functions of the psyche).

Section 1, with respect to the Fundamental Principle of Living Beings, found the function, goal, and meaning of morality – to flourish. In terms of the many factors influencing ethical environment as states of affairs and states of the self (exemplified in spirit), moral truths are conditionally objective with respect to their contributing elements affecting states of well-being. The success of morality and normativity rests with the mechanisms and dynamics of the Highest Good and, in particular, the adaptive cycle of values.

Moral standards correspond to definitive states of the world that ordain their fate through Nature's Laws. If morality and normativity command insufficient and incompatible values through vectors and utility, such as material utility, thereby neglecting the functions of reason and spiritual fulfilment, then morality and normativity will be limited, will suffer, and may even fail. Moral authority is that which draws on the supreme functions and values of real and prevalent dynamics of Natural Law and the conditions of the Highest Good to facilitate greater positive ethical effect. Moral authority is the function of reason and force of the greatest value in respective conditions of ethical environment and individual agency. Where morality is objective with respect to a sense of well-being and the pathology of the human psyche, so that there are clear answers to what makes us fulfilled and will effectively utilise structures of ethical vectors and tangents through certain rules of behaviour, righteousness turns into the authority of ethical value and interest.

The adaptive cycle of values is a central feature of civilisation's development, rise, and collapse. The normativity of regressive and insufficient ethical values, therefore uncompetitive, loses out to greater values commanding greater force. The adaptive cycle affects Nature, as well as changes with it. Moral authority is the value of a morality and normativity in its implemented, engaged, functional form. Certain values, principles, convictions, and beliefs fit into the conditions and narratives of particular demands and conditions of ethical environment. Moral authority is that which appeals to the values of well-being with respect to the demands and concerns relating to an ethical environment. There are of course many elements that affect the dynamics of values. Environmental, social, psychological, medical, economic, political, civic, cultural, and technological factors are just some of the influences on the determination of ethics and ethics' causality. The given conditions and circumstances a person or community confront are most usually intimidatingly complex. Nevertheless, the truths of morality and normativity in terms of the Highest Good always persist in any and every multidimensional structure of ethics.

Moral truth is complex and fickle, but where the functions of our interests and values are set, such as with a structured framework in reference to an ethos and primary ethical disposition (e.g. Fear and its base morality), agenda-setting and core values become coherent. There will always be a highest moral truth that works with all frameworks of human nature in respective conditions of environment and stages of development. To identify these functions and primary values, then integrate them into structures of ethics on par with normativity and secondary dimensions of ethical utilities, can be excruciatingly difficult. However, the social sciences, combined with the natural sciences, give us some clues and insight to begin working on normative innovation and study.

Moral authority is the most befitting value and principle guiding actions and goal-directive behaviour in terms of morality's command of human interest. Accounting for and studying the dynamics of ethics' structures, such as with its various mechanisms and tangents and vectors, enables not only more coherent goal-directive behaviour, but also binds the command and unity of interest through moral authority presiding over all ethical elements. Thus, where values compete, so too does morality and its authority. Due to the nature of ethical values and their contingency of material utility, reason becomes the foundation of moral authority. As such, reasoning also allows to find, study, and shape morality and moral authority, but only where it is in harmony with functions of the psyche. Moral authority is the word of Natural Law and the Highest Good which the Imperative of the soul is compelled to. It is the most fundamental power on humanity, provided it is given a voice that can be heard or the power to enforce it.

To illustrate the point of competing values, consider two hypothetical communities: one, community P, places moral emphasis on peaceful cooperation, whilst another, community V, places moral conviction in violent domination, including among members of its own community. Community P would arguably be more stable without constant infighting and without the destructive forces of violence distracting and undermining social progress and prosperity, assuming that the members of the community possess a nature that does not value conflict above all else. Community P would function more productively to achieve its people's goal of stable flourishing by focusing their efforts on work and development. In contrast, community V would likely face constant struggle of its own members being set against each other rather than working together.

Our history has shown us that unity and cooperation towards a common goal generally prevail. Human natu1re is malleable and does not necessarily restrict itself to a single conception; this is the adaptation of high-reason. It is conceivable for either community, P or V, to correspond to the framework of human nature. However, we clearly objectively function better when we work together, when we have unity and the ability to collaborate. This phenomenon can be explained in terms of maxims of values. Where a mode of values becomes integrated and maximised in its efficacy and is effectively channelled, such as through the institutions of modern societies, its force becomes greater. This can be considered as a moral truth in mathematical terms consistent with normativity employing material utility in sum terms or by virtue of efficiency.

However, if more variables are included in the illustration of the two communities, the moral truth of the Highest Good becomes much more distorted. If community V could become absolutely dominated by a single individual, the community could expand by the desire and ambition of their unifying leader. The tyrant could unite community V to then subject other communities to violent domination, reflecting hostile human civilisation throughout history. On the other hand, if communities were to unite against a common foe, i.e. community P and another against community V, then their combined efforts could defeat the force and value of the opposition. Along such reasoning it is intuitive how the ambiguities of this P-V community example could quickly expand if other real variables are considered.

What is important to draw from this illustration is how the moral authority of functions of flourishing can bind the will of people. If the normative culture and disposition of a people draws towards a particular ethic, whether violent domination and control, or peace of social cohesion and prosperity, and functions of the psyche align themselves with these values, then moral authority will imbue corresponding values. But only in consideration of the tangents of these values can their piety be properly evaluated. If a violent community striving for domination has only its own secluded ethical environment to affect, then its power-struggles will tear it apart. However, as is the case with war and strife, dedicated endeavour against suffering may be extremely ethically costly and developmentally unstable. A community of peace, collaboration, empathy, and compassion, on the other hand, might be more fulfilled. Yet if it cannot protect itself or maintain developmental pace, it will suffer.

This illustration demonstrates how values in communities and individuals can function. Moral authority is the authority of being right. Where one is right about morality in terms of principles that lead to greater well-being, they command moral authority as the fundamental force affecting people's actions through guidance. Subsequently, the respective moral authority possesses greater value and power. However, if this authority is not functionally synchronised with mechanisms of the Highest Good, notably the adaptive cycle of values and Natural Law, then its vulnerability will be challenged by other values and will suffer or decease.

We often adapt, change, and interpret laws or rules to achieve the best conceivable way to be better off. Societies and nations that are more progressive and open-minded about their moral outlooks are consequently more adaptive, hence likely to be more successful, even though mistakes will be made. In a disordered world lacking effective direction and vision consistent with the demands of circumstances, moral progress is vital to the well-being of any community, society, and nation. However, this necessitates the moral authority of reason, which has been consistently disfigured and corrupted by strong influences of base-reason rooted in the vices of Fear. Those who find the moral truth in their given circumstances and follow it thrive by the moral authority of the Highest Good. If an individual ignores the moral truth, he or she condemns themself to suffering. All people and all moralities adhere to this moral truth of lesser ethical values yielding to greater values of a higher moral authority by the Highest Good. This is a *Natural Law*.

Understanding Natural Law is integral to appreciating moral authority as more than a mere force of opinion. First, Natural Laws are unbreakable and are binding. Within the structures of ethics, from bodily processes to entire societies, behaviour is conditioned by the functions of reason – of logic and information, whereby the Natural Laws are the sovereigns conditioning actions. The psyche of reason is mental, physiological, deterministic, and mechanical. Natural Laws of ethics are those which condition, mediate, and set the parameters for the mechanisms of actions and their functions. If an ethic did not abide contending values, such as it was unable to sustain life, then it will erode and collapse.

Where people need fulfilment to live engaged and happy lives, Natural Laws as exemplified mechanisms of internal and external ethical environments affect the modes of ethical functions and corresponding behaviour. The Natural Laws of morality build on moral laws as principles of ethical tangents and vectors. Where moral laws are narrower in reference to specific causal ethical tangents and vectors, Natural Laws are the greater sum manifestations of moral laws extending into secondary spheres of ethical structures. Respectively, Natural Laws have an especial bearing on normativity, the implications of which are far more serious than basic views of morality might have presumed.

Considerations of normativity and Natural Law can lead to progress or devastation. A society and political culture negligent of, or ignorant to, Natural Laws will make poor decisions and implement ineffectual or incomplete civic policies. For instance, neglect of the Natural Law of the adaptive cycle of values, with emphasis on the concern of degrees of liberty being necessary for development, will lead to stagnation, degeneration, conflict, and destruction. Mediating ethical tangents through mindfulness of the Natural Laws is necessary for wiser normativity. Where normativity is successful with reference to considered criteria qualifying and measuring success, it will exercise power through moral authority. Insight into, and mastery of, the Natural Laws of ethics is instrumental to normativity. Where one commands good and strong normativity, ethical value is cultivated and wielded to emphasise the moral authority of a normative function through its respective functions of Natural Law. Ignoring and neglecting good normativity will lead to suffering. Where a moral authority is strong enough and in greater comparative harmony with the Highest Good, it produces flourishing which can attract new tangents of values. As such, Natural Laws are the arbiters of moral authority, and people would be wise to choose carefully, for positive moral authority leads to great promises.

The reoccurring issue of diverse, deviating, and contradictory morality and normativity remains. In terms of Natural Law and the dynamics of adaptive ethics, the circumstances and conditions of ethical environments form respective moral and normative policies. Their merit is designated to particular functions of respective ethical environments and demands. The basic mechanism of moral diversity then transmutes to richness of normativity as ideology and philosophy.

With respect to Natural Law and the dynamics of values, every civic utility, whether of political, social, or economic ideology, has its merits in terms of certain functions of reason and corresponding values. Moral authority of embraced values borne of experience, impressions, insight, and knowledge form and bind to normative principles and ideologies. The logical possibility of an ideology and its moral authority moves theory into practice, whereby Natural Law then mediates its fate. But only moral authority of higher virtue, consequently greater value, triumphs and flourishes.

The role of moral authority and its normative and moral power is foundational to ideology and civic utilities and policies. Only understanding of ethical environment and mindfulness of the human psyche can truly enable effective normativity, granting and using the supremacy of moral authority. Where moral authority does not influence other ethical vectors and their spheres, Natural Law and coercion of the adaptive cycle of values weeds out vice and regressive values, crippling and destroying lives and societies. Commanding reason and ethical interest is the nature and utility of moral authority and normative power, the greatest asset of which is Natural Law and its sovereignty of the Highest Good. Where religious preaches may aspire to call down God's wrath to smite the sinful, Natural Law needs no attention for its mechanisms to exercise self-causal power and to balance values.

To fully appreciate the power and relevance of moral authority in tandem with Natural Law and the Highest Good, especially relating to civic utilities, philosophies, and ideologies, requires understanding of the anatomy of reason in normativity. Instinct can be straightforward in its functions. However, where instinct is convoluted with multiple tangents of desires and interests, goal-directive behaviour enriched with forethought, insight, and knowledge leads to complexity and even complications in agendas of primary interests. Primacy of base morality in Fear has been argued to be particularly vulnerable to this aspect of ethics where unmediated instinct and sentiment fundamentally contradict ethical values, interests, and desires. These phenomena may be accounted for through the anatomy of human psyche.

Where base-reason performs its basic, automatic functions, the faculties of high-reason diversify basic functions. New possibilities and a wealth of information perplex base-reason. Contingently, the structure of reason dealing with stupendous amounts of information, further amplified with contending interests and values, at times being fundamentally ethically contradictory, makes morality and normativity diverse and complicated. Any ideology, philosophy, and normativity will usually only be a partial reflection of reality and concern itself with a very narrow view of ethical tangents and vectors. Discipline and mindfulness in both categories of reason are necessary to shift through the abundance of information and concerns. Only then can harmony in all-reason make coherent study and mediation of normativity possible.

It is not easy to distinguish between, as well as systematically structure and account for, interests and values of instinct and their multipolar functions through interlinked high-reason. No single person can effectively do this, as the personal quality of virtue will always be subject to self-examination and the available amount of information will elude even the most capable minds. Naturally, moral authority as guidance and leadership appeals to any and every person, even if as a lonesome principle lacking greater vision and philosophy.

This is the origin of moral authority drawing on organic dynamics of ethical values. High-reason leads to the inevitable synthetic contingency of diverse normativity found on basic values and concerns. And as all things that are ethically synthetic, synthetic normativity is fickle and troublesome, while also extremely rewarding and necessary for development. Balancing and mediating synthetic tangents and vectors is necessary for normative success and ethical prosperity. This, however, is an actual skill and discipline that must be learnt and practised. Normativity and secondary spheres of ethical concern are not simple things and require a great deal of insight, knowledge, and personal ability. Presumptions misjudge, and blind biases disfigure, the Highest Good. As such, moral authority can be a capricious and even volatile force in ethics with respect to its incomplete values driven by reason. This brings one to consider a concentrated form of moral authority embodied through ethical vectors – that is, the agency and character of people. Moral authority leads to *moral power*.

The notion of *moral authority* can be rather straightforward and intuitive, even if it lacks a dedicated conceptual account. In structures of ethics, moral authority is taken to be a force acting on reason through and in terms of ethical values. Moral authority specifically relates to causal ethical tangents as an element of ethical force in reason relating to Natural Law, whereas people *draw* on moral authority. Where moral authority becomes engaged directly in ethical vectors, moral authority transitions into another conceptual qualification as *moral* and *normative power*.

Moral power is that which is being used, is active, whereas moral authority is something that can be present in active human endeavour, as well as a transcendental function of reason yet to be discovered or integrated into the dynamics of ethical structures. The essence of moral authority and moral power is the utility of moral knowledge and insight which translates into reason affecting people's dispositions and behaviour. Moral authority represents the tangents of ethical activity, whereas moral power is the vector of the ethical interests of and among people. Where morality dominates people's concerns by the imperative of life to flourish, moral authority and moral power are the fundamental forces shaping human activity.

The point of distinguishing between moral authority and moral power is to highlight the *relational* nature of power in morality and normativity. Where moral power is the active embodiment of moral authority as the directive of reason, it only ever draws on ethical values in certain spheres and structures. Moral power and moral authority are apparitions of reason and their anatomical functions, which the soul or character never possess, only embody until vice or death. Moral power moves with people and the character able to herald it, just as its moral authority is carried by a host vector. Moral authority and moral power then do not possess people, but only influence them through respective values towards particular modes of conduct.

For example, the knowledge that smoking harms one's health, subsequently vitality and well-being, becomes a form of moral authority over people. A medical practitioner can then draw on moral power as a medical professional to engage other people's concerns for well-being to influence attitudes towards smoking. But this moral power is never possessive in either the doctor or the person cautious of smoking. Neither vector possesses moral authority, as that authority is of reason and its moral knowledge. Then, moral power is only drawn from moral authority which can reflect onto another person as influence of people's moral and ethical dispositions. This is the relational nature of moral authority and power.

The final and pivotal point of the nature of moral authority and normative power is as such – relational power of morality manifesting through the will and reason of people as the source of all legitimacy to wield the power of change. Through moral authority and the will of people, institutions and individuals are granted legitimacy of government to exercise power on people. Any force of change among people, whether of government or community, is of morality and normativity bound to reason influencing people's minds. Moral authority is the force underlying all endeavour of goal-directive behaviour exemplified through, and embodied by, reason. The relating spheres of vectors and agency of moral authority as *moral power* warrants a whole other discussion, because it is more specific to central activities of normativity among people and in structural dynamics.

Moral authority may refer to functions of Natural Law, while moral and normative power are part of engaged and prevalent elements of moral authority. Moral power is more practical in its nature, therefore necessitating its own focus of study than moral authority. Moral authority is the seat of power, the source of all legitimacy and influence over people; moral power is its action. To leave this Chapter, the mindful reader would know the organic nature of moral authority in terms of power-knowledge of the Highest Good above all affecting oneself. Where one's mind and spirit are at Liberty, moral authority of the Highest Good is inviting, calls to us, whispers, and none so much so by the liberty of mindfulness by the Void and the balance of Harmony. Thought becomes mindful meditation of wisdom found in spirit and ethos.

Chapter 25:
Moral Power

A dedicated study of moral power in structures of ethics would benefit from building on other literature. Part 3 will be more focused on revision and innovation rather than fundamental restructuring (as seen in Parts 1 and 2 of Section 3). Jal Mehta and Christopher Winship at Harvard University published a relevant paper "Moral Power" (2010) on the social nature of moral power. In parallel to Mehta's and Winship's paper, drawing on much inspiration, this project adopted the term *moral power* as *the ability to influence through reason*. Much of this Chapter will develop an understanding of moral power with reference to Mehta's and Winship's paper. After all, this project is dedicated to establishing a social science of ethics and morality, which in practice would be achieved through actual application of the model of structural ethics.

However, efforts of this Chapter are not intended to put forward a formal analysis of Mehta's and Winship's essay, and neither will familiarity with the respective paper be necessary. Instead, I will put forward another account of moral power borrowing inspiration from the referred paper to then reinterpret, criticise, or reform it where appropriate, but within a conceptual framework of structural ethics and its metaphysics.

Mehta's and Winship's work examined the role of individual power to influence others by virtue of character. The subsequent ambition here is to expand on initial work to contribute towards a comprehensive theory of moral authority and moral power. Building on Section 1, morality and normativity are objective. This insight and knowledge, understandably, however, was not available to Mehta's and Winship's efforts. Their stance was more conventional in adopting a more subjective view on moral standards that reflects the subjective practice of morality in various communities and between individuals. For clarification, the view adopted throughout this project in light of the adaptive cycle of values and conditional moral authority is that moral subjectivity arises from distortion in complexity. By looking at the functions of values and principles, then accounting for them through a respective ethos and ethical core, they can be understood better. Hence, agenda and narratives of goal-directive behaviour become more coherent and objective.

Where all ethical matters factor into well-being, with the sense of well-being (spirit) established in functions of the psyche primarily in terms of base-reason and an ethos of pain-aversion, then convoluted through high-reason, morality is objective in relation to values of well-being. Morality concerns itself with well-being, with moral power being the force corresponding to effects on states of being. Combined with the adopted concept of moral authority drawing on the mechanisms and functions of Natural Law, moral power is objective in terms of the anatomy of the psyche and is also predictable, corresponding to causal states of affairs affected by the human psyche and material dynamics of Nature. Reason is the 'putty' of human activity and the dynamics of ethics affecting, as well as affected by, material substance, with reason being composed by the substance of logic contingent on causal qualifications of material and physical forces (see Section 4). Essentially, reason is not a mere abstraction or faint mental phenomenon. As such, reason can have real causal power, as is clear in retrospect even without a foundational account. Therefore, moral power can be defined as *the ability to influence through reason,* or alternatively – *the causal power of actions,* where actions serve ethical, then moral, ends of imperative concerns of well-being.

Without the aforementioned assumptions and conceptual frameworks of ethics and morality, Mehta and Winship define moral power as *"the degree to which an actor, by virtue of his or her perceived moral stature, is able to persuade others to adopt a particular belief or take a particular course of action"*[1]. In retrospect, this notion of moral power bears greater relevance to the sociopolitical and normative, whereas the former structural ethics interpretation is more metaphysical, then normative. Mehta's and Winship's conception of moral power could benefit from an understanding of the dynamics of normativity in terms of moral authority. Moral authority is found through reason and Natural Law, whereby moral power is then granted through 'power-knowledge' of moral authority. The will of people binds to moral authority perpetuating reason of greater well-being, consequently vectors of moral authority are granted legitimacy by people following a respective ethical tangent. Whilst Mehta's and Winship's paper does not acknowledge moral authority as such, their understanding of moral power seems to focus on the relational role between a voice of reason and adherence to it. They effectively outline interpersonal and social dynamics of people being able to persuade others and whether people listen to what others are saying. As they wrote: "[it is] *moral power of the specific actor making the claim that is important in determining the outcome*"[2], referring to the moral quality of the individual making the claim and its relation to the effect such a voice can have on influencing certain outcomes (focusing analysis on ethical vectors). This analysis can be expanded on through a conceptual framework of structural ethics' metaphysics of morality and ethics.

To introduce some context, Mehta and Winship 'develop an outline' of moral power as *"a function of whether one is perceived as morally well-intentioned, morally capable, and whether one has moral standing to speak to an issue"*[3]. They define the three mentioned categories of perception. *Intention* concerns itself with the issue of *"whether an actor is perceived to be promoting a particular position out of concern for what is morally right or good, as opposed to being driven by self-interest or other motivations, and [...] whether that actor is perceived to be trustworthy"*[4]. *Capability* reflects the question of whether *"an individual is seen to be both generally wise and knowledgeable in forming moral judgements and appropriately informed about the specific issue at hand"*[5]. They take moral standing to refer to *"the degree to which the actor is understood to be a member of a relevant moral community"*[6]. These conceptual categories clearly assume certain moral standards with respect to the characteristics of individuals, that certain traits are indeed good. It is apparent that Mehta and Winship wisely tread in the territory of studying moral power by embracing moral subjectivism. In light of new arguments throughout this project, hopefully we can dispel some moral ambiguities and find more concrete answers to moral authority, to then build on Mehta's and Winship's preliminary theory.

First, consider the category of *intention*. The primary element ascribed to it is the relation between the person with moral power and the individual who agrees to be influenced by power, in other words the receiver of power binds to the moral authority the person of influence draws power from. The mind and spirit of an individual will only ever abide a morality that nourishes the imperative of flourishing. For one to agree on what is morally right or good is for his or her body of reason to acknowledge its sense of well-being. As is formalised by the Fundamental Principle, people are fundamentally self-interested even if not selfish. Mehta and Winship undervalued the role of moral power and moral authority by not giving them the power they truly warrant within ethical functions of morals and values bound to *self-interest*. Where morality fundamentally concerns itself with the self-interest of well-being, in whatever form well-being presents itself in spirit, moral power affecting states of well-being is absolute in moving the intentions of self-interest and the soul's imperative. Particularly relevant to intention is how people bind to moral authority and grant its vectors moral power through reason and values of well-being. If a person senses that those who influence his or her life don't do so righteously and with worthy virtue, then the ability to command through any power is lost, or rather taken away by the commanded.

It may seem that various sources of power are distinct to moral power. For instance, it may be counter-intuitive to argue that a violent dictator subjecting the will of a community through forceful coercion does so with moral power. However, because the will of the commanded is set to obey the oppressive regime and its agency, members of a community allow themselves to be governed by violent tyranny. If the psyche and spirit is bound to the rule of Fear, then actions will conform. Through the terror of pain and death, a society may relinquish liberty and accept a dictator, binding to a regime in spirit of Fear. But if a person is courageous, is pressed to desperation, or delves into madness, forming other tangents and vectors of moral power, then the person will defy the command of oppression. Violence can command great moral power in Fear because it moves people either in defiance or subjugation. Intention might not be benevolent, yet it can command people's actions even if perceived to be characterised by vice. Intention is consequently subject to a great deal of ambiguity in congruence to the ethical, as moral power can affect people's values and dispositions without righteous intent. This, as many other topics discussed in this Chapter, could benefit from dedicated and specific study. However, an introduction to the matter at hand, inviting clear sense and intuition of the fundamental ambiguity of moral power, will have to suffice for now. Nevertheless, the component of moral intention in moral power holds.

Intention is also characterised by another related and vital aspect – *trust*. Trust can be implemented to differentiate between moral power and the ambiguities of its forms, i.e. power through free consent rather than false consent of forceful coercion. It could be argued that the notion of moral power portrayed by Mehta and Winship is one of power exercised over people through the liberty of will, contrary to influence through the will of coercion. When people bind to moral authority, they do so in the belief that this arrangement will make them better off. This inevitably requires trust that giving a person the legitimacy to influence others is done so in accordance with the function of the fundamental will. People may elect a certain government in hopes that their consent will benefit them through their mandate, whereby trust is essential for the placement of moral power. However, this same trust applies to coercive or malevolent power. A person may obey an oppressive government in the belief that appeasement will be rewarded. One might think that by obeying a violent dictator he will not get killed or tortured, but if he thought that an action would result in suffering, then the person would probably try to escape the despot. Therefore, trust works with all ambiguities of moral power, yet it does not cast away the universal reach of moral authority through variations of moral power.

In general, the category of intention in moral power holds, particularly within the scope of self-interest in goal-directive behaviour. However, it is difficult to draw a line between moral power and any other form of power to influence, making the concept of moral power and its authority run in parallel to all influences on human conduct and activity. Any source of power rests on its force of reason on a person. Perhaps what is deemed moral power is the pinnacle of influence over people, the apex of all forms and sub forms of power, the purest and most fundamental essence of influence on reason. Even where an action may sever any potential of action in a person through death, the consequent vectors and tangents will be just as potent as the judgement on an individual. In reflection, one may argue that Mehta and Winship underestimate the extent and capacity of moral power, as well as mistake its fundamental and metaphysical nature. Moral power does not just come with the perception of benevolent intent – moral power is absolute. If the intention of an individual binds to the motives and desires of others, there will be moral power. Then again, other powers, such as coercion, may be subject to the conditioning of moral authority by Natural Law. Moral power is only itself if the individual binds to its moral authority of reason. The power of coercion could be a mode of moral power if the person sets his or her will to it, but coercion loses its stature of moral power if an individual does not submit to it.

On the other hand, the voice of reason can carry with it moral power ever-greater than the moral power of coercive force, as the efficacy of the power of reason through symbols and words has greater, longer-lasting, and more stable influence. Then again, competing thoughts can hold power, but only that which best conforms to Natural Law will be accepted by the psyche and can succeed. Contingently, understanding reasoning that fuels ambition and moves life allows to identify appropriate concerns and then complimentary intentions of representative moral power. Where the driving values of a vector are identified in terms of their structured ethics, specifically with respect to an ethos and Central Principles, then active values will highlight morality, its authority, and subsequently the intention open to power. Thus, reason – specifically the psyche and its global structures – is the essence of moral power and its parallel forces. The most significant power of reason comes with the voice of moral authority projecting liberty of reason appeasing the soul, a force without unstable, unreliable power coercing reason that fails to channel complimentary intention. However, this moral power of reason through the force of meaningful words can only bind a person's will to a certain moral authority with honesty and trust as the prime virtues of intention. Only through benevolent and sincere motivation of good faith and goodwill can moral power convince or compel a person to a worthy and righteous moral authority, if such is the determination of liberty and autonomy of will. Then, one may be granted moral power, but never can it come in its full potential and greatest form where intention is false and unvirtuous; one must first find the worthiest of moral authorities to follow, through which to then inspire others.

It becomes clear that if the empowerment of virtue in liberty of goodwill is to succeed, then no blind personal ambition suffices for the worthiness of moral authority. Mankind does not need paternalistic figures, it does not need patriarchs or matriarchs, it does not need supreme leaders, or moral tyrants, or exalted messianic leaders of unsubstantiated wisdom. Any vector of moral authority, whether a philosopher king or prince, is only ever a conduit within a given structure. A shaken structure of ethics will not benefit from vectors carrying its sickness on a grand or small scale. While great change and structural reform of ethical environment can only occur through each and every virtue of a person, its vectors and tangents can only be set in motion by a leviathan changing the ways of the world and imprinting on Natural Law itself. But no such vector lives or perhaps ever has. If mankind is to embody and fulfil its virtue of humanity, it can only do so in virtue of common goodwill through the justice of moral rule, Natural Law, and the Highest Good – not ambition of any individual seeking power under the guise of dishonest intentions. For moral virtue to empower people beyond Fear and towards greater ambition, they need not a ruler of moral authority, but a peer in moral authority and justice that inspires as one of their own. For moral and spiritual liberty to succeed, there ought to be liberty in commonality and goodwill, all facilitated by the virtues of good faith and mindfulness of Harmony, in duty to the Human Imperative. It is easy for God to live up to His innate piety, yet the challenge of people's Fear makes their piety ever-more worthy and inspiring. Only common ground and common good faith, all bound to empathy, can move virtuous moral power through intention. These sorts of frameworks of virtues and principles illustrate the diverse influences on the dynamics of moral intention in moral power.

Mehta and Winship consider another category of moral power – *moral standing*, mainly associated with relevance to a 'moral community', which the structural ethics interpretation would consider in scope of an ethical environment and its active values as principles and agency. In terms of people listening to a particular voice of reason, relevant relations among individuals and groups are often key influences on people's willingness to listen. Following up on *intention* needing common ground and good faith for mutual understanding, *moral standing* can be considered the formal category of an inspiring ethical vector that can reach out to people. *Moral standing* can come in many forms and with many origins; sometimes it can be justifiably rewarded, whilst other times it can be taken for granted and found through ignorance. People will listen to whoever they want to listen to, yet sometimes conscious intent can be overridden by unconscious desires, muting a fair and valuable voice. Where the base morality of instinct and Fear is dominant, value will be found in 'relevant communities' and its voice of appeasement and gratification will flatter vice and withering character. One cannot deny the prevalent aspects of status and belonging influencing moral standing, just as one cannot ignore the bias of Fear that brings to attention preferential and comfortable views. However, relevance to specific communities as a vector of 'fitting' value nevertheless can be extremely broad. Moral standing as part of a moral community is ultimately global and universal in terms of the fundamental nature of the soul's imperative to flourish adhering to reason, as true wisdom has no bounds but those of Natural Law and sensibility. As such, moral standing is more than lonesome relevance to specific communities, for even an outsider can earn great standing if moral authority and other criteria of moral power are accommodating.

Moral standing accompanies the beliefs and views of people, which are then associated with relevant communities characterised by corresponding moral and/or sociopolitical principles. Moral standing can, for example, correlate with left or right political views, religious beliefs, economic opinions, cultural or social affiliations, and all sorts of ethical dispositions. Moral standing is found through the will of people who relate to a certain moral authority. There are always particular causes for the convictions people uphold. The reasoning driving an individual reflects the moral authority a person binds to, thus the moral power placed in people. Moral standing, just like any ethical system, functions absolutely by the determination of reason. Therefore, any form of reason with strong endowment of Natural Law can overpower the reason placed in one standard of moral principles and shift them towards another moral authority, consequently affecting the moral standing of individuals. Moral power in terms of moral standing moves with the authority of values and reason. Moral standing mainly depends on the quality and character of reason, which base morality may commonly ascribe to base elements of reason such as in terms of belonging to a particular community.

Mehta and Winship categorise moral standing in terms of social functions and relevant perceptions. However, moral standing is in many ways secondary to the systems of reason moving individuals. It is undeniable that moral standing can exercise great influence on the determination of the moral authority people bind to, especially where perception is involved. Nevertheless, moral standing is a secondary category of perception and moral power rooted in the functions of reason, for standing as perceived moral power or relevant opinion (voice of reason) is only as inspiring as the corresponding value, capability, and judgement of character. Moral standing comes with moral power and moral authority which are subject to the mechanisms of reason rather than perceptions alone. Moral standing is the continuation of moral judgements and an extension of moral power rather than a primary cause moving the vectors of power. Young generations will only listen to old wisdoms if the standing of a moral authority is deemed virtuous in its value. Furthermore, a tradition of listening to elders only bears relevance in an ethical environment laden with moral principles of valuing elder's wisdom, at times a blind function of base morality and not of liberty of will and wisdom. Where the quality of character is questioned, such as with acts of vice, standing can be lost. But such occurrences would primarily depend on the effects of and on reason, whereby standing is lost where people put in question the intention and *capability* of an individual. Moral standing as a root of perception, while significant in the intuitive way of expressing sincerity and valued virtues, whether empathy or wisdom, that affects perceived intention and capability, is only as good a utility as its reason and respective virtues. This then links other aspects of moral power into its sum manifestation.

The aspect of moral standing is central to the dynamics of moral power, yet by virtue of its fickle and dualistic nature it also seems to highlight the complex nature of moral power's variables. Just as the category of standing can be extremely elusive and then momentarily shine, its impression can endure a history of imperfection and vice, as has always been the case with revered and great people. Many influences contribute to the dynamics of moral power, which becomes intuitive and practical, more than theoretical, through virtue and mindful empathy. It is beyond the scope of this work to put forward a full and detailed account of the many niche aspects of moral power's dynamism. Instead, here I will settle on exploring the main tangents of moral authority and power. Hence, one must narrow down the discussion of moral standing to what has been presented, to then emphasise its naturally complex and dualistic nature relating to the state of environment and ethical tangents. For instance, where moral standing may seem to be only relational and socially constructed, this context is structured in a framework of emphasised base morality. One can intuitively understand how the component of moral standing affects the states of moral power in terms of base morality and Fear guiding the concerns of well-being. Employers will always have moral standing over their staff while the staff do not wish to be fired, because they still need to earn a living or occupy themselves. Stature and position of power is always relational in terms of people's individual interests of well-being moving actions, providing the essence of morality's convention in ethics' structures in terms of moral standing. Moral standing as a central feature of power warrants more than a mention that this work must settle for. However, as a foundation to a framework of moral power concerned with ethical vectors and the tangents roused by moral authority, these points should suffice for an intuitive understanding of *moral standing*.

The other category of moral power recognised by Mehta and Winship is *moral capability*. They define *capability* largely in terms of perception, consistent with the social functions of tangents of moral authority. Perceptions among people are a function of the mind as any other phenomenon of reason. While people are different and predisposed to particular talents and skills, morality and wisdom are very specific ones. Those seeking advice and guidance often look up to, or gain inspiration from, others they deem wise, virtuous, righteous, or otherwise *morally capable* – a perception especially conditioned by moral standing. Moral capability is a characteristic of an ethical vector – a character and person. The essence of moral capability can be identified as *the ability to reason and debilitate on what is morally good*. Moral capability, in short, is the capacity of character to identify, draw on, and meditate on what is good and what is the right course of action, achieved through many virtues. All moral capability is based on one's aptitude for reason and moral insight, knowledge, and wisdom.

Where the convention of moral standing may reserve capability for a select few, this is far from the actual norm of moral capability. Even a naive child can live according to principles of moral truth, regardless of how or why the child acknowledges his or her convictions. Even children can inspire moral righteousness in an adult confused by deep wounds. Even the most vicious criminals can speak moral truth through their regret and sorrows, of vice commonly inherited from hostile environments of social and family perils. Moral capability arises with every virtue, but only the most disciplined, mindful, insightful, and dedicated individuals gain wisdom heralding great moral capability and its empowering standing. Where moral capability is conditioned by the circumstances shaping moral reasoning, it comes in varying degrees to all. Every person is morally capable to offer wisdom and insight by virtue of experience, for even a mistake can be more useful than an old tradition. Every person is able to move, as well as be moved by, reason, whether through argument or mere perception; as such, moral capability, just as moral authority, can affect all. But then the features of standing and intention become central to how moral capability can exercise power on an open mind. Opening up the mind is the trickiest part of moral power, and different circumstances require different measures, all contingent on perceptions. Where intentions factor in, sometimes a carefully crafted and borderline manipulative facade of capability and standing becomes a benevolent vector of moral goodness and righteousness, even if base morality leaning towards a tradition of selfless intent may find this odd. These elements and insights all factor into the grand truth of morality and ethics, and moral capability is the ability and virtue of alignment with the glimmer of moral truth in particular circumstances. Moral truth is everywhere, even if only as a partial truth. Yet the main difficulty is not only reasoning with people, but knowing when you are truly right and not deceived by a partial truth. Where partial truths appease biases, petty moral capability can lead to great standing, all to people's loss or for comparative gains for the virtuous. But then the greatest capability leads to timeless standing, and vice versa.

The relation between the individual and society, then as part of a global ethical environment, works on many levels through a myriad of mechanisms. Moral capability could be the main component in moral power, as it directly corresponds to the dynamics of moral reason. Yet it is nothing without its other elements – moral standing and moral intention. Moral capability grants a mind the ability to conjure and affirm positive judgement on actions and virtues. If moral judgements conform to Natural Law and moral law, then ethical profit ensues. Positive moral judgements may bolster the well-being of the self, but if they are extended to the minds and actions of others, moral power is implemented through a moral authority of good spirit. Good moral capability leads to positive moral judgements; the successful application of such judgements can then build the trust of intention and the loyalty of standing. If somebody makes the right choice, then people will be disposed to trust the capability of the person making a sound and good judgement. By continuously reaffirming the trust of others and nourishing one's moral capability, the bond between people and the ethos they incorporate grows, consequently strengthening the ties between vectors and the tangents of moral authority. This trust and loyalty can grow to the point that one may turn a blind eye to, or forgive, mistakes and blunders of moral negligence. Mistaken judgements might not win a person any favours, but it doesn't inherently become the end of moral power, as is always seen with biases in contrast to occasional disillusionment from strongly held views provoked by powerful negative reactions. We forgive loved ones and look past their flaws because we see something more valuable and precious. Where moral capability is subject to widespread and even grand considerations, such as with global rather than only local issues, capability can lead to judgements that many would find difficult to understand, not least to actually agree with. This could be ascribed to politics, where some difficult choices must be made with tough consequences which the ordinary citizen might find morally disgusting, unappreciative of the necessity and difficulty to make such choices.

Mindfulness by the Void lends its discipline into moral capability, even if as mere speculation and study, to make tough choices in grim and dark circumstances. Morality in grand schemes is an inherently gloomy and corruptive effort. But Harmony can offer much when darker aspects of morality are necessary, especially in establishing a synchrony between micro and macro spheres of ethics' structures. As some may begin to appreciate, there can arise a conflict between mindful rationale drawing from Harmony by the Void and healthy fulfilment of spirit in synchrony of base and high faculties, undisturbed by the necessity of moral duty; mastering this is part of Liberty in grander schemes. Mindfulness by the Void complimenting rationale, but mindful of excess detachment, can be hugely beneficial, but it must only succeed as a disciplined mindset and attitude within specific circumstances. If such mindsets beg for control and power, twisted from their proper form of Defiance and Discipline, then they lose touch with their truest potential in spirit of Liberty. Greater forms of moral capability with respect to an ethos and ethic of Liberty will require discipline to distinguish, mediate, and be mindful of the transitions of moral utilities in one's mind and character. Where a person feels conflicted, he or she must first meditate on why there is conflict, as well as be mindful of intent, desire, and the state of self. These features of moral capability threaten any intention and standing, with the lack of coherent moral authority leading to evident conflict seen in much of the world or in oneself as the discord of reason. Just as any component of moral power, capability, while in many ways the primary characteristic of moral empowerment, is fickle, complex, and dualistic.

Where global morality and ethics turn to darker undertones, as can always be expected, and many individuals in society become tormented and vexed by Fear, a strong positive moral authority is necessary. But for this authority to prevail, its conduits and vectors must be exceedingly virtuous and morally powerful through, towards, and by themselves. A strong, positive, and *adaptive* moral authority, upheld by able and worthy individuals moved by more than Fear, is necessary for strong spirit, ethical environment, individuals, and society. Where humanity is bound to the Highest Good beyond borders and governments, a righteous and sustainable moral authority is crucial. This sustainable and just authority can only arise through the moral power of the virtues of citizens.

The relation between moral capability and intention and standing is a central feature of moral power, yet there is more to be explored on this dynamic. I want to look at the cause of people changing their views. People will follow an ethic that fulfils and gratifies in spirit. However, it comes to no surprise that people change their minds. In terms of morality, there must be a specific function of reason that shapes moral conviction. For a person to follow another morality means there was a fault with their previous beliefs that led them to seek another path, to pursue another tangent. This disparity of reason in moral authority is a cause of moral division in conjunction to moral progress and contention. To change the moral outlook of others there must be a void in the reasoning of their moral authority, conscious or unconscious. If a person has the ability to recognise these faults in reason and improve them, hence finding other tangents of moral authority, he or she can cultivate moral power by influencing and reasoning with others. If the individual assimilates new thoughts, then the person will live according to another moral authority. The deprivation of spirit and reason by a given moral authority can carry great influence on societies. For example, some people may ignore national laws because they disagree with them; consequently, they may commit crimes like avoiding taxes or consuming banned substances. There are reasons for why laws are set into hierarchy. But as people's morality develop, their thoughts may diverge from the moral authority of the status quo, foregoing tradition and out-dated hierarchy. As such, moral authority of Natural Law supercedes political, institutional, and legal powers, with morality reigning over the sociopolitical and every individual. But only that which betters the lives of others through benevolent influence is granted the power of alignment with people's attitudes and reasoning.

Ultimately, true moral power of Natural Law comes with the ability to empower other people and improve lives. An ethos that moves a person to greater flourishing is one that holds moral authority over that person, with the moral power of reason being the primary force of influence over behaviour, known through sensation and perception of living. Only through the moral capability to bring positivity into people's lives, respectful of the autonomy of the soul and spirit, will a person have the trust and loyalty of others to command moral authority.

Mehta's and Winship's work on moral power focused primarily on the social dynamics of power among people. However, their understanding of morality and ethics, I believe, was insufficient to construct a more unified theory of moral authority and moral power as their insight into the metaphysics and anatomy of actions, ethics, and morality was limited. Through my efforts I hope I have built on initial work and provided some context of a more comprehensive and detailed structural theory of moral authority. The final test, and contingent application of a theory of moral authority in the context of a structural ethics' interpretation, is to see how effectively such a theory can be applied to other sociopolitical, individual, moral, and ethical matters. The three qualities of moral power – intention, standing, and capability – have fundamental power over moral authority and social dynamics, regardless of the type of relational power involved. People are governed by the moral authorities they are driven towards through common moral accord of mutual ethical interest. Thus, moral authority supercedes and births all other authority and power. The essence of this revision of moral power and moral authority builds on the metaphysical account of people's reason and spirit being bound to the Imperative of the soul to flourish. The intuitive nature of the mind and its actions in the pursuit of well-being is fundamental to not only the individual but all society and global ethical environment. This is what moral authority and moral power constitute, involve, and affect.

Regarding the scope of the force of moral authority and its power, of the many notable propositions made by Mehta and Winship, one in particular comes to attention. They claim *"moral power is fragile"*[7]. I argue that moral authority and moral power are beyond any other form of power. Whilst moral power *can* be fragile even where the authority is potent, it is only fragile in relation to the quality of its vector. However, the quality of character and its moral power are determined by the influences of a moral authority acting on and through a character. A religion of blind standards and appealing only to certain aspects of human nature will fail where other aspects of the psyche and spirit are neglected or unfulfilled. If a person deviates from moral authority and Natural Law, or a person's character succumbs to vice, then moral power will abandon him or her. Moral power is not fragile – its fluidity occurs where vectors may lack the necessary virtues to hold it, conditioned by moral authority and its sovereign Natural Law and the Highest Good.

The fluidity of power is the justice of the liberty of morality. Mehta and Winship suggest a related thought concerning the flaws of character and use of moral power by saying that *"because moral power is fragile it is easily attacked. [...] As such, ad hominem attacks can actually be very powerful"*[8]. When the character of a person is weighed in people's perception commanded by a particular moral authority, vices and virtues are considered. People's judgements then qualify the traits of a person to determine whether or not a person is worthy to be listened to via the three categories of moral power. Ad hominem arguments can influence the judgement of standing, intention, and capability, but if an individual of authority commands enough moral power, then even the biggest mistakes and personal flaws can be forgiven. If a person is important enough in your life, you will forgive what you are willing to forgive to secure future interests. As would be intuitive to suggest, any attacks or competitions among moral authorities and its vectors are deeply contextual. Ad hominem attacks and attempts to undermine moral power will always be complex and deeply conditional phenomena. Only the cynical and disillusioned will easily follow ad hominem attacks to relinquish faith in any individual; only the blind and arrogant do not acknowledge criticism; only attacks against character within the context of particular ethical tangents can be powerful, and only the truest, sincerest, and sharpest of moral attacks are powerful. It is another aspect of moral capability to identify and use the faults of a moral authority and its individual characters for constructive ends as just, righteous, and warranted ad hominem attacks, especially through humour.

Well-founded and valid criticisms of individuals' capabilities and character can be very influential in determining people's station of moral authority. Moral power in many ways is high-risk, high-reward. It can either topple regimes and align societies to a moral authority, or it can invite hatred and many enemies. Those who identify, pursue, and abide by the Natural Law of the Highest Good will be able to hold moral power in accordance with the demands of circumstances. With success, their range of influence can grow to become timeless. Great character, especially of sacrifice, sustains a moral authority through the end of a noble life, with one great act often overshadowing a long history of mistakes and vice. In this manner, acts of martyrdom and sacrifice can generate extraordinary moral power to a moral authority through the inherent virtue found in the great strength necessary for such deeds. If a person commits to a moral authority, in death they could become far more powerful than in life, or rather that moral authority becomes far more powerful. But such an authority is only ever just and its vector virtuous when it is committed righteously for genuinely good ends and not self-righteously. Where personal sacrifice is involved in tandem with a moral authority nourishing one's spirit and inspiring goodness in others, only an act of sacrifice committed in goodwill and good faith carries a truly righteous moral authority. Where sacrifice is just and righteous – committed in empathy and duty for others and in pursuit of eudaimonia of spiritual liberty through and for others – it is of a higher moral authority. These remarks are noted to contrast between good sacrifice and the self-righteous sacrifice of malevolent intent and tormented spirit, as a moral authority is only ever truly just, righteous, and worthy of its virtue as a greater and higher authority when it helps the world and oneself with greater justice.

There are many case studies that can be considered in studying the continuity of moral authority through acts perceived to be great. Legends and historic figures are born of such principles of the dynamics of ethics. The sacrifices and miraculous deeds of Prophets are a testament to lasting moral authorities and great moral power. But then even the sacrifice of the ordinary person, perhaps ever grander through a common lack of expectation for great courage in people, is defiance against injustice and oppressive wrong-doing. One person's act of courage can be immortalised as an Ideal of virtue through a single story or photo, becoming a Paragon of inspiration. When people inspire and evoke goodwill and good faith, their moral power rises with the people looking up to them with an expectation of righteousness, justice, hope, and goodness. This becomes a key element in cataclysmic sociopolitical and ethical changes through acts expressing the spirit of a moral authority and its virtues. A neat and perhaps unexpected way of summarising such a notion of the great power of morality and virtue is to quote (and reinterpret) Obi-Wan Kenobi from Episode IV of the *Star Wars* saga: *"You can't win [...]. If you strike me down, I shall become more powerful than you can possibly imagine."*

While moral power can exercise profound force, it is true that it can be fickle and fragile. One must also consider the nature and dynamics of moral power where values compete and conflict. For instance, religious morality can be both fundamentally moving while simultaneously completely negligible. Every act of every individual represents and stands by certain principles of morality. When people live and act according to an ethic and morality, they are only as good as an ideal and its authority. Take away, dismantle, and extinguish that which inspires and moves people, and their morality will be lost. The only surest way to tear down that which moves one's spirit is to annul its authority in just and righteous acts of virtue, which can only be done through the authority of the Highest Good by affecting the spirit and psyche with goodness. People act in self-interest; where such interests conflict, often subject to biases and flaws in base morality and vulnerable psyche, only that which sets people free in spirit and grants peace of mind is a worthy and powerful moral authority. And, of course, this must all be conditioned in acceptable bounds of ethical and moral liberty.

In the secondary spheres of ethics and its utilities, formally exemplified as the Secondary Principles, philosophy is a fundamental asset. In all society, globally and locally, values and ideas compete. Understanding the dynamics of moral authority and moral power is instrumental to such causes and for one's own sake of fulfilment and happiness. Sometimes, the virtue of moral authority is its power to justify and guide actions in a clear direction, something often lost in difficult circumstances. It is not enough to presume understanding of others and oneself; one must also understand the world and its Laws. As such, philosophy and morality are the grandest power over humanity. But their implementation is both an art and science, known through the behaviour of people and mindfulness over one's own state of mind and spirit, achieved through empathy and all the elements of Harmony and relating disciplines, academic or practical.

Moral power can be categorised as a form of normative power, if not the apex of normative power from which the latter is derived. As was shown in Section 2 through the discussions of the elements present in the contention between the West and Russia, one interpretation suggests that normative concerns (as individual concerns for well-being) were fundamental. Understanding normativity and morality in this context of the structures of ethics and their mechanisms and driving forces is categorical for normative insight and wisdom. Where morality may have been thought to be negligible, or rather only as relevant as ruthless selfishness of hostile international and interpersonal environments dominated by fear and uncertainty, moral authority is nevertheless present and central. Moral authority and moral power can not only be utilities for the traditions of morality with respect to benevolence and justice, but can also be used in parallel to conventional power in politics and society fundamentally affected by Fear and morality. Normativity is a far-reaching subject and discipline from which any and all could benefit, not only those of greater moral ambition of the Highest Good.

Moral authority connects the will of people; those who command moral authority can command or appeal to the will of particular people. It is needless to say that moral authority can be highly rewarding. Mehta and Winship, through the works of George Akerlof, claimed *"high moral status can result in high social status"*[9]. They suggest the view that people perceived to be of high moral character by others are trustworthy, which positively influences social and economic success. Trustworthy and morally upstanding people can certainly attain social and economic well-being. Society and culture can largely function in terms of competitive deceit among people unregulated by traditional virtues. A world can function largely in terms of virtues placed in greed and clever, ruthless tactics that do not allow the virtues of honesty, compassion, and mutual respect to grow and flourish. The conditions of ethics and morality are set by Natural Law; so if a person is morally upstanding with respect to the valued characteristics of a given society that serve a useful function, then, and probably only then, can the individual be successful.

This view in particular applies to contemporary Western society which may commonly seem to have little clear moral sense on a daily basis. This gap in moral authority largely caused by perceived moral subjectivity leaves a lot of room for suffering, social divide, and moral and spiritual corruption. Then, on another note, where people act selfishly and against each other, a moral authority of Fear's vice spreads along its vectors and respective moral power. In these contexts, moral authority and moral power can be definitively illustrated to be crucial to individual and civic success, because their neglect can lead to mass suffering, degradation, war, and other undesirable civic inefficiencies. However, as was stated previously, those who identify gaps in moral authority and build on them can ultimately gain a lot of moral power through reformed moral authority. If that moral authority accurately corresponds to the Highest Good and Natural Law in relation to the demands of ethical environment, it will evoke flourishing. This can then become a normative and moral utility and asset in social, political, cultural, and economic spheres.

In support of the above-mentioned thought, Mehta and Winship write that *"moral power is like the other forms of capital: it is a resource which allows actors to do things they wouldn't be able to do without it,"[21]* a sentiment that largely seems to have been neglected in societies of moral uncertainty and excessive, thoughtless moral liberty. By cultivating moral authority, one can align people to an ethical tangent and common will, which can influence many things, even on the most personal level. Moral authority of the Highest Good is everywhere: between friends, families, teachers, doctors, corporations and consumers, political representatives and their supporters... If one can effectively implement moral authority and use moral power, he or she can find and act in accordance with greater flourishing through and for themselves, others, and society, especially where common interests are fulfilled. Normative power is fundamental to all things of the secondary sphere of ethics. However, for the power of moral authority to be utilised, it ought to be remembered that moral power ought to always serve the interests of people in accordance with the Imperative. The Natural Law of the Highest Good conclusively functions in terms of the human condition, which fundamentally pursues the determination of the will to flourish. The greatest moral authority truly of the Highest Good is one that empowers people and makes them better off. I will apply this concept of moral authority throughout the proceeding studies of the Secondary Principles.

On a final note, relating back to the heritin ethos of Liberty, moral power can be seen by some as primarily a social asset, a form of capital in relations of power. Such views would misconceive the greatest of rewards of moral power – virtue of character and good spirit. Honour and nobility may have once been significant aspects of social dynamics. Some people are of better character and greater virtue than others, entailing their immediate value lends greater social status and moral capital. But base morality deceives us of the true worth of moral power where it relates to society and self-interest driven by Fear and the lust for power and social status. Honour and nobility of virtue, borne of moral power inspired and moved by a worthy, righteous, and just moral authority, is an asset to one's spirit of Liberty. Honour to oneself and with respect to others is the virtue of Liberty evoking noble character resilient to Fear; nobility is the testament to the character we reflect on during sleepless nights. Being comfortable in one's own skin and mind, beyond the torments and quick temptations of Fear, is the measure and worth of nobility and honour – to be happy with oneself. Where habits and behaviour are a related matter, true honour and nobility, known in spirit through meditation on the self and sensation of the self, are evoked through actions raising virtues of the mind. Moral power through and of one's own character, living free from and in the corrosive effects of Fear, moves one's state of living in accordance with values and morality. To allow moral power to move through oneself, through habits and intuitions of virtues and goodwill, is power's greatest reward, the status of which comes in spirit of nobility and honour foremost to oneself and one's sense of living.

Chapter 26:

The Nature of Policy, the Civic, the State, and Governance

Politics and government are the hub of the sociopolitical; a figment of an inherited social contract shapes this state of affairs. The regime of a society is founded on the character of its people – on people's *moral culture*. The psyche of a populace is cast by its ethos and reigning moral authority. Rather than explore particular orientations of thought, such as left or right leaning views, normative studies (at least at first) could benefit more from normative analysis in terms of ethical dynamics and moral authority affecting the sociopolitical.

Political science and empirical evidence are necessary for any serious discussion concerning government, which an account of the human psyche and moral authority in structures of ethics would complement, at least even if only as a framework of study. Any political or economic theory may present itself with a degree of truth drawing from an aspect of human nature. Understanding human nature in its great diversity, central to ethics, lends much insight into the normative and sociopolitical spheres of structures of ethics. The proceeding study of Secondary Principles will primarily focus on the dynamics between liberty and authority, central to the sociopolitical and normative. However, the main concern is not to dedicate effort to particular views, as might be tempting to impatience. The matter at hand is to understand how normativity affects sociopolitical dynamics and their tangents and vectors of moral authority with respect to key categories – liberty and authority; but first, one must account for human nature.

A common theme arises among major works on political theory setting a foundation based on a view of the human condition. Thomas Hobbes in *'Leviathan'* (1651) argued human beings are physical, sophisticated machines. Hobbes develops this view towards the conclusion that people are wholly self-interested, then he brings attention to the animalistic nature of man. Certain inspiration from said work has translated into the metaphysics of heritin ethics, especially in terms of the self-interested, but not inherently selfish, Fundamental Principle. Consequently, an interpretation of Hobbes suggests that he argues for a pessimistic outlook on the human condition without a social contract to bind us together under law and order – under a common moral authority. In contrast, Jean-Jacques Rousseau argued in *'The Social Contract"* (1762) that human nature is inherently good, pure and free until it is corrupted by the chains of social life and politics. Also, John Locke put forward the view in *'Two Treatise of Government'* (1690) that we are naturally moral beings, free and equal under the rule of God. These three classical views of human nature are plausible and to a degree true if they correspond to the character of at least one individual. However, the model of the human psyche is incredibly complex and is not bound to a single identity.

The body of reason is shaped by the world around it, to which its mould serves as a conduit of force reflecting back into global ethical environment. We are creatures of two formations of reason – base and high – the synchrony of which corresponds to our spirit, mentality, morality, identity, psyche, and condition; the reason of man shapes his world. We are diverse and influenced by different ethical conditions and parameters. We discover and enact various parts of our natural entity, the traits and characteristics of which develop through particular nourishment. The fundamental of human nature is the force of reason, base and high. The power of reason corresponds to external and internal environments, such as sensation pressing on the machinations of instinct and mediation of greater rationale. Reason and human behaviour are consistent, predictable, and mechanical. Everything we are is the determination of reason.

Due to the adaptive and malleable formation of reason in the psyche, our nature is diverse. Classical theorists and their students often restrain themselves to a dogmatic view of human nature and mankind. However, the nature of mankind does not bind itself to a single identity beyond the potential alternatives of reason and characteristics. In all deviation and difference there is always a reason for why people are the way they are. These disparities in human nature, qualitatively and quantitatively, however, arise and present themselves in episodes, as is observable with normative developments contingent on the societal and material spheres. Base-reason is made tremendously more complex by its relation to high-reason, which is accompanied by a diverse framework of the human condition. Some orientate on the view of the duality of man – that we are either good or bad. Whilst there tend to be opposites in nature, in the human framework the two conceivable opposites are base-reason and high-reason; however, they are part of the whole body of reason and are inseparable. In the configuration of reason there is no absolute duality in human nature, only a multitude of variations in the synchrony and manifestation of reason. Every aspect of the human psyche is a single component of the whole. Violence, pleasure, pain, happiness, suffering, grief, love, hunger, rational thought, and every acknowledged passing moment or impression in the conscious mind are singular elements of the conscious mind's entire potential. It is because of high-reason that we take on many identities and characteristics often stemming from a foundation of the base faculties, especially as coping techniques with pain and suffering. Consequently, humanity becomes diverse in thought and belief respective of the nourishment and inheritance of circumstances and traits.

To look at one aspect of mankind in order to find Natural Law is a mistake, because the entire framework of the human condition in specific contexts has to be taken in mind. Hobbes, Locke, and Rousseau may be right in their own way, but their views mostly exemplify only certain aspects of the grand potential and nature of mankind. To find a plausible and valid theory of the sociopolitical is to identify the psyche and ethos of mankind; to argue how mankind ought to be governed is to structure prevailing ethics; to implement civics is to embrace and employ a respective moral authority; everything then conforms to conditioning of Natural Law and the Highest Good, for which we can only be so prepared.

The complexity and diversity of the human condition makes it counter-intuitive to establish an absolute natural state of people. Where ethical circumstances nourish particular dispositions of belief and rationale, with habits and upbringing influencing the base faculties, human activity and values can be categorised differently. First, to understand and evaluate the nature of values, behaviour, and character, one ought not to rush to moral judgement. Being mindful of the soul reaching into the world through its mental and moral utilities of actions, borne of certain characteristics, offers much insight for further evaluation. Structuring behaviour and activity in a framework of ethics, driven by the soul's Imperative, formulates a useful model for understanding the human psyche, especially in terms of Fear, instinct, and base morality. Some might suppose that emotions are irrational and wrong, that mankind's animalistic and baser elements are undesirable or somehow 'bad'. It could be said that focus on revered rationality is commonly symptomatic of desynchronised reason and corruption in its functions, for the arrogant and elitist pursuit of status through rationale can be ascribed to animalistic social behaviour vexed by Fear.

For what it's worth, the vice of mankind's 'rationale' is worse than the viciousness of the common beast innocent in its instincts. The vice of mankind, augmenting instinct through high-reason and making it ever more powerful, is of greater malice than that of any common animal. Yet this same effect can translate into impeccable virtues, befitting our humanity. The heritin ethos strives for harmony and synchrony between sentiment and greater rationality, in doing so teaching much about the human condition. These insights then reduce thought and mindful sensation to the foundation of all active living – spirit and soul. Where all actions are inherently bound to the Fundamental Principle, and with respect to the Highest Good there is no such thing as an absolute evil, one may begin to think of mankind as inherently good. The better conclusion to draw from this thought is that the foundation of the human condition and the innate quality of the soul are *amoral*. Only when the soul develops and engages with the world, relevant to ethics, does it become subject to moral evaluation. The practical connotation of the suggested thought is mindful study and analysis of human behaviour, activity, endeavour, and condition, as is useful in terms of the conceptual framework of heritin ethics that equally views people as mechanical vectors and as living things of distinct inherent value.

Where the foundation of evaluating people is found on the amorality of the soul, considerations of value and morality with respect to individuals and society can become more coherent in ethical structures and frameworks, especially in the context of the adaptive cycle of values and the operating ethos of the human psyche. Where moral values and ethical valuation drive society, people necessarily employ utilities of high-reason to adapt to new conditions of ethical environment. This gives rise to laws, rights, and what may be described as social contracts. In the context of this work, the aforementioned elements can be categorised as moral utilities, as active and engaged manifestations of reason. As such, social contracts and governments, their reigning laws and rights, are a structural form of the soul's Imperative to flourish. A social contract is a metaphysical and veiled token of moral authority. Social constructs are structures and causal cascades of the soul. Society and civilisation have grown with people's imperative to flourish, extending and amplifying our abilities, possibilities, and influence. Society is natural to mankind; civilisation is natural to humanity. But where high-reason may appeal to a social contract, and philosophy develops through social contracts, social contracts are only as ethically synthetic as their design of high-reason.

A social contract, as well as a law and right, will only be successful if they comply with the organicism of ethical principles and values. Therefore, rather than providing definitive moral valuation of human nature and society, it is more productive to first be mindful of ethical context. Values, attitudes, and the spirit of modernity are comparatively different to pre-industrial normativity. From this point of view, one can better understand the needs and necessities of and for values. This feeds into organic and intuitive understanding of the human condition and society at large, according to which philosophy and the science of normativity become ever-more useful, practical, realistic, intuitive, and straightforward. This value is imperative for all political thought and civic and policy development, for successful and effective policy must come from and with proper normativity compatible with ethical demands. Perhaps the main point to draw from this Chapter is the nature of policy design and social, political, and economic thought and philosophy as fundamentally contextual to the conditions of an ethical environment and people's related moral culture. Every political philosophy has its merits and partial truths, but only in broader context and considerations of ethical environments do they become truly effective as civic and moral utilities. All political orientations – conservative or liberal, right or left – have their merits and utility, which are only just and good in specific circumstances and conditions demanding policy initiatives – reactions.

The organicism of human nature led to formation of society and civilisation. Society is natural to us, even if developed modern society is intellectually, normatively, civically, practically, mentally, and spiritually challenging. The dominance of base reason and its primacy over morality may have created the modern world. Yet it can be argued that the utility of base morality is becoming deficient, with greater balance and civic and moral effectiveness achievable through higher morality. For example, mindfulness that leads to the moderation of reactions through discipline can serve as an essential virtue for sustained happiness in the modern world counter-acting the corrosive and often corruptive effect of the negativity bias. But normative development towards modern society was organic up to a point; whether it is organically sustainable in terms of the adaptive cycle of values remains to be seen.

The introduction of synthetic utilities, such as social contracts, laws, rights, and their corresponding philosophies, flow with ethical and moral values. These aspects of human society are further affected by organic and synthetic dynamics, with synthetic intervention necessary for the sustainability of society and civilisation, but only achievable through complimentary organicism of values and conditions of ethical environment. As human nature and its condition adapt to ethical environment, these events reflect onto the normativity and morality of society at large, subsequently influencing governments and the political sphere. Where ethical development and change occur, society becomes ethically convoluted, diverse, at times conflicted. Here synthetic social and political measures are employed to deal with social issues and challenges. Social contracts, laws, and rights become the foundation of society and governance, contingent on normativity and morality. However, as is evident with the many challenges of modern society turned fiery through Fear splintering and fracturing not only views and social cohesion but also humanity, a social contract's effectiveness diminishes with rifts and voids in moral authority and its power. An emphatic insistence on a blind social contract, even if resourceful, is an inefficient, limited, and ultimately only a temporary normative utility.

Conceptual confusion may surround the precise nature and essence of social contracts, laws, and rights. From a model of structural ethics, these aspects of the sociopolitical can be categorised as tangents and vectors of values and moral authority in the secondary spheres of ethics. Social contracts, laws, and rights, in whatever form they take, can be summarised as agreements and parameters of social endeavour and activity bound by moral authority and moral power. The basis for this point, while not ultimately essential for future discussions and arguments, is the nature of moral authority influencing society and people as a whole. Laws are set in place and upheld only by agreement and compatible values and interests. For instance, a police force will only be effective so long as people fund government agencies. A law will only be a condition of behaviour and activity so long as people agree to it and uphold it, tacit or dedicated. The normative foundation of social contracts, laws, and rights can be considered in such a framework of moral authority and its vectors and tangents in a social ethical environment.

The valuable implication of this view is its ability to account for the fluidity of normativity and society at large. Where one may wonder how society came into being and how the informal social contract bound society and led to the formation of civilisation, an organic view of normativity and moral authority serves as a point of insight. Social contracts and their laws and rights are derived from the reason producing respective behaviour, activity, and endeavour. The manifestation, design, and culture of social contract societies are contingent on the foundation of all human activity in terms of people's concerns for well-being and ethical profit or security. Therefore, where people and civilisation have flourished through society, managed and moved according to the authority of morality and the state, a social contract as an explicit normativity of moral authority becomes instrumental, organic, and intuitive. To live together and reap the rewards, contention and conflict in normativity must be settled with a greater authority able to secure order and justice – a social contract's state and government. Social contracts pertaining to centralised moral authority of law, state, and government arise through the dynamics of environment requiring such measures for greater well-being. Therefore, the state and the authority of governance, above all through moral authority formalised as an overt social contract forgotten to attention, are legitimised through common concerns for well-being and relating values and normativity.

Society and state are not always just, as their normativity may elude the justice of ethical values and virtues. Where utilitarian maxims are considered, the strength of any social contract's moral authority is the sum moral power of its vectors. Popular performance in liberal democracies is the clearest manifestation of this. Where moral authority is undermined by the state itself, and moral communities in a society turn against each other, civic disorder and discord undermine human endeavour. A social contract is only as relevant as its moral authority and normativity affecting society. A social contract is only that which becomes an accepted, prevailing norm in the politics of governance and culture of morality. Only moral power of a truly just and virtuous moral authority can secure and reinvigorate a worthy social contract, achievable only through its vectors of virtue. But this tangent of moral power is antecedent to a social contract and works on a more foundational, metaphysical level to the normativity of a social contract. Hence, wise authority would be mindful of its legitimacy found through bettering people's lives and contingent moral authority and power. Formality only dictates appeal to social contract; the underbelly of any ethical structure is the normativity invoking a particular social contract and episodic manifestation of the state of the human condition reacting to the adaptive cycle.

The moral authority of the Fundamental Principle brought us to our modern state. Society and people require leadership and guidance through moral authority, whether through influential people or established laws. Environmental conditioning and opportunities motivated us to come together and organise ourselves to ensure greater chances of survival and well-being. Hence, certain people gain power. The natural example of this is how children instinctively look for approval from their parents and elders, thus bestowing moral power to their guardians. The resolution of base and high reason forms the basis for governance over people, whether through personality, law, or morality. As social and civilisational development is organic, any civic, social, and political development would be wise to follow suit while devising synthetic utilities. To identify and employ synthetic social utilities with respect to their values – that is, *civics* – one must study, understand, and embrace organic aspects leading up to the necessity of synthetic intervention. Social contracts are secondary to their foundation of normativity. Thus, in devising civics and binding them to a social contract envisaged through the state and government, built on a particular ethic and morality, one must consider many relevant views and expressions of human nature and character; one must consider elements far beyond a fundamentally biased or impressionable view of people, instead focusing on the mechanical basis of the soul and its Imperative.

Here the purpose of the state, governance, society, and normativity become clear – they are utilities in the pursuit of ethical interest. The state and its politics, like any moral utility, is an extension of the primary ethical dynamic driving all and any behaviour – a mode pursuing well-being. Perhaps a forgotten, obvious premise, normativity, politics, society, state, and government are utilities of the soul's Imperative, an extension of ethical tangents into secondary spheres and grander ethical environments. It is in this context that all matters of state and governance, whether of law or social contracts, ought to be examined. However, any mode of authority or liberty is found on its ethical premise, basis, and principle, just as the character of a society's and nation's people – vectors in an ethical environment and sphere – determine the species of a regime. The context of the adaptive cycle of values, other Natural Laws, and moral laws are pivotal for matters of normativity, state, and society. Where plurality of values' tangents and their many forces arise, a centralised institution, whether personalistic (primitive or basic) or progressive and of a higher sort (such as of rule of law), becomes instrumental to people's needs and concerns. Ethics, normativity, and the sociopolitical bridge the reason guiding actions, thoughts, and convictions. Structuring ethics should hopefully provide some clarity with regards to the utility and purpose of state. However, even with this clarification, the problem of complexity disguising itself as subjectivity remains.

The state will always face tough and unclear choices with regards to policies and missions. Priorities must be assigned and core values and interests found for guidance. Therefore, a hierarchy of values must be considered, as this work does by structuring Core, Central, Secondary, and Tertiary Principles. The state itself is a mere utility for normativity of the values that forge it. The moral authority and power of particular values, subsequently their normativity, are central to the performance of governance and the purpose of the state. Where one may question the merits of positioning normativity at the centre of the sociopolitical – the secondary sphere or level of ethical structures – the reason for this view is found through considerations of the moral authority that creates this sphere. But due to the nature of moral authority, as well as discussions raised throughout the Central Principles, both society and the individual are of equal worth with respect to well-being and ethical value. The basis of the state and governance in the context of normativity can hitherto be formalised in such a framework. Yet structuring a hierarchy of values and studying ethical values competing in different circumstances is still an art and science that remains to be explored and understood, which will be the guiding motivation of the following Chapters.

People need guidance and leadership; it can be philosophical in the form of pure moral authority, or it can be normative through legal institutions and government. Governments arise through the reason binding us to social contracts. The prevailing moral authority of a society thus constructs the occupying regime. As people are diverse, behave differently at certain times and under various circumstances, and act as vectors in accordance with active values, all political thought is at least partially true with respect to the context of ethical environment and people's characteristics. Social contracts are aligned with moral authority striving for goodness in times of contention, threats, and conflict; social contracts are an agreement to order, even if agitated, so as to withhold from ethical contention leading to vicious and bloody conflict. This service and right is bestowed on the *state* and *government* as the formal structure and institution of moral authority. The only chains put on mankind are those of reason, and only the state, by virtue of moral authority, exercises this power legitimately in a society at odds, but only in so much as the state is of law and morality of the people and merit in accordance with the Highest Good. If the state is immoral or amoral, it no longer becomes an authority. When authority is unjust and wrong, people must look to themselves and morality to secure justice and create greater well-being. Which moral authority best conforms to Natural Law and the Highest Good remains to be said, with most answers being conditional and partial to circumstances and conditions of ethical environment. A government's purpose is to organise, manage, and lead a society and its people, a dynamic that often arises among people without institutional intervention. As such, society and civilisation will always be subject to the powers of the state and morality, bringing to light the fundamental duality of normativity and sociopolitical thought – liberty and authority. This leads to the question of how people ought to be governed. Should people be free or bound to strong authority? Henceforth I shall engage with the classic question of liberty and authority, freedom and control.

Chapter 27:

The Utility and Limits of Liberty

The Secondary Principles of liberty and relevant discussions on the normativity of liberty will stem from the Central Principle of liberty:

People ought to have liberty to practise different moralities so that the Highest Good and mankind with it, through the Human Imperative, may develop and progress through stronger moralities, thereby producing flourishing for the individual and relevant ethical environment through moral development. When opposing moralities give cause to unnecessary and unjust suffering and lead to conflict with the Central Principles or other moralities in a destructive manner, then that particular ethic is not to be tolerated and must be addressed with effective and just practice of morality, but only in accordance with justice.

Much of what needs to be kept in mind and said on the normativity of social, political, economic, and cultural liberty can be found through this Central Principle in conjunction with other Central Principles and considerations of moral authority and moral power. The Central Principle of liberty concerns itself with moral development of individuals, then societies. This principle focuses on moral liberty – liberty in moral choices and actions as part of the growth of character and freedom for people to make their choices. The Central Principle of liberty builds on the metaphysical account of the liberty of morality – the systemic ethical aspect of morality reflecting and corresponding to the dynamics of values, particular with reference to the adaptive cycle of values. The Central Principle of liberty outlines a foundation of moral authority that values the autonomy of individuals by appealing to the virtue of the fundamental will of a person and the organicism of autonomous judgement. An individual who willingly binds to a particular moral authority does so in pursuit of flourishing, serving as the foundation of harmonious and stable synchrony (particularly with respect to convictions and loyalty) and sustainable activity in terms of both the tangent and the vector. Only where a person's conviction is fulfilling and rewarding, as well as of its own determination and volition, will its agency, and subsequently effect on environment, be truly virtuous and positively strong. This empowerment of any moral authority is essential to its own and its host's well-being.

The other aspect of the Central Principle of liberty concerns itself with empowered and effective agency absent the inefficiency and volatility of Fear's extreme civics such as coercion and the direct threat of harm. A lack of liberty will sow stagnation and degeneration, the fragile order of which can never be sustained through self-cannibalising measures of doomed authority and corrupted ethical environment and its vectors. These elements of the Central Principle of liberty are the cornerstone of stable autonomy through virtue. However, if free autonomy opens up influences of vice, then the positivity of liberty can be undermined. This leads one to examine the sociopolitical dynamic of liberty and authority, which follows from the ethical foundation of the corresponding Central Principle.

While the Central Principle of liberty concerns itself with moral freedom, this liberty is distinct to social, political, legal, civic, and economic liberties. Moral liberty is conceptually different from normative liberty, as the latter, with respect to the nature of its secondary sphere of ethics, engages many ethical dynamics and aspects beyond specific liberty of morality forming particular values. For most part, the Central Principle of liberty focuses on morality and the individual. Ethics serve as the foundation for all things social, political, legal, civic, and economic, with core and central moral principles underlying their corresponding secondary manifestations. The natural consequence of the Central Principle of liberty is liberal or libertarian political thought.

Liberal disciplines and schools of thought have been studied extensively. Certain discussions and ideas on the normativity and ethics of liberty would benefit from revision of the basic tenants and principles of liberal thought. In particular, the normativity of liberty would benefit greatly from reference to the classical text of John Stuart Mill's *"On Liberty"* (1859). Any discussion of normative and political liberty could borrow much from Mill's philosophy. The goal of this Chapter is to study the normative structural ethics interpretation of Mill's thoughts on liberty. The value given to Mill's thoughts on social, political, and economic liberty should be intuitive in the context of the Central Principle of liberty – liberty is necessary for flourishing and development, socially and individually. Liberal political thought and philosophy are not mere policies and civics of a feel-good factor of independence and autonomy; liberty's utility is fundamental to the adaptiveness of values, progress, and development. However, in the grander scheme and in the context of diverse ethical environments, liberty requires balance and moderation. Furthermore, moral authority and moral power are only environmentally sustainable through vectors independently and autonomously giving corresponding causal tangents force and relevance. If the Highest Good is to thrive in an environment, then it must be sustainable, which ultimately can only be accomplished through normative liberty.

The foundation of any political thought is found on its corresponding values, morality, and normativity. John Stuart Mill developed his political philosophy on the ethical basis of the principle of utility *"as the ultimate appeal on all ethical questions,"*[11] which then gave progress to secondary normative formulations of ethics – that is, ethics of the sociopolitical. The central ethical concern of Mill's utilitarianism that influenced his political philosophy was, broadly speaking, the concern for the greatest amount of happiness and higher pleasure[12]. Utilitarian thought is intuitive in terms of well-being, and the influence of utilitarianism on moral intuition and reasoning is fundamental to heritin ethics and normative combinatorialism. It is rational, intuitive, and emotionally liberating to consider the most happiness for oneself and for others.

However, as is common for utilitarian considerations, other criteria and guiding principles must be satisfied. The combinatorialist framework emphasises the relevance of character to guide utilitarian considerations, then exemplifies virtue with duty. The measure of well-being is the spirit borne of the psyche. Thus, utilitarian considerations are only as good and valuable where their virtue – good utility – is met and spirit is worthy. Balancing and mediating utilitarian considerations with reference to other normative criteria, especially in consideration of the tangents of certain actions and their moral authority, is key. Normative combinatorialism and the Central Principles will guide utilitarian and other judgements with respect to the sociopolitical. This point is crucial where moral liberty, concerning the liberty of people's decisions and society's future, can lead to the necessity of inaction on suffering. The Natural Law of the adaptive cycle of values requires liberty and organicism. Subsequent suffering is not ideal and is undesirable, yet it is a consequence that one must accept in just measure. In these cold thoughts it may be tempting to lose oneself, spirit, and virtue to apathy and delusion. It is for this reason that a combined approach and ethical principle, not merely utilitarianism and limited insight of rational estimation, must be adopted to guide the concerns and interests of liberty, or else moral liberty will degrade into brutality and selfishness.

Morality liberty leads to normative competition and adaptation. As was argued in Chapters 17 and 18, the individual and society deserve equal consideration. The basic argument is that care for the individual and society serve the Human Imperative, and therefore maximise individual interests. Synchrony and harmony are vital for a healthy, good, just, and efficient ethical environment. Individualist and communitarian ethical principles and philosophies excel in particular circumstances. Society is better off with a stronger and more virtuous constituency; the individual is empowered through duty to others, society, and the Highest Good. The virtue-duty of Liberty's spirit of duty, struggle, sacrifice, and care for people and society can be phrased in the following way: duty to society is an expression of an individual's will and power – the virtues of great spirit. It can be difficult to withstand apathy and be steadfast under the pressure of mass suffering; where virtue does not submit, it turns to duty and nobility, fulfilling the self with grand spirit of character's strength. However, the relation between the individual and society is complex and often contentious. Different needs demand different approaches. As such, it is imperative for ethical valuation to prioritise – to lay out a hierarchy of values and interests. However, neither the community or the individual inherit primary value, as both must be in harmony if each is to thrive through the highest virtues. It would be wise to first consider the nature of individual autonomy and its liberty in society.

John Stuart Mill emphasised individuality and the growth of moral character for society to thrive[13]. Mill's arguments for autonomy are constructed on the premise that individuals often know what is best for them according to their own judgement. As he wrote: *"It is for him to find out what part of recorded experience is properly applicable to his own circumstances and character"*[14]. This thought reflects the arguments on the genealogy of values with regard to functions of people's psyche forming values through experience and impression. The moralities we adopt are invoked by the psyche in accordance with the information we absorb and the conditions to which we adapt. Autonomous judgement always functions through the determination of the fundamental will; this principle is essential for the success of any moral authority. To set an individual on a virtuous path through a corresponding moral authority can only be done when character is empowered by its resolve and determination through the soul at liberty of ambition.

When virtuous autonomy is combined with sensible judgement, the individual forms and learns greater moral sense and coercive control is not necessary for justice beyond the intuited reason of moral authority guiding people's moral reasoning. This is the great value of liberal autonomy – a moral agent acting ethically positive and morally upstanding according to their own will; this is intuitively more efficient, more stable, and in terms of governance perhaps even easier than exuberant or excessive authoritative control. The throne of power is an appealing position in Fear; notable character and the mindful individual will know the true worth found in harmonious society at liberty from oppression and corrosive and corruptive Fear. It is better to have a golden society than a golden throne, as the former is of priceless spirit, and the latter is of futile effort. The success of a society placing conviction in the freedom of autonomy rests on the virtues influencing the determination of autonomous judgement and action. This is suggestive of an understanding and definition of a liberal society as one that can flourish through virtuous autonomy.

Western thought often considers liberty a fundamental and basic right, essential to any prosperous society. In consideration of virtuous character and autonomy, which require development and nourishment, liberty can be difficult to achieve and sustain. As such, liberty is a luxury. Liberty is a privilege that must be earned, and only when a community is able to embrace it can autonomous freedom succeed. When the resolve of a people is strong and their will is of great virtue, liberty is embraced and not-easily surrendered. Only when Fear or general vice fester in a society does liberty become restrained or rejected, consequently the luxuries of liberty are set aside for lesser development, provided the circumstance benefits from a truly just authority. Liberty can be a complex sociopolitical utility to foster and sustain effectively; it may be burdensome, but its benefits are extraordinary. Where virtue feeds and sustains good character, and society's individuals grow, develop, and mentally, spiritually, and morally evolve, a society can become more adaptive and therefore stronger. However, as is evident in modern times, corruptive disparities in values, driven by ignorance, foolishness, pettiness, and the vices of Fear, give rise to *unjust* contention and conflict in values. The value of authority, especially moral authority, becomes obvious as a utility for social cohesion, harmony, order, stability, and security where social harmony is abrupted by the tangents of lesser moral authorities.

The great advantage of liberal autonomy is the cultivation of virtue in society as a whole. The influence of the adaptive cycle of values and its reign of Natural Law always puts pressure on any government and society. Decades of endeavour and new generations of a globalised world have catalysed ethical dynamics to form a far-reaching, interconnected, truly global ethical environment and its causal cascades. Through times of peace and prosperity, values have transformed through the globalised world and modernity's unprecedented liberty of thought. This stage or cycle of development is now threatened by the madness of idleness. Where degrees of stability and material satisfaction led to idleness and opportunity, values developed with individuals. Ethics, morality, and philosophy have revolutionised. Now, moral ideals and values compete more than ever.

With vast amounts of easily accessible information, even if plagued by misinformation and ill-discipline, and with prevalent literacy and education, value formation and development has become swift and hectic. Whether these values are good or bad, or constructive, degenerate, impulsive, or unfound, is a whole other matter. In these circumstances, capable autonomy through virtue of character and coherent guiding values become necessary. Any developed and prosperous modern society will become subject to the pressure of values adapting to new environments; the opportunity to develop through liberty becomes an absolute necessity if a society is to adapt and sustain advantage. Virtuous autonomy – that is, the character and psyche of values suitable to ethical conditions producing good actions – is the means to harmony with change in Natural Law and the Highest Good, of individual and social ethical adaption. For this, degrees of civic, social, and fundamental liberties are necessary. A liberal society can adapt more successfully to values corresponding to the conditions of ethical environment than any authoritative state restricting the growth of the individual. The fundamentals of liberalism, such as free thought, free speech, and free practise of *just* values, are instrumental to the progression of the individual and society. A government would not need strong command over a liberal populace where the individuals of a society are capable of doing the right and good thing without the necessity for inefficient and corruptive coercive control. An excessive authority of government stripping away at the development of individuality will eventually undermine the potential of its people, leaving the nation to degrade and stagnate under the pressures of the adaptive cycle and through the lack of ingenuity or eccentricity driving progress. The self-governance of autonomy is thus, in modern conditions of the adaptive cycle, ultimately the most efficient mode of governance. However, it can only succeed when the virtues of a community enable successful freedom of virtue.

Mill argued that morality and the individual should develop. Where development through and of ethical values is desired, this is only achievable by appealing to virtuous and just autonomy of proportional liberty. As Mill wrote: *"Human nature is not a machine to be built after a model, and set to do exactly the work prescribed for it, but a tree, which requires to grow and develop itself on all sides, according to the tendency of the inward forces which make it a living thing."*[16] Not only does Mill affirm the positive utility of individual judgement when it is morally effective, but he also identifies the need for a person to adapt to his or her experiences. These parallels hint at the Natural Law of the adaptive cycle of values, yet not to the degree explored in structural ethics. Mill's thoughts give much attention to the development of ethics, reciprocal of the complications of utilitarian ethics considering consequences and estimating ethical maxims. Where one is mindful of ethical vectors and tangents, utilitarian considerations of consequences and ethical maxims become more intuitive and coherent. As Mill wrote in regards to individuals' value-formation in empirical terms of experience and impressions influencing values: *"It is the privilege and proper condition of a human being, arrived at the maturity of his faculties, to use and interpret experience in his own way."*[17] This emphasises the condition of the individual character *'arrived at the maturity of his faculties'* (that is, of developed character) as a means to fulfil the *'proper condition of a human being'* (or function of life and the human psyche with respect to the Human Imperative), which is satisfied in Mill's thought through the *summum bonum* (highest end good) of the higher pleasures. The heritin interpretation favours this value not only in terms of global interest, but also in terms of the mechanism of fulfilment satisfied only through the cultivation of virtue nourishing spirit and character.

To clarify where the main point might be distorted, the parallels between the thoughts in this work and Mill's should only serve to expand the understanding of that which seems intuitive and accepted in some spheres and communities. The metaphysics and theoretical framework of this project should complement the greater understanding of that which is only subjectively or minimally appreciated. The utility of civic liberty is not only of a subjective sentiment in terms of a feel-good factor; it is a utility imperative for flourishing with respect to the concrete mechanisms of Nature conditioning states of affairs and living conditions. The rift between Nature and mankind is only of egotistic illusion, yet humanity can never submit to Nature or allow its brutality to overwhelm our virtue. While this conversation must be reserved for another time, it is important to put forward the notion that while humanity and mankind are best in harmony with Nature, we are not the supremacy of Nature, nor God's idolised perfection of higher virtues stripped of instinct. Yet it is our ambiguous and amorphous humanity that makes us notable and of a distinct destiny and position to question.

In short, values and moral principles must adapt according to the pressures of the cycle of values, otherwise Natural Law takes its course of coercion and conditioning. Strong moralities can heavily influence the determination of the Natural Law through the force of moral authority. Allowing strong character to develop through autonomous pursuits accentuates the moral authority of an ethos and the moral power of an individual and their morality. If such an authority and its value is just, righteous, and virtuous, this leads to social prosperity. This is the utility of individuality and its liberty, of civic, civil, social, and fundamental liberty. Society and generations must adapt to the times; this is how people organically behave according to the compulsions of the soul and the necessity of Natural Law. The adaptive cycle of values constantly mediates the enterprise of human civilisation and people are bound to its principles. Some may defy the prevailing state of Nature to such a degree to author profound influence over the Highest Good, changing the conditions of Nature. But even such feats of moral leviathans are only achieved through the determination of Nature and the Highest Good, as any must humbly admit.

Individuality is key to human development. Human development changes the world and influences Nature. Accordingly, we are forced to adapt and change if necessary, with positive virtues prevailing. Even dissatisfaction with a moment of shame is enough to move values towards positive growth. Our will to flourish gives us the purpose of the Human Imperative, and to achieve our goals we can only do so by developing, flourishing, and progressing. This implies there are various paths we can take, the liberty of which is necessary for the succession of values and good practices. Moral truth of Natural Law can, at times, be too complex to identify through introspection alone in reflection of current states of affairs. Liberty, autonomy, and individuality are instrumental for human utility and the Human Imperative. It is, therefore, in the interests of developed and capable societies to encourage and protect individuality. It is vital for mass society that the autonomy of individuality succeeds where it is of imperative utility and just, both in terms of moral sense and ingenuity encouraging progress, as change in the character of society ripples across spheres of ethical environment, for better or worse.

Mill extensively wrote on the protection of minorities, particularly those of 'eccentric' genius[18]. It is a common theme in contemporary Western societies to protect individuality, or at least it is encouraged in social culture valuing, perhaps overvaluing, the individuality of notable persona, whether in terms of trends, beliefs, attitudes, or labels of identity. Where the health of such occupation can be questioned (extensively), identity and individuality are invaluable instruments. For society to develop it needs liberty of intellectual and moral deviation, something that only a minority of particular character can achieve until these attitudes succeed and apparent minorities balance with the majority, resulting in an atmosphere of creative ingenuity no society of prevailing vice could achieve. Where the strong values of virtue, justice, and righteousness are born, their power will only succeed if the corresponding authority succeeds in terms of the Highest Good. For every success there have been ever-more failures, yet even a single breakthrough can bring about necessary change. Liberty can sow social and civic inefficiencies in terms of mentally, morally, and spiritually unsound or immature individuals. Liberty has a cost. However, for all such deviations that strike the attention of Fear's biases and impatience, the best of humanity can arise in the most surprising of times and places. It is this liberty of individuality and, supposedly, eccentricity that drives progress and development, achieved best in a welcoming environment able to confidently mediate subsequent positive and negative influences, for even negative influences have an organic utility and value by driving progress through Fear in those lacking self-sufficient, autonomous motivation.

Where a virtuous society develops when it begins to accept and tolerate certain deviations, the minority and majority can achieve synchronised development at liberty of their values and goals. It is as Mill wrote: *"Genius can only breathe freely in an atmosphere of freedom,"*[19] from which both the minority and majority can benefit greatly. Without undue coercion of social or institutional authority, a person can focus on doing what he or she does best, balanced with greater needs of justice through a benevolent and mindful authority, the beginning of which is bound to morality and common understanding and good faith. But insecurity and immaturity can undermine social and civic cohesion of the majority and minority, disrupting necessary development, undermining adaptation – undermining change for the better, improving outdated traditions and a mediocre status quo.

Despite Mill's attention to the minority of genius, minorities involve more than brilliant mind and eccentric identities. Even a minority practising an unusual way of life absent any intentional genius can have a positive influence on the majority by teaching a little new quirk or offering insight towards discovering something ethically useful. Genius and brilliance possesses incredible utility for any society through the virtue of ingenuity and development, for it is greatness that makes the greatest break-throughs. However, combined endeavour and collaboration over time can achieve great results even without genius. Nonetheless, the liberty of opportunity absent distraction and excess Fear are pivotal for greater ingenuity and development. As Mill wrote: *"Person's of genius, it is true, are, and always likely to be, a small minority; but in order to have them, it is necessary to preserve the soil in which they grow."*[20] It is further evident beyond Mill's exclusive terms that good social, ethical, and mental nourishment is necessary to encourage ambition and inspiration. Any empowered will of a vector set to test the limits and advance humanity requires material and human resources, the cultivation of which requires civic and interpersonal liberty. The liberty that provides opportunity and increases moral luck sows the resources of its spheres' growth and prosperity.

Prevailing majorities can offer a framework for existence, identity, value, and desire to those who do not value eccentric individuality or to those who are otherwise not born to a sporadic and turbulent destiny of oddity. It may seem as though some people disproportionately strive for individuality without the necessary characteristics to support their wishful identity. A strong sense of self and a healthy ego are necessary in social dynamics to fulfil one's potential and to protect oneself from the harm of being mistreated and misused, as the connection between confidence and status in baser terms is quite obvious and often belligerent where sensitive and weak. Ego is the difference between slave-master relations, and no worthy virtue uses slaves or is willing to have slaves. However, excess concerns over individuality harms the self more than it protects. It is the death of liberty where the sense of self is squandered to Fear and the corruption of deceitful security in conformity. It is far worse to be something you are not than to be honest with the self. But honesty to oneself is fulfilled only in virtue to improve in nobility of character overcoming vice. An unhealthy obsession with individuality does not resolve the root of its spirit's sickness – the fragility of identity.

The majority may seem to some as ordinary, average, mediocre, as something to be looked down upon and superceded. The majority serves its positive utility to those who are not born to difference and to whom happiness and personal function can be satisfied with established ethical tangents and expectations. There is grace and beauty in their happiness of simple living. Others' hunger and ambition is of its own sort and value, but not exclusive as a species or above and beyond the common ancestry that gave it life. The morbidness of greatness is, truly, of suffering. Drawing on the Central Principles of ethical value, we all have our roles, places, talents, and value. Where one contributes by any means righteous, just, and virtuous, even with minor effect, this is worthy of honour and respect. Any work contributing with goodness, no matter how seemingly menial or insignificant, is worthy, respectable, and *good*. No effort contributing to the Human Imperative is valueless or meaningless; no soul of the Highest Good and aligned with the Imperative – of humanity – is demeaning.

Individuals of blessed talent may be of great significance, yet their roles are usually only enabled by the many contributions of the majority sustaining the virtue of societies at liberty capable of ingenuity and significant change. Both minorities and majorities, when just, righteous, and virtuous to a satisfactory degree, are worthy of respect and good faith. Eccentricity is not always a thing to be feared, just as the tyranny of the majority is not always a threat or a sign of undervalued humanity and mediocrity. And while the two aspects of any society will contend and compete, harmony can be found beyond Fear and in humility and good faith between persons. Ultimately, however, the tyranny of the majority is supreme up to the point of the determination of Natural Law and the Highest Good. Negative characters of minorities will be stumped if disfavoured by the majority. So, any voice of a minority, in all its humility and mindful thought, should consider the consequences of its effects on people in greater terms. The majority is good at testing the resolve of moral authority, setting a standard for anything the minority might create. Yet the courage of eccentricity should not be blind to the dysfunction and moral corruption found in itself or in the majority.

Where one has questions concerning individuality, its civic and social aspects benefit from oddity and eccentricity as a mode of diversity and a means of change. Regardless of whether deviation is spiritually and morally positive or negative, deviation influences ethical adaptation, whether through development or cause to develop. Only when the liberty of deviation exceeds the threshold of justice and tolerable moral liberty does it warrant a reaction that curtails liberty. A study of the ethical dynamics between majorities and minorities is, for now, best restricted to the present context beyond a comprehensive dedicated study. The discussion of the value of individuality ought to be, for most part, left to the Tertiary Principles as principles concerning themselves with the broad effect of identity and personal values on character. Nevertheless, in the present context it is best to settle the topic of individuality by establishing the relevance of degrees of eccentricity, individuality, and deviations from established norms as a necessary means for development and social and civic adaptation through the liberty of ingenuity and morality. A detailed account of this would benefit from further revision and study of Mill's original work.

Liberty can cause or lead to conflict; this is not its utility or justification. Even though liberty enables degrees of negativity, it does not permit or tolerate unjust immorality or excess vice. Liberty's primary utility is intended to enable righteous actions absent coercion or excessive authority to do the right thing, which culminates in greater development and positive autonomy of character. Liberty of the spirit and mind, combined with autonomy of the soul's higher ambitions, leads to liberty of empathy. This capacity to understand and put oneself into another's place, to be mindful of others' experiences and pain, can be the beginning of amendment and positive change. Where empathy prevails even as unfocused compassion, common ground of good faith can be established and harmony can supercede Fear. This is applicable not only to interpersonal dynamics of individuality and the rigidity of the character of the majority, but also to the subsequent dynamics between liberty and authority. Where measures of authority are understood and the graces of liberty appreciated, synchrony in endeavour and ambition can be found through empathy's liberty, insight, and virtues of patience and understanding.

Some may cling to the sentiment of love as a grand normative power, a panacea to suffering. While love holds great worth, its value to normative power is mute and feeble as a deeply personal emotion moving spirit but not civic utilities and the determination of societies and nation-states. Blind hope appealing to love as a source of peace is unreliable and inefficient with respect to the difficulty of cultivating corresponding feelings and employing relevant moral utilities as a resource of power, especially where hate spreads like a disease through Fear and violence. Tolerance and social harmony do not require love, nor even notable degrees of compassion; above all else, society benefits from empathy questioning good and bad intentions and by building common understanding towards faith in others to do the right thing and appreciating others' adversity.

For society to thrive it must confront all its vices, even if one at a time. This requires sufficient empathy to understand other people's troubles. Where issues are addressed and common understanding prevails among the citizenry, across spheres of income and opportunity, social harmony can be cultivated and sustained beyond the seeming disparities caused by liberty. It is then intuitive that the democratic performance of a nation can become more effective where self-interest is mindful of social and civic troubles demanding immediate attention. Base concerns divide individuals, community, and society through persons' lust for status and false security moved by the fragility of ego. Status comes not through external objects marking and symbolising the perception of authority, but through nobility of virtuous character possessing power beyond the character subdued by Fear. Where the corruptive influence of Fear is mediated or diminished, perhaps where Liberty of spirit and morality succeeds in moving greater ambition, empathy nourishes the individual constituents of a society. Individualistic concerns for status that undermine personal ambition give way to more noble interests and ambitions of greater and more powerful character. This sows the tangents of social and civic harmony and synchronised development in societies at liberty.

Personal virtue is instrumental to alleviating, or at least mediating, the short-comings of liberty. But only the liberty of character, as liberty to grow from vice and suffering, can sustain the advantages of civic liberty. And only the liberty of character at greater ambition than lesser interests of corruptive Fear can drive more effective social development. Liberty's social and civic function is to improve people's lives; such is the only concern of the soul for any civic utility. Thus, liberty is only as good as its performance for society and the individuals affected by ethical environment. Only liberty of common accord, as opposed to coercion, can sustain social harmony, peace, and greater forms of security, stability, and continuity.

One must then consider a core question in matters of civic liberty. How can any individual and society know that its values are right and good, and others right and wrong? Objective study of ethics' structures allows us to evaluate good and bad values, right and wrong principles. Indeed, as has been argued, values are deeply conditional and circumstantial with respect to their relevance in an ethical environment. Where the character of a society is unvirtuous, unable to embrace and sustain effective social and civic liberty, it will suffer from defective values. The genealogy of values contrasted between societies of developed and immature characters and moral culture can demonstrate that greater degrees of authority are necessary to sustain society up to the point when it can develop to sustain effective degrees of liberty. After all, societies only developed freedom and liberty when its citizenry enabled such civic accord and ruling values, where, for example, the will of the people was determined to revolutionise its society against oppressive and unjust authority. Only when values effectively serve a society can their merit be established, the ultimate appeal of which is the condition of well-being. The circumstances of people's living are conditional in terms of the environment, and degrees of well-being can be qualified by a variety of conditions. However, these are not grounds for subjectivity, only points of inquiry and reference to states of affairs and living. Where the psyche and its hierarchy of values can be structured through the study of people's mental and spiritual functions, and accordingly the goal-directives of respective values, states of well-being can be evaluated and the quality of values structured.

The standard of any value is its scope of justice. If the sum of a value and principle is positive according to the measure of its goodness, or at least greater than comparative ethical negativity, then the justice of a value can be established with reference to ethical circumstances and conditions. However, because circumstances and conditions shape actions and values, a higher standard of justice comes through reference to ethical conditions. A prosperous society of developed moral character will have higher standards of justice than a disadvantaged, brutish society. A prosperous society will have greater opportunities and realistic prospects to act with higher morality where the presence of Fear is less severe without, for example, the prevalence of poverty and mass hunger. Formalising the genealogy and anatomy of the values of a society allows the study of values' goal-directive functions that make it possible to objectively evaluate the merit of respective values serving an ambition. Subsequently, the justice and goodness of a morality can be qualified and evaluated. Where a value sows social peril and civic inefficiency or deficiency, the value's worth can be considered bad and its principle wrong. A view, principle, and value are not made good by the determination of a majority and prevailing tangents; the determination of civic normativity and its virtue or vice is found through reference to considerations of Natural Law and the functions of values. Accordingly, the model of structural ethics and its combinatorialist framework are the means of normative evaluation.

When liberty enables negative influences, the character of vice undermines the freedom of autonomy, causing suffering of society and the individual. If the tyranny of the majority coerces the individual, limiting his or her potential to change and restricting positive free development, Natural Law and the determination of the Highest Good will condemn the society to suffering through the pressures of the adaptive cycle. If the character of a majority is of vice, the entire sphere becomes dominated by vice and its performance corrupted. Do not mistake this thought as implying divine intent or retribution – such is the concrete mechanism of the Natural Law of the adaptive cycle of values, and it cannot be prayed to or bought. The suffering perpetuated by the tangents of vice and their causal effects are enabled through respective characters and vectors. The effects are felt in the individual, and society experiences the perils of vice demanding the attention of governance. It is common for withering characters to blame the Gods for ill-fortune or plead for answers as to why their fate is one of suffering. In doing so, people are too often blind to their own mistakes and faults, for much of the suffering we experience is the doing of mankind's vice. The punishment and condemnation to suffer for vice is not by reason of transcendent judgement, but only a cause of individual or social character exhausting its utility. The lack of virtue that withholds the courage and mindfulness to admit faults, as well as deficiency in empathy to identify suffering, all contribute to the inability of society to improve on its vices, the beginning of which is peoples' character and actions. The lack of courage, mindfulness, and empathy hinders proper adaptation, leading to personal and social stagnation.

Competing values and interests between the majority and minority can lead to social discord and disrupt civic harmony. Even though this is a necessity for liberty's utility of development and progress, it comes with a cost that, if immoderate, undermines justice. In particular, the issue of offence can be very evocative and divisive. Where people take offence, one begins to question the virtue and extent of liberty, as is common with provocative acts of freedom of speech and related civic elements tacitly permitting bad values. This aspect of liberty's normativity would especially benefit from ethical development. Currently, it seems as though no *definitive* and *absolute* prescriptive principle guides freedom of speech and related actions to moderate liberty, prevent harm, and provide security. Many arguments concerning freedom of speech are unstandardised and too vague or contradictory. Suffering is a notable aspect of social life, even if social life is a vast improvement of the brutish states of primitive societies and communities. Natural suffering cannot be subjected to just or unjust evaluation, as it is beyond mankind's direct control. We only cause ourselves natural suffering where our mistakes lead to misfortune. Establishing a home in the zone of impact of a live volcano could lead to self-inflicted disaster, yet considerations of the justice and morality of an active volcano does not particularly benefit from study – when we are familiar with natural suffering we know it is bad. The merits of establishing a settlement in such places, however, is subject to evaluation in terms of people's actions that led to corresponding states of affairs. Where people's *judgements and actions* cause harm, the effects of their activity become relevant to ethical valuation. As such, where the matter of harm comes to attention, its justice is relevant to ethical inquiry. The offence of natural suffering doesn't need to be questioned; however, man-made suffering is relevant to evaluation of offence.

Harm inflicted by people on other people is a cause of offence. However, there are varying degrees of justice in acts and affairs, including those who inflict suffering, which means that the justice of offence varies. People are not at liberty to cause others direct harm; even indirect harm can in certain cases, such as with accidents, legitimise the restriction of liberty. However, where the extent of the harm caused by an action is more ethically positive than negative, the action can be considered with a positive, or at least tolerable, degree of justice. Where such utilitarian maxims may seem to suffer from intuitive and familiar problems of utilitarian thinking, one needs to refer back to the combinatorialist framework to comprehensively account for the merits of liberty's justice. For instance, being mindful of the conditioning of vectors and related ethical tangents is central to sophisticated utilitarian maxims, for even a single act of vice, even if under harsh circumstances, can introduce a corruptive tangent of immorality of negative sum ethical value. This being said, certain injustice of people inflicting harm on one another are just in the grander scheme of liberty's utility. Liberty may enable suffering, which is not ideal or fulfilling of our ethical interests. But it is clear that, in present times, the motivation borne of suffering is of a certain imperative value for ethical development and progress. Thus, certain forms of actions that cause harm can be just, as suffering itself can be just if we make it so. However, suffering can only be just if it becomes positive and if it satisfies the criteria of just suffering (see Chapter 19) such as the immediate pain of exercise producing sum positive gains in the long-term. Therefore, for instance, the offence or harm of constructive criticism is just in cases of free speech.

The inclusion of vectors and tangents has more to offer for the evaluation of the justice of harm and offence. When suffering is experienced, its functions can be evaluated in the context of the psyche and spirit, or broadly speaking, in terms of the *source* of suffering. Sometimes suffering is caused by a state of affairs, such as natural disasters, while other times it is rooted in the vice of character – suffering borne of vulnerability and weakness, triggered by defensive impressions. The suffering of states of affairs is different to the suffering of vice interpreting offence, which the unmindful and undisciplined mind and spirit are often unable to distinguish. Where offence is related to the fragility and immaturity of ego disrupting the necessary dynamics of liberty to grow from suffering, these cases of offence are more personal than of an actual social peril and injustice. The suffering experienced originates from the vice of character more so than actual negative aspects of states of affairs. For progress to be achieved, issues in states of affairs and vices of character require attention, with respect to which offence borne of disproportionate insecurity is not of primary concern. The harm of offence related to vulnerable character is not more important than the offence and harm caused by immoral behaviour. Therefore, the harm of offence felt in the vice of character can be comparatively just among considerations of general offence and harmful presences.

However, where an action, including speech, leads to direct harm, such as by provoking and directly encouraging harmful and unjust actions, its origin and presence as a state of affairs suggests it is unjust and ought not to be tolerated. When the ethics of an act of provocation is unambiguous, such as with provocation triggering legitimate offence beyond simple vulnerability, directly rousing unjust and intolerable actions such as murder, valuation focuses on the most ethically negative aspect. Ethically negative provocation, that is unjust and intolerable, is defined in terms of directly inspiring morally intolerable and unjust actions, in relation to provoking offence by supporting legitimately intolerable and morally reprehensible actions. The proportional and just action responding to such occasions is a whole other matter. Of course, that which provokes vice of character to commit immoral deeds is itself an offence bound to triggering vices in people. In such cases, however, the provocation of vices that triggers immoral actions, such as by calling on unjust violence, and relating states of affairs of actions' causal cascades are different to the provocations of offence related to personal impressions of harm. The former is wholly unjust and cannot be tolerated, as its offence is unjust because it causes harm without giving precedence for vice's amendment. The offence of the latter, on the other hand, originates in exaggerated vice that would benefit from improvement, with the intended justice of the experienced offence and suffering being to improve, heal, and grow. Where the intent of an action is unclear, the function of the act and its relating values can be studied to evaluate their corresponding ethical value.

Mediating and affecting the reach of liberty and its consequence of harm and offence must serve a purpose. Restricting liberty is only just in so much as this accord produces positive ethical value. Restricting the offence and harm of liberty is only just if it produces greater ethical interest and fulfils the value of its utility. The pressing question then concerns whose ethical interest, or which category or faculty of interest – society or individual – should to be fulfilled in certain circumstances. The individual and society must be fulfilled and in harmony for greater ethical interest to be achieved. If offence is sensed by one person, then the idealised maxim of interest, involving the sum terms of social and individual welfare, cannot be satisfied. It then goes that the root of offence must be examined and studied. Individuals ought to be respected with basic decency of virtuous character, but not necessarily tolerated or appeased. Greater justice is served where ethical development is fostered. Hence, individual vices that unjustly and unnecessarily stunt ethical development in the self and society are unjust or at least of lesser justice than tolerable or purposeful offence.

Where offence is raised in emotions and personal impressions, one ought to look inward to virtue and strong character to feed on such suffering and grow. The voice of injustice only affects spirit where the nobility of conscience is mute. The function of liberty is intended to produce goodness; if this utility is disrupted unjustly and unnecessarily by a personal inability to grow in virtue, then liberty withers and the goodness of a society and the character of its citizenry is undermined. If the source of offence does not to produce goodness and is rooted in the suffering of a personal inability to grow, then this offence is not a justifiable reason for disrupting the piety of liberty. Even though individual liberty and suffering must be considered, greater ethical interest is often found and fulfilled elsewhere by focusing on what produces greater value for all. An individual might not be ready or mentally, spiritually, and morally equipped to embrace virtue and duty. But when an inevitable choice affects others, greater sum interests are fulfilled by supporting the goodness that facilitates the most prospective growth.

To conclude these discussions, one can formulate a *standard of liberty's offence (and harm) – harm and offence as a consequence of liberty are just, tolerable, and permissible in so much as they perform the justice of producing positive ethical value in sum terms (for individual and society); impressionable offence, as opposed to the offence of unjust states of affairs, deemed unjust by reference to the Central Principles of morality, is not a just reason to hinder the positive utility of liberty.*

Whenever a voice calling to its own vision of justice is found to be of lesser ethical worth and lesser justice and moral authority, it will be ignored. Where a claim's standard is found wanting, it is best set aside, archived, and not given wasteful attention. The mindful scholar and ethicist will listen to folk wisdom and embrace the burden of mindful empathy, yet would be disciplined to disregard a morality found wanting in a vocal character festering in its own vice. Then, virtuous character is wise to understand and accept its lonesome limitations, always attentive to any available insight.

Values, moral sense, and individual's fears and ambitions can set people against each other, inciting competition and conflict imposing a state of heavy, unsustainable moral disorder. When liberty gives rise to the freedom of debased autonomy and grants freedom to negative social and individual influences bred by vice, liberty is undermined and may even become unsustainable. If a society and nation wish to rejoice in liberty, autonomy and individual responsibility must be righteous or of prevailing character. However, no society is perfectly virtuous, just, or righteous. Therefore, governance and authority are compelled to take measures to regulate the dissent of vice. The dynamics of transitional values must be mediated and balanced (a means of justice) for maximum effect of nourishing progress and well-being. The necessity of just authority cannot be denied in balancing the beneficiary of liberty. Laws, rules, standards, guidelines, compelling motivation, and established authority of basic morality are necessary for the function of any society. Society is a beneficial mode of human organisation to our common greater aspirations which demand collaboration and functional relations. It may be argued that where liberty motivates good performance in the citizenry, a basis of organic authority, whether of instinct or the necessity of circumstance, can push for desired ends among those not driven by the liberty of higher and more dedicated ambitions. Ethical development and corresponding values require mediation and balance, a function which an established authority can, to a degree, perform. Democratic regimes enable the implementation of different ideologies and values, in doing so usually achieving sustainability unless democratic performance is degenerative by a majority's poor choice. Where these dynamics of values at liberty become unsustainable, liberty reaches its limit and authority receives its merit.

Societal demands, the pressures of Natural Law, and common sense and practical wisdom familiar with vice lead any reasonable thought to the conclusion that measures of authority are necessary. When conflict and emerging vice demand intervention, authority reins in its intuitive value. The application of authority can present itself as coercive and extreme, sometimes even unjust, or it can be tacit, passive, superficially coercive, civil, and civic. Different degrees of authority are used through the conditioning of judgement and prevailing moral principles of the time. Just as no utility is inherently evil, authority itself is not wrong so long as it fulfils positive utility and is exercised justly and righteously. Where liberty is sustainable, lesser measures of authority are applicable. However, some societies and ethical environments demand greater application of authority where virtue and autonomy are unsustainable. Whilst prevailing liberty proportional to the character of a populace which upholds effective freedom can warrant greater stability and prosperity, which would only be hindered by the inefficiencies of excessive authority, too much freedom can equally be a burden to society. As such, balance between liberty and authority – *the justice of liberty and authority* – ought to be found. This leads to a discussion of the utility and measures of *authority*.

Chapter 28:
The Merits and Measures of Authority and Normative Power

The bottom line of any civic utility is its prospect of ethical interest. The civic utility of liberty is conceived, in most part, as a means to development and progress through adaptation enabled by the liberty of deviation and interacting values including contention and competition. Authority is a utility for preserving stability, sustainability, moderation, and order; authority is a civic utility for mediating liberty to ensure its efficiency, effectiveness, and sustainability. This is the outline of the matter to be discussed in this Chapter.

The issues and interests of authority are intuitive in the context of liberty in the global ethical environment that lacks coherent moral authority and effective normative power to sustain an effective order. When life becomes chaotic, we naturally want order and stability; this is the purpose of authority. When social and civic liberty is founded on Fear, values hold people to no higher standard than morality restricted in spirit, ambition, and potential. Where values, interests, and desires are only those concerned with self-preservation and the wish for comfort, vision is restricted and morality is blind. This accord of morality, restricted in its sense and of lesser service to the Human Imperative, undermines normative power and moral authority, resulting in restraints or losses of ethical interest through inefficient values. In the instance that moral authority fails to synchronise rationale and sentiment, nonetheless of concrete authority by Natural Law and the Highest Good, and Fear sets its own standards producing values and interests at odds, morality and its justifications are condemned to a state of little meaning and menial power. Normative power rewards where it is drawn from the moral authority of Natural Law and when civic utility, character, and policy are aligned with the Highest Good. The degenerative and destructive consequences of the global discord of immoderate moral liberty, where common ground and good faith are only found on mutual Fear lacking compelling morality, suggest the absolute value of the authority of unconditional morality appealing to sum interests of all souls. In a time of great uncertainty and threats, the authority of morality is a means to a definitive order without institutions binding policy and actions in common good faith towards common interests. Nevertheless, the necessity of liberty must be accepted and embraced.

Where the justice of liberty becomes undermined by excess liberty and vice, measures of restoring justice become instrumental. Thus, the order of authority is reined in. Authority is raised where its necessity is sensed; order is established by the order of discipline and values. Moral authority influences and mediates the inherent anarchic and interpersonal aspect of institutional authority and material power. Calls

to order and demands for authority arise when characters of vice and their causal vectors disrupt harmony of social and civic goodness. Where *people* contend and
conflict, sowing disorder, values compete through their vectors. As such, the core of
the demands of authority involve dynamics between individuals, bringing attention
back to individuality.

A regime of liberty is enabled by effective individual autonomy, while authoritarian governance is imposed in proportion to failing liberty and in response to the
vices of society. Civic liberties are made possible by the character of virtue; authority
is necessitated in response to the influences of vice. Positive ethical values are consolidated by effective, righteous, and just authority as the morality of individuals
and institutions of values. Lack of virtuous and able authority enables negative influences to undermine the sum of goodness. Mill's work acknowledged the value of
authority, which he used in consideration of characters not 'arrived at the maturity
of their faculties' of questionable utility and value. As he wrote: "*It is, perhaps, hardly
necessary to say that this doctrine is meant to apply only to human beings in the maturity of
their faculties.*"[21] Furthermore, Mill wrote: "*Despotism is a legitimate mode of government
in dealing with barbarians, provided the end be their improvement, and the means justified actually effecting that end.*"[22] Mill built on arguments appealing to the moral character of
autonomous individuals by acknowledging the aforementioned and following limitations: "*Liberty, as a principle, has no application to any state of things anterior to the time
when mankind have become capable of being improved by free and equal discussion.*"[23] The
formal structure of these arguments can be intuitively expanded on through the application of the model of structural ethics appealing to vectors enabling and invoking
certain tangents of values that could prove unsustainable. Where immoral character
leads to wrong-doing, sowing negative ethical interest in an ethical environment, the
liberty of these tangents and respective vectors could be unsustainable and therefore
unjust. Where sustainable liberty is found through the character of people and the
corresponding moral culture, the degree of imposed and accepted authority reflects
the character of a nation.

The usual condition of authority is bound to what can be classified as the *harm
principle*. As Mill argued: "*That principle is, that the sole end for which mankind are warranted, individually or collectively, in interfering with the liberty of action of any of their
number, is self-protection. The only purpose for which power can be rightfully exercised over
any member of a civilised community, against his will, is to prevent harm to others.*"[24] As the
civic utility of liberty has imperative value for well-being in terms of progress and
development, it is intuitive to suppose that it is in our interests to uphold and preserve as much liberty as practically possible. A guiding principle to justify and enable
authority as a necessity of sum well-being makes more sense than a justification of
principles of authority found on valuing authority for authority's sake. Therefore,
enabling authority and subverting liberty as a means of preventing harm (protecting sum ethical interests) as a 'rule of thumb' of civic liberty and related degrees of
authority is a good and intuitive fulcrum for normativity. Suppose the use of the
harm principle in the concerns of liberty and authority – that is, justifying authority
as a means of sustaining liberty and its positive utility by, first of all, preventing and
protecting from undue, unjust, wrong, and intolerable suffering (or harm) – as the
fulcrum of authority.

The fulcrum of authority is contentious. The primacy of security, as a means
of self-preservation and normativity of Fear, can undermine the positive utility of
liberty where security is disproportionate. As was suggested in regards to the issues

of freedom of speech and liberty's consequence of offence, certain harm entailed and consequential to, but not necessarily caused by, the civics of liberty is necessary and just for the purpose of liberty's utility of development. The standard of liberty's offence performs its service in this context to balance harm and well-being. After all, certain forms of suffering must be endured and embraced for the justice of liberty's utility to be achieved. Liberty serves a purpose in insecurity, as it is an adaptive means to prevailing over threats and rising from vice. Where Fear may set a standard of values by the fulcrum of authority prioritising self-preservation, such as in terms of comfort and aversion to pain, greater ethical interest of liberty can be lost and competing values lose sight of sum interests. Therefore, normative principles, such as the standard of liberty's offence, are useful for wisely balancing and moderating the degrees of liberty with measures of authority. Certain forms of harm must necessarily be endured for the civic utility of liberty to be performed, even if they are not themselves necessary for growth where an ethos of Liberty sows ambition. Where suffering consequential to the liberty of actions is compatible with the justice of liberty by producing sum positive ethical interest, it becomes an exception to the fulcrum of authority or harm principle with respect to the reasoning that it serves greater interests of well-being, therefore being compatible with the principle. Where any civic utility, as right, principle, or law, is intended to serve ethical interests of well-being, its formality (such as an institution or law) is wholly dependent on the reality of its application corresponding to the production of positive ethical interest. The pragmatism of normativity is valid in so much as it viably serves practised values. Where liberty is surrendered to protect people, and the protection of people is suspended by justification of ensuring realistic opportunities for growth *in* people's and society's combined interests, then both aspects of a general normativity of authority are viable.

Liberty that causes harm is not the justice of liberty's utility to facilitate positive ethical accord. Being able to grow from suffering and vice does not justify actions perpetuated in their character. Suffering and succession from it are only just where the individual embraces these aspects of life in the moral liberty to do so; the justice of suffering is determined by the personal ambition responding to suffering. These standards do not apply to matters of authority relating to the state and governance. Therefore, suffering in society corresponding to civic utilities and normativity does not, in its own, right permit the liberty of actions to cause others harm, yet accepts the necessity to tolerate certain events of suffering for greater sum interests when it comes to the liberty of individuals' actions responding to suffering.

The main consideration here is attentiveness to the adaptation of values and the conditional necessity to accept and tolerate suffering for ethical progress. While it is a matter of ambition in the individual whether he or she chooses to embrace suffering or avoid it, this choice is not applicable to matters of state, law, and governance, as their concerns ought to focus on the performance of authority's function to preside over sum terms of ethical environment. The choice of action as policy, right, law, and principle in matters of governance does not correspond to the same structures as individual choices; the choice of an authority is not the choice of an individual. As such, the justice of liberty and its restriction through authority, with respect to the function of the state as an institution (vector) of authority, is not to blindly tolerate or wholly eliminate suffering. The justice of authority dealing with suffering ought to balance and moderate suffering, to achieve greater sum interests of progress and development by mediating and influencing social and political affairs through civic utilities at an authority's legitimate and rightful disposal, including laws and rights.

These thoughts draw from their respective core and central ethical foundations. When suffering is invigorating, frustrating, and empowering, it becomes a moral utility, transferrable to respective civic and normative utilities. When suffering is crippling and depressing, it is corrosive. The former ought to be used with Discipline; the latter ought to be made peace with in Harmony or accepted through other measures of spiritual upliftment and fulfilment including pleasure. Similarly, certain forms of society's suffering can be tolerated, accepted, and even used towards a positive end, while other forms of suffering ought not to be ignored and ought to be bound to measures of justice. Then, however, if striving for peace becomes self-righteous, deceiving intent and suffocating good spirit, where one ought not to be at peace, Discipline takes precedence. Sometimes one may rightly disfavour peace, may not want it, to instead embrace drive and ambition to pursue the maxim goodness of happiness, relief, and fulfilment after even a smallest appreciation of their potential sought to be infused into the world. The prescription of this combined normative principle of the fulcrum of authority and the standard of liberty's offence depends greatly on a given issue and its circumstance; the application of this combined principle rests on following the model of ethics' intuitive thinking and principles guiding moral reasoning.

How policy is implemented with respect to particular challenges is a matter of other disciplines studying aspects of social, political, and economic spheres. The guiding principle and framework warranting the malleability of values in relation to the demands of circumstances in a coherent manner allows for normativity to then lend a hand in prioritising values, interests, and desire in the implementation of policy. For example, freedom of speech must be permitted to enable development, such as through the discussion of ideology and competing values, even at the cost of the possibility of offence, to then restrict this freedom when acts of speech lead to the unjust practice of values such as by directly instigating unjust and wholly immoral actions. Whether this freedom ought to be restricted by laws of the land or rules of conduct and etiquette is a matter of context. Furthermore, where particular rights and laws bear relevance to a civic and normative utility with respect to their effect on an ethical tangent, such as policy affecting a community or the founding principles of a nation, considerations of their value allow the prioritisation and implementation of ethical values and interests knowledgeably, intelligently, creatively, and wisely.

A good case to consider for illustrating the discussion so far can be found in issues of internet neutrality and state surveillance. While this is a very contentious and complex matter, it involves a fundamental question regarding rights and laws and the corresponding relation between liberty and authority. In terms of the fulcrum of authority, mass state surveillance can be justified if it is effective for ensuring social and national security. With respect to the standard of liberty's offence, it is arguable that freedom from authority's infringement on individuals' private affairs is worth more than the risk and subsequent events of society experiencing harm. The reasoning for the former is straightforward, while the latter is a bit more complicated. Where the causal cascades of ethical tangents are considered, surrendering some founding principles of liberty for security can be very causally ambiguous. For one, where values and interests lean towards Fear and self-preservation, liberty and its potential of short-term insecurity, but greater sum gains, can be threatened in a given circumstance. However, a measure of surrendering liberty can ensure the sustainability of liberty. For example, if continued terrorist attacks and threats persisted without being addressed, and the mass culture of a society responded to such threats with greater degrees of Fear and subsequent caution, bias, and bigotry, then the goodness of liberty can be undermined. Where people surrender one fundamental aspect of liberty, liberty becomes more susceptible to renewed change, with good or bar consequences. But much of this change depends on the character of people. The guiding values and ethos of people will reflect on the outcomes of a policy.

Where Fear is a more prevalent ethic and subject to greater influence of base-reason's sense undermining mindfulness of greater vision, the primacy of security is established. The justice of this ethic can be evaluated and moralised, but this is not the current goal of studying the general dynamics and structures of ethics. So, as a basic illustration that would benefit from further study, differentials in values of security and liberty in matters of governance and policy-making are subject to the conditions of ethical environments and the variables in certain circumstances. Liberty is inherently of greater justice and ethical value in policy-making, but only in so much as it is effective in terms of the normativity of a society able to sustain effective civics of liberty. However, even fundamental normativity of a society can change where the character of its people develops according to the dynamics of values, with greater authority and the suspension of liberty being necessary in response to the conditions of an ethical environment. So even the founding normativity of a society is not concrete in its justice and ruling principles. As such, democratic principles and democracy as a mode of governance demonstrate their intuitive utility with respect to social, political, and economic change reflecting the adaptation of values, moral character, the mass psyche of a populace, and the culture of values – moral culture.

Where opinions are divided and subsequent conflict of interest is volatile, one needs only to remember that views and values are only as appropriate as the circumstances they adapt to. Whether views lean towards liberty or authority, their merits are true in so much as they are appropriate responses to a particular concern, issue, impression, and challenge. Any party and political faction, true to goodwill and democratic values, aspire towards the betterment of society and nation. The foundational normative political and social predilection – liberty or authority, left or right – is not a point for hostility, for these values are reciprocal of people's circumstances. These are not irreconcilable differences, and strong emotions of either love or hate are unnecessary for a functional society. It is sufficient for people to understand the most basic element of a certain view and be empathetic and attentive to others' concerns for functional accord of values to rule the performance of government and institution. Any political view may be viable up until its value is studied in sincerity and mindful discipline not to warp values through subversive influences of Fear. Only then can justice be truly established and appealed to in order to mediate truly reprehensible values and ideologies wholly inappropriate to the state of affairs and developmental stage of society and civilisation.

The development enabled by liberty increases the adaptiveness of ethics, values, and their related elements, including philosophy and ideology. Where the global ethical environment is undergoing a new phase of swift mass development, adaptiveness becomes crucial. As such, liberty is a means to greater security through offering the utility of development and adaptiveness in synchrony with social and national challenges. Normativity is not merely a factor guiding and mediating the institutions of authority, but is also a means to agreement, dominance, and self-preservation. The utility of normativity, in relation to Natural Law and the sovereignty of the Highest Good, is its prospect of enabling states of well-being. The greater the well-being on offer, shaped by the sense of living and states of affairs, the greater the power of a moral authority and its normativity. This is the ultimate power of any civic utility, whether in terms of domestic or international influence. Where an international actor may seek to influence other ethical spheres, such as other societies, its right to do so comes by virtue of the Highest Good found through mindful meditation on, and study of, ethical values and functions behind policy and actions. As such, normativity and moral authority have a tremendous bearing on matters of security and authority.

It is in the interest of security, with proportional and conditionally appropriate measure, to sustain and protect what liberty an authority can for long-term security. For instance, cultivating an adaptive (in other words autonomous), skilled, and progressive citizenry can support society by ensuring the global competitiveness of a nation by virtue of domestic development. Measures of institutional authority attentive to the liberty of development, such as good education and healthy moral authority, are a major aspect of security and effective dynamics of authority. Subsequently, a citizenry of nourished moral character reflects into social affairs, with society and nation benefitting from a moral character of able and effective autonomy.

A harmonious society needs not a homogenous entity to be functionally adaptive, for good faith and goodwill are sufficient where the predominant vector of the public's character is ethically positive and morally sufficient. Where judgement and performance of a nation's citizenry is virtuous and well-nourished, it should positively influence the performance of the state with respect to the issues and concerns demanding attention. The citizenry sets the appropriate measure of authority by shaping the government and the character of its vectors of authority (as the character of people in positions of power), especially in representational liberal democracy. For the sake of an ethical environment as society and nation, it is in the interest of all for authority to be fashioned as a good, righteous, virtuous, and just constitution. This principle, however, seems to be very elusive in spirit of Fear where individuals are vexed by corrupted base morality pursuing unnecessarily excessive power as a means to control in weakness to Fear.

The Natural Law of the adaptive cycle of values is central to any sociopolitical thought. Any mode of governance must be appropriate to the demands of ethical environment and its pressures to adapt to internal and external forces. One must accept the inevitability of making mistakes, whether as an individual or as an institution. The will of the majority, if immoral, ought to be accepted even where its judgement is mistaken and against its own wishes, for such is the machination of liberty. The presence of the immorality of others can be just if intervention would only cause further harm, which is a common consequence of oppression and mistakes of compassion and impulsiveness. When the majority acts immorally, then it is the arbitration of Natural Law to seal its fate, as all vice cannibalises itself. The individual's contrary moral sense must then find its place and dedication, to assist or to abandon. The desire to preserve civil society can originate from good intentions, but the question must always be raised whether that particular society can be saved from itself, whether its civility is sincere and worthy. Only the greatest moral authority can save the world from itself. By the determination of liberty, self-inflicted decay of society must be accepted if just and proper in consideration of the Central Principles, with the liberty of morality being prime. This does not excuse the individual from the responsibility, duty, and spirit of basic decency, yet this does appeal to considerations of values and global ethical interests. According to the heritin interpretation, all ethical values and interests must be examined in reference to the Human Imperative. The citizenry is above all established on individuality and virtue, with nations being subsequent organic constructs of social behaviour. Only the liberty of meditation and insight grants the wisdom to attain the truth to guide normative concerns and advise the performance of authorities.

The truth is pivotal to liberty's success and society's welfare. Where the truth is difficult to establish, or governance on complex matters demands prolonged and strenuous procedures, authority can seem slow and inefficient; liberty's democracy can be slow. However, the efficiency of authority's many institutions and branches of power leads to good and effective performance through competent and informed judgement. Swift decisions and executions of power are not necessarily, or even usually, better than strategy and dedicated effort. However, some decisions of governance are unforgiveable and unwinnable, least one settles for a policy of damage reduction. Time can be an elusive luxury that does not permit ideal conditions fostering agreeable or even careful judgements in challenging moments and pressing concerns. The efficiency of liberty and democratic authorities then rests on the character of individuals. Popularity contests for figures of authority are in the public's interests where strong, wise, and virtuous leadership is imperative for a society's and nation's well-being in terms of institutional performance. The strings attached to competitive politics then require another discussion. However, in general terms of major or global dynamics of liberty and related authorities, the primacy of authority's success depends on good judgement. As such, wisdom, insight, and knowledge are imperative for authority, achievable only through degrees of truth and disciplined, mindful thought. The virtues of the citizenry then transfer into the dynamics of authority through character able to moderate thoughts with discipline and mindfulness.

Many issues accompany authority and power, especially in terms of corruptive base morality surrendered to Fear. In whose interest is authority? What is the merit of a good social environment? These questions have been addressed previously, but refreshing their moral principles and ethical values in this context will be useful. A healthy ethical environment, such as in terms of the state of society, is in all persons' interests. A divided society, for example, will subject people to discord, contention, and potentially violent conflict. Extreme divides, especially encompassing ethnic, cultural, political, and economic factors, are susceptible to the corruptive effects of Fear with respect to social perils. Where crime is improperly and ineffectually addressed, it will produce an ethical environment of greater risk of unjust harm. A person of notable wealth can only do so much to protect themself, with the desire for excessive wealth and obsessive need for security being its own source of insecurity and suffering. The state's investment in societal development could be argued to entail much greater draw backs than the liberty of personal investment in security and welfare. Of course, the dynamics of liberty and authority in governance and policy-formation are always dualistic and causally complex. The complexity and dualism of values are the merit for the devolution of authority.

The concern of this project is not to engage discussions on specific policies, but rather humbly remark that any policy initiative and success will be determined by the conditions of their implementation and circumstance. Particular emphasis is given to studying the ethical environment encompassing variables such as a populace's moral character and moral culture. Human nature is diverse and shaped by near-incomprehensible influences; however, certain functions of the psyche can be realistically and practically established in a framework of understanding. However, the contribution of the appeal to structural ethics is found in highlighting the value-formation of the ethos leading to particular policies and actions.

Where Fear influences values, decisions, actions, and policies, the function of a value might never be fulfilled through a particular course of action. A decision made in base Fear, such as one that mainly appeases a personal sense of security without fairly attending to security's broadest scope, will not guarantee the fulfilment of the goal of a value and action – freedom from fear and pain. Where Fear and corrupted base morality cloud judgement, policy ambitions and effective civic utilities will be blocked from their conception and practice because of what values make us pay attention to – the scope of awareness. Social issues may seem distant from a high-castle's view, but social causal cascades are the foundation of the walls of a moral throne. Then, as has been argued in the appeal to empathy, losing sight of social issues and people's suffering will only neglect real sources of suffering that will affect everyone and their ethical environment in some form or another. On a more personal note, a strong influence of Fear guiding civic concerns, or lack thereof, is not as fulfilling as the spirit's relief through the virtue of duty – to do what is right by others, for such characteristics mark strength and the worthiest moral authority than an authority of cowardice and moral weakness. How these concerns are to be addressed effectively ought to be dedicated to more focused subjects studying policy and social life; the nature of desires, values, and interests, however, can be evaluated through structural ethics to inform related subjects.

To clarify the argument, in a globalised world and hugely interconnected ethical environment, one cannot afford a narrow vision of concern and ambition. Even the consequences of individual actions are widespread and significant. For instance, the lack of domestic social investment can entail the potential of undermining general economic potential by, for example, undermining development, moral or social and economic. Where the entire economy struggles, it is self-explanatory how this may affect anyone in an ethical environment. The liberty of adaptation and competitiveness further enables the diversification of societies and communities through normative appeal. A thriving society appeals to opportunistic and ambitious individuals, whereby successful governance mindful of its normative image, achieved through moral power, can relish in the diversity of human resources internally and externally. Where a nation assists and defends others or imbues policy with dutiful concerns, such as aid or investment, its moral power can grow through mutual trust or interest. Ignoring these normative aspects of governance and implementation of authority affects even the opportunity to diversify a society where its needs may require foreign financial or human investment. A good society will invite characters of greater virtue, the norm of which, if retained and not diluted, should mediate the conduct of its citizenry and mass psyche. However, even a single act of immorality can hinder a considerable degree of goodness.

The immoral action of a single person in a position of governance and authority will undermine the normative power of the entire institution in some measure. Yet it seems such occasions are the measure of ethical liberty and adaptation in terms of shifts in power. Furthermore, as has been argued in Section 2, the ethos of Fear carries with it, in modern times, with respect to a lack of ethical and moral development, many inefficient, deficient, and unfulfilling, thus corrupt, goal-directive functions (ambitions). The subsequent global ethical environment inherits fundamental flaws, as is seen with global issues that demand serious attention with no simple, clear, or even plausible solutions in the circumstance of the given ethical environment. Greater consideration of ethical environment is in every individual's interests by virtue of both the state of affairs and the spiritual and mental effects of noble and virtuous character. Selfishness is but a form of foolishness.

The Human Imperative is an idea and principle that formalises the aforementioned thoughts and concerns and makes moral reasoning and normative guidance more intuitive and straightforward. All consequences affect the self and others. We must be diligent, mindful, and concerned for others' welfare if we are to live in a truly better world and if we are to create a better world to live in. The effects of certain consequences might not impact the ethical environment greatly and might not immediately improve one's surroundings, but they will reflect our character, mentality, and spirit. Caring and being mindful and empathetic is more rewarding than the moral, spiritual, and personal restrictions of selfishness imposed by the vices of Fear, as these virtues are far more empowering, resilient, ambitious, liberating, and fulfilling; duty is its own reward.

As was argued throughout Section 2, the consolidation of entering a sustainable new era of a globalised world and ethical environment is very challenging. With this development comes potential shifts in power-shares, of new countries emerging and meeting power-potentials of major countries and the superpower-state. Globalisation and global development can lead to a multipolar world order of balanced world powers and their guiding values, the competition of which could prove unsustainable, inefficient, immoderate, and unjust. Where Fear in its basic form continues to affect the foundations of human civilisation and its social environment, the risk of conflict and unsustainable, inefficient contention can be heightened. Where powers are left to their liberty of unmindful morality derivative of mere sophisticated impulses with no presiding sovereignty of wise virtue, righteousness and just moral authority are undermined, and mankind is left blind to its own judgement. But by virtue of the soul and reason, moral authority of the Highest Good is binding and achievable, if only we find glimmers of its insight, wisdom, and knowledge.

Truth is pivotal for moral succession, and the worth of truth is sacred. In a world without an inspiring and convincing moral authority and its vectors of normative power, whether as actions, individuals, communities, or institutions, we are left to the mercy of Natural Laws without our own counsel or arbitration. Where a single member of a major global institution acts immorally, judged without appeal to mindful standards of a global society unbound to the Highest Good's authority as a Kingdom of Ends, disorder and contention ensue. A degree of goodness in this chaos comes as the liberty of ethical development. Where an establishment of incredible power withers through the vices of institutions of corrupt values, and its society wanes through the character of its citizenry, a single provocative act undermines the institution's and its agents' moral authority.

A superpower arises by virtue of circumstance and appropriate response to fortune's potential. Where it fails to adapt and prevailing moral character degenerates, Nature erodes ethical values that are not worth preserving – vices. A superpower spanning and affecting global environment loses its moral authority, normative power, and relevant sum elements of power where vices and immorality are allowed and tolerated. Its security is undermined by vices that are not held to a greater standard of sovereignty of moral authority reigning through individual's conscience. Wisdom and virtue elude those surrendering character, spirit, and will to Fear's base mode, for true power is found in character employing power of the will in harmony with virtue and righteousness, as a means to an end appreciating the merit of authority, and not surrendering self-worth under the promise of power's security poisoning the spirit, enslaving character, and deceiving the will's intent. As such, even the smallest of immoral actions and gestures of a global superpower affects all, for permitting one act of immorality and corruption creates the foundation of an institution left to the design of its own vice. Where immorality undermines said institution's power and authority, it will be affected externally and from within, fostering greater risks to its own prized security.

Where an established authority begins to dissolve, other forces affect the power vacuum. However, this is when values compete in some of their fiercest ways, giving rise to swift developments in values. As always, suffering is one the greatest catalysts for ethical and moral development, succeeded only by pure ambition usually borne of, or learnt through, suffering. Then, only the worthiest and most competent moral authorities take hold of a power-share, with nature and character determining the future of a morality and its authority and vectors. Even a single policy and individual decision can become historic and lead down a tangent that shapes the destiny and character of an authority's vector and body. But the mindlessness and ill-discipline of mankind maintain the madness of repeating mistakes of history, for moral authority of individual ego malnourished by Fear's base form, as well as people's general vice, overshadows the wisdom of the Highest Good found through its science of ethics and art of morality.

Values form ideology, and ideology cultivates and appropriates values. Values and ideology become part of identity. Disruptive, unhealthy, and defensive ego shaped by Fear becomes threatened when ideology and one's values are tested. It is important to stand up for one's values, to protect one's interests, but Fear's vision and vulnerable ego can spur overly defensive and even aggressive reactions. This leads to the corrosion and corruption of adaptation through difference and deviation. This is natural and common to all people, but it must be moderated and harmonised. To bring justice and order to the liberty of different views, ideas, and opinions, one ought to be mindful and disciplined, which can only be effectively sustained through personal virtues and a society that values appropriate and complimentary principles.

A sensible tradition of philosophy values just and righteous authority. Persons seeking its position, however, seem to rarely befit the ideals people project onto them. The demands of authority and governance – the great responsibility and burden of their duties – mandate particular character of a distinct species of virtue. Leadership means making the tough choices that must be rightfully made, then dealing and embracing the consequences and cost. Whichever iconic and inspirational figure found in history is examined, whether it is Gandhi or Mandela, their stories often tell of great cost and sacrifice. Tales of legend and greatness ask for much in return, the suffering of which is of its own sort and often of little clear victory. Some aspirations, especially in positions of no clear achievable resolution, such as with top figures of governance, will bestow on persons of responsibility great suffering. But such is the cost of duty for duty's profound reward in spirit and worldly goodness. Doing the best one could in an unforgiveable circumstance is not always good enough, and the virtue of mankind is only so great. But with an issue that must be addressed, only certain people of able autonomy and character are fit for the task. Where their character is not of conventional virtue with respect to ordinary folk, their virtue is found in another hierarchy of duty, and it is not necessarily one to be envied.

Ruthlessness and callousness, ideally balanced with mindful empathy nurturing understanding and appreciation and expanding the scope of attention, become important, if not necessary virtues for such persons; they cannot afford absolute harmony in and of spiritual liberty, for their discipline must be found in duty. Great suffering and profound experiences carry weight, and only persons of tested character stand a chance to not yield under the exhausting pressure of great responsibility and duty. Then, the lessons of humanity and suffering give promise – emotional scars hold together one's humanity, least one turns into a monster, and lingering pain proves and reminds of humanity. Or, a particular species of monster is made to perform a necessary function, hollow in its humanity. And if this leviathan of suffering is given a clear direction and purpose – something worth doing to indulge its monstrosity, then it becomes a catalyst of great change and moral power. When those who have been profoundly hurt, those who are enraged and accustomed to emptiness, are given a purpose – hopeful or retributive – there is a lot that they can achieve. Then, through the virtues borne of suffering, struggle, ambition, and composure, one becomes mindful. Mindfulness leads to empathy and its humility, stirring the great spiritual and moral power of Harmony with the Highest Good.

Herman Melville wrote: *"All men tragically great are made so through a certain morbidness. Be sure of this, O young ambition, all mortal greatness is but disease."*[25] Mindful intentions of brutal honesty know the following: greatness is the disease of dissatisfaction; righteousness is the hedonism of virtue; nobility is the redemption of shame. All is good or bad by measure of justice and sincerity, one only needs to be willing. The only fulfilling motive of power is found in the imperative of the soul and the spirit's lure of freedom. Fear only has so much to offer, and corrupt base morality, of Fear or not, neglects the potential of power where instinct is simplistic and unappreciative. The individual must have a personal and spiritual imperative to call on authority to move values in the image of one's identity, or power for power's sake will consume intent and goodwill. Only a principle of virtue and righteousness can give power the justice it warrants, least to keep it stable. This, however, is found in its purest form through the individual's honesty with the self to accept flaws of character, from which duty then arises. It is common for intent to be moved by wishful thinking of bettering the world, that one's actions are righteous by virtue of character; it seems few possess the strength to acknowledge otherwise, as ego and the self are possessed by Fear, limiting people's reach and withholding greater power.

In the heritin ethos, great value is dedicated to strength and power by the credence of Discipline. However, Discipline's utility is only as good as the justice of an intent. Discipline, like any moral utility, is only as fulfilling as the dedication of the will. Only where the ambition of an action and way of life is established in a harmonious and healthy function of the psyche can the spirit flourish and ethical environment thrive. Discipline and Defiance are means to this end, with power and strength being drawn from pain and suffering, using Fear against itself through itself to achieve greater sum gains. Moments of power, experienced in the capacity to control in accordance with one's will, are exciting. There is a rush to be found in moments of strength. However, like any pleasure or excitement, not all are equal. Power exercised in corrupt spirit of deficient functions of behaviour in excess Fear are unfulfilling and unhealthy, also often unconstructive and inefficient. Only the power that addresses the core concern of an ambition can fulfil its design. For this, mindful reason, dedicated intent, and harmony with sensation and sentiment can imbue the spirit with power and channel goodwill through the power to achieve greater ethical interest.

Where the character and the will are strong in and by themselves − of a truly autonomous soul focused on the liberty of its ambitions − power becomes a utility complimenting the ambitions of duty and justice, of virtuous character and right-eous discipline. Positions of social responsibility become a dedication; positions of great responsibility with respect to duty of authority, whether to friends, family, or institutions, grant the dutiful character the opportunity to enact its character if such is the discipline it strives for. But only through mindfulness by the Human Imper-ative and Harmony can Discipline guide the execution of power in the spirit and image of Liberty.

These values are found in the everyday practice of power, responsibility, and duty, by how one treats others, especially the vulnerable and those one stands noth-ing to gain from, and by abiding dedicated principles of morality. How these virtues translate into the brutal sphere of centralised vectors of power and grander aspects of normative dynamics are another matter demanding a particular concern for broader considerations of ethical interests, for dutiful virtue then involves the discipline of making a punishing and costly choice. This ambition subsequently tends to seem as only that of a disease, for the dedication of truly virtuous and righteous character may struggle with decisions that have no clear guidance, those of limited knowledge, wisdom yet to be found, and constant personal struggle. There is no simple solution to the issue of power's allure than that of personal responsibility and honesty, as the Fear that makes it all too appealing is easily misconstrued for benevolent intent. Liberty is just another excuse to value power. Only duty grants power its worth in Liberty, for only power gained through opportunity by the determination of the cy-cle of values, bestowed on an individual through the self-determination of the flow of values in accordance with principled actions, is a power righteous and just with respect to the conscience and spirit of goodwill. Power of and for goodness is the only power and authority worth its justice and fulfilling of its potential; this power is only achieved in the liberty attaching moral authority to the intent of goodness, not the intent of a lust for power.

The desire to control the world in any degree is commonly found in Fear, and so power can be corrupted with and through Fear. Power itself is not inherently evil - it is only the vice of man that corrupts it. *"It is not power that corrupts but fear. Fear of losing power corrupts those who wield it and fear of the scourge of power corrupts those who are sub-ject to it."*[26] It is natural for us to fear, for us and anyone to want control over our lives. But sometimes Fear becomes so strong that obsession and lust for control clouds piety and the virtue of the individual, disfiguring the essence of power. The virtue of power is not found in Fear but the Liberty to act beyond Fear and seize greater ethical interest. Power has the utility to defend, but only when people are honest with power and sincere with themselves. The order of power mandates virtue and duty.

The moral conditions and demands faced by individuals at the centre of power and global ethical dynamics are wholly different to those of the ordinary citizenry, and so the virtues of the great and powerful are somewhat different. But no matter what height one achieves, as is the case with virtue of great character, the essence of duty is always found in its elements of justice and righteousness. No matter how great or powerful a person is, duty and virtue of basic humanity are expected, for this is the key to position and significance as figures of authority. Patience, disci-pline, mindfulness, and empathy are fundamental to both vectors of authority and the institution's effects on the citizenry. The best to be expected of such characters comes in terms of performing their duties and nourishing what goodness of spirit can be found in the performance of duty, even though the baser self might suffer greatly. It seems as though such is the cost to be expected, marking great character and righteous authority. That being said, there are intuitive and clear differences between morally upstanding, even though ambiguous, actions in seats of power and cases of clear-cut immorality and negligence, of which corruption and the abuse of power are elementary.

Cynicism conjoined with apathy and pessimism are a feature of living for many generations. Optimism and hope, or their relating courage as defiance, inspire far and wide even where the cynic's expectations are humble. Even an opportunistic cynic has a beginning. Authority and liberty should inspire, as their guidance ought to be of justice, righteousness, and virtue. Disillusionment of the citizenry where governance lacks morally strong authority causes social discord and related perils and deficiencies. This sows divide in mutual understanding and authority, with impressionability fostering the character of cynicism and selfishness across society.

It is not only the citizen that becomes disillusioned by a morally corrupt figure of authority, as the person performing his or her duties will become disheartened where understanding and common good faith cannot be upheld with genuine good intentions. The figure of authority will become disillusioned in the character of people where their vices show the worst in people, exaggerated by Fear's bias. The relation of vectors of governance – that is, between citizens and the agents of an institution, between those subject to power and those exercising it – is dualistic, with impression affecting all. But where the relation is troubled, a single act of great spirit can inspire goodwill and restore justice. Any person upholding moral values must be mindful of his or her state of mind and character, so as to hold themself to account before giving the state its substance as citizens and individuals of a certain moral character. This mindfulness must be practised and become habitual, for the loss of mindfulness will lead to mistakes or even moral corruption, for Fear and vulnerability are easily swayed and influenced; all people are organically susceptible to Fear until empowered. Then, the nation's state ought to mediate its actions and policies through individuals' adherence to the duty of governance by fairly reflecting on intentions and consequences. This is a virtue-rule for all responsibility and power.

For harmonious and healthy social dynamics, a moral authority of binding normative power is in all people's interests, upheld by the authority of the soul moving all intentions, antecedent to all actions, values, laws, and institutions. This could prove necessary for the better performance of an ethical environment, fulfilment of one's concerns, and perhaps instrumental for overcoming contentious times and bring justice to unsustainable discord of values. But the proof of any such claim is intuitive when the relevant discussion concerns itself with relations between people and the elementary aspect of common goodness or common courtesy for a functional and healthy relation. Of the most evident consequences of a morally weak authority – one that is careless with, or wanting of, principles of normative and moral power – are people's nonchalance of laws instilled by uninspiring and unconvincing institutions, and dramatic rifts in understanding and values between generations, with the latter having an especially notable influence on democratic performance. While different world visions and understanding are to be expected between generations, the health of this difference is another aspect worth considering. Where elders ascribe many vices to younger generations, one ought to consider that tradition and ancestry serve as role models for their successors. Where the sins of our forefathers leave us in dismay and with a legacy to be redeemed for, it is the greatest act of a generation to overcome vice and succeed in virtue, not submit to despair and antipathy.

Insight into the limits of able individual autonomy can be found with respect to current affairs. People's judgements are not always very wise or mindful, further worsened where impressions are swayed and malformed by devious and irresponsible institutions and persons of authority. The general public can be attentive to its needs and set the agenda for competitive politics and economics. However, the public's capacity for judgement is never ideal where proper education on complex matters is practically unachievable. People have their own specialisations and the social roles they adopt. It is the authoritative responsibility of the able and appropriately skilled to perform the function of informing, advising, and guiding normative concerns of a social, political, economic, ethical, moral, and cultural nature. Nevertheless, the effectiveness of these roles and their agencies are usually far from perfect or incorruptible. Information cannot always be broken down into a simple and digestible form while retaining its true meaning. Subsequent malformation and even misinformation, whether by negligence or opportunist scheming, undermine normative endeavour and performance across society. The general public might not be the best at making political, social, and economic judgements for a variety of reasons, yet this is the inevitable medium of the adaptive cycle of values. As vectors, people cause and carry ethical development, becoming a near mindless leviathan of ethics through society. Having a clever and smart general public can be idealised, but this is not essential for positive democratic performance if there is ample variety of specialists and sufficiently educated citizens and if positive moral authority, especially *trust*, prevails in advancing synchronised agenda adhering to public interests and the principles of effective execution of power.

The correctness and measures of response to social and normative deficiencies through policy and behaviour can only be determined in the context of specific variables and the cause of deficiency. Ethics and matters of governance deal with near limitless variables, many of which cannot be accurately measured. Nevertheless, certain causal tangents and their underlying functions and vectors allow objective study and prediction, or to some extent at least. However, specialists and members of authoritative responsibility can make mistakes. Furthermore, the biases of the educated and politically dedicated can be more obstructive and damaging than the concerned scepticism of the common citizen actually experiencing the numbers that are otherwise laid out on spreadsheets. Where mistakes have been repeated and the guise of good faith dissolved in the tears of betrayed and abandoned citizens, society and the state suffer fundamental discord. Where the words of the wise and able cannot reach the public by the vices of faulty and corrupt institutions, whether of news outlets, sources of funding for governments, or various agents of weak character and morality, all suffer. The shortcomings of one nation can affect all and undermines the global human potential. This does not satisfy duty or the authority of the Human Imperative.

Just as the general public can ignore wise and well-informed counsel, the public can also become deceived by specialists, innocently or deliberately. People who place trust in a person with moral power can become misled to act or vote against their actual interests, either by deliberately selfish ambitions of a person in a position of authority or as an innocent lapse in judgement on behalf of the individual in power. In such a manner, a person in a position of moral authority can threaten and undermine liberty in power cycles. For example, if a person of moral authority comes to command very significant moral power, gestures or actions that disclose their political alignment could potentially be damaging for many people. One person's impression, however informed and wise, might not be reciprocal of others' circumstance. As such, one view can be absorbed and regurgitated without fair appreciation of the guiding value, as people can then be misled into voting against their actual interests. So it would be wise for persons of moral power to be cautious and restrained in their advocacy of political affairs, but not so much social affairs.

This isn't to say that persons of moral power should not be politically active. Persons of moral authority can and should be mindful of political and social affairs in proportion to being versed on the subjects they engage. Furthermore, as is argued, normative guidance by those sufficiently skilled is instrumental for governance and socioeconomic performance. There is no definitive formula for responsible use of moral power, especially in regards to law, but caution should be emphasised, particularly for those who may come to influence societies profoundly. On the other hand, sometimes a cataclysmic moral authority can be instrumental for positive development, as historic figures demonstrate. Moral power should be empathetic, mindful, and be understanding of others' circumstances, while also cautious of its ambitions and the consequences.

Waves of anti-establishment attitudes, disillusionment, and populism of simplistic policy have sown much dissonance across the Western world. The fault lies with many, symptomatic of failing moral authority. Blame can be ascribed to poor ethical performance of the citizenry and the state's deficient governance. The central point for reflection is the failure of virtue, with the sentiment of people overwhelming them and, above all, authority failing people. Incompetence, negligence, breach of faith, and corruption have torn apart functional relations between authority and the citizenry in many spheres of society. A generation or community felt unheard, ignored, failed, and abandoned is the epitome of failures of moral authority and weak governance. Where governance might have been led by selfish intent and ignorance, a greater threat is not the anger of an emerging generation, but individuals and groups looking for power where their spirit is otherwise hollow and of questionable moral sense. Where pessimism and cynicism turn away from hatred and create monsters beyond common instinct, vectors of power become gilded with a new species of callousness and brutality easily provoked into vengeance and moved by a higher form of Fear.

The lack of binding normativity and its front of authority are without a doubt a significant contributing factor to social discord, highlighted by the example of figures of government mistreating and ignoring their constituents, the impression of which trickles into a deep pit of resentment and antipathy. Proper governance is an extremely demanding profession. Even though clear victories seem impossible, measures of preserving justice through exemplary actions should nonetheless be worth consideration. Excuses and apologies are relevant to dynamics of moral authority, but they are only substitutes for acts of confidence and inspiring leadership conscious of sum gains and mindful of relations between the state and citizenry. Dubious behaviour by members of the state taint authority's righteousness, which, when combined with incompetence and poor performance lacking proper competition, undermines institutional performance and society's well-being.

Abuses of power or questionable executions of power impress on the common citizen disagreement with a decision of government that is perceived to be overshadowed by strings attached to bodies of power that do not clearly hold much concern for the public. Lobbying and political decisions formed in the shadow of a design to personally profit are the most obvious examples, especially due to how common they may seem. The vices that undermine effective authority and harmonious society are found across spheres of society, from institutions and to the public. Both greater liberty and sterner authority can be appealing as viable solutions to institutional and personal corruption, with one view preferring to eliminate the power that could be abused and the other subjecting people to greater accountability and less room for errors and abuse. This issue is reducible to the question of autonomy, in other words concerning the vectors of power and values.

People make mistakes. The state is undermined or fails where its agents make poor judgements; societies suffer when their constituents are unable to make good judgements and concerns for public interests are mute or insufficient. At the heart of these troubles are the capacities of individual characters. It is intuitive to think that greater authority should be granted in guiding people towards their own betterment. Suppose that an authority can legitimately exercise its power for the betterment of society. Indeed, such successes are far from rare. The subsequent problem is the lack of empowerment of the public where it cannot properly hold its authority to account. The parallel element is the lack of synchrony in the dynamics of the adaptive cycle of values, for the lack of effective liberty to develop values leads to contention, discord, and even conflict of volatile actions craving control, self-determination, and satisfaction of justice. The violation of civil liberties without consent and common accord entails great risk of heightening tensions and undermining social harmony in terms of tangents and vectors of change.

With respect to the principles of liberty's normativity, people must be allowed to make mistakes. Where the parent can assist his or her child, the state has no such power – only figures of moral authority do, which the state can only collaborate with and embrace for the sake of its own performance and purpose. Society must adapt and develop, which excess authority will hinder. The state cannot follow the same principles of liberty as individual morality in its general form, as it is the necessary function of the state to protect civilisation in appropriate measure of justice. Voluntary and necessary mistakes must be enabled if values are to be adaptive and in harmony with Natural Law and its manifestation of the Highest Good. However, if a measure of authority is realistically plausible in achieving the goal of serving society with greater justice through stronger measures of authority, even if only as momentary security for future prospects of growth, then a strong measure of authority is just and warranted. However, this can only be the case if it is compatible with prevailing values through the consent of the citizenry. Furthermore, as is clear in reflection of common history, anyone ought to be very cautious of justifications of strong means of authority and authority's judgement and execution, especially as people are very easily deceived by Fear. A dual relation of power and trust is necessary for functional and healthy institutions of authority. Only a common source of moral authority can fulfil this function, which does not require a sovereign of morality other than basic moral principles leading to empathy, goodwill, and mutual good faith.

This work does not seek to propose simple solutions and quick fixes. Nonetheless, the intended purpose of this work is realistic and concrete in suggesting points of insight outlining useful thoughts in helping guide policy directives and their execution. The first point of inquiry is to consider the correctness of basic assumptions, to evaluate what is taken for granted and posit any goal-directive function in a coherent and structured framework. Where the functions of behaviour are understood, and their influence on secondary ethical spheres are accounted for, normative elements of authority and governance become much more intuitive and their agenda better structured in terms of core and central values. When we know what we want, what is truly in our best interests, and how to effectively achieve this, individual, social, and political behaviour can become much more coherent. This is the main point sought to be made on the issue, on top of exemplifying a hierarchy of values and its respective moral authority, with Natural Law and the Highest Good exercising real power on the determination of mankind's future.

No authority of institution is above the Nature that conjured it and gave it a function; no person is beyond the constitution of the soul's directive. Lending its insight into the application of liberty through democratic authority, where contention and conflict between values ignite passions, and where passions overwhelm sensibility, leadership ought to mitigate negative ethical elements through moral power. Only moral authority can build solidarity. But where policy is surrendered to emotion without heed, it is led astray of higher moral sense. Then, even the seed of sensibility and humble self-doubt can restore functional balance and justice. Nurturing virtues of individuals in positions of power and responsibility – *all people* – is the most achievable and empowering of all policies. Moral authority can inspire this through gestures of genuine care, kindness, strength, and goodness; its leadership and power come through vectors of virtues shaping the world in the image of the Highest Good.

The plurality of values and moralities makes society and authority compete. The mediation of values and interests is the function of institutional authority and governance. Sometimes people mistake multiculturalism for multinormativism – an inescapable and necessary feature of modern societies. Multiple vectors of values at odds with others constantly subject societies and civilisations to change. Sometimes values can coexist harmoniously and functionally, balanced through the authority of the state. However, certain values are completely incompatible. Where the function of a tangent of values is irreconcilable by the standards of a society and its local vectors, measured and evaluated with reference to established ethical values and moral principles in accordance with the state of ethical environment, the presence of incompatible and destructively competing normativity may have to be suppressed. It can prove difficult to establish the full structure of a value and principle in a given context through which judgements can then be effectively made.

As was highlighted previously, once unacceptable values proved to be right another time. While no simple argument can be given on this topic, a suggestive remark will have to do for now in that lessons learnt can perhaps now turn into an effective science of establishing the merits of seemingly arbitrary and subjective moralities. After all, for justice to succeed it needs to formalise parameters of conduct and guidance. Principles of liberty may herald tolerance and acceptance, but there are degrees and limits to such attitudes that must be enforced. Through appeal to the fulcrum of authority, in tandem with the principle of liberty's offence, certain values cannot be given liberty. And so the authority of a nation's laws may object to certain values, even at a cost of increasing social disharmony. However, this is only if the restriction of liberty is compatible with sum maxims of liberty through positive values known to be righteous by Natural Law and the Highest Good, regardless of a value's origin with respect to an ethos in so much as its consequences on the state of affairs are good. Then, only a just source of moral authority above dogmatic, arbitrary, inconsistent, and inefficient conviction, mindful of the structures of ethics in service to mankind and bound to the Human Imperative, is adequate to serve the purpose of normative guidance.

This is not intended to propose that the heritin interpretation is in and of itself worthy of such a position. The argument is simple in that only the most fit in ethical dealings and matters, whether as people or ideas, ought to mediate, balance, and guide normative endeavour. Only functional institutions can advise in proper form the normative and moral parallels of any secondary manifestation of ethics. Reason and the intuitions of sentiments ought to be the centre of any moral authority, with sensibility and mindfulness paving way for development and action.

Where agenda are confident and rhetoric engaging, solid arguments are better than rich but unsubstantiated words. A case analysis studying acceptable and unacceptable values, in tandem with the dynamics of authority and the public, would be beneficial. For this, the authority and moral weight of violence manifesting itself through actions, practice, and policy serves as an engaging topic. Any act of violence can be deeply moving and terribly provocative. Furthermore, where emotions run high and base morality is convinced of the fairness of impulse lacking discipline, violence corrupts authority and undermines society, whether through illegitimate use of force by the state or by citizens.

Much has been written on the morality of violence, yet its moral power warrants a special note. Violence is destructive, costly, chaotic, and less efficient than other conceivable modes of ethics. Violence projects suffering and pain into the world, through which it reflects onto and off people in a lingering cycle of pain and destruction. Violence divides people and opposes mutual understanding where disciplined empathy lacks virtue. The scars of violence tear the body, wound the earth, poison spirit, and tarnish moral authority. To this day a single ambiguity of thought can cast a wave of destructive violence. In the condition of people bound to the compulsions of base-reason and impatience, unjust violence finds its way into the world through the exploited vulnerabilities of Fear. Violence often manifests itself as one of the greatest forms of suffering, but its suggested evils are not absolute, although nonetheless overwhelming and disturbing.

It is striking that the message and wisdom of non-violence have to be constantly reminded even now, to then be lost to attention by distractions of instinct's excitements lacking higher spirit. Acts of violence are usually compulsions of Fear, at times disguising sophisticated instincts through compulsive strategies of policy acting against truer interests and values unknown in the veil of Fear. It is rare for violence to become bound to higher utilities commanding violence and fury. But then the consequence of violence affects people differently, hardly ever giving greater fulfilment or satisfaction when its suffering lingers. Liberty of spirit can only be achieved by conquering the suffering of violence, both by embracing it and, when necessary, handling it with composure. The psychological and mental effects of violence are often greater than their physical force, requiring distinct strength and virtue to remedy their affliction. Mastering and coping with violence is imperative not only for spiritual fulfilment and growth of character, but also for health and the mass psyche of society, starting with a clear moral sense and intuitive conscience. The virtue of restraint in violence, but not cowardice, is learnt from adolescent squabbles and immaturity and insecurity in adulthood.

Violence leads to goodness when the resolve of humanity succeeds the vicious cycles of suffering and violence. However, this goodness extinguishes its ethical interest where it encounters the limits of people's strength. Mankind has extraordinary potential found in its humanity, achieved only in the liberty to overcome our fear and enjoy the liberty of free and good spirit. Nonetheless, violence is often a catastrophic influence on positive moral authority crucial for any ethical environment.

Violence committed for sociopolitical gains or change, motivated by the desire for justice parading as instinct's compulsion for control, is too commonly a corruption and vice of Fear. Any 'just' cause that instigates violence as a means of direct political influence loses higher moral authority, belittling authority to a state of subdued character and spirit heeding to a corrupt morality lacking notable autonomy. Extreme patience and discipline championing over violence, enduring the suffering of violence with indomitable composure rejecting Fear's lure, is unequivocally good by the standard of any moral authority. Resisting the vices of violence empowers a cause more than any Fear. The greatest of all is a moral authority, morality, and ethos mastering the use of violence – for protection and growth. Violence is a circumstantially necessary means to justice and righteousness. As such, resisting violence and alleviating it by whatever means appropriate to the circumstance is the path to commanding Fear and pain. Furthermore, the adaptiveness of pragmatic moral utilities preserves and facilitates Harmony with the Highest Good. Dogmatic guidance is not the worthy autonomy of Liberty, with the integrity of the Ideals realising itself through established moral principles of virtue and duty manifesting themselves through individuals – vectors of Paragon virtues truly in accord with the Highest Good.

The wisest society and leadership are those that know the limits and merits of violence as a form of moral and spiritual power. Underhand and deceptive tactics employing measures of violence against enemy combatants or rival factions, even if this deceitful plot is never revealed, could very well be the better initiative, but it will reflect back onto its vector, changing its nature and character. As with all intentions as the reasoning behind any policy and exercise of power, the presence of vice will persist with the psyche that feeds it. Intent can make any acceptable utility right or wrong, just or deplorable. Where moral sense justifies excess and unjust violence, drawn to its deceitful spirit of power, consumed by a lust without fulfilment, the power of righteousness and goodness is forgotten. The only righteous use of violence and coercive execution of power is found in mindful intent and disciplined, harmonious goodwill. Fear can create its form justice, but the corruption of Fear warrants great suspicion, just as the freedom of Liberty's great ambition demands tremendous balance through discipline and mindfulness. Suffering-love – loving other souls through the suffering they inflict – is the cure to violence and the measure of its power. The justice of violence and coercive power is empathy towards others and care for the world, but only in so much as the freedom of spirit to be in harmony with the world is greater than any pain its humanity may have to endure, noble beyond any and all Fear, awe-inspiring in its dignity of will, grandiose in its ambition and faith in the Human Imperative.

What good has ever come of violence against innocents, the ignorant and unwise, against the non-combative? What has mindless violence ever achieved for a moral authority? What has violence ever done to the spirit of an individual? What is the cost of violence on humanity? Conflicts and wars requiring just retaliation and violent opposition have their use and have bolstered moral authority by sustaining it when its worth of virtue is tested. Morally upstanding individuals benefit from acts of violent self-defence, but flourish in the clemency of empathy's suffering defiant against the presence of violence. Even targeted killing as necessary a last resort to abrupt devious plans of a disturbed individual or group have a degree of good utility in very restrictive moral conditions. But by maiming a body or reducing a life to char and ash in a decree consumed with Fear, the spirit only gives into vice. Destroying civil society, sowing death and mass suffering, causing awful grief, and sustaining a presence of Fear only serves the corruption that Fear is itself averse to.

Society and civilisation can be profoundly affected by violence, provoking the worst of conflicts or epitomising the best of humanity through suffering-love and resilience under the great pain and fear of violence. In moments of strife, especially where the pain and threat of violence chases us, values are subject to extremes. Authorities are always compelled by the demands of violence – its use or in response to its provocation. The fundamentals of state power are moved in accordance with the values of people embodying its institutions, even when the founding principles of one's constitution is discarded in favour of changing values and character. But Laws of Nature and universal wisdoms of the Ideals supervene any intuitions and compulsions of an emotional moment or brutally rational estimation. The values appealing violence always demand great meditation and reflection. Authority must always balance these values. Leaders might know the wisdom of non-violence, but desperate and poisonous urges may spur the heard with momentarily powerful sensations. A dichotomy arises – feed the lust of the masses, or exercise authority to compel higher sensibility and conscience? Should the public's emotions be adhered to in response to the anguish of a violent act? Should policy be retributive or vengeful? Will restraining public outcries appealing to destructive and corruptive policy initiatives be met with greater distain, or with eventual admiration and understanding beyond momentary anger and fear? Is the response proportional and necessary? Only the conditions of an instant can provide clues that inform normativity and morality. Only in a specific case can a person estimate and evaluate the consequences of policy and exercise of authority. No universal arbitration can be made beyond individual circumstances, with the only practical reality being intuition and conscience guided by Core and Central Principles forming one's Ideals. One such principle is clear and simple – any exercise of power employing or responding to violence requires laborious and exhaustive consideration and study, for its ethical values and dynamics are exceptionally complex.

Violence is a special case of the plurality of values active in a single ethical sphere. As was sought to be shown, in matters of plurinormativity, while it could be clear which value is right or wrong, or which consequence is the most predictable, only a model of ethical structures can effectively advise the performance of authorities. Only a clear understanding and appreciation of the dynamics of ethics and its concreteness as values, formalised as principles of right and wrong guiding decision-making, can receive insight relevant to authority and power. Answers are possible and real, but they require dedicated combined effort that supercede individual's limitations in vision, insight, wisdom, knowledge, and overall ability and character.

The plurality of values is present in the globality of our common ethical environment, as is seen with contention between degrees of liberty and authority, conflicting values of autonomy and justice. Champions of freedom base their justice and righteousness on values helping mankind, heralding a view of the Highest Good and its own version of the Human Imperative by appealing to the normativity of civil liberty and freedom. The liberty of the champions of liberty is a value in itself, subject to all of base morality's influences, good and bad. The righteousness of any such mission is only found in the reality of its contribution and in measure of the Highest Good.

However, while intent can seem good, right, and just, nonetheless demanding honest introspection, consequences and states of affairs necessitate even greater evaluation.

The ambition of human rights and just liberty is admirable. The heritin ethos is bound in duty and conviction to the betterment of mankind and protection of humanity, for which civil and civic liberty are essential. Any analysis of the actuality of this mission as foreign and domestic policy, however, unveils many uncertainties and flaws. It is not currently the case for argument whether or not successes of liberty's global ambition have outweighed the damage. The guiding presumption is that while progress has been achieved, more could be done and ethical development could be more efficient and sophisticated. There are many deep self-inflicted wounds that must be healed for the most developed and richest societies of civil liberty to be stronger and healthier. The second decade of the second millennium has revealed deep troubles in the most developed societies, with ethical and moral vulnerabilities undermining success. Pessimism, optimism, cynicism, apathy, delusion, ignorance, and hopefulness can ascribe different values. But no bias or impression can dodge the conclusion that mankind's civilisation is not the healthiest or claim that its most advanced communities and spheres are not invulnerable.

Fear has allowed the ambition of humanity as its rights and liberty to decay. Pessimism and cynicism may influence study, yet even though the successes are many, much work remains and the wounds of a weak moral authority are striking. The cause of liberty and justice lacks the power it heralds where its own societies cannot live by their own example. By the authority of the Human Imperative and its Highest Good, the ambition of global human betterment towards liberty is admirable and worthy, but its vectors of power are weak and insufficient in their present state. Only moral empowerment through conviction and principle can restore the justice and righteousness of global well-being and progress, for liberty is only worth its weight of applied goodness. But if history has anything to say and principles are convincing, then liberty and just measures of authority that serve the ends of liberty are the pedestal of the Highest Good, crown utilities of the Human Imperative in their global and institutionally, socially, politically, and economically established forms. This liberty also entails the liberty of alternative means of growth appropriate to the circumstances of an ethical environment, as any state of liberty can only be cultivated, not installed.

The premise of liberty's justice finds the beginning of legitimate authority in self-determination. It is the dedicated right for any person to defy illegitimate and morally weak authority of personality or institution, for this is a mark of virtuous character and a principle of justice by the Highest Good. A disagreement in moral authority evoked by ideological differences does not grant legitimacy or moral empowerment to disproportionally resist against sensible and just authority. An authority of the majority can only be defied when the authority of a regime exceeds its legitimacy by law, by the will of the people, and tolerable bounds of morality. Until the elements of genuine civil and civic liberty remain and democracy has a shred of power, violent revolt and volatile uprising have little-to-no legitimacy or moral justification. Disparity in views calling for violent struggle can only find justice in clear vision greater than the immediate veil of fear and pain. This claim does not entitle people to defy the authority that their opinion or sentiment merely deny or disagree with, as the will of the majority and of other people, no matter how much one might disagree, if within a tolerable standard of key moral principles, is to be respected. This respect also manifests itself as care through civic activity towards the betterment of oneself and others, as all endeavour fulfilling of the Human Impera-tive in whatever degree or form is good and respectable. Even the simplest of acts like getting out of bed and doing something nice for yourself and others whilst subject to torments of the mind and spirit nourish character and spirit with goodness, keeping it going, keeping up the good fight. Even resting to gather strength or putting in a lit-tle bit of productive effort through restraints of a damaged body is good. Producing and spreading goodness is admirable, yet this path also needs moments of care for oneself by accepting goodness.

One might not be able to do anything about injustice on the other side of the world, but goodness can be cherished by doing *something* good, no matter how seem-ingly insignificant, even if only as an act of kindness to oneself, a loved one, a friend, a stranger, or someone never to be met, appreciated in the silent care of empathy's diligence and personal responsibility. Even the cleaning task of a mundane job can contribute to global goodness by not feeding people dirt, appreciated in the mind-ful moment of meditating on disciplined action, inspirational through the strength of confident character. But only the truest intent in goodwill is rewarding with this principle, not gluttony of unsatisfying, endless consumption of goodness inviting pity, lacking admiration of autonomy of virtuous and strong character. Nourishing the goodness of character by improving and making more of oneself for the good of oneself and in duty of the Human Imperative are the steps of duty of righteous intent. Consumption for blind and unfulfilling hedonism as distraction from a suf-fering life is an objection to this principle, nevertheless warranting empathy and de-grees of compassion. These sorts of values are the foundations of a just and righteous authority influencing the global state of civilisation. Simple gestures of unity found in common good faith and goodwill, as kindness and decency, are elements of good and just social living, reflective of the Human Imperative and its Highest Good fulfill-ing the individual with meaningful spirit and purpose appreciated in *raw* sensation.

The surest measure of creating an ethical environment compatible with greater civic utilities, such as functional and healthy liberty, comes through nourishing the goodness of individuals. Where such a covenant cannot be implemented properly, the implication is that inaction and passive normativity are a legitimate mode of in-ternational conduct with respect to values in accordance with the Human Imperative. Social, political, economic, and cultural elements compose the normativity sought to be influenced through the values of national initiatives. All aforementioned var-iables influence relevant policies and actions. Inaction is sometimes equated with wrongdoing; this judgement is only as valid as the circumstance demanding action. In immediate circumstances, it is not always clear which action is good, because any case can be ambiguous. Appropriate reaction, including enduring inaction, requires justification in measure with conditions and related ethical tangents attached to a potential action. Ambiguity will always exist and the lack of information will always be relevant. But inaction when immediate action can foster goodness is wrong, just as action more destructive than inaction is wrong. In all normative ambiguity, certain clarity persists. For greater normative goodness, restraint and passive action or even inaction are plausible and legitimate modes of conduct. When good actions are real-istically achievable, such as by influencing the normativity of a local ethical sphere, and when ambiguity recedes, then it is right to exercise authority on another sphere of authority such as another nation-state. Power is only legitimate in the Highest Good of the Human Imperative when it serves the interests of *all*. Inaction is far from ideal, as it may enable states of suffering, but ideal outcomes are rarely fulfillable.

Undesirable and deficient values persist in the world by the determination of Nature's ethical mechanisms and dynamics. It is in the interest of the Human Imperative to create and sustain goodness to its greatest possible degree. Competing values that do not serve the greater interests of the Human Imperative will always be relevant to ambition's concern. Where these values may be tolerated or synchronised in accord of functional values, sum positive ethical interest can be achieved. However, some values are incompatible, and their vectors of power must be neutralised. Appropriate action should then only be taken where greater interest can be served positively – that is, righteously and justly. Destructive and gravely corrupt values demand attention and a response, for righteous values are only those concerned with the justice and goodness of all mankind and in duty to the Human Imperative, in whatever form these values present themselves. Any ethos that settles for less than the maxim of the Human Imperative lacks the reach and esteem of an ethos of Liberty, but values consistent and compatible with the Imperative are worth preserving and studying. Any ethic above all else valuing goodness for all mankind and in service of human civilisation, resistant to Fear's corruption and excess, is agreeable with the Human Imperative. Then, the practices and insights of any interpretation of spirit's Liberty, found in the essence of the human psyche, can interact and grow through and from one another, moving humanity closer to the Highest Good we all seek and need.

Other morality and ethics found wanting in their value require development or a response. For example, the values that favour unjust violence and selfishness are inconsistent with the Human Imperative. Where moral authority and normative power can assist governance and human well-being, other means of power are necessary to counter-act the degenerative elements of violence, selfishness, and excessive Fear. Only a select few figures in history have exercised such great power to shape the moral character of a society, to become the conscience of a nation and people, to bring harmony to tangents and cycles of violence or giving communities and societies the opportunity to heal from their pain and succeed their Fear. Political, social, cultural, and perhaps most importantly economic means carrying civic utilities in human interests are key for harmonising the plurality of values and their everlasting fluidity and evolution. For this, a distinct mode of ethics and morality must match the demands of a new world.

The ambition of achieving harmony in values, at least defined by the lack of active conflict, is an endless one, an impossibly complex one, and the most enduring of spiritual incentives, for this is the essence of all ethical dynamics and duties in accordance with the Human Imperative and the Highest Good. When greater values can be established as common, agreeable, and functional moral authority, won only in the liberty of self-determination and healthy mind and spirit, then a design befitting the Human Imperative can be sustained as civilisation in its name – humanity's essence of living and all living's ambition. This does not call on the heritin interpretation to reign; these arguments and hopeful wisdoms only suggest a model for all mankind's wisdom to understand ourselves and the world around us. But as with all valued wisdom, a silver tongue and compelling word are never enough.

The first intuition of discipline is to reconsider emotionally intuitive policies – to pursue a coercive and intrusive justice, or a rational strategy that can be chilling. Policy must be appropriate to a given circumstance. Reason, sensibility, patience, and mindfulness must guide any reactions in moderation with the most human sentiments known through and as the Human Imperative. Policy direction is just and righteous in as much as its implementation and results, with the consequences deemed good even if the intention held true to virtue but lacks idealised achievement. Damage mediation combined with the growth of character could prove to be the best outcome in an extremely demanding situation. The success of a strategy reflecting idealised ends could potentially be achieved with blunt and straightforward means, provided their measure is combined with the vision of an adequate strategy. However, coercive means of achieving any normative end warrants utmost scepticism and caution, even if their economic, political, cultural, normative, or even military measures are subtle.

The tangents of coercion can be extremely evocative, with their utilities too commonly sowing divide among people rather than fostering good faith. But such is the necessity of maximising positive ethical interests, for the preservation of healthy and prosperous ethical environments above others derives its right from the ability to protect itself from competing corrupt values. Promising civic states, liberty, and healthy ethical environments *must* be preserved before their inevitable causal tangents influence other spheres, to at least protect themselves from other spheres' antagonistic competing effects. Goodness must be nourished, preserved, and protected by its worth of goodness and ethical health and harmony, which can be achieved in unexpected ways including taking risks that could undermine material security, yet risks that cherish the virtues and uphold the principles that made such action and environment possible. A righteous normative sphere and ethical community requires sustenance of its goodness in a multitude of forms, just as a person has many needs. Along these lines one can begin to appreciate any society's deficiencies and vulnerabilities, to be remedied or exploited. Tacit approaches or even defensive isolation and seclusion (with respect to causal tangents) can be favourable and respectable initiatives and principles of domestic or foreign policy. For example, any international actor and ethical vector ought to attend to its own vulnerabilities before engaging with another opposing or outright competing vector. Normative power has at times not been used with attention to this principle of ethical or normative *protectionism* – a basic tenant of global ethical dynamics. However, its worth is not in survival for survival's sake, as the grandness of its purpose is only befitting if aligned with higher ambition and justice. Adaptive intuition serves this purpose well by guiding sensibility to appreciate discipline behind any action and life's dedication.

To emphasise the role of structures of ethical environments with respect to their social dynamics, the recognition of the legitimate and institutional authorities of societies is imperative for guiding normative global and intentional policy. Being attentive to the many dimensions of power and influencing the inherently many causal tangents shaping any ethical sphere are examples of ethics in practice. Influencing individuals through institutional power, sometimes through underhand means, is evident in much of political affairs. While political and social practices responding to concrete threats might require deception, and pragmatism will always have to consider such policy orientations, all normative aspects must be considered, or else concrete gains could undermine the core interests of moral authority. The citizens of society have a greater capacity for moral conduct, especially with respect to legitimacy, in their respective environments. This conduct can include revolt, protest, uprising, and insurrection. Appealing to these ethical elements – vectors of power – are instrumental to normative ambitions of national grand strategies seeking favourable change. But the rightness and goodness of any such ambition is only realised if it assists people's interests and is compatible with principles of morality. Therefore, the liberty of people's determination, especially where beyond the jurisdiction of a national authority, ought to be respected. Other people's interests ought to be included in any normative dedication drawn from the Human Imperative. This concern also entails the principle of self-sacrifice for harmonious transitions in power and value, such as in the case of the decay of societies by poor democratic self-determination. One ought to find harmony with the liberty of values leading to change, as an opposition acting with excess authority against inevitable change will only produce an end more volatile than a soft development. Accepting inevitable change can help with balanced transition without further destruction. Change can be unfavourable, yet this is a rite of Natural Law, and through it one can find peace, virtue, and even opportunity. One community's loss is the potential for another to gain ethical interest, with sum ethical interest still preserved or even increased.

Duty of the Human Imperative can foster good faith in these transitions of power and values. Mediating Fear and base morality through good values and principles can assist human welfare and development. Moral power and normative stature, such as by leading with example and influencing through alluring moral principles, can become concrete tools of policy by influencing the foundations of power. Or at least this is more favourable than provocative and intrusive displays of power, or complimentary to the moderation of coercion where coercion is sophisticated and morally correct. Combined approaches employing different types of power assist all ambitions of authority. No state or grand power ever settles for mere survival and continuity, for when mankind sees potential and opportunity it becomes hungry for more than settling for Fear – *Liberty* excites ambition. Both care for humanity and the ambitions of authority can rouse the most elemental aversion to idleness. But only some of these ambitions are truly befitting of the spirit and virtue of Liberty. Liberty is but one option where the veil of Fear is lifted, and in Liberty, combining the motivation of both empathy and ambition, authority and its reach grow.

To reiterate the promising element of ethics of Liberty in respect of their focus on seizing ethical interest, balanced with sensible concerns for sum gains and practicality, Liberty grants opportunity. Naturally and intuitively, any ethic of Liberty entails risk, but a risk no greater than the limitations of an ethic of Fear exhausting the efficiency of its utility. An ethic of Liberty grants new possibilities and modes of fulfilling actions, revealing unforeseen options and overcoming the vulnerabilities, limitations, and insecurities of other ethics. Liberty's promise is sensed and appreciated where one is beyond the reproach of vice, enshrining itself in a different set of rules to ethics of subdued potential oppressed by Fear. The moral authority found in non-violence is such that its character and spirit does not submit to the Fear that moves others to violence, *if* this is fulfilling of our greater interests – this is Liberty. Ambition and the sense of power offer a form of spiritual fulfilment, yet Liberty offers far more. Liberty is great in its higher ambition driven by a higher form of hunger and a spiritual incentive superceding and freeing oneself from non-critical needs, in turn arousing eternal personal empowerment and awakening an unprecedented clarity, focus, certainty, meaning, and purpose. Where one achieves such Harmony with oneself and the surrounding world, enabled through Discipline, one elevates the self beyond Fear's common rule. The potentials of ethical interest become much greater, particularly as absolutes of fulfilment, happiness, and eudaimonia conditional only on the determination of will and capacity of character, of incentives and drives beyond common pettiness and menial power games. Where the sense of self is in a realm of its own, unyielding to zero-sum games of Fear's basic mode overvaluing simplistic and lesser fulfilments of power conditional on others, Liberty succeeds all. This empowers character and strengthens a moral authority's vector. Where a vector becomes morally stronger, in time, the entire sphere stands to gain. Then, the reach of ambition grows.

The intricacies of policy and their circumstances, combined with the lack of a coherent ethical model for decision-making, render normativity inconsistent and to a degree arbitrary, even powerless in the most basic vision of policy. Previous arguments have sought to show the relevance and importance of normativity in all dynamics of power, from domestic social cohesion to foreign policy dealing with competing vectors. After all, opinions are not immune to causes. And illustration will benefit the adopted model of understanding and structuring of competing values. What values are to be prioritised in terms of the pursuit of liberty and human rights? Which principles and resources hold the greatest value? Normatively speaking, how can and should interests be maximised? The case of competing values in the mission of spreading liberal democracy and concerns for protecting national interests is an excellent case to consider in seeking insight on the dynamics of power and their normativity and morality.

First, the means are as much the end as the end's objective, because the neglect of normative and moral principles of an envisaged end reflect the character and nature of a vector pursuing that end, setting the conditions for a vector's self-determination. Competitive democratic governments influence policy outcomes in relation to competing values, interests, and priorities. Acting in accordance with respective values, interests, and priorities affects domestic conditions and foreign affairs. For one, nation-states value status as a normative resource, as the status of a country affects its citizen's individual and collective self-esteem and influences the shaping of national identity and unity[27], as was explored throughout Section 2. A global presence of a nation as a major power will affect national ego, as any sense of empowerment in localised or grander scales can bolster the sense of status, at times becoming a plague and a corrosive addiction. Even though public concerns can manifest themselves primarily in terms of domestic self-interest, such as the concerns for affordable living and housing and accessible education, public pressures to some measure do influence government international dispositions. People have interests in and for the world, whether as straightforward national security or a sense of justice and duty. Strong reactions are stirred by evocative threats such as terrorism and opportunist groups taking advantage of power-vacuums in zones of civil strife and war. People can put great pressure on the orientation of states in response to natural disasters, whether starvation or disease, or to events of, for example, genocide and mass murder in developed countries.

Proactive foreign policy is an extension of the function of aversion to idleness. The Cold War – a period of major normative and ideological competition – is a good example of national security concerns being combined with the reach of normative ambition. The continued mission heralded by the West to spread the civics and normativity of liberal democracy, which it is convinced, after the perceived victory over the Soviet Union, is a priori better[28], is a modern example of effort dedicated towards a normative goal. Combined factors of self-interest in national security and the desire for greater meaning or purpose in power can be attributed to ethical functions of the mass psyche. Few with power, it seems, settle for their comfortable state, to be driven by concerns to preserve this state, bolster it, or relinquish it. However, where these interests differ, their values, priorities, and principles compete. For instance, domestic economic comfort can compete with international missions of an idealised normative principle, according to which the two values can appear wholly contradictory, suggestive of hypocrisy, ignorance, foolishness, and weakness. For context, consider the ties liberal democratic countries have with nations of alternative values and civic establishment, whether it is Russia, China, or other alternative species of regimes and mass normative vectors. Political ties can be strained by conflicting interests and normativity, yet nations are moved towards forming a contract by greater economic interests in each party's favour. In such cases, it is the purpose of governance to lead by organising strategy and policy among competing interests, with the lack of effective normative guidance crippling the process and leaving outcomes less efficient. Furthermore, the public's lack of vision and understanding complicates matters for governance and policy by making it difficult to reveal and organise perceived incompatible interests. Contradictions in desires then demand resolution and mediation for effective action and policy. Hence, authorities are forced into a political, economic, and normative zero-sum game. Authorities take charge, as might be intuitive in any position of leadership.

Democratic performance compels governments to extend the authoritativeness of representation beyond the mode of a democracy with greater direct civil participation in policy formation, with persons in positions of government making decisions on behalf of their constituents. The value of such a system is conceived in measure of satisfying majority interests, a system that could benefit from strong moral authority balancing values where all people's interests realistically cannot be completely satisfied. Not empowering the public by reserving command to secluded institutions and individuals without proper measures of accountability and balance of power sows normative discord. Neglect of the public and of moral authority leads to negative domestic effects on unity, solidarity, motivation, inspiration, and overall domestic performance. For instance, this may be observed as youth disillusionment producing apathetic generations necessitating excesses recreation and spiritual self-remedy, as well as producing underperforming democratic processes as certain tangents and vectors exercise greater, unbalanced power than they should.

The overreach of authority can manifest itself as deep-rooted vectors of establishments that fail to adapt by fault of individual characters and vectors of power, further worsened by the lack of electoral turnout and activity subjecting authorities to greater pressure. An example of this phenomenon is the narrowing of individuals' and agencies' priorities where lack of leadership, fair cooperation, and organisation disproportionally emphasise a select group of values and interests. People have talents, skills, knowledge, and social roles; where unmediated, people's concerns and interests can become self-centric and self-serving. Where concern and vision are reclusive, and government authorities function in zero-sum terms of competing interests and values, state powers are emphasised. Institutionalisation in this form can stabilise ethical tangents, as the state may stabilise society by creating order in competing values and interests.

However, a value that is given too much power, prioritising itself over other pressing interests, without proper conditioning, can cause disturbances in normative performance. For example, people may be concerned with both national security and personal comfort of living. If the state prioritises one of these values to a disproportionate degree, the adverse effects could become too significant and costly. The lack of domestic coherence, such as by the neglect of a compelling moral authority, undermines greater interests by failing to organise and lead people in their own interests in accordance with their own interests. Not being able to highlight the values in people's favour and compelling the public to act in its own greater interests – achievable only through moral authority – is a civic, social, and national vulnerability. This measure of authority or authoritativeness is only righteous and just when performed in a framework of civic and civil liberty through individual autonomy and social self-determination.

Consensus is the foundation of coherent normativity in governance. The lack of mediation and stability can also produce negative consequence in terms of the overreach of authority and false justification inclining vulnerable morality to selfish intent and actions. This can enable severe institutional and moral corruption crippling the state, nation, society, normativity, moral authority, and the sanctity of power itself. A combination of the explored elements can undermine a normative vector, its cause, its status, its power, and even render its mission obsolete in spirit and value. Therefore, discord in authority between the state and society undermines the cohesiveness of policy and reduces its potential and power through unbinding normativity corresponding to the concreteness of ethical causation. The fulfilment of ethical interests is then less efficient and less satisfying.

Considering the matter at hand in terms of national security interests and the normativity of liberal democracy, the paradigm can be outlined as follows. For liberal democracy – a civic utility treasured by the Human Imperative – to be sustained, it needs sufficient economic and social virtue. In terms of the modern necessities and cost of living of developed societies, especially in terms of energy, liberal democracies must engage with other nations of alternative values, sometimes at odds. To further the cause of liberal democracy, nations must protect themselves and their allies, as with the initiative of NATO and the powers striving to protect the free world. One step and policy at a time, the mission of the champions of liberty is intended to come closer to a truly free, righteous, and just world. However, this grand calling has not benefitted from a healthy normative parallel of power, with the consequence being that the public and its institutions may have the reach but not the grasp, impaired by vices of character.

The mission of peace and freedom can unnecessarily and unintentionally instigate conflict, whether through negligence or underestimation. These faults undermine the goodness of intent, effort, and ambition, but they are not without the potential to be reformed. Nations may claim to protect human rights and humanity, but are seemingly forced to concede these principles where they must engage with vectors of alternative values or as part of a coherent grand strategy momentarily tolerant of injustice. Where understanding, coherence, and order between the state and society are at odds and in a state of discord, authoritativeness is normatively weakened by the lack of support and maximised efficiency of a given power. The state can move its resources abroad as part of a broader foreign policy that the common citizen may not appreciate fully, yet in conflict with domestic concerns that are narrower in their scope of interest. Then, with this divide in understanding comes excess such as policy enacted by authorities profoundly at odds with public values. For example, security initiatives spying on its own citizenry can be deeply at odds with people's value invested in civil liberty, yet satisfy the value of security and initiatives protecting citizens (if policy is effective in protecting people). A nation may establish a global presence to protect itself and its allies, but then relinquish this trust and alliance through disproportionate underhand measures and deception. Nations need logistical and strategic advantages to serve their security interests, such as military bombing campaigns requiring operable and sustainably supplied launch sites, and so governments invest according to far-reaching interests. But then the focus of these costs and initiatives, if unmediated by accountability, transparency, and proactive electoral considerations – the basics of liberal democracy – can detract from a greater balance in terms of domestic investment, contradict normative principles, and possibly undermine policy arrangements with other nations. Security is sensible and also as a measure of Fear. Disproportionate fear undermines liberty *and* security, while the lack of concern for security forgoes strengthening and defending liberty. People are not yet adequately equipped emotionally, intuitively, practically, or academically to structure, with absolute certainty, the values that guide tangents of power. These are all matters of power and authority that show the fundamental conflict in values that move and invoke these powers. Until interests, values, and principles are structured in a coherent framework – given hierarchy, the sum of power and ambition will not fulfil their ethical potential.

Now, to illustrate the application of structural ethics as a discipline and study. With reference to the fulcrum of authority and the standard of liberty's harm, and through reference to a given structure of ethics and its hierarchy, values can be posited in a useful, intuitive, and coherent manner. First of all, spheres of liberal democracy ought to be protected and nourished. When liberty leads to degeneration, this consequence must be mediated through the standard of harm, suggesting the merits of a policy that allows vice to consume itself in a manner sustaining the maximum goodness in losses of ethical interest. Policy that furthers the positive ethical interests of liberty and spreads its positive contribution through normative power is good in terms of a grand strategy and ambition. However, the means by which this end is achieved are central to success.

For one, long-term goals of the normativity of liberty should not compromise the foundations that invoke relevant objectives. Effective measures of security, including those of considerable authority bordering on intrusiveness, can be just and ethically positive in terms of sustaining and protecting the long-term ends of liberty and liberty itself. However, the lack of moderation in such policies domestically and internationally undermines the normative power of liberty. Policies of liberal democracies warrant active liberty in their formation, including measures of accountability and self-determination, not excess authoritativeness turning to corruption. So, only an agreeable and compatible accord of domestic governance in line with the normativity of liberty ought to be practiced as a regime calling itself a liberal democracy. This primary value states the principle of first protecting liberty, with development and growth of liberal environments being part of this principle. It is in human interests to maximise ethical positivity, starting with the preservation of what good there is. Then, the tangents of liberty's normativity and civic utilities can grow and expand from a solid basis in accordance with harmonious liberty of ethics. Liberty can only be cultivated and instilled – not installed. Thus, liberty's normativity must first grow on its own terms of liberty through reciprocal values and vectors, being another primary or central principle of policy orientation and normativity in liberal democracies with proactive foreign policy.

Suppose this foundation of a protective and tacit, even withdrawn, mode of normativity of liberal democracies as *normative libertarianism;* the alternatives of such conduct can be explored at another time. Essentially, where a liberal democracy must primarily focus on sustaining its own goodness, at times demanding self-sacrifice to bolster its moral strength and character, it can engage with non-liberal democratic states if it serves the greater ends of justice. Rather than forcing normative and sociopolitical change in an unstable and volatile manner, the first approach of normative power is tacit by being inviting and inspiring, by nourishing and consolidating vectors of change in greater interest of all mankind. However, comprehensive accounts and studies must be done for any policy to be implemented effectively.

The basis of a libertarian normative approach, defined by central values of protection and tacit approaches, or any normative guidance of the policies of liberal democracies, will inevitably encounter the duality of interests – growth or protection, risk or security? Both conservation and progression are necessary for the sustainability and wellness of an ethical sphere. Respective policy is best implemented under the most appropriate conditions. There is no concrete answer beyond the priorities of central values. The only guidance to be offered is contextual on the measure of success that can be achieved in respect of risk assessment. For example, supporting democratic movements in other countries can be a good thing, but only when performed in a non-provocative demeanour. Regimes sensitive to liberties are made so for a reason, and so only domestic vectors of positive change ought to focus on creating change, the justice of which is only found through constructive utility and appropriate self-determination – that is, determination in the demeanour of liberty and democracy. Violent revolution can be a just measure of transition towards liberal democracies, but only when instigated by the passions of the people defying authority, not by foreign vectors driven by ambition and illegitimate exercises of power.

That being said, non-violence is ideal and preferable in all circumstances, although restricted in practice. Authorities can employ this principle through tacit and soft approaches such as non-military, economic, and direct normative measures of power, distinct to the normative elements of militarism, authoritarianism, and their variants of coercion rather than harmonious influence. Favour is given to principles of soft normative power and values based on the assumption of their greater degrees of stability as opposed to the usually chaotic tangents of violence and forceful, evocative policies and civic and normative utilities. So, instigating and heavily supporting destabilising regime changes without sufficient support and concrete normative influence is unadvisable, whereby proper and effective normative influence is only achievable through the willingness and determination of a people without active promises of support other than through appealing normative incentives such as of an economic and social nature.

The risks of destabilising regimes are too great, as their consequences will affect the international ethical environment and potentially undermine domestic cohesion. Where a policy undermines domestic social cohesion, such as with respect to the concerns for security or its ambition given disproportionate value, its worth contradicts greater sum interests encompassing all necessary elements of broader normative health. In other words, neither security nor selfish self-centric policy are legitimate in terms of the priorities of a true liberal democracy. The fear that finds strong authority and security appealing will gnaw on itself, as the lust of ambition's growing reach can poison the goodness of its endeavour and intent. These core ethical elements of morality and normativity must be balanced if their initiatives are to fulfil their potential and succeed.

The basis of any solution to conflict in a hierarchy of values, interests, and principles is mindfulness in policies attentive to ethical tangents and vectors from which the prioritisation of values becomes intuitive. For example, it becomes just and normatively correct for states to concede the limits of liberty's normativity in spheres that are not yet compatible with such values and principles. Where a nation must protect itself and its liberty, it is normatively permissible to interact with other species of regimes in order to preserve the greatest goodness, determined by Natural Law and the organic liberty of ethics' dynamics. However, the principles of liberty ought not to be undermined by countries of a similar orientation and disposition.

The concern for security ought not to be given detrimental focus at a disproportionate cost to combined normative policy amplified by alliances and combined resources. However, if the potential ally and supposed liberal democracy loses its character, then two mass vectors (nations) become less normatively compatible, shifting the focus of value towards more compatible vectors. A liberal democracy of lesser moral character is not as valuable to a liberal democracy as an alternative species of regime with a more compatible moral character and set of values. Although, in practice, one would expect this principle to be rare, as the moral character and culture of liberal democracies would tend to reciprocate each other more than alternative regime types by virtue of necessary social, economic, and normative contributing factors. Where unity is undermined between liberally democratic nations, value is to be sought through the next best source of positive ethical interest, which can rightfully be through another culture.

Nevertheless, ideally, common values and interests are amplified through combined effort and mutual understanding, all in service to, and in harmony with, the Human Imperative. This, however, is not always achievable, as moral character, virtue, and humanity is still incomplete. In the meantime, policy ambitions and values must work in their given paradigm according to which Fear requires greater mediation through the moral authority of normative guidance and moral intuition found in the discipline of ethical sciences. Opinions and actions have consequences and are not immune to consequences. Understanding these tangents and how they relate to and reflect their vectors is key to normative guidance. The bottom line for any authority dealing with competing values and interests is that the values sustaining, protecting, nourishing, and that characterise the nature of an authority are prime and central. However, their legitimacy, justice, and righteousness can only be established through honest introspection, study, and discipline. In time, this can become intuitive, and practice can make perfect.

This dedicated Chapter has explored the ethics of authority and power. Still, there are many unexplored elements and aspects of this perplexing and convoluted theme central to life itself. An analogy will sum up the arguments and thoughts. Where a precious and beautiful flower is borne of dirt and a seed, appreciated more where surrounded by a familiar desolate land, ambition sets itself to supplant a desert with a kingdom of life, forever fed and enriched by a faint memory of a sensation most uplifting. All soil becomes the province of hope for the greatest of life's beauty. If a weed surfaces, it must be severed without killing the roots of the flower sought to be preserved, or least to save the lot. But the fear of losing this prize will poison its grace, for the scent and spice of a flower can become the seed of a soul's tree of life. It is good and right to desire this growth, want it, pursue it. But such intent is only true where it grows from, and is moved by, high spirit longing for the purest moments of spirit's relief and elevation.

One cannot always be in a state of eternal peace, for its greatest form comes through struggle nourishing spirit and psyche in accordance with the ethos of spirit's fulfilment, then giving the momentary sensation of eternal peace sustained only by suffering in its image. The greatest of Harmony and eudaimonia is achieved in sum terms – in the self *and* the world to which one is bound to, to which detachment is only a beginning of something far more. Then, the most ordinary elements become divine. However, the soul, spirit, mind, and character must be whole and complete for the Highest Good to conjure its dream of life's richest vivacity, clearest in all questions and worries, compelling by any and all sensations and sentiments.

This divinity can emanate as a greater happiness of the freest and sincerest love, stronger than any and all anguish bound to the love itself. Its tears of joy and relief of having known the wonder of a part of one's soul in another will salt the earth of all pain's growth, for this earth from which such awe was born heartens with gratitude for the impression, inspiring to be vigil for all those who find a part of this soul in others. When one sobers from a lucid attachment and affection, with only the impression remaining, it grants impeccable insight. The utility of the past attachment unbound to the conditions of the presence of attachment can continue to exercise its positive power without corruption of Fear, to focus on positive elements in others, oneself, and the world without the cloud of Fear objecting to a greater goodness and strength. Power is the movement through which this growth realises and concludes itself, but only as a power of soul and spirit guiding the substance of its reality, not yielding to power disturbing, poisoning, and corrupting the spirit eternally moved by the soul's hunger for fulfilment and relief.

In Liberty, power serves the ambition borne of, and moved by, good spirit; this greater and higher power allows good utility, such as a form of love and attachment, to continue its positive effect without Fear sealing away its pain, to then use that insight, that pain, and its suffering's reward, leading to positive change in the world. A central value of any higher goodness forms the function of action exercising power. A set hierarchy of values is instrumental to any authority serving the purpose of bettering states of affairs and improving quality of living. The dynamics of power then affect those values, shaping the authority that makes an ethical environment the way it is.

But this power is bound to the material of the body and land.

Chapter 29:

Social Justice and the Ethics of Material Utility

Living and movement require power for their sustenance and continuity. The ambition and power of goodness require substance. Accordingly, material utilities as material resources are central to normativity and ethical endeavour. Human civilisation has thrived through the use of Nature's substance. We live in a material world that has integrated basic and complex technology into our being to the point of dependence. Mankind's hunger and ingenuity changes the world around it. This power is only utilised through ambition and desire in accordance with an ethical function. The consequences are global and profound. Modernity and future development will only be possible through a key element of opportunity through material capacities. As such, the ethics, normativity, and morality of material utility – that is, how we use material resources in accordance with moral values – is a critical and urgent subject to study.

Modern times are vibrant with discussions of the economic sphere and subsequent ethical connotations. The topics of social justice concerning the distribution of resources, fair and just societies, and civilisation's intrinsic reliance on material for development and livelihood are extremely complex and equally fascinating. Core elements of social justice and the ethics of the use of material relate to themes of economics and finances, subjects that deserve serious consideration. Material innovation and utilities support the foundation of global civilisation and individual welfare. Wealth has a fundamental value for people's well-being and its considerations are compulsory for any ethic and morality. The issue of 'moral luck' as the dilemma of moral judgement on, and the valuation of, persons committing wrong-doing in unfavourable circumstances, such as a starving child stealing, is a core example of the ethical significance of material utility. Moral discourse mandates the consideration of the capacity for action and associated influences on ethical vectors that are shaped by the *physical* possibility and potential to act. For instance, economic factors shape society and ethical environment, having profound influence on the formation of character and individuals. Questions of social justice require consideration of economic aspects. Any subsequent moral judgement and principle will have to be mediated with considerations of practical policy, as was argued to be the case in matters of governance and the normativity of liberty and authority.

This Chapter will focus on the fundamentals and basic principles of material utility; I hope to return to the subject another time to include more insight and knowledge on the relation between economics and ethics, to structure a *practical* ethic of material utility. Current efforts will focus on raising notable questions and points for inquiry to excite future studies, as well as outline fundamental moral principles of material utility. The present work will discuss the ethics of material utility and moral judgements concerning material utility such as 'poverty is wrong and undesirable', but will not discuss in-depth how exactly policy and practice ought to be integrated to achieve ethical goals – how poverty should be addressed. This study will inevitably consider the ethical tangents involved in the normativity of material utility. What is particularly interesting is how ethics and morality can serve the ends of profit and sustainability in terms of both material and sum ethical interests of the individual and society.

Discussions on the philosophy of material utility in terms of distribution and justice are incoherent without a convincing fundamental guiding value and principle. The Fundamental Principle of Living Beings functions to structure the ethics of any utility. The foundation of all aspects of material utility is bound to *ethical interest* in terms of ethical gain or profit (making ourselves better off) and the security of well-being. Any matter of justification, justice, or distribution of material utilities is found on the respective ethical interests of well-being. Key aspects of the ethics of material utility are based on the conditions of relevant ethical interests and desires. Justifications for material distribution accompany the tangents of ethical growth through the use of material. All such growth is found on self-interest, which can manifest itself or be maximised through individual focus or the focus of social and communal dedication. Self-interest can be maximised through focused individual welfare, or individual welfare can be maximised by focusing on the development of a good ethical and social environment. For example, the justification for equality is found on the belief that a more equal society serves ethical interests better.

The reasoning and thoughts behind the justification of modes of material utility and related preferences are diverse and numerous. To achieve and mediate greater material interests, the concept of *justice* is appealed to. Justice in ethics is the applied principle or value of mediating ethical interests and their causal tangents for harmony, balance, moderation, and efficiency in ethical development, all for the sake of greater ethical gains. Justice is supposed to make ethical activity and endeavour more efficient and more rewarding. To say that poverty is unjust is to claim that poverty does not make us better off. In terms of material utility, poverty is unjust because it is symptomatic of people's suffering, as well as causes suffering. Poverty further causes other social problems, such as crime, and is related to other imperfect aspects of society, including poor education. However, deep inequality is usual a consequence of the necessity of inequality for the sake of greater development. Liberty in people's entrepreneurialism leads to ingenuity and the diversification of free markets. People who are driven by profit, often related to the desire for financial security and comfortable living, are encourage to innovate and produce something useful for the public through liberty. This can lead to inequality. The justice of this inequality then depends on the balance between progress and making people better off, such as development in proportion to the suffering of inequality.

Entrepreneurialism and liberty in production can enrich people's lives, whereas deep inequality can lead to suffering. Justice is then balance between what enriches people's lives in proportion to the subsequent suffering. The production of wealth is unjust if it causes more suffering than goodness. The *social justice* of material utility is, accordingly, concerned with mediating and balancing welfare and resources towards fulfilling greater ethical interest. For example, a position of social justice may favour social investment to alleviate the symptoms of poverty through appropriate policy in order to make society as a whole better off. All and any discussion of the ethics of material utility is a discussion of well-being influenced by material resources, measured and valued in reference to a particular ethic and ethos. The goodness of any mode of material utility, such as a theory of social justice, is judged by the goodness of its effect on well-being in particular conditions of an ethical environment and stage of development and ethical adaptation.

Applied principles of social justice are found on property rights. A *right* is an applied value and moral principle and a civic utility – an agreement – invoked and guided by moral authority. Rights are employed as normative principles shaping civic, social, economic, and political well-being. Property rights are civic utilities affecting and constructing the parameters of how society and individuals deploy, and engage with, material resources – the material sphere of ethics. Property rights are not mere figments of hypothetical social interactions and agreements, but are concrete ethical elements and tangents of moral authority according to which respective vectors operate. When moral authority is contested, conflicted, or unconvincing, the dynamics of property rights are subject to competition in and through values. These powers are subject to Natural Laws. Accordingly, greater liberty of individual property rights is more associative of the efficiency of individual autonomy, whilst more authoritative measures are reserved for the societal trends of less capable autonomy of the citizenry. Where individuals can self-sufficiently maximise their ethical interests through given resources, such as responsible and effective consumption, institutional authority can permit greater liberty of property rights and generally greater civic liberties. Authoritative measures, such as taxation and redistribution, or restrictions in individual and conglomerate rights, are enacted to moderate and mediate deficiencies in imbalanced liberty of material activity. Neither normative and ideational material orientation is inherently wrong; however, both are dualistic.

Sometimes the liberty of individual property rights and the initiative of production can lead to more authoritative and elitist states of wealth distribution, made so by the will of the majority at liberty to support a particular enterprise through individual consumption. When uncompetitive monopolies form to the detriment of society, and wealth distribution is inefficient, liberty may have been the cause of this authoritative state of affairs. When competition in material utility and enterprise is immoderate and uncontrolled, hierarchies and monopolies inevitably form. Economic activity in modern societies is very synthetic. Modern economies are established on the organic dynamics of exchanges in values – if people find use or value in something, which applies to both consumers and producers, they will buy it or invest in it (exchange their available ethical value and resources, labour or money, to get something worthwhile). However, in modern societies this dynamic is very synthetic, mostly due to technological advancement which includes advertisement and modern technologies, particularly the internet.

The global consequences of modern economic activity are far more sophisticated and synthetic, especially in relation to the consequences of economic activity on the natural environment and the issues of the sustainability of modern societies. Natural Law is in itself incapable of moderating modern economies for everyone's benefit, as the uninformed consumer will be deceived by a company, biased government lobbies, and corrupt information outlets, all to the detriment of everyone's greater interests. It is our responsibility to moderate the modern economies we have created, as the inherent synthetic structure of modern economies consists of sophisticated vectors (people), which can only be effectively and efficiently influenced through human means. Information and ethical insight guiding material activity become particularly relevant. The Laws of Nature apply in the sense that the lack of competitiveness leads to the stagnation of a society, nation, and economy, but only if competitiveness is the means to innovation and progress. If the liberty of competition and innovation bestows power and wealth to particular vectors and groups, which liberty inherently does or is supposed to do, then the shares of power, through material resources, become concentrated, creating a less free and more authoritative state of an ethical environment. In relation to the utility and merits of both liberty and authority, freer or more authoritative states of material utility and the distribution of wealth are good or bad depending the circumstances and conditions of an ethical environment.

Democratic and authoritative modes of social justice can restrict individual liberty to achieve greater social balance and more effective wealth distribution, supporting the necessities of liberty and development as a whole. When liberty benefits an individual at a disproportionate (and unjust) cost to everyone else, therefore damaging the ethical environment, then this liberty is inefficient, possibly unsustainable, and not good. Governments, public groups, and social movements can enact policies or influence certain interests to mediate the dynamics of values, including the exchange of values. This is more authoritative than liberty. However, this measure can moderate liberty and competition, therefore making them more sustainable and efficient. The relation between the liberty and authority of values and ethical interests is at the centre of the ethics of material utility. Any policies, principles, and values are measured in, and with respect to, their given circumstances. Rights, laws, and policies are the utilities influencing, enabling, and causing material states of affairs and wealth arrangements. Their purpose is to generate ethical profit and positivity – to make people better off. The value and quality of any mode of material utility, whether it is more authoritative or liberal, more equal or unequal, depends on its ability to generate ethical goodness.

Any notion of property rights suggests *ownership*. Mankind owns nothing, with notions of ownership only found on the power of what we can move. Where people's reach over material is global, societies combine their efforts for common greater gains where this is just and righteous. These conglomerate vectors then become shaped and influenced by moral authority and ethical forces. All material is inherently of the universal substance of reality, over which mankind can only claim ownership through the moral authority to do so in terms of our values. The opportunities created by material utility and the capacity of material utility grant mankind the right and legitimacy to use material substance in accordance with the soul and its Imperative. This premise is not established on the thought of 'doing something simply because we can', but suggests our right as living things to use the world we inhabit, and are created by, towards our ends in accordance with the Human Imperative. The justice of any such right in practice, however, will be mediated by Natural Law enforced through, say, environmental consequences of malpractice and negligence.

Mankind does not own the world or its substance, yet we are of the same essence and made from the same substance, and so we are part of it. As the body can use its own arms and legs, so too can the body of a living thing use the substance of the world. Mankind can claim a utility through what we can command, but any such power or ownership is lent from the world itself, of which we are but another part. Therefore, when it comes to individual person's claims to ownership and using certain material or representations of material value, we inherently do so through

Nature and the Highest Good. This dynamic of values is then mediated through the relevant presiding moral authority. Claiming ownership and the use of certain material is based on individuals' claims that their use of material makes them *and* mankind better off – benefits them *and* others. The foundation of the ethics of material utility rests of Natural Law and moral authority, which means that respective and antecedent principles and values apply.

The design of this principle of humility and commonality is intended to foster harmonious dynamics between substance and the intent of the soul, as objects and material ought to only serve the betterment of the will to flourish, not suffocate it. Then, what mankind can command is determined by the power to do so through values and morality. These natural rights operate differently in more sophisticated ethical structures including society and institutions. Moral authority, which underlies the agreement with rights, laws, and just practices, becomes the essence of material activity, as any relevant value will affect actions and behaviour employing a material utility, whether this utility is a necessity or a luxury. To say that the individual has particular property rights is to concede or consent that the individual's will to influence specific objects or substance is reserved for his or her own determination. Claims of individual or social rights of material or enterprise suggest unity or commonality in the mutual or combined ability to influence material. To grant individuals greater property rights is to place trust in the liberty of their autonomous virtue. When this mode of material utility and distribution is undermined by vice, then the liberty of autonomous production and consumption becomes corrupted by lesser values and character. The intended end of all modes of activity is well-being, the justice of which can only ever be truly found by appealing to the Human Imperative and when satisfactory in terms of maxim interests.

The matter of equality is a common issue in discussions of wealth distribution, social justice, economic activity, and material utility. To claim that equality is good or valuable is to posit that its applied utility is beneficial with respect to the Human Imperative. Human nature is diverse and its moral culture is determined by majority values and the contingent mass psyche and moral culture. Only a society with a majority valuing equality can sustain it, which is only achievable through coherent and complimentary values and principles guiding behaviour compatible with established civic utilities of society's institutions. Only a society that agrees with equality and embodies compatible values can create sustainable equality. The same idea applies to liberty and an unequal society. The intentions and values behind any movement – towards greater equality or liberty – will shape the corresponding structures of ethics, determining their fate. However, the character of the citizenry is often at odds with absolute equality and complete freedom, with pragmatism sometimes settling for the base and natural ethical value of recognising *fundamental* or *basic* equality and liberty. Liberty and equality require each other in different degrees for the sake of greater progress in advanced stages of ethical development.

In accordance with the Fundamental Principle, any mode of social justice and the corresponding degree of equality or justified inequality is only as good as the mode's efficiency and fulfilment of ethical interest – that is, ethical profit and the capacity to generate goodness. Therefore, any principle of equality is only as good and valuable as its capacity to fulfil ethical interest. This, however, is conditional in terms of the character of the citizenry and dominant values. Greater degrees of equality are only as good and fulfillable when dominant vectors can cultivate and sustain material interest according to the corresponding mode of economic activity – one compatible with, or complimentary of, equality. Equality is only possible when people not only desire it, but when they are genuinely capable of it. Due to the complex nature of concrete manifestations of the civic of equality, it is something to be achieved, like liberty, but not taken for granted. Equality is more synthetic than narrower individualistic ambitions and self-interest, as the latter is easier for the undisciplined and fearful mind. Hence, the first or base mode of social justice is inclined towards valuing the liberty of progress and competition over equality. Until people are capable of effective and sustainable equality, the inequality of ambition and ingenuity will succeed. Then, the ethical value of greater degrees of equality, as well as the measure of the goodness and justice of equality, is found in its utility to generate greater ethical interest for all in terms of the sum maxims of ethical interest. If a better state of ethical environment can be cultivated through lesser degrees of equality but greater material efficiency, then this is more ethically valuable and more just. The same applies to equality, which has notable ethical benefits in terms of securing a stable foundation of society and normativity, as well as providing the basis for maximising the efficiency of civic and civil liberty. These points will be expanded on in due time.

Life consists of material substance and is fundamental to the soul and continued living. However, the insight of structural ethics finds ethical interest to be determined by more than financial statistics alone. One becomes stronger and richer in spirit when material utility is known to be but a single part of the soul and not the absolute definition of well-being. Ethical, material, and social ambitions function in accordance with the pursuit of well-being. The issues of sustainability and stability with respect to ethical environment and civilisation's reliance on material substance are grounded in the intended use of material – to cultivate well-being. The desire for sustainability and stability in ethical, social, and natural environments is based on the desire to profit – to achieve well-being, which inherently involves both the individual and society. Modes of greater equality might not be the most efficient in a purely economic sense, yet the relevant tangents are of much greater value and ethical interest. For example, greater degrees of equality might invest more directly in society and its development, thereby nourishing the greater goodness of liberty, social cohesion and harmony, healthy moral authority, and a generally more stable ethical environment. The truth of this, however, depends on the reality of the circumstances.

The profit of any material enterprise is key to the enterprise's success and sustainability, but excess profiteering can undermine other elements of ethical interest by failing to enrich oneself in other important ways. Great insecurity can only be resolved from within. It is *how* one uses material utility that generates the most ethical profit, which is what material profit is supposed to do in the first place. Ethical profit consists of more than just wealth and its corresponding desire manifests itself in many ways. Greater degrees of equality in terms of the pragmatism of ethical interest, not equality for the mere sake of equality as a principle lacking social utility, can serve greater ethical interests with respect to the foundations of harmonious society, individuals, and authority. The application of equality as a policy in response to the conditions of ethical environment, however, is more circumstantial and case sensitive than any hypothetical principle idealising the use and distribution of wealth. The Natural Law of equality and social justice depends on the conditions of Nature and ethical environment.

The role of every individual acting on the global ethical environment and society is meaningful, relevant, significant, and important. Every individual influences the world around him or her, and every living thing is of a soul of the world and its Highest Good. People are not of equal value in relation to other people and the Highest Good of the Human Imperative. Yet, nonetheless, every person has a fundamentally notable and consequential value. This value can be observed in many ways. Others people's value is inherent even in terms of how we treat others and how this reflects and shapes our character, especially with respect to how we treat those from whom we have nothing to gain, yet everything to gain through virtue. Every action affects and shapes the global ethical environment. The personal sense of significance in relation to the Human Imperative is not the foundation of personal happiness and fulfilment. True happiness and fulfilment are found in the virtues of good spirit and goodwill, which only use the Human Imperative. The Human Imperative is a utility; its promise of fulfilment comes through the humanity it evokes in us. Individual values, principles, ambitions, interests, and hopes affect behaviour and reflect character. Subsequently, ethical causal tangents are produced by the corresponding ethical functions and their quality. Some interests and ambitions are driven by the desire for profit and security, while other values reflect a greater view of ethical profit and security. Neither is inherently evil; only in objection to Natural Law and when morally corrupt do attitudes lose their positive utility. The global welfare of human civilisation is the primary interest of the Human Imperative. This necessitates individual welfare in proportion to global ethical welfare, as every individual is part of our shared ethical environment in terms of cause and effect, gain and loss, fulfilment and suffering. The consequences of one person's habit on the other side of the world in relation to the natural and social environments are real.

An individual's ambition to profit can in theory be structured to benefit the Highest Good. Indeed, while this point may be contended, modes of material utility have succeeded in advancing mankind to the modern age. The self-interest of profit is as good as its capacity to cultivate goodness. The corruption of self-interest – selfishness – is caused by the lack of virtue and unwise morality. Excess Fear leads to corruption and self-deceit. The self-interest of profit and security is only as good as its security from self-corruption and self-decay by undermining greater security, welfare, and well-being. The value and utility of personal profit is borne of the desire to succeed, which is central to Liberty. With this comes the fear of failure. This fear can be corrupt in two ways: by making us too idle or by feeding insecurity.

The fear of failure keeps us in a diminished state; insecurity further reduces character, leading to the fear that craves status; both are natural reactions. By acting on each type of the fear of failure, rather than making them *a part* of ambition and success, we betray ourselves. Trying to succeed in Fear without overcoming it never quenches the motivating desire and is ultimately futile. The fear of failure stops us from growing. When we act on its insecurity, we lose parts of ourselves to Fear. By striving for personal profit without care for others, in order to gain status and power over others, people only feed Fear and reduce themselves. In doing so, people enslave themselves to Fear and gain no virtue or identity of notable worth. By giving away a part of ourselves to the corruption of Fear, we gain nothing of worth, as this satisfaction is vain and hollow. One may feel unstoppable in a moment of success in Fear, yet that person is only being used by corrupt Fear enslaving him or her to act without final fulfilment.

Profiteers that act without regard for others' welfare and the Highest Good are weak and cowardly. The consequences of individual suffering on behaviour and state of mind then affect ethical dynamics, leading to the stagnation or loss of everyone's ethical interest. For instance, the act of an insecure, petty man leading to another's frustration can cause another to smoke to deal with stress. The psychological harm inflicted by the character of vice can fundamentally damage someone, preventing the harmed individual from fulfilling his or her potential and picking up some bad habits. The long-term consequences of mental self-medication, which become necessary for the immediate survivability of people living with great distress, affect social performance in terms of health and individual capacity to act on virtue, as well as affect wealth distribution when people squander their greater long-term interests in favour of the perceived immediate necessity to self-medicate.

Profit for the sake of security and comfort is valuable, intuitive, and essential for the foundation of individual well-being and maximising individual potential through opportunity. This book was only possible through sufficient, although uncertain, financial security. However, the ambition of Liberty aspires for more than basic security alone, willing to take risks to gain more, finding fulfilment in the challenge and in the journey. Liberty thrives through adversity, including financial insecurity. It is good for people to experience moments of uncertainty and threats to financial insecurity, as this builds character and insight. However, as a lasting state, this is not good. Profit, as a measure of sustainability and utility, and personal financial security are vital for welfare and development. However, their value is based on the ends of ethical profit. Risk-prone behaviour and the desire to profit over the concerns of security are not prevalent or dominant attitudes, and perhaps for good reason with respect to cognitive biases. Development and progress would be hectic without order created through aversion to loss and uncertainty; the lack of concern for security would in general terms lead to greater losses through recklessness. Concerns for financial security, particularly in relation to moral luck and the state of an ethical environment, generally lead to better ethical development of both people and their ethical environment.

Financial security and sufficient wealth generally produce better ethical activity and increase the chances of moral behaviour. However, excess wealth can also be corruptive when people pursue great wealth in accordance with a disproportionate desire for financial security. Sometimes good intentions and good faith are not enough for moral behaviour, especially when people don't have financial security and are starving. This sets the precedence for alternative, pragmatic, and circumstantially more efficient values and modes of sustaining goodness in endeavour – wealth, profit, and financial security. Sometimes the best way to encourage moral behaviour is to provide it with, or to consolidate it with, a solid incentive. In certain cases, if not the usual trend, good material utility and moral conduct are achieved through personal profit and security. This is not wrong, unless this ethical disposition is corrupted. Personal profit can be structured to fulfil many greater ethical interests, but only through moral authority and compatible incentives. The concerns of personal security and profit can be structured into social and civic concerns and incentives where their ethical interests are outlined and highlighted.

Values and orientations of ethical attitudes towards material utility differ. Integrating the desire for personal financial profit and security into a structure of ethics is wise. However, the desire to profit and to be financial secure is far from perfect, as is clear in free market modern capitalist societies. On the other hand, orientations of values in material utility focused on societal welfare, focusing on social security, also aren't perfect. In accordance with the Human Imperative, any mode of material utility, personal or social, is as good as the utility it provides and how it makes us better off. The two major modes of material utility focus on the personal or social aspect. Respectively, these modes focus on liberty or authority – capitalism or socialism. The success of either material attitude depends on the dominant values and characters – on people. Socialism would intuitively seem to satisfy the Human Imperative more. However, there are some notable issues. For one, excess equality can undermine the effectiveness of liberty's organic utility. After all, entrepreneurs and talented individuals require sustainable liberty to maximise their potential in all people's interests, achievable only through the socially just inequality of liberty. Some people's work is more important for everybody's welfare. This point that is intended to challenge the idea of absolute equality, however, isn't intended to challenge pragmatic interpretations of social orientations of material utility.

The desire for personal success through great wealth and financial security is symptomatic of instincts, especially in relation to social status and significance. The desire for equality is also often symptomatic of instincts and concerns for social status and opportunity. The satisfaction of Fear, instinct, and base ego is not just if this minor satisfaction undermines ethical efficiency and effective material utility. More so, base interpretations of justice are usually corrupt and can be very divisive. Base claims of justice can lead to deceitful claims of entitlement lacking or even obstructing justice. The conclusiveness of such claims, however, can only be established in practice and in the reality of states of affairs, with ethical wisdom and moral principles providing guidance for the evaluation of what is just. The malleable and impressionable nature of mankind shapes the character of people in relation to a given ethical environment and individual experiences of life. The character of people, the stage of ethical development, and the conditions of ethical environment determine the effectiveness and efficiency of any mode of material utility. Modes of material utility, people's attitudes towards material substance, and corresponding values and their integration, implementation, and the structures of their ethics depend on people's character and nature. Individual values and dispositions, expressed and embodied through people's character and values, are central to modes of material utility and their structured values. Material utility is competitive by virtue of competing values, interests, and desires, shaped by the adaptive cycle of values. Social justice as an authority must then balance competing values, vectors, and dynamics.

Every tangent of material utility is enacted by the attitude of the individual towards consumption. While a person still lives he or she requires degrees of material attachment in order to sustain livelihood. There is wisdom in traditional practices of material detachment including fasting and humility. However, there is little strength to be found in constant starvation. Mankind suffers when it is impoverished in wealth and spirit. Material attachment to, and the security of, the basic needs of survival and sustainable living are good. There is virtue to be found in the wise use of substance. There is spiritual fulfilment to be found in a dual relationship between the soul and its substance. Harmony can foster a profound connection to substance and material. Harmony evokes a sense of universal unity, commonality, and belonging, through which even the experience of something simple like the refreshment of drinking water can become more meaningful and fulfilling. Self-centred personal satisfaction is not as satisfying or meaningful as returning goodness through the goodness being consumed. For example, not only does the self-sacrifice of charity foster the spirit of Liberty, it also develops Harmony with the world through care and love for the substance which gave birth to one's soul. Consumption should never be about guilt, and never should one feel guilty about the Fear that arouses the desire for security that is instrumental to sustainable good living. Fear in itself is not bad; moral corruption – the failure of ethical functions to fulfil goals and achieve well-being, which inflict and maintain suffering – are bad, which can apply to both Fear and Liberty.

However, there is much more to material consumption than just sustenance. Physical substance, whether it is a drink or digital art, can enrich people's lives with fantastic experiences. Certain philosophies value detachment and material humility. Letting go of these values, of their guilt and restriction, while balanced with values of harmony and compassion, allows oneself to experience other great joys that are not spiritually corrupt. Everything is a matter of utility and ethical interest – our bodies are, we are, other people are, and the things around us are all utilities serving our ethical interests and the desires of the soul. A straightforward principle is found: every action is an investment in ethical interest, in oneself and others; choose wisely.

Every experience created by the use of material is an experience of living and of the soul. However, all such goodness is only as good and free from Fear as it returns this goodness into the world as investment performed in goodwill. With respect to the Human Imperative, we have a duty to protect and nourish the world we live in, according to which consumption becomes necessary as an investment for greater return. Investment into the ethical environment through oneself and others, in accordance with the Human Imperative, creates a better ethical environment. Even if the consequences aren't immediately sensed and the rewards aren't immediate in terms of the broader environment, the investment in one's own character and spirit is. Charity and acts of undermining direct financial security work by investing other aspects of ethical interest into something that produces greater rewards. By acting against the reluctance to destabilise financial security, particularly through charity, a person strengthens his or her character to act beyond Fear and despite the subjugation of Fear. However, this is only good when it is wise and when it is not reckless. In turn, however, this inner strength of spirit, character, and morality can then lead to discipline and wisdom that enables better financial performance, such as the discipline to not spend on vain and unfulfilling things. We have a duty to do the best we can in our given circumstances – to do what we can. The measure of virtue in material utility and wealth distribution is the amount of ethical profit produced through one's endeavour for others in proportion to oneself. It is moral and good to give more than one takes. One day, when we fulfil the Imperative, perhaps we will no longer need to consume. However, until then we must consume in order to reinvest material and channel it towards something greater, to achieve greater returns in ethical interest.

When the use of substance exceeds necessity, and when material utility begins to exhaust its ethical positivity due to corruption, greater flourishing is undermined. There are many positive aspects of material consumption and production, such as medicine. Social and financial security are good in many respects, especially in terms of social development by nourishing future generations. Some may oppose a link between spiritual fulfilment and materialism, yet the connection between the body and spirit is the embodiment of the connection between the soul and the substance it is made of. It could be said that material attachment contradicts the mindfulness of detachment. However, finding balance between the two and employing material utility with mindful ambition should lead to greater wisdom and ethical interest. Moderation and balance are necessary for the best use of material. Virtue and spiritual liberty come through willpower and autonomy. This growth cannot be achieved through attachment to material consumption in disproportionate Fear, especially when attachment is a distraction from emptiness. Mindless and impulsive consumption often lead to the loss of greater ethical interests. For example, consumption that damages the natural environment and the unsustainability of certain habits are real threats caused by people's lack of discipline and awareness. Then, the other major elements are the ignorance, apathy, and lack of self-discipline of consumers that don't hold enterprises accountable to moral standards. The individual's decision always has consequences. Where a decision enables corruptive tangents of bad enterprise through bad consumption, the world suffers. Every dutiful individual has a moral responsibility in his or her habits of consumption. The liberty to act on said duty is an expression of virtue, character, spirit, and the power of autonomy. We often fail to act on our greater ethical interests, whether in terms of the natural environment or civil society, by supporting companies with bad policies through our consumer habits. Fear holds us back and deceives us through comfort and ease. By having the power to overcome Fear, we can fulfil our greater ethical interests.

Spiritual liberty is felt through the sense of strength and autonomy to act on our greater interests and desires, to defy fear and pain. Sometimes we want to be entertained and distract ourselves. This in itself is by no means bad. However, this can lead to certain bad habits, particularly when it leads to spiritual stagnation, neglect of our greater well-being, and settling for lesser happiness. It is good to be happy and to do what makes one happy, but only when this happiness is true and not a mere distraction from true happiness. When we want to comfort ourselves and experience joy, we can be easily deceived. We can buy things that make us feel better for a moment, but in doing so we don't necessarily improve our condition and don't become stronger or grow in spirit. Other people can exploit our unhappiness, and none become better for it. By failing to properly deal with our unhappiness, we can consume material substance, whether through buying luxuries or consuming food that is bad for us, without actual fulfilment and resolution of suffering, sometimes to the point of recklessness.

Momentary joy can be good and it can enrich one's life; distraction is good for a moment of rest and relief; but this is only true while it leads somewhere, while it serves a greater purpose. Distraction and joy are only good up to a point. Rising above depressive and unfulfilling habits is good and awakens a sense of inner strength through autonomy that becomes fulfilling. We better ourselves and act with greater virtue by not succumbing to the Fear that preys on us, that betrays us and itself. By resisting temptation and momentary distraction and by standing up for our greater interests, such as not supporting a company with bad values and of poor conduct, we enrich our spirit and live better lives. The discipline to act righteously in the face of impulse and compulsion evokes a strong sense of self and the subsequent spirit of Liberty. But then not overburdening oneself with responsibility and duty, to simply enjoy a given moment, is also good.

Many things are good in moderation. Basic pleasures are good when they are not corrupted through excess and disproportionate Fear. However, temptation of material consumption can lead to wrong-doing or actions against one's greater interests. Not enabling immoral or undesirable modes of enterprise by withstanding temptation, steadfast against the nuisance of immoral material activity, is more fulfilling and more rewarding. The momentary spiritual and emotional fulfilment of pride, strength, and power then leads to better environmental consequences.

The immorality of enterprises, profiteers, and free market economies is not unnoticeable. It may be easy to criticise and assign blame to conglomerates abusing their positions of power. However, often it is the consumer that enables such practices and corresponding states of affairs. It is the citizen of a nation affecting the state of governance and socioeconomic order that enables the corruption of material utility. Apathy, symptomatic of the lack of moral authority or the weakness of authority, leads to social and individual suffering. Immoral and ethically inefficient material utility leads to everyone's loss. The selfish mind consumed by Fear and greed will never be fulfilled, as selfish behaviour is created by Fear and suffering that cannot be relieved through selfishness. Selfishness can never lead to contentment, as excess Fear will always linger.

The order of Fear and corrupt base morality often values selfishness as a virtue. Being manipulative, cunning, greedy, ruthless, selfish, and egotistically competitive may seem the tradition of competitive markets and their socioethical environments. Their consequences may lead to the fulfilment of the basic goal of immoderate wealth accumulation, yet leave one bereft of many key aspects of ethical fulfilment and profit. Selfishness alone cannot nurture a truly good ethical environment. The only worthy power is power of goodness and virtue, which selfishness and its veil of Fear can never achieve. The only worthy power of wealth is found in the ability to create goodness for the self *and* others, to build and nourish what is truly good, to express virtue through goodwill and not submit spirit and humanity to moral corruption. Power is more valuable than wealth, and the worthiest power of wealth is found in goodwill and good spirit to make the world in the image of virtue. The guiding values and principles of material utility are found in this sentiment and virtue-rule: the values of responsibility and duty. The lack of duty is a lack of virtue; the lack of virtue is a lack of strength and is of lesser spirit. The true worth of wealth is the ability to use it with goodwill and beyond the restrictions of Fear. Yet material utility is necessary for growth and life. Therefore, we ought to be mindful of duty and responsibility in our consumption. Personal responsibility and duty also means being mindful and restrained in our anger. Public outcries and backlashes can be mindless. Where anger is provoked by the perception of injustice and immorality, of power given to persons undeserving of its piety and responsibility, one ought to be mindful of the intuitions of Harmony – defy the vice and find peace through empathy. This is the true power of virtue and good spirit, through which better material use and conduct is achieved.

Competitiveness is an instrumental part of wealth accumulation in modes of material utility characterised by liberty and self-determination. The Human Imperative encompasses the individual and global society. People are inherently individuals, and mankind is still fractured, lacking a binding common authority. As such, competition is inevitable. Competitiveness as a utility regulating ethical development and free markets has its merits of organically balancing values. When material innovation, progress, and liberty is undermined by uncompetitive monopolies threatening the liberty of enterprise, the utility and value of material liberty is diminished. Nonetheless, the achievements of modes of material utility at liberty are many. The moral, ethical, and spiritual element of competitiveness, however, is another matter, which this work will focus on.

Competitiveness may ordinarily be ascriptive of instinct and base morality. Many elements of competitiveness are good, although susceptible to corruption when lacking virtue. But the greatest aspects of competitiveness are the ambition, motivation, and drive to improve the self and to grow. Furthermore, ingenuity thrives through adversity, including constraints and the need for resourcefulness. Sometimes constraints, such as an authority, and restricted financing help drive good competition.

Friendly competition in good spirit and goodwill can benefit all involved. However, competitiveness can be extremely corrosive, especially where ego is fragile and sense of self is not empowered by virtue. Where unhealthy ego erodes the good spirit of competitiveness, further threatened by an immoderate desire for power and status, the efficiency of competitiveness is undermined. Competition can be sensible and good, but only if just. The justice and utility of competitiveness is only as good as its fulfilment of ethical interest, which is evaluated by a number of contributing factors and ethical elements. The lack of moral authority that should guide the performance and conduct of an enterprise and any endeavour leads to ethical underperformance where values are deficient. By failing to act with greater ethical interests in mind, both the consumer and producer suffer from ethical deficiency or loss. The goodness of material utility and its competitiveness needs ethical and moral development. The virtues of discipline and mindfulness can help balance competitiveness in both the individual and socially.

Global competition as an ethic guiding material utility and enterprise has led to success and progress. This ethical dynamic, however, is created by inequality and has inevitably enabled degrees of inequality. Some inequality allows for positive utility, while also casting the shadow of severe inequality such as poverty. The economist will raise the valid and appropriate discussion of which policy direction serves best the interests of alleviating poverty. The present effort is not dedicated to this matter. Ethical evaluation and moralising concerns itself with different matters.

A certain line of argument may validate the case that momentary inequality and even poverty, while far from ideal, are conditionally good. Wealth concentrated in a just and righteous mass vector, such as a prosperous nation or company, can lead to smart, wise, and good investment in regions desperately requiring development. Alternative modes of material utility and their distribution might not be able to achieve the same level of development or as efficiently. In the present context, it cannot be conclusively argued which mode of material utility is better, furthermore as the truth of economic philosophy is conditional on the state of ethical environment and the stage of the adaptive cycle. The insight or principle to extracted, however, is that social justice can be maximised through flexibility and adaptiveness in material utility. Competitive material utility and its justice involving inequality are just and good in proportion to the utility's capacity to generate ethical interest, particularly in terms of global development. Competition may be good and just despite the momentary existence of poverty, provided this is intended to be a momentary state of development, if the concentration of wealth is *reinvested*. Wealth ought to be reinvested, and not merely redistributed, as the former is aligned with the Human Imperative and individual interests of a good and healthy ethical environment. However, selfish and egocentric values driving competition can warp the justice of competitive material utility. Competition can give rise to its own form of indirect global cooperation and collaboration through mutual development and organic exchanges of ethical values and interests. The harmony of this mode of justice is threatened by immoderate Fear and vice. The safety net of opportunity and basic equalities can secure a foundation from which the liberty of ambition thrives. Moral authority as common good faith, empathy, and goodwill can mediate the skew of corrupt elements of competitive ethics.

How exactly ethical interest is maximised through the practices of material utility and relevant policies, such as how poverty can be eradicated, is a different subject matter which cannot be fairly addressed in this project. However, economic policies benefit from ethical insight and a hierarchy of values serving the fundamental goals of policy initiatives and their formulation and coherence. Individual concerns of welfare can fulfil common interests through profiteering and development. Material utility is intended to benefit development, progress, security, and growth. The pragmatic aspect of material utility – how ethical profit is created from and through material – is the most important. People inherently value material, and certain individuals are very capable of generating material profit and development. But the material sphere, which consists of dynamics of exchanging and interacting values, is inherently competitive and fluid. People are at the centre of this, and when people want security or growth, in global terms, people's liberty allows them to fulfil their own interests and benefit others. People's liberty in consumption and production is far from perfect. The inefficiencies of liberty in material utility can be amended through clear moral values and interests to the benefit of the individual and society. Even though certain inequality and the liberty that leads to inequality, by virtue of ambition, can be beneficial to all, certain degrees of inequality lead to other forms of inefficiency in material utility and social prosperity. Equality and inequality are not inherently good or bad; moderation and balance of the two is more flexible and adaptive. The merits of inequality as a consequence of the liberty of ambition are intuitive in terms of development and progress. However, this principle and value should not lose sight of the issues of inequality and the problems of immoderate and unjust inequality.

Deep inequality can only be tolerated as a necessary state for the ultimate goal of global development. Inequality could be made sense of, and justified, in utilitarian terms; if certain inequality leads to everyone's long-term global benefit, then it is just. However, poverty is an immoderate form of inequality, it does not serve the Human Imperative, and it ought to be addressed in equal consideration of development. Poverty is only justified in proportion to the distribution of wealth; if no one is rich and the availability of resources doesn't make anyone particularly well-off, then poverty can be justified. Concentrating wealth in a certain utility or group, creating a degree of inequality, is then just if it serves the end of alleviating the suffering of poverty. The justice of inequality or equality depends on the efficiency and effectiveness of corresponding ethical profit. It is best to invest and concentrate wealth where it can be used with the most ethical efficiency. However, the suffering of poverty and the further deficiency caused by poverty challenge the justification for inequality and the corresponding liberty.

The troubles, deficiencies, and suffering of poverty are many. Poverty is fundamentally related to conflict, extremism, stagnation, dehumanisation, inefficiency, weakness, powerlessness, and immorality. Poor people are not inherently immoral or weak. But considering that people are usually susceptible to the influence of extreme Fear and pain, especially when people are not given the opportunity to grow through education and good and stable socioeconomic nurture, trends of immorality prevail in poverty. Immorality grows through ignorance and disempowerment. Accordingly, does the existence of poverty justify its related liberty? Poverty causes fundamental global ethical instability. An impoverished individual on another continent turning to extremism can fundamentally affect the course of a nation through Fear and terror. Severe inequality can undermine the growth of a generation and certain communities. People in neglected and impoverished communities find a way to survive through crime or gain a sense of power through extremism. The consequences are divide in society and distrust among people, causing certain classes of people and elites to protect themselves, leading to further insecurity and deficiency. This is not ideal and is far from good. Whether poverty in relation to the liberty of growth is proportional and ethically, socially, and economically effective in relation to inequality is not something that can be concluded on here. But considering that poverty is such a fundamental factor influencing society and ethical environment, it warrants central consideration in ethical evaluation and the practice of material utility and economic policy.

Justifying poverty can lead to a slippery slope of moral reasoning and corruption. Relieving poverty can create better social cohesion, alleviate extreme ethical tangents, can increase innovation through giving talent and genius the liberty to emerge and grow, among other benefits. Society and human civilisation are shaped by the adaptive cycle of values and mandate the order of adaptation. Adaptation happens through vectors, whereby the chances of good adaptation thrive through liberty, by giving people a better chance to act autonomously, and by allowing good values to be consolidated. Making the concern of relieving poverty a central aspect of the ethics of material utility can fulfil and maximise people's utility otherwise wasted to crime, suffering, and despair. Paying attention to poverty evokes and cultivates other related virtues such as empathy, compassion, wisdom, and duty, rising above Fear.

Using one's position to help oneself and others in goodwill is of noble character. People may strive for status and security through it; nobility is the truest answer to that end. Where both the rich and the poor are divided, the moral authority of empathy and nobility can bring greater harmony and justice to these practically inevitable inequalities. The disadvantaged may simply wish for a better life, to give their loved ones and children what they never had. The prosperous and those with opportunity may seek more in life than unsatisfying security and the shroud of Fear. People with the opportunity to act on the greater good can enjoy the power of the Highest Good and reap the rewards of its great spiritual strength and nobility, finding a notable place and eminence in society by virtue of duty to the Human Imperative. Those who help people and society become more valuable because they offer more and produce greater goodness. This nobility can then inspire hope among the disadvantaged, align people with a good and benevolent moral authority, and truly help them through opportunity and empathy. People usually embody certain values of pride and strength, which can include virtues or the vices of ego and spitefulness. It can be somewhat common for people to refuse help when they need it or could have benefitted from it greatly; I have certainly been guilty of this. These attitudes can be addressed and relieved through Harmony as humility and empathy, through compassion to oneself and others, to find unity in the kindness of absolving common pain. Often the people who want to help others are driven by a certain desire that can only be satisfied through kindness and compassion; it is wise to accept their help, in doing so helping them, oneself, and other people.

An environment of good faith and goodwill can be cultivated through moral strength. This accord is righteous and effective not when people are forced into action, but through the self-determination of a concern for humanity and duty of the Human Imperative. This self-determination could potentially manifest itself through persons launching initiatives aligned with moral authority, enriching the spirit and ego with far more than anything Fear could offer. This point is not intended to suggest any preference in policy or political orientations. The point raised is a moral and ethical one that stresses the great value of self-determination and liberty to act with goodness as a more promising mode of noble, just, and righteous use of wealth. One must then consider the competing values between liberty and equality in another framework of understanding.

Liberty can lead to inequality by enabling mistakes. Poverty may be the fault of society and of individual vice. Liberty to make mistakes, however, is necessary for the organicism of adaptive values, the suffering of which is acceptable but far from ideal or gratifying. Personal vice may be a major contributing factor to states of poverty, especially in terms of poor personal finance. First, these vices are bad when the person affected by them suffers; judgement ought to be reserved and patient. It could very well be the case that persons unable to secure a solid financial position are victims of high social costs including the need for significant spending to alleviate pain. Material utility can provide comfort that is instrumental for good development of character, whereby this investment is good if it leads to the cultivation of virtue. Higher morality would argue in favour of good and responsible personal spending producing the most achievable welfare and holding competitive enterprise to account. But the reality of states of affairs is hardly ever ideal.

People are unable to care for a higher sense of morality where they can't afford to live with decency and basic comfort or where this comfort is constantly threatened by a hostile social environment. Enterprises can achieve advantageous social positions to the point that people depend on certain products and cannot easily hold enterprises to moral account. When the basic needs of modern societies, including energy and the internet, become monopolised and uncompetitive, people cannot act on higher morality when their basic needs can't be fulfilled through competitive consumption. It may be the case that people struggle to eat healthily because the circumstances of living make this difficult or practically impossible. The fact that people aren't able to provide for themselves does not warrant judgement or scorn towards them. People's disadvantages leading to strenuous financial circumstances does not make people any less deserving of humanity, empathy, and decency, or that their suffering can be ignored. Wealth can grant power and opportunity to pursue and abide higher morality, while more challenging circumstances make higher morality more rewarding and more meaningful. Pain can make people depraved and wicked.

However, in pain people can also show the best of humanity, validate the greatness of virtuous character acting in greater justice, and demonstrate the steadfastness of virtue challenged by anguish, making people evermore noble; such is the virtue of the damned. When corrupt enterprise monopolises on the basic needs of modern societies, and government institutions are ineffective and competition is unbalanced, it will take dire, desperate, if not deranged virtue for the moral consumer to reject a great part of his or her life. Practically, though, this is impossible and cannot be appealed to as a moral standard. But telling a person that can barely afford to feed his children, or who cannot live a mentally sound life without significant recreation, that his spending habits are wrong is unwise and probably wrong. Indulging a warped and primitive sense of status and nobility in terms of financial advantage is ridiculous and petty. The sense of status found in personal pride of the strength and courage to help others is a sign of nobility.

Excess personal wealth may seem unjust. The present discussion is not intended to vilify fair abilities and ambitions that led to major success in wealth accumulation. There is absolutely nothing wrong with the endeavour and ambition of accumulating great wealth if this is done righteously and virtuously, with any talent warranting a degree of admiration. Furthermore, the ambition of certain individuals and groups leads to the creation of enterprises from which all society and humanity can benefit.

However, the concentration of wealth in people who fairly achieved their wealth can lead to the idleness of wealth and to vanity. Material utility is unjust if it is not used mindfully and reasonably, which includes not sitting on a pile of gold without investing it into personal betterment and development in accordance with the Imperative. Idle wealth beyond basic needs and proportional comfort does not serve the interests of the individual or mankind. A foundation of wealth is not idle when it serves the purpose of sensible and proportional security. However, excess security is a corruption of material utility. There are many ways idle wealth can be used for both personal and social welfare. The use of wealth in accordance with personal values and needs, which may not be known to others, is valid and good provided it is just. Possession of great wealth is not something warranting or deserving any guilt or shame, but only if such a position was achieved through righteous ambition and just conduct.

However, the justice of concentrated wealth can be dubious. The natural inequalities of people's abilities and strengths that produce states of major financial disparity, subsequently consolidating unequal distribution, may be justified and just, yet of lesser justice and less efficient. The circumstance of one's birth and the associated moral luck are often a key factor in the determination of a person's future. However, the power of one's will, ambition, and perseverance can make more of oneself than the circumstances of one's birth. This attitude can evoke virtue rising above the unfavourable circumstances of one's fate, further strengthened and made the most use of through fundamental equality of opportunity. Justifications can be made on any state of justice or injustice, but it is the ambition of the individual that elevates him or her beyond settling for the justifications of the state that can be overcome – if this state can be overcome. This is the prize of liberty, but not its promise.

The spirit of Liberty thrives with ambition when Harmony is too complacent and idle for a person's own good. Liberty in material utility and its inequalities are the most organic path in the modern state of Nature and human civilisation. Those deserving of greater goodness are made so through the liberty of their efforts and work that bestow on them their value. Some may inherit fortune and certain advantages from birth. But the liberty of morality moves character to act in accordance with corresponding values, forming the consequences of a state of living shaped by moral fortune. Where the fortune of new generations is undeserving, fortune will be lost through vice, recklessness, and unfitting moral character. Those who do not learn the worth and power of wealth, accustomed to comfort and lacking the strength to pursue ambition, will lose it. This same liberty enables the justice of the ambitious to seize opportunity befitting their virtues and abilities. When those born rich squander their wealth, the ambitious and those deserving of greater material utility can benefit from this. This is the liberty of material utility and the adaptation of values in material utility. This point is central to any enterprise where people's incompetence will inevitably become an issue, especially where leadership is weak and unskilled. Those unfit for a certain role, who are ineffective in a certain position of the production of ethical value, can then abide liberty and fulfil their proper role and value elsewhere. Liberty is instrumental to functional and efficient competitiveness of material utility and the vectors producing it. And so, liberty and ethical organicism brings harmony and justice to unequal states of ethical environment.

Persons performing a highly valuable function may require significant reward to make their great effort sustainable. The mental and spiritual demands of strenuous responsibilities may necessitate great relief, such as holidays, making it just to spend and invest a lot to fulfil a vital but highly demanding role. Levels of stress ought to be reciprocated with necessary measures of relief, as all pain, especially of the body and baser self, ought to be relieved. Good health, physical and mental, is best to be maintained. Following the same principle, where practically just and achievable, every person's function ought to be rewarded sufficiently and proportionally in order to maximise efficiency. It is ideal, although practically difficult, for all mankind to live with decency and basic comfort and security. However, the state of the world, as well as the liberty of individuality and values, does not allow for such ideals to become reality, with the supposition and hope being that this state is momentarily necessary for development towards a reflection of something ideal. If the capacity of a person's behaviour is unable to mediate his or her earned resources in a sufficiently just world, then it is the liberty of the person's judgement to create the justice he or she experiences. If people are unable to spend wisely even though they are realistically given the opportunity to do so, then the subsequent suffering they may experience is just in terms of moral liberty. This wisdom is an extension of the insight that too commonly our own mistakes bring about the adversity we dread, giving rise to a cycle of suffering only to be relieved through goodness of spirit and will. Material utility is just, fulfilling, and rewarding when it does the goodness of relieving suffering in the most efficient way. Extensive material utility and capacity are of little worth without the virtues and justice of the Highest Good and Natural Law. A prosperous economy is weakened without accompanying good moral culture and social justice to uphold order, goodness, and secure a foundation for people to find a meaningful place, purpose, and function. It all begins with the ambition of self-improvement through the liberty of opportunity and ability.

The goodness of liberty in material utility and its proportional degree of inequality is not based on the vast wealth it enables for the few, but the positive influence it can have on development. The autonomy of wealth and its liberty in accordance with Natural Law is valued in terms of the positive influence of the organicism of values and their gift of talent, ambition, and innovation. The utility of profit is not in material obsession and vice, but excitement of reward through effort to better oneself and the world, to work and sacrifice in endeavour of the Human Imperative as the worthiest goal of all souls. The utility of liberty to profit is not in enterprise passing the costs of consumption on to others. The virtue of material autonomy is in pushing development and progress in all human interest; when this utility becomes eclipsed by inefficiencies, such as inequality, its justice is squandered. Of the core elements of these values is the certainty that the cost of enterprise and profit should not jeopardise the prospects of our children, as future generations should surpass their forbearers, not repeat the same mistakes. Society ought not to suffer from severe and dysfunctional inequality by the coercive determination of corrupt vectors of power or the institutions they influence, support, or subvert. Any distribution of wealth or its mode are only just if the consequences of self-determination produce greater goodness through fair inequality. However, failures and mistakes then should not become definitive of a person's life or become the absolute condemnation of a person to a life of poverty without access to opportunity for new beginnings, which may be the case for poverty. Imposing a system that rejects and undermines these principles will ultimately fall to its own corruption by suffocating liberty through authority lacking endowment by Natural Law. Liberty for the common citizen can allow him or her to rise to great wealth through their talents and ambitions, in harmony with adaptive and organic dynamics of values.

States of unjust wealth distribution, created through liberty of material utility, are consequences of values guiding and moving wealth. Any enterprise is only as lively as consumption allows it to be. Liberty may enable an unjust state of unconscionable and recklessly inefficient allocation of wealth in concentrated groups and few individuals. The values being considered are not designed to harbour contempt for successful individuals that have fairly come to possess extraordinary wealth; the designation of wealth is not in and of itself a point of judgement on character and moral valuation, as it is not the essence of spirit. The liberty of competitive enterprise is of a dual relation with respect to production and consumption. People buying into an enterprise enable its value. This dynamic of ethical values in material utility between production and consumption is governed by *moral authority*. People who find value in the material they consume influence the distribution of material through the liberty of consumption and production. While the individual consumer's degree of influence is contentious and minor in the grand scheme, it is nonetheless relevant and important in more ways than the individual might know. Every action of an individual becomes a tangent of ethics, with every characteristic becoming a vector of ethical causation invoking and responding to the influences of tangents. An attitude buying into a product – a tangent – shapes the vector that produces other subsequent tangents. The judgement to consume one product and support its enterprise will in some way reciprocate similar judgements, subject to exhaustive variables shaping judgements and their moral quality. What the individual does and how the individual behaves are important and matter, and the power of the consumer cannot be understated.

Attitudes towards particular elements of material utility set the foundation for subsequent and related values. Values that shape consumer habits are reflective of other character traits and mental and spiritual states. Where these values and characters affect ethical environment, they carry the tangents that others react to. Acting a certain way may suggest for others that this behaviour is appropriate and permissible. For example, this point can be summarised with a common notion that 'if I don't do it, someone else will'. Some may suppose that not acting in a certain way is pointless since majority attitudes and values will not change. This highlights the weakness of morality based on social contract. However, self-interest and the intent of virtue are served best when they are focused on self-improvement, not when fulfilment is based on the conditions of bargaining and contracts. The sacrifice of comfort and opportunity fulfils autonomy and grants great spirit to the ambitious, righteous, and deserving. However, this morality and its goodness, in general terms, thrives through a strong base of emotional fulfilment and good health, whereby actions committed in the character of hard morality are rarer and insufficient to be established as moral norms. The choice in accord of higher morality and of fulfilling spirit and autonomy will influence the state of an ethical environment that *will* invariably affect other people and their values and attitudes. Identity and character are sensed through actions; actions of nobility and strength influence the self and other people.

Is it wrong to allow or enable people to consume a product that is not in their best interests? Is enabling people's unhealthy or bad habits moral? A person will consume that which gives him or her value in the individual's judgement. That value may not be in the greater interests of the person; the person might be unaware or may disagree. Similarly, other people might not be informed enough have specialised skills and knowledge to make a truly good judgement concerning what is good for another person in his or her circumstances. A person with a destructive addiction suffers, meaning this habit is bad. A person with a bad habit might be resorting to a lesser, but necessary evil in a strenuous condition. It is the principle of liberty that people ought to find and live in accord with their values provided suffering is just – if suffering does not eclipse goodness. If people's bad habits lead to social decay, and if this is just, then this liberty that leads to decay might have to be accepted if none else can be done without causing further damage, to then start anew with a firmer foundation of values. For an enterprise to produce something that is not in people's best interests, yet compatible with certain good interests, is a just form of liberty. As such, in principle, this form of enterprise and consumption can be tolerated and is acceptable.

However, the principle and value of liberty leading to unideal enterprise and consumption can be susceptible to moral corruption and slippery slopes of justifications. It must be stressed that while this liberty may be tolerated, this far from makes it truly right. However, every case of justifying certain enterprise and consumption will be different with respect to its causal structures and variables. The current study can only strive for a framework through which ethical and moral considerations can be effective, coherent, and intuitive. For instance, while supporting, assisting, and creating enterprises that do not give people the most value might not be completely right or of higher goodness, certain arguments can point out alternative values. Society and people have certain needs that only enterprise can fulfil. Competition makes enterprise adaptive through the liberty of the tangents of values and vectors. An enterprise that does not serve people's greater interests, yet of greater value and more aligned with people's interests than another enterprise – outcompeting an enterprise by providing more value – can be better and more just. The estimation of value in terms of the best of two choices applies here – in other words, the lesser of two evils. If 'I don't, another will' is a reality that *must* be dealt with, then it is best to be pragmatic. Then, the morally favoured tangent and vector, such as a conglomerate enterprise, profiting from an unideal enterprise can redeem itself and facilitate greater social justice and harmony by investing its fortune in other improvement.

The pragmatism of ethics and morality is not above PR stunts. Similarly, the individual can at times only do the best he or she can in unideal circumstances such as by working for a conglomerate of questionable morality, yet in doing so providing the security to nourish children with goodness and strong morality that will lead to a better future. To mitigate the effects of cynicism and suffering in society that may counter-act the positive effects of good upbringing and role models, or for society to support positive base influences, a moral authority is necessary, whether as ideals of morality or inspirational figures. Social elites of goodwill, good faith, and of moral power in accord of a just, righteous, and ethically appropriate moral authority can then create greater positive change for humanity through people who enable a moral and social elite's advantageous position.

The advantages and disadvantages of liberty in material utility have been discussed, yet insufficient attention has been given to matters of equality running against principles of autonomy and liberty in material utility. Any discussion of social justice and wealth distribution will have to address the common critique of welfare benefits and infringement on individual rights to liberty. Can the authority of the state exercise power over individual's wealth and earnings for common interests and to redistribute wealth? Is it right to support a public where it could encourage complacency and idleness – ethical inefficiencies? Any such questions will ultimately have to be weighed with respect to the variables of an examined case and in relation to the conditions of an ethical environment. Nevertheless, certain insights can be outlined to guide the intuitions of ethical evaluation and moral reasoning. Social security through welfare and systems of redistributing wealth may be argued to enable ethics lacking ambition and incentive. Certain cultures may find shame in living on welfare, while other cultures are shameless and irresponsible. The reality of any such claim depends on the moral culture of the majority of a citizenry, yet the thought is valid as its value is possible. For one, people's lack of ambition and incentive to succeed is often rooted in another function of ethics rather than mere laziness. The depressing and unfulfilling consequences of idleness are punishing for society and especially the individual. People suffer in unemployment. Stumbling through life without direction, illuminated by distractions of pleasures void of fulfilment, leaves spirit in the limbo of misery. Not enabling these ethical attitudes would be ideal, with the proposed solution being a compelling moral authority giving meaning and purpose behind actions. However, the lack of welfare also leads to insecurity in ethics, society, and material utility (such as in terms of opportunity and diversity). The final judgement must then be made in reflection of a state of ethical environment conditioned by whether or not basic welfare benefits are sustainable.

There is merit in the value of welfare benefits providing basic security for the public and consequently for the entire ethical environment. The principle conclusion is, therefore, that while public welfare benefits are balanced in terms of social and economic development – that is, welfare benefits and social security are sustainable – then this mode of material utility is just. The legitimacy to tax people's wealth in order to support society and nation is found in its utility and relating promise to redistribute and invest in the interest of all people and in terms of sum maxims of common betterment. It is the function of governance and institution to implement and mediate this in practice. As for individual attitudes, however, the ethos of Liberty would value the opportunity to invest in society towards the Imperative. The power of generosity, mercy, and duty to enact greater goodness is the most rewarding aspect of all material utility, with the provision of assistance to others being a privilege. Charity or institutional measures are relevant when it comes to considerations of the most appropriate mode to fulfil the end of social security. The more cynical and realistic approach, however, in line with previous arguments, would favour the institutional, authoritative mode, with charity being supplementary. That being said, excess authority, such as disproportionate taxation, can be divisive and cause discord in moral authority.

In conclusion to the matter of the functional relation between material liberty and equality, the two ethical functions and utilities ought to be balanced in terms of effectiveness and efficiency in the production of ethical interest and value – ought to be *just*. Justice includes the conditions and circumstances of an ethical environment and its Nature, particularly the state of the cycle of values and its stage of ethical development. Sometimes greater liberty is necessary, or greater equality is necessary for sustainable and effective liberty. Wealth distribution ought to be harmonious, fulfilling of human decency, and effectively sustainable, yet wealth distribution should not be strict and coercive, meaning liberty and authority ought to be just and proportional. Proportional degrees of equality and liberty are instrumental to one another and their ultimate function of material prosperity. Of all the insights to be taken in mind from the discussion thus far, moral authority and normative power as resources are imperative for the ethics and practice of material utility.

If society and state elect material profit over instruments of moral authority, the consequences can be terrible. If people choose material profit over sensible and just morality, neglecting other central aspects of well-being, then ethical interest is undermined. The result of a declining and failing moral authority can manifest itself as social discord and strife, leading to disengagement, apathy, and dissent in the form of tax evasion and corruption. Some ethical losses are too great and the security and profit of certain material utilities cannot outweigh moral value, affecting the success of enterprise. Some costs to moral authority are disproportionate, and the security or profit of certain material utilities cannot outweigh their normative influence. Consider the social utility of nationalised healthcare. The taxation necessary to support nationalised healthcare may be argued to infringe on individual rights of liberty and autonomy. Furthermore, the case may be made that nationalised healthcare could be economically and socially inefficient. Yet the benefits to social welfare and its positive impact on the security of moral authority and its mode of social justice and development can be tremendous. If a state is sufficiently wealthy, financially secure, and socially harmonious to have nationalised healthcare to look after its citizens through the use of common wealth, the moral authority of the nation can be seen to be good, just, and benevolent. The power that enables an authority to save and better lives encourages happiness and loyalty among the citizenry, even if this point requires rhetoric or reminding where it is taken for granted. Considerable financial expenses of national budgets can result in greater security of moral authority, subsequently producing greater social cohesion, harmony, and effective performance. The same principle applies to investment in education and fulfilling other basic needs through social security. However, any such claim would depend on a given moral culture and ethical environment. The practicality of these policies is relevant to the concreteness of applied ethics, yet the present context is focused on outlining a framework formalising the principles and hypotheticals of the fundamental ethics of material utility.

Where the moral culture of the majority orientates on the attitudes and vices of disproportionate self-entitlement and lack consideration for the common good, social benefits and welfare through institutionalised enterprise become threatened. Social, material, and ethical efficiency is further undermined. Accessible healthcare and education may be seen as basic rights in advanced modern societies, yet similarly to liberty, these rights are a luxury that must be developed and sustained. A strong moral authority and its support through and of positive affirmation of social and ethical successes can be used to address the inefficiencies of individual vectors of vice. The utility of a strong and virtuous moral authority can inspire in others a sense of pride, fortune, and facilitate loyalty to a righteous and noble moral authority. This ethical efficiency can further manifest itself as, for example, a person's belief in the goodness of a nation and society, worthy of an individual's labour and stress, including the willingness to pay taxes and follow laws. This moral order fosters a better ethical environment and social, civic, and ethical performance, establishing security and opportunity which invite investment and further development. Therefore, transactions involving short-term losses in wealth for the sake of ethical and social development can lead to greater financial and social security through moral authority, and therefore be more valuable.

The moral authority carried by culture also has a significant effect on society, nation, ethical environment, and moral culture. Setting aside the arguments of the economic benefits of certain cultural projects and instead focusing on the exchange of wealth for ethical and normative gain, culture is another aspect of investment affecting states of justice and related influence on people's performance. The prestige of art that turns the substance of the mind into physical form is precious to moral authority by influencing the world, people, character, and identity through the senses and the mental realm. Moral culture and its authority are channelled and expressed through art. Furthermore, art may influence sociopolitical dynamics by evoking certain sentiments and experiences that lead to good impressions, insight, and values. A wealth of culture affects states of values and influences moral authority. Culture is a fundamental aspect of humanity in spirit and psyche. More so, cultural influence can serve as a utility of moral authority beyond the borders of a nation and the reach of a government, to serve as a utility and medium of normative power. International economic arrangements can have positive effects on anarchic global relations by binding people to a common goal of mutual prosperity or common dependence. Through a cultural influence that is able to provoke shared sentiment and attitudes among people without significant financial material utility, certain political goals can be achieved, particularly when the jurisdiction of a sovereign authority restricts policies. Culture affects history and identity; investment in it rewards with other elements of moral and normative power in terms of a moral authority.

Culture in all its forms affects mass psyche and consumer culture. With the emergence of a globalised world, increased rates of education and literacy, and unprecedented access to information via media and the internet, consumer culture is evolving in accordance with values. People are in varying degrees concerned with social issues. Questions of sustainability and the environmental impact of consumer habits and the normativity of international trade are just some examples of people's concerns of social justice and social issues. It must be stressed that the present work cannot offer definitive judgements on the role of particular social issues and their ethical value, or claim which social issues and values are the most important to the consumer culture of certain countries. However, according to the theory of structural ethics, moral authority presides over consumer-producer relations and dynamics, with values guiding social awareness being a relevant factor. Even the disregard for social issues in favour of immediate comfort and basic interest is a parameter of ethical dynamics and moral authority in consumer behaviour.

Moral authority makes a product appealing and valuable to the consumer. With cultural, social, and ethical development, such as in terms of rates of education, literacy, technological innovation, prevalent ethical dispositions (e.g. apathy and the need for hedonism), dominant morality, and the distribution of wealth, greater ethical tangents will begin to affect consumer behaviour, dispositions, and values. Where the consumer might be primarily concerned with the quality and cost of a product, greater personal development bound to socioeconomic development will also expand the scope and measure of quality and cost. All products are based on ethical value. Quality may encompass socioethical concerns, and cost may consider long-term costs such as with respect to broader consequences. The interests of morally and socially aware consumers can then pressure competitive enterprise towards conforming and adapting to the liberty of morality. Moral authority between consumers and producers and the values and interests that guide consumer behaviour become a point of interest for competitive markets, notably where competition is particularly tense. The supposition is that ethical and socioeconomic development will influence consumer demands pressuring industries and services to adapt to the developing nature and quality of ethical values – what people see as valuable to their interests.

Good conglomerate moral authority in terms of values and *image* will become increasingly more important, with branding and common interest leading to loyalty and continued or renewed subscription to the product of an enterprise. However, only in greater virtue of autonomy can this ethic and mode of material endeavour truly succeed, contingent on consumer culture responding to the circumstances of an ethical environment. The extent of the ethics of apathy and distractive hedonism, or other ethical attitudes, further influence the state of consumer culture and prevailing moral authority corresponding to consumer-producer dynamics. Where scepticism is raised, further arguments will highlight the practicality and relevance of an initial hypothetical thought that consumer behaviour is developing in its scope of interests and concerns.

Ethical development is relevant to the interests of consumers and businesses. The most relevant foundational aspects of consumer ethics and interests have been explored above, allowing for the consideration of conglomerate interests. An enterprise can profit from the practicality of good moral authority and a normative image that attracts consumers. Investment in moral authority in relation to normative power through image and branding is another aspect of self-advertisement. Ethical interests and normative guidance of good moral authority can assist policy-formation and make company policies and functions more efficient such as in terms of human resources. Without extensive discussion and in-depth analysis, the following modes of investment can assist an enterprise through fulfilment of ethical interests and utilities. Charity is a traditional aspect of moral image. Yet social investment can be taken further and with the potential for profit where a company uses its profits for further wealth accumulation and social betterment through more specialised investment than charity. Benefits for workers, such as medical ones, may be an example of the suggested form of investment. The parallel interest of these benefits is potential improvement of the workforce such as in terms of healthier, more vigorous, and mentally sounder people.

This point, however, is very hypothetical. Nevertheless, additional incentives and motivating factors, including bonus opportunities for employees, can be good for an enterprise. Investment in the employee that assists the individual, and hence the public, is a form of social investment. Policies that follow the law (notably of taxation) and are attentive to public concerns and social issues are also points of ethical investment in moral image. The ethics and morality of material utility and enterprise need not be formalised and considered in terms of traditional or stoic morality, as coherent morality is found in pragmatic ethics analysing ethical interests and values that affect behaviour and socioeconomic dynamics.

Questions of sustainable profits will be immediately raised, and rightly so. Profit is a determining factor of an enterprise's value and sustainability. An excessive and erratic pursuit of profit in narrow consideration of ethical interest can jeopardise long-term and global sustainability, including the sustainability of the enterprise itself. The dull ambition of immoderate and unsophisticated profiteering can jeopardise the normative image of a company, having a cost where consumers and investors are deterred and uninspired. A balance between profit and investment is instrumental to moral authority and its form of normative image. A specialised or better social and moral image can attract particular character and consumers. Normative image is a form of moral power and ought to be seen as an asset to be invested in when possible. Material utility serves ethical interests; transactions in ethical values should be sustainable, profitable, and just. An imbalance in policy can lead to a company's deterioration, which means loss of jobs, loss of a potentially valuable source of material utility, loss in material wealth, and failure of a comparatively more normatively upstanding enterprise of greater value than its competitors. The reckless use of budgets can raise questions among investors that would be reluctant to use their wealth in areas of uncertainty. Among the competing interests of normativity and wealth, eventually, one will succeed over the other, subject to Natural Law.

An unsustainable enterprise will eventually stop; contingency plans are necessary. Where one enterprise ends, it can transform into another. Material interests can re-emerge through further investment succeeding an initial enterprise. The normative element that unites the interests of consumers and the workforce is another parallel of financial success and survivability. But where the material resources of production end, the normative image remains, the interest of which may foster new beginnings through the promises of a good reputation and the loyal support of common interests based on moral power. The value of the former is intuitive, but the latter is perhaps less so.

Good moral authority is valuable in terms of a continuous and loyal consumer base. Where brands are competitive, there are trends in human favour and interest, with the fashionable and familiar being examples of such trends. Loyalty is understood to be a form of attachment to a brand and a form of favour beyond occasional and singular purchases. This ethical feature of material enterprise has the potential of cushioning prolonged and stable profits, conditioned by the availability of wealth in the citizenry and consumer public. Normative enrichment and sophistication may increase the financial cost of a product and service. To mitigate this consequence, consumer dedication to a brand can be driven to accept the cost and continue supporting a product where common interests are satisfied. The virtue of consumer autonomy can influence behaviour to fulfil material needs and greater ethical interests, but potentially at a cost to material comfort and a base sense of security, yet more gratifying in valued virtues. Where practical and realistic, quality over quantity is a wise ethic. The fortunate are then at a financial, ethical, and social advantage to exercise power of and in goodness and noble status by using their wealth to support normatively better enterprises and maximise ethical interests for all. Where the leaders of a company are concerned with profit and wealth as the measure of worth, wealth in itself is a minor definition of status, as wealth is only a contributing factor to the normative power that enables fulfilment of spirit and ego.

Wealth leads to power, but the power of one's character aligned with the opportunity to exercise greatness and nobility is the most rewarding of people's autonomy and certainly stronger than Fear and solemn base compulsions of uninspiring ambition. Greater status is found in having something to give to others, something valuable. This personal balance and discipline in the vectors of an enterprise – responsibility among producers, consumers, workers, and profiteers – facilitates other ethically contributing factors that positively influence individual and conglomerate performance. These attitudes may enable broader intuition and insight that contribute to self-composure and ethically coherent company policies and actions, which include positive relations with consumers.

The other aspect of the beneficial effect of solid and coherent normativity is in terms of investors and market performance. Trade markets can be very anarchic and uncertain; security, risk factors, and the interests of profit are the guiding values (and very sensible ones) of wealth accumulation. An enterprise with a solid consumer baseline and the performance of which is effective, efficient, stable, and sustainable, risk factors can be mitigated and promote certainty. Normatively sound enterprises might not be the most materially profitable or at least in the short-term in the given global culture, but certainty in some form should nonetheless be appealing for investors. However, this greatly depends on consumer behaviour and culture, which is shaped by the structures of ethics, and the application and practicality of consumer loyalty is a complicated matter. Where the mass vectors of the consumer base influence company performance through ethical interests and concerns, the subsequent focus of development in competitiveness would include the product itself. The normative development of a product aligned with consumer values and interests would achieve an edge over competitors of lesser normative image and power. The hope is that this mode of material enterprise would encourage innovation that benefits enterprises, consumers, society, the individual, and mankind.

The benefits of normative enterprise can be highly practical. Conventional normativity of companies may be focused on survival at all cost and maximum financial profit. Just as Fear and base morality may shroud judgement and hinder greater ethical interest, the same effect translates into an ethical tangent influencing company performance. Here one can further discuss normative practices affecting company performance, which one could even argue aren't definitively normative. This discussion will make previous arguments more intuitive. Employees care about their work environment; conscientious people care about the morality and value of their employment. Both factors are relevant to keep human resources satisfied and effective, strengthening company performance. This point should be intuitive; its practice is beginning to evolve into new forms even as considerations of investment, as employee sentiments factor into their productivity[29,30,31]. Where moral authority is harmonious and normative image is binding in terms of both the consumer and workforce, the potential benefits to efficiency and effectiveness, such as through loyalty, are self-evident.

Morally upstanding people – of strong character and, in certain respect, better workers by the virtues of discipline and decency – are comparatively more valuable employees. While certain views may consider morality to be correlative of intelligence, wisdom is found everywhere. Less intelligent and less educated people are more than able to possess a good conscience and be of virtuous character. The opportunities and circumstances of people's education are not wholly definitive of their intelligence and moral quality. Intelligence in itself is not definitive of moral capability and the goodness of one's character. Where character is good and responsible, it is valuable as a human resource. These individuals would be more attracted to normatively upstanding companies and ethically harmonious work environments. Many disciplines and areas of study may contribute to the practice and betterment of good work environments, but a normative dimension is inherent. Formalising policies with specialised knowledge of ethical dynamics is useful for company performance, with the ethical and normative aspects of enterprise, in terms of the consumer and investor, becoming promising areas of improvement and investment.

In relation to the ethical dimension of employee performance, consider the following. States of affairs and the character of people produce and invoke values that correspond to particular behaviour. For example, hostile, aggressive, apathetic, and generally bad social and ethical environments fundamentally affect the quality of the citizenry and human resources. A majority of the public with such characters, probably of vice regardless of the circumstances, will affect work environments and interpersonal dynamics. A workforce of individuals easily provoked into conflict by insecurities and vice will have a negative impact on company performance. Impulsiveness and poor stress and anger management techniques, reciprocating and reflecting ethical dispositions and moral culture, will have consequences on a person's work ethic and his or her productivity. Vectors susceptible to the destructive influences of stress are vulnerable and may crumble. Measures that address such concerns should be of great interest for an enterprise seeking to maximise the productivity and efficiency of its work force, especially where talent and ingenuity are the foundational resource. The normative dimension of these policy initiatives is but one of the subject areas relevant to human behaviour. Social investment having a positive influence on an ethical environment lays the foundation from which human resources are employed, once again highlighting the dual relation between the public and enterprises, or rather between the consumer public, human resources, and conglomerates.

The discussion of the ethics of enterprise has intended to be introductory. The circumstances of this project could only afford to outline the foundation of structural ethics and its application. The main ambition has been to introduce a new understanding of applied ethics. Basic intuitions and assumptions will, hopefully, pave way for future in-depth study. The concern has been focused on creating a model of studying and evaluating material utility and maximising the ethical interest of material utility, as well as structuring what is in our greatest interest. I intended to show the possibility of greater normative coherence in modes of material utility, wealth distribution, and financial dynamics. However, one must be mindful of the importance of consumer culture in achieving any designed goals. Before any ethic of material utility is developed into a tool of normativity – a particular area of interest for further study – the influence of morality ought to align consumer culture towards a disposition exercising greater influence on enterprise and corporate ethics. Only with a basis of strong interests and incentives is this hopeful endeavour truly worth developing further.

The possibility has been hypothesised; theory should then be applied into practice and be tested, to then develop initial insights. More information is necessary to develop a greater model of material structural ethics, as the complications and intricacies have been noted even through basic suggestions. A focused work is more appropriate to the subject area. When an authority can begin to centralise, and influence, the vectors of consumers through values and coherent standards and rules, above all else as a trustworthy source and institution, then new development can begin to mediate and influence the liberty and dynamics of material utility. This development should improve on inherent inefficiencies and nurture a better global ethical environment in terms of modern civilisation's intrinsic reliance on material. Only the normative dimension of values and morality can shape and influence consumer culture towards a more efficient and functional mode of behaviour.

The public might not yet be sufficiently equipped to maximise its ethical interests in current ethical modes of economic utilities; some people simply don't care when they really ought to. Some people will be more normatively proactive when their competing interests and conflicting values are structured. The authoritative word of a moral institution that is trusted may be instrumental to the success of autonomous and liberal modes of material utility. Where consumer behaviour can be better understood and made more predictable by structuring values, dispositions, and behaviour, global economic performance can become more orderly and simultaneously adaptive. This, however, must all be considered within a disciplined study mindful of the potentially disastrous consequences of excessively synthetic intervention in the organicism of material dynamics at liberty. Ethical insight and moral knowledge have not been developed enough to make the normativity of economic and social performance coherent and effective through objective claims – through authoritative claims. Too many questions and points of inquiry must be integrated into a coherent and practical ethic of material utility, the study of which is severely restricted in the scope of this work, as knowledge and insight aren't sufficiently developed yet.

Normative power through wealth can be dangerous. Power enabled through wealth, particularly in the ethics of Fear and base morality, is susceptible to corruption. Where the main ethical interest is determined by immoderate and imbalanced values based on material profit, the vectors of these values can become very socially powerful and harness major synthetic power. People and conglomerates driven by vulnerabilities in Fear gain power through the mutual interests of profit and security at a cost of ethical and moral security, turning into weaknesses. Society may suffer when the synthetic power of immoderate wealth influences the state and governance; society suffers when this synthetic power is corrupt. The *lobbying* of government by conglomerates preserving their often-selfish interests are of great concern to society, material utility, and welfare. Conglomerates and corporations – mass vectors – can exercise tremendous ethical force, especially where the disempowerment, apathy, and ignorance of the consumer public and electorate enable such states of affairs and their causal tangents. Corporate interests and values can then become at odds with the ethical interests of a society and nation. Wealth accumulation and economic development ought to be in the interest of all people, but only in so much as these interests encompass greater sum ethical interests. Material profit is designed to serve an ethical function of profit above all else, which often becomes corrupt when immoderate. The modern age has made extraordinary wealth and quality of living possible; consequently, our vulnerability in Fear can become a weakness. The lack of discipline and mindfulness fails to moderate our excitements, whereby we lose ourselves and our character to Fear and hedonism borne of material luxury. The issues of the subject at hand have been explored in Section 2.

The potential consequences of excessive synthetic power affecting society should be intuitive. The bottom line is that lobbying of government to protect corporate interests at odds with the public, but only if said interests are at odds with public interests, is bad and does not serve maxims of ethical value. The main concern is that synthetic material utility that influences governance and authorities through proxy values can be detrimental to a society and nation, as economic success is but one sphere of ethical welfare, albeit significant. Lobbying follows the dynamic of competitive values and interests; this can be good and bad. The lobbying of values themselves is another area of industry competitiveness in terms of reciprocal consumer values and interests.

The problem at hand is that social and political performance requires material utility and resources. Every principle and value corresponds to, and requires, power in and of substance. Where modes of material utility are given liberty, the lobbying or influencing of sociopolitical performance will happen in some form or another. However, as these powers are tangents of values, they can be used towards good ends for sum maxims of ethical interest, but only by the vectors and moral culture enabling certain tangents. One especial concern is deceptive advertisement and misleading, manipulative information taking advantage of the public. These are synthetic influences categorically and intolerably eroding the truth of information, which is imperative for the success of liberty and the adaptive organicism of values and corresponding ethical development. Corrupt lobbying of media and disingenuous, biased, or erroneous information are detrimental to society and enterprise. The lack of ethical order in information is consequentially bad.

On another note, to further the case of the normative element serving the interests of enterprise, good normative practice and a good image of media outlets rewards with moral authority in terms of trustworthiness and loyalty. While intrinsic biases and inefficiencies will remain in any media service and company, normative awareness can assist in a crucial way by emphasising a value directly relating to the successful performance of an enterprise. However, due to vices and limitations in people's judgements and character, media outlets may profit from detrimental values and ethical functions. For example, the negativity bias may corrupt information and news by skewing it towards an audience reacting to fear through impulsiveness. Corruptive forms of Fear can move a person to focus on information egotistically confirming their beliefs, biases, and prejudices. In an environment of material dynamics at liberty, influence on consumer culture and investment in accordance with a good normative image are potential directions of policy initiatives. However, there is also the viability of authoritative measures involving regulation of industry and economic liberty; the value of such policies is only as efficient as its actual success of regulation. Scepticism is relevant and appropriate to both the liberty of individualistic enterprises and authoritative policies open to corruption and poor normative performance. Both liberty and authority can suffer from certain inefficiencies and flaws.

The liberty that enables the explored states of affairs and people can be used advantageously and efficiently. Corporate interests influencing the state and society are only made so by the wealth bestowed on them by a consumer base. Where consumer interests are opposed, value will be found elsewhere. Lobbying can be used to find favour with consumer culture and orientations, thereby giving a normative edge over competitors. This may come at a cost to enterprise, illustrating the point raised previously concerning competing material and normative interests. An enterprise's determined end is a reason for setting plans for future continuity. The seeming loss of short-term profit in favour of normative enrichment can balance the concern of prosperity by finding favour with a supportive consumer base, the profits of which can translate into innovation and industry development in a new direction, promising continuity. For example, people's anger and spite can be appealed to and monetised on against a competitor, whereby the value of one's product grows by virtue of simply not being produced by someone that is more hated. This is not ideal in terms of ethical interests, but it can be effective in the short-term.

Where people are aware that their consumption habits lead to positive investment, their greater interest may be satisfied, making them more willing to follow through on this investment. For example, unsustainable energy sources detrimental to the natural environment have an expiration date and do not fulfil all consumer interests. Yet these sources of energy are of imperative material value and are necessary for modern society. People's greater interests can be satisfied where profits are reinvested in new, innovative energy sources that are more satisfactory of consumer interests. The interests of an energy company built on unsustainable resources will have to innovate and evolve to survive. Considering that energy is necessary for modern life and consumers, reinvesting profits into sustainability can also appeal to consumer interests, whereby short-term interests can be aligned with the long-term interests of all people. Where companies and products compete, people's interests can be appealed to with the premise that, although the consumption and production of unsustainable energy is not ideal, at least a certain company is using its wealth towards something better, making it the lesser of two evils, so to speak. Accordingly, normativity in material enterprise can be compatible, useful, and profitable, as well as pragmatic.

Where lobbying is problematic, it can be used to bolster normative image and be rewarding through lobbying appealing to consumer interests. A company can secure its and the public's interests through lobbying the state in accordance with public interests, making the consumer public more willing to invest in that particular company, mediating profitability. But this is a necessity of pragmatism in liberal modes of material utility, and perhaps a better way can be found. This mode of lobbying is more organic and symbiotic of ethical dynamics, moderating synthetic influences. However, consumer culture and corporate practice have to be shaped into such a mode, which demands greater attention and further study before the practice of lobbying can be implemented properly, as well as be sustainable.

Consider the case of the United States' Federal Communications Commission's (FCC) decision to repeal Net Neutrality in 2017. The decision was very controversial and shady. The repeal of Net Neutrality would in theory financially benefit major Internet Service Providers (ISPs) by allowing them to monetise more on internet traffic. However, this would come at a cost to companies relying on the internet for their business and would cost the consumer more. Competition would take place between conglomerates. The interests of major conglomerates that would stand to lose from the repeal of Net Neutrality could lobby the decision just as much as competing conglomerates could. The lobby that was aligned with consumer and public interests could benefit itself *and* consumers and the public. This form of lobbying, counter-acting corrupt lobbying of government as well as actually being aligned with the public's interests, would benefit normatively and in terms of moral authority, attracting consumers through common values. If an ISP criticised the repeal of Net Neutrality, it would have gained support from consumers. Then, if Net Neutrality was repealed and certain companies decided to monetise on this, the ISP that is supportive of public interests, if it stood by its word and didn't repeal Net Neutrality in its company policies, would out compete other ISPs. If the profit of ISPs undermines the entire economy's performance, such as by undermining the profits of other major companies and small and medium businesses, on top of reducing consumers spending power, then this is economically and ethically bad and nonsensical. This is an example of normative lobbying and the application of ethics and normativity in material enterprise.

How can values, normativity, and morality be theoretically structured into a practical mode guiding consumer and business practices with positive effect? How can the *lobbying of lobbies* be implemented and used? A centralised, established, and perhaps institutionalised moral authority is a promising start to coordinate normatively positive enterprise and consumption. To influence the inherently anarchic element of free markets and the human factor of autonomous consumption, moral authority appealing to people's interests in terms of individual material needs and broader, even global concerns can be employed to produce the designed end. Measures compatible with the autonomy of consumers – that is, non-coercive ones – are forms of moral authority guiding consumer behaviour (hopefully) without immoderate synthetic power. Morally conscientious people who are aware of social issues may desire easily accessible, informative, and fair guidance on the ethical quality of a product.

However, not all persons are able to perform extensive research and complex analysis of volumes of difficult, biased, or deliberately misrepresented information. A reliable and trustworthy source of normative information categorising and qualifying the ethical value of a product, within full compliance of the liberty of autonomy, is a conceivable enterprise to satisfy such ends. Prior to the renewal of objective morality and normativity, and when ethical insight was limited, this wouldn't have been possible, complicated further by the necessity for a significant enough moral authority. A *normative rating system* or *moral rating system* evaluating and scoring normative performance is to be suggested as a medium for such an enterprise and service. Its dedicated purpose is to structure and formulate definitive values presiding over, and guiding, consumer-corporate dynamics and interests, to make the liberty of material utility, involving both consumers and producers, more efficient and effective.

There are existing industries and services that provide ethical evaluation, and ethical committees are not a new idea. However, the point raised in this book, and one that I would suspect many would agree with, is that ethical development and coherence have been lacklustre. My efforts have been dedicated to revising and strengthening normativity and morality through structural ethics and by appealing to the Fundamental Principle. I hope this work will provide the necessary ethical development and innovation of our values. But the other pivotal aspect of this goal is reinvigorating people's sense of morality and morally empowering the individual. Our values are based on incentives, and morality is no different. Due to the subjective views and understanding of morality and ethics, a binding moral authority has hitherto been practically impossible. Through structural ethics and Natural Law, this impediment to moral empowerment can be remedied. Or, at least people might be better-off settling for the next best dominant moral authority that has at least some binding moral power.

Challenges to initiating such an enterprise are many. The tangents of any value and ethic in practice are causally complex, demanding extensive study to get the facts straight and claims right. The development of a normative rating system deserves more attention and effort than can possibly be made in this introductory work. The ethical analysis of economic performance has a lot to consider in each and every case, with trends being circumstantial and temporary, similar to ethical conclusions concerning the political level of the structures of ethics. In simpler and isolated tangents, normative evaluation of enterprise and industry is contingent on right and wrong. Where we know what's good or bad, we can evaluate, judge, and decide. This, however, becomes infinitely more complicated when values interact. The most valuable thing is determined by the greatest ethical interest. Then, building on certain values, forming a hierarchy, competing values and interests can be mediated. However, certain material cost is too great to social and normative interests. So how can this be measured and evaluated? Only through quantitative study and by estimating the effects of certain practices and behaviour on sum ethical value, subject to risk-assessment, factoring in the economic consequences of ethical functions can this evaluation be coherent. This text acknowledges the question raised as the main challenge of establishing a practical ethic of material utility. Yet even the intrinsic uncertainty of risk-assessment does not make the conceived enterprise of the normative evaluation of industry impossible. Despite the significant challenges, a theoretical foundation should be outlined.

First, any normative and moral evaluation needs to establish values and principles guiding the judgements of right and wrong, good and bad – requires a hierarchy and structure. That which harms more than produces positivity is bad, with bad influence solemn being of utter evil; that which produces positive ethical interest in sum terms is good or tolerable, with higher and greater positive fulfilment of ethical interests being of greater goodness or even of the Highest Good. Then, these values must be considered in terms of broader considerations of justice and competing values. Where degrees of goodness are divergent or even contradictory to one another, justice is the measure of balance between ethical influences and values. Ethical analysis and evaluation must consider primary tangents relevant to a phenomenon or process in the world. If a material enterprise causes bad consequences that are not balanced by positive gains, then it can be concluded to be of negative ethical interest, and therefore bad. Bad consequences must consider the social as well as economic effects of an enterprise, meaning social performance and lobbying become relevant. This basic outline can serve as a prototype formula for the normative evaluation of enterprise. The model will be applied in a case considering the environmental impact of an industry to illustrate how it could work.

Damage to the natural environment can harm people; therefore, a policy that damages the environment can be wrong if it damages people. Where it does not harm people or its risk of harming people is minor or negligible, then it is tolerable and may be good if ethical profit is greater. Nevertheless, enabling even minor forms of normativity can grow into more significant tangents. Hence, even seemingly insignificant practices are relevant to evaluation and analysis, but only in comparison to primary and dominant ethical causal tangents. Uncertainties and the limits of insight into trends begin to factor in. An environmentally unsustainable practice is wrong as it will threaten the habitat and harm mankind. If development reaches a point that, say, mankind is able to inhabit other environments or colonise other worlds, then the positive gains are greater than the destruction of environment in terms of the exchange of values, therefore tolerable even though not ideal. That being said, mankind cannot yet fully or practically colonise other worlds; thus, relying on this positive outcome is very uncertain. Concern and interest should be placed where valid and reasonable judgement is more certain. If one can be more certain that damage to the environment will be detrimental to human welfare before mankind can overcome the corresponding negative consequences, then the normative conclusion is that the damage caused is unsustainable and wrong. Individual concerns of a disproportionate and unsustainable cost to global ethical and social environments is not the most fulfilling of individual interests. Therefore, these concerns can be negligible if they are established to be corrupt by reason of detracting from sum ethical interest. So individual interests of profit and unreasonable financial security are not sufficient reasons to justify corporate success over social welfare, unless company success also benefits society overall.

The interests of social and national welfare and prosperity, especially in terms of international competitiveness, are relevant to the evaluation of corporate interests in relation to the public. Dependence on energy makes energy companies important. Relations with other countries may be necessary for energy security and prosperity, conflicting with social normativity. Developed nations, if just, take primacy of ethical interest in terms of the Human Imperative, granting them legitimacy and the right to preserve their goodness – a goodness constituted by the positive effect of their enterprise and the goodness of their endeavour for the sake of mankind in accordance with Natural Law. The material security of one nation may supercede normative concerns influencing other nations, but only when just and of good normativity. This judgement enables the values of social security over certain normative ones, with the harmony of this normativity then becoming contributing factors to the domestic success of an ethical environment and material enterprise through the quality of the citizenry and human resources. Therefore, the interests of energy security as social interests are greater than the interests of harming the natural environment, giving the former primary value.

However, this merit is only true if social interest harming the environment is sustainable and of greater interest than social interest inherently dependent on the natural environment. Social and national needs of energy security justify their subsequent damage to the natural environment, but only in so much as the degree of damage is profitable and sustainable – that it is just. These aspects of ethical valuation and analysis of interests encounter the challenge of deeply contextual theoretical and hypothetical considerations, as effects on states of affairs and their justice are measurable in and of the world. Normativity and morality must develop through and from insight of the real world and be based on concrete facts; this requires empirical study, which can be challenging. Certain company policies or consumer behaviour may be unsustainable, but the effects must be considered in the concreteness of their practice for relevant ethical evaluation to be complete.

The use of energy has been instrumental to the development of modern societies, nations, and economies. However, questions of sustainability have now become central to ethical and pragmatic concerns. Balance between profit and damage can make competing interests normatively neutral. Hence, policy that causes less damage or invests in the development of efficiency becomes normatively positive, increasing the rated scales of an enterprise's normative stature. However, concrete study must be performed with respect to each tangent and each relevant industry to evaluate and measure where they stand on the balance of profit-damage interests between society and society's dependence on the natural environment. These considerations allow for the following general conclusion on the normativity of enterprise having an effect on the natural environment. Harming the natural environment is wrong because it harms people or has the potential to harm people, thus producing loss in ethical interest. However, the profit of ethical interest at a cost to the interests of an ideal natural environment may legitimise the primacy of material and social ethical profit and their corresponding values. Therefore, certain practices of material enterprise causing harm to the natural environment can be normatively permissible, classifying them as normatively neutral or positive. However, enterprise harming the natural environment and of lesser social interest – that is, unsustainable and unjust – is of negative ethical interest, and therefore normatively negative.

Consider another enterprise – information, news, and the media. The media, news, and other mediums of information outlets are necessities of developed, modern societies. However, consumer culture and the lack of company responsibility can lead to normatively negative modes of information distribution. Specific to this concern are skewed, misrepresented, or false news. People's confirmation bias feeds the medium of biased and ethically deficient and corrupt news, because this news fails to fulfil the ethical interest of truthfulness, which is imperative for the liberty of autonomy. The negativity bias turns news into sensationalism deprived of the virtue of disciplined and mindful information distribution, producing a scope of awareness focused on perhaps inappropriate and less important ethical concerns and interests. Consumer behaviour and interests that support the nature of enterprise abusing people's interests leads to negative ethical consequences unfulfilling of civic and public interests. It is apparent that biased media negatively influencing people's opinions and world views is ethically negative and wrong. However, the liberty of consumer habits produces the corresponding states of affairs, according to which it is arguable that enterprise only feeds on people's vices in the liberty to do so. In other words, it is the fault of the people and their ill-discipline that grants corporate corruption its perceived normative neutrality, in relation to which the enterprise is only performing its organic function. Therefore, the liberty of such an enterprise justifiably sustains it, as it seemingly serves people's interests. This point is only applicable where its negative effect on society is minor or negligible and only applicable to non-necessary products and services.

A product or service that is not of imperative value or is not a necessity may be granted greater leniency from strict normative evaluation. News is a necessity of modern and democratic societies. This necessity has been abused by corporate interests with a great cost to greater public interests of fair and proper autonomy, with the civic cost being greater than the profit of having certain media outlets – sum ethical profit is undermined or negated. Therefore, untruthful news can be evaluated to be ethically negative and bad. The social cost can be considered along one of the tangents perpetuating apathy and dismay instigated by sensationalised news and lies feeding off undisciplined and unmediated biases. The profit of this irresponsibility and maliciousness is wrong. Which causal tangents are primary in considerations of evaluation are determined by the potential and concrete consequences of a civic and material utility, even with individual reactions factoring into what ought to be investigated.

On another note, the nature of news selection, such as the selection of headlines and front-page material, is another aspect of the intuitive qualification of value and ethical hierarchy. What we think people will find most interesting and important, while quite subjective, is somewhat intuitive but susceptible to bias. The same principle, within a framework of normative guidance and the metaphysics of ethics, applies to normative evaluation as part of a system of rating. However, this system would benefit from greater coherence and structure.

Competing social interests and values particularly complicate normative evaluation and judgement. For instance, domestic public concerns may be focused on affordable luxuries, yet not desire for the working conditions producing these luxuries to be appalling. People might not want child slavery to be involved in the production of the phones they buy. Ignorance in interests and values creates ethical deficiency, with apathy leading to many subsequent bad ethical effects. Certain interests of consumers have to be prioritised, with the judgement of moral authority becoming greater than the judgement of the individual, permissible and possible through Natural Law. A normative rating system should point out the relevant ethical concerns, structure their consequences and effects, then strategise how to achieve the greatest possible ethical profit in a given circumstance. If it is better to buy more expensive phones that are not produced through child slavery, then this should be a primary concern in the evaluation of a product. Some people have the right to say what is good or bad, right or wrong by virtue of moral wisdom through objective ethical insight.

However, to mediate such judgements and not presuppose arrogance, the liberty of values must be maintained and respected, with any influence of a normative rating system serving as guidance and recommendation to be utilised by consumers and those interested. The service of normative guidance and recommendation should not be enforced. If the production of phones through child slavery is morally tolerable or permissible in people's views, then this liberty ought to be respected and accounted for. Policy can then be designed through established values. If cheaper products are made so by unfairly cheap and extortionate labour abroad, then the normatively better policy would be to pay a fair and liveable wage proportional to the needs of workers abroad and in proportion to economic conditions and possibilities of those societies such as by reference to their GDP. If a product's or its components production cycle is done abroad in a less affluent region, then the amount payed for this labour ought to be proportional and just. If a phone is being produced by impoverished workers in dire working conditions, and exporting this cost of labour to other nations is far more costly and unsustainable, then it is at least better to pay the price of the average difference – to pay slightly more for good ethical quality. In this case, it would be better to pay extra for workers to not have to suffer as much. But this has to be pointed out to consumers and producers. This, however, requires further information concerning the factors and circumstances of these states of affairs and relevant judgements. The implication is that many issues will be raised, demanding specialised study and evaluation. So for any system of normative guidance in the form of categorised rating and valuation to be effective and coherent, a forum and council as part of a general systematised thinktank will become necessary. Or, specialised knowledge and a database accompanying a hierarchy of values will be necessary.

The normative rating system is designed with the intent to also mediate and balance the influence of wealth on governance and vested interests – to mediate lobbying of the government. First, is it good for corporate interests to be relevant in the formation of policy? Is lobbying and heavily influencing state performance permissible? The mass vectors influencing government policy initiatives and their orientation of values is another area of ethical competition. The practice of governance and its politics, like most things, are contingent on material utility enabling vectors' efficacy and power. As such, lobbying and influence of material capacities become inevitable features of society and necessities of democratic performance. Democracy is built on funding. In the present context, I will develop arguments around this premise and focus on the normative aspect above other policy initiatives dealing with the issues of lobbying.

It would be ideal for intrusive corporate interests to not meddle in the affairs of the state and civic performance. However, this is not the reality of modern democratic societies. Moreover, the liberty that enables lobbying as a tangent of values can be used towards producing and consolidating positive ethical interests. The liberty of values and interests that underlies the functions of lobbying is a medium through which better values and greater normative interests can be promoted. Lobbying can become a means of satisfying consumer interests by counter-acting contending corporate interests through enterprise itself, with the vested interest of an enterprise being greater normative alignment with its consumers through trust and normativity. In this fashion, normative guidance in lobbying can show which values and policies competitive industry ought to embrace. As society and culture develop, values change. This change and the predisposition of values are subject to trends. Identifying these trends and their moral quality, such as whether or not certain values are good and sustainable, can provide companies with information useful for relations with the public and consumers.

The last aforementioned point raises the pivotal question of how to encourage and inspire people to *care* about such initiatives. The dedicated reader may see reason in the argument promoting the common interest of a better ethical environment. But the non-reader and the uninformed general public will not be persuaded in the same way. Furthermore, cynical attitudes towards mankind's state of moral culture are very relevant to realising the profound challenges of nurturing virtuous autonomy. Moving vice against itself by affecting people's emotions and ego – by appealing to base ethical attributes and functions – towards greater ends is a possible medium of influence.

The basis of this thought is that influence on moral culture and the mass psyche is necessary for greater normative change. Manipulation of base interests in compliance with higher values causing just or no harm to the person is a legitimate means of achieving the goal of guiding consumer behaviour towards good ends. People have desires and goals they act on, which can be observed in their behaviour. Helping them achieve those desires and goals through 'giving them a nudge in the right direction' is morally permissible if just. After all, is this not the nature of leadership? If people primarily act based on emotions, and the structure of this moral culture is fully understood, then appealing to the emotional aspect of people and their desires for the theirs and the public's greater interests is just. However, this sort of structural change is extremely challenging to pull off. Any such cause and trend can only be initiated, encouraged, and sustained through appealing values and interests that satisfy individual autonomy.

However, the people who think that they know what is best for others can be wrong. Therefore, any counsel of a normative guiding authority must be based on liberty, honesty, disciplined virtue, and adaptiveness. Structural change on such a scale may perhaps only be achieved through the influence of material utilities and their dynamics including lobbying. Values guided by and implemented through economic powers moving structures of ethics may be the best mode of structural – top-to-bottom – change that satisfies greater ethical interests. Thus, the liberty of lobbying may be the just medium to achieve what may seem impossible – to change the moral culture and character of a society. Lobbying is a medium of moral power. This power is subject to moral authority and Natural Law. Lobbying the consumer, enterprise, the general public, and government will be instrumental for the industrialisation of morality.

I will outline a basic blueprint or formula for a normative rating and evaluation system. The purpose of this initiative is to balance and mediate ethical inefficiencies and deficiencies of modes of material utility. First, one must establish primary interests and values, to then formulate guiding principles employed in normative evaluation and its practice. Values of contending interests must be structured by looking at their causal tangents, then measure or qualify their trends in states of affairs. These processes may include, for example, analysing political attitudes through democratic performance or examining the profit of an industry in relation to the social cost of damage to the natural environment. Categories of normative values then factor in other relevant ethical aspects including degrees of certainty, risks, effects on vectors and tangents of values, or unknown or obscure contributing factors. This sets the foundation for a system of normative guidance and evaluation.

1.   Consider a normative value and formalise it as a moral principle.
2.   Examine the interests of and in values, including relevant competition in values.

3. Qualify interests and values by studying their ethical causal tangents.
4. Consider factors of certainty, risk, and other relevant variables.
5. Through reference to relevant principles, conclude the primary and most applicable ethical interests and priorities.
6. Formalise values and interests into a digestible and applicable form reciprocal of specific challenges, concerns, and policy initiatives.
7. Integrate values into policy format as rules and advisory principles or guidelines in reference to the ethical purpose and value of an industry and/or service (e.g. luxury, basic or advanced need).
8. Evaluate company performance with reference to applicable values, interests, and concerns with respect to the degrees of an enterprise's effect on relevant spheres (e.g. energy companies' effects on natural and social environments, or the media's influence on society).
9. Conclude on the normative rating of an enterprise by studying its performance.
10. Outline areas of promise, interest, and value to the enterprise (use ethical insight and normative guidance to assist company performance such as by expanding the services provided and the quality of the product).

Normativity can be coherent and effective in guiding values, interests, and policies. Its application is relevant and useful to material utility. Liberty is important for the positive function of material utility, with corresponding inefficiencies having been discussed. This Chapter has sought to introduce some subject areas of ethics that could improve economic issues and concerns. The conclusiveness of these theories is to be contested. However, a start may be promising. All secondary ethical spheres – individual, social, political, cultural, economic, and so forth – are fundamentally interrelated and causally entwined. These dynamics and forces of a secondary ethical nature are found on the effects of the structure of an ethos (Core Principles) and key interests of, and behaviour in accordance with, Central Principles. Central interests and values inevitably compete through many mediums and across ethical spheres; the purpose of the Secondary Principles has been to understand and use these ethical forces to fulfil the functions of the Fundamental Principle – to people and the individual in society better off.

Part 4:

The Tertiary Principles

Chapter 30:
The Divine, Spirituality, and Ego

This Chapter will consider Tertiary Principles of the structures of ethics and their heritin interpretation. Tertiary Principles are intended to categorise personal, individualistic, or even private features of ethics and morality. As an illustration, the distinction between Central Principles and Tertiary is that the former is of the realm of moral law and, in a sense, supervenes individual interpretations. (The Central Principles may be understood better as analogous forms of Kantian Categorical Imperatives). Tertiary Principles are not as rigid.

The general theme of these principles encapsulates moral culture and relevant interpretations compatible with moral law of Core, Central, and, to a degree, Secondary Principles. Prior discussions have included points relevant to the design of Tertiary Principles and inevitably touched on moral judgements of a tertiary ethical nature. This Chapter will explore these themes further, with ethical and moral practices and beliefs being key aspects of study. Accordingly, the discussion will focus on religion, spirituality, and ego. The three mentioned tertiary aspects of ethics are not exclusively tertiary and are not the only major elements of Tertiary Principles. However, they will more than suffice as themes to explore and from which key insights and understanding can be found. Furthermore, it is a principle in itself that these aspects of life should be kept private.

The following meditations and study will not just consider heritin interpretations of morality and their judgements, as broad considerations befit proper discipline of structural ethics. General trends and insights are of primary interest. However, the heritin interpretation is found on core metaphysics of morality, with the discussion of religion, spirituality, and ego (as the element of psyche and spirit measuring the self) involving core themes of ethics and metaphysics in individualistic terms. The dedication of this Chapter is to examine the nature of beliefs and subsequent practices and values as part of moral culture arising from core and central moral judgements. Religion and spiritual practices, as well as their effects on mentality, worldview, and spirit, are excellent mediums for analysing moral culture. Furthermore, religion in itself is a fascinating aspect of ethics, morality, and philosophy in general. It deserves its own dedicated study. Spirituality is also deserving of a more personal note.

Liberty in morality and moral culture is an inevitable consequence of its function and a necessity for ethical and moral development. Where moral liberty is just and righteous, harmonised through tolerance, understanding, empathy, and personal discipline, moral culture benefits from diversity. Religious beliefs and spiritual practices are extensions of the liberty of morality and major elements of moral culture. Religion and difference in belief may lead to conflict where moral authority is deficient, personal virtue is lacking, and states of affairs are unjust. Thus, principles mediating differing beliefs and their morality are important for society and personal attitudes and growth.

Contingent on the principle of liberty and its justice, if a person follows their beliefs and does not harm anyone or disproportionally interferes with prevalent social trends and moral culture to a point of conflict, then the person's liberty and his or her diverse values and beliefs are to be tolerated and can be good. (For relevant values and principles, refer back to the principles of liberty). The personal attitude, then, is to treat such persons with absolute decency, rightness of virtuous character, and with humanity. Where character is at odds with others' values or people's attitudes are fundamentally different, then it is not a moral imperative to develop friendships, with appropriate and decent treatment of others being sufficient. The guiding wisdom of empathy is that there is always a reason for why people are the way they are and why their pain may lead to vice. Beliefs are products of experiences, impressions, and degrees of reflection and thought. The two contribute to the state of mind of an individual, to which a culture of virtue must respond by being understanding of others and to only intervene if justice of liberty demands it. Only where a value of a religious belief, formed or warped by an impression and function of the psyche, leads to immoral action does it require intervention.

Even characters of vice warrant patience and a disciplined approach. Religious beliefs as a part of moral culture are usually an extension of character and mindset rather than a binding authority of its own compelling character. Formal beliefs are not necessary for positive interaction or are definitive measures of a person's character. Extremes in morality and attitudes, derivative of interpretations of ambiguous and unconcise religious values, can be ascribed to modes of Fear, base morality, and discord in high-reason inflamed by vice. However, even morality aligning itself with higher functions can lead to lesser values or even immorality, as with corruption through the Void and unjust complacency and idleness of Harmony.

As with all and any belief and value, reason is primary. Interpretations of beliefs are derivative of character. Where base morality, Fear, and pain influence the psyche, moral culture and religious beliefs can easily suffer from corruption. Religious belief in Fear is a utility dealing with elements of Fear. However, this is not the greatest merit of spirituality. Merely being good out of fear of reprisal and punishment by the divine for committed sins is not a testament to true virtue; liberty of a person's will in dedicated accord with the pursuit of goodness beyond Fear is of greater virtue. Religion or other forms of spiritual beliefs may serve ends of both the ethos of Liberty and Fear, with the ultimate end being satisfaction of spirit through relief from suffering. Insights of Liberty have much to offer to that end.

Universally good ethical practices beyond moral formality – good by virtue of functions of shared intrinsic humanity – can benefit any ethic. Fear itself should not be judged, but its effect through character and action ought to be evaluated. Mindfulness is a means to balance, self-improvement, inner peace, and synchrony in all-reason, formally known as the discipline of Harmony in the heritin ethic. Fear ought to be made peace with and harmonised in thought, emotion, and morality for higher and greater spirit, as Fear will always be there, only dormant or set aside in relieved states. Belief as a mere substitute of Fear is not the greatest reward of spirituality and not most fulfilling of the self. Whilst Fear in religion is not corruption, with Fear in religion being a utility of pursuing fulfilled spirit through the succession of suffering in and of Fear, liberty of spirit is the ultimate end to any purpose invoked by spirit. Fear is not the end of religion and spirituality, only a state to be overcome.

Character, values, beliefs, and sense of self grow together into one's spirit as state of living. Where Fear and suffering are so prevalent in the world and among people, beliefs conform to these impressions as well as shape the experiences of these impressions. Accordingly, any belief closely bonded to ethics and morality, especially of a deep spiritual nature as religion may sometimes, but not always, be, is susceptible to corruption of suffering. This is a point imperative for all people and any ethic. One ought to always be mindful of personal limitations and maintain realistic expectations for others, with empathy, sincerity, honesty, fortitude, courage, and patience serving as prime virtues. Religious belief is not a species of corruption, yet like any ethic and utility of morality it can be corrupted. The cause of corruption, however, comes through core and central ethical influences or those responding to forces of secondary ethical spheres. Corruption of belief is only a consequence of underlying mental functions of ill-wisdom, suffering, vice, and vulnerability.

Any discussion of profound and personal beliefs bound to notions and senses of spirituality warrant excruciating self-discipline in mindful reflection, meditation, and analysis. Spirituality and its religious aspect is another mode of reason and an element of the psyche, suggesting that analysis and objective study are just as much a part of spiritual experience, or unless Fear and base morality corrode truthfulness and protest Liberty leading to particular beliefs and insights useful for any ethical, moral, and spiritual practice. Discussions must be careful concerning the philosophy of practiced beliefs, religion, spirituality, and the self that grows through these influences and continues them. However, this vigilance and patience is rewarding.

Beliefs and values bound to spirit can complete all and any doubt, make sense of values, and unite rationale and emotion. Belief is not only of hope and faith. Where liberty is brought to spirit and one finds a sense of self bound to the essence of the world and living, a species of spirit is evoked, one greater than its variant characterised by hope. Spirituality, conviction, and ego in harmony with Liberty produce something extraordinary and, in terms of the heritin interpretation, may prove to be the path completing the pursuits of Liberty and eudaimonia. This enlightenment, however, is only found as a consequence to virtue and dedication, as an aspect of spirit able to sense and understand it. Spiritual liberty cultivated through active and engaged living leads to a special state of mind and worldview formalising what has been called the heritin interpretation. It begins with the *soul*, with questioning what one is doing, why one is doing something, and what one desires.

All behaviour and actions can be reduced to the functions of the psyche and the Fundamental Principle – to pursue flourishing, well-being. The continuity of living in accordance with the fundamental guiding function – to flourish – as a substance of the body and element of the world is formalised in this work as the *soul*. All functions of the psyche corresponding to actions are aspects of the soul, embodiments of the soul, phenomena of the soul. Accordingly, as with all apparitions and phenomena borne of the psyche, beliefs are of the soul, are parts of the soul. The soul is not the mystery of consciousness; the soul is the substance of the world from which the individual conscious world – the spirit – is born. Understanding of the soul does not require any mysticism, while understanding the nature of spirit is a question of philosophy of mind and consciousness. This work is averse to mystification. A rational and emotionally balanced account of the soul, spirit, and psyche, mindful of sensations, leads to further insights. These insights are relevant to ethical study because their meditations allow us to apprehend the soul, form certain notions on the nature of human life in the world, and examine how some fundamental aspects of the psyche operate.

Certain functions of the mind lead to philosophical thought reflecting on living and forming religious beliefs. Mankind is distinct to the common beast by virtue of intelligence and the faculties of high-reason, even where undisciplined and under-nourished. Comparatively advanced intelligence and developed faculties of high-reason, coupled with baser faculties of the psyche, have ultimately enabled inward thought and for people to self-reflect. Mankind's uniquely amplified and deepened ability to cogitate in unison with self-awareness sets us apart from common animals. Meditation and profound thought creating the discipline of philosophy, consistent with mankind's more complex nature through high-reason, brought about elaborate beliefs, ethics, values, and sense of being. Religion and elevated spirituality as a function of the psyche may be reducible to humanity's unique traits. Evidence of this can be found in spiritual practices, be it fasting, meditation, prayer, or philosophical thought. These spiritual practices are not simplistic functions of instincts, even though their goal may be derivative of base morality. An instinct may spark curiosity of discovery and travel, it may motivate; yet instinct alone does not and cannot provide the efficacy and ambition of grand discovery and personal growth.

Clarity, peace of mind, and the sensations of Liberty can be instilled through spiritual practices. Where spiritual practices are performed correctly, they harmonise oneself and instil and inspire greater connection to the world in sense, concern, thought, motive, and ambition. It is not a blind assumption to consider the aforementioned elements as heavily engaged with and by the higher faculties of reason. Maybe this model accounts for certain religious interpretations being averse to the baser self and to what may seem as debasing instincts, with such shame being an aspect of the baser self suffocating higher spirit at liberty. Any accentuated phenomenon, process, and function of high-reason evokes higher states and sensations of spirituality. Any practice of mindfulness dabbles in this sphere of the psyche. Where mindfulness focuses insight and attention on experience of the self as part of the world, a great degree of self-awareness is generated. Accordingly, the nature of spirituality and its contingent beliefs must be a general sense of living, of feeling alive as part of the world.

Impressions left by moments of heightened self-awareness, mindfulness, and their spirituality shape the mind profoundly. Respectively, beliefs and values become influenced by these experiences and become extensions of the self as part of the world. Impressions found through personal growth and thoughts and beliefs influenced by ego create a state of mind projecting itself into the world and seeing itself as a particular piece of the world. Self-awareness and its cognitive functions are the catalysts for respective beliefs and states of mind and spirit. Thus, spiritual practices and religious beliefs are expressions of self-awareness, continuations of the self in and as part of the world. Where the mind and spirit develop a greater sense of synchrony between the world and the self, the numerous higher faculties of ego – the elements of the sense of self – are forged. By meditating on the soul and practising meticulous and extreme mindfulness, one discovers rich, higher sensations towards the self, beyond instinct and Fear. The soul and self are understood and sensed differently.

Through the metaphysics of the Fundamental Principle and by practising core heritin principles, the conceptualisation of the universalisability of the soul assists empathy, mindfulness, and self-discipline. This principle and notion of the universalisable soul offers many helpful insights and treasured moral utilities. Understanding and appreciating that which underlies the functions of life and the origins of the will comes with, as well as further inspires, spirituality. While different views may define the soul differently and disagree on its nature, if the soul is what gives a thing its life, then it is bound to the body. Immaterial consciousness and its figment of spirituality are only experiences of living, consequences of that which breathes life in the first place. (A dedicated discussion on the nature of conscious experience and the relation between consciousness and the substance of the world is found in Section 4, further studying metaphysics of ethics with regard to consciousness and the mind). The body is the host and hammer of the soul, with continuity of living as every movement, process, and function being a part of the soul. Everything that is entwined with the fundamental will to flourish is of the soul. The material and substance that compose the body, through which life sustains itself, are of the soul as well, or rather the soul is of the world that creates and nourishes it.

The will to live is in and of the body; it is created by the same foundations of substance as the lifeless rock. Harmony assists the practice and discipline of empathy by conceptualising the soul in this manner. Where one is able to let go, whether through finding common value in and through others or by finding peace with the world and fate, the world and living feel differently. Degrees of complacency and idleness may arise, corrupting goodness of Liberty by failing to cultivate more of that goodness achieved best by appreciating the littlest of the best and accepting it as it is and as much of it as there is. But Liberty is diverse and fluid, fluctuating in all values and spirit. Being mindful of these changes and finding harmony in instability, familiarising oneself with tranquillity, is the duality opening the Void through which greater liberty of spirit is found. Being mindful of the Void and sustaining discipline to not succumb to it are the path to greater Liberty. Along this journey one grows and discovers much insight on the nature of the self and the soul.

The coldness and profound detachment inspired by the Void is pivotal to understanding the soul. For where life is seen through detached value and concern, seen as mere moving things, the same vision looks inward and outward to see the same movement everywhere as part of everything. Then, where Discipline further emboldens emotional composure and Harmony instils wisdom and mindfulness in emotional states, all in healthy synchrony of higher rationale, the three aforementioned core aspects influence the fourth (base) state and aspect – the aspect of the heart. Focus of impression and insight achieved only through accord of the four core aspects reveals another sense of the soul, living, and the world. Every soul is a conduit of force acting on the world, shaping it, experiencing it. Every soul has a fundamental unity in value and purpose. The world acts on itself through the will of a living thing made to act in accordance with the soul's imperative *by* the world itself. Higher and baser aspects of the psyche are of the world and of the soul. Where all things are connected and fluidity of the fundamental will is of the soul and its bondage to the world, life and its substance are of the same soul.

This abstract thinking may be misunderstood as mystifying, quirky, fanciful, but the conclusion is very real. If nihilistic understanding reduces living to nothing more than the continuity of bodily functions, not giving any meaningful value or belief to misunderstood, distorted, and inflated sensations, then the substance of the function of the fundamental will is found as well. The origin of the Fundamental Principle and the fundamental will as the soul are bound to the processes of the world itself, antecedent to conscious life as we know it, perhaps even prior to any conscious sensation and spirit. After all, if the Fundamental Principle is true (the functional nature of which is yet to be finally concluded), then all conscious experience of living is only that – an experience.

The soul must be of the world itself, a formation created by the world through development, continuity, growth, and evolution. The soul is universalisable in life and in seemingly ordinary substance. The will to flourish is not just of conscious living. The will to flourish is a function of the world creating it. The fundamental will is exemplified in continuity of functions as behaviour striving for well-being, yet this continuity is only of that which enables its intent. The origin of the fundamental will is self-enabled continuity antecedent to a formal Fundamental Principle. Actions invoked by the mind are only the way they are because of a deterministic psyche forced to act in a deterministic manner. The will to flourish is only formal in the intentions of actions, with the setup being purely mechanical. The Fundamental Principle is non-causal, it is simply a label for provoked causes, with the experience of deliberation being an experience of contributing causes. The fundamental will manifests itself in varying degrees, starting with the sustained bond of the molecules of the body. The will to flourish is woven into the nature of substance itself. (For a more dedicated study, see Section 4). So the pursuit of flourishing is either the will of the world or of a transcendentally greater soul in all substance of reality, perhaps as a principle and Law of Nature.

A suggestive thought may consider that there is no will at all. This would be an extension of hyper nihilistic thought, but it is not invalid for general consideration. The fundamental will is defined as a complex consequence, not an intentional or deliberative mechanism moved by freewill. The existence of the fundamental will can only be through and of the body – of substance. To claim there is a 'will' to flourish is to claim that substance is deterministically moved towards states of flourishing or the continuity of such states. As was argued in Section 1, if such a principle did not exist in mental programming and the mechanism of goal-directive behaviour guided by the Fundamental Principle of Living Beings was not effective or active, then the continuity of living in challenging environments prompting reactions might not have been possible.

The basis of the argument thus far has been moving this concept away from moralising and back towards metaphysics and further into the world – into substance beyond the experience of living. According to such a paradigm, one cannot contend whether or not a 'will' as a mode of sustained material processes towards growth and development of living things is real – it absolutely is by virtue of sustained existence. One can only contend whether or not this principle is applicable towards the whole universe of substance and whether or not its success as universal flourishing is possible, achievable, or inevitable. The other question is then whether universal substance might have a 'spirit' or consciousness of its own. These questions warrant intense and utmost scepticism, for all existence and its continuity may be momentary and coincidental.

Equipped with this conceptual lens seeing behaviour and life through a universal mechanical soul binds high-reason to practical perception. For one, it bolsters the capacities of empathy through non-judgemental, emotionally balanced, and unthreatened listening to people, understanding of people. For instance, universalisability of the soul and empathy are realised where people find commonality in mutual experience of pain, for all are of the same soul in our pain and Fear. Expanding this view further allows a particularly useful attitude in trying to understand the world without Fear. The universalisable soul transcends beyond its applied perception among living things and allows one to see the world as a living thing and see oneself as a lively conduit of the world itself. Where Discipline builds character and spirit to the point that Harmony becomes intuitive, perception of the universalisable soul becomes intuitive, the meditations of which grant new insights, or at least become integrated into the sense of self. This brings me to a discussion on Nature and God.

In Liberty's discipline and mindfulness, the influence of base morality and Fear recedes and becomes balanced. Where instinct's perceptions and influences on rationale and belief are detached, greater clarity, sensibility, and coherence become accessible. Stemming from the heritin interpretation of the metaphysics of morals, the universalisable soul may be extended in principle to suggest a universalisable will to flourish or a *Universal Will* (or simply *the Will*), familial to a notion of God. This notion of godliness is suggestive of its nature being above all else as a force moving the substance of reality. The dynamics of the world and its Laws of Nature moved material to turn into living things which then shape the world around them. The Universal Will would be recognised as a force orchestrating and embodying all such change and development. The Universal Will, or God, is a prime cause, a principle of causal cascades self-designed towards fulfilling the principle found in the movement of living things – continuity and flourishing. How this metaphysical idea or entity applies to the real world is of great uncertainty and perhaps impossible to know.

Every movement of matter or energy and every chemical reaction or physical dynamic is part of the continued Universe through which life has grown. This 'will' of substance, clear in living things but intuitively absurd in lifeless substance, can be interpreted to be driven by a force mediating all things towards continuity and growth as life knows for itself. The Universal Will, as a causal consequence like the fundamental will, would be conceived as a principle and Law of Nature where the existence of the world could only have been possible through a factor able to sustain itself, as a principle balancing and mediating universal causal cascades against collapsing tangents unable to sustain the continuity of existence. This is the Universal Will; this is God. Accordingly, everything is of the Universal Will, especially life itself. The Universal Will flows through its greater conduits as heralds of complex, sophisticated causes – living things.

What can be said on the nature of the Universal Will, on the nature of God and the divine? Within the given narrative of heritin metaphysics of actions and living things, especially in terms of the soul, the Will is considered as the continuity of the universalisable soul in substance itself (or vice versa). The Will is a principle, a law. It is not a force – it is a parameter of how any physical force manifests and works. The Will is not a living thing in the familiar sense. One may contend that the Will or God are the life of the entire Universe, that they are a sum of consciousness. This suggestive argument, however, is very sceptical and ultimately ethically irrelevant. If the Will as a conscious being is a sum or maxim of all things, then it would be an embodiment of all things, infinitely amorphous. The Will's absurdly diverse nature would then only be definable in terms of its function – continuity of existence. If substance can only exist through principles sustaining substance's continuity and movement, which is the function the soul performs for living things, then the Will's nature in all its diversity would apply itself towards the maxim of that end.

Living things could only survive and grow through instinct, through baser attributes. The Will, in all its eternity and automation, is fundamentally different. What use would it have for instinct? It does not operate through a conscious mind of instinct such as our own; it does not have a brain like ours. However, just as information compiles in our minds through the laws and operations of logic, the same would occur on a universal level of logic encompassing all causal cascades. But no such operation would be deliberative, in freewill, and most definitely it would not be of the same function as instinct or at least of the same sorts of instincts as our own. The Will is beyond instinct. As a metaphysical fundamental of the substance of reality, the Will would have no identity, no character, no sentiment, no emotion, or at least it would not actively use these utilities to perform its primary function.

As is very intuitive and common, the divine is ascribed with something greater, something 'higher'. The operations of the Will would be wholly characterised by high-reason serving the function of the Universal Imperative. God is a leviathan of pure reason, beyond vice and virtue. The Will is not of mankind's character; the Will is eternally what it is. It is the embodiment of the Highest Good in substance, that which conjures the moral laws we must find for ourselves and use to guide one another in our best judgement, always ambiguous by the necessity of the Natural Law of adaptation. Where the Will's function is its own and we are part of that function – conduits of its force acting on the world, to change according to the environment – everything would happen according to its design, to its scheming, according to its function. Never should we or could we understand its universal scope, the ambiguity of which is necessary for our function and living. Where the Will has no use for an ethos, where its function is predetermined, and where it doesn't need instincts, the Will has no use for punishing or rewarding, in bargaining and granting favours. Its fortune and interest through individuals is only for the mutual concerns of the soul and the soul's Imperative. Nothing is personal for or to the Will, as can be the case in our base perception and understanding. The Will is a leviathan of pure reason, absolute in its Law, wholly mechanical.

An immediate issue arises with this interpretation. If all is of the Universal Will, where does that leave individual liberty of autonomy? The subjective sense of self and functional mentality are derivative of the Fundamental Principle and are logically harmonious in terms of structuring an ethic – the fundamental will is one's own, of oneself. To introduce an aspect of a Universal Will underlying the will of the self threatens sense of autonomy. Weak, unmindful, and unwise characters may then blame personal vice and irresponsibility on another, including the Universal Will. Disheartening fatalism may become the natural reaction. However, the first concern of the fundamental will is the quality of living we experience. We experience living as a state of mind and spirit through attitude, mentality, and behaviour. Regardless of the thought underlying it, the primary concern is how actions and living make us feel in spirit. The underlying schemes of God are ultimately irrelevant to immediate experience of living. Even the sense of responsibility is only of relevance to us as judgement of ourselves, key to good discipline.

More technically, the soul of a living thing is an extension and a part of its Universal Will. People embody the same will as God; we are all part of the Will. The experience of living, however, is our own in spirit and consciousness, and this is what we value. There is no need for us to hold ourselves accountable to God, because we all *are* a part of God through the soul. We are thus only accountable to our own ambition, to our own will, and to each other's souls as constituents of God. The goodness of any such account is qualified in terms of the Highest Good known with greater certainty than any notion of godhood. The final account is of righteousness, justice, and goodness of will. Any account of the influences on our actions, such as by God or causes that change our world, is useful as a pivot for mindfulness in terms of the Human Imperative and the Highest Good. Personification of this mindfulness and awareness is useful and valuable as a simplification, but its greatest value is found in dedicated practice supervening basic meditations. Determination of living and actions by the Universal Will does not threaten autonomy or accountability, as inherent interests are nonetheless compatible and are of the same consequence regardless. Furthermore, the nature of willpower and ambition is no different where the origin of the soul is still the same, as the functionality of the soul and human psyche remain the same.

This pragmatism of ethical interest and moral utility refers back to the Central Principles of suffering and liberty where the conclusion was that individuals cannot be justly subject to suffering against their will or interests by the determination of other individuals and their ambitions unless the circumstance is just and compatible with the principles of liberty and greater ethical value. Wrongdoing or acts of inflicting harm on others cannot be justified by appealing to the Universal Will, even though such phenomena would be the Will's determination. There are definitively better modes of ethical development and personal growth than through actions of excess Fear, for suffering is best relieved and channelled than inflicted unreasonably on others.

Not shying away from the potential difficulty created by fully accepting the Universal Will grants more. Fulfilling of both Discipline and Harmony, letting go of the concern for well-being paradoxically serves the interests of well-being more by releasing the will of its corruptive aspect of excess attachment. Relinquishing the self to something greater is to release ego seeking to protect itself, moving oneself to a new realm of Liberty and Liberty's spirit through the self. Embracing the Universal Will in all its aspects, even if as a mere personification, grants an unprecedented level of mindfulness and awareness through its respective conceptual lens. To some spiritual and religious practices, releasing the ego offers inner peace; this is also a wisdom of Harmony. However, a healthy ego has much promise. By letting go of one's ego a person may be content, but they will simultaneously lose an invaluable utility in terms of Discipline and Defiance – ambition.

The ego is best developed beyond just inner peace and made to be in harmony with ambition of Liberty and Discipline. The release of ego may sow complacency, idleness, and apathy, with just and righteous struggle feeding virtue of character enabling a healthy and mindful ego, through which easing the concerns of ego grants clarity and virtue. Then, where one preserves good ego and finds harmony with the world, he or she can achieve unity through and with the Universal Will in an extraordinary way. The Ploy of Consciousness – the greatest known Liberty in this interpretation – is further realised where one's ego and sense of self becomes part of the world itself, becomes in line with the Will. Ego is not surrendered where it once may have been – it is nourished. The spirit and mind become consciously part of the world, of the Universal Will, and of the self not tormented by suffering. One's ego becomes eternally stronger and more satisfied where its fulfilment comes through a strong self and strong spirit of self-sustaining moral conscience.

To offer a simpler illustration of the Ploy of Consciousness, people may not be afraid of death, yet in doing so they are subject to a greatest fear of living. Where this kind of sentiment is a sign of great and profound suffering, it is also an opportunity for extraordinary growth. By finding peace with such suffering, one succeeds over one of the greatest fears, beckoning Liberty. The mindfulness and personal discipline, virtue, and insight required for this personal development fosters an attitude and mental state that beckons intuition on a certain view of a Universal Will. The Ploy of Consciousness ultimately becomes an ethic and mental state that is comfortable with change, thrives through change and its momentary suffering, that is satisfied in the hunger for growth inherent to an ethos of Liberty. Where one is at peace with change and is able to overcome great adversity, these insights shape the perception of change around oneself. The self is strongest through the Will personifying all change and all reality one experiences. Where on feels in harmony with the Universal Will, with change, with Fear, with suffering, with Liberty, with happiness – with everything – the sense of self can no longer be threatened by anything it sees as part of itself, a self that is in harmony and at peace from Fear. Where one accepts unity with the Will, they become closer to it, more mindful of it and subsequently of the world and others.

Through the Universal Will, godhood becomes irrelevant, as one receives the graces of the divine through the Highest Good of virtue and goodness of spirit, through a sense of self found on righteousness and nobility. This is the panacea to Fear, breaking its corrosive hold over ego, liberating sense of self to be with and of the Will igniting virtues of the Will's Highest Good. Then, one can take pride and strength from not submitting to Fear where it can be so tempting in immature character and spirit, to enjoy ever-freer spirit, as being at liberty of spirit is to be of the divine beyond and through suffering, for divinity transcends Fear and Liberty while preserving their utility. However, it is the baser self that doesn't like to suffer, and that is the part of the self that requires the most healing, least one's humanity is starved and the whole self is deprived in spirit. Where one is more determined than afraid, they are at liberty to care. Thus, nobility and harmony of ego are complete through the baser self. Every individual is a story of pain, suffering, and Fear among all other aspects of living. Only by moving past one's Fear and suffering and achieving greater liberty of spirit does a person become more than Fear and instinct, simple rationale and vision, and more than immature spirit, thus finding an ethereal strength and virtue through the Highest Good of all things and the Universal Will and, most importantly, receive the relief and fulfilment every ethos strives for.

The conceived nature of the Will involves suffering. Suffering in the world must be of the Universal Will, of the will of God. However, if the Universal Will is envisioned as a principle and mechanism promoting flourishing, what role does suffering play, and what implication does suffering have? The familiar arguments on the compatibility of a benevolent, merciful, and kind God with suffering are not of interest. The present concern is innovation.

First, the argument that nothing is inherently, absolutely evil in human activity, although degrees of wrongness and badness are valid, suggests that people's deterministic nature causing suffering is not incompatible with the conceived Universal Will. However, suffering is antagonistic to well-being, with suffering by itself perhaps being an element of evil incompatible with the existence of God. With all the mass and seemingly pointless suffering in the world, especially of innocents, it is difficult to conceive of a God where great suffering persists. Through and in Fear as a conduit, suffering serves as a catalyst for growth and progress. As such, suffering is compatible with the Will as suffering leads to growth and ethical development.

However, if the Universal Will is designed to promote maxims of flourishing, and a harmonious mode of development is theoretically conceivable, then suffering may not be a necessary utility or a utility befitting a Universal Will. The Universal Will is established on a prerogative principle that its dynamics and mechanisms are dedicated to facilitating the greatest flourishing, with relative or arbitrary degrees of positive ethical growth exposing inconsistency and randomness. Therefore, any lesser modes of positive ethical development than hypothetically conceivable ideal modes could theoretically contradict the interpreted nature of the Will. Suffering is not necessary for the imperative of our will yet it supplements our growth and development up to a point. One may only guess whether the current model of global growth is necessary for ultimate success.

A perfect design of structural ethics may require adaptiveness of life, in which the seeming inefficiencies of pain and loss become necessary for growth through motivation. However, these sorts of discussions and wonderings are overshadowed by fundamental uncertainties. Ultimately, impressions and biases will profoundly influence interpretations and conclusions. For now, the study is inconclusive as to whether or not the global mode of ethical development influenced by suffering's effects is compatible with the Universal Will. However, the implication is that neither is suffering incompatible with a Universal Will as it is conceived. Then, how we experience suffering, what impressions suffering leaves, and parallel goodness in the world all contribute to an understanding and interpretation of the nature of the Universal Will. Where morality is balanced with discipline and mindfulness beyond base Fear, complimented with insight of profound detachment, God can be seen in a very different light.

Impressions involving the Will can portray it to be brutal or merciful, callous or compassionate. Structures of the Will have no interest in the opinions of living things as manifestations of the Will in its own world. Furthermore, the conceived understanding of any divine species is suggestive of a whole other sort of consciousness or 'mind' to that of any ordinary living thing. This isn't to presume any conclusions on its nature beyond the definitively arguable that it is by all measures different to the mind of instinct. Our conscious experiences are only dreams of the causes that move us. Our attitudes and mentality conceive the Will's nature, and so the mind makes use of the Will through related interpretations. Where the Will is seen to be brutal, the mind looks into the world accordingly, or the other way around. Where the Will is seen to be benevolent, this gives hope. In truth, however, the Will's nature is of a single function – to guide the greatest flourishing and, presumably, to sustain continuity of existence, with people's concerns being only as relevant as means to an end. It is up to us to find commonality in one another to fulfil our own interests, not to depend on divinity other than of our own nobility and virtue.

Written commands can be simpler and easier to follow than thinking for oneself, but this doesn't make it better. Older ethics succeeded where they were adapted to their respective stages of the cycle of values. All prophets and ethical and moral teachers were right in some way or another. Now, in some respect, the global ethical environment is sufficiently developed to enable greater autonomy, to which the nature of the divine has to change in accordance with its own Natural Laws as aspects of its divinity and function. Prospective divinity is morality of spiritual liberty from Fear and suffering, of virtuous autonomy – not bound to Fear, to pain's corruption, not to people of lesser virtue, and certainly not to blind dogma. Where autonomy is nourished and spirit, character, and mind are strong, the Will's nature and intent become irrelevant to deliberative interest and instead becomes a supplementary utility in living.

The Will can forever be in one's favour, but only if virtue, discipline, and mindfulness enable such mentality and utility. Where one can find positive interest in all bad circumstances and not succumb to Fear, relentlessly pursuing interest of well-being in spirit of Liberty, pain, corruption, malevolence, suffering, and mistakes become resources for growth. It is then that the Will reveals its grand utility as a focal point of mindfulness and discipline. The Will serves our interests where it does not become a necessity, where it is not the root of hope that everything will work itself out. The Will serves as a realm of focus and perception assisting nurtured ambitions of the soul and virtues. The self must be ready to embrace this utility, for only certain types of character can attain such Harmony with the Will that in all its cruelty and goodness it still binds mindful thought to unity with change, for the Will is nothing more than a personification of change, a pivot for attaching the soul to all else in absolute empathy and ambition. Metaphysical truths of the Universal Will are subsequently irrelevant.

Where mysticism and ambiguity abound to any argument on religion and concerning spiritual experience, the study of spirituality requires discipline. Experiences and developments in the higher faculties of the mind are vivid in terms of their very real sensations. Subsequent interpretations, however, are a science and art. Logic, reason, and a balanced psyche are necessary for success in these studies. Spirituality and its many experiences are not faint or mystical – they can simply be misunderstood and misinterpreted. Where the mind and its activity through ethics are understood and structured, so too can its spiritual aspects be studied in a disciplined and coherent manner. After all, spirituality is understood to be the sum sensation and feeling of the state of living.

The argument conceiving the Will is straightforward, intuitive, and rather simple where sufficient insight is available. Applying knowledge of the physical sciences interprets the nature of substance to be structured and mechanical. The same is applicable to people. Where the mind and its conscious experiences are stripped down, where insights of the structures of ethics are employed, people are understood to be mechanical; so too are our experiences. The movement of living things is part of the movement of all substance. All deliberative thought and all living things' 'willing' are machinations of sophisticated information-processors reacting to change in the world. People have a 'will', yet it is only a continuity of change and development in accordance with the world and continued existence – it is part of Nature and its substance. Therefore, the same conception of change and movement is applicable to Nature itself. Subsequent spiritual conscious experiences are merely natural conscious experiences bound to change and development – nothing wholly mystical, only requiring further study.

An example of the 'higher' experience found in metaphysical and quasi-religious thought is the sensation of personal growth and expansion of sensation through self-awareness and mindfulness. The relation between the self and the world becomes balanced through focus of self-awareness and mindful thought. All spiritual revelations and sensations only begin to serve the soul in the way it sees fit. It is never a question of what God expects of us or what we can do for God, it is always about the soul and our ambitions, directives, and desires. Moral development then fosters a relation asking how harmonious self-interest can be served through the utility that is God and the Will, for we are the Will and the utility we see in it is the Will seeing its own utility in the moment. But this utility can only ever be executed and properly employed where thought is balanced and mindful, not selfish or perceived in Fear. The Will is a utility demanding an ethic mindful of all its organic, synthetic, and extremely diverse aspects. Where virtue guides mindful thought amplified through the Will, thereby extending empathy and goodness further into the world and goodwill's scope of interest, self-interest is maximised, for divinity is a utility found in universalising the soul.

Traditional religion may scorn such a view, criticising it for being narcissistic and selfish. But in terms of the Fundamental Principle, all ethical matters are bound to self-interest. The argument does not presume humanity to be greater than divinity. Humanity is the conduit of divinity. Humanity uses divinity as a utility just as the divine uses humanity for its purpose. The relation is symbiotic, or at least best serves the mutual imperative found through structuring the ethics that underlie all such movement. The suggested nature of God as serving mankind is of no concern for the divine, for the Will has no ego, but people do. At different stages and times of the adaptive cycle of values and its state of affairs, the nature of divinity adjusts to people's needs and mental states. *This* is the ultimate nature of the divine – of the projection of humanity onto the world, as this is all that divinity is.

Divinity is not of individual personhood to be used as an authority to dominate. Divinity is the highest of authority of Nature and its Law that supercedes mankind. Divinity can be found anywhere, but not all of it is of its truest form as the Highest Good. Only the Highest Good is the authority of that which is seen to be divine, for this is the nature of the divine. The realisation of these insights and subsequent practice of relevant valuable utilities can only be achieved through a basis of virtue and goodness, with humility and mindfulness being prime. Only in humility and harmony of sincerest humanity – in balance of higher and baser faculties – can the Will be appreciated fully in the way it is portrayed and be employed for mutual interest. It is this practice of high-reason that leads to a greater mindful awareness of that which spirituality sees to be divine. But as one may see, it is only through personal practise of virtue and goodness that one is able to herald the divine in experience and sensation, with all divinity only being personal satisfaction and fulfilment in living, spirit, and ego. In the end, humanity has always been strongest when it took its fate into its own hands, when it pursued its ambitions and imperatives, when it embraced the autonomy of its virtues. The divine is a guiding authority for humanity, serving as a parent when mankind was young, supportive when we commit any sort of leap of faith, a partner when we have grown into our virtue. The Will is anything it has to be and anything our values make it to be, just as the soul.

A personal note as a case study will benefit the discussion. The notion of a Universal Will to exemplify change and living is simply used as a coping mechanism constantly adapting to experiences and values. In my personal experience, the Will has been used as an idea formalising change and the experiences of living into a singular, focused aspect. Rather than seeing it as someone's 'will' acting on life, the adopted view is that any such force is merely that of natural cause, of reasons leading up to the moment that affect living and states of affairs. The Will is a personification of causal cascades and respective fortunes and reasons for easier introspection. Where people may wonder why something happened, the idea of a Universal Will or any divine intervention becomes a tool to try understand or even rationalise events that are otherwise simple occurrences over which we can only act in hindsight, learn from, but never change.

It is a mistake to blindly accept the events of one's life. The Will is designed as a personal utility used as a conceptual and focal lens to study and understand the causes which led to an event of interest or concern. Emotions, especially those of suffering, motivate one to explore states of affairs and try bring relief where the spirit and mind are in pain or dissatisfied. Subsequently we learn and ethics develop. It is arguable that the mind has a natural inclination towards learning from pain. This beckons meditation and reflection on events that caused suffering.

The same goes for behaviour that brings pleasure, relief, satisfaction, and happiness. In trying to make sense of things it is easy to look at reasons for certain causes or even reasons for what may appear as divine intervention. Trying to rationalise suffering or fulfilment by considering the reasons for something, such as with questions of why and for what reason something happened, can push thoughts in many directions. Presumptuous thought would assume that the rationalisation of reasons for something happening in terms of the Will would be to think that it was all for a greater good, all for the Highest Good, to fulfil a maxim of universal well-being. After all, is the function and nature of the Will not to fulfil its imperative of continuity, of maxims of goodness, of the Highest Good? Should we not simply accept everything that happens as part of divine design? Any such ethic would not perform a greater service to humanity or perform a necessary justice.

The Will by its nature is incapable of 'revealing' its scheming to us, neither is there any purpose in this. All things happen as they should do. Our only concern is to cope and to grow. We do so in the liberty of morality and innate or general ethical inclinations towards autonomy and adaptation, as per the mechanisms of the soul. Over-rationalising in attempts to understand and learn can divert attention away from the most basic elements of the mind and spirit that require adaptation, that require healing. Where suffering requires healing, only sustained progress in a good direction can bring about positive influence that allows healing and growth through the causal tangents of virtues. By focusing on changes and developments in states of affairs by understanding them in terms of the Will assists self-reflection, helps a person to understand that there truly is a reason for why something has happened and *what* has happened; any such reason is only of a particular deterministic cause. However, any such reason that might be devised by the Will is irrelevant to the person in the moment, for it is only the immediate quality living that matters to the individual, not the design of any higher power – this would distract. In terms of the soul, any divine intent and schemes are only as relevant to us as we see them to be. The Will's reasons and reasoning are irrelevant to us, only useful as a way of thinking about and for ourselves.

To explore the matter of reasons, it may be true that everything does happen for an intended reason by a power of its own will beyond human power. Everything may indeed happen for a reason. However, any such reason may not directly involve oneself or be for one's own benefit or goodness. A random event seemingly acausal to the self may profoundly affect another. One person's great suffering or death may mean nothing to another, yet it may be key in the grand scheme. On this subject one has to be made aware of any such reasoning. Liberty and Harmony seek to make peace with that which cannot be used in Discipline for greater growth. Some forms of great suffering should be accepted and made peace with, but never should their relevance and power be dismissed. No suffering should ever be simply dismissed or ignored if its sensation is real, and one ought not to numb themselves and detach from very real and meaningful suffering – this is unhealthy and ethically inefficient.

There are times when circumstances and immediate reactions will beckon all sorts of responses, but detached and numbed modes of spirit, mind, and their subsequent ethics are far from the best. First of all, while such mental states may protect, they do not allow healing and may easily produce corrupt ethics. Second, their insight and potential are limited as opposed to mentalities and ethics that have been tempered by, or are otherwise familiar with, the suffering that may lead to numbness. Excess rationalisation that does not allow one to learn is particularly susceptible to over-thinking and over-protective diversion of attention away from that which seeks to be amended and healed. Reasons are not excuses. Change is always real, and we can only do so much about it. At times the best we can do is to channel change towards something positive through ourselves in thought and action. Then again, as has been argued, there are uses to detached and unemotional analysis of states of affairs and reflection on the self.

Focused, objective, and emotionally uncompromised thought has imperative uses. Where reasons for deplorable events ought not to sow idleness and apathy, for this would not serve our greater interests, degrees of detachment assist in understanding and studying the causes producing a moment of suffering. These modes of thinking and their mindfulness were categorised as *mindfulness by the Void* – that is, mindfulness void of compromising influences detracting from necessary practice and permitting alternative lines of thought and intuition. Sometimes, the necessary decision or even its realisation can only be possible by combining disciplined detachment with our most basic inclinations, as horribly difficult as this may be. As should be intuitive in this discussion, any such practice is delicate and dangerous, because suggestive thoughts and vocal opinions can cross lines that shouldn't be. Harmony is a close peer to such thought where one has to understand their limits and be mindful of balance, especially in terms of the virtues of humanity. Where spiritual reflection ascriptive of Harmony may concern itself with the divine, it can be swayed and corrupted by imbalanced and undisciplined thought.

Humanity may seek to understand the divine, to emulate it, but this is too easily a path to excess detachment, great suffering, decay, or possibly even madness. Even a reaction turning to such a mental state can be a sign of great distress and declining mental health. A madman's knowledge can be useful for our common well-being, but it can demand a heavy price that might not be worth it. Never should humanity be characterised as an emulation of the divine, for the divine is of no humanity. The divine is not good or bad, while people are a whole other species subject to the many drives and experiences, especially emotions, of our conscious living in all its diversity. Our concerns, interests, and what we value, in terms of Natural Law and the Highest Good imbued with divinity, are subject to moral evaluation and judgement, as is part of our nature and autonomy.

The divine, as the Highest Good and its moral law, guides us, but only virtues in humanity are something worth striving for. Striving to emulate something with no humanity or morality is unwise and wrong. The great deeds of noble and strong character that inspire us are human, are of personality that the Will is not and never could be. Where people may embody and herald the most admirable virtues, these ideals are made so because of the dedication and struggle it takes to achieve such a state of mind, spirit, and overall character, as well as aspire to its rewards. We are not born to be ideal; we are born to be adaptable, changing, with the potential to become more than we were at our first breath. The Will and the divine are not ideal – they simply *are*. Mankind, on the other hand, must change and grow. So we ought to pursue the Ideals we find for ourselves, with the Will being a mere conceptual tool – and not even a necessary one – towards that end. We can only borrow from the Will, use it. Even though we are part of it, we are not divinity itself. In all humility of our mortality, we should look to ourselves, to find strength in our spirit and through one another, in doing so pursuing the goodness laid before us by the divine. The Universal Will should only serve the Human Imperative – according to its own design – through us, as a moral utility amplifying and focusing empathy, mindfulness, and awareness; never should it consume or define the individual.

To put this into context, I often ask myself why something happened. It can be easy to come up with reasons and to overthink. I have my reasons for doing so. This entire project is a dedication to ethical study borrowing from personal experience and insight, the ideas of which remain to be tested and applied further. The point is that rational thought is mindful of such considerations and the reason for questioning is not blind in investing in something divine. If the theory or divine stops working and performing favours, when it ceases its greater value, or where it is no longer coherent or intuitive, then it no longer performs the good it should do, losing its value in terms of the Highest Good. The interpreted Highest Good, morality, belief, or divinity must adapt or be replaced, as with all utilities and values. However, flexibility is not valuable where it undermines worthwhile persistence; the difference is found through moral wisdom.

In such a manner, this ethic, discipline, and philosophy has developed, changed, has been rewritten, and keeps evolving. The conceived nature of the Will followed this trend. Clearly, the nature of the divine is to be amorphous, befitting its prime and necessary law of the adaptive cycles. Many causal tangents shaped the character and mental state explored throughout this project. This journey began from discord, disquiet, and a hunger for more, then consciously and deliberately carried by lingering dissatisfaction and ambition mindful of the justice it seeks to preserve and nourish in humility of sincere humanity. Many events shaped the impressions, experiences, and respective thoughts poured into this project, especially pain, grief, acceptance, forgiveness, and relief. The conceived notion of the Will developed accordingly and was employed to channel experiences and all their emotions towards a pursued ambition. Where the Will, as all divinity, is an extension or projection of self-awareness, it can serve a purpose.

This project was created and carried by many motivating factors. It became imbued with a sense of purpose and duty, with meaning, became a mission to help others and oneself. Accordingly, many contributing factors to personal growth carried into this work in accordance with the sensed purpose. Certain events and experiences were very painful, which were made peace with through trial and practise, granting insight or used as motivation. Where seemingly random events were given reason befitting the narrative of an ambition, they not only assisted the endeavour, but might have been necessary. A sense of purpose and meaning certainly amplified the pain and detracted from the basic fulfilment that is very desirable, but it also pushed for progress, channelled negative experiences and made something far better of them.

This project and all these ethical ploys are mere devices for dealing with the realest of emotions and living on. Spirituality only becomes a technical term, considering any mysticism, uncertainty, and anxiety as things that remain to be studied, as something unexplored, as something that remains to be tested, as an inevitable complication. Every experience demanding significant enough attention fit into this narrative and was exploited until something valuable was taken from it. Many contributing factors pushed towards an end by a deliberate design. The self-given purpose is simply a product of the soul and its Imperative, with any actual divine scheming and reasons being irrelevant. The Will was and is only used to compound various influences into something digestible, useful, something fitting the desire and its narrative. The key to this success is being aware of the liberty not to do so, to abandon this mission and its purpose.

This project was seen with much hope and promise, but it was always equally seen without absolute necessity, with much scepticism and doubt. And so the narrative of the ambition aligned in accordance with the Will and reciprocated a sense of purpose, but never was it absolute, never was I obliged to do so. *This* is the strength and use of a divine moral utility such as the Will. Intuitively, its nature or metaphysical truth is irrelevant where sufficient ambiguity can be employed towards the ends of the Human Imperative. The exploitation of God is, of course, of His own design, for the Imperative is performed through us as we are conduits of the Will. Due to the conceived nature of the divine, stripped of baser attributes unnecessary and inapplicable to it, correctness or judgement on the nature of divinity is ultimately irrelevant, for our opinions about the Will are irrelevant, for it has no purpose for judgement. The divine has no care for praise or appeasement; God is a silent, undiplomatic arbiter of the Highest Good. That being said, the heritin interpretation on the metaphysics of that which could be suggested to be divine, especially in terms of God and/or the Will, is fairly rigid in its suggestions on the nature of the divine. What is to be made of it all is only as relevant as ethical concern and interest.

The metaphysical possibility of the Universal Will is plausible, especially since it is uncertain and ambiguous. This is sufficient, and any other truth other than absolute rebuttal is only as useful as its role in a given narrative. One can choose to believe that everything happens for a reason towards something better, in accordance with the Highest Good, even if that choice is made for us through prior conditioning. Hopeful thought and intent would always admire such devotion, but only as much as this devotion is good, just, righteous, and virtuous. Yet the application of the Will in ethics as a moral utility would always be shrouded in valid uncertainty. This agnosticism is paradoxically the most enlightening of the Will, most appropriate of its amorphous nature. Because where one focuses on pragmatic and dedicated ambition rather than mere subscription and hopeful prayer, one finds insight – through oneself – on the nature of change and development, inscribing it all with *the Will*, which is ultimately our own and what we make of it. I believe in some form of the Will, not necessarily by choice, to believe that good can be made from terrible things, but not that good necessarily comes from the worst. This belief nourishes and sustains inspiration, motivation, spirit, and maybe even goodness. It is useful. Just as the prayer is always met with silence, meditation on the Will as meditation on the self, surroundings, and states of affairs, within a narrative projected onto the world, is a way to focus and self-motivate. Thinking in a way that constructs causal cascades and respective reasons for events is a way to personally align one's ethic and ethos. Ultimately, where a value or utility serves the ends of human betterment and produces states of well-being, it is an aspect of the Will, an act of the divine.

Belief in fate is intrinsic to a deterministic and mechanical view of a world structured by Natural Law. The subsequent belief that deterministic causal cascades are structured towards a certain predetermined end is subjective, although there will always be an end. Wondering what that end may be is only as relevant to us as our preconditioned mentality implementing and embodying an ethic serving our own ends. The Will is a focal point for such thinking, of a conceived and/or desired end. Healthy ego in its higher and baser aspects grants insight into the nature of the Will, which can then be used according to our ambitions. In doing so, in pragmatism and liberty of this morality and spirit, the Will is understood as it is. The Will can serve Discipline and Harmony. It may be unconventional to suppose such a nature of the divine befitting our own ends, despite the argument that mankind has intrinsically always done so with all divinity. Where ego and virtuous character lead to such an understanding of the divine, ego and the self grow further, evolve mentally and spiritually. One may begin to feel more in tune with their surroundings, with change exemplified through the Will, be more aware of themselves and causal cascades affecting one's own and others' living, be more aware of others' mental states and the nature of their character – such is a product of mindfulness and its form of emotional intelligence. Through mindfulness accentuated by the Will, core practices and ethics of Liberty cultivate further virtues by extending them into states of affairs with full awareness of one's inner world and its nature – that is, one's character and mentality. The Will assists in developing a greater sense of autonomy, of being more in control of oneself responding to change, especially with regards to suffering. The Will helps one to surrender control, to let go and receive the relief of dissolving Fear. However, in terms of the most basic moral wisdom, we can't always afford to do so, as some pain, concern, and Fear are good and their utilities noble. Where this aspect of the Will is appreciated it brings relief to ego, recalls humility and joy in our humanity, and evokes the simplest, yet most profound, happiness as the liberty of spirit not having to be bound to the Universal Will or being obliged to the expectations and pressured desires we may impose on ourselves in misery of unnecessary duty. *This* brings balance and beckons Liberty.

One narrative of the Will assists Discipline, teaches to channel change through oneself towards one's own ends. The other aspect, through which one channels responses and impressions of change in Harmony, assists the art of letting go, of acceptance, of making peace with that which is worth making peace with. Moments of suffering may lead to progress and growth if one chooses or is able to. Then, one can become grateful for such a resource and make peace with it, let go of its pain that is no longer of value. However, where pain is too great, where it is to permanently scar a person, dismissal of such suffering by rationalising it as part of divine design will not truly allow oneself to let go of that suffering. The design of suffering may be for a universal reason, but where it cannot be used as a resource for growth and that pain plainly stings and hurts, one ought to find humility in it, turn to the best of humanity, to accept misfortune and try heal in what way one can. It may help to know that no such events of profound suffering are ever personal or malicious, thereby introducing the humble thought that misfortunes are an inevitable part of life. And so the Will may help in this practice of dissolving pain by opening a channel for other insight, for positive thinking through humility and acceptance of what we cannot change. Only wisdom can teach us how to apply these ways of thinking. The only general rule that can be prescribed is to contrast frustrating pain, which can be used, and depressive pain, which is best to be made peace with. Following ambitions and desires may alter such narratives and change attitudes, but henceforth the circumstance changes and so too its most applicable values. In the end, through the Will, one can focus on change and what has happened to oneself through a non-judgemental, emotionally detached mindfulness. Where one meditates on states of affairs and the self without judgement, through high-reason reciprocal of the Will accentuating the soul, non-judgement enables empathy and understanding, beginning healing and introducing inner peace. The Will can extend peaceful awareness of one's surroundings that reflect back inward to create a calmer inner world that positively influences the mind and spirit. It starts with meditating on the soul, by feeling change in the body and around oneself, and relating to it all as part of the same thing. Being mindful of underlying metaphysics through meditative thought binds sensation and self-reflection to a mode of mindfulness enabling Harmony. It begins with harmonising thoughts and creating positive influences and variables that foster a psychological environment more at ease, that is calmer by perceiving the world as non-hostile, as something without emotion, bringing attention to one's own sensations and feelings, then using them in ambition.

The practices and utilities entwined with high-reason, such as those of a religious-moral nature, may have complex relations with pleasure, between the higher and baser self. Religious thinking and feeling may find certain pleasures to be demeaning, shameful, degrading. Mindful non-judgement would dissolve any judgement on innocent pleasures. The principles of morality apply to such judgements and ought to mediate them. There are good and bad pleasures, but the best way to balance them is to judge through oneself, which can be difficult where people are easily dishonest with themselves and their habits. Pleasure is by no means inherently wrong. Pleasure is an essential part of life and good spirit, especially for mental well-being. However, if pleasure is ridden with guilt in the shadow of divinity, then something is wrong with one of the two mentioned ethical elements. The best pleasure is pleasure in and of healthy relief. Joy is good provided it does not take away from oneself a part of character's and spirit's goodness. Sometimes, however, such as to get through tough times, immediate sacrifice of physical health may be necessary for long-term interests of mental health and sustainable good character; after all, people aren't omnipotent. Where corruption of, or discord in, base morality makes certain natural and morally acceptable pleasures guilty or uncomfortable, their Fear objects to greater mindfulness and connection with the divine. There is great spirit and insight in enjoying (in healthy measure) life's pleasures. So long as mindful thought is nourished in good spirit and this positivity is sustained, one can appreciate pleasures in extraordinary spirit through Liberty where pleasures are seen as the world giving itself joy through itself. There is something profoundly spiritual in appreciating and experiencing the substance of the world from which one is made. However, these great pleasures are only possible where Fear does not cloud their sensation and good, positive judgement prevails, including judgement to let go in good spirit and character – to simply have fun. Pleasure is a key part of building a healthy link between the baser and higher faculties, to ground and balance spirit and mental state. A healthy ego and mind is the promise of the most fulfilling pleasures. Divinity can be a pleasure in itself, but the greatest of such pleasure is incompatible with the corruption of veiled inner suffering, even though pleasure can be a valued utility in immediate coping and balance.

Pleasure is important for balancing one's mindset, to ground oneself in reality and not get carried away in over-thinking or over-zealous unhealthy practices. Beliefs about the world and divinity are an expression of the self, of many complex aspects of human psychology. Exploring these beliefs and parts of human nature, as was done in this work, can be very demanding. Pleasure is one of the best ways to bring balance to such thoughts. However, if the conditioning that produced obsessive exploration of the divine and the spiritual is of suffering, pleasures momentarily relieving this suffering might not bring the balance or goodness advocated. This project has been very tiresome and very mentally and spiritually costly. The ethic devised in this work is fulfilling in its self-perpetuated and self-established goals, but that doesn't mean it is necessarily fulfilling in all cases in terms of the part of the self most in need of goodness through, firstly, above all else, basic relief. This basic relief is just as much a part of the divine as the deepest meditation. The reasons and influences underlying this project are also of a terribly peculiar delusion in a fantastic, comical, seasonal mild depression, responding to feelings as though one is to be as a guinea pig of God's experimental phase of dark, but not distasteful, humour.

All that is wanted is to humour oneself in basic of compassion and humanity. In a time of monetised, advertised, and marketed mass absurdity and cynicism, humour is perhaps the healthiest, most human cure, the perfect utility of the divine. To heal, some cycles have to be broken and their spheres burst. Depressive ways of thinking need to be abandoned; one needs to get out of them. The depressive state is tricky and deceitful, but sometimes a certain state of misery and suffering in rage is better than desolation or death. Ambitions defying apathy and torment can guide the self out of darkness and allow oneself to grow into extraordinary character in pride of conscience and virtue. Happiness is then the dutiful justice it can bring to the world and the happiness its character can give others through the strength found in uplifting oneself. But its truest fulfilment will only be found in balance of making good on one's own pain and finding peace to accept happiness and relentlessly try to find it, beginning with dissolving suffering by accepting non-happiness. Some of those first steps of helping oneself are to help another, so show another person kindness and compassion. The most human of things, in all our empathy and humility, is the goodness that overcomes Fear. Where Fear creates its mental traps that continue causal tangents of a questionable nature, where synthetic influences of high-reason are excessive, freedom through joy's relief is the best thing, the best ethic. Over-indulgence in the divine and possessed philosophising can become a trap, an addiction, a way of coping through distraction and denial. Good can come of it, but only so much. Humanity becomes that wonderful absolution to the darker aspects of divinity made so only through disharmony of the mind. And so, in the end, Fear and the baser aspects of human nature serve us well to sustain goodness and give relief and fulfilment in living. This is what good spirituality and sense of self are all about.

By allowing oneself to act on a simple desire to no longer be in a dark place, to not be miserable, one can let go of a need to make sense of life through distraction of divinity, to let go of a way of living perpetuating and holding onto internal suffering thought to be a way out through ambition yet only causing discord. Accepting change without imbuing it with divinity and special reason, achieved through mindfulness relating itself to the Will, grant the soul, spirit, and mind their freedom in living, their relief. The Will, the self, others, and plain living can be appreciated with lasting freedom from suffering and fear. Letting go of ambition and grandiose psychological desires can become the surest path to realising them in the most humble, simplest, and most efficient of ways. Being mindful of the world through the Will by being mindful of oneself, by letting go of the grandeur of divinity, can serve its and one's own ends better by allowing oneself to be happy. This is true divinity.

It seems that suffering can only be dissolved by goodness succeeding pain. Making good of pain is the path to absolution from suffering. Ambition of extraordinary goodness can be borne of extraordinary pain. But the greatest reprieve comes through mercy of sincere love and acceptance through oneself and others. Ambition may dismiss love from others to focus on the emotional charge of pain to create goodness, but the graceful touch of another soul is the greatest clemency from the world healing itself. All the bad leading to a moment of time can conjoin two souls in empathy, friendship, and love to bring mutual happiness by showing that suffering can be absolved by evoking compassion, understanding, and acceptance through common pain. In all gloom of life in a cruel and vile world, it is the way of the world to make good of itself through the soul – through the Will of all souls. The torment of one's soul can absolve the same torment in another's soul and become the beginning of all their future life's happiness and goodness, giving oneself relief by seeing the great and genuine happiness created from one's painful past, lifting the weight of the world off one's shoulder, making it all worth it. And when such souls must part and can no longer give each other the happiness they once did, the callous mind will know it to be mere transaction of value with vivid impression. But in this brutality of the soul, it can be known that it is the world and its Will that makes such goodness – a goodness that heals and nourishes spirit where all that may have been seen was darkness and suffering. Even a memory of such love and happiness can last a lifetime, be a glimmer of *eudaimonia*.

Any and all decisions in life and on living are preordained by the vast causal cascades affecting each and every one of us to some degree. No matter how we choose to look at life's events, what attitudes we adopt, all of it is causally determined. The Fundamental Principle and modes of ethics are Natural Laws of human conduct. By experiencing change and being mindful of change through oneself, it is clear that all events of one's life would've and will happen, not that they are meant to. The variables aligning causal tangents through its many vectors include our own characteristics, state of psyche, morality, and ethical dispositions. Past events and our responses to them set up the future we will live. One's fate is not meant to happen, but it will. In reflecting on a past made meaningful through our sensation of it and in spirit, it is good to embrace a following attitude: all events would have and will necessarily happen, but there is no necessity in them meaning to happen; everything would and will happen, but none meant to. This is fate; this is the Will. Nothing has to happen for a reason, but anything can be given a purpose. We can embrace our fate to then find that the suffering of our fate, or its gift, are in our hands. It is up to us to do what we can with the life and responsibility we are given through fate. If something is our fate, then it can also be our fate to change a given future, to change the variables that bestowed on us our fate – good or bad, to bring others joy or relieve others' pain. This is the exploitation of the divine – the exploitation of God. There is no greater purpose than one born in Fear and at Liberty; only then do the Will and humanity become one. Through the Ploy, we become free of it all and in everything, which is achieved by not being afraid of losing our humanity yet having something that always remembers it. The divinity of humanity is consciousness beyond holiness and evil, a species of conscience betwixt vice and virtue, and good spirit above happiness and misery.

Friedrich Nietzsche prophesised the *Last man;* the Last man is the species of modern base morality, of idleness, excess comfort, superficial happiness, weak sense of self, spiritual stagnation, denial, suffering, and Fear. The Last man will destroy himself and the world with him. Through the Last man will rise the divine human, forged in suffering, tempered by peace, transcending both, of spirit in harmony between the animal and the soul. This divinity is defined by the ability to empathise with others and by something serenely liberating – a good heart, understanding, and love, caring for the whole world. This species of reason and humanity becomes global and adapted to a world beyond the convention of instinct.

Pain teaches humility and enkindles the spirit of humanity when pain is made into goodness. The greater the pain, the greater the release; the greater the suffering, the more profound the serenity; but only if goodness can be found and made. Through humanity and its virtues of empathy, humility, and willpower, we bring the sensation of their spirit – relief and peace – into the world and connect to the Will. But along with the Will is its parallel – the Void. We come to the Void through great pain and relief from pain, great suffering and joy. The Will presides over all life and all aspects of life. The Void is the shadow of life. Only through humanity and the conscious soul do the Will and the Void become connected. Their integration in the soul allows life to use both these moral utilities. Through the Ploy of the soul's consciousness, humanity usurps its destiny, and the Will and the Void become our equals – parts of our soul. The kingdom humanity usurps must be dedicated to our hearts. But to achieve this one must always adapt and the soul must transform, as all virtue must rise. The Will is of all elements and aspects; through adaptation the Will is found and its mindfulness strengthened. Barriers must be crossed for mindfulness and its Will to expand and one's willpower to grow. At the core of this principle is ethical pragmatism, manifesting itself as the deliberate use of language engaging with, and appealing to, high-reason.

The core assertion of this philosophy is that psychological fear and aversion to pain can weaken the ego, which when combined with a fragile ego leads to spiritual stagnation and suffering. Fear and ego are not inherently bad, yet they become morally corrupt when they lack balance, moderation, and positive nourishment. The remedy is discipline, mindfulness, and positivity – joy, pleasure, love, peace – but all in harmony and balance. To change patterns of thought and behaviour requires adjusting the variables, introducing new ones, whereby even a single moment engaging a certain part of the mind, whether of the higher faculty or of the core of someone's pain, can lead to change – can awaken a tangent of virtue. By dedicating attention to our hearts and basic selves, such as to our inner child, then connecting it with a greater sense of existence beyond the veil of instinct, the beginning of new growth can be inspired. To reach out to something deeply spiritual and morally higher – the divine – people can get a point of reference from which to think, reflect, and be mindful. To aspire for something more than what Nietzsche described, and criticised, as the Last man – one that has conformed and settled for a spiritually diminished state subdued by suffering – is to grow, to surpass the former self, to rise above vice, and rekindle dying spirit.

There is a definitive point in practising and applying mindfulness through the Will. In time, mindfulness heightens the capacity for self-awareness and general awareness. This helps a person to understand what is going on around or inside him or her; it brings to attention sentiments, feelings, emotions, and utilities of the mind that are essential to good living. Then, through ethical practice and being mindful of the soul's metaphysics, one can begin to channel mental utilities through actions, developing one's abilities and character through virtue. A balanced, healthy, and strong ego is one that is in harmony with spirit and the soul – unconflicted, not in discord of suffering, autonomous and independent through conscience. The body becomes an extension of one's will – not its headless arbiter. In due time this growth focus inward. Self-discipline can alter mental states through thought alone. It may seem absurd as though mental, rational thought alone can change one's way of thinking, the entire mental state, or even attitudes towards living. Mindful rational thought is only able to do so through a cultivated sophisticated mechanism using many pinpointed and established strategies which may involve memory triggers, music, habits, and much more. Habits of self-discipline can be broken, and the argument isn't that rational thought alone is sufficiently able to influence mental states, attitudes, and sentiments.

The argument is that *habit* and *self-discipline* are a way to learn how to channel internal states. The internal world cannot be wholly controlled – it can only be channelled; certain actions and compulsions can be controlled through cultivated mediums of channelling interest and desire. But it is very much possible to influence mental states and emotions through mindful, disciplined thought through an established structure of mindfulness and habit – through virtue. The overall state of living and its perception through spirit can be influenced by conscious thoughts. This is what heritin ethics ultimately tries to achieve and make habitual, intuitive.

It is extraordinarily difficult to see things from another angle and try to channel negative and evocative thoughts during times of great distress; it can take longer than a single moment, than a month, than a year. Cultivating certain habits and triggers for such adaptability and flexibility of the mind can be done through many utilities and the liberty of autonomous judgement and morality will prove instrumental for these developments. The core of this practice involves self-questioning, especially of desires and behaviour. The Ploy is the pinnacle of this ethic, of reflexive mindfulness and self-awareness. The Will, as a projection of mindfulness, spirit, and sense of self onto the world, has been proved very useful and very practical towards these ends. However, it is only as useful as it channels mindful thoughts inward and through the deepest parts of the mind, then doing the same outwardly with change and states demanding action. But this whole deterministic and mechanical account of the psyche, of spirit, of soul, of the mind and of consciousness will only make most sense through further study of the metaphysics of ethics and its relation to the conscious mind.

Section 4:

On Consciousness

Chapter 31:
Origins of the Mechanism of the Fundamental Will

The mind lives through the brain. Somehow and somewhere the complex physical network of the body gives rise to consciousness, subconsciousness, awareness, and the mind. This physical network and its mind embodies and performs the functions of the fundamental will. So how does the mental phenomenon of the conscious mind come into 'existence' through the physical body? How do complex structures of atoms and molecules become conscious, become something very distinct from the rest of the physical world? How have mechanisms of physical substances constructed complex operations such as actions, thoughts, and desires?

The Fundamental Principle of Living Beings and the 'will' to flourish are the core of all behaviour and underlie all processes of living. The ability to interact with the environment through the Fundamental Principle requires a form of information-processing, which is performed through mechanisms of the brain and operations of the mind. Hence, in relation to the discussions in Section 1 and the conceived nature of the fundamental will to flourish – to gain positive ethical interest and value – I consider the 'will' of flourishing as the foundation of the mind or as that which exemplifies the Fundamental Principle of the mind's operation. How has the physical brain developed this core mechanism to sustain living and activate behaviour, to pursue ethical interests?

The following discussion will concern itself with developing a functional understanding and view of the mind's operation. The function of the will to flourish is ingrained in conscious life. One could argue that a body capable of interacting with its environment with a degree of intention is enough to consider the body to be of an operational mind or organ able to process information. This claim does not equate the mind with self-awareness. More so, consciousness may be associated with the mental phenomenology of experiences and sensations, with the experience itself, such as of colour, being a form or manifestation of consciousness[1]. However, another aspect that may be associated with consciousness is cognition or deliberative thought[2] – the ability to process information – or perhaps relevant awareness[3], whatever that awareness may be. All these functions are to at least some degree related to the physiology of the brain. This suggests two parallel aspects of the conscious mind and its operations – the physical and the mental. So how is the Fundamental Principle bound to both these faculties? How does the conscious mind operate?

A developmental or evolutionary account, befitting the genealogy of the human psyche, could be helpful in structuring functions of the mind in terms of ethical development and growth. Pressures of Natural Law and natural selection have shaped human nature. People do not have the greatest natural advantage of claws, fangs, or the fastest legs. However, our intelligence, our minds, and our social nature are our main assets for surviving. Mankind has risen to the top of the food chain and our civilisations have flourished through our adaptiveness and ingenuity. Language and communication as part of our advanced social nature have been key utilities. Spoken and written language is one of mankind's greatest assets as a social species. This allowed for thoughts, information, and wisdom to be passed on to other generations and people.

The ingenuity of written language is not of simple instinct – it is a utility of high-reason. Yet how did an original thought spark into existence in the first place? How did our ability to speak develop? Language is particularly interesting because it carries with it very complex information that involves both baser and higher faculties. Everything discussed and studied uses language dealing with information and meaning. The prerequisites of physiology enabling such activity of the mind and body involve very sophisticated aspects of the fundamental will. Language exemplifies meaning and information; information engages the world and instigates, as well as conditions, responses. All ethics and behaviour operate through information, the operations, functions, mechanisms, and causal structures of which are represented through language. How does information affect the determination of the will and its understanding of circumstances demanding action? How is the physical aspect of information operational in the mind?

People are able to learn and use language, with the ability to learn language apparently innate. Functionally speaking, how does the brain wire itself for language? How is the brain capable of connecting thoughts to movements of the tongue and mouth, of the fingers and wrist? How do sounds and written structures begin to allocate or assign meaning? At the core of these questions rests the idea that somehow the wiring of the brain is capable of connecting mental phenomena (meaning and information) with and as part of the physical body. Somehow the brain and mind are easily able to perform complex information-processing and cause equally complex behaviour. Regardless of whether the physical and mental realms are of separate substances, their operation is natural, fluid, and fundamentally connected. The Fundamental Principle of Living Beings could prove intrinsic to these finer aspects of behaviour and living beings' operations.

The fundamental will dictates and directs behaviour, conditions our responses through and with information, and provokes responses in accordance with given information, or rather the fundamental will exemplifies the purpose and function of behaviour. But all behaviour of the Fundamental Principle is entwined with the computational reasoning underlying all mental behaviour. For instance, reasoning in our brains and minds, on a physical and mental level, somehow goes: "If this is better for my well-being, then I will do this," thus producing actions. This way of thinking and mental operation underlying actions is of a goal-directive nature, as was argued in Section 1, and is thus *computational*. Reason and logic are fundamental to all behaviour. Language exemplifies information and meaning, which is operationally only coherent and functional through reason and logic. Therefore, where goal-directive operations of the mind and body are bound to reason and logic, the Fundamental Principle is present both mentally and physically, aligning these operations through reason and reducible logic. Computational operations of the physical and mental faculties may be analogously distinguished as hardware and software, with electricity that embodies all operations acting as the equivalent of logic constituting pieces of information. The Natural Law of the operations of living things to pursue ethical interest illustrates both physical and mental behaviour. The mind seeks out the preferred outcome as is desired for well-being, which must have a physical correlate, while the body acts on such determination. The Fundamental Principle embodies both mental and physical operations.

People's capacity for language undoubtedly developed with the brain and its connection to the body. The evolutionary advantage of social creatures sharing information is intuitive, whether through written language or body language. Information affects behaviour. The senses gather and transfer information, which is then represented with language. It is important to note that all information affecting behaviour, or information that we are directly aware, of is *meaningful*. Meaningful information can be transferred in different ways, as sounds of a spoken word or through symbols of a written thought. Information can have a 'raw' form of meaning adapting to different types of mechanisms dealing with information. For instance, the number '2' consists of the sounds of the word /tu:/, the grammatical structure of the word 'two', and the numerical symbol of '2'. Underneath all this is the central, raw meaning of the idea of '2'. New ideas and meaning can form without an innate functional structure representing that information until phonetic or written structure is assigned to it. Those instances of epistemic satisfaction, those 'ah-ha!' or 'eureka!' experiences of instantaneous clarity and understanding, are indicators of the inner dealings of the mind with raw meaning that is not yet ascribed to specific language. This central raw thought or meaning is important for understanding developments and operations of the mind, because it demonstrates raw information. It can be very familiar to think in terms of assigned meaning, such as with language, but an underlying form of information and meaning is definitely always present and consequential.

Development of language accompanied the development of the brain. As our intelligence developed, so too did our chances of survival. Our brains gained extra capacities and material to perform more complex operations with information – that is, developed higher modes of reasoning beyond simple 'I am hungry, I must eat, so I must get food'. Subsequently, those what, how, and why questions arose. How has the anatomy of information-processing, essential to the operations of the fundamental will, developed? What role or relation does this development have in terms of raw information?

Considering the human brain requires a lot of nutrition and sustenance for its proper function, the nutritional aspect of the brain as a material substance corresponding to operations of the mind may hold some clues to understanding said operations. Of particular interest is Richard Wrangham's work *'Catching Fire: How Cooking Made Us Human'*. In short, the hypothesis proposed by Wrangham is that cooking food made it more nutritionally efficient, more digestible, which in turn allowed for greater brain development[4]. The hypothesis will not be evaluated here, but the suggestive thought, regardless of how hypothetical, can serve as an account for the main point sought to be made. As newfound material was digested and tried to be placed in the body, one part of it certainly must have involved the growth and development of the brain. After all, as with all bodily growth, energy and nutrition are essential. This extra material possibly allowed for the creation of spare neurons that might not have served a direct purpose of any kind. Regardless of how this specifically happened, the brain began to grow and store extra material. This material, whether of white or grey matter, or of neurons or glial cells, was the foundation for advanced brain functioning and information-processing, including that of greater rational thought. But any such material or parts of the brain would be adjacent to the base parts of the brain, built on the physiology operating through instinct. Fitting in with this idea is the inherent functionality of a healthy psyche (and balanced state of living) that necessitates both baser and higher faculties to be synchronised and satisfied. The two modes of thinking must also be interconnected on a physiological level.

Section 1 argued that the mind and psyche wholly operate through reason. Base-reason guides the functions of sentiments, feelings, and emotions, even if non-deliberatively, while high-reason is ascriptive of traditional deliberative reasoning or of rational thought. In the past, base-reason of instincts could have gotten muddled up and confused in the reasoning produced by the extra material of the brain that was not directly assigned to one functional task of an instinct, bridging various parts of the brain. With the need for action, morality was created through a combination of high-reason and base-reason. This new material connected different parts of the brain, diversifying states of mind and the capacity for thought.

It is not a strange thought to suggest that an excess of liberally assigned neural structures allowed for greater information-processing and mental operation. Subsequently, new thoughts and questions accompanied expanded information-processing. Reducing the constant burden of survival allowed for early humans to explore their minds, the world, and living. Some bored fella may have sat on a rock and couldn't occupy their thoughts with anything meaningful. So they began procrastinating; they picked up a stick and started hitting the sand in front of them. Thus, in boredom, art was created. Of course, this thought is only intended to be humorous, with inspiration obviously being a key factor in the creation of art. When this act of art was given a functional purpose – as in, the brain figured out that markings in sand or tree bark could aid our needs by transferring information – written language was created. With reference to the Fundamental Principle, the conscious mind has to stay occupied in fulfilling its directive of pursuing positive ethical interest, which led to the creation of various practices including philosophy. The main point of these suggestive thoughts is to highlight the relation between the conscious mind and the physiology enabling its function. Physical structures have a fundamental role in influencing mental activity. This idea will become more apparent as it is developed towards the conclusion that the physical is wholly deterministic of corresponding mental functions. Furthermore, it is interesting to propose some account of the physiology of the psyche in terms of its baser and higher faculties of reason, with less restrictive aspects of the brain enabling greater channels for thought and expanding the resources of core systems of information-processing.

To explore the interconnectedness of the brain and the mind's complex and rich internal states, consider music. Music is able to trigger the most profound and perplexing feelings and emotions. Music can trigger old memories; its rhythm can appeal to something primal in us; its choir can ease our minds, while its beats can uplift our spirits when we are close to tapping out. The exact physical mechanisms of music's influence on the brain and mental states may not be fully understood, yet its fundamental moving quality is real nonetheless. The clearest mechanisms of music and related perception operate through hearing and soundwaves. A soundwave with certain properties is heard, and then the mind interprets it. Music affects people very differently, no doubt setting off our convoluted emotional structures. Emotional states directly affect our overall mental state and phenomenal perception. Where the physical mechanisms of music affect certain emotional triggers, those physical causes also affect our mental states and fundamentally influence how we think. The ability for music to quickly and fluidly evoke very diverse mental states, emotions, and sensations is a testament to the complexity and deep interconnectedness of the brain. It would be a very sceptical argument to ascribe this interconnectedness to the suggested model of neural patterns undefined by rigid mental organs, which then allow for operations of information across many spheres and levels of the mind. But, nevertheless, it becomes apparent that mixed and complicated emotions affected by music are suggestive of a deeply interconnected nature of the brain that directly corresponds to the mental realm. Music is a type of information for the physical senses or that carries with it certain physical information, which can then profoundly affect the mind and states of consciousness. Therefore, it is not at all absurd to consider the physical and mental aspects of the mind's functionality and consciousness to be interconnected, with information being of two mutually operative forms – causal in terms of both the physical and mental.

Regarding the Fundamental Principle, it is a function present in the direction of actions, but not necessarily thought. Thoughts structure the parameters of actions through a goal-directive function shaped by the Fundamental Principle. But it is the absolute directive to pursue positive ethical interest, determining which action is committed, with thoughts only conditioning the parameters of actions. By their nature, thoughts are operations of information, but they are not necessarily the complete causes of actions. After all, there is little we can do to control our thoughts, for they have a will of their own, it seems. For instance, the subconsciousness can often bring to our awareness random, irrelevant, or unhelpful thoughts or memories. However, these are just thoughts, just jittering of neural connections and not calls to action. The Fundamental Principle somehow regulates thoughts and channels the most productive ones towards actions – the Fundamental Principle is present in the conditioning of information relevant to a tangent of an action. The behaviour of thoughts then moves focus on learning from our greatest pains and perceived failures, creating repeating and at times inconvenient thoughts, with depressive thinking patterns becoming habitual, triggered by relevant influences.

A paradox of causality arises between these faculties of physical and what appear to be mental influences on the determination of actions. On the one hand, the physical structure of the brain and nervous system prompts certain actions, then on the other, mental structures of the mind regulate and cause other forms of actions. Alternatively, some function enables habits, such as of healthy lifestyles, which incidentally produce good outcomes. This paradigm of behaviour draws on the understanding of the interactions of the brain's functions loosely related to instincts and actions primarily aligned with base components of the brain. So the question now is how do these faculties interact? Or more precisely, how do rational and conscious thoughts and base processes of the brain interact with one another? What underlies the mechanism of thought?

It may be helpful to differentiate between *organic* and *synthetic* thoughts. Organic thoughts characterise immediate, basic information formed through observation of the world. These are the most intuitive thoughts. For example, by seeing a blue pen, 'this pen is blue' would be an organic thought. Synthetic thoughts are thoughts compounded through antecedent, more basic information – thoughts and information produced by inner mechanisms of the mind. Interpretations of information, such as scientific theorising and moral evaluation, are clear examples of what can be classed as synthetic thoughts. The way we see the world and interpret change through fundamental beliefs and impressions is often constructed in the mind, suggesting world-views are synthetic in their nature.

This model of thought is not intended to be strictly defining or completely certain; its idea borrows from organic-synthetic aspects of the model of structural ethics explored in Section 2. The operational nature of thoughts is particularly relevant to present interests. The immediacy of a circumstance provoking a reaction instigates instinctive thoughts such as of self-preservation. Base-reason takes affirmative control over the mind; high-reason only becomes supplementary by providing additional information in a narrow base mode of operation. For instance, very stressful or dangerous situations take hold of the mind's concern. Thoughts become focused on the immediate circumstance; they do not drift towards day dreaming or deeply reflective thought. The mind engages with present, most evocative information; this way of thinking is intuitive and *organic* in its functionality. When stressful or threatening circumstances are overcome, the mind naturally begins to learn from the experience, to reflect on it, try to understand it. The mind focuses on *synthetic* operations with information.

As would be known, moments of self-reflection and attempts to understand very stressful or painful experiences can be very confusing, emotional, and difficult. The processes responsible for these operations of the mind are organic, but their sophisticated mechanisms are best described as synthetic in their nature, because they are much more ambiguous and less certain. Synthetic thought may seem more rational and deliberative, whereas organic thoughts are intuitively clearer. Organic thoughts may appear self-causal, self-propagating. Synthetic thoughts, however, appear more controlled, intentional, at liberty of their functions. Synthetic thoughts – as rational, deliberative thoughts – are functionally peculiar.

The mechanisms that synthetic thoughts operate with, such as reflective and analytic thoughts, are not as intuitive or clear as organic thoughts focused on immediate information. Organic thoughts are rather structurally simple – the senses are focused on the circumstance and thoughts fit into the narrative of a given focal lens. The scope of awareness is narrower and more operationally engaged, with the Fundamental Principle presiding over these functions. The capacity for freedom of deliberative thought is restricted where concern and interest is more defined. This isn't the case with synthetic thought – there *is* greater freedom of information and impression in analytic and reflective thought. It may seem as though we are 'free' in our thinking, that we can somewhat control thoughts. Deliberative thought, such as with traditional rational thought, may seem consciously controlled – a conscious will moves synthetic thought. However, to any external observer and any scientific investigation, never does an 'operator' of thought appear – a soul or spirit is not observable. However, self-aware experience forms the impression and respective thought that there is an 'operator' of the conscious mind.

Freedom of thought and liberty in deliberative thought are illusions. An operator of the mind is a misconception and misinterpretation of self-awareness. Operations of thoughts, even synthetic ones, are self-causal and self-propagating. They operate in terms of their own potential for operation through corresponding functions and mechanisms. Operations of the mental realm must be functionally bound to their physical parallel, according to which a mystical operator is fundamentally counter-intuitive. Observing two events simultaneously or the potential of two distinct courses of actions does not necessarily entail that we have freewill or *freethought* (causal freedom in thought). From a physical point of view, we know that neural activity of the brain relates to mental processes including thoughts. Certain elec-tro-chemical functions may occur that connect various parts of the brain where-by different connections are established and corresponding mental states manifest themselves. Thoughts accompany and/or are created by physical processes.

But if the conscious mind is a distinct substance to the physical brain, then how can there be something driving thoughts? How can two fundamentally different sub-stances be causally obligated? A fanciful operator of the conscious mind is too caus-ally ambiguous to fit into the clearest model of the operations of the conscious mind bound to physical processes. While mental thoughts definitively affect and corre-spond to physical operations, the dynamic of this activity can be misleading. Men-tal thoughts do not precede the physical processes of thoughts, but rather mental phenomena *accompany* the physical processes of thoughts as equal parallels. Where deliberative thought is equally tied to physical processes, it must be causal and deter-ministic. Deliberative thought, by its very nature, cannot be of its own causal liberty. The accessibility of information is conditioned by environment, experience, impres-sion, and internal capacities for mental operations with information. The way the mind deals with information is heavily conditioned by deterministic factors. Peo-ple's dispositions for creative and analytic thought are a testament to the determinis-tic nature of thinking and operations with information. The intellectual capacities of people, levels of education, and available information are deterministic of our cog-nitive capacities, ways of thinking, and thoughts themselves. Thought has none of its own causal and behavioural liberty – it is deterministic, mechanical, and conditional. Thought must follow certain structures, or else it would be incoherent, with incoher-ence being a symptom of decaying and dysfunctional organs of thought. Consider this argument as the *necessity of causal coherence*. Freewill is an illusion, and so is free-dom of thought. This supposition should be explored further.

How are the mental and physical faculties of the conscious mind causally paral-lel? If the mind did possess freethought, then how would it be capable of processing information in the first place? If there was a sea of information and thoughts, how could the mind interact with it? How could the mind function if there was complete acausal liberty of thought? Without particular mechanical structures of influence in place, there would be complete chaos of thoughts and ideas. Yet the mind functions quite well in terms of the primacy of ethical interest. There are faculties of influence that direct elements of thought encompassing logic, creativity, available knowledge, memories, experiences, impressions, beliefs, and so on. It can be argued that in a free-for-all of information countered by the suggested view of the impossibility of freedom of thought, coherence and functional structure are imposed by the laws of logic, by laws of the mental realm and its conscious mind. Regardless of the meta-physics of such views, the functional account still requires the mental realm to be causally coherent with respect to the physical. But if the physical aspect – that is, the brain – has any degree of involvement with the mental, a causal account becomes necessary in terms of both the mental and the physical. Broadly speaking, this chal-lenge is known as the *mind-body interaction problem*. Insights of the Fundamental Prin-ciple as the core function of behaviour may offer new areas worth considering for the study of the mind. Can the Fundamental Principle be applied metaphysically to both the mental and physical aspects of the conscious mind?

It is sufficiently clear that a mystical freedom of thought is impossible in opera-tions of the mind. The mental account of the Fundamental Principle as an evolved and established Natural Law of goal-directive behaviour is credible. The physical account, however, is more ambiguous. How does the Fundamental Principle engage physically or is functionally parallel to the physical? We can be certain of the following – sensory impulses carry with them energy that activate various parts of the brain. If my finger is cut, then the nerve stems receive a signal that travels to my central nervous system, accompanied by or triggering the experience of pain. Energy reflected from or channelled through the sharp object caused my skin to tear. That energy then spreads across tissue and activates the nerve. This causes certain reactions that result in a current of energy shooting from the finger towards the brain. This in turn triggers the physical mechanism related to pain, such as the release of pain-related signals, and activates a response or engages deliberative thought as a complex reaction to pain.

Within these models of behaviour one can draw out a principle of purpose and function in behaviour – the preservation or cultivation of ethical interest, of well-being. A deliberative response to the experience of pain is an example of the fundamental will in practice. In terms of behaviour and active living, the Fundamental Principle is an absolute directive present in all relevant functional aspects. The Fundamental Principle must have some physical aspect beyond its manifestation as a principle in continuity itself – it must have a physical correlate to cause something. Furthermore, spirit as the general sense of living must have a particular physical mechanism. Perhaps these suggestive thoughts in themselves are not the right ones. The precise physical nature of the Fundamental Principle and its functionality remains unanswered and there is still too much ambiguity.

What physical element causes or is causally parallel to the fundamental will to flourish? It would be helpful to revise ideas from Section 1 on the practical metaphysics of ethics. The Fundamental Principle of Living Beings and Actions states that *all living beings' actions and the dynamics of mental functions move in accordance with, and are determined by, the pursuit of the greatest or highest mode of well-being and flourishing, with the determination of mental functions subject to mental states and functions of the mind in accordance with relevant and available influence on the will; all actions are functions or contingencies of the will to flourish.* In simpler terms, behaviour of living things is determined to follow its greatest conceivable ethical interest, conditioned by information and thought – the mental aspect. The possibility of this principle was found in the nature of goal-directive behaviour pursuing circumstantially positive ethical interest. As was argued, this function of behaviour, which is necessary for sophisticated behaviour in terms of deliberative actions, is derived from observed continuity and sustainability of behaviour. After all, where behaviour is unable to sustain an organism's well-being, it suffers. The metaphysical conclusion of Section 1 in regards to the Fundamental Principle was that the will to flourish is found in continuity of sustainable behaviour. The Fundamental Principle, in this sense, is best understood as an orientation of intent and desire. However, the physical parallel of this function isn't clear; there must be some relevant physical property. Keeping these insights in mind is crucial for developing any sort of coherent or sensible complete account of the metaphysics of ethics.

One potential view is that the fundamental will is a conglomerate will of reducible component 'wills', that every individual reducible particulate, whether cell, molecule, or atom, has a potential for willingness. A metaphysical principle of substance to move towards some sort of growth is conceivable. As there are certain mental laws, such as of logic, the same may be true for physical laws of continuity. It is certainly true that existence mandates conditions sustaining its continuity. However, to claim that there is a predetermining factor shaping substance towards continuity as a Natural Law is a very sceptical undertaking. To apply this sort of a metaphysical rule to physical substance is dubious and unscientific. Ultimately, unsubstantiated, unprovable, and leery appeals to metaphysics or mysticism are epistemically unsatisfying. The study of the metaphysics of reality is instrumental, but any functional account of the mind would certainly benefit from more precise study. A better approach is preferred. Any Natural Law of existence and reality necessarily being sustainable, applicable to the foundation of material substance, is not convincing. For any argument that reality continues to exist because conditions necessarily enable it to continue existing does not mean that prior conditions will necessarily apply or be effective in the future.

One may argue that universal causal cascades would inherently nullify unsustainable models of existence – that causal tangents leading to disaster would cancel themselves out. But any such claim is ultimately very ambiguous. A fairly simple counter-example is that people form memories and experience the present, but then when the moment passes that reality fades or is forgotten. Everything before our deaths existed and was 'real' to us, but death could very well cancel all that existence out. But then this example applies to reality perceived in consciousness and not to the metaphysics of substance of reality that may be subject to wholly different Natural Laws. These discussions could lead down many tangents of thought, but this effort isn't promising for present concerns. A different model of an account of the physical function of the Fundamental Will is preferred. In conclusion, it is unprovable and too ambiguous to consider any argument that every individual particulate functionally involved in operations of the Fundamental Principle have a will of their own.

The alternative approach is to reductively develop insight by examining functions of the Fundamental Principle. In conscious deliberation on actions, intentions and desires set the precedence for goal-directive operations of behaviour encompassing both thoughts and actions. There must be some physical mechanisms through which desires and intentions are possible and operate. Regardless of the precise science behind the mechanisms of desire and intention, directives of the Fundamental Principle command behaviour. But as was concluded, an unphysical operator of the mind – of desires, intentions, and behaviour – is unconvincing or outright impossible. Yet it is clear that the Fundamental Principle and its will is found in continued functions of the brain, in the actual operations of the brain. Is the Fundamental Principle antecedent to operations of the brain and mind? No, because the Fundamental Principle only has functional purpose where it is concerned – that is, in terms of actions. But actions are only provoked by a causal power demanding them, for if there was no need for actions, then they would not take place. Established patterns of actions as sophisticated and structured reactions then become habitual, compulsive, *behavioural*. It is then sensible to ask a following question of whether, during the evolution of goal-directive functions of the mind, desires and intentions preceded actions. In goal-directive functions beckoning actions, did the first instance follow a desire, or did the desire develop with habit?

Basic neural structures can invoke reactions as reflex-based actions or as responding actions functionally centred in base elements of the psyche and even wholly subconscious faculties, hidden from deliberation. Deliberative actions may appear wholly different to simpler reactions. The appearance of distinction is possibly rooted in the conscious awareness of deliberative actions and the subconsciously rooted instigators of reactions lacking deliberation. This dynamic and difference, as well as the very nature of deliberation, ought to be studied. Small organisms may interact with the environment through reactions rather than actions, whilst humans can act with conscious deliberation involving *desire* and *intention*.

Reactions are functionally rather straightforward to understand as pure mechanisms. Deliberation is a more sophisticated process, which must be accounted for physically parallel to the mental aspect. The view opposing freethought implies that deliberation is not a function at its own liberty, that it is subject to the conditions of thought and necessities of causal coherence, because thoughts are necessarily deterministic, mechanical, orderly, and structured. Where information conditions and shapes thoughts, and deliberation is not functionally indeterminate, deliberative actions must therefore be structured and deterministic as well. In practice, there is no choice over the choices of actions, with conceivable courses of actions only being available in terms of the conditions of circumstances and ingenuity conceiving possible actions and outcomes, with the Fundamental Principle shaping the final action.

Thoughts can be spontaneous or seemingly irrelevant, but their application and range of interest and concern is influenced by the Fundamental Principle. Focusing on a situation beckoning action is a function concerning itself with well-being that demands action. However, the processing of information and thoughts themselves are not direct applications of the concern for well-being as actions are. That being said, the precedence of thought in terms of relevant concerns is invoked by interests of well-being which dictate the concern of thought. The Fundamental Principle is relevant to deliberation and the function which thoughts try to fulfil. For example, this study tries to understand how the mind works. By understanding how the mind works, greater insight can be found and then applied in future deliberation. All development, whether developing habits or learning from experience, is relevant to the functions of the Fundamental Principle. Deliberation is subject to its deterministic conditioning, consequently suggesting that deliberative actions are conditioned by structured and orderly mechanisms. Desires and intentions are part of the mechanisms of deliberation, being part of the process of deliberation by setting the precedence and motivation for thoughts and concerns. Therefore, desires and intentions are deterministic in themselves. If all deliberative processes are deterministic, mechanical, structured, and orderly, then deliberative actions are procedural. Reactions are procedural as well.

Accordingly, the only difference between reactions and deliberative actions is that the latter is a more sophisticated mode of the former. Where high-reason may serve ends conceived by base-reason, such as with base morality, deliberative action is only a mode of reaction dealing with greater degrees of information and more complex information. *Actions are intricate, sophisticated reactions.* Conscious desires and intentions are consequences of complex and competing information. Deliberative actions are consequences of desires as competing interests and information; deliberation is a reaction to competing desires.

Desires are functions of the fundamental will; desires are engaged ethical values and tokens of our will. Desires are not merely mental phenomena and are functionally physical. Ethical values, as aspects of desires, and their functions of goal-directive behaviour have a physical body of operation. Simple reactions, such as of microscopic organisms, would seemingly have no ethical values or desires in their movements. It would seem counter-intuitive to suppose that a body's reflex – the simplest form of reaction – is of any sort of desire or functionally bound to some ethical interest.

However, all deliberation that concerns itself with an ethical interest is only a complex reaction, therefore, in a sense, a compound reflex. Deliberation is a deterministic mechanism following the precedence of desires. But for the immediate interest, it has been concluded that the Fundamental Principle must be antecedent to deliberation. The Fundamental Principle is evident even in the simplest of desires and ethical interests by their very nature, as it is necessary for their successful function. Further reduction suggests that all reactions are extensions or composites of their simpler forms. Reactions and actions follow deterministic mechanisms subsequent to information; reflexes are the same. The only difference is conditioned by varying degrees of information such as sensory information and relevant knowledge. Thus, reactions and actions can be understood as levels of reflexes, as actions are procedurally determined by the conditions of available information, with the manner of information represented in the form of thoughts being deterministic in itself. Actions can be viewed as reflexes to choices, interests, and conditions of information. The Fundamental Principle is reducible with every ethical interest. However, no ethical interest is, strictly speaking, functionally independent in the sense that ethical interest is a consequence of continuity (as the fundamental will is). The Fundamental Principle is derived from observed functions and continuity – it is observable behaviour as developed functions of physiology and psychology. This observation is made in terms of actions which are reducible and applicable to reflexes as well. Ethical interests and desires aren't mere mental figments mystically influencing behaviour – they must have a concrete base. That base is reducible to the simplest form of reflexes.

It is not that the Fundamental Principle exists in its own realm independent of the physical, but that the Fundamental Principle is an observable phenomenon or function borne of the simplest continuity of physical processes. A simple physical process may cause a physical body to move deterministically, unintentionally, and non-deliberatively. Where that process, such as a reflex, was sustainable and successful, it could grow, then evolve. In this sense, the physical component, element, aspect, or mechanism of the Fundamental Principle is simply sustainability and continuity of bodily functions. The Fundamental Principle does not necessarily have to exist or be true. But just as continued existence has to be true of existence itself, movement of the body has to be sustainable for it to continue moving. Therefore, the Fundamental Principle has to be physically true of the continuity of life's movement for it to also be true in terms of its mental aspect.

The truth of the Principle's physical nature is metaphysical, but its function is as real as observed continuity. The physical function and the nature of the Fundamental Principle are its own continuity through the body; even the smallest of non-voluntary movements of the simplest of organisms is a manifestation of the mechanism necessitating flourishing that is then known as a 'will' to flourish. The 'will' or 'soul' referred to in previous Sections of ethical study was intended to be fully deterministic and physical in its nature describing mere uncontrolled movement, only conditioned by the forces influencing the mechanisms of behaviour. The soul is not a substance of its own, but rather a mere manifestation of continued physical processes. This point is crucial to the structuring of ethics, as it suggests actions to be wholly deterministic, not disengaged from the natural world.

While it was assumed from the beginning that operations of the mind are contingent on the physical, further argument has now established that operations of the mind can be accounted for in wholly physical terms parallel to the phenomena of mental processes. However, the precise mechanisms of parallel operations remain to be illustrated further, and the proposed arguments are not yet intended to provide a hypothesis on mind-body interaction. The physical aspect of the mind's functionality is conceived as operation of and through the body, particularly the nervous system (the brain and sensory systems). The mental, on the other hand, concerns itself more with informational processes of the mind itself, correlating with physical processes but not necessarily defined by them.

Conscious experience – the first point of familiarity with everything – is the medium of all information that we are consciously aware of. *Phenomenal experience* is the quality of consciousness and the information we deal with, for everything that we experience is phenomenal as part of our awareness of experience[5]. The phenomenal is equivalent to experiences such as of colour, of sound, of pain, and so on. The physical is the medium of the process that led to the actual phenomenal experience – the experience through which other information is interpreted and is known through our awareness of said information. The mental can be of its own sort as well where we are not aware of the mind's activity such as in subconsciousness. Henceforth, when phenomenal experience or phenomenology is mentioned, it is a term restricted to the conscious quality of an experience, of a process, of an operation, and relevant information. To any phenomenal experience, such as of the sight of something red, there is a physical correlate of sensory information, in this case the information corresponding to the physical property and quality of the colour red. Physical functions and phenomenal experiences are subject to their relevant criteria of function and order, for all functions of the mind are subject to certain structure, order, and deterministic mechanisms.

The mental faculties have been considered to function wholly in terms of reason and its resources such as information, knowledge, and memories. Mental operations must have a physical correlate. Therefore, reason must have a physical element. Physical processes that grew into sophisticated reflexes led to the development of the brain and its mind. Therefore, to account for functions of the conscious mind and its Fundamental Principle, a physical correlate or aspect of reason is necessary. Previous discussions on raw meaning or raw information suggested a brute form of information through which the mind operates but only knows of through conscious experience. The mental and phenomenal aspects of consciousness are conceived as non-physical substances. After all, no conscious thought or experience would in itself, such as with the feeling of self-awareness, be of physical substance even though it operates in terms of physical structures.

This work will not delve into specific literature debating the subject, because it finds it disagreeable. Furthermore, it would be more useful to undertake a study to try make sense of how two different substances – physical and phenomenal – may interact, rather than denying the challenge by categorising it all into a single substance.

Phenomenal awareness only experiences the processes and products of thought, yet none of its deliberation is of its own consequence or operation. Consciousness has no direct effect on the operations of the mind; consciousness is only the medium of awareness of the mind's and body's functions, yet it does seem to follow certain causal order and with its own operational structure. Conscious experience, as was discussed earlier in terms of language, can be broken down into a simpler form of raw information or meaning. Raw information through which the mind operates must also be physical. However, because conscious experience does not operate the mind, such as through an invisible operator, raw information is functionally independent of its conscious experience, or at least primary functions of raw information cannot be based on conscious phenomenology.

Section 1 concluded on the nature of mental operations and the psyche as being wholly functional in terms of reason and reason's element of logic; logic is considered to be the natural foundation of mental operations developing reasoning. All operations of the mind can be structured through computational and mechanical functions of base-reason and high-reason. This view was built on a goal-directive nature of behaviour and its Fundamental Principle. However, this view was focused on the mental aspect of behaviour. Reason guides mental behaviour, but it does not strictly or directly apply as an account of physical processes. The Fundamental Principle and its reasoning was interpreted, not directly observed.

Thoughts and mental processes are necessarily connected to their physical counter-part. What is the physical counterpart to reason and logic? What is their simplest form? What is the particulate of logic, if there is one? How does reason structure itself mentally and physically? If reason is a necessary part of the mental, or at least if this is the case in describing the mental, then reason must be a necessary aspect of physical operations as well. After all, thoughts can influence behaviour in some ways, so reason and logic must have a physical correlate as well. There are many theories on cognition and reasoning, but the present effort is more concerned with finding a physical parallel to, or aspect of, logic as the foundation of reason, to consider logic as having or being a *substance* according to which reasoning occurs or is performed.

Reason and logic are computational, orderly, and structured, similar to mathematics and as seen with logical arguments. We can be certain of proper reasoning due to its orderly nature such as with $2+2=4$. Reasoning is built on logic putting two and two together. Reason and logic manifest themselves in conscious experience – are phenomenal – as thoughts. The certainty of some rational thoughts must have a concrete physical base, as we know that all thoughts follow relevant neural processes. Logic, as compounds of raw information and raw meaning, can be found in everything that we can analyse or is relevant to reasoning. There must be accessible and relevant information for reasoning and thought to occur. As such, logic is the compounding of information through the inherent qualities or properties of compatible, combinable information. Information, such as sensory data leading to impressionable thoughts, is the particulate of logic and subsequently reason as structures of logic. The reasoning that $2+2=4$ consists of many different particulates of information, in this case '4' meaning 'four of something'. This opens up many channels for discussion, but present efforts should focus on what is considered the *anatomy of logic*.

The certainty of reason goes hand in hand with the certainties it tries to explain or describe; mathematical order in the sciences is a testament to this. That being said, ambiguity is abundant in rationalising thoughts. Fundamental worldviews and core beliefs can influence thoughts towards absurd interpretations and wild assumptions. The thought that everything can be somewhat structured or that everything follows certain mechanical patterns is itself biased. But even reasoning that seems absurd, such as in terms of a fundamental view, can be structured through a particular logic, with opposing thoughts subdued by defensive mechanisms of the mind. There is a physical aspect according to which these operations of logic are performed flawlessly or questionably; there is a physical parallel to reason that works as the 'two and two together' nature and model of logic.

All certainty and ambiguity in logic must have a bodily anatomy. Visual data retrieved by the eye stimulates the respective organ of information and passes that sensory data through a neural pulse. A neural pulse passes visual data along until it reaches a point of information unified into conscious awareness, becoming phenomenal or directly known through consciousness. Conscious *awareness* here is intended to mean the phenomenal experience and activity of the mind and body that we are most or are directly aware of. If something in sight is significant or impressionable enough, it may dominate attention. If something dangerous is perceived, it will take hold of one's mind. That information may then become reflexively, predictably, and habitually relevant to behaviour responding through action or thought. Natural or synthetic thoughts, or both, may become active and open to conscious awareness. An immediate danger may be known mentally and rationally understood, such as by structuring its (base) reasoning through ethics primed by an ethos of instinctive aversion to pain, while also having an underlying physical mechanism through which that reasoning operates. Visual data combines into a conscious representation and mental impression of an object known to be dangerous.

For example, a happy dog can be very loving and helpful, while a growling dog may be associated with danger to oneself or an impending threat. A physical structure is causally parallel to respective conscious and mental reasoning and information. The physical aspect of information fits into relevant physical systems in terms of the anatomy of logic to produce or align relevant mental conditions of reasoning. Reasoning on such dynamics is representative of the neural pulses operating in reason's systems and serving as a conduit for all thought. A neural pulse of visual sensory data fits in with the systems of information-processing responsible for reactionary behaviour conditioned by relevant information. Seeing a dangerous dog fits in with subsequent reasoning of conditioned reactions to the perceived threat. Fundamental beliefs suggest a core informational aspect through which neural structures operate, with flexibility of the mind, such as with cognitive dissonance, demonstrating its mechanical nature where sufficiently vigorous neural activity can fundamentally change one's attitudes and views.

This account makes sense in terms of childhood impressions influencing attitudes and thoughts in adulthood. Nonsensical reasoning and thoughts are possible in the mechanical mind where its narrative and preconditions of information are interpreted on the outset of received sensory data affecting the mind through established core neural structures and their categories of information – or knowledge. The model of logic as 'two and two together' or analogous to puzzle pieces fitting together must also have a physical basis in logic's anatomy as part of the brain, sensory organs, and the capacity to perceive. The anatomy of logic must consider appropriate, compatible, and consistent qualities of impressions and experiences leading to their respective thoughts along with a physiological (neural) basis. There must be a concrete physical substance corresponding to information imbued with deterministic and structured causal properties.

Consider the following model and illustration. A red apple is red and apple-like. Seeing a red apple creates a vivid phenomenal experience of an apple with all its qualities. The redness of the apple is itself a particular phenomenal experience. That redness is experienced in correlation with physical systems causing activity in the brain. A ray of light corresponding to the apple bears specific physical qualities that can be mathematically described such as with the ray's wavelength, frequency, and intensity. These physical qualities distinguish red from, say, blue rays of light with their own physical characteristics. Light reflecting off the apple hits the eye and leads to the formation of relevant visual data, which is then translated into neural activity as information digestible by the mind correlating with conscious experience.

Physical properties of red light correlate with qualities of the experience of redness. The visual data of redness correlates with information and phenomenal qualities of redness. This illustration can be formalised in terms of P and Q. The physical properties of red light P (as visual data in/of the object and corresponding neural activity carrying and/or inferring that data) causally relate to red's phenomenal qualities and properties Q. Alternatively, physical properties of red P correlate with visual data and its respective neural information Qd, which then corresponds to the qualities and characteristics of the phenomenal experience of redness Ql. In a healthy and fully functional physical sensory system, its ability to realise and discern sensory data is structured and coherent. There must be concrete physical properties of respective sensory data that differentiate causal influences acting on neural systems and information correlating with vividly distinguishable phenomenal experiences. Judging by the systems of sensory information and the order of subsequent mental operations and conscious phenomena, or said systems being structured and orderly after the point of receiving or interpreting visual data, there is a definitive causal framework in the physical, mental, and phenomenal – that is, respectively, of the brain, of the mind, and of conscious awareness. Information of relevant properties and qualities is an ascribable feature of real events, coherent in describing real differences in causal mechanisms of sensory systems and their conscious phenomena.

Phenomenal qualities – properties of what it is like to be something or what the experience of something is in or as consciousness – are otherwise known as *qualia*[7]. The explored framework of operational systems between the brain (sensory systems), the mind (information and knowledge), and consciousness (phenomenal experiences) outlined deterministic causal structures between relevant properties and qualities of related events. Qualia are considered to be strictly appropriate only to qualities of phenomenal experiences and consciousness. However, the systems and substance of qualia must also have a physical parallel correlating with orderly differences and causes. Phenomenal data and information must have reciprocal physical information and data. But because our first point of awareness and familiarity with information manifests itself in phenomenal form as consciousness, phenomenal qualities must have underlying physical properties. In the case of light correlating with the colour red, the quale of redness has an underlying physical quality with its own information that is causally differentiable in physical systems able to operate with that substance, to operate within that unconscious world. The physical correlative qualities or properties of qualia can be defined as *quidia*. Quidia are defined as follows – information or data of causal attributes correlating with qualia. The conscious experience of redness is the *quale* of red, while the properties of red light correlating with subsequent sensory and neural activity corresponding to the experience of redness is its *quidam*.

Quidia describe the physical aspect of information in causal systems and the phenomenal correlate to neural activity. It is crucial to understand that quidia are considered to be metaphysical, not strictly physical. Quidia are used to describe and categorise information relevant to causal systems of information involved in consciousness and operations of the mind (not exclusively in terms of cognition). Similarly, numbers and abstract concepts are used to describe physical phenomena.

While applying numbers to describe something doesn't necessarily imply that numbers are in or of the world itself, it doesn't deny the reality of described deterministic and orderly causal structures. Quidia are of the same nature, used to describe phenomenal events in conjunction with their physical correlates such as with redness or any colour necessarily being causally related to sight and visual sensory data.

Sensory data allows us to experience the world and gather insight. The senses are the source of some empirical information and knowledge. Therefore, quidia underlie operational information of the mind involving empirical knowledge. However, as has been argued, all mental operations have a physical correlate. Quidia concern themselves with information linked to sensory data, thereby becoming relevant to associated mental empirical information directly or through interpretation. This same empirical information constitutes relevant thoughts. It goes, then, that quidia are the substance of certain thoughts.

Thoughts concerning empirical observations and impressions correlate with physical dynamics of neural systems. The neural aspect engages with differentiating criteria of information and may include empirical information as sensory data, which is describable in terms of underlying quidia. Information engages logically with compatible information, forming lines of reasoning as logical arguments and synthesised information combined in the mind through inherent characteristics (as per the impossibility of freethought). Sensory data may produce empirical knowledge through the compatibility of information describable in terms of quidia. Then, synthetic thought can be logically and causally structured in association with other premises, memories, or beliefs, and so on.

The seemingly random thought 'pink elephant' pops into my conscious awareness in association with reflection on synthetic thought because it is a memory from previous experiments with random thoughts. The creative element of that random thought can be tracked down to the impression of a pink elephant from a childhood book. Creativity and imagination may seem to be a challenge to the orderly nature of the mechanical mind built on quidia, but the randomness of creativity can be accounted for via habitual thinking patterns (or lack thereof, or their flexibility) and a history of impressionable experiences. The representative mental image of art is itself a mental construct, seemingly different only as a distinct conscious experience to, say, a sound. Infinite regressions and associations in ideas and synthetic thoughts can be accounted for through antecedent information and respective quidia.

On this note, it is worth mentioning that memories and stored mental information, in terms of quidia, might be nothing more than stored and recycled quidia. An impression or experience is stored or replicated in the mind, forming a memory, which then adds to the entangled informational structures of quidia. In this sense, knowledge and the mind can be imagined in terms of a whirlpool to which objects are constantly added. These objects – information and quidia – are then recycled in the operations of the mind, setting the foundation for cognitive operations. The puzzle model of logic exemplifies its computational nature; quidia can describe or note the causal properties differentiating between specific patterns and behaviour of the nervous system with regards to correlating mental activity. Conscious experience of thought involves an underlying 'raw' form of information, with reasoning constituted by pure logic. Particular behaviour of the nervous system can be accounted for through properties of its electrochemical activity, with parallel systems being describable in terms of quidia. Thus, quidia can serve as an account of the physical substance of, or substance correlating with, logic and describe logic's functionality.

Quidia are the answer to the structured and orderly nature of thought, providing the necessary piece to understand the dualistic anatomy of logic in terms of its physiological mechanisms and mental operations.

The main question of this Chapter concerning the functional origins and nature of the Fundamental Principle in terms of the conscious mind can now be directly addressed. The Fundamental Principle is not in itself a causal principle as a conscious thought influencing and conditioning behaviour and functions of the body and mind. Usually, we are not even directly consciously aware of our desire for well-being; rather, the directive of well-being is preconditioned, precognitive, assumed, and innate. The Fundamental Principle is unconscious and is not directly observable – it is deduced and, as such, is metaphysical and abstract. However, it is metaphysically – that is, *ontologically* – necessary. For example, for something to exist, it must necessarily be able to exist. For behaviour and life to exist, it must necessarily be able to continue existing in a given moment of its existence – while it is still alive. The Fundamental Principle is derived from observed continuity, thereby being ontologically necessary as a condition of behaviour and living. However, it then becomes an observable influence at least as a conditioning factor, ascribable to both mental and physiological aspects of behaviour. How is this possible? Furthermore, how is this possible where it must be independent of direct consciousness and must have a concrete causal base?

All bodily and mental operations, functions, and mechanisms are structured, deterministic, and causally coherent. Consciousness has been stripped of causal power as physiology has been argued to be the primary cause of operations – conscious awareness only observes bodily and mental movements. Regardless, the physical and mental, even as distinct substances, necessitate causal coherence in their functionality. The mechanical nature of the body and mind are suggestive of causally coherent properties and categories like puzzle pieces fitting together. An account of this has been put forward in terms of *quidia* as self-computational categories and components of operational functions of the body and mind. Different functions of the body and mind must be coherent for their proper, orderly execution, according to which there must necessarily be certain categories and properties to differentiate causes. This point is an application of our thoughts to describe the information and sense data producing those same thoughts. While quidia are ultimately abstract, they are valid and appropriate in describing observed differences in behaviour of both the body and mind. Quidia describe and account for categories of different causes and the orderly causal structures through which the body and mind operate.

Operations with reference to the Fundamental Principle, such as thoughts or bodily movements, have been argued to ultimately be non-deliberative, wholly computational and deterministic, even reactionary and reflexive. Continued behaviour and living is only possible through successive accidents adapting to circumstance and environment. Sustainable and effective behaviour led to its growth and evolution conditioned by the necessity for sustainability, with the basis remaining the same – non-deliberative, computational, and reflexive. Behaviour through the Fundamental Principle, thought to be consciously deliberative, is no different, as is necessary with the rejection of freewill and freethought. Self-causal sustainability – that is, non-deliberative or absent freedom of will and thought to do so – of continued operations and behaviour, which is described in terms of the Fundamental Principle, can be made ontological sense of in terms of quidia.

The Fundamental Principle is necessarily applicable to the continued functions of both the mind and body, as its ontological certainty is necessary for observed sustainability of operational causes and living. The Fundamental Principle can be a principle or parameter of functions and mechanisms describing bodily and mental functions at least as parallel causes operating by the same principle as is necessary for the order of coherence. Even if the body and mind are wholly different substances, their continuity and sustainability necessitate parameters of behaviour described in terms of the Fundamental Principle.

Both faculties operate necessarily in terms of the Fundamental Principle, applicable as a description of the functions and operations of the psyche. Causes of the mind and body don't necessarily interact; rather, their understanding can be made sense of through a common operational rule, principle, or parameter. But in terms of the necessity of order of causal coherence and the impossibility of freethought, the mental cannot be independent of the physical. The mental aspect as rational thought and deliberation is only a faculty of the brain's operation, only different through consciousness; the mental is only another operation of the body. Causal coherence can nonetheless be found in both the mind and body, consciously or not, in terms of the structures of computational categories and the properties of causes – in terms of their *quidia*. The phenomenal aspect of behaviour – its conscious form as that which we are aware of – is functionally accountable through structures of causes compounded through relating quidia.

In conclusion, the Fundamental Principle is not an observation in the continuity of causes, but is an ontologically necessary feature of all continuity of bodily and mental operations and their behaviour. The Fundamental Principle exemplifies sustainability of behaviour and respective functions, as well as illustrates necessary conditions for said behaviour. As such, the origins of the Fundamental Principle are found in sustained and continued behaviour and living, and ontologically necessary as a Natural Law applying to behaviour as physical movement. Then, regardless of whether the body and mind are of separate substances, their functions must abide the Fundamental Principle. The nature of bodily and mental operations is not without its own conditions of orderly causal coherence.

The question of whether or not the body and mind interact is wholly accountable in terms of common conditions of their operations, mechanisms, and functions through the Fundamental Principle. That being said, the arguments and thoughts put forward dismiss the mind in its common sense, relating it to the brain and all cognitive processes to physical systems. However, conscious awareness of behaviour and living, as well as of bodily and mental operations, is vividly distinct. Causal coherence in the body and mind has been accounted for through quidia, which are abstract descriptions of concrete events subject to their own parameters and principles of dynamism and operation. Even mental operations ascribing quidia to operations of the mind that we are consciously aware of is an operation of the mind itself, giving rise to what we may know as the *conscious mind*. However, the mind and its behaviour can be unconscious as well. The Fundamental Principle can account for operations of both the body and the mind regardless of whether or not they are wholly distinct substances.

That being said, quidia and qualia *are* wholly different substances. Qualia as properties of phenomenal, conscious experiences are all that we are ultimately aware of and know, but they do not seem to have causal power. Structures of causal influences relating to the conscious mind can be made sense of through an alternative account arguing that consciousness has no direct causal power and operations of the conscious mind can be coherently structured through the mind parallel to behaviour of the brain by appealing to causal coherence and respective quidia. Nonetheless, consciousness and its phenomenal nature and qualia are fundamentally different to quidia and the body and mind. For a full understanding of the functions of behaviour and operations of the mind, one must then understand consciousness itself and the relation between qualia and their quidia.

Chapter 32:

Qualia

The nature of qualia has been widely debated. Some argue that they are physical, others suggest they are purely mental or metaphysical, and some question their very reality. This study will work with the view that qualia are very much 'real' but are unphysical, although correlative of physical causation and physical properties in terms of quidia. There are physical processes and corresponding quidia that underlie the behaviour of qualia. However, consciousness, in its most direct sense, operates in terms of qualia and phenomenal experiences rather than their underlying physical causes – we are directly aware of qualia, not quidia.

Conscious experience is the necessary reality we deal with, as it is the front of all information, observation, and experience. The previous Chapter argued that consciousness and qualia do not have direct causal influence on behaviour. However, even if they did, their operation would be bound to the Natural Laws of behaviour according to the Fundamental Principle. If qualia and consciousness are indeed acausal and do not serve any definitive function of behaviour, then why do they exist? How do they exist, especially in relation to quidia? What is the nature of qualia and consciousness? It would help to begin by looking at the fundamentals of conscious experiences.

David Chalmers argues that qualia and consciousness should be considered fundamental aspects of the universe, similar to matter and energy, even though qualia are subjective and non-physical[7]. Chalmers argues that certain aspects of the universe, such as space-time and electromagnetism, are taken as fundamental elements of the universe we inhabit because they are irreducible. These elements are considered fundamental without due appropriation – they simply are considered fundamental. As Chalmers wrote: *"No attempt is made to explain these features in terms of anything simpler"*[8]. He then proceeds to suggest that: *"a theory of consciousness should take experience as fundamental"*[9].

Whilst there are reasons for considering certain things fundamental where they are not further reducible, these arguments in terms of consciousness are weak. It may seem that phenomenal experiences simply are the way they are and are irreducible, thus fundamental, but this hardly offers profound understanding on the subject. As Brian Earp wrote, Chalmers' arguments do not offer 'epistemic satisfaction', they do not give rise to that 'eureka!' moment of profound understanding[10]. It is not promising to assume the nature of qualia and to take them for granted. By then applying this fundamental understanding to the hard problem it only offers a solution through defining the question as a tautology or reducing the idea into a circular argument. Saying that consciousness is the way it is because that is the way it is hardly explains much. Claiming 'red is red' is a tautology, yet saying that 'redness in the world is red because it is red' involves connecting perceptions with the external world, whereby little is certain anymore. Are qualia fundamental? If so, what part of their nature is fundamental or how are they fundamental?

Chalmers explored the potential variations in the phenomenology of qualia[11]. An in-depth analysis or critique is not necessary for the present context, but a suggestive thought is raised on the nature of qualia – how they present themselves. He discussed the question of whether or not the same experience could potentially alternate in different physical systems, concluding that different material structures replicating the same causal system would not change the quality of the experience itself. However, this does not explore the presentation or manifestation of the experience itself in its most basic form or the consistency with which phenomenal experiences present themselves.

It is without a doubt that phenomenal experience is a type of information. We are aware of our understanding of the world in terms of conscious experiences. When one sees the colour and shape of an object, the conscious mind portrays the properties of the object through and with different mediums such as visual representation and linguistic representation (like an inner dialogue describing the mental image). Certain processes occur in the world that transfer and interpret physical changes, which are then picked up by the sensory organs. The functions of the sensory organs – the *senses* – provide consciousness with relevant information correlating with their phenomenal forms of *perceptions*. Consciousness understands the world around it through perceptions – the actual phenomenal experiences corresponding to sensory information, but the reality and nature of those perceptions is questionable. It is a self-evident thought that perceptions can be hugely deceptive and are limited in their access to certain knowledge. We can see colours, but it is reasoning performed by the mind that suggest the knowledge of the true nature of light.

Scepticism over perceptions is valid, but in practice this can neglect the constant quality of the presentation of repeated occurrences of perceptions' information. If a person opens his eyes, provided the eyes work properly, he can see – receive visual sensory data. Perceptions and the phenomenal experiences are fluid and constant. If I look at an object of the physical world, such as a red blanket, my perception of it will not change unless something happens. If I leave it in the same place, it does not move; if I do not tear it, it maintains its shape; if I do not wash it, it keeps its colour; all of which corresponds to my phenomenal experience of the red blanket. If the physiology of my eyes does not decay and fail to function properly, and the properties of the red blanket are not interfered with, then my perception of the blanket won't change. Yet when something does change in the world, my perception accompanies or accommodates that change. Every passing moment is portrayed through a perception, and perceptions of active changes consistently reoccur. A previously unfamiliar experience, either a colour or shape, usually comes naturally to conscious awareness. The sight of a few rays of light peering between the branches of a Christmas tree, the flickering and movement of a candle flame, the movement of a ball through the air, all such phenomenal experiences just seem to occur with ease.

Considering the difference in phenomenal experiences, qualia extend to beyond mere colours and shapes. Qualia are the very foundation of perception, including the movement of objects, the feeling of raw thought and meaning, and self-awareness itself. Everything we know of the world naturally is rooted in the perception of qualia. We then know of qualia's respective quidia through the mind's introspection on perceptions, as properties and categories corresponding to the particulates of events. The orderly causal coherence of physical systems and their quidia also applies to coherence in phenomenal experiences. Unless the physiology of a sensory organ undergoes certain changes, it seems to maintain a contingency of identical and coherent perceptions. Phenomenal experiences of perceptions are subjective; even so, consciousness doesn't tend to suddenly switch the quality or category of perceptions without a corresponding change provoking change. If I stare at a red blanket without interfering with my eyes and sight, then the perception of the red blanket would remain the same. Phenomenal experiences are constant, consistent, and orderly within functional systems with fixed properties; they are natural and fluid in consciousness. We do not have to focus or concentrate on what we are perceiving – our consciousness is abundantly stimulated with phenomenal experiences without having the need to make sense and categorise a phenomenal occurrence. We do not have to put in any effort to experience perceptions; phenomenal experiences just happen. Causal categories of phenomenal experiences, in terms of their respective quidia, are a way to structure and categorise the phenomena of consciousness.

The fluid nature of phenomenal experiences is suggestive of their inherent, fundamental properties. These fundamentals can be attributed to the world itself – qualia being mind-independent – or to operations of the conscious mind – mind-dependent or *mentally synthetic*. The former view suggests that qualia exist as fundamentals of the world and are fundamentals independent of the functions of the senses, perceptions, and the conscious mind. According to this view, phenomenal experiences are non-representative, purely reflective of a degree of reality corresponding to the world. The latter view is that qualia are properties formed by the functions of the senses and perceptions operating through schemes or blueprints enabling the qualities of experiences – not reflections of the world. As sense data triggers activity demanding a conscious form, it is the functions of the senses and perceptions that create qualia to interpret and represent information – the mind or sensory functions *synthesise* qualia. Essentially, as our senses begin to operate they conjure a conscious form where necessary. These forms can be of the world itself as the objects we directly observe the way we do, or representative through our minds filling in the gaps.

Suppose the view of qualia as fundamentals of the world independent of mental synthesis and interpretation as the *realism of qualia*. Qualia do not exist outside of consciousness because they are qualities of consciousness itself. The realist view of qualia would argue that qualia are fundamental properties in relation to quidia, not that consciousness assigns the qualities of experiences to sensed quidia. For example, a deaf person may have never heard sound properly due to damaged sensory organs. However, give that person a hearing aid and he or she can begin to perceive new sounds with ease. As with all perceptions, new phenomenal experiences would come easily, intuitively, organically. The radical change in perception through synthetic intervention may suggest that phenomenal experiences are beyond just structures of the mind or aren't purely mind-dependent. As the physiology of a sensory organ changes, its perceptions adjust accordingly, absent clear metaphysical tuning of the interpretation of phenomenal experiences. Simply put, conscious experiences manifest themselves without any awareness of deliberate operations making them 'real', suggesting that the properties and qualities of phenomenal experiences are natural to the mind and not made up. In this way, if phenomenal experiences do not rely on metaphysical structures to interpret the qualia of physical processes underlying perceptions, qualia can be argued to be fundamental of the world itself. Accordingly, perceptions are reflective of reality, not representative.

An immediate issue raised by the idea that perceptions are reflective of the world itself is familiar in terms of the common response to any form of realism – the illusion of perceptions. Perceptions rarely offer absolute certainty in what we see. Visual illusions can play tricks on the mind and the mind itself can sometimes distort what a person sees. This fair point may seem to challenge the position of qualia as being objectively fundamental. However, this is only an issue raised by the limits of sensation and perception. People cannot see x-rays directly, but we can know of their existence through other methods of interpretive perceptions such as through science. The reality of perceptions can be distorted and limited, however, this does not entail that all perceptions are illusive. Rather, it is an issue concerning the limits of non-synthetic perceptions of sensory organs. Occasions of conflicting quidia may reflect strange outlier qualia that do not truly represent reality. Yet this does reflect a degree of reality corresponding to the present quidia. In this sense, distorted perceptions are not a flaw of phenomenal experiences, but are undermined by the limits of received sense data and relevant qualia. Actual physical mechanisms malfunction in relation to reality, the accompanying perceptions of which consequently are also distorted.

If qualia are fundamental, then they are reflective properties of *degrees* of reality, but perhaps not of absolute reality. To relate this thought to observable changes in the perceptions of deaf people through hearing aids, one may not hear a certain note, thus not be naturally aware of it beyond other knowledge such as through vibration. The ears might not detect a soundwave with the properties of a C-sharp, but then easily experience the sound in conscious form if the ears are adjusted to hear it. These new perceptions may open up consciousness to new aspects of reality, yet perhaps not to the entire degrees of reality such as other sounds or other possible perceptions of sound through the other senses. The senses pick up on physical changes and perceptions tap into respective qualia. Therefore, it can be argued that qualia are fundamental to objective reality.

Alternatively, one may consider the view that qualia aren't properties or qualities inherent to quidia. Fundamental categories of qualia in terms of quidia as categories of perception-formation may be understood as blueprints for interpreting sensory data and forming or invoking corresponding perceptions and respective qualities of perceptions. The blueprints of qualia with respect to respective quidia are embodied by the sensory organs themselves and related mental functions, not as inherent fundamentals of objects of the world and their forms of information. The mind synthesises, assigns, and/or associates qualia with their corresponding quidia. All perceptions could be interpretative fixtures of the mind; thus, perceptions are not reflective of fundamental qualities of the world. The qualities of phenomenal experiences can be made what they are through their correlating blueprints of perceptions that conjure qualia. Therefore, qualia are mentally synthetic. More so, blueprints for the interpretation and formation of qualia may be the primary faculty of the mind able to perceive and experience phenomenal qualities in the first place. For instance, without a scheme in the mind that is capable of identifying the colour red, red light might not be able to be identified through purely organic perceptions. Such a metaphysical stance would face significant challenge from a physical and material understanding of the world because claiming that there are causal abstract 'things' in the mind that are the primary mechanisms for identifying the qualities of experience is highly sceptical, a point also applicable to the notion of quidia. However, there is a great deal of scepticism in discussing the mind and consciousness, as both these categories of enquiry depend on inherently metaphysical identities and qualities.

If mentally synthetic schemes are responsible for the identity of phenomenal qualities, then this hypothesis would have to account for the radical and fluid changes in perceptions and phenomenal experiences. New and reoccurring perceptions in a similar category of association, such as colours, are constant and consistent in their qualities of familiarity: red is always red, green is always green, blue is always blue, and so on. The established qualities of perceptions constantly reoccur in their same degree of familiarity. In this sense, conceptual schemes of phenomenal experiences can serve as default configurations for the identifiable qualities of phenomenal experiences. So whenever new sets of perceptions are introduced to consciousness, their corresponding qualia are subject to the establishment of default schemes for perceptions. A previously unfamiliar perception comes naturally to the mind, even though certain experiences may feel a bit strange or odd at first or could evoke awe and excitement. Encountering a previously unseen colour comes effortlessly to the mind and consciousness. The schemes of perceptions underlying or corresponding to the qualities of perceptions are thus either synthetic in accordance with the physiology of the senses, or innate to the interpretation of sensory functions. Default configurations of qualia are either mentally synthesised by consciousness to identify the quality of a perception, or the quality of a perception is preordained by innate schemes of the mind.

Concerning the latter, it can be argued that whilst the physiology of the senses is assisted with synthetic mental mechanisms, consciousness has hidden innate configurations for identifying the corresponding qualities of phenomenal experiences. This position of innate default categories for identifying qualia is more sensible in terms of the contingency and fluidity of organic perceptions. On the other hand, in regards to conceptual schemes of perceptions being mentally synthetic in some categories, it is difficult to convincingly argue that consciousness is able to instantaneously set a parameter for the quality of an experience without glitches or bugs analogous to computer software distorting the appearance and function of the phenomenal experience.

To explore the nature of phenomenal or conscious schemes (blueprints of perceptions) or their equivalent as default categories for the qualities of perceptions, it is reasonable to believe that people tend to experience the same or similar perception of the exact same object. Suppose two people have more-or-less the same operational systems of sight. They would likely report to see the same colour of an object. If there is a clearly red cube in front of two people, the people are likely to report seeing the same colour, or at least they will sense a similar shade of the cube. This thought could suggest that phenomenal schemes of qualia are default in their relating categories. However, this interpretation of the relation between quidia and qualia wouldn't be correct. A person may receive certain physical sensory stimulation that carries with it objective forms of information, but the assignment of qualia to those sensations does not necessarily correspond to the reality of quidia – qualia can be mentally synthetic constructions. The people seeing the red cube may receive the same physical stimulation and the same quidia, yet this does not necessarily mean that they perceive the same phenomenal experience, which we ultimately wouldn't be able to tell. It may be that the phenomenal schemes of one person actually assigned the colour blue to the senses corresponding to red. It is vital to make a note that quidia and qualia are inseparable; similarly, any phenomenal schemes corresponding to qualities of perceptions are inseparable from the physical processes of corresponding sensations.

To ease ambiguity, schemes assigning qualities of perceptions and all meta-physical or mental constructs of conscious functions must relate to physical senso-ry mechanisms conditioning perceptions and enabling their coherent structure. To resolve the question of the origins of default qualia or of conscious schemes, these faculties can be mentally synthetic or innate to perceptions. Mentally synthetic prop-erties of phenomenal experiences suggest the view that the qualities of perceptions are created in the mind after sensory organs find a source of perception.

In this sense, new forms of perceptions, particularly those the mind is wholly unfamiliar with, are accompanied by phenomenal experiences with qualia being as-signed, associated, or represented through physical processes. This evidently has to occur instantaneously and through perfect mechanisms of consciousness, or other-wise glitches and inconsistencies in perceptions could be problematic, which evi-dently is not the case. The alternative view suggests that conscious schemes underlie default configurations of phenomenal experiences, whereby perceptions can only appear in conscious awareness by having an access point for interpreting sensory functions of physical mechanisms.

This view can be challenged by considering the development of physical systems enabling perceptions such as with the evolution of eyes. When an organism evolved to have eyes and to see, it was likely able to see as quickly as its physiology allowed it to. More so, the primitive organism that developed its first eye probably didn't pos-sess a sophisticated mental faculty in order to 'assign' or 'create' conceptual schemes for its perceptions. If the defaults of qualia are set innately within the mind, then how did the first perceptions form? What was the first conceptual scheme that allowed other schemes to emerge and perceive different sensations? Narrowly focusing on this position isn't promising or sensible. In regards to focusing solely on either of the two views, to suppose that the phenomena of perceptions are wholly mentally syn-thetic or absolutely innate to the mind is unconvincing and problematic.

A feasible alternative to addressing the question of the origins and nature of qualia is that processes identifying qualia are fundamental to perceptions themselves and their relation to sensations. In this sense, default configurations of the qualities of phenomenal experiences are entwined with the physical systems of the senses and not with the faculties of consciousness itself. Quidia and qualia are inseparable; similarly, conscious perceptions and physical sensations are interchangeable. The focal point of this discussion is the constancy, consistency, coherence, and fluidity of phenomenal experiences, henceforth referred to as the *argument from fluidity*. Qualia do not necessarily have to possess the exact worldly characteristics that we are famil-iar with. They are not objective in relation to the external world, but they are funda-mentally subjective to consciousness. Perceptions are wholly tied to the sensations they correspond to. Yet in conscious awareness perceptions are constant and possess consistently identical characteristics. The synthesis of qualia in consciousness cannot account for the origin of conscious phenomena.

In other words, conceptual schemes and default configurations of phenomenal qualities could not pre-empt the influx of new perceptions – the scheming of qualia would have to be fundamental of sensory functions. Also, qualia cannot be solely mentally synthetic at the point of sensation because perceptions follow clear stand-ards for the reception and interpretation of experiences. If qualia and phenomenal experiences were 'made up on the spot', then this would likely result in some varia-tions, inconsistencies, or 'glitches' in the same quidia of a perception, implying there is at least a certain degree of fundamental categories for the synthesis of perceptions such as the equivalent of conscious schemes of perceptions. Therefore, I suggest an alternative that qualities of phenomenal perceptions are fundamental of sensations themselves and that qualia manifest themselves through the physiological functions of sensory mechanisms.

It is evident that perceptions are subject to the functions of the senses. The manifestation of qualia is greatly dependent on their corresponding quidia, whereby any state of quidia that we are aware of is accompanied by a corresponding phenomenal experience. The manners in which perceptions present themselves are constant and fluid in consciousness. New, unfamiliar experiences are natural to the senses and perceptions, but both the senses and perceptions of new experiences require a relatable trigger and default or basic configuration. A system of categorisation is essential for perceptions and consciousness, suggesting that phenomenal schemes of mental phenomena and qualia are not innate or synthetic in the mind or consciousness alone, but are intertwined within the sensory functions that permit the influx of information. Perhaps the interpretation of conscious schemes of phenomenal experiences is misinterpreted. Rather than default configurations of perceptions being innate within the mind, they are actually innate or fundamental to sensory systems enabling perceptions.

This position would accept that the origins of the qualities of perceptions are automatically enabled by the predisposition and configuration of the senses in relation to their corresponding perceptions. So as soon as the first eye was able to see, the primitive form of consciousness was able to perceive the subjects of visual sensations because the configuration of those perceptions was innate to the bodily system of sensation. In other words, qualia and perceptions 'attach' themselves to the processes of sensations. This view could also account for the constant, consistent, and fluid nature of unfamiliar experiences, as the universal default qualities of perceptions accompany all the various systems of sensation. Thus far the position that perceptions are fundamental of the physiology of sensations is sensible, but this idea has to be examined in relation to other faculties of consciousness. More so, qualia and phenomenology extend to internal states, beyond the imminent sensations of eyes and ears.

To illustrate the aforementioned view, I will outline an analogy of the conscious schemes of perceptions as being similar to a telescope. A telescope's lens is able to alter the properties of light before light hits the eye. In analogy, the telescope itself can be seen as the sensory organ, such as the eye, which is capable of interacting with the substances of the external world – with light. The lens of the telescope interacts with light and changes its properties. In this case, the lens is equivalent to the schemes of perceptions identifying or constructing qualia that then manifest themselves in consciousness. As of yet, I will not explore this analogy further to draw implications on the nature of qualia as substances beyond the realm of consciousness.

So far this study has focused on external sensations, yet what of internal states? Emotions and internal feelings are also major constituents of conscious phenomena. Sensory organs outline degrees of reality concerning the external world in accordance with states of quidia, and processes within the body are no different. In terms of consciousness and its sphere of awareness, everything outside of conscious awareness is foreign, unconscious. The body and the influences acting on the body shape consciousness as we experience it. However, phenomenal consciousness itself is the primary substance of our awareness. Everything beyond conscious awareness is external until it reaches consciousness in the form of phenomenal experiences.

Pain travelling through the body is triggered by the nervous system connected to a section of our anatomy, but the phenomenon of pain is presented to us as a conscious experience. Emotions are known to be the result of certain mental states triggered by chemical and biological processes. The physical systems underlying mental states have particular states of quidia which by themselves are external to directly phenomenal consciousness and only when they reach conscious awareness do they correspond to the internal appearance of phenomenal consciousness.

Accordingly, all physical mechanisms of internal states form sensations just as the physiology of sensory organs evokes perceptions of the external world beyond conscious awareness. Mental states that are produced by bodily functions such as pain, temperature, balance, hunger, exhaustion, or by emotions such as anger, love, envy, sadness, joy, all these phenomena of consciousness are very distinct in their nature. Sometimes they may over-lap, can even be unfamiliar and confusing; nonetheless, they are usually distinct. Each state is triggered by very particular processes within the body and corresponds to exclusive circumstances. Pain results from harm to the body, the sensation of balance adjusts movement when the body is unstable, the feeling of heat from intense sun-light spreads throughout the body. There are very particular functional mechanisms and components that correspond to each of these sensations and relating perceptions. Phenomenal experiences and qualia manifest themselves directly through operations of the sensory systems, and they do so consistently and with definitive organicism. The most sensible position to account for the presentation and nature of qualia as metaphysical mental phenomena is that they are created through conscious schemes of perceptions inherent to sensory systems and that qualia manifest themselves directly in relation to the quidia of sensations taking hold of and/or replicating in consciousness.

All qualia emerge directly in relation to sensations, however, not all sensations become phenomenal or conscious. Our perceptions often adjust to sensations. For example, our visual experiences tend to ignore the nose and move focus on more important observations. A physiological explanation can account for this presentation of conscious phenomena such as the mind's mechanisms focusing attention. Now that I am thinking about my nose, I am focusing my line of sight on it – I notice it more. Then my mind decides to focus on writing, and I begin to ignore my nose once more. Other forms of sensations, particularly emotional ones, can pass consciousness completely unnoticed. Sometimes we act without thoughts and motives we are consciously aware of. The subconsciousness often directs entire functions of our bodies absent direct conscious awareness of the corresponding intent and desire, as is especially the case with reactions. Perceptions and qualia of sensations *only* appear and come into 'existence' through conscious awareness of them. More so, it is clear that phenomenal experiences are not necessary for the computational behaviour of the mind or body. Sensations can occur absent qualia, but perceptions necessitate conscious awareness. Subliminal influences and subconscious states most commonly move the direction of our lives, they make us what we are without our conscious awareness even recognising this. Much of the computation of the mind goes beyond conscious awareness, with thoughts and patterns of behaviour revolving around spontaneous and transparent exchanges between internal points of information.

Internal states of qualia also concern thoughts in terms of 'raw' meaning and thought. The identity of thoughts, the substance of meaning underlying many mental phenomena, such as words, mental images, and ideas, are phenomenal experiences of internal information perceived and understood through qualia. Raw meaning and thought *are* another form of qualia. The conscious perceptions of thoughts do not control computations of the mind; they are simply the *phenomenal awareness* of the processes going on in our minds. The subconscious mind can come up with ideas that then become available in conscious awareness, yet awareness itself has no role in the mechanical computation of mental systems – awareness is the central observer, but not necessarily the operator. If relevant stimulation of various mental states is strong enough, then corresponding mental states appear in the forms of qualia and perceptions in conscious awareness. So in regards to computational thoughts of internal high-reason, if a thought is strong enough and particularly relevant to the activity of the senses and the awareness of them, then that subconscious thought will or may become accessible to the reach of conscious awareness. The same goes for all phenomena of conscious awareness. If the vigour of a sensation is tenacious enough, then it will move close enough to the reach of conscious awareness to manifest itself as a conscious perception.

A long-standing issue in the study of mental phenomena is the distinction between mental faculties, particularly of consciousness, awareness, self-awareness, subconsciousness, and the mind. I have not been forthright concerning the conceptualisation of these distinct mental phenomena, and for good reason. There are no clear definitions for the many points of interest regarding our mental qualities, largely because we do not fully understand our own minds and consciousness in general. Now that a certain view on the many processes of mental systems, something we are so deceptively familiar with, has been put forward, one can begin to categorise our notions of its many components.

The general term for consideration of our phenomenal mental substances is 'consciousness' – the thing we seem to be mainly familiar with. Phenomenal experiences appear as the dominant quality and subject of consciousness and awareness, whereby phenomenal experiences are the 'substance' of consciousness and, at the same time, conscious awareness gives substance to perceptions. However, perceptions are at the mercy of sensations and depend on the interests of awareness. There are physical processes that underlie phenomenal presentation, including the computation of reason. The nature of thought and mental computation is wholly influenced by physiology, as part of the argument of causal coherence in thought and the impossibility of freethought. In this paradigm, it appears that *consciousness* is the observer of mental functions, the phenomenal manifestation of underlying processes, particularly those corresponding to mechanical computations of reason. Thoughts pass through our conscious awareness and only become 'real' through perceptions when conscious awareness allows this through the determination of computational functions. As I have shown, reason is the primary faculty of causal influence on consciousness and the entire mental system. In this sense, *consciousness* can essentially be understood to be awareness, the centre of mental phenomena, the core of mental entanglement. Everything we 'know' is only known and cognitively acknowledged through conscious awareness, but the substance of conscious awareness is only made up by the functions governing it. Consciousness is the central observer, the hub of the mental.

On the other hand, the computational and mechanical properties of consciousness are those of reason. The reach of consciousness is often limited, and there are latent, subsidiary masses at the disposal of computational processes before they materialise in conscious perception. The vast stores of inactive, non-phenomenal properties of consciousness fall under the branch of *subconsciousness*. Memories, beliefs, hidden activity that does not present itself to and through awareness until its potential is activated to reach consciousness, all forms of presently dormant information are the veiled substance of subconsciousness. When the appropriate mechanisms are triggered and the corresponding types of influences are utilised, the computational mechanisms of mental systems can push subconscious entities into conscious awareness. More so, certain secluded subconscious processes can offer sudden revelations, whether it is a scientific break-through or a personal realisation. The psyche and the computational functions of reason are what can be categorised as the *mind*. The mind *is* the computational faculty of the mental system embodied in our nervous system, the primary mechanism of metaphysical reason and its associate quidia. It is evident that the mind can be both conscious and subconscious, whereby familiarity with it depends on the reach of consciousness. Furthermore, one should distinguish between the *conscious mind* and the *subconscious mind*, with the mind being the governing faculty of mental processes where subconsciousness harbours dormant capacities and secluded workings of the mind, while consciousness is the centre of familiarity and perception of the mind.

Qualia are subjective in individual consciousness and are only accessible to the individual experiencing phenomenal perceptions. These discussions have concluded that perceptions and their characteristics are determined by their default identities corresponding to conscious schemes of sensory mechanisms. The qualities of phenomenal experiences are default in terms of their determinations of quidia and the physical mechanisms that underlie mental phenomena. This fundamental and universal presence of conscious schemes of sensations suggests that qualia should be identical. If one person sees the colour red as it appears, then in due consideration of the characteristics of perceptions, it can be argued that another person experiencing the same visual sensation should see the same colour.

However, qualia nonetheless maintain their subjective position in individual consciousness and are not objective with respect the external world, as they are only found through perceptions tied to conscious awareness. Consciousness is not linked to other bodies of consciousness, and so the qualities of perceptions will only 'exist' to conscious awareness raising qualia. The conceptual schemes of the default configurations of perceptions are not known objectively through the external world, but they are metaphysical components of active sensations. Whilst the identities and characteristics of qualia may be universally fundamental of sensations, their perceptions are only fundamental of consciousness itself. Qualia are not fundamentally objective of the external world – they are fundamental of consciousness itself. Metaphysical aspects of the universe are the extensions or manifestations of conscious influences acting on the universe, with qualia being fundamental parts of the conscious realm. Considering that qualia are fundamental of the qualities of perceptions, it may be argued that qualia are objectively fundamental of consciousness itself, but phenomenal consciousness is inherently subjective in individual awareness.

To make these arguments more relatable, the theory of *panpsychism* suggests that there are conscious properties and degrees of consciousness tied to each physical element of the universe[13]. I have sought to show that whilst every material state has a corresponding state of quidia as data that can be sensed, even if dormant, similar to a mathematical identity describing physical behaviour and properties, each sensation we pick up on poses its own state of quidia. Qualia are constituents of perceptions that only manifest themselves through conscious awareness of sensations, which does not suggest that qualia are fundamental of sensations themselves – they simply correspond to particular quidia, activated through consciousness. Therefore, every physical element may possess latent capacities for qualia and perceptions, but it is the sensation and perception of them that ultimately forms the qualia we are so familiar with. The nature of qualia suggests that they are fundamental of *actively perceived* quidia and this is where the existential presence of qualia is limited. Therefore, I argue that qualia are fundamental properties of consciousness alone and not fundamental of the universe beyond perception and phenomenal experience, but are nonetheless fundamental. As for what exact place consciousness occupies or has in the world is not absolutely clear and remains to be studied.

Chalmers argued that qualia are fundamental aspects of the universe. I have sought to demonstrate how qualia are, indeed, fundamental of the universe, but they are not objectively fundamental of the external universe itself – they are objectively fundamental of subjective consciousness, which may be understood as part of the world. In other words, qualia are fundamental parts of consciousness, but consciousness is a universally subjective element of the universe. Now I consider that the nature and understanding of qualia does not have to be taken for granted and that there doesn't need to be profound confusion regarding their place in the universe. What remains now is the more difficult question – why do qualia exist at all? Their existence depends on perceptions that are themselves only realised if awareness grants them presence in, or relevance to, consciousness. The sensations and computations of the mind are predominantly physiological functions, and in terms of the proposed understanding of consciousness, there is no need for consciousness to exist in order for a body to function. Or is the claim of consciousness being unnecessary correct? Why does consciousness exist? Why is the mind conscious? Why does the body perceive rather merely sense? The subconscious mind can do the work of the conscious mind, but nonetheless conscious awareness 'exists'. This *hard problem of consciousness* will be the next subject of study.

Chapter 33:

Consciousness

The phenomenal aspect of consciousness is harder to explain. The central theme of this chapter is how quidia coexist with, or manifest themselves as, qualia. I have suggested how qualia are raised through perceptions and why the characteristics of phenomenal experiences are the way they are (in terms of configurations of the senses). I have sought to coherently place qualia within the framework of the universe and found that they are objective properties of an inherently subjective world where the realm of phenomenal consciousness is their home. However, I have not found exactly how or why we are phenomenally conscious at all. I have not figured out why qualia arise. The relation between sensations and conscious perceptions determines phenomenal experiences and qualia. Yet how does consciousness even come into existence? The circular relation between the substance of consciousness and the selection of conscious perceptions remains to be explored.

Explaining how and why we are conscious – why and how we have phenomenal experiences and sensations have qualia instead of being blindly operational without conscious awareness – is known as the *hard problem of consciousness*[14]. David Chalmers formulated the problem:

"It is undeniable that some organisms are subjects of experience. But the question of how it is that these systems are subjects of experience is perplexing. Why is it that when our cognitive systems engage in visual and auditory information-processing, we have visual or auditory experience: the quality of deep blue, the sensation of middle C? How can we explain why there is something it is like to entertain a mental image, or to experience an emotion? It is widely agreed that experience arises from a physical basis, but we have no good explanation of why and how it so arises. Why should physical processing give rise to a rich inner life at all? It seems objectively unreasonable that it should, and yet it does."[15]

The hard problem is contrasted to 'easier' problems of explaining the nature and behaviour of the conscious mind. Scientific methodology can be reasonably and successfully applied to the study the brain and its observable properties such as cognition. We can know of active thoughts by linking mental activity with observable neural activity. However, consciousness is its own subjective realm that cannot be directly observed beyond personal, subjective experience. Furthermore, the adopted view in this work is that consciousness is acausal. As such, without a direct function, the 'existence' or manifestation of consciousness, especially as the dominant form of awareness and experience of function, seems odd. What makes the problem 'hard' is because there seems to be no precise, scientific way of studying consciousness, because it is wholly subjective. Studying consciousness as a non-physical substance parallel to wholly physical operational systems cannot be performed in any conventional or structured way other than through metaphysics, which can be wildly ambiguous. Then, it is not certain where to even start to explain and understand operationally pointless consciousness or whether consciousness is pointless. This Chapter is dedicated to finding an answer, and developing insights into, the hard problem of consciousness. This Chapter will build on the understanding of the functional nature of the mind, categorised divisions of the conscious mind, and insights into the character of qualia and quidia.

Consciousness may not have any notable causal power on behaviour and mental functions. It is then conceivable that we or others could be 'philosophical zombies' – functional, moving things without consciousness[16]. As an example of the hard problem, there is no actual way of saying with certainty that others have conscious experiences – that they aren't zombies. It is reasonable to suppose that we all have conscious experiences, however, this can't be sufficient for studying consciousness. We often act through the subconscious mind absent conscious consideration or conscious decision-making. The computations of the mind occur deep in our subconsciousness absent phenomenology. To a certain degree, we are indeed philosophical zombies. In sleep, our bodies move around and the brain processes information, but our consciousness can only dream. We wake up with no direct awareness of what happened during our slumber; the only thing we can more-or-less remember is the darkness of absent dreams or a faint phenomenal experience of a dream. There are real instances of behaviour without conscious awareness of intent and desire. It is evident that we are to a degree 'philosophical zombies'. Why are phenomena of consciousness selective and temporary? Why is consciousness the way it is? Why are we aware of certain things?

The view that consciousness is acausal should not be disregarded without further contextual revision. Consciousness might not be computationally necessary, but it might play another role. A greater capacity for mental operation and subsequent integration of information results in advanced cognition and scopes of awareness – that is, what we can be aware. People's developed intelligence and sophisticated brains are the source of our heightened awareness. Simply put, the greater the intelligence, the greater the potential for complex knowledge and information-processing, thus increased integration of information in the mind. The more information we can process and hold, such as sense data and corresponding synthetic thoughts, the more aware we can be of our surroundings and ourselves, becoming more conscious. Giulio Tononi's Integrated Information Theory (IIT) portrays a neat theoretical framework for the degrees of consciousness and awareness, giving a formal account for the intuitive claim that greater intelligence and information-processing can result in heightened awareness or greater consciousness[17]. As the computational ability of the brain and mind develops, awareness may also gradually turn to self-awareness and consciousness. This work will not delve into a specialised scholarly analysis of IIT, as the present interest is proposing insight and introductory alternative thoughts on consciousness. The Integrated Information Theory may offer insight on the capacities of the mind, but the theory is, unfortunately, incomplete as a fundamental account of consciousness in terms of the hard problem, even though very promising.

The learned reader may spot the similarities between the arguments for quidia and IIT. This work is mindful of its place as a more metaphysical rather than scientific approach informally adding suggestive thought. A parallel philosophical and metaphysical argument may be necessary for any equal physical account of consciousness. No matter how conscious information is reduced to a physical substrate, such as with quidia, there is an epistemic and ontological gap between quidia and qualia. The idea of integrated information and information-processing being correlative of degrees of consciousness is a starting point to explore the function of consciousness.

Faculties of intelligence and the anatomy of logic are responsible for the computations of the mind, but what if consciousness aids this computation in some way? Moral deliberation and ethical inquiry are mainly conscious. When it comes down to very complicated questions, conscious awareness is immediately present in analysis and thought upon a subject of focus. As has been illustrated previously, consciousness presents itself to us as the centre of information and thought, bridging latent unconscious thoughts. What if consciousness and qualia are necessary for advanced information-processing of greater integrated information? What if phenomenal consciousness is the centre-point of information-processing of all-encompassing, complex questions?

The faculties of intelligence are responsible for computations of the mind. Developments in the psyche greatly influence moral reasoning and the functions of intelligence and logic. All reasoning is dependent on the computations of the mind, which is ultimately physiological. The computational mind can account for all reasoning, complex and simple, so consciousness is not necessary for complex thought. However, with greater intelligence and greater integration of information comes more advanced thought, accompanied by the conscious phenomena of perceptions of those processes. Phenomenal consciousness is that – phenomenal, not intrusive. More so, many bright ideas or sudden revelations can present themselves to consciousness without awareness of antecedent thought-processing – they just appear like a light bulb turns on. Often ideas just pop into our heads without due course of their conscious formation. It is evident that the unconscious mind does a lot of, if not the majority of, complex information-processing. The processing of emotions and memories is often subconscious. The bottom-line is that phenomenal consciousness does not seem to be necessary for computations of the mind.

An alternative might be to suggest that phenomenal consciousness *aids* computations of the mind. In this sense, the function of consciousness can be posited as a subject or tool of efficiency rather than necessity in computational functions. On deep reflection and consideration, the computations performed in the mind are incredibly complex, mentally and physically. For instance, how are neural structures able to easily recognise and categorise faces whilst digital computers find such functions incredibly difficult? To consciousness, cognition can be simple, easy, fluid, and flexible. It could be suggested that consciousness functions as an efficient means for computations of the mind. Is phenomenal consciousness an efficient mode for complex integration of information?

Consciousness somehow arises through the many cells of the nervous system. The phenomenal properties of information residing in neural networks are difficult to explain in purely physical terms, because the subjective, transcendent, and metaphysical elements of our minds are inaccessible to others. Within the operations of the mind, phenomenal experiences surface in the conscious mind vividly or faintly. The picture of a memory presents itself very faintly in comparison to the immediate visual perception. Even recalling the perception of a passing moment is nowhere near as vivid or clear as the original content of direct perception. The mechanisms of the senses deal with huge amounts of information. Seeing a simple object involves many things, such as the turning of focus of visual sensations, recording the influx of various colours, recognition of shape, acknowledgment of the object's location, and so on. Even the apparently simplest idea can be linked to countless other points of knowledge and reduced nearly infinitely. Every single word carries with it the potential to evoke conscious meaning, elusive to the objective observation of the content of others' consciousness.

In the vastly complex structure of the brain and mind, with all the integrated information residing in the unconscious and conscious mind, consciousness deals with information rather easily. The meaning of a single word may bear with it several links between neurons, or maybe an individual cell constructs the word's meaningful entity. The electrochemical processes within the brain are responsible for the causal mechanisms driving the mind. Through these elaborate interactions between physical objects, complex integration of information takes place. In everyday life, our conscious minds can deal with incredible amounts of information very quickly. In dangerous circumstances, the mind can swiftly consider many actions, then promptly act on its best judgement and assessment. These hugely complicated processes of the mind occur very easily to consciousness. It is apparent that in all functions of the mind, phenomena of mental states are correlative of quidia residing in the vast physical networks of neurons.

The substance of consciousness is restricted to the content of the mind and the degree of accessibility depends on the category and quality of influence. If visual sensation has strong influence on the mind, then focus of conscious content is centred on visual perceptions, as is the case with sensations in dangerous circumstances. It is clear that consciousness is the imminent collaboration between vast components of information – of interlinked quidia. These packets of information are then made easy by access through qualia, so qualia may just be the more efficient model for the interactions of quidia. From an evolutionary standpoint, a quickly functioning mind would certainly provide benefits to the survival of a creature. In this sense, intelligence may be correlative with a brain's access to qualia – a fundamental substance of the conscious realm of the universe. By being able to arrange information in correspondence with qualia, by allowing quidia to take on the simpler shape of qualia, the mind is capable of performing complex functions easily, thus giving a computational advantage of efficiency.

The consideration of the function of phenomenal consciousness as aiding computation of the mind through more efficient means in comparison to interacting quidia absent unifying qualia can warrant a degree of sense. Qualia may be fundamental elements of the universe, whereby their presence may assist information-processing in organic systems of integrated information. Tangled packets of data and reasoning become easily accessible to consciousness through the presence of qualia, thus giving a functional account. This way, consciousness and qualia can be considered fundamental types, elements, or substances of information, but in their purest, non-representative state, rather than as with secondary aspects of consciousness assigning meaning to properties external of qualia themselves. A universe absent qualia or consciousness could be envisaged, but what if the absence of consciousness and qualia was a huge disadvantage to conscious operation due to the inefficient computation of the mind absent unification and integration of information through phenomenal substances?

Developing this view further is not promising, as subsequent ambiguities are immediate and circular. These ideas of some kind of metaphysical substances mysteriously latching onto consciousness and consisting of an ineffable, transcendent fundamental part of the universe is a very sceptical hypothesis, especially with the implication that this substance could somehow interact with the physical brain. More importantly, however, computations of the mind are most definitely dependent on the physiology of information processing and integration. Phenomenal aspects of the mind are present through the processes underlying their arrangement. Unconscious thought becomes conscious by its degree of influence, but the initial creation of that subconscious thought pre-empts its phenomenal existence.

Granted, when an idea or thought becomes conscious, it also becomes accessible to other information. Yet this is only how consciousness presents itself rather than necessarily suggesting this phenomenal presence is linked to any other computational functions of the mind. All processing of information and all computations of the mind are determined by neural behaviour, and phenomenal consciousness does not seem to be in any way necessary for this processing. To suggest there is an invisible, unobservable 'thing' within neural patterns that also somehow influences the behaviour of objective, physical elements only invites ambiguity and scepticism. Consciousness is separated from this category of ambiguity because it is itself the most real thing to us. Everything around consciousness and its physical operation is not as certain as the reality (but not necessarily truth) of conscious experience. It may seem as though phenomenal consciousness is easy to awareness and that qualia make it simpler for quidia to become digestible for the physiology of integrated information, yet there is no necessity for them. The computational capacities of the mind are wholly responsible for the dynamics of reason and the physiology of information-processing is in fact what determines the efficiency of mental computations, as well as the substance of phenomenal consciousness. (Or, at least this is a more coherent and sensible account in the present context.) The ease with which the mind is able to process and integrate information is down to the faculties of intelligence, the phenomenal presentation of which is secondary to physical functions. The phenomenal efficiency of consciousness is nothing but an illusion that corresponds to the capacities of computation. The bottom line is that there does not seem to be any particular function for phenomenal awareness in regards to the performance of the mind. Conscious awareness and its qualia are phenomenal and ghostly.

The impossibility of freethought should be reiterated and expanded on in direct terms of consciousness. Mental operations must be structured and causally coherent, but this doesn't in itself deny the possibility of consciousness having causal properties. Mental operations may follow their own structures parallel to physiology in terms of their own set of complimentary models of functions bound to the Fundamental Principle (although the preferred view is that the mental is wholly causally dependent on the physiological). The suggested irrelevance of consciousness in mental functions does not deny with certainty its possible degree of functional influence. For instance, as was considered, consciousness could be a utility of efficiency in cognition. At this point, a mere aversion to the idea of an unphysical substance influencing the physical is not satisfactory. The account of mind-body operation in terms of the anatomy of logic may be more appealing, but this doesn't necessarily make it right.

Can the causation of consciousness – the causal power of consciousness – be outrightly denied? Simply put, it can't be. Questions raised later will demand a flexible understanding of consciousness. However, the causation of consciousness does not appear to be necessary and applying a causal view of consciousness to physiology would mostly only create avoidable explanatory gaps. It may seem as though denying the causal relevance of conscious experience, such as pain or pleasure, is counter-intuitive. Yet there are sensible arguments that support an acausal view of consciousness, which will be discussed in due time. Physiology must follow coherent causal order; consciousness may provide a level through which physical operations are complimented. Random causal systems can be observed in Nature, such as with behaviour on a quantum level, hence causal interference of consciousness could be possible. However, seemingly random influences of consciousness on physical performance would be disruptive. An evolution of the psyche and consciousness through trial-and-error of conscious influence is hypothetically conceivable, but if so, this seems to be redundant or unobservable. Moreover, it could be suggested that consciousness is subject to the rules of the Fundamental Principle as well, but the nature of consciousness in terms of qualia is fundamentally different. Consciousness is not constant or stable like the operations of the body in the sense that the content of consciousness is more spontaneous. The Fundamental Principle is necessary for operational sustainability, but consciousness always changes and can even switch off, such as during sleep. The behaviour of consciousness does not require the Fundamental Principle to describe it. So while it cannot be absolutely denied that consciousness has causal power, it is not really appealing and is somewhat an unreasonably difficult view.

If phenomenal consciousness does not serve any distinct function, could consciousness simply be an accident or an evolutionary by-product? Could it really be that phenomenal consciousness really doesn't have any particular function or purpose? This would suggest that consciousness and qualia are inconsequential fundamental components of the universe. This can't be right, as nature does not make accidental fundamentals; every fundamental element of the universe serves a purpose – does something. Fundamental elements of the universe, such as matter and energy, all serve a function. Qualia are fundamental elements of the subjective realm of consciousness with respect to considerations of their default nature and serve the function of phenomenal consciousness. Qualia make information and quidia accessible to awareness when consciousness grants the privilege of the phenomenal manifestation of quidia. One certain function of consciousness is tied with the manifestation of qualia and phenomenal experiences, but their function in the first place remains a mystery. Consciousness and qualia are fundamental components of the universe correlating with the functions of other fundamentals of matter and energy. The force acting on the chemistry of the brain sustains the mechanical mind, which is then subject to phenomenal experience. Consciousness has a function; it may not have a causal influence over information processing, integration, or computation, and neither is it necessary for the functions of the body and mind. Nevertheless, consciousness is persistent and is the first point of familiarity.

The human mind is capable of holding great amounts of information and knowledge, as well as able to perform extraordinary mental functions in order to deal with the vast information stored in the unconscious mind. It has the intrinsic potential to integrate and bind very complex knowledge into something noticeably simpler or lead to even greater cognition. A thought can trigger sweeping neural activity, bridging many points of information, connecting many memories, beliefs, and ideas. Knowledge and phenomenal experiences are united with physical systems through interconnected neural structures. Quidia bind together in neural connections to harbour complex experiences, sensations, and integrate tremendous amounts of information. A single idea can be the product of many neurons coming together to construct one single entity of knowledge or experience. There are many components and faculties of integrated information, but in consciousness they become comprehensive in their presentation under the scope of qualia and phenomenal experiences. Visual experiences are subjected to many phenomenal schemes that configure the content of perceptions including informational organisation of the influx of sensations. All aspects of a single observation consist of many reductive components unified in/as conscious perception. The constant sensations received when the eyes are active are usually accompanied with phenomenal experiences in conscious form, even if focus is not moved to address those visual observations. When an idea or thought develops a strong enough charge, it will invade our awareness and thus become conscious. Everything we know is centred in conscious experience and beyond direct experiences we know little, especially when further knowledge requires deduction and interpretation absent direct perception.

Qualia are composite in their nature, binding quidia into a concentrated or comprehensive phenomenal substance. Physiological functions and computations of the mind are responsible for conscious activity, where consciousness itself is the product of the functions determining its content. The mind and body directly cause and build the conscious states we experience. However, it is clear that consciousness is the centre of all awareness, therefore of all the cognitive and phenomenal states we can be aware of. Atoms and molecules construct the cells that then exchange energies, thereby integrating information and collaborating in their functions. The tiniest of connections between the material of the mind conspires with larger domains of neural networks, binding colossal degrees of quidia of integrated information. Perhaps this is the function and purpose of consciousness – as an *informational binding force or state*. The stupendous amount of information received by the mind and senses is bound into a concentrated entity in conscious form. Where neural activity bridges multiple points of information that correlate with consciousness, that information is no longer secluded – it becomes *singular,* forms its own *identity of information.* Qualia and consciousness might be the product of integrated information bound into a singular form.

The basis of this idea stresses the nature of qualia as compositions of quidia. Where points of information and sense data are bridged as stable, continuous neural activity and interlinked states of electro-chemical activity, that information adopts a centred, singular arrangement. Quidia are no longer divided but are wholly collected into a new form. That form is defined as being active, employed, and as an entirely different state to idle quidia in/of the world. In the world, quidia are separated and disengaged, but in the conscious mind quidia adopt a new form. A square is a collection of four lines, but that shape, its properties, and identity are different to those of a single line or four lines running parallel to one another. In this sense, consciousness is not a causal function, but rather it is the product of causation. The bonding of integrated information and its physiology produces a singular entity constructed by many individual posits which produce the conscious phenomena corresponding to the presence of active sensory quidia. Even the seemingly simple interaction of a single molecule with another can cause an imminent causal or informational union. A single photon hitting the eye can spread its energy across many molecules, thus causing a particular state of sensation and physiological activity. That state is then recognised by the mechanisms of visual sensations and translates it into the perception we are most familiar with. Those exchanges between energies and matter through sensory functions are contingent on the elements of quidia and no individual sensation is simple in its nature. Consciousness is then the product of centred quidia and integrated information – the binding force and core of the mind's content. This explanation of consciousness as a phenomenon of collusion of information as or by a binding force – the *united format theory of consciousness* – will be given further consideration.

We know that consciousness is the product of integrated information, the result of neural activity, so how does the proposition account for the hard problem of consciousness? The hypothesis suggests that the connection between material itself forms a distinct entity. Conscious states are constructed similarly to their specific entities of/as quidia. The notion I envisage is of mental states being fundamental elements of non-representative information functioning of its own accord absent synthetic mechanisms. Just as matter can take on multiple shapes and forms, qualia and consciousness are the imminent bond of many points of quidia – a unity of information as its own format. A phenomenal experience does not linger absent physical causation; just as a thought appears, it instantly disappears from its phenomenal familiarity unless called on again, even though the information remains functionally accessible where provoked. Pleasure lasts as long as chemistry sustains it. Collaborations of quidia form their own entities, their own distinct substances and states. Consciousness is the product of those entities coming together and having a strong enough influence on the core of the mind.

Consciousness is more than just integrated information – it is a distinct state of information. A light diode may be characterised by certain information and data that convert into qualia through respective quidia. However, information of the light diode is divided in the object or is causally related but not singular. In consciousness, that information becomes a single entity or format, becoming more than just integrated information. The united format theory of consciousness would claim that consciousness does not exercise causal power of its own, but exists necessarily because compounded formats of information can no longer sustain their primitive form of individualistic points of information in their own dimension. As a further analogy, quidia are two-dimensional, while qualia are three-dimensional. Consciousness arises necessarily from quidia because their united form in the mind changes their nature and structure in a way that causes a new order and species of information. The necessity of consciousness can be formalised in terms of a *binding principle of mental information,* according to which a change in the structure of information in the mind and senses generates a new format of mental information. A computer may operate with information through computational processes of cause and effect, but consciousness is distinct where the nature of that information necessarily changes as a consequence of unity. The focus of this idea is inspired by the observable stable connections in neural activity, whereby individual neurons or components of the brain create a particularly identifiable informational structure and entity.

Qualia are states reflecting the reality of states of quidia, which are conditioned by the functions of the senses. These bound quidia aren't just causally linked – they are uniform congruencies of objective states. A study by Aaron Schurger found that conscious phenomena require a stable connection between physical components of the physiology of the brain[18], complimenting the view of consciousness in terms of the binding principle ascribed to neural activity correlating with consciousness. The oscillations between neurons carry, communicate, and connect stored or received sensory information; while that unity persists, a formulation of qualia to corresponding quidia is created. The senses pick up on objective packets of reality and morph into conscious forms as they become entangled with an informational core imbedding quidia. Conscious substances are quidia that are bound into singular forms, whilst the objective world relying on the interpretation of our own senses can never grant the satisfaction of phenomenal appearance beyond the unified realm of subjective, personal consciousness.

The Integrated Information Theory and Schurger's study fit together to help understand the computational mind and consciousness. However, these scientific investigations rely on preordained fundamentals. Qualia have been argued to be informational fundamentals of the universe, the knowledge and understanding of which then falls to metaphysics. The metaphysics of informational unity is the core of the hard problem, for phenomenal consciousness is essentially a fundamental substance of information. In terms of the binding principle, the senses interact with objective states of quidia which are then bound to an informational core. The unity between systems of informational integration and sensory mechanisms creates a distinct state of information (quidia). This information becomes a uniform substance, different to 'wild' quidia disconnected outside of the brain and consciousness. Sensory data and mental information are not just causally interlinked in consciousness – they are a singularity of unified quidia that correspond to other causal influences with their own states of quidia. Beyond consciousness, no quidia are bonded and no knowledge has unity – they only have purpose in their relation to causal systems. But through the anatomy of consciousness, quidia form distinct new entities which we know of as qualia. These qualia reflect the world and serve as manifestations of singularities of integrated information in the brain, the corresponding quidia of which are utilised in physical systems of causation and computation. This deduction then fits into the narrative of IIT and consciousness as a phenomenon of stable neural activity.

Mental activity becomes 'real' to us through the awareness of it. There are subconscious processes and mechanisms that can trigger certain actions beyond conscious decision-making leading up to the execution of particular behaviour. However, mental activity can be unconscious and awareness can elude mental activity. Why is it that some quidia become phenomenal as qualia, while other information-processing does not become conscious? Why are qualia selectively applied in information-bonding?

What of the varying degrees of consciousness in terms of recurring faint experiences of a first impression such as with memories? A phenomenal experience occurs instantaneously, but it recedes into memory soon after where it no longer exhibits the same phenomenal force. A visual sensation can trigger certain physical states and leave an imprint on neural structures that results in the memory of the visual sensation. The immediate sensation is vigorous, but thereafter the mind can only access a small degree of the sensation's initial power, only able to draft a faint impression. Yet when a visual sensation is sufficiently evocative, triggering its memory could cause distress or even flashbacks. In these cases, it could be that the degree of sensory imprints can determine their influence on phenomenal awareness. Just as an unconscious thought may need to build up sufficient 'charge' or degree of influence to become conscious, a similar process applies to all faculties capable of mobilising phenomenal awareness beyond initial sensations. Relating to this point, mental images and other faint perceptions recalled in memory, I would argue, are qualia of less-detailed copies of the imminent quidia responsible for the initial phenomenal experience. The level of influence and charge sensed by the eyes and the corresponding degrees of (emotional) reaction shape the brain's networks, and the corresponding quidia can be evoked if similar or correlative states of quidia again affect the mind. This model can apply to any triggers and influences acting on the mind in regards to thoughts and memories – any internal mental states.

In relation to the question of active mental states and unconsciousness, it could be the case that the failures of physiology to continue sufficient connection with other components of the brain and mind are responsible for the limitations of conscious awareness. Experiences in early childhood may influence us towards a certain predisposition of behaviour, which then becomes a deeply in-grained part of the psyche that eludes consciousness. We sometimes react before conscious deliberation. These are indicative of subconscious mental elements influencing activity of the conscious mind. We cannot always recall all our memories at once; we cannot be open to all thoughts and influences acting on the mind. Interest usually determines the focus of awareness. It is often the case that we need to deeply reflect on our own minds to understand more about our intentions, our latent thoughts, and ourselves. These secluded components of the mind are hidden in the subconsciousness absent phenomenal awareness, because their degree of influence might be insufficient to evoke awareness. I can stare at a blank white wall and at the same time engage in reflective thought, but all other components of my mind are set aside by the focus of awareness.

This mechanism suggests an anatomical faculty of the mind responsible for conscious awareness. There are parts of the brain that dramatically influence our degree of awareness such as with the mechanisms that shut down consciousness in sleep. One may speculate that there are dispersed points of the brain responsible for evoking conscious awareness. Nevertheless, this thought or any relevant speculation doesn't negate the idea that consciousness is the phenomenal product of a binding force of integrated information within the mind. Certain influences acting on the mind determine what reaches the core of awareness, but thereafter the connection of corresponding influences interact and collaborate with other vast points of information. There can be a lot of neural activity going on in the mind with a number of pathways being simultaneously active. These then feed into the centre of conscious awareness.

The centre of conscious awareness may be considered to be the cerebral cortex, as Giulio Tononi wrote: "Widespread destruction of [it] leaves people permanently unconscious"[19]. The defence of any claim on the physiological centrepiece of conscious awareness and its functions requires a scientific account. The hypothesised binding force of consciousness considers connections between systems of integrated information (composites of quidia) forming a unified entity of information distinct to their separated parts. Phenomenal states are the manifestations of the connections between various posits of information forming one single informational structure that presents itself through phenomenal consciousness. These connections can seclude themselves from the conscious centre, thus affecting the mind without any phenomenal companionship. But when these influences bind to other integrated points of information, they make up a significantly more complex weave of quidia. These sets of quidia come together in contingency with other networks, creating the content within reach of conscious awareness, which then binds them all into singular forms as phenomenal qualia. However, while complexity may give rise to consciousness, the distinction isn't so clear with simpler composites of quidia. Suppose some unconscious thoughts are not complex and are merely causally interlinked rather than of their own distinct entity. Simpler formations of quidia should still be conscious if their more complex forms are. The issue of selective consciousness hasn't been resolved.

This work considers consciousness to be *epiphenomenal* – that consciousness has no causal power over physical and mental behaviour and that its content and state is caused by physiology. Where consciousness is not strictly necessary for operations of the body and mind, the causes of relating quidia do not necessarily mean that quidia must adopt a conscious form for the mind to continue functioning. The necessity for consciousness arises from qualia replacing quidia where information's simpler state can no longer be idle. However, how can we know of qualia and consciousness if they are acausal? That is, if qualia do not influence behaviour and are of a separate substance, how does the brain know of them, pick up on them?

To ask why we are aware of some subjective experiences is to ask why we are aware of ourselves. Acknowledging qualia is only possible where we know we are experiencing something, subject to the coherence of mental order. Thinking about qualia is implicit of two affiliated mental activities, of two similar sets of data conceived as two groupings of quidia. I am analytically self-aware when I think about awareness. Discussing the experience of consciousness is only accompanied by conscious phenomena of analytic thoughts and not by a double experience of the same sort. The content of the experience and the experience of thinking about the quality of the experience are two related, but not identical, mental and conscious events. After all, just as water in a lake is never the exact same, no experience is ever the exact same in terms of content, time, location, and the state of self. So how are we aware of qualia and single instances of consciousness? Well, we never experience or know of qualia through their double forms – that is, any awareness of qualia responds to raw information and conscious thought such as the mental sound or image of thoughts respective to qualia. We consciously know of qualia *reflectively and representationally, not directly*. We only know we are experiencing something, and 'what it is like' to experience it is an experience accompanying a cause.

We don't innately know of qualia – we only 'know' of qualia when we experience them and are made aware of them through parallel awareness and acknowledgement. Rather than understanding knowledge and awareness of qualia in terms of the consciousness of qualia, it is more appropriate to consider and structure these themes in respect of quidia. We can be aware of complex quidia, then replicate and represent them in alternative, subsequently phenomenal forms. But this awareness is strictly compatible and conceivable within physiological terms. Neural activity can interact with correlating neural activity through identical raw information of a particular phenomenal quality, but not of the exact same conscious experience. We know of qualia as and through related information, not as a simultaneous experience of the indistinguishable experience. Awareness of a phenomenal experience is distinct to the experience itself, attuning the epiphenomenal nature of qualia with their respective quidia and physiological function. Therefore, it is possible to know of qualia within an epiphenomenal framework in terms of quidia and their specific, non-identical qualitative properties. Essentially, the argument is that knowledge of qualia is possible with respect to corresponding physical parallels of consciousness that acknowledge and make aware the same information but in different forms. When we talk about qualia, we talk about their derivative and corresponding forms, whereby the knowledge of qualia is knowledge of quidia.

Causal structures in the brain and mind in terms of the composition of quidia (information) are finite, requiring a stable final form that can be accounted for in terms of epiphenomenal consciousness. The physical parallel of consciousness must have phenomenal substance and not mere cause devoid of a structural format as phenomenal substance precisely because consciousness appears to be acausal, or else structural causes would not produce a composition necessary for consciousness. To break down this quirky claim, if physiology was not the final front of cause, and qualia were, then cause outside of physiology would arguably not suffice as comforting conditions for informational integrity, because additional composition would be required for phenomenal states of unified sensory information. But because we are indeed conscious through the medium of phenomenal experience where qualia lack causal force on physiology, this means that the final product of causes of sensory information can only culminate in acausal substance of phenomenal substance, as continued causal structuring of (sensory) information would continuously bind quidia without a consistent form. Sensory information and quidia keep stacking, multiplying, and composing our sensations, perceptions, and phenomenal experiences.

However, without having a limited immediate form of combined, unified states of sensory information and their quidia in a causal chain, there could not be a truly bonded immediate state of information that grants qualia their rightful presence in consciousness. Continued causes without a product would keep instantiating an ever-changing form of information without any consistency that can grant a unified state of information that becomes clear as a phenomenal experience, for, after all, our conscious states are arguably the pinnacle of the immanency of information as we do not know anything beyond the immediate content of our conscious minds (which does not negate the potential for latent information that can flare into consciousness if provoked). If the equation kept infinitely adding up quidia without a stable format, sensory or mental data would never be able to be coherent or digestible. Consciousness is, thus, a peak of information and is coherently acausal.

Conscious experiences, such as of pleasure and happiness, appear to influence behaviour. If something makes us happy, such as pleasure or love, we can be drawn to it. Without an emotive quality of a conscious experience, it seems counter-intuitive to think of consciousness as having no direct causal influence on behaviour. Most intuitively, we pursue something pleasurable and what makes us happy because of their emotive quality. Without the pleasurable experience, it may seem difficult to see behaviour as being moved wholly in terms of physical, unconscious processes. However, emotional states can be viewed just as any mental and conscious state – a changing, fluctuating, fluid state.

One argument may focus on the physiological causal cascades involved in behaviour, setting aside emotional features as mere contingencies. Another counter-intuitive thought is that the observable fluidity of conscious states and emotions is the transparent evidence of their powerlessness. We can interpret and act on a single emotion in a multitude of ways. We can then act according to an emotion without its direct influence or sense of it. One can act in pursuit of happiness without caring to be happy, as alternative senses of well-being are conceivable. Emotions in themselves do not always set the paradigm of goal-directive behaviour. Emotional satisfaction can come as a consequence of behaviour and not through a corresponding direct intent. The desire not to be in pain is bound to rational thought averse to pain, but not necessarily bound to pain itself. It is possible to act in the absence of direct emotion, and so emotions do not necessarily exercise power on behaviour. Imagine an ancient tribal community; times are harsh and survival is a constant concern.

Now, just as back then, love may be something that aids living through survival, but it is not necessary. Love can uplift living, yet life can carry on just as usual without love. One can similarly continue living without a real concern for, or want of, happiness. Where this sense is found, flexibility of the mind makes one aware to the plausible view of emotions not having direct force on actions.

In some cases, emotions do appear to exercise power where they are relevant. Emotions provide powerful drive and motivation for behaviour. The aforementioned argument and the fluid nature of conscious states shake up the intuition that emotions have causal power on behaviour. Love is among the most powerful emotions. However, even this power is determined by physical processes, with relevant consciousness accompanying the chemistry that affects the rationale. Fixation on emotion is always momentary. According to such an understanding, then, change in intuition makes alternative views of behaviour and emotions most plausible. Unconscious thoughts can drive behaviour in patterns and cycles, with emotions only being events. This intuition forms a particular idea on the nature or distinction between thoughts and emotions.

Emotions and thoughts appear to be fundamentally different, but are they really? In Section 1, I argued that even though behaviour operates entirely in terms of reason, emotions are different to reason or thoughts. But the difference between emotions and thoughts is only in appearance, and not fundamental. Emotions are felt, yet we don't seem to think of ourselves as *feeling* our thoughts. Emotions are, in a sense, *raw*, whereas thoughts have images, sounds, and complex meaning. The phenomenal distinctiveness of emotions, in comparison to thoughts, is the same with all things phenomenally and consciously different – of different states and orders of quidia. All qualia are different in their appearance, but their operational basis in the brain and in terms of quidia is the same. The conscious mind operates through the brain's anatomy, which involves electro-chemical neurological processes. Emotions and thoughts are both products of chemistry and signals of the nervous system. Both thoughts and emotions are a state of quidia – in other words, are types of information. For thoughts and emotions to be consciously and phenomenally *perceived*, they must be *sensed*. Just because certain sensations appear differently to us and are rooted in different categories of sensation does not mean that they are *fundamentally* different. The same applies to thoughts and emotions – the two are different types and categories of sensation, which does not mean that they are completely opposite. As was argued with respect to raw meaning and raw thoughts, epiphanies are sensations of raw meaning – of raw thoughts. Epiphanies *feel* very similarly to the experiences of raw emotions – epiphanies *feel* like some sort of movement without being described by specific words, even though the corresponding categories of sensation, and the sensations themselves, are different. Thoughts are *felt*.

Emotions are primary sensations of base-reason, while thoughts are primary sensations of high-reason. Emotions aren't naturally felt with an accompanying word, because the sensation or identification of certain meaning or information with images, sound, and movement is based on the operations of high-reason. High-reason is not inherently as evocative, powerful, or dominant as base-reason – the foundation of high-reason. Because thoughts are sensations of information relating to the faculty of high-reason, their information is inherently composite, or more composite than information formed in, or relating to, the base faculty. For this reason, thoughts are sensed with accompanying images, sounds, words, and other related meaning or information. Emotions can be similarly sensed with accompanying bodily sensations such as butterflies in the stomach. The fundamental difference between thoughts and emotions is phenomenal; the anatomical foundation of emotions and thoughts is the same, with the aspects or areas of corresponding physical behaviour setting emotions and thoughts apart. Thoughts and emotions are derivative of quidia, but different only in terms of their qualia. Thoughts and emotions are different kinds of sensations and feelings, but this doesn't mean that the fundamental nature of sensation and feeling makes thoughts and emotions acausal or disjointed. Thoughts, emotions, and all sensations deal with information, the difference being the type or form of information being dealt with. The way in which emotions and thoughts influence behaviour is fundamentally the same, but different in terms of the *channels* the effects take. Therefore, the perceived influence of emotions on thoughts, and vice versa, does not contradict the epiphenomenal understanding of consciousness.

To relate another aspect of selective conscious states with considerations of further themes of consciousness, consider death. Death may disband consciousness, and thus all that remains is the blackness of non-existence, similar to sleep. However, 'blackness' of missing consciousness is only 'there' when it is acknowledged after subsequent conscious states are able to confirm or recognise missing moments of awareness. Consciousness is not aware of its non-existence; I cannot think if I do not exist or cannot think. It seems that gaps in awareness are only palpable or have any sense of meaning or substance after consciousness acknowledges them. Furthermore, the idea of *conscious time reference* relating to themes of chronoception that puts consciousness in a certain place in time and seems to 'jump' through gaps of awareness towards immediately following conscious states poses some interesting questions about the nature of consciousness in correspondence to time itself and the properties of awareness. Also, the linear function of phenomenal consciousness in congruence with time – that is, phenomenal consciousness always being of immediate experience of the 'here and now' and not being stuck in a past or future state – is intriguing. This consideration of the properties of consciousness, whilst sensible in a physicalist and materialist perspective, raises questions about the *selective locality of consciousness*, whereby it becomes odd, yet fair, to ask: Why is my consciousness my own? Why is my consciousness here and now? Considerations of the physical counter-part of the conscious mind may provide a solution by claiming that, since consciousness is body and mind dependent, any conscious state is attached to a part of physical substance in the world and its properties and states of affairs. However, this supposed response only complicates matters by not specifying why exactly consciousness is attached to a certain body, more so attached to the here and now by an *anchor* of consciousness. It is too early to ask such questions until a foundation of consciousness has been formulated by addressing the hard problem. Even if a seriously contending theory addressing the hard problem has been put forward, this only gives rise to even harder and more counter-intuitive questions that shatter sensibility and plant confusion and disorientation.

The suggestive thought of an *anchor of consciousness* applies to the question of selective consciousness. Selective consciousness is, essentially, a feature of awareness, as the issue is poised by certain mental activity and information being conscious while other is not. First of all, it would help to consider our scope of awareness. We are always focused on certain sensations even though we can still sense other parts of our bodies and the world around us by shifting focus. However, sense-awareness is seemingly different to computational awareness – awareness of our thoughts. Selective focus and awareness through the senses can be explained physiologically; the conscious content of cognition and unconscious mental activity is different to the functions of bodily senses. Accordingly, the issue of selective consciousness is best examined with respect to the different faculties of awareness – sensory and cognitive. Why are some thoughts unconscious?

Awareness of subconscious mental activity only surfaces when thoughts achieve a conscious state or reach the centre of conscious awareness. The content of conscious cognition involves information warranting the most attention by the determination of suited mental functions, as seen with the deliberative nature of conscious awareness and its norm of cognitive competition. In central awareness, previously unaware information becomes available to immediate judgement. After all, conscious cognition does not seem to be the only or even primary source of learning or synthesising new information, which seems to be more spontaneous through unconscious cognitive processes. Furthermore, all complex cognition is only conscious as phenomenal awareness, with phenomenal experience being acausal on cognition. Central awareness that makes information available for complex cognition and deliberative judgement allows for combined information to be passed along to all concerned faculties. However, subconscious cognition, even though able to provoke reactions and influence certain aspects of conscious thought, is a mental realm of its own. The subconscious mind may operate in terms of causal tangents of information-integration constantly adding and compiling mental data, which can eventually become conscious. However, mutual effects of information may not be sufficient for full informational unity, implying that subconscious quidia are not united formats beckoning qualia. Any composite information, with respect to the binding principle, must become conscious, and yet consciousness is phenomenally selective. Then again, subconscious cognition may be poorly understood or entirely misunderstood. This much is clear – subconscious cognition may be concerned with its own operations and influences, but a centre of immediate information seems necessary for bridging thoughts such as with deliberation.

Conscious awareness centralises the categories and magnitudes of the senses. Furthermore, conscious awareness can maintain focus of information and sensation, as well as disband it through meditation. For unconscious cognition to be relevant to conscious awareness, it must follow relevant parameters of orderly causal coherence – it must be triggered and tapped into. In this sense, conscious thoughts are those that can be *sensed*. Certain features of consciousness are suggestive of a necessary *grounding* characteristic described as the *anchor of consciousness*. Qualia require a stable format of neural activity. Subconscious thoughts may only become conscious where the relevance of information and the principles of cognition and reasoning enable this, with continued awareness only being possible as the maintained stability of neural connections and their quidia. The *hub* of conscious awareness could prove to be the object that holds and sustains neural activity rather than merely passes along thoughts and connected information. Thoughts that achieve conscious awareness are disbanded when they are no longer deemed necessary by the focus or object of awareness. As with any connection and continuity, there must necessarily always be something perpetuating its causal singularity. However, unconscious thoughts that aren't grounded must still be composites of quidia by their nature as complex information. Therefore, they must have qualia or phenomenal properties outside of awareness.

But then this would suggest separate units of consciousness outside of our conscious awareness, which is very ambiguous. Without a grounding aspect of consciousness, thoughts are difficult to be considered with degrees of unrelatable consciousness. In an internal world rich with many simultaneously active conscious thoughts, the content of conscious cognition would be hectic and causally complicated if not for the functions of awareness and focus. For thoughts to be conscious, their quidia must be bonded into a stable format with appropriate properties that can be sensed, requiring a certain 'grounding' feature nevertheless. The suggested nature of conscious awareness indicates a system of mental and informational organisation through which the content of consciousness and its phenomenal character are a consequence of informational dimensions. So for thoughts to be conscious, they must be sensed by the relevant and appropriate functions of the senses, as is common with the mind's schemes of association and cognition. Frameworks of sensation give weight to information relevant to consciousness and enable their phenomenal presentation through stable forms. The central body of consciousness – perhaps the cerebral cortex – is what gives neural activity sufficient potency and stability to be conscious and maintain the sensations of united formats of information causing a phenomenal state. Then, a physiological account must test this.

The concern was how and why consciousness is selective in terms of united formats of information that would theoretically be present outside of conscious awareness. The conclusion is that while there may be parallel conscious states arising from the mind, which isn't an attractive or impossible view, centralised awareness is necessary for stable and behaviourally coherent neural activity. This is because unconscious cognition can only become conscious if causal order allows its content to be sensed. Consciousness is grounded in or through awareness, and cognition relevant to awareness is maintained in consciousness through sensation, both of which depend on an aspect of consciousness able to anchor down the content of consciousness.

As is ontologically necessary with all continuity, the continuity of consciousness and its pieces (united formats of quidia) requires something able to sustain it. The order of causal coherence of the mind and senses mandates principles of structural dynamics where thoughts and mental activity are relevant to engaged interests and information. Accordingly, all content of consciousness is conditioned by the order of relevance and compatibility, according to which unconscious information is made relevant or behavioural applicable through the senses triggering it. In the hub of conscious awareness binding cognition directly to the environment, information becomes especially composite, demonstrating a clear unified format. The structure and behaviour of subconscious cognition isn't perfectly clear or understood, so it can be difficult to precisely argue when and where quidia can or can't be phenomenal. Perhaps unconscious thoughts are purely causally connected but not fully informationally active or integrated. If they are behaviourally disengaged or consciously irrelevant, it is possible for them to be parallel pieces of consciousness immediately inaccessible to central conscious awareness.

However, this doesn't fundamentally contradict the structure of central conscious awareness and the principles of its functions and orderly causal coherence. The continuity of stable consciousness requires a feature grounding mental activity correlating with consciousness further acting as an anchor of consciousness in the present moment. Now, this thought is astonishingly puzzling. Nevertheless, not knowing how consciousness is grounded into its state the way it is doesn't refute the decisive argument that consciousness requires continuity for its substance to be phenomenal, although this does cast uncertainty. Not fully understanding the physical laws governing the quantum level doesn't completely refute what other understanding has been achieved. In short, one part of the argument can be summarised as claiming that subconscious thoughts might be conscious, just not consciously aware, only to be made aware through reciprocal senses and sensory mechanisms.

Or, all unconscious activity is of *latent* phenomenal quality until tagged into awareness, or a combination of the aforementioned views. This makes sense where not all subconsciousness is simultaneously active at all times, and so certain parts can be made conscious where the senses focus on them without being overwhelmed by an excess of mental activity. Alternatively, it might be possible that unconscious thoughts aren't fully qualified as united formats of quidia necessarily manifesting themselves through qualia where engaged by conscious awareness. But this view suffers from the theoretical idea that they should be conscious. Either way, the binding principle of mental information holds and the united format theory on consciousness is plausible.

The discussed theories on mind and consciousness have proposed a full explanation of behaviour and functions of the psyche in a way that does not challenge the primary interest of this project – ethics and the Fundamental Principle of Living Beings and Actions. Section 4 was devised to fully account for the metaphysics of ethics and morals with respect to their hub of operation and activity – the conscious mind. Structural coherence, integrity, and order has been maintained in the theories put forward. According to these theories, the activity, operations, and functions of the conscious mind are compatible with the deterministic and mechanical nature of ethics. Ethics was the main subject area of study and effort in this project. Section 4 has defended the metaphysics underlying all themes discussed throughout. As it stands, for now, nothing more can be added, but further work is invited and will prove instrumental.

Bibliography

INTRODUCTION
1. Brey, P. A. E. (2014) "From moral agents to moral factors: the structural ethics approach." *The moral status of technical artifacts,* P. Kroes; P. P. C. C. Verbeek (Eds.), *Philosophy of engineering and technology*; 17:124-142.

SECTION 1

1. Aristotle; Ross, W., D. (1999) *Nicomachean Ethics,* Batoche Books, Kitchener.
2. Kraut, R. (2016) "Aristotle's Ethics", *The Stanford Encyclopedia of Philosophy,* Zalta, E., N. (eds), URL=<http://plato.stanford.edu/archives/spr2016/entries/aristotle-eth-ics/>.
3. Hume, D. (1739) *A Treatise of Human Nature,* Selby-Bigge, L.A. (1896) Oxford: Clarendon Press.
4. ibid:244-245.
5. Wilson, D.S.; Dietrich, E.; Clark, A.B. (2003) "On the Inappropriate Use of the Naturalistic Fallacy in Evolutionary Psychology." *Biology and Philosophy,* 18:669-682.
6. ibid.
7. ibid:671.
8. Hurka, T. (2015) "Moore's Moral Philosophy", *The Stanford Encyclopedia of Philosophy,* Zalta, E., N. (eds), URL=<http://plato.stanford.edu/archives/fall2015/entries/moore-moral/>.
9. Aristotle, *Nicomachean Ethics,* Ross, W.D. (1999) Batoche Books Kitchener, p.32-33;
10. Hursthouse, R. (2013) "Normative Virtue Ethics", *Ethical Theory: An Anthology,* 2nd Edition, p.645.
11. Aristotle, *Nicomachean Ethics,* Ross, W.D. (1999) Batoche Books Kitchener, p.97-102.

SECTION 2

PART 2
1. Urnov, M. (2014) "'Greatpowerness' as the key element of Russian self-consciousness under erosion." *Communist and Post-Communist Studies,* 47:317.
2. Nye, J.S. (2003) *The Paradox of American Power: Why the World's only Superpower Can't Go it Alone.* Oxford University Press, p. 5.
3. Hudson, V. (2014) *Foreign Policy Analysis: Classic and Contemporary Theory,* 2nd Edition, p.50.
4. ibid.
5. Sakwa, R. (2008) *Russian Politics and Society,* 4th Edition, Routledge, p.392.
6. Rutland, P. (2015) "An Unnecessary War: The Geopolitical Roots of the Ukraine Crisis." *E-International Relations,* URL=<www.e-ir.info/2015/04/09/an-unnecessary-war-the-geopolitical-roots-of-the-ukraine-crisis/>.
7. Larson, D.W.; Shevchenko, A. (2014) "Russia says no: power, status, and emotions in foreign policy." *Communist and Post-Communist Studies,* 47:272.
8. Sakwa, R. (2008) *Russian Politics and Society,* 4th Edition, Routledge, p.83.
9. ibid:84.

10. ibid:85.

11. ibid:398.

12. Larson, D.W.; Shevchenko, A. (2014) "Russia says no: power, status, and emotions in foreign policy." *Communist and Post-Communist Studies*, 47:273.

13. Lukyanov, F. (2008) "Russia-EU: The Partnership That Went Astray." *Europe-Asia Studies*, 60/6, p.1108.

14. Sakwa, R. (2008) *Russian Politics and Society*, 4th Edition, Routledge, p.386.

15. ibid:398.

16. Maslow, A.H. (1943) "A Theory of Human Motivation" *Psychological Review*, 50:370-96, *Classics in the History of Psychology*, URL=<psychclassics.yorku.ca/Maslow/motivation.htm/>.

17. Urnov, M. (2014) "'Greatpowerness' as the key element of Russian self-consciousness under erosion." *Communist and Post-Communist Studies*, 47:317.

18. ibid.

19. ibid.

20. ibid:320.

21. Gerber, T.P. (2014) "Beyond Putin? Nationalism and Xenophobia in Russian Public Opinion" *The Washington Quarterly*, Fall edition, p.118.

22. Putin, V. (2016) 4th of April, ONF (Obsherossiyskogo Narodnogo Fronta) Media Forum, Video Interview, URL=<https://m.youtube.com/watch?v=jg-qoDWOdG8>, '3:10' onwards with emphasis on the '3:35' mark, accessed: Aprial 2016.

23. ibid.

24. Gerber, T.P. (2014) "Beyond Putin? Nationalism and Xenophobia in Russian Public Opinion" *The Washington Quarterly*, Fall edition, p.115.

25. Kemp, R. (2006) "Moscow", *Ross Kemp on Gangs*, Series 2, Episode 3.

26. Putzel, C. (2009) "From Russia With Hate", Video Documentary.

27. Gerber, T.P. (2014) "Beyond Putin? Nationalism and Xenophobia in Russian Public Opinion" *The Washington Quarterly*, Fall edition.

28. ibid:125.

29. ibid:128.

30. ibid:129-30.

31. Harris, S.J (1953) "Purely Personal Prejudices", *Strictly Personal*.

32. Urnov, M. (2014) "'Greatpowerness' as the key element of Russian self-consciousness under erosion." *Communist and Post-Communist Studies*, 47:315.

33. Forsberg, T.; Heller, R; Wolf, R. (2014) "Status and Emotions in Russian Foreign Policy." *Communist and Post-Communist Studies*, 47:263.

34. ibid:263-4.

35. ibid.

36. Forsberg, T. (2014) "Status Conflicts Between Russia and the West: Perceptions and Emotional Biases." *Communist and Post-Communist Studies*, 47:325.

37. ibid.

38. Urnov, M. (2014) "'Greatpowerness' as the key element of Russian self-consciousness under erosion." *Communist and Post-Communist Studies*, 47:309-11.

39. Dawisha, K. (2014) *Putin's Kleptocracy*, Simon and Schuster Paperbacks, p.154.

40. Urnov, M. (2014) "'Greatpowerness' as the key element of Russian self-consciousness under erosion." *Communist and Post-Communist Studies*, 47:317.

41. ibid:306-7.

42. Sakwa, R. "Russia on the edge of change", p.36, URL=<rusemb.org.uk > P36-38RichardSakwa.pdf>.

43. Urnov, M. (2014) "'Greatpowerness' as the key element of Russian self-consciousness under erosion." *Communist and Post-Communist Studies*, 47:309-12.

44. Dawisha, K. (2014) *Putin's Kleptocracy*, Simon and Schuster Paperbacks, p.313-4.

45. ibid:315.

46. Sakwa, R. "Russia on the edge of change", p.38, URL=<rusemb.org.uk > P36-38RichardSakwa.pdf>.

47. Dawisha, K. (2014) *Putin's Kleptocracy*, Simon and Schuster Paperbacks.

48. ibid:94.
49. ibid.
50. ibid:313-7.
51. Urnov, M. (2014) "'Greatpowerness' as the key element of Russian self-consciousness under erosion." *Communist and Post-Communist Studies*, 47:309.
52. Dawisha, K. (2014) *Putin's Kleptocracy*, Simon and Schuster Paperbacks, p.315.
53. ibid.
54. Urnov, M. (2014) "'Greatpowerness' as the key element of Russian self-consciousness under erosion." *Communist and Post-Communist Studies*, 47:309-11.
55. Kirschbaum, E.; Sobolewski, M.; Ireland, L. (eds) (2014) "German minister compares Putin's Ukraine moves to Hitler in 1938." *Reuters*, URL=<uk.reuters.com/articles/uk-ukraine-russia-germany-idUKBREA2u0140331.>
56. Faulconbridge, G.; Carbonnel, A. (2014) "Prince Charles provokes diplomatic row by comparing Putin to Hitler." *Reuters*, URL=<uk.reuters.com/articles/uk-britain-putin-prince-idUKKBN0E20P920140522.>
57. Dawisha, K. (2014) *Putin's Kleptocracy*, Simon and Schuster Paperbacks, p.144.
58. ibid.
59. Sparks, J. (2016) "Russia's 'Secret Syria Mercenaries'." *Sky News*, URL=<news.sky.com/story/revealed-russias-secret-syria-mercenaries-10529248.>
60. ibid.
61. ibid.
62. Aung San Suu Kyi (1991) *Freedom From Fear*, Penguin Books, p.180.
63. ibid:181.
64. Stein, J.G. (2012) "Decision Making: Rational, Psychological, and Neurological Models." *Foreign Policy: Theories, Actors, Cases*. Smith, S.; Hadfield, A.; Dunne, T. Oxford University Press.
65. Lukyanov, F. (2008) "Russia-EU: The Partnership That Went Astray" *Europe-Asia Studies*, 60(6):1107-19. Routledge.
66. ibid:1114.
67. ibid.
68. Sakwa, R. (2008) *Russian Politics and Society*, 4th Edition, Routledge, p.382.
69. ibid:420.
70. ibid.
71. Rutland, P. (2015) "An unnecessary war: the geopolitical roots of the Ukraine crisis." *E-International Relations*, URL=< http://www.e-ir.info/2015/04/09/an-unnecessary-war-the-geopolitical-roots-of-the-ukraine-crisis/.>
72. Mearsheimer, J. (2014) "Why the Ukraine crisis is the West's fault." *Foreign Affairs*, URL=https://www.foreignaffairs.com/articles/russia-fsu/2014-08-18/why-ukraine-crisis-west-s-fault.

SECTION 3

PART 1

1. Mill, J., S. (1863) *Utilitarianism*, Batoche Books, Kitchener, 2001, p.19.
2. Descartes, R. (1641) *Meditations on First Philosophy*, Translated by John Cottingham, Cambridge University Press, 1996, p.16-17.

PART 2

1. Aristotle, and Ross, W., D. (1999) *Nicomachean Ethics*, Batoche Books, Kitchener.
2. Kraut, R. (2016) "Aristotle's Ethics", *The Stanford Encyclopedia of Philosophy*, Zalta, E., N. (eds), URL=<http://plato.stanford.edu/archives/spr2016/entries/aristotle-ethics/>.
3. Mill, J., S. (1863) *Utilitarianism*, Batoche Books, Kitchener, 2001, p.19.
4. Mill, J., S. (1863) *Utilitarianism*, Batoche Books, Kitchener, 2001, p.11-2.
5. Mill, J., S. (1863) *Utilitarianism*, Batoche Books, Kitchener, 2001, p.6-8.
6. ibid.
7. Mandela, N. (1995) *Long Walk To Freedom*.

PART 3
1. Winship, C.; Mehta, J. (2010) "Moral Power", *Harvard University*, p.1. URL=<scholar.harvard.edu/cwinship/publications/moral-power/>.
2. ibid:4.
3. ibid.
4. ibid.
5. ibid:4-5.
6. ibid:5.
7. ibid:12.
8. ibid:13.
9. ibid:14.
10. ibid:21.
11. Mill, J., S. (1863) *Utilitarianism*, Batoche Books, Kitchener, 2001, p.14
12. Mill, J., S. (1863) *Utilitarianism*, Batoche Books, Kitchener, 2001.
13. Mill, J., S. (1859) *On Liberty*, Batoche Books, Kitchener, 2001.
14. ibid:54.
15. ibid: Chapter 3.
16. ibid:55.
17. ibid:54.
18. ibid:62.
19. ibid:60.
20. ibid.
21. ibid:13-4.
22. ibid:14.
23. ibid.
24. ibid:13.
25. Melville, H. (1851) *Moby Dick*, Penguin Popular Classics, 1994, p.87.
26. Aung San Suu Kyi (1991) *Freedom From Fear*, Penguin Book, 2010, p.180.
27. Urnov, M. (2014) "'Greatpowerness' as the key element of Russian self-consciousness under erosion." *Communist and Post-Communist Studies*, 47:306.
28. Lukyanov, F. (2008) "Russia-EU: The Partnership That Went Astray." *Europe-Asia Studies*, 60(6):1114.
29. http://uk.reuters.com/video/2015/04/08/happy-employee-happy-company-happy-inves?videoId=363782766.
30. http://uk.reuters.com/video/2015/04/08/considering-employee-sentiment-for-inves?videoId=363783522.
31. http://uk.reuters.com/article/2015/04/08/uk-investors-workers-sentiment-insight-idUKKBN0MZ01T20150408.

SECTION 4
1. Chalmers, D. (1996) *The Conscious Mind*, Oxford University Press, p.4.
2. ibid:26-8.
3. ibid:28-9.
4. Wrangham, R. (2014) *Catching Fire: How Cooking Made Us Human*, Basic Books, retrieved from: https://archive.org/details/pdfy-DDoNCJJ_Wt0qOH7e.
5. Chalmers, D. (2010) *The Character of Consciousness*, Oxford University Press, p.497-8, 503.
6. Chalmers, D. (1996) *The Conscious Mind*, Oxford University Press, p. 4.
7. Chalmers, D. (1995) "Facing Up to the Problem of Consciousness", *Journal of Consciousness Studies*, 2(3):200-19, URL=<http://isites.harvard.edu/fs/docs/icb.topic1462521.files/Week%203/Chalmers%20-%201995%20-%20Facing%20up%20to%20the%20problem%20of%20consicousness.pdf>.
8. ibid:209.
9. ibid.
10. Earp, B., D. (2012) "I can't get no (epistemic) satisfaction: Why the hard prob-

lem of consciousness entails a hard problem of explanation", *Dialogues in Philosophy, Mental and Neuro Sciences,* 5(1): xx-xx.

11. Chalmers, D. (1995) "Absent Qualia, Fading Qualia, Dancing Qualia", *Conscious Experience,* URL=<consc.net/papers/qualia.html>.

12. ibid.

13. Seager, W.; Allen-Hermanson, S. (2015) "Panpsychism", *The Stanford Encyclopedia of Philosophy,* Fall Edition, Zalta, E., N. (eds.), URL = <https://plato.stanford.edu/archives/fall2015/entries/panpsychism/>.

14. Chalmers, D. (1996) *The Conscious Mind,* Oxford University Press, xii-iii.

15. Chalmers, D. (1995) "Facing up to the problem of consciousness", *Journal of Consciousness Studies,* 2(3):200-19.

16. ibid:94.

17. Tononi, G. (2012) "Integrated information theory of consciousness: an updated account", *Archives Italiennes de Biologie,* 150:290-326.

18. Ananthaswamy, A. (2015) "A stable mind is a conscious mind", NewScientist, 3016, 226:5-57.

19. Tononi, G. (2012) "Integrated information theory of consciousness: an updated account", *Archives Italiennes de Biologie,* 150:293.

Life for life's sake is never enough